THE STRUCTURE
OF COMPUTERS
AND COMPUTATIONS

THE STRUCTURE
OF COMPUTERS
AND COMPUTATIONS

VOLUME 1

DAVID J. KUCK
Professor of Computer Science
University of Illinois at Urbana-Champaign

JOHN WILEY & SONS

New York • Chichester • Brisbane • Toronto • Singapore

Library of Congress Cataloging in Publication Data:

Kuck, David J
    The structure of computers and computations.
    Includes bibliographical references and index.
      1. Computer architecture. I. Title.
QA76.9.A73K83   621.3819'52   78-5412
ISBN 0-471-02716-2

10 9 8 7

NOTATION

The following notational conventions are used throughout the book:

$\log x = \log_2 x$

$f(x) = O(g(x))$ means there is a constant $r > 0$ such that $\lim_{x \to \infty} (f(x)/g(x)) = r$.

$\lceil x \rceil$, the ceiling of x is the smallest integer greater than or equal to x.

$\lfloor x \rfloor$, the floor of x, is the greatest integer less than or equal to x.

$\log^2 x = (\log x) \cdot (\log x)$

$K = 1024$

P denotes the fewest processors needed to obtain the best known speedup of some computation, while p, $1 \le p < P$, denotes any number of processors used for some computation.

PREFACE

Art is I
Science is We
Engineering is They

Much ado has been made about whether the design of computer hardware and software is art, science or engineering. The above expansion of Claude Bernard's "Art is I, Science is We" seems to capture the essence of the matter. Computer system design is all three.

A good computer system designer must first heed the problems of the intended system users, the technology from which the system will be built, and the people who will carry out the construction and programming of his design. All of these considerations form the "They" of the above quotation and constitute the engineering aspects of computer system design.

Various physical and mathematical principles must be followed in carrying out the design of a system. The "We" of the above quotation represents the collection of people who, as computer system design has evolved, have developed various guiding principles. Both theoretical work and experimental work have been done in a scientific way, to give us a useful set of computer system design principles.

Finally, with "They" and "We" in mind, the individual designer of a piece of hardware or software must employ his own creative talents to produce a new design. The "I" of the above quotation often creates a distinctive, individual design. The "artistry" of designers is obvious when one considers the variety of different types of machines and software sold to the same market. Indeed, the artistry extends to whole companies, which develop "corporate styles" of hardware and software design.

As we discuss throughout this book, there is no "one best way" to design a computer system. Many tradeoffs within and between the artistic, scientific, and engineering levels must be made. The goal of this book is to clarify these tradeoffs by pointing out what they are, how they can be analyzed, and how they affect one another. Abstractions as well as practical computer design topics are considered.

The title of this book describes its contents and its purpose. The structures of both computers and their computations are examined, and the importance of understanding the close ties between them is emphasized. A computer's structure obviously consists of a collection of interconnected hardware devices.

But, despite the fact that most computers are called "general-purpose machines," in recent years computers have become more and more specialized. This specialization is reflected in their physical and logical structure, but it is motivated by the uses to which various machines are put. Indeed, the computations to be performed by a machine *should* lead designers to the structure (or architecture or organization) of the machine. Examples of different structures are minicomputers, supercomputers, and time-shared computers.

This leads us to the second half of the title: "The Structure of Computations." Although this phrase may be less exact than "The Structure of Computers," the different uses of the kinds of computers mentioned above do indeed lead to computations of widely different structures. Examples are the dominance of short, integer arithmetic versus long, floating point arithmetic; the heavy use of scalars, one-, two-, or more-dimensional arrays, or trees as data items; the sizes of these data structures and the amount of input and output required; the relative frequency of branching instructions, arithmetic, stores and fetches; and the users' view of the machine as a quick response, small-problem solver or as an overnight, large-problem solver. Each of these features, and many of the other features discussed in the book are closely related to the structure of the computer itself. Obviously, a machine should be tailored to match the characteristics of the computations that it is to perform.

Most of the qualities mentioned above are useful for characterizing the structure of an individual user's program or computation. Also, certain characterizations of the structure of the system software (compilers and operating systems) are relevant here. For example, hardware features that can aid in compilation include various types of word formats and arithmetic (for number conversion), push-down stacks (for parsing), and hardware register management (to avoid scheduling complexities). Operating systems can be greatly aided by hardware for handling interrupts conveniently and by virtual memory and other input-output hardware, and the like. Again, the type of software anticipated for the system may be an important consideration in designing the computer's architecture.

The theme emphasized throughout the book is that unless computer system designers appreciate and understand both the structure of the computer and the structure of its computations, serious design errors are likely to result. They may show up in the cost, speed, usefulness, or reliability of the resulting hardware and software system. I do not claim that such errors can be totally avoided, but the book's goal is to spell out the issues and to clarify the tradeoffs and solutions that are known. These points are important for software designers as well as hardware designers. The book discusses a number of structural features of computers that must be taken into account by compiler writers and emphasizes the program transformations that form the basis of compiler algorithms for various computer structures.

GOALS AND ORIENTATION

This is a book about how computer systems work and why they are organized as they are. It includes the history of real machines to explain how system organization arrived at its present position, and also projects what may lie ahead, based on current knowledge. The purpose is to provide the reader with facts about *how* things are as well as good intuition about *why* they are that way.

This is not a book about logic design, at least not in the traditional sense. Nor is it an attempt to explain a number of different, real computer systems. However, I believe that readers will come away from the book with a good idea of the important issues of logic design as well as a clear understanding of the operating principles of most current computer systems.

Traditional logic design books are concerned with abstractions about Boolean algebra and switching theory, and with concrete examples of many different kinds of useful circuits. However, most of these abstractions are of little use in modern logic design, and the study of half a dozen different adder circuits, for example, overkills such a problem. In this book I instead develop some theory that can be used to estimate the speed and component counts in a wide variety of useful circuits. With this background, the relative costs and speeds of different designs for a given circuit or for various parts of a processor can be easily estimated. This is just one example of our approach to the material.

Books that explain real computer systems in detail are valuable references, but it is often difficult to extract any general principles from them. In this book, individual chapters on processors, control units, memories, interconnection switches, and memory hierarchies provide background material, with examples drawn from real systems. Some principles are also given to explain why these devices take the various forms they do. Thus readers will be able to compare various machine features in a detailed way, and they will also be able to compare these features with certain absolute measures of speed and cost. The quality and usefulness of each of these parts of computer systems are also discussed in each chapter.

Frequent references are given throughout to manufacturer's model numbers, even though there is a risk of being outdated by new announcements. Actually, most manufacturers make few fundamental changes in a 5- to 10-year period. Thus, the earliest model numbers usually refer to a sequence of machine families. For example, the IBM System/360 and System/370 had few fundamental differences, and I sometimes use "IBM 360" to designate all of these. Similarly, I refer to the CDC 6600 and 7600 frequently, but without mentioning the more recent but structurally similar CYBER series machines. Also, I use the PDP-11 to reflect the DEC minicomputers.

The machines I discuss as examples are typical of those sold by major manufacturers. Of course, much of the computer market involves special-purpose digital devices or a dedicated use of general-purpose machines. Frequent examples are given of unusual machines that are effective in particular areas. For a survey of recent high speed computers, including discussions of the structure of their computations and performance, see [KuLS 77].

It is expected that users of this book will have a good background in programming computers. The intuition about how computers work, which is gained in this way, makes it feasible to avoid various detailed explanations. No background in logic design is assumed.

In Chapter 1, I first present criteria by which computer systems can be judged. Next, I attempt to coordinate the backgrounds of all readers with a brief discussion of some elementary hardware and software topics. As a preview of the later chapters, I then give an overview of computer system organization. A rather detailed history of computers is given, which provides some interesting and useful facts about real systems. Moreover, knowledge about how much had been built before 1950—and, indeed, how much was known before 1850—should instill a good deal of humility in all computer people. I conclude the chapter with an overview of the rest of the book.

All readers should scan Chapter 1 to determine the kind of background material that is assumed. Selective reading should be used to fill in any gaps in background at the beginning or later during the study of particular chapters. This leads to an important question: For whom is this book intended?

For university courses concerned with computer organization, computer design, or computer architecture, this book can serve as a text. These are the courses that are usually designed for advanced undergraduates and beginning graduate students in computer science or electrical engineering. There is more material in this book than can be included in a normal one-semester course. In fact, depending on local circumstances, there is enough for two quarters or perhaps two semesters; if enhanced by readings from research papers, parts of the book can be the basis for an advanced graduate course on computer system theory and design.

The students who take an introductory "computer organization" course may have one of several motivations. First, they may be interested in a career as a computer system designer. For these individuals the book provides a broad, solid background for further work. A second type of student may be interested in system software design, including compilers and operating systems. For such students it is very important to have a good working knowledge of the details of computer systems. The hardware background provided here should carry over to aid system programming on any real computer. Finally, there are students who are interested in computers from the point of view of machine users or owners. That is, they want to be aware of tradeoffs that exist in comparing machines, and they want to have a general background about the architecture of computers. By selectively reading this book, they should be able to meet these goals.

The statements above, although explicitly concerned with university students, are equally valid for professional people who are not formally students. Sufficient background material is provided throughout so that the book can be used in a self-study mode.

It is important to realize that there is a great deal of interdependence between various parts of this book. For example, the control unit chapter assumes, from time to time, that the processor chapter has been read, the memory hierarchy chapter assumes that a number of previous chapters have been read, and so on. A number of explicit cross-references are provided in the chapter discussion, and I suggest that if a reader is confused, he or she consult the book's index or table of contents for earlier references to background material. Since a goal of the book is to present an integrated and coherent view of the structure and operation of whole computer systems, such interdependence seems a necessary and, indeed, important fact of the book's organization.

Chapters 3 to 7 discuss various parts of computers: processors, control units, main memories, interconnection networks, and memory hierarchies, respectively. Chapter 2 presents some theoretical background that reappears at several places throughout the book. Most students at the level for which this book is intended may find Chapter 2 "hard" or "unusual," and to shorten the time spent on it this chapter may be treated lightly. However, it should not be avoided entirely. The introduction is fairly long and gives the idea of the chapter. To reflect the type of course being taught, this and selections from the four following sections may be chosen.

Much of the material in Chapters 3 to 7, with Chapter 1 used as needed and parts of Chapter 2 used to set as much of a theoretical background as is desired, can be profitably used in courses given in computer science and electrical engineering. More comments about the book's contents appear in Section 1.4. of Chapter 1.

The homework problems provided with each chapter are given in two groups—"easy" and "medium and hard." Within these groups they are arranged roughly to follow the sequence of the chapter discussion. Some of the problems are theoretical and others are design-type exercises. Any finer distinction than "easy" and "medium and hard" would be difficult because of the diversity of the subject matter; the backgrounds of individuals have a wide range. A number of the problems are included to fill in gaps in the text, where it seems appropriate to expect students to be able to fill in these gaps. For example, some problems relate the general ideas of the chapter discussion to one specific computer or another. In this case, the problems are intended to be self-contained, but for more background about one machine or another, manufacturers' literature may be studied.

Many of the problems have been written in the spirit of their accompanying chapter, with certain built-in assumptions. This is sometimes necessary to avoid even longer problem statements. Students should make and state any assumptions needed to make the problem clear for solution. The problem statements contain numbers that are more or less realistic; however, simplifications and idealizations are often used. Detailed solutions to all of the problems may be found in the Instructor's Manual.

Only a few problems are included in Chapter 1, since this chapter is intended as background material. However, for a good understanding of the material in this book, a number of problems should be solved in each of the succeeding chapters.

David J. Kuck

Many complain that the words of the wise are always merely parables
    and of no use in daily life,
    which is the only life we have.
All these parables really set out to say
    merely that the incomprehensible is incomprehensible,
    and we know that already,
But the cares we have to struggle with every day:
    that is a different matter.

Concerning this a man once said: Why such reluctance?
If you only followed the parables you yourselves would become parables
    and with that rid of all your daily cares.

Another said: I bet that is also a parable

The first said: You have won.

The second said: But unfortunately only in parable.

The first said: No, in reality: in parable you have lost.

On Parables
Franz Kafka

ACKNOWLEDGMENTS

I am indebted to many people for help with ideas that led to parts of this book as well as for help with the material as it appears in the book. First, I thank the many anonymous students and teaching assistants in CS 333 (and its predecessors) at the University of Illinois who asked questions and made suggestions that improved my notes over the past ten years. I am also indebted for ideas or help with the presentation of the book's material to Walid Abu-Sufah, Dan Atkins, Utpal Banerjee, Richard Brent, Paul Budnik, Roy Campbell, Donald Chang, Milos Ercegovac, Dan Gajski, Lee Hollaar, Sharon Kuck, B. Kumar, Bruce Leasure, Kiyoshi Maruyama, Yoichi Muraoka, David Padua, Stott Parker, John Pasta, Michael Schlansker, William Stellhorn, Richard Stokes, Ross Towle, and Michael Wolfe.

The entire manuscript was read by Richard Brown, Won Kim, and Duncan Lawrie, and they made many very valuable suggestions about the presentation. Robert Kuhn made many original contributions to the homework problems and helped put all of the problems in their final form. I am especially indebted to S. C. Chen, Duncan Lawrie, and Ahmed Sameh, for background ideas, comments about the book, and endless discussions about the material.

Finally, my sincerest thanks are reserved for Vivian Alsip, who typed the manuscript several times and suffered without complaint a good deal of abuse. She always produced the highest quality drawings and typing, quickly and pleasantly.

D. K.

CONTENTS

CH

1

However, if I had waited long enough I probably
 would never have written anything at all since
 there is a tendency when you really begin to learn
 something about a thing
not to want to write about it but rather to keep on
 learning about it always and at no time, unless
 you are very egotistical, which, of course, accounts
 for many books,
will you be able to say: now I know all about this
 and will write about it.

Certainly I do not say that now; every year I know
 there is more to learn, but I know some things
 which may be interesting now,
and I may be away from the bullfights for a long
 time and I might as well write what I know about
 them now.

Death in the Afternoon

Ernest Hemingway

Anyone who says he knows how computers should
 be built should have his head examined!
The man who says it is either inexperienced or
 really mad.

Computer Architecture

James E. Thornton

AN OVERVIEW
OF COMPUTER
SYSTEMS

1.1 INTRODUCTION

1.1.1 Computer system design criteria

All computer systems may be characterized in terms of five broad criteria:

1. Cost.
2. Speed.
3. Quality and usefulness.
4. Design assurance.
5. Reliability.

These ideas are interrelated in many complex ways. In what follows, we will merely scratch the surface in explaining them—the remainder of the book will develop some of their details. Some aspects of these criteria are quite well understood in the context of computer system design, whereas others are still being developed. But we will be guided by one or more of these points in almost all of the discussions in this book.

One can imagine the criteria being used in any of a large number of contexts. There are perhaps three such viewpoints which we will assume at various times in this book. One is that of the designer and builder of the computer system. In the long run, the designer seeks a system that is useful and can be sold competitively. However, he or she must first be concerned with available technology and current design practice. Furthermore, the designer must design something that is reasonable to manufacture and which will not be too confusing or complex for those who do detailed logic design and those who must program it.

The second point of view we can take in interpreting the criteria is that of the salesperson of the system or its owner. Here there is less interest in what is inside the machine than in how much it costs to buy and to operate, how much physical space it occupies, and in superficial ways how well it performs relative to the competition. Reliability may be quite important here also.

The third point of view is that of a user or general critic of the machine. Here, the quality of the machine's computed results is very important, as is the ease of using the machine. Speed is important in that users want their answers quickly. They care about system efficiency only as it affects their cost of computing.

Throughout the book we will discuss the design and performance of parts of computers as well as whole computer systems. From time to time we will take one or another of the above three viewpoints, so the reader should keep them in mind. The five criteria listed above will also guide most of our later discussions, but in order to clarify what we mean by them, a few details are given now.

Cost

Basically, the cost of buying or leasing and operating a computer system has three components: hardware, software, and people. The relative costs of these have changed over the years and vary from one manufacturer to another; they are also strongly related to the size and type of computer installation in question. In the early days of computing, every new computer was a super-computer (i.e., the biggest and fastest available). Most of the expense was in the machine itself; little software was available and few people were involved.

As time passed, computer systems became specialized in many ways. Some continued to do large scientific jobs but others were used in banking, in education, for airline reservations, to handle payrolls, and so on. Advances in technology and ever increasing uses for computers have led to a range of computers—from microprocessors that fit on a single semiconductor chip, through minicomputers, to multimillion dollar supercomputers. Minicomputer systems which have a full complement of peripheral equipment may now be purchased for only a few tens of thousands of dollars. Microprocessors can be bought for only a few dollars, although this is just the cost of a semiconductor package; memory and peripheral gear increase the price of a system substantially.

Just as there is a wide range of hardware costs today, there is also a wide range of software costs. In some applications, software packages have been developed and optimized over many years, so competition between software houses has led to reduced costs. Other software must be developed from scratch at very great costs. It is important to note that the costs of producing software are mainly people costs. These are sometimes borne by machine manufacturers, sometimes by companies which deal exclusively in programming, and sometimes by the owners of computers who write programs to fit their own specific needs.

It is often pointed out that software costs are rising much faster than hardware costs. Although this seems to be true in general, it should be remembered that some standard application codes can be reproduced for the cost of punching a deck of cards. The costs attributed to software usually include the cost of programmers, who range from system programmers to applications programmers of all kinds. Clearly, the size and type of computer installation influences the cost breakdown. A very small computer system may require a programmer whose annual salary is equal to the cost of the system, whereas in a very large computing center the cost for hardware may be many times more than that for people and software.

Speed

Two fundamental kinds of questions determine the speed of a computer system—some physical and some logical. Physically, the speed of a computer is constrained electrically by the time required to switch a device (e.g., transistor) or to propagate signals along conductors, and mechanically by such constraints as the rotation time of a secondary memory device (e.g., a disk motor's speed). Logically, the speed of a computer is determined by how the elementary physical devices are organized to build circuits that perform the desired functions and how these are interconnected to form a complete system. At the lowest level, one is concerned with the time to perform such functions as AND, OR, and NOT; whereas at higher levels, one is concerned with the time required to access a word in main memory or a block from secondary memory, to add two numbers together, or to decode an instruction for execution.

In this book we will be concerned mainly with questions of logical speed. Physical speeds are dictated by manufacturers who produce devices, research in physics to discover new devices, or properties of the universe (e.g., the speed of propagation of electromagnetic waves). By various design tricks, however, faster and faster schemes have been determined for carrying out computations—even assuming that device speeds do not change. For example, adders can add two bits at a time serially, or they can use fast parallel carry lookahead schemes. Throughout the book we will make the assumption that devices and circuits have a fixed speed. This is equivalent to saying that we will study devices and circuits at any fixed point in time. Then we can study questions of designing fast computers using such components of fixed speed. We will discover that there are logical limits as well as the above-mentioned physical limits on the speed of computations.

The costs of various parts of machines will also be related to their speeds. In general, it is instructive to consider a criterion function such as the product of the total number of components used and the time to carry out a computer function. Often such a criterion function is more or less constant over a wide range of designs—as the cost increases, the time decreases, and some kind of overall parity is maintained. For example, a slow adder can be built inexpensively using few components, whereas a fast adder needs many gates and is expensive.

Of course, viewed more globally the speed of a computer system may involve complex interactions between many parts of the system. And different people may view speed in different ways. For example, a machine's owner may be interested only in the number of jobs per day which can be pushed through the system. Or, a user may be interested only in the turnaround time for the job. These questions are related to each other and to the lower level ones mentioned above in complex ways which we will consider throughout the book.

Quality and usefulness

Cost and speed are relatively well-defined and rather well-developed notions in computer systems study, but the quality and usefulness of a computer system are more nebulous. In one sense, these are quite subjective points—individual users may have different personal tastes and demands. On the other hand, there are a sufficient number of different machines and users today so that in some areas a consensus may be reached about certain good and bad points.

For example, almost everyone would agree that compatibility between machines is a good idea. If a particular program can be run at any computer center that desires it, software costs can be reduced. Of course, if this drives up hardware costs too much, then legitimate complaints may be registered. Similarly, designing a family of machines—large to small—all of which can execute the same instruction set, reduces the difficulties of interchanging software and upgrading the machine in a computing center.

Another topic of importance here is the ease with which compilers and operating systems can be written for a computer. Have hardware designers given sufficient attention to these software matters? In some computer systems the answer is clearly no, whereas in others it is yes—at least in some respects. Particularly in the design of control units, a number of such points are important. We will discuss several of these in Chapter 4, but it is almost certain that this is one of the weakest areas in present computer systems and one of the most important for future research and development.

Another aspect of the quality and usefulness of a computer is the results it produces. Particularly in numerical computation, if the numbers emerging from the machine contain large errors, the machine designers may be at fault. Whereas any machine computation is approximate relative to infinite precision computation, designers should do their best in choosing number systems, word formats, arithmetic algorithms, rounding algorithms, and so on. These areas are rather well developed, although there are still a number of unsolved problems.

There is obviously a wide range of quality and usefulness questions in real computer systems. We will deal with a number of them and the discussion will continue throughout the book.

Design assurance

This is a subject of concern mainly to the designers and builders of computer system hardware and software. After the speed and cost as well as the quality and usefulness of a design have been agreed upon, there is still a very important open problem. This involves successfully implementing what has been designed. We use the term *design assurance* to refer to efforts in the design and implementation phases that are aimed specifically at this problem.

The difficulties of implementing a hardware or software design are manifold. First, the design may have some flaws which appear only when low-level details are worked out; at the level of overall system design these may not appear. Second, even if there are no design bugs—a very unlikely event—how is the overall design to be communicated from a handful of system designers to several dozen or more system implementers? Finally, assuming the design has been communicated perfectly to the implementers, how can the implementers or the designers tell if the resulting system meets its specifications? These questions are very important and very difficult to answer.

Answers to these questions—techniques for design assurance—are available in various intuitive ways. But there are no clear-cut procedures which, if followed, will guarantee a smooth transition from design to implementation for hardware or software. Moreover, it should be remembered that in fact, hardware and software design must often proceed together, further compounding the problem.

In the hardware area, various design assistance programs are available for circuit board layout and simulation of logic designs. Then breadboard (i.e., prototype) hardware layouts can be built and tested in more or less exhaustive ways. Finally, the entire system can be assembled, and again test procedures are available for systematic checkout, but many bugs can slip by these procedures.

In the software area, the situation is no better. Traditionally, a few simple system programs could be designed, written, and debugged by a few expert programmers. Because few people and not much time were involved, little concern was expressed if these programmers used obscure programming tricks to speed up or reduce the size of their programs. As programs grew in size and complexity, more and more programmers had to work together on one project. In a large programming project, quirky programming leads to disasters. When this was recognized, more systematic design and implementation techniques began to appear in the software area—structured programming being a catchall label for a number of techniques. Presently there is a great deal of interest in attempting to prove the correctness of programs or to debug them systematically. In one sense, program debugging is more difficult than logic design debugging because in the latter, logical tests and simulations as well as hardware probes may be used to make tests. Program testing is often inadequate due to failures in considering certain possible combinations of input data. Thus the "essence" of a program may be more elusive than that of a piece of hardware; however, hardware bugs can be quite bizarre too.

In this book we will give some ideas about design assurance, particularly at the interface between hardware and software. An important goal is to allow hardware and software designers to communicate their designs to each other from the beginning to the end of the project. This allows the rational evaluation of design changes on both sides. We will present a few ideas on this subject, but a good deal more thought is necessary in developing good design assurance techniques.

Reliability

The reliability of computer system hardware and software is equally important. Both hardware and software bugs can cause wrong answers and either can go undetected for long periods of time. In fact, when a machine malfunctions, there is often confusion about whether the difficulty is in the hardware or software.

Clearly, this subject is an extension of design assurance as discussed previously, since some system malfunctions were either designed into or built into the system! Other bugs, especially in the hardware, appear after the machine has been operating for a while. Transistors fail, solder joints open, pins and sockets corrode, and so on. Some of these are "hard" failures, but the worst ones are transients which come and go. These intermittent failures are often very hard to locate and indeed difficult to distinguish from obscure software bugs.

Whereas program bugs cannot spontaneously appear in correctly operating programs, such programs can become "incorrect" for another reason. If a number of programs which have complex interactions are used together and a programmer makes a change to fix one program, the fix can cause another program to malfunction. Finding the error can be difficult if the inter-communication paths between the programs are intricate. Such programs must be classed as unreliable because they were poorly designed in the first place.

Hardware reliability can be studied from a number of viewpoints. Statistics and probability can be used to estimate system reliability in terms of component characteristics. Coding theory can be used to design error-detecting and error-correcting codes to enhance system availability by attaching parity bits to all machine words. Logic designers can provide "fail soft" systems with redundant subsystems that allow whole subsystems to fail and be switched off for repair. Careful attention at the time of system design can aid in the writing of programs to detect and locate errors.

Basically, these are all aimed at providing the maximum system reliability or the maximum time of system availability. The important parameters are the mean time between failures and the mean time to repair the system once an error has been detected.

The study of probabilistic reliability theory and of fault tolerant logic design are well-developed subjects. Although they are of obvious importance, they require a good deal of specialized background and for that reason we will largely ignore them in this book. We will superficially discuss some aspects of the reliability problem, but the reader is referred elsewhere for the details of the subject.

1.1.2 Background ideas

Overall, this book does not assume that the reader has any hardware or logic design background. The reader is expected to have an understanding of computer programming and thus some intuition about algorithms and machine organization. In this section we provide some background about hardware and software for readers who may be unfamiliar with them. The points we will discuss here are intended to serve as a glossary of elementary terms which we will use, and in most cases expand, throughout the book. For more information about any of the topics in this section, it is suggested that the reader check the index for later references to the topic in this book, or consult one of the introductory textbooks available. A good source of definitions and brief introduction to many ideas is [RaMe76].

1.1.2.1 Hardware ideas

At the lowest level, we use the term *hardware* to refer to the elementary devices used in computer circuits. In earlier times, relays (in the 1940s) and vacuum tubes (in the 1950s) were used as switching devices and they were interconnected with wires and solder joints. By the early 1960s, transistors were used in computer circuits. Passive components such as resistors and capacitors were also included in these circuits. All of these devices were mounted on some kind of circuit boards, the most complex of which consisted of a number of layers of conductors and insulating material. These provided interconnections between the elementary devices as well as their mechanical support.

By the late 1960s, integrated circuits (ICs) were in use, providing in one silicon chip several transistors, the required resistors and capacitors, as well as interconnection paths. The trend is to place more and more components on one chip. By the mid 1970s, large-scale integrated (LSI) circuit packages (less than 1-inch square) contained several thousand transistors and related components. The actual number of components in one chip depends on the speed of the devices and the regularity of the pattern used to lay them out on the chip. Generally, slower circuits and ones with simple, repetitive geometric patterns can be produced with very high levels of integration.

These packages are interconnected by attaching them to printed circuit boards just as was the case with discrete transistor circuits. One of the design problems for LSI circuits is the mechanical attachment of pins to the LSI packages. Although a package may contain thousands of devices, typically 16 to 32 or at most a few hundred pins can reasonably be attached. In the future these pin numbers may increase, but the gate to pin ratio will probably always be an important measure. IC designers attempt to maximize the gate to pin ratio, while still providing system designers with packages that satisfy their needs. They also attempt to get by with as few different types of packages as possible, thus minimizing their production costs.

TABLE 1.1   Logic Truth Tables and Gates

INPUTS		NOT	AND	NAND	OR	NOR	EXOR
A	B	$\bar{B}$	$A \cdot B$	$\overline{A \cdot B}$	$A+B$	$\overline{(A+B)}$	$A \oplus B$
0	0	1	0	1	0	1	0
0	1	0	0	1	1	0	1
1	0	1	0	1	1	0	1
1	1	0	1	0	1	0	0

NOT   AND   NAND   OR   NOR   EXOR

Regardless of the technology involved, transistor circuits are used to implement a fairly standard set of elementary functions. At the lowest level are logic functions. For example, AND, OR, and NOT functions (see Table 1.1) may be implemented, with each function requiring several components. These are called *gates* and they may appear in many forms. An AND gate may have two or more inputs and its output (the AND of its inputs) may be sent to one or more destinations. The number of inputs allowed in one gate is called the gate's *fan-in* limitation and the number of destinations to which its output may be sent is called its *fan-out* limitation. Real circuits have various fan-in and fan-out limitations which must be observed. A small amount of time is required for electrical signals to pass through a gate; this *gate delay* depends on the type of circuits used, but faster gates usually have lower fan-in and fan-out limitations.

Other logic functions are also used. The exclusive-OR (EXOR) function is also shown in Table 1.1. In practice, NAND and NOR logic is common; Table 1.1 gives truth tables defining it and shows the standard logic gate symbols. These are popular because they are easy to implement in hardware and they are logically complete; that is, any logic function can be implemented solely by making combinations of either of these functions. In the case of the NOR, this was first shown by C. S. Pierce [Chur56], and in the case of the NAND by H. M. Sheffer [Chur56]. In a sense, using only NANDs or NORs simplifies the hardware design as well as the logic design rules because only one kind of device need be considered. For example, by constructing truth tables it is easy to show that (A AND B) = (A NAND B) NAND (A NAND B), whereas (A OR B) = (A NOR B) NOR (A NOR B). A one input NAND or NOR gate serves as a NOT gate and this allows two gate OR and AND implementations.

Given some type of elementary logic functions, computer designers are interested in combining them into more complex circuits. There are two kinds of circuits at the next higher level—combinational logic circuits and sequential logic circuits. A *combinational logic circuit* consists of a network of elementary

Register 1   Register 2

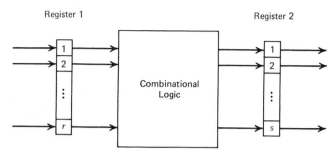

FIGURE 1.1   **Combinational logic.**

logic function devices without any logical feedback loops.[1] In other words, we can imagine a black box which accepts r input bits and produces s output bits, as shown in Fig. 1.1. Assuming the box contains combinational logic, if we trace a path from input to output, we will not encounter the same gate twice because there are no feedback loops. This must be true for each path from each input to each output. Thus we can think of each output as some kind of complicated, multistage fan-in from a number of inputs.

In a real computer, a combinational circuit's inputs must come from somewhere and its outputs must go somewhere. Normally, such sources and sinks are registers. A *register* is a memory device that holds one or more bits until they are changed by new register inputs. A register is made from another kind of logic circuit, generally called a *flip-flop*. There are a number of different kinds of specialized flip-flops, but they all have the property of holding a bit until externally signaled to accept a new input. The two registers of Fig. 1.1 show an input wire to each bit and an output wire from each bit. A register's contents are always available at its outputs; thus, we can regard the inputs to the combinational logic of Fig. 1.1 as originating as the outputs of an r-bit register, and the outputs as going to an s-bit register.

In practice, a combinational circuit may take its inputs from more than one register. For example, an adder could be implemented as a combinational circuit which takes two d-bit numbers as inputs, forms their sum via combinational logic, and delivers the sum as a $d+1$ bit output to another register. The output register of an arithmetic unit is often called an *accumulator*, particularly when it can be fed back and used as a later input.

The driving force of any computer is a *clock*, which is an independently operating device that produces control pulses at regular intervals called the *clock cycle time* or *period*. These pulses are distributed throughout the computer system to *control points* to regulate the flow of information. Clocked logic is sometimes called *synchronous* logic and, although essentially all modern computers are synchronous, certain parts of computers may be *asynchronous*. For

---

[1] Although it is possible to construct combinational circuits that have feedback loops, for practical purposes our definition is adequate.

example, inputs from external devices may come at random times, but as we shall see later, they are assimilated into the system in a synchronous way. Unless we specify otherwise, this book will be concerned with synchronous logic throughout.

Typically, as shown in Fig. 1.2, the output register of one combinational logic circuit is the input register for another. Thus, control points at registers between combinational logic stages regulate the flow of information through the system. When a register is clocked, it accepts a new input which is then held in the register. The contents of the register are available at its outputs, and these signals form the inputs to the next stage of combinational logic. Notice that with a clock and control points, feedback loops in logic circuits cause no problems, whereas without them a feedback loop in a combinational circuit can lead to undefined results, or results that are intricately dependent on various gate and wire delays in the circuit. For example, in Fig. 1.2 register 2 could be connected back to register 1, or register 3 could be connected to register 1 or register 2.

In a real computer, there are a number of registers and combinational logic circuits. Abstractly, it is convenient to lump all of the combinational logic in a system into one box and all of the registers into another box, as shown in Fig. 1.3. Thus the combinational logic makes simple transformations of the data in the registers. The clock pulses allow information to enter the registers and flow through the next stage of combinational logic, and the clock period is determined by the longest time delay around the loop—from the registers back to the registers. Because the data is repeatedly transformed on successive time steps, such a scheme is called a *sequential logic circuit.* This is the second type of circuit mentioned earlier.

We pointed out above that an adder could be implemented as a combinational circuit. What about multiplication? One way of regarding multiplication

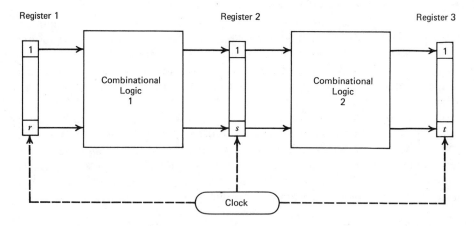

FIGURE 1.2   **Two-stage clocked logic.**

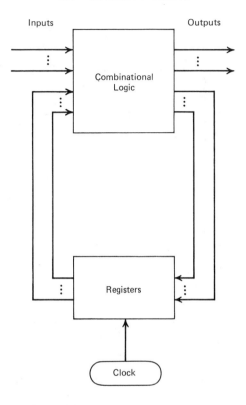

FIGURE 1.3 **Sequential logic circuit.**

is as a sequence of additions. Thus an obvious use of a sequential circuit would be to implement multiplication using an adder. Somehow we would have to feed back the output at each intermediate step and add it to a new input until the entire multiplication was complete. Taken together, combinational logic and sequential logic form the basis of all real computer logic design. We will return to a more detailed study of these two important ideas and their applications.

The box labeled "registers" in Fig. 1.3 is sometimes called the memory of a sequential circuit. Indeed, a register is a memory device. In modern computers, however, the system memory usually contains a much larger number of storage locations than the number of registers associated with the combinational logic of the processor.

In particular, consider the block diagram of Fig. 1.4, which shows three components found in every computer system: the control unit, the processor, and the main memory. Generally speaking, the processor carries out the arithmetic and logical operations of a program. The program and data to be operated on are stored in the main memory. And the control unit, under the

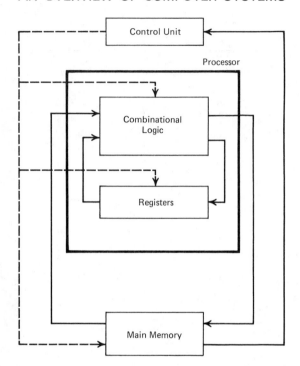

FIGURE 1.4   **Elementary computer model.**

direction of the program, causes the entire system to operate properly. Traditionally, the term *central processing unit* (CPU) has been used to refer loosely to the control unit and processor in order to distinguish the combinational logic parts of a machine from the main memory and other peripheral memory devices.

The system clock is physically located in the control unit as are a number of registers and the combinational logic which handles the decoding of program operations and processing of addresses. The processor is composed of another set of registers together with combinational logic (cf., Fig. 1.4), which carries out arithmetic and logical operations. The memory can be regarded as a very large collection of registers.

The processor in Fig. 1.4 is shown as a sequential circuit of the type displayed abstractly in Fig. 1.3. We pointed out that the clock located in the control unit is used for timing throughout the system. In the abstraction of Fig. 1.3, the control points were associated with the set of registers; however, the more realistic diagram of Fig. 1.4 also shows control lines from the control unit to the combinational logic of the processor. These lines carry decoded instruction signals to control points in the combinational logic. For example, when the clock pulse triggers a register to accept a word of data and thus presents it as an input to the following combinational logic, we may wish to gate that word to one of several destinations, depending on the particular operation being performed. Control points in the combinational logic are used to control the path taken by such words. Other control points may be used to select a destination register for the outputs of the combinational logic. It is also obvious that we sometimes wish to select inputs from memory and sometimes wish to switch outputs to memory rather than processor registers. The above level of abstraction (combinational logic and registers) is often called a *register transfer* level of computer description.

In short, the control points in the processor are the control unit's points of contact with the processor. They allow the control unit to influence the sequence of events carried out in the processor. Other control points in the memory serve a similar role, and still other control points within the control unit allow the control unit to control itself! This is not a circular definition because certain control unit events, for example the clock, are free running, and ultimately the control unit can be controlled from the console switches on the outside of the cabinet by an operator. In Chapter 4, we will discuss more details of this.

This section began with a discussion of technology. The sequence has gone from relays to large-scale integrated circuits between 1945 and 1975. Recently, it has been exciting to observe that the question about what to put on a semiconductor chip can now be answered: Put a computer on a chip. Entire processors of 8-bit or 16-bit words called *microprocessors* are now available in this form. Whereas longer word floating-point arithmetic is not now available in a single chip, it may be some day. Furthermore, microprocessors are usually implemented in slow technologies. But the tradeoff between inexpensive microprocessors and more costly custom-designed LSI is becoming more and more difficult. In those applications where short, fixed point words are sufficient, the choice of microprocessors is an obvious one.

At this point, it is appropriate to point out several standard distinctions made between different sizes and speeds of computers. Traditionally (in the 1950s), there were standard, *general-purpose machines* and *supercomputers*—the biggest, fastest machines available. As time passed, the ideas that proved successful at the supercomputer level trickled down to standard computers of the next "generation."[2] With wider and more diverse use of computers came more specialization in machine size, speed, and function. Presently, a number of different classes of machines can be distinguished, ranging from supercomputers, through standard and *minicomputers*, to the microprocessors of the above paragraph. Minicomputers, an interesting outgrowth of the 1960s, are usually 16-bit word machines with a full set of peripherals that sell for under $50K. Indeed, the advent of minicomputers was in part responsible for forcing

---

[2] Various attempts to define "generations" or "classes" of computers have been popular from time to time, but they are so vague and ill-defined that we will eschew any further discussion of them in this book.

down the prices of a number of I/O devices to make them compatible with memory and CPU prices. Minicomputers have in turn spawned *midicomputers,* which are generally 32-bit machines with more comprehensive I/O facilities than most minis provide, and which are in the price range above minis.

The advent of LSI has had its biggest impact on memory design. Semiconductor memories can be laid out in regular patterns, so high densities are possible. The number of bits per chip has been quadrupling every few years; in the mid-1970s, technology passed through the era of 1K-, 4K-, and 16K-bit memory chips. The cost of semiconductor memories is competitive with traditional magnetic core memories in many cases—particularly, fast main memories. Cores remain competitive for large, slower backup memories. It is interesting to observe that we are returning to a situation where processor and memory technology are of the same type, a situation that has not prevailed since the early 1940s, when relays were used everywhere.

The main system memory is usually organized as a large number of words, any of which can be accessed in some fixed time. This ability to access any word in a memory in a constant amount of time characterizes *random access memories* or RAMs. Other memories have the property that the time required to access a particular word depends on the location in which the word is stored. Magnetic tape drives require moving the tape to the desired position, for example, and rotating magnetic drums and disks require at least the rotation time of the drive motor to access some words. Such devices are slower than random access memories and are referred to as *sequential access memories* (SAMs). Because random access memories are faster and more expensive per bit than sequential access memories, most modern computer systems have a random access main memory and a sequential access secondary memory. Such a *memory hierarchy* allows the storage of larger quantities of information at low cost although in a less accessible way on secondary memory devices.

Figure 1.5*a* shows the general organization of a random access memory. The address of a word to be accessed (α here) is loaded by the control unit into the memory address register. If the access is a fetch, the memory is cycled[3] and the contents of the addressed location are read and placed in the memory information register. If the access is a store, the word to be stored is first loaded into the memory information register (MIR), the memory is cycled, and the word in the MIR is written into the addressed location. Words to be stored and fetched are gated between the memory and the processor through the MIR, which is usually physically located in the memory.

A sequential access memory works in a similar way. The main difference is in timing because we may not be able to access the memory immediately, depending on the position of the desired location relative to the access

---

[3] Cycling a memory refers to the process (which varies from one technology to another) of electrically causing the address to be decoded, selecting the addressed location, and reading or writing a word at this location. A fixed time, called a *memory cycle*, is required to carry out this process.

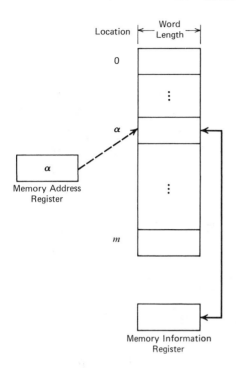

FIGURE 1.5a   **Random access memory.**

mechanism. In Fig. 1.5b, we sketch a sequential access memory which could be implemented as a rotating magnetic disk or drum, or as a *shift register* type memory using magnetic bubbles, charge coupled devices, and so on (see Section 7.3.4).

Basically, the idea is the same in all of these cases. An address placed in a memory address register is decoded in several stages. First, one of several separate units is selected. The data stored in these units are constantly rotating, passing the read/write heads periodically. One track in the selected unit is chosen next. In some disks, the heads must be moved to access the proper track. In other disks and shift registers, each track has its own head. After the head is properly positioned (if necessary), we must wait for the correct word to pass the head. When it does, we read or write it using the memory information register to hold the data. Whereas random access memories can be accessed in a few hundred nanoseconds, shift register sequential access memories require a few hundred microseconds and on the average rotating disks or drums require a few tens of milliseconds. Because the access time is so long, it is normal to read or write a large block of contiguous words in one transmission. The costs of these devices also cover a range of values, which make each attractive in different applications. More details about sequential access memories will be given in Chapter 7.

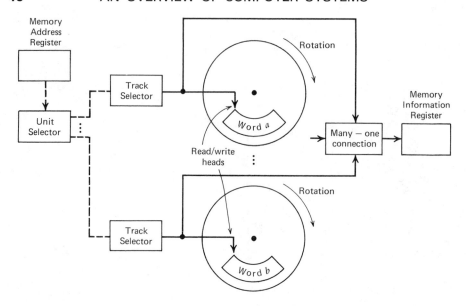

FIGURE 1.5b   Sequential access memory.

The number of bits used in a computer word varies with the applications for which the machine is intended. Word lengths usually range from 8 bits to 64 bits in real machines,[4] although occasionally an even larger word is used. Sometimes a memory is provided with facilities to address half words or bytes as well as full words. Often this is done by providing logic for gating parts of the memory information register (Fig. 1.5) to processor registers for use. Most machines must handle alphanumeric characters which are represented with a 6- to 8-bit byte. This leads to word lengths of 1 to 10 characters in most machines. Real computers use several representations for numbers; we will discuss the details of this in Chapter 3.

The memory devices discussed above share two important properties; they are accessed by specifying (1) an address and (2) whether to read or write the location addressed. There are useful memories which work differently in each of these respects. Some memories can be written once and then read repeatedly. They are called *read-only memories* or ROMs and are useful in various ways in computer systems. The idea is that a designer writes the ROM as desired and then users may read this information. A ROM is often cheaper than a read/write memory and usually is faster. The simplest form of ROM is

---

[4] In the past, 1-bit processors were sometimes used to operate on longer words one bit at a time (bit serially), and in fact some current machines (e.g., STARAN IV, see Section 1.2.1.6) contain a number of bit serial processors operating in parallel. Bit serial microprocessors may also be useful in low-speed applications.

the traditional punched card. Once a programmer punches the card, it can be read repeatedly but it cannot (except with great difficulty) be changed. High-speed ROMs are made from various semiconductor devices—some of those (read-mostly memories) can be read quickly but rewritten very slowly by some special procedure.

ROMs can be used in various ways in computer systems. For example, a fixed program can be stored in a ROM and accessed quickly. Also, tables can be stored in ROMs; for example, numerical values to begin iterative computations of special functions can be so stored. A very interesting application of ROM-type memories is that they can sometimes be used in place of combinational logic. For example, to perform addition we can use combinational logic which transforms the arguments to get their sum, or we can use the arguments as a ROM address and simply look up the answer. Of course, this is impractical for adding long words, but it is practical for short words. Indeed, multiplication algorithms may use a mixture of combinational logic and ROM lookup (see Section 3.4.3). ROMs which users can program, called PROMs (programmable ROMs), as well as PLAs (programmable logic arrays), are quite popular in this respect.

We can observe ROMs and RAMs serving in two very different roles in computer system design; one is the more traditional memory subsystem role (e.g., to store programs or data) and the other is as a logic component. The latter role has been made possible by the introduction of integrated circuit chips; we gave several examples above and will give others in Chapter 3. Traditionally, a combinational circuit element might have been an AND or OR gate, but now it may be a complex integrated circuit or a ROM (or PROM, or PLA) chip. Similarly, flip-flops traditionally were used to introduce time delays in sequential circuits via their role as memory elements. Now, whole arrays of flip-flops in one integrated circuit serve as RAM components or other types of register components. The static nature of ROMs and the time-varying nature of RAMs are brought into focus by the above analogies with combinational and sequential logic circuits, respectively.

Another useful type of memory is one that is accessed not by specifying an address but by specifying part of the contents of the word desired. Suppose we want to fetch all words in a memory whose first bit is a 1 or whose first character represents a T. Such access is provided by a *content addressable memory* (CAM) or *associative memory*—either name may be used. Such memories take different physical forms but they are usually read/write memories which are somewhat more expensive than a RAM (see Section 5.4.2.3). Furthermore, provision must be made for the fact that many memory locations may respond to a single request—imagine requesting the telephone numbers of everyone whose last name is Smith! Later we will see several interesting and important uses for associative memories in the design of computer systems. Associative memories are too expensive to use as the main memory except in special-purpose machines.

The speeds of various parts of computers are expressed in terms of bandwidth. By *bandwidth* we will mean the number of bits per second passing some point in a system. Generally, we will refer to the maximum possible bandwidth of some part of the system; on other occasions we will discuss averages.

1.1.2.2   Software ideas

Now we turn to some basic software ideas which will be assumed throughout the text. At the lowest level, programming a computer and designing its logical organization are the same thing. Indeed it is essential that certain fundamental software and hardware ideas be formulated hand in hand. If care is not taken, the machine may perform incorrectly or it may be very difficult to use. The decisions made at this level can be reflected throughout the machine.

Computer "languages" exist at a number of distinct levels. The lowest level language consists of the signals that cause the control points to take various actions. These signals are contained in *control words* issued by the control unit. Each control word contains bits for all control points in the machine. The clock signals can also be regarded as part of this lowest level machine language.

At the next higher language level are the assembled and loaded instructions. These are arranged in some instruction format that usually contains an operation code field and an address field, as well as several other possible fields. The control unit processes these instructions—one after the other—by separating the address and operation code and then taking appropriate actions. The address is used to access memory for data or as a location from which to fetch the next instruction in case of a jump. The operation code is decoded and causes one or a sequence of control words to be issued. These control words cause the specified operation to be carried out in the memory, processor, and possibly the control unit.

The assembled and loaded instructions referred to above originate in a user program. Users may write assembly language programs, which are quite close to the operation code/address format discussed above, or they may write in a higher-level language which is oriented toward the applications area for which they are using the machine. Popular languages include FORTRAN, ALGOL, and APL which are oriented mainly toward scientific algorithms; COBOL which is oriented toward business applications; PL/I which is a combination of these; and many other languages. Regardless of the language used, the programs produced by the user are *translated* (assembly language is *assembled*, higher-level languages are *compiled*) into the operation code/address format by system programs. Then, when the user's program is to be executed, it is *loaded* into the machine and *linked* to other programs by system programs.

Another option here is to leave the program in some kind of high-level language format, or translate it from a high-level to an intermediate-level language. In any case, the resulting program is not in machine language. This program is loaded and linked and then executed by *interpretation.* An interpreter may be a program which does the final stage of decoding and then causes machine language instructions to be executed. Or an interpreter may be a combination of hardware and software which does this final translation. The latter approach may be carried out in machines with microprogrammed control units (see Section 4.2.2). In any case, interpreters allow additional flexibility in the use of programming languages.

Thus an individual program can be observed at a sequence of key points in time. These are *translation time* (when the program is compiled or assembled), *load time* (when the program is linked to others and loaded into memory), and *execution* or *run time* (when the control unit decodes and executes each instruction). It is often important to observe the earliest time at which the value of some parameter is known or the latest time at which it may be specified. If specified by the programmer when the program is written, it is known at translation time. If specified by the user when the program is to be run, it is known at load time. If computed by the program, it is known only at execution time.

As examples of the above consider the following. Most programming languages include executable statements which are translated and later decoded and executed, as well as nonexecutable declaration statements which direct the translator in its work. Thus, a statement like DECLARE X (10,50) will cause a compiler to allocate 500 memory locations for the array X. This is easy for the compiler to do, but it means the space may be idle a good deal of the time while the user's program is in main memory.

A run time approach to this, which usually ties up memory for less time, is to allocate the space only when a block of code that uses it is active. Thus the program segment

> READ(M,N)
> BEGIN PROC
> DECLARE X(M,N)
> .
>
> .
>
> .

will at run time set M and N and then enter a block of code (or call a procedure) called PROC. Now, a run time system procedure that carries out dynamic storage allocation can be invoked to set up X as a 10 by 50 array. Later, when PROC is exited, the X array will disappear, so the memory space is released. Load time procedures using control cards to declare array sizes can be implemented in ways similar to the above.

There are a number of ways in which hardware and software interact with respect to program translation, linking, and loading. For example, when programs are translated for a relatively simple machine, the translator can be relatively simple. Suppose that more registers are added to a processor. Then the translator must do more work to allocate the registers properly (if not optimally) for the storage of intermediate results; this saves memory accesses and speeds up the program execution. Next, suppose that more hardware is designed which can make run time decisions about register allocation. This would allow certain translator decisions to be eliminated, thus speeding up program translation. The history of computer system design is full of such cycles in which complexity and speedup pass back and forth from hardware to software.

In almost all real computations, a number of programs must be linked together for each user at load time. If the user has a relatively long program, good programming style will force him or her to write it as several separate procedures, that is, as a main program and several logically separate subroutines called by the main program and each other. Moreover, users may require system-supplied procedures for special computations to be linked to their own programs.

Traditionally, computers executed one program at a time under the supervision of an *operating system* (OS) program which causes a user's programs to be translated, linked, and loaded. Then it allows the program to compute, perhaps for a maximum time specified by the user or until it halts naturally. During execution, the operating system aids the user in executing input and output operations. In particular, system programs which deal with specific input and output devices remove from the user the burden of understanding the details of various devices. These traditional operating system functions have become much more elaborate as computer system organizations have become more elaborate and as the services provided to users have become more diverse. Several of these extensions will be outlined now and expanded later.

Even though just one user at a time was being run, the notion of multiprogramming arose through such uses of operating systems. There are two main reasons for *multiprogramming:* first is the desire to carry out computation and I/O operations simultaneously, and second is the desire to provide quick response to users. In multiprogramming the main memory is shared by several jobs; the processor runs one for awhile, and when it stops to do I/O, for example, the processor switches to the next job, then the first, then another, and so on, overlapping the processing of small jobs with I/O for a large job. Thus, an attempt is made to exploit a fixed hardware configuration by sharing the memory. Although some time is lost due to overhead, any time saved is passed on to the users. Even better user response can be achieved by processor time-sharing (in addition to memory sharing), which we will discuss shortly. In early multiprogrammed machines, the operating system would initiate tasks of its own, interspersed with a user's programs. Whether or not these tasks were servicing the user, they could be regarded as independent of the user because they were not linked to him or her and were loaded into different areas of memory.

A number of software and hardware problems had to be solved to allow several independent programs to be commingled in this way; we shall discuss these matters in more detail later. For the moment we want to emphasize that once certain elementary multiprogramming ideas were worked out, the sharing of a single computer by several distinct users became possible. This caused some new hardware and software problems, but the basic idea remains the same.

Another way of sharing main memory, as well as the memory hierarchy (together these amount to more than half the cost of most systems), is to build a multiprocessor organization. In a *multiprocessor computer*, several processor-control unit pairs are attached to the same main memory. Separate programs can be run in the individual processors, and they may be derived from the operating system and one or more users (see Sections 1.2.1 and 1.2.2). When viewed at the system level, a multiprocessor computer is also a multi-programmed computer. As we will see in Section 1.2.1, there are a number of other approaches to speeding up computations by architectural changes which allow processors to perform several operations at once, without changing the memory configuration substantially. Several criteria for evaluating multi-processor or multiprogrammed machines will be discussed in Section 1.2.1.2.

Clearly, the operating system of a multiprogrammed computer is more complex than that for a monoprogrammed computer, but it is not difficult to imagine extending a multiprogrammed system to a time-shared system as follows. In a *time-shared computer* system, each of several users is given short, fixed length bursts of processor time in rapid succession. Thus, in addition to sharing the memory as in the multiprogrammed case, the users are also now time-sharing the processor in short intervals, which allows very fast responses to users sitting at keyboard/display terminals attached to the computer. To contrast them with time-sharing systems, traditional operating systems are called *batch processing* systems, either in the monoprogrammed or multi-programmed case.[5]

Now if the users have relatively simple computational tasks, or larger tasks that can be broken up into a sequence of smaller ones, a time-shared system can provide an important class of new services. If a number of user terminals (keyboard/display devices of some kind) are attached to a time-shared compu-ter, those who sit at the terminals can use the machine as if it were working only for them. For example, they can type in programs, attempt to have them compiled, and get compilation errors displayed immediately. Then they can edit their programs, recompile, and so forth. When the program is compiled without error, it can be executed and the results can be displayed while the user watches.

Such users of a computer system are said to be *online* users in contrast to batch processing users who are designated *offline* users. Since the computer and its online users communicate back and forth in an immediate way, such systems are often called *interactive systems*, particularly when software is available which makes communication easy.

---

[5] The terminology we are discussing here is rather loosely defined, but widely used, although it may vary from one manufacturer or set of users to another.

Computer systems that respond quickly to the outside world are also called *real-time systems*. Interactive systems are real-time systems. Other real-time systems may be connected to various kinds of physical devices such as laboratory equipment, industrial processes, and so on, and are called real-time *process control systems*.

Of course, time-sharing cannot be effective among a number of users with heavy computational loads, because each such user may need the whole machine. Operating systems often run small users in a time-shared (or foreground) way and service big users in a batch (or background) processing way by allowing the big jobs computation bursts from time to time, mixed with the small jobs. Thus some users can be served in real-time, whereas others receive slower service.

The systems we have mentioned involve various overheads. In most cases, additional hardware features are required. In all cases, various kinds of special software are necessary. Often, very elaborate operating systems must be written to provide these services.

One hardware consequence of any memory sharing between several users is that more main memory is required. Although the originally stated motivation for multiprogramming was to make better use of a fixed hardware configuration, the full development of such systems has led to much more elaborate memory hierarchies than were previously needed.

An important idea in this respect is what has come to be called *virtual memory*. Here the idea is to allow users to imagine that a very large virtual memory is available to them. The hardware and software systems maintain mappings between the realities of physical memory and the users' abstract notion of virtual memory. Roughly speaking, the method used is to break up physical and virtual memory into a set of small *pages*. At any instant of time, the contents of main memory hardware pages may be any set of program and data pages from any active users' jobs. None of the users has any idea of where his or her pages are in physical memory—only the system knows. When a user's job tries to access a page of virtual memory which is not in the hardware main memory, a *page fault* occurs. The system then corrects the page fault by fetching the needed page from secondary memory, replaces some page of main memory with this one, and continues to execute the user who generated the fault. During the time required to correct the page fault, other jobs can be run in a time-shared way.

We have mentioned several circumstances in which it might be useful to bring telephone lines into the computer system picture. For example, time-sharing user terminals could be located anywhere, given that some kind of data communication link to a computer existed. Telephone lines, microwave towers, and satellite communication systems all have been used for this purpose. The only real problem here is having a sufficiently high bandwidth for transmission. But, because most terminals are rather slow devices—as are most human terminal users—the available speeds often serve quite nicely. Thus, airline reservation systems, commercial time-sharing systems, information retrieval systems, and so on, all use such *remote computing* facilities.

Examples of remote computing that use a process control machine at some distance from the process are easy to imagine. For example, oil pipeline control stations spread out over hundreds of miles can all be coordinated by a central machine. Ground control of missiles or satellites is another obvious example.

If terminals can be remote from a central computer, it is clear that multiple computer systems could also be geographically distributed. Computer *networks* are collections of computers and users interconnected by a (telephone or other) communication system. Networks can be quite useful in several ways. One obvious use is in a large company with several offices in different cities. They could share data bases and programs via a network. Such schemes have been used in many companies. The ARPA Network is used by a number of universities and government agencies with Defense Department affiliations. In Tokyo, in the early 1970s some 60 banks were interconnected for the instantaneous transfer of funds.

In the case of computer networks, data transmission rates become more critical than with remote terminal users. In order to achieve sufficiently high bandwidths, multiple leased telephone lines or microwave transmission systems are often used.

Other problems in computer networks involve their operation and management. Since a number of different types of machines may be involved, some kind of standard network interface is required. Also, some kind of network operating system must ensure that messages are routed to their destinations properly, perhaps in spite of certain network nodes being temporarily down or busy.

One happy consequence of networks and remote terminals is the reduction of computer costs. If a local computer center is providing services at a higher rate than one some distance away, users now have the option of dialing the distant computer. Although some users may find concomitant inconveniences in using the remote system, many users find it best to use the cheapest, fastest computer available. This has led to the spawning of various commercial time-sharing services, some of which are brokers of excess computer capacity in various large centers. In a sense, we are approaching the use of computing facilities as a public utility. As with electrical power, excess supplies of local computing capacity can be sold in other areas via computer networks.

1.2 COMPUTER SYSTEM PRINCIPLES

Here we will look a bit more closely at some of the ideas of the previous section. In Section 1.2.1, we will survey a number of types of computer organizations. We will see how a simple program can be executed on each of them at faster and faster speeds. The entire range of current machines will be spanned by this discussion. We will also consider compiling programs for various types of machines. High processing speeds as well as efficient memory hierarchy management questions will be discussed.

We turn to some philosophical computer system design points in Section 1.2.2. How do machine design, compiler design, and program design fit together? We discuss several aspects of the present state of the art and suggest future possibilities.

1.2.1 Machine organization and computation structure survey

This section contains a brief introduction to most types of system organizations found in current computers. We begin by discussing traditional uniprocessor machines; this is followed by a survey of more complex machines, from multiprocessors and multifunction processors through pipeline and parallel machines. In each case, we will present the machine's structure and describe one or two computations running on the system.

The emphasis in this section is on speedup of processing through architectural changes. Aspects of memory organization are mentioned, but only in a subordinate way. We assume that the memory and control unit are well designed and always keep the processors supplied with work. Further discussion of processors can be found in Chapter 3, of control units in Chapter 4, and of main memories in Chapter 5.

In this section we will provide a number of references to books and papers that describe various machines in more detail. Two books which contain reprints and discussions of a number of real computer systems are [BeNe71] and [Ens174]. We will give references to original sources as well as books for the reader's convenience in finding reprinted papers.

1.2.1.1 Uniprocessor computation

The basic computer system of Fig. 1.6 is shown for historical completeness and to introduce our notation. Solid lines indicate data flow, whereas broken lines indicate control flow. Arrows indicate the direction of flow. We will not explain exactly what "data flow" and "control flow" mean at this point, but the general idea should be clear from the following discussion.

In Fig. 1.6, instructions are fetched via the solid line from memory to control unit. The control unit has various wires connected to control points in all parts of the machine to effect changes of state in the machine. In other words, the control unit causes data and instructions to flow through the machine. For example, it can command a card reader to read a card, and receive a reply when the task is complete, via the line to the input box. Similarly, it can cause a card to be punched in the output box.

Furthermore, the control unit sequences the events in the memory and processor. For example, consider the source language statement $X \leftarrow A + B$

which assigns to X the sum of A and B. This might be compiled as:

Opcode	Argument
FETCH	A
ADD	B
STORE	X

These three assembly language statements[6] would, of course, appear in the machine's memory as a sequence of bits in some standard format (see Chapter 4 for a discussion of instruction formats). In executing these three statements, the control unit first causes the fetch of A from memory to the processor. Then B is fetched and added to A, and finally the result is stored in X. Implicit in this is the fact that the control unit is continuously keeping itself supplied with instructions by fetching them from the memory whenever necessary.

There are a number of shortcomings in a machine organized along the lines of Fig. 1.6. For one thing, the control unit is kept busy managing the entire system; for another, the processor is involved in all *input and output* (I/O) activities. Also, the memory size may be constrained by cost to be too small for some computations. Figure 1.7 represents an enhanced machine organization which avoids these shortcomings.

Figure 1.7 shows a secondary memory device, which is usually a rotating magnetic disk or drum. This allows much more data and program storage in an "online" way. In other words, we need not enter information via slow input devices each time we use the computer. We can simply keep it stored in files in secondary memory.

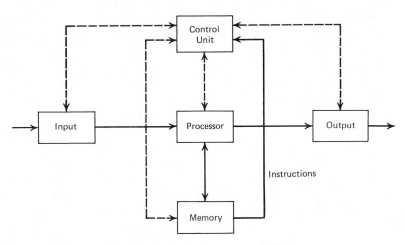

FIGURE 1.6   **Basic computer.**

---

[6] Here and elsewhere in this book we will introduce computer instructions informally. For more details of real instruction sets, see any manufacturer's manual or [Katz71], [Thor70], or [DECo71a] for typical sets.

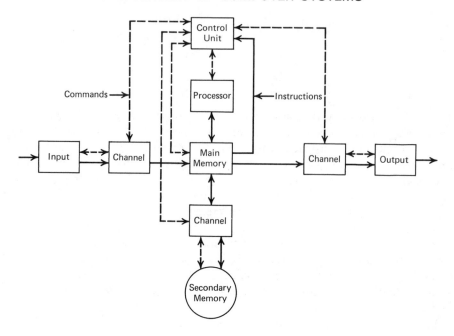

FIGURE 1.7   **Uniprocessor system.**

We have, in Fig. 1.7, also changed the I/O device connections to access main memory in a direct way. This allows the processor to compute at the same time I/O and secondary memory activities occur. Such "overlap" as this is a key idea in designing faster computer structures, and we shall see other examples of it shortly.

Finally, we have introduced channels between main memory and the slower units with which it must communicate; the main memory is still directly connected to the fast processor and control unit. The point of this is that the control unit can give commands to the channels and then forget them until they complete their tasks. Meanwhile, the control unit can devote its attention to the main memory and processor. Thus, a channel is a kind of auxiliary control unit which is assigned a task by the main control unit. It can be quite simple because it is dealing with devices that are much slower than the processor and main memory. When a channel transaction (e.g., input or output of a file) is completed, the channel informs the control unit which then decides what to do next.

We will refer to the main memory, secondary memory, and certain I/O devices collectively as a *memory hierarchy.* Note that the secondary memory can be used to hold files that back up a computation in progress, or it can be used to hold files between one run and the next. If runs are infrequent, magnetic tape, for example, can be used as an output and input medium. Thus tape provides a longer-term, slower storage medium in the memory hierarchy than do disks or drums. Magnetic tape can be regarded as an I/O medium which is part of the memory hierarchy.

There is another difficulty which we have not mentioned in Figs. 1.6 and 1.7. While the required control unit speed was decreased by moving from the system of Fig. 1.6 to that of Fig. 1.7, what about the main memory speed? In fact, what about the balance of processor and main memory speeds in Fig. 1.6, *before* the memory hierarchy demands were made on the main memory? The statement executed earlier, $X \leftarrow A + B$, is simple, but fairly typical of the statements found in many numerical programs. While the processor performs one addition, we must fetch two operands from memory and store a result as well as fetch the instruction (or several instructions in assembly language). Thus the total number of words per second demanded of the memory may be substantially higher than the processor data rate measured in operations per second. And we have not mentioned the added bandwidth required by the memory hierarchy for I/O.

The typical solution to this problem in well-designed, high-speed computers, is to use a memory with a total bandwidth matched to the sum of the bandwidths of the processor, control unit, and I/O devices. One way to do this is to buy one memory unit with a very high bandwidth, but this could be quite expensive, or it could be impossible if the machine is very fast. If, for one reason or another, such a fast memory unit is not a feasible choice, an alternative is to operate several slower memory units in parallel. For example, in the statement $X \leftarrow A + B$, if A and B are stored in two distinct memory units, we can fetch them simultaneously and effectively double the memory bandwidth over a single memory unit. The use of parallel memory units in a main memory is quite common, and we shall assume such a memory is used whenever needed. In Section 2.5 more details about balancing the bandwidths of various parts of the system will be discussed, and Chapter 5 will give more details about fast memory systems.

Many real programs deal with arrays of data. This is true of a commercial program updating a file or sorting a file, as well as a numerical program inverting a matrix or doing numerical weather prediction. The fundamental characteristic shared by such programs is a statement defining an iterative calculation over a sequence of subscripted statements. For example, in a FORTRAN-like language

$$\text{DO} \quad S_1 \quad I \leftarrow 1, \ 100$$
$$S_1 \qquad X(I) \leftarrow A(I) + B(I)$$

defines a sequence of 100 scalar additions.

All modern computers contain special indexing hardware which allows easy indexing through arrays and also permits accounting for loop iterations. Instructions are provided that set and test index registers, and which use these registers to modify addresses before they are used for memory access. The index registers and index arithmetic unit can be regarded as part of the control unit. Although we will not illustrate this in our figures, indexing hardware plays a key role in high-speed computation, and extensions of this idea will be discussed as we consider more complex machine organizations.

Before leaving the traditional machines of Figs. 1.6 and 1.7, we will briefly consider the compilation and execution of a simple program for such machines. The following program computes the inner product of vectors A and B of dimension N, and assigns the scalar result to T:

Prog. 1

$$T \leftarrow 0$$
$$DO \ S_1 \ I \leftarrow 1, N$$
$$S_1 \qquad T \leftarrow T + A(I) * B(I)$$

This might be compiled for a computer of the type shown in Figs. 1.6 or 1.7 as follows:

Prog. 2

Address	Opcode	Args	Comments
	STOZ	T	Store zero in T
	SETX	I,0	Set XR(I) to zero
LOOP	TESTX	I,N,OUT	Add 1 to XR(I); if $C(XR(I)) \leq N$ continue,[7] else go to OUT
	FETCH	A(I)	A(I) from memory to register
	MPY	B(I)	Fetch B(I); multiply A(I) and B(I)
	ADD	T	Add T to $A(I) * B(I)$
	STORE	T	Store result in T
	JUMP	LOOP	Jump to LOOP
OUT	·		
	·		
	·		

In terms of this simple program, some insight can be gained about the relationship between control unit, memory, and processor in various machine organizations. Figure 1.8 shows a time sequence of events in executing this program on a very simple computer. We assume that each memory, processor, and control unit operation takes a single time unit. Notice that the execution of each instruction begins with the fetch from memory of the instruction itself and is followed by a step in which the control unit examines the instruction. At this point the control unit may cause memory activity, for example, a store of zero

[7] We use C(X) to denote the contents of X.

Step	Instruction Fetch	Control Unit	Data Fetch	Processor	Data Store
1	STOZ T				
2		STOZ T			
3					T
4	SETX I,0				
5		SETX I,0			
6	TESTX I,N,OUT				
7		TESTX I,N,OUT			
8	FETCH A(I)				
9		FETCH A(I)			
10			A(1)		
11	MPY B(I)				
12		MPY B(I)			
13			B(1)		
14				A(1)*B(1)	
15	ADD T				
16		ADD T			
17			T		
18				(A(1)*B(1))+T	
19	STORE T				
20		STORE T			
21					T
22	JUMP LOOP				
23		JUMP LOOP			
24	TESTX I,N,OUT				
25		TESTX I,N,OUT			

Inner Loop (steps 6–23)

FIGURE 1.8   Nonoverlapped system.

for the STOZ instruction on step 3, or the fetch of A(1) for the FETCH A(I) instruction on step 10. Alternatively, at the end of the control unit step, the control unit may have finished the execution of the instruction, for example, setting XR(I) to zero on step 5, testing an index register, and performing a conditional jump on step 7 or executing an unconditional jump on step 23. More complex instructions require a control unit cycle, followed by a memory fetch, followed by a processor operation, for example, the MPY B(I) on steps 12, 13, and 14, or the ADD T on steps 16, 17, and 18.

It is important to note that each instruction's execution begins with an instruction fetch and control unit cycle. During the control unit cycle, the control unit decodes the instruction to determine what steps must be taken in its execution, and if the execution can be carried out within the control unit itself, this is done at once. Then the control unit proceeds to sequence the memory and processor in their performance of steps necessary to execute the instruction.

Now, consider the time necessary to execute this program. In Fig. 1.8 the inner loop may be seen to run from step 6 to step 23; thus it consumes 18 steps. We have been assuming that each step required the same amount of time, but in real machines this may not be so. For example, multiplication may be slower than addition, or a memory access may require more time than an addition. But to avoid complicating matters at this point, we will continue to make the relatively realistic assumption that each step does indeed correspond to the same unit of time.

Another important timing consideration is the *overlap* or parallel execution of some of the steps. For example, in step 2 of Fig. 1.8 the memory is idle and we could be fetching the next instruction. This would eliminate step 4, overlapping it with step 2. It is common practice in many real machines to operate in some kind of overlapped way. This tends to make the machine more complex, but in modest doses such overlap can be an inexpensive machine speedup technique.

In Fig. 1.9, we redo the diagram of Fig. 1.8 for Prog. 2, again assuming that each step corresponds to one time unit, but now we overlap the memory, control unit, and processor operations. We even allow several memory accesses at once—a realistic use of parallel memory units—with an instruction fetch and

	Step	Instruction Fetch	Control Unit	Data Fetch	Processor	Data Store
	1	STOZ T				
	2	SETX I,0	STOZ T			
	3	TESTX I,N,OUT	SETX I,0			T
	4	FETCH A(I)	TESTX I,N,OUT			
Inner Loop	5	MPY B(I)	FETCH A(I)			
	6	ADD T	MPY B(I)	A(1)		
	7	STORE T	ADD T	B(1)		
	8	JUMP LOOP	STORE T	T	A(1)*B(1)	
	9		JUMP LOOP		(A(1)*B(1))+T	
	10	TESTX I,N,OUT				T
	11	FETCH A(I)	TESTX I,N,OUT			
	12		FETCH A(I)			
	13			A(2)		

FIGURE 1.9   **Control unit, memory, processor overlap.**

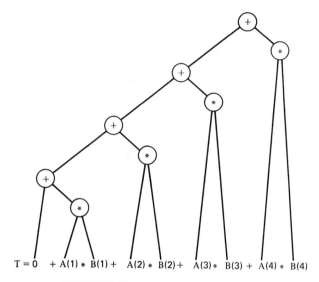

T = 0   + A(1) * B(1) +   A(2) * B(2) +   A(3) * B(3) + A(4) * B(4)

FIGURE 1.10   Serial inner product.

data store on step 3, an instruction fetch and data fetch on step 6, and so on.
Note that the inner loop now runs from step 3 to step 9, so its length is 7 steps.
This represents a speedup of $\frac{18}{7} > 2.5$ over the nonoverlapped machine of Fig.
1.8.

Recall, however, that there are only two arithmetic operations in the original
inner product loop of Prog. 1—a multiplication and an addition. Thus, the
seven steps we are using to perform the two required arithmetic steps may still
seem wasteful. This is reflected in the large amount of blank space in the
processor column of Figs. 1.8 and 1.9. It will be shown later that other overlap
techniques could be used to squeeze the seven steps closer to the two really
needed for arithmetic.

The execution time of Prog. 1 can be estimated in terms of a parse tree, as
shown in Fig. 1.10, which reflects the assumptions outlined above and shows
that a serial computation of Prog. 1 requires $T_1 = 2N$ steps. We will return to
this same program later and see how its execution can be speeded up using
more complex machine organizations. In real machines, actual computation
times are often proportional to the total number of arithmetic operations in
programs that have a significant amount of arithmetic. On the other hand, for
programs with little arithmetic, the computation time may be proportional to
the number of memory accesses or the number of I/O transmissions. Later we
shall discuss these points in more detail.

The ideas discussed to this point are far from new. In one form or another,
machines that developed these principles were built before 1960. Indeed, most
of these ideas were known to Babbage in the first half of the nineteenth
century, as we shall see in Section 1.3. Most manufacturers build machines

along these lines, or with more advanced features to be discussed in subsequent sections.

Typical of today's uniprocessors are the Digital Equipment Corporation's PDP/11 family [StSi75] or the IBM System/370 [Katz71]. The IBM System/360 was the predecessor to the System/370 and each represents a family of machines ranging from very small to very large computers. They are all compatible in the sense that they execute one instruction set. The PDP/11 family consists of a number of computers that cover the range of mini-computers. Throughout the book we will refer to various models of the System/360/370 as well as the PDP/11, since these are widely used machines. It should be pointed out that, for example, mentioning the "IBM 360" usually means all models and also includes the System/370 since there are so few architectural differences [CaPa78]. When an important difference exists we will make that explicit. The original descriptions of the IBM System/360 are found in [IBMS64] and [IBMJ64]. A candid, retrospective discussion of the PDP-11, including its design, flaws, and evolution is presented in [BeSt76].

1.2.1.2 Multioperation computation

The two types of systems presented thus far have had a single processor and a single control unit. We have discussed ways of balancing systems in terms of bandwidth, that is, the number of bits per second generated or consumed by a particular element (e.g., processor, memory). But what about increasing the overall system bandwidth? How can we make a faster computer? Basically there are two approaches; one is to use faster components (switching devices, memory elements, etc.), the other is to use a different machine organization.

For the moment, assume that faster components are not available to us— they may be too expensive, or our system may already be using the fastest components manufactured. So we turn to other machine organizations. The obvious way to improve the speed of a single processor which carries out one operation at a time is to execute more than one operation at a time. There are many ways to organize such a machine. The following is an outline of a few of the most commonly used approaches to this design problem, which emerged in the 1960s and 1970s.

Although there is no generally accepted name for all such machines, we have adopted the term *multioperation computer* to refer to them all. Each of the machines discussed in the following sections shares the characteristic of being able to execute more than one operation at once. However, the machines vary widely in how these operations are specified (by the user, the compiler, or control hardware) and how they are carried out.

First, we should clarify what we mean by a "faster computer." To a computer center manager, a faster computer is probably one which allows more jobs per day to be processed through the computer center, whereas to a user, a faster computer is usually one which returns the answer more quickly.

These two notions, *throughput* and *turnaround time*, are indeed two commonly used measures of a computer's processing speed. Although they share some common points, they may call for different speedup techniques.

A simple way to increase throughput is to install two complete computers. In theory, two machines can handle twice as many jobs per day as one machine. But for individual users, the absolute execution time of a single job is not speeded up by this approach. However, user queue lengths may be reduced so the turnaround time may drop for some users.

In principle, one way to decrease turnaround time would be to install a single computer capable of simultaneously executing more than one instruction for a user. This may speed up each user's job, although some programs may not be able to take advantage of the multi-instruction execution feature. But, in general, turnaround time will be decreased and throughput will be increased this way.

Another important point that we should emphasize here is the cost of I/O equipment and a memory hierarchy. The cost of this part of a machine such as the one in Fig. 1.7 represents more than half of the equipment investment. Hence, it is desirable to share these costs among several processors.

The great appeal of a single faster computer which could increase throughput, decrease turnaround time, and also share a memory hierarchy and I/O equipment has indeed led to a number of diverse machine designs. Now we shall sketch several typical organizations which were motivated by these ideas, after giving several definitions.

For each of the machine organizations considered, we will assume that the given computer can perform $p \geq 1$ arithmetic operations at once. We denote the time to perform some computation A on this computer as $T_p[A]$, or simply as T_p when no ambiguity can result. The time to perform the computation on a traditional serial machine (uniprocessor) is denoted $T_1[A]$.

The *speedup* of a p operation computer over a uniprocessor is denoted

$$S_p[A] = T_1[A]/T_p[A] \geq 1$$

for algorithm A. The *efficiency* of this computation is defined as

$$E_p[A] = S_p[A]/p \leq 1,$$

and we can interpret this as the actual speedup divided by p, the maximum possible speedup using p simultaneous operations.

1.2.1.3 Multiprocessor computation

The system represented by Fig. 1.11 has p processors, each with its own control unit. Thus each control unit can execute an independent program using its processor and sharing the memory hierarchy. The processors can communicate with each other through the memory (one reads what another wrote) or by some kind of direct path shown as a broken line at the top of the figure.

The main memory box here represents a number of parallel memory units. To meet the bandwidth requirements mentioned earlier, such a system probably has two to three times p memory units in its main memory. When a number of memory units are shared by several processors and I/O devices, the question of conflicts in accessing a particular unit becomes serious.

We show an interconnection network which allows the various units to communicate data and control signals to each other. The details of this network pose a major question in the design of any real computer system. Its speed and cost are obvious matters for concern as are questions of conflicts when, for example, two processors want simultaneous access to secondary memory. Physical implementations of such interconnection networks range over a wide gamut. Note that the units may be "tightly" or "loosely" coupled.[8] For example, there may be two tightly coupled processors working on two subroutines for one user, with all of the equipment dedicated to that one user. At the other extreme, loosely coupled processors could be scattered about in several computer centers, each running independent jobs which share a common data base occasionally.

If we restrict our attention to a tightly coupled system (roughly speaking, something that is contained in one room with one operating system), then there are two major limitations on performance. The first, as mentioned above, is degradation due to conflicts. These include conflicts in accessing main memory, secondary memory, and I/O devices. The second limitation arises in scheduling and synchronizing jobs on the multiple processors. This becomes more acute when attempts are made to run a single job on several processors at once, say, with one subroutine being executed on each processor.

A simple example of the use of a two-processor multiprocessor is the following. Suppose we wanted to multiply two $N \times N$ matrices together. This requires the computation of N^2 inner products. Thus Prog. 1 could be invoked simultaneously in two processors.[9] If a different row-column pair were processed in each processor and each of these pairs was stored in two distinct memories (or sets of memories), then the computation would proceed as if two separate computers were involved. Approximately $N^2/2$ inner product times would be required to multiply the matrices.

Two important questions are raised by the above discussion: How are the simultaneous invocations of the inner product program specified? Special language statements such as FORK and JOIN (see Section 2.4.3) can be used by a programmer to cause two control paths to be followed. Or, we could

---

[8] The terms *tightly coupled* and *loosely coupled* will be used in this book—as they are by computer people generally—without a rigorous definition. They only connote a feeling about a system as should be clear in these paragraphs; thus most multiprocessor systems are more loosely coupled than most parallel processor systems (see Section 1.2.1.6). The amount of synchronization and memory sharing between the processors is often an indication of how tightly coupled they are.

[9] Although most multiprocessors execute distinct users' jobs in distinct processors, we consider the more interesting case of running one computation in several processors.

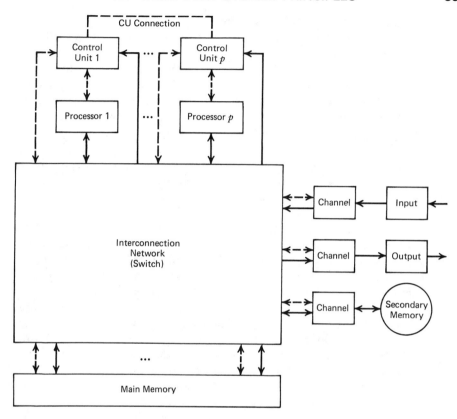

FIGURE 1.11   **Multiprocessor system.**

expect a compiler to discover such parallelism (a subject we will consider in Chapter 2). How are the arrays stored in the memories? Either a programmer or a compiler can decide this, and we will return to this question in Chapter 5.

Because of the various difficulties in utilizing them effectively, most real multiprocessor computers have at most four processors, with two being much more common. Most modern multiprocessors have several identical processors. An early example is the B5000 [BeNe71], the Burroughs D825, followed by the B6700 and B7700 [Ensl74]. Also commercially available are the Univac 1108 and 1110 [Ensl74], the IBM 370/158 and 168 [Ensl74], and the Honeywell (earlier GE and MIT) MULTICS systems [Ens174] designed for time sharing. Up to ten processors are provided in the very specialized Bell Laboratories CLC, a radar signal processing control computer [Bell75]; up to 16 PDP-11's are included in the experimental C.mmp at Carnegie-Mellon University [WuBe72].

Sometimes the processors are not identical, as in the early Pilot project [BeNe71, LeNS59] or an IBM 360/75 with an attached 360/50 for various support computations [Ensl74]. Quite often very large or specialized computers have a simpler, "front end" machine to interface with the outside world.

As another example, the Honeywell 8200 [Hone71] has a standard operation (arithmetic, logic, etc.) word processor for full-length (48-bit) words, and a separate character processor which operates on 8-bit characters, integrated into one CPU. In fact, each of these processors is compatible with a separate line of earlier Honeywell machines, so the 8200 represents an upward compatibility with two quite different earlier architectures. These two processors share a memory hierarchy and, together with an I/O controller, are under the overall control of a master control facility. The master control hardware and software carries out a number of system management functions.

The performance of a multiprocessor varies greatly, depending on the tasks to be run. If all of the tasks are known well ahead of their execution, then degradation may be less severe than if a number of random jobs appear in real time. For a normal mix of jobs, presented randomly, however, one can expect a p processor multiprocessor to exhibit a throughput which is substantially less than p independent computer systems should have. Firm figures are difficult to obtain, but probably a two-processor system could be expected to have a throughput of about 1.5 to 1.7 times a single processor, whereas a four-processor system may have a throughput of about 2.5 times a single processor.

These are figures which are justifiable on cost grounds, however, because memory hierarchies frequently account for more than half of the system cost. Thus, if duplicating the CU and processor and adding a memory unit increased the hardware cost by 50 percent, a performance increase of 1.5 would be justified. A similar argument holds for four processors, which might increase the system cost by 100 percent or even 150 percent.

One of the consequences of having several processors share a memory hierarchy is that the main memory size and cost go up in proportion to the number of processors used. In the above paragraph we mentioned adding one CU, processor, and *memory unit*. The idea is that a little memory added to a relatively big existing main memory will be enough to sustain an added processor. We could not hope to add a processor without adding *any* main memory, in general, but it is reasonable to assume that different processors are handling different sized jobs, and by chance (or by using some scheduling algorithm), some processors can be handling relatively small jobs if one processor has a very big job. Thus, the main memory may not have to grow as fast as the number of processors. On the other hand, as more users must be handled at once, more system software is needed; the users need different compilers, for example, and multiprocessor/multiprogrammed operating systems tend to be much more complex than those for uniprocessor/ monoprogrammed machines. There are several ways of partitioning and sharing memory hierarchies, however, including the use of paging and virtual memory systems. We will explore these methods of exploiting memory hierarchies later (see Chapters 4 and 7).

Conflicts in memory accessing can be a serious source of degradation. We will discuss the details of main memory access in Chapter 5 and those of interconnecting switches in Chapter 6. Various language and software features have been developed to aid in exploiting multiprocessors. We will discuss some of these in Section 2.4.3.

We can conclude that multiprocessing with a shared memory hierarchy is indeed more cost-effective than multiple independent computer systems, just because there are so many multiprocessors in use. On the other hand, one should be aware that the limits of this approach in real-world, general-purpose computing have been four processors. Most major manufacturers provide multiprocessing—but none of them promise more than four processors in the mid-1970s.

Another advantage of systems with several identical processors is quite important, namely, the redundancy that provides high reliability. If one memory unit or one processor fails, it is often the case that the system can continue to operate, at a reduced speed. For systems in which reliability is more important than speed, multiprocessing is also a good solution. The first multiprocessor operated (see Section 1.3.3) was constructed largely for this reason. For roles such as interplanetary space vehicle control, machines of this kind have also been designed [AGMR71].

1.2.1.4 Multifunction computation

Machines designed along the lines of Fig. 1.11 deliver more processing speed for the price of more processors and control units. But, can we in some more delicate, less straightforward way achieve higher speeds without so much hardware? If we could speed up single programs by performing more than one operation at a time from a single stream of instructions, then the scheduling and access conflict problems of the multiple instruction streams of Fig. 1.11 should also be reduced.

One approach to such machines is illustrated in Fig. 1.12. Here we have a single control unit and a single processor, but the processor can carry out more than one "function" simultaneously. Each function unit has a few registers associated with it to hold its operands. A set of general registers is shared by the function units to buffer operands and results for the main memory. They also hold temporary results computed on one step to be used as operands a few steps later. The registers are tied together by an interconnecting bus, which allows fast data transmission from point to point. Several real computers have been built along these lines, with various interpretations of what a "function" is.

Typical function units are a fixed-point adder, a floating-point adder, a floating-point multiplier, a shifter, a Boolean logic unit, and so on. For example, if a machine has independent floating-point adder and multiplier units, the statement $X \leftarrow (A*B)+(C+D)$ can be executed by simultaneously

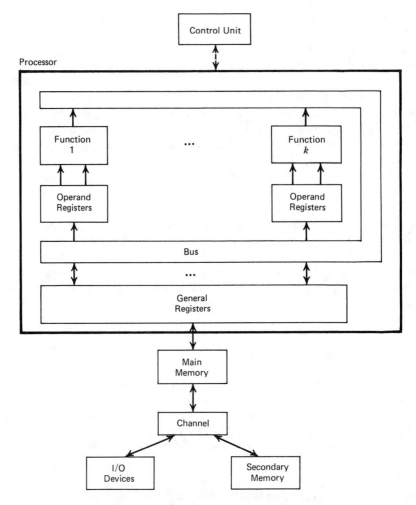

FIGURE 1.12   **Multifunction processor system.**

forming $(A*B)$ and $(C+D)$, and adding these results when they are completed. This obviously speeds up certain programs, but there are some drawbacks as we shall see.

To illustrate this, let us return to the inner product program of Prog. 1. The parse tree of Fig. 1.13 shows how this might be executed for $N=4$ using an independent adder and multiplier. Except for an initial multiplication and a final addition, we can use both operation units on each time step. Thus, the total execution time has been reduced from $2N$ steps to $N+1$ steps, achieving a speedup of $S_2 = 2N/(N+1) \approx 2$ at an efficiency of $E_2 = N/(N+1) \approx 1$.

It is important to notice here that we are achieving a higher processing speed for a single program, with higher throughput (as in the multiprocessor) and also

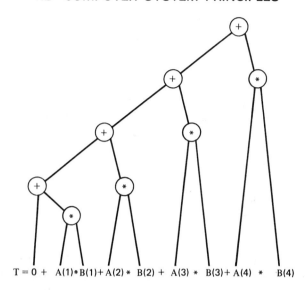

T = 0 + A(1)*B(1)+A(2) * B(2) + A(3) * B(3)+A(4) * B(4)

FIGURE 1.13   **Multifunction inner product.**

lower turnaround times for single jobs. Furthermore, in addition to sharing the memory hierarchy (as the multiprocessor did) we are also sharing the control unit here, between the several functions. In fact, the functions may be said to be sharing the general registers as well, although the number needed in a standard uniprocessor may be substantially less.

An additional complication is that parallelism between operations must be discovered. This can be done using a compiler, using hardware at run time, or by some combination of the two. In fact, because the simultaneous execution of instructions depends on their order in a program, hand coding in assembly language often is very effective unless a good optimizing compiler is available. In any case, the control unit and processor become more complex than in the simple machines mentioned earlier, because now two or more distinct simultaneous operations must be performed. This is in addition to overlap between processor, memory, and control unit activity as in the machines of Figs. 1.6 and 1.7. This control unit must be prepared to sequence a number of distinct operations at once, whereas in Fig. 1.11 we had p separate instruction streams. We are also led to wonder at this point about how many operations we could expect to perform at one time for one program. How many independent operations do programs exhibit? Also, how many independent operations can be handled with a reasonable amount of hardware? Later we will return to these questions.

Despite the difficulties alluded to above, several real computers have been built with this type of organization. They were first introduced in the early 1960s, some time after multiprocessors had appeared. The highly successful

CDC-6600 [Thor70], its successor the CDC-7600 [Bons69], and the CYBER models derived from them [Ensl74] have such organizations.[10] Also, the IBM-360/91 [IBMJ67] and 360/195 [MuWa70] were organized along these lines. The number of function units in such machines ranges from 2 to 10.

Another similar organization is found in the PDP-11/45 minicomputer when a floating-point arithmetic unit is attached. This unit is attached to the standard processor, not to the Unibus described in Section 6.3.1. When a floating-point instruction is encountered, data is fetched through the standard processor to the floating-point processor, which then proceeds simultaneously with the standard processor to execute the instruction.

We have now sketched a number of machine organization ideas which, in one way or another, invoke simultaneity of operation to achieve faster processing speeds. These have included simultaneous processor, main memory, and secondary memory operation. We have also seen that several control units and processors may operate at once or one control unit can drive several simultaneous functions in a single processor. Regardless of the data structures involved in the programs executed by any of these machines, the processors execute the programs as if the data consisted entirely of scalar quantities.

It is true that index registers and index arithmetic units have long been used to access memories in a way that takes advantage of the nature of arrays. But individual arrays were accessed one element at a time and processing was carried out on one or perhaps a few elements at a time. The machines we will consider next access a large number of elements of one array simultaneously, and they also process a number of elements at once. As more and more memories are used in parallel, the nature of memory indexing becomes more complex, but the question we will deal with first concerns the processor's role in executing programs on array-type data.

1.2.1.5 Pipeline computation

The first method we consider for speeding up array computations is pipeline processing. The basic idea in a pipeline processor is to introduce some simultaneity of processing by breaking a complex, time-consuming function into a series of simpler, faster operations. For example, any floating-point operation involves exponent handling and various shifts of the fractions as well as an arithmetic operation. Furthermore, multiplication, for example, may require a sequence of additions.

Although some real pipeline processors may involve several pipelines, let us consider the simplified model shown in Fig. 1.14. Suppose our longest operation (say multiplication) can be broken into k segments. Shorter operations may skip some of these segments, but assume all operations use the same pipeline.

---

[10] As with the IBM System/360 and System/370, there are few architectural differences among the earlier CDC-6000 and 7000 series machines and their successor models in the CYBER series. For that reason, this book will refer to CDC machines by their traditional numbers.

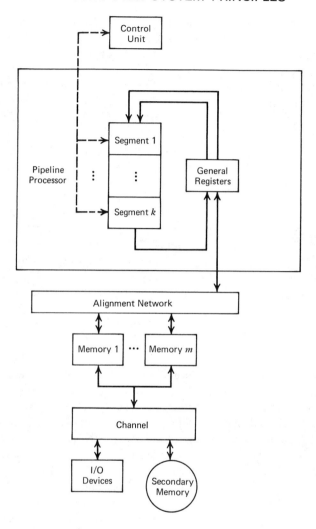

FIGURE 1.14 **Pipeline processor system.**

As a first example, we consider executing the following simple program.

$$\text{DO} \quad S_1 \quad I \leftarrow 1, \ 100$$
$$S_1 \qquad X(I) \leftarrow A(I) * B(I)$$

Initially, the A and B arrays are fetched from memory to the general registers. Processing begins as A(1) and B(1) are sent from the registers to segment 1 of the pipeline processor. When segment 1 processing of these two operands is complete, the results are sent to segment 2, and so on, until the result X(1) emerges from segment k. But when the intermediate results of A(1)*B(1) are passed to segment 2, two new arguments, A(2) and B(2) can enter the pipeline through segment 1. Thus, by the time X(1) emerges from the pipeline, the nearly completed results of A(2)*B(2) are entering segment k and so on up the pipe to segment 1 where A($k+1$) and B($k+1$) are entering. Notice that this process is very much like an assembly line, where each segment does a little further processing of the intermediate result, and segment k emits the completed product. Each segment consists of combinational logic followed by a register to hold the intermediate results.

Now, if we assume that the time to pass through the entire pipeline is approximately equal to the time required to multiply two numbers in a standard processor, then for scalar operations, nothing has changed. But for a vector of operations this time has been divided by k, the number of pipeline segments, if the vectors are very long. This follows from observing the rate of flow from segment k. A new result appears in the time required to traverse one segment of the pipe, not all k segments. We must also pay k delays to fill the pipeline initially. So if the vectors are short relative to k, then pipelining is not very effective.

The speedup of a k segment pipeline over a k clock serial version of some function is

$$S_k = \frac{T_1}{T_k} = \frac{nk}{k+n-1}$$

for n pairs of arguments. The denominator follows from the fact that the first pair of arguments leads to a result in k clocks, and the $n-1$ subsequent results appear at the output in $n-1$ subsequent clock periods. If the pipeline inputs are not all independent of one another, as in the summation of n numbers, for example, the speedup formula degrades from the above. But it is clear from the above equation that $S_k \rightarrow k$ for $n \gg k$, and this is the best possible speedup for a k segment pipeline. We will consider this in more detail in Section 3.6.

As in the case of a multiprocessor, conflicts may arise in accessing arrays from the m parallel memories of Fig. 1.14. If the data must be rearranged between the memory and processor, an alignment network is shown for this purpose in Fig. 1.14. Otherwise, the memory hierarchy may be a standard one. A number of existing computers have pipelined arithmetic units, including the CDC-7600 [Bons69], the IBM 360/91 [IBMJ67], the CDC STAR 100 [HiTa72], Texas Instruments ASC [Ens174, Wats72], the CRAY-I [Cray75], and the Manchester University MU5 [Sumn74, LaTE77].

1.2.1.6 Parallel computation

Parallel processor computers have an array of simultaneously acting identical processors driven by a common control unit. Besides sharing the control unit, the processor array shares a memory hierarchy as shown in Fig. 1.15. Here we show an alignment network that allows data to be transferred from one

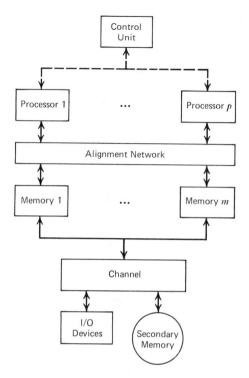

FIGURE 1.15   **Parallel processor system.**

processor to another or back and forth between memories and processors. This is similar to the interconnection network of Fig. 1.11, except that we are now dealing largely with uniform alignments of one entire array of data at a time, rather than one or two elements of several arrays for several subroutines at once, as in Fig. 1.11. It is important to note that this machine executes only one program at a time. The control unit causes each processor to execute the same instruction at the same time, so p elements of an array of data can be computed at once.

For example, if $p = m = 100$ in Fig. 1.15, then the program

$$\text{DO} \quad S_1 \quad I \leftarrow 1, 100$$
$$S_1 \qquad X(I) \leftarrow A(I) + B(I)$$

is executed by fetching $A(1)$ and $B(1)$ to (say) processor 1, $A(2)$ and $B(2)$ to processor 2 and so on, with $A(100)$ and $B(100)$ going to processor 100. Then in only one add time, all 100 sums are formed. The results are then returned to 100 memory locations $X(1), \ldots, X(100)$ in parallel.

In practice, it is often necessary to perform several variations on the above.

If an array is smaller than the number of processors, or if some elements are to be skipped, certain processors may be disabled by the control unit. Also, it is sometimes convenient to *broadcast* a single scalar to all processors, either through the alignment network from one memory or processor, or directly from the control unit in the case of constants compiled into the program. A program which could use a broadcast instruction efficiently is

$$\text{DO} \quad S_1 \quad I \leftarrow 1, 100$$

$$S_1 \qquad X(I) \leftarrow A(I) * B$$

The inner product program of Prog. 1 (Section 1.2.1.1) can be executed in parallel, and if specified as Prog. 3, this is easy to recognize. In Chapter 2 we will show how to detect such parallelism even in the form of Prog. 1. Prog. 3 gives an indication of several desirable features for a high-level, array-type machine language. For example, we can consider compiling Prog. 1 using the array instructions of Prog. 3.

Prog. 3

$$\text{SIM}[T(I) \leftarrow A(I) * B(I); I \leftarrow 1, N]$$

$$\text{TOT} \leftarrow \text{SUM}[T(I); I \leftarrow 1, N]$$

The SIM statement indicates simultaneous execution for the entire index set I (see Section 2.4.3); all of the multiplications can be executed independently of one another. The SUM function fans in the $T(I)$ elements for the entire index set I; it can be carried out in $\log N$ addition[11] times on a parallel machine, as shown in Fig. 1.16 for $N = 4$. A well-designed control unit would handle such instructions directly, executing the program for any size arrays, without the programmer or compiler writer performing any additional work.

[11] Throughout the book we use $\log x$ to denote $\log_2 x$, and here we assume $N = 2^k$.

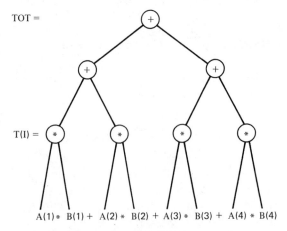

FIGURE 1.16   **Parallel inner product.**

The parse tree of Fig. 1.16 shows how to execute Prog. 3 using four processors in three steps, the fastest possible time for this program. This achieves a speedup of 7/3 over a serial processor at an efficiency of 7/12, because we are using four processors. Assuming N is a power of two, the multiplication step requires one time unit and the summation $\log N$ time units, in general. Thus, given N processors we can perform such computations in $T_N = 1 + \log N$ (see Chapter 2 for the details about this) for a speedup of[12]

$$S_N = \frac{2N-1}{1+\log N} = O\left(\frac{N}{\log N}\right) = O(T_1/\log T_1)$$

at an efficiency of

$$O\left(\frac{1}{\log N}\right) = O(1/\log T_1).$$

Note that on successive steps the number of processors required is halved. Also, intermediate results must be aligned properly for the calculation to proceed.

Clearly, parallel machines can achieve substantial speedups over a single processor. If the number of processors p, is substantially greater than the size of most arrays to be processed, however, this organization is quite inefficient because many processors may be idle. For purely scalar operations, the machine's efficiency is disastrous.

When compared with a multifunction processor, a parallel processor may be much faster due to the simplicity of controlling a large number of identical processors. The multifunction processor's control unit must sequence a number of different functions at once. Although Fig. 1.15 is similar in appearance to Fig. 1.11, the two machines operate quite differently. Recall that the multi-processor of Fig. 1.11 actually executes p distinct programs (including perhaps several subroutines for one job) at the same time. Each has its own control unit. Thus the cost of a multicontrol unit machine may be greater and the access conflict and scheduling problems may be more difficult to resolve.

On the other hand, it is not obvious how array operations can be discovered in ordinary programs, so the compiler problem is more difficult for a parallel processor computer, assuming users have been running FORTRAN programs on a serial machine, for example, and wish to compile them for a parallel processor machine. The question of program parallelism detection also arises for pipeline processors, as well as for other organizations discussed earlier, although to a lesser extent as the machines exhibit less parallelism. Since program transferability is often a precondition for purchasing a new computer, this is an important subject and it will be discussed in detail in Chapter 2. As we saw in Prog. 3, another option is to add language features that explicitly specify parallelism, but this requires reprogramming and puts the burden on the users.

---

[12] Throughout this book we use the notation $f(x) = O(g(x))$ if there is a constant $r > 0$ such that $\lim_{x \to \infty} (f(x)/g(x)) = r$.

Parallel machines, and to a lesser extent the other organizations discussed earlier, also may have hardware mismatches to the set of programs intended to be executed. Inefficiencies may arise due to mismatches between array sizes and the machine size, as discussed earlier. There also may be serious memory conflicts in a parallel processor, although because arrays are being fetched in parallel, it may be easier than random fetching for independent programs in a multiprocessor. More details about these points will be presented in Section 3.6 and in later chapters.

Several parallel processors have been built and are reasonably successful in particular applications areas. Illiac IV [BeNe71, BBKK68], designed both at the University of Illinois and at Burroughs Corp. and built by Burroughs, is a scientific-numerical machine with 64 processors of 64-bit words each. The Goodyear Aerospace STARAN IV [Ens174, Rudo72] is an associative processor of 1-bit words, and is built in multiples of 256 processors. STARAN may be regarded as an associative memory (see Section 1.1.2.1 and Chapter 5) when accessing data in its memory, and as a parallel processor when transforming data. A special-purpose parallel processor for radar signal processing connected to the Bell Laboratories CLC (see Section 1.2.1.3) is the PEPE system [Ens174]. PEPE was originally designed by Bell Laboratories and built by Burroughs. Also, ICL has a parallel processor [Redd73].

In 1977, Burroughs announced the Burroughs Scientific Processor (BSP), which has sixteen parallel processors but is also pipelined from memory to memory [Burr77]. Thus the memory, alignment network, and processors are all overlapped and are sequenced as pipeline segments of high-level macroinstructions.

1.2.2 Matching machine design and users

The purpose of designing computer systems is to serve some class of users. It seems eminently sensible to consider these users' computations before undertaking a machine design effort. In one way or another, designers have considered users in the past, but often in superficial ways. In this section and indeed throughout the book, we consider how the end users' desires can be taken into consideration by computer system designers.

Figure 1.17 shows an overview of how computer systems are used. Given a problem or problem area, an analyst studies the problem, draws on known methods and somehow produces an algorithm to solve the problem. All of the criteria of Section 1.1.1 may be brought into play in making such a choice. For example, fast algorithms are always desirable and the memory space requirements are also important. A numerical analyst may be concerned mainly about the numerical quality of the results. A business analyst may be concerned about the ease of preparing inputs and understanding the results produced by the computation. Thus, many algorithms may be considered before one is chosen.

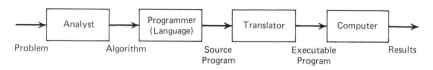

FIGURE 1.17   **Computer system use.**

After a complete algorithm to solve a problem has been specified, the algorithm must be programmed. The programmer has a choice of languages, and will choose one in which the algorithms and associated data structures specified by the analyst can be expressed. Each programmer will produce a program in his or her own style. Thus, many possible programs could result from a specified algorithm.

Next, the program is translated. There are also many possible outcomes of this step. Naturally, the machine on which the program is to run determines one level of choice. Another class of choices concerns the degree of optimization to be carried out in translating the programs. This, in turn, depends on how much speed and efficiency are desired when the resulting programs are run.

The executable program is finally run with some data to produce results. There is even the possibility of a variety of computations resulting from a given executable program. For example, on the IBM 360 and 370 series, a wide range of machines can execute the same machine language through the use of microprogramming (as will be discussed in Chapter 4). Results can be obtained much faster by using a high end of the line machine rather than a low end of the line machine. And if the same source program were translated for the machines of two different manufacturers, for most numerical computations, different results would be obtained in the two cases. Different word lengths, different number representations, different rounding schemes, different I/O conversion programs, and the like, all contribute to such discrepancies.

Thus we see that for one given problem, a tremendous number of different solutions are possible; clearly, some are better than others. The goal of computer system designers should be to make it easier for users to get better results with less difficulty, taking into account all of the criteria mentioned in Section 1.1.1. Toward this end, let us reconsider Fig. 1.17 from the standpoint of machine design.

From the user's standpoint, the logical flow of events in Fig. 1.17 is from left to right. In fact, users would like to defer any options they may have until the last possible moment. This is as it should be. For example, defining the size of some array should not have to be done until execution time. It would be impractical, for example, to have the analyst choose an algorithm for which array sizes were fixed.

On the other hand, from the standpoint of computer system designers, the sequence of design events has traditionally flowed from right to left in Fig. 1.17. First, a machine was designed, then languages and compilers were designed, and finally algorithms were studied and programs written. Of course, if a proposed design performed poorly on benchmark programs, it was often redesigned, that is, patched up somehow to run the benchmarks better. As we will see shortly, there have been certain notable exceptions to the exaggerated statements above, and over the years, designers have become more enlightened about the overall machine design process.

The ideal situation might be to allow machine design to flow from left to right, as shown in Fig. 1.17. This might lead to a totally new machine design for each problem—an absurd proposal for the foreseeable future! Compromises can be found in two different ways, however.

First, it *is* possible to have a collection of machines available for a user via a network. Even in a single computer center there can be special-purpose pieces of equipment for special users. As we traverse Fig. 1.17 from right to left, more obvious flexibility is possible. For example, there may be various compilers for each language, various languages for different applications, and so on, as mentioned previously. Thus, instead of designing a new system for each user, we can provide many options by building and operating many different hardware and software configurations. However, this dodges the original question of how to design systems well-suited to various kinds of applications.

Our second compromise in designing a new system for each user is to study classes of users and their problems and try to design computer systems proceeding from left to right, as in Fig. 1.17. As soon as high-level languages appeared, machine designers began to design with certain language features in mind. FORTRAN and COBOL were developed in the mid-1950s, and by 1960 ALGOL 60 was announced. In 1962, the Burroughs B5000 was introduced, and this machine was very well matched to the ALGOL 60 language. The push-down stack of the B5000 was also well-suited to compilation of ALGOL programs. Thus, in designing the B5000, three aspects of Fig. 1.17 were considered at once—the programming language, the compiler, and the computer itself.

Such an approach has been attempted to some degree in the design of many other machines. The notion of microprogrammed control units, introduced by Wilkes in 1951, was very influential in this respect. By the late 1960s, the use of fast, inexpensive semiconductor ROMs and RAMs allowed many designers to build language interpreters into control units. If a RAM is used, the interpreted language can be changed from one job to the next in an otherwise fixed machine. This has led to an activity called *firmware* development—designing and writing control unit microprograms—and has led to a great deal of flexibility in machine design and use.

An early design that used wired-in control logic instead of microprogramming for a FORTRAN machine was carried out by Bashkow [BeNe71, BaSK67].

A number of other similar efforts were made for other languages [ChuY75]. In the early 1970s, a machine called SYMBOL was built which could directly execute a source language also called SYMBOL [RiSm71].

The above were attempts to consider the programming language and/or compiler in designing machines. It is a more difficult task to attempt to design machines on the basis of the actual source programs to be run on the proposed machine.

First, we must establish exactly what this proposition means. "Machine design based on programs to be run on the proposed machine" can be interpreted narrowly or broadly. In a narrow interpretation, such machines have always been designed. Hardware improvements from the beginning of computer design history have been included to make programs run "better." Index registers were added to allow easy indexing through arrays. Other address mapping hardware was added to provide virtual memory machines. Floating-point and double length arithmetic operations were added to aid in numerical computations; and so on.

On a more global scale, specialized processors have been built. For processing time series data, array signal processors are commonly used [RuCo69]. Picture processing and other kinds of associative processing can be performed well on various proposed and real machines [Rudo72, McCo63]. For string processing and code breaking problems, the HARVEST system was designed and built [CaHP62]. Other machines have been proposed to solve specific partial differential equations or to play checkers, for example. In the limit, this approach goes to the left end of Fig. 1.17 and defines a special-purpose machine, exactly for one problem. Clearly, this leads to machines that are so specialized they are not cost-effective. Most manufacturers would not consider building a machine that was useful to only one or two customers' needs, although this occasionally happens.

Thus there is no clear practical distinction between "general-purpose" and "special-purpose" computer systems. Or, put another way, there no longer is any such thing as a "general-purpose" computer. All machines are specialized in some way, simply because there are now so many uses for computers. Just on a speed basis, machines can be classified as "special-purpose"; indeed the IBM 360 and 370 lines were designed to capitalize on exactly such speed differences between users.

The idea was to provide each class of users with a suitable machine, but one which was logically equivalent to all other machines in the family. Thus, when the user outgrew the present machine, transferring to a bigger machine would be relatively painless. This is an extremely important point in the practical, real world, and has been a great aid in IBM's sales efforts.

Another approach to specialization is to consider the programming language as well as typical source programs in the design of a computer system. This has been done abstractly for FORTRAN, COBOL, GPSS, and certain aspects of information retrieval and file processing [Kuck76]. The proposed machines all had special features for processing as well as control units which catered to the types of algorithms used in these languages.

Throughout this book we will be considering the relation of hardware features to program characteristics. The final answers to questions concerning the design of the best machines for various kinds of computations are not known. However, several general principles which do seem to be true will be presented. Chapter 2 gives transformations intended to reduce the number of time steps required in program execution (e.g., by discovering array operations) and also intended to localize in address space the data address sequence produced by each executed program; this will be expanded in Chapter 7. Although we will be discussing examples from FORTRAN-like languages, it should be clear that the ideas are useful for programs in such languages as GPSS, COBOL, and even SNOBOL.

By FORTRAN-like languages we mean those reminiscent of most traditional serial programming languages, for example, FORTRAN, ALGOL 60, PL/I, COBOL, and so on. These languages are well established, and most existing programs are written in them. Whether or not they will ever be replaced by new languages is an interesting question. It seems that for a new language to become established it must either

1. have expressive powers beyond most existing languages; or
2. be strongly supported by a machine manufacturer.

The arrival of new languages, however, does not mean the departure of old ones. This is true, mainly because

1. many debugged programs exist and are in regular use in older languages,
2. many programmers are content with languages they understand and have been using, and
3. new language features are sometimes sneaked into old languages.

For the above reasons, it is probably safe to state that FORTRAN and COBOL, to name the two major workhorses among programming languages in the United States, will never die. Rather, they will be amended to include new ideas, and they will be supplemented by other languages for other types of programming.

In any case, throughout this book we will deal with programming examples written in such a programming language. This does not make our discussions vulnerable to being outdated, because even if such languages were to disappear, new languages would have to be able to handle the mechanisms we discuss. Perhaps these would be hidden from the user in new, higher-level languages, but the problems would still have to be faced by compiler writers. We regard the language we discuss as the lowest level language above assembly language in which it is reasonable to perform the transformations we will discuss. To attempt to transform traditional assembly languages would be a much more difficult undertaking, because much of the obvious detail in a higher-level language is obscure in assembly language.

A number of real-world programming languages provide array operations directly. The most comprehensive such language is probably APL. If programs were written in such a language, some of the tranformations we discuss would not be needed. We will see in Chapter 2, however, that for maximum speedup of more complex programs, even with an APL-like language, more complex transformations will be required.

Regardless of the source language used, the transformations of Chapter 2 lead to structures whose execution can be carried out using many operations simultaneously. This also has implications for the design of control units; array-type machine languages and control unit hardware to process them rapidly are of great interest in this regard. Some aspects of this will be presented in Chapters 3 and 4.

Finally, we must consider machine design for the execution of programs other than user programs. Compilers and operating systems occupy a good deal of machine time in certain computer installations. Compiler structure is reasonably well understood and designing special-purpose compiler machines would be a relatively straightforward task. However, such efforts are usually aimed toward the direct execution of high-level languages—either by microprogramming or some kind of special logic (see Chapter 4).

Operating systems are not as well understood, but in some installations, operating systems account for more machine time than user programs. Thus, there would be enormous payoffs from the introduction of hardware which aids in the execution of operating system programs. In real machines, various attempts have been made along these lines. The SYMBOL computer [RiSm71] had a hard-wired operating system which ran on certain special logic modules. In many machines, certain control unit registers and logic are available that aid operating system designers.

In the long run, we might imagine a control unit consisting of a number of microprogrammable special processors. Each of these would correspond to an operating system module. They all could operate simultaneously as well as communicate with each other, which would speed up the running of the operating system. It would also free the processor, which presently is used for many operating system functions, to engage in executing user programs.

We close this section by returning to Fig. 1.17. Our discussion has been aimed at widening the machine designer's scope and by including more aspects of Fig. 1.17 in the design process. In the past, languages often have been taken into consideration, but actual programs and their characteristics should be considered in more detail. Of course, it can be argued that the algorithms used are program- and language-dependent and hence it is a mistake to look at existing programs. Although this argument has some plausibility, it is not very convincing in the real world. New machines are built to replace existing ones. It is extremely difficult to sell a new machine that requires much reprogramming.

Thus, being able to recompile old programs for new machines is a useful idea. More fundamentally, whereas programming languages may influence algorithms to some extent, this influence seems to be mostly on a superficial level. Indeed, the fundamental aspects of programming languages that will be discussed in Chapter 2 seem to exist in almost all programming languages. They are masked with different kinds of higher-level structure in different languages; nevertheless they are present, as will be seen later. In fact, even in research on algorithms, the kind of program constructs we consider are fundamental.

In the final analysis, one might expect some kind of iterative process to hold in finding the ideal machine design method with respect to Fig. 1.17. Thus, the analysis of programs for machine design leads to certain fundamental building blocks which will be discussed in Chapter 2. These could be fed back and made more explicit in programming languages, and in this way, machine design could influence language design and algorithm design constructively. Of course, machine design has influenced all of the others from the beginning, but the influences should continue at higher and higher levels.

1.3 HISTORY OF COMPUTER DESIGN

The design and construction of the world's most powerful computer has never been easy, and in many ways the nature of the struggle has been constant through time. It has taken at least four or five years to get every major new machine into operation. Typically, financial crises arise, regardless of whether the undertaking is in a university or in an industrial setting. And the speedup over the fastest previous machine has never been much more than a factor of ten, and often much less. Still the cumulative results from the mid-1940s to the early 1970s have led to an impressive speedup factor of 10^6.

Just as impressive, but more bewildering, is the growth in complexity of computer organization. Early machines contained a few thousand relays or vacuum tubes, but modern ones are approaching 10^6 transistors. One of the designer's main trade-off problems has always been between the number of parts used and the speed of each individual part. Because, for a fixed cost, the designer wants the fastest machine possible, he or she can choose a simple organization with very fast parts or a more complex organization with slower parts. The fewer the parts, the higher the reliability, but fast parts cost more than slow ones and producing them may be very difficult. The designers of the most powerful machines have always pushed both reliability and cost to their limits. One reason for this is that from the early 1950s on, there have usually been two or more groups in competition to build the next big machine.

In this section we outline the history leading to modern digital computers. We do this for several reasons. First, despite their great number of parts, computers are quite simple in functional terms and it is interesting to learn when various ideas were first proposed or implemented. It is also revealing to note how few really big innovations have occurred.

References to source material will be given throughout this section, but there are two particularly noteworthy general references to the early history of computers. An entertaining, illustrated volume that covers roughly the period discussed in this book is [EaEa73]. A solid reference work that contains many of the original papers is [Rand73]; we will not refer to it explicitly below, but the interested reader can find papers covering most of the material there.

1.3.1 The world's first computer designer

Although present machines are direct descendants of ideas of the mid-1930s, Charles Babbage designed his Analytical Engine, the world's first general-purpose digital computer, nearly 150 years ago [MoMo61]. He also built a prototype of the world's first special-purpose digital computer, his Difference Engine, which he evidently first thought about in 1812—ten years after the invention of the steamboat! The ideas that he and a few colleagues had about computers and programming over some 30 years are overwhelming. They touched on a great many of the ideas used in modern computers. Nor were his thoughts limited to computers, as we shall see later.

Not surprisingly, Babbage had to face many of the above-mentioned difficulties that present-day designers encounter. Several of these proved so overwhelming that he never finished anything but a prototype of the Difference Engine. His major problem seems to have been an overly ambitious plan—a barrier over which every designer must stumble at least once. This led to financial problems and difficulties with his chief engineer.

Babbage himself wrote down few details about his machines, and it was said that his lectures about machines were largely incomprehensible. Fortunately, an Italian army officer named Menabrea, who sat through a series of lectures Babbage gave in Turin in 1840, published a good account of the Analytical Engine. This was later translated into English and, at Babbage's suggestion, annotated by his colleague, Ada Augusta, Countess of Lovelace. On reading this paper as well as several by Babbage, one is depressed by the relatively small progress made by thousands of modern computer scientists. Or, more accurately, one is annoyed by how often the same problem is discovered, worked on, solved, and breathlessly discussed in the current literature.

Babbage had been motivated as early as 1812 to consider a machine that could evaluate polynomials by the method of differences. He was annoyed by the fact that human computers of astronomical and other tables were usually people of some intellectual accomplishment but that such computations really required only mechanical skills.[13] He was also bothered by the large numbers

---

[13] The history of mechanized arithmetic predates Babbage by nearly 200 years (see [Rand73]). In 1642, Blaise Pascal designed and built a mechanical adder and subtracter. In 1666, Samuel Morland adapted Pascal's idea to build a machine that could multiply by repeated addition. Independently, in 1671, Gottfried Leibniz designed a machine that could add and multiply; it was completed in 1694. This design led to a sequence of other machines, none of which achieved commercial success until the Thomas Arithmometer in Babbage's time (the 1830s).

of errors that occurred in published tables as well as errata in errata sheets. So, between 1820 and 1822, he built a 6-decimal digit Difference Engine capable of evaluating any second degree polynomial. Initial conditions were placed on wheels by hand. Spurred by his success with this project he obtained government funds for a 26-digit, sixth-degree Difference Engine. This was a much more complex machine. It was to have automatic rounding, provision for double precision arithmetic, various alarm (interrupt and completion) bells, as well as a method for engraving copper plates for printing the computed results. The latter would preclude transcription errors. Concerned about inherent mechanical errors, Babbage arranged various roller and conical bearings that would jam if certain mechanical tolerances were exceeded. If completed, the Difference Engine certainly would have revolutionized the tabulation of mathematical functions. It must also be noted that Babbage was developing a complex design notation for communicating his ideas to his engineering and construction people.

This project dragged on for about 10 years until 1833, and consumed 17,000 pounds (£) of English government money and perhaps as much of Babbage's own fortune. During this period Babbage engaged in a series of fund-raising activities and became increasingly at odds with his chief engineer, Clement. Evidently he proposed many design changes but the exact details of the collapse of the project do not seem to have been recorded. In any case, by the early 1830s he was interested only in obtaining funds for the construction of his newest idea, the Analytical Engine. Before discussing its details, we shall set these events in historical perspective by noting the following. The chronometer of Harrison, which was the first one suitable for precise longitudinal trans-oceanic navigation, was produced in the 1760s after a very long and trying experience. It took Harrison three years to produce a *copy* of his first successful model. Interchangeable parts were not to come for some time. In fact, Whitworth, who later introduced standard screw threads among other things, lost his job with Clement when the Difference Engine project collapsed. Babbage worked at a time which was sparked with great inventions—the steam locomotive in 1825, the electric generator in 1831, the reaper in 1834, the electromagnetic relay in 1835, daguerreotype in 1839, and telegraphy in 1844. Of course, no thought of an electrical computer was possible then. But one is impressed by Babbage's courage to attempt so complex a mechanical device given the state of the art at the time.

Babbage's machines were all designed to be driven by a hand crank, but in one of his accounts of his first inspiration he quotes an early conversation with John Herschel. They were checking some tables and Babbage said, "I wish to God these calculations had been executed by steam," to which Herschel replied, "It is quite possible." Herschel, Babbage, and George Peacock had been friends as Cambridge undergraduates, where they formed the Analytical Society. Later Herschel became a famous astronomer and Peacock a leading algebraist at Cambridge. Babbage later had many discussions about his machines with these men and many of the leading scientists of the day.

Laplace, Bessel, and Jacobi (not to mention the Duke of Wellington) all had extensive discussions with him.

It is fascinating to note that Boole and DeMorgan were both contemporaries of Babbage, but no interaction between them concerning machine design has been noted. However, Ada Augusta Byron, the poet's daughter, studied mathematics under DeMorgan for many years. Mrs. DeMorgan notes that on an early occasion, she took Ada to visit Babbage and that Ada quickly understood what was going on. Some years later, as Lady Lovelace, she translated Menabrea's paper on the Analytical Engine and collaborated with Babbage.

The Analytical Engine that Babbage designed in the 1820s and 1830s was spectacular, even by the standards of the 1950s. His design methods and his ideas for the machine's organization and use demonstrate Babbage's genius. The immense complexity of what he hoped to build demonstrates his kinship with many of today's designers. By pushing funds and technology to the limit—and often too far past the limit—he faced a long series of frustrations.

The Analytical Engine was to be a 50 decimal digit machine. Its "store" or memory was to hold 1000 of these words (about 165,000 bits) in decimal form. These words could be written from or read to the "mill," or arithmetic and logical unit, via some mechanical linkages. The whole system was under the control of a process which was described on two sets of punched cards. One set, the "operation cards", contained the series of operations to be performed. The other set, called "variable cards", indicated which store locations were to be operated on by the operation cards. Babbage was quite familiar with the Jacquard loom which was controlled by a sequence of punched cards. In fact, the punched card idea dated back to the early 1700s, although Jacquard's famous loom was not developed until 1804.

Although the Analytical Engine did not have a stored program, it was able to perform various kinds of condition tests and then branch on the outcome. In particular, it could move its card sequence forward or backward a fixed distance. Furthermore, there were an index register and index adder available for loop control; to quote Menabrea, "When the number n has been introduced into the machine, a card will order a certain registering apparatus to mark $(n-1)$, and will at the same time execute the multiplication of b by b." This is in a discussion of evaluating b^n. Note that the indexing arithmetic was apparently carried out in parallel with the multiplication. The index register was evidently not used to index through memory, however.

The arithmetic unit was designed to perform fixed-point, 50-digit calculations at the following speeds: add or subtract in one second; multiply or divide in one minute. To achieve such speeds Babbage devised, after years of work, a parallel addition algorithm with anticipatory carry logic! He was very proud of that accomplishment. As in the Difference Engine, Babbage provided for multiple precision operations, automatic mechanical fault prevention and detection, and automatic rounding and overflow detection.

Babbage was bothered for some time about the provision of standard function values (for example. log x, sin x) to the machine. Finally he concluded that either the recomputation of such numbers, essentially via a subroutine, each time they were needed or their provision from external cards would work. He was willing to let the decision rest on operating experience. His table lookup procedure was arranged as follows. The machine's operator would be provided with drawers full of such cards punched with both x and $f(x)$. When a bell rang, the operator would read a dial and pick out the corresponding card. The machine would check to see that the correct card had been supplied by testing the argument, and if an operator error had occurred, would ring a louder bell. He was quite proud of this idea because the problem as well as its solution had evidently perplexed Bessel, Jacobi, and others for some time.

When reading Babbage, Menabrea, and Lovelace, one is amazed and delighted to see how far the questions of mechanical computing were explored. It is tempting to read things into their statements from time to time. On some occasions they are exasperatingly brief, and sometimes they are ambiguous or mildly contradict each other. Such matters as the self-checking mechanisms, which would jam when too much mechanical error accumulated, are hard to understand, and the writers state they will not attempt a complete explanation. On the matter of parallel arithmetic operations they make several passing remarks. We quoted Menabrea above about index calculations. At another point in his summary, which seems to indicate the importance of the idea, he is discussing the speed of the machine and says, "Likewise, when a long series of identical computations is to be performed, such as those required for the formation of numerical tables, the machine can be brought into play so as to give several results at the same time, which will greatly abridge the whole amount of the processes." This seems to be a clear statement of parallelism between arithmetic operations! Parallel operations do not seem, however, to have been part of the Analytical Engine design.

Both Babbage and Lady Lovelace discuss programming questions, but she exhibits great insight in her notes on the Menabrea paper. She was quite concerned about languages for expressing programs. One was a kind of assembly language notation on large charts. These were translated from another notation very much like compiler assignment statements. All variables were denoted by V_i where i indicates the storage location from 1 to 1000. To avoid the confusion of writing $V_1 = V_1 + V_2$ she introduced another index and wrote $m + 1_{V_1} = m_{V_1} + n_{V_2}$ to indicate that the right-hand side values were the mth and nth values to occupy their respective storage locations. Her machine level language was a kind of zero address operator language, although a separate operand stream was specified to the machine. Thus, to evaluate

$$x = \frac{d'm - dm'}{mn' - m'n},$$

$$y = \frac{dn' - d'n}{mn' - m'n}$$

she would use these three operation cards: $6(\times)$, $3(-)$, $2(\div)$, where commas separate the cards. Note that the common subexpression in the denominator is evaluated just once. Locations were supplied by a three-address scheme using three variable cards, two for the arguments and one for the result.

She finally suggests a loop notation using the Σ sign to denote loop control. She also allows for an index variable and nested loops! Her notes contain several complex programs, but she and Babbage were not bothered by long programs. In fact, they both were heartened by the fact that Babbage owned a Jacquard tapestry that had required over 20,000 cards for its production. She does remark that from the standpoints of the time required and ultimate accuracy, some numerical results would be impossible to attain in any practical sense.

We noted earlier that during the course of the Difference Engine project, Babbage had received 17,000 pounds (£) from the government. He had spent perhaps as much of his personal inheritance from his banker father. Thus, by the time he was deeply involved with the Analytical Engine, sources of funds were scarce. Evidently, Lady Lovelace and her husband were fairly wealthy and both were interested in horse racing, as was Babbage. Consequently, at one point they devised betting procedures, evaluated them on the prototype Difference Engine, and lost a good deal of the Lovelace fortune.

On another occasion, Babbage studied the possibility of game playing (including chess) on the Analytical Engine and designed a tic-tac-toe machine. He proposed to put several of them on the road with admission charges. Perhaps he had heard of Mälzel's "automatic chessplayer" which was revealed to contain a man. One is also reminded of Mälzel's collaboration with Beethoven, which resulted in "Wellington's Victory" but no machine. In any case, Babbage dropped this plan.

On the whole, Babbage's life was a very interesting and creative one; his computing activities formed only one facet of his career. Because he regarded them as an annoying distraction, he carried on a lifelong battle with street musicians—hauling them into court on several occasions. As a result, his home was the scene of frequent retaliatory concerts. Being much interested in the heartbeat and respiratory rates of all animals, he took every opportunity in his travels to measure these rates. On one occasion he had himself sealed inside a 265°F. oven for about five minutes to study the effects on himself. Railroads, a new invention, were a great interest and he is credited with many ideas including the invention of the first recording speedometer as well as the first cowcatcher. A contribution of which he was very proud was a notation for describing the motion and "logic" of his mechanical drawings for his engines. Earlier in his life, he and his Analytical Society friends had been instrumental in getting English mathematicians to drop Newtonian notation for the calculus in favor of that of Leibniz. We conclude this discussion with an abbreviated list of other writings and work: an operations research type study of the post office system; meteorological and tree ring observations; electricity and magnetism; a widely adopted lighthouse occulting system; various other signaling schemes; and a study that convinced him that the Analytical Engine could play chess with a "3 or more" move lookahead! In short, whereas Babbage may occasionally have been in error, he was seldom at a loss for ideas about a subject.

He was Lucasian Professor of Mathematics at Cambridge for nine years, but bitterly remarked that that was the only honor conferred on him by his own country. Babbage's entire life was filled with the frustration of having only a few of his ideas appreciated and even fewer adopted. Toward the end of his life a friend noted, "He spoke as if he hated mankind in general, Englishmen in particular, and the English Government and Organ Grinders most of all." In his book, *The Exposition of 1851*, he expressed his feelings quite clearly when he wrote:

Propose to any Englishman any principle or any instrument, however admirable, and you will observe that the whole effort of the English mind is directed to find a difficulty, a defect, or an impossibility in it. If you speak to him of a machine for peeling a potato, he will pronounce it impossible; if you peel a potato with it before his eyes, he will declare it useless because it will not slice a pineapple. Impart the same principle or show the same machine to an American or to one of our Colonists and you will observe that the whole effort of his mind is to find some new application of the principle, some new use for the instrument.

In 1871, the London *Times* noted in his obituary that he lived to be almost 80, in spite of organ grinding persecutions.

Actually, Babbage lived to see some small successes for his ideas. Inspired by a published account of his Difference Engine, a Swedish printer, George Scheutz, and his son, Edward, built a machine. Scheutz spent a good deal of his own money and had some government support. In 1854, he exhibited in England his fourth order, 8-digit difference machine with a printing output mechanism. Babbage and his son received Scheutz warmly and after a good deal of publicity the machine was sold to the Dudley Observatory in Albany, New York. Whether or not it was much used seems to be in question. In any case, a copy was made in 1863 and the British government used it to compute actuarial tables for the newly emerging life insurance business—a topic on which Babbage had discoursed in earlier times.

Babbage's son, H. P. Babbage, continued to work on the Analytical Engine and after his father's death managed to construct some working parts of the mill between 1880 and 1910. At a demonstration this machine computed and printed a table of 20-digit multiples of π.

In the 1880s, another interesting forerunner of modern computer equipment was under development. Working at the U.S. Patent Office, Herman Hollerith, an engineering graduate of Columbia, constructed a punched card tabulating machine. By 1890, Hollerith machines were in use at the U.S. Census Bureau for processing returns of the 1890 census. Hollerith later went into business for himself, manufacturing a variety of card processing equipment. He was quite successful, and as we learn below, his company became a basic building block in the modern computer industry.

1.3.2 C-T-R et seq.

In 1892, young Thomas J. Watson launched his sales career on a horse-drawn wagon, peddling sewing machines, pianos, organs, and caskets out of Painted Post, New York [Roge69]. Before long he moved to Buffalo and Rochester, and became a star salesman for the National Cash Register Company of Dayton, Ohio. His record was observed by J. H. Patterson, the head of NCR, and Watson was elevated to various positions; by 1914 he was the number two man at NCR, which by then was the largest cash register company in the United States. His position in the company and the company's position with respect to competition caused Watson some difficulty.

First, Patterson was a manager who ruled with an iron, if somewhat bizarre, hand. His executives had to engage in various Patterson designed regimens (e.g., prework group horseback riding and special foods) and were fired for various kinds of real or imagined insubordination. Occasionally, instead of firing someone, Patterson would provide him with a "fresh start" by moving the entire contents of his office out on the front lawn, dousing it with kerosene, and touching a match to it. So, after almost twenty years with NCR and the survivor of many earlier purges, Watson was fired by Patterson in 1914.

The foremost market position of NCR was due in large part to Watson's efforts, but this was his second difficulty. Some months before his firing, a number of top management NCR people, including Patterson and Watson, had been taken to court for a number of illegal business practices. They had essentially eliminated all competition in the new and used cash register business by strong selling, price cutting, industrial espionage, personal harassment, and their ultimate weapon, the "knockout machine." This was a cheap, inferior copy of a competitor's machine that would be sold as the real thing and would soon break down. Watson, at the time of his firing, was appealing a fine and one-year jail sentence. In spite of this, Watson asked Charles R. Flint for a job [Roge69].

Flint was a New York tycoon who had invested in practically everything, and in 1911 had formed one of the early conglomerates of diverse product manufacturers—the Computer-Tabulator-Recording Company, otherwise known as C-T-R. This included several companies that made equipment which could be called business machines, and included Herman Hollerith's Tabulating Machine Company. When Flint proposed Watson to the Board as manager of C-T-R, there were some raised eyebrows, but Flint prevailed. Later, the jail sentence and other litigation disappeared. Watson moved rather slowly at first, but became C-T-R president, and by 1924 was solidly in command. In 1924, he changed the name of the company to International Business Machines.

In many ways, Watson ran IBM as Patterson ran NCR. He was once referred to as a "benevolent despot," but he was more rational and, if not intellectually inclined, he did enjoy and had good intuition about making money. IBM flourished and by the mid-1930s Watson was the highest paid person in the United States.

Watson's interest in developing new products as a way to greater profitability caused him to support various new machine development activities within the company. He also enjoyed talking with people inside and outside IBM about possible uses of his equipment. Thus, in 1928 when a young education professor at Columbia, Benjamin D. Wood, telephoned him Watson said he could spare an hour for a lunch meeting. The meeting went well and Watson stayed until 5:30 listening to the problems and ideas Wood presented. In short, Wood had been developing intelligence tests for college students and had 35,000 to process. With a room full of girls and some equipment he had designed, the processing of these tests was costing at least $5 each. He explained how these tests and similar material could be processed for perhaps 10 or 20 cents using IBM equipment—perhaps with some modification. Two days later, Wood had a room full of IBM equipment at his disposal, free of charge. His predictions were correct and he continued to offer suggestions to Watson, including one that the mechanical parts should be eliminated in favor of all electrical equipment. This association led to a line of IBM equipment for education, and Wood remained an IBM consultant for many years. More importantly, the equipment attracted the attention of other Columbia faculty and students. Wallace Eckert, an astronomy graduate student, talked with Wood and Watson, which later led to another gift to Columbia, the T. J. Watson Astronomical Computing Bureau. One of Watson's top engineers, Clair D. Lake, built a special machine for the Bureau. It was the first IBM machine that could multiply, and it also had a sequencing mechanism. It was used for the computation of astronomical and navigational tables—the latter were very important in antisubmarine warfare in the North Atlantic in the late 1930s. Later, Eckert joined IBM as the first director of the T. J. Watson Laboratory, which was located near the Columbia campus.

Eckert's earlier astronomy calculations had attracted a good deal of attention and among his visitors were Harlow Shapley, astronomy professor at Harvard University, and James B. Conant, the president of Harvard. Shapley discussed the Columbia work with Howard Aiken who was teaching mathematics in Harvard's Graduate School of Engineering. Aiken had known about the state of the art in computing and had been thinking about building a more complex machine. Shapley prompted Aiken to visit Eckert at Columbia and, later, to discuss his ideas with James W. Bryce of IBM. Bryce had been one of IBM's key inventors for thirty years, and as a result of these discussions, Watson put up a million dollars to build a machine for Aiken.

1.3.3 Modern machine beginnings

Four men ushered in the modern digital computer era in the 1930s. They were Howard H. Aiken of Harvard University, John V. Atanasoff of Iowa State College (now University), George R. Stibitz of Bell Telephone Laboratories, and Konrad Zuse of the Technische Hochschule in Berlin. Aiken, Stibitz, and

Zuse designed and built a number of relay machines and by the 1940s, each had completed a general-purpose programmable digital computer. They all apparently worked independently of one another, although Aiken used the engineering talent of IBM to build his machine; in particular, three men were his co-inventors: B. M. Durfee, F. E. Hamilton, and C. D. Lake, who had designed a good deal of earlier IBM equipment. Atanasoff began work on digital electronic circuits in the late 1930s and by 1939 had produced a breadboard model of a special-purpose digital computer. By 1946, J. P. Eckert (no relation to Wallace Eckert) and J. W. Mauchly of the Moore School of Electrical Engineering at the University of Pennsylvania, had successfully completed ENIAC, the first operational electronic digital computer. This attracted the attention of John von Neumann, who, as a consultant with Eckert and Mauchly, proposed EDVAC—the first stored program computer. This design was modified and embellished by a number of people, and by 1950 there were more than a dozen big machine projects under way. Actually, by 1950 so many of the ideas used in current machines had been proposed and experimented with that it will take us a good deal of space to outline the details. It is, of course, impossible to pin down who first had each idea, but we shall attempt a rough chronological ordering based on various published documents.

Zuse [MTAC47, Hoff62] evidently began first (he had his first ideas in 1934), but his influence outside Germany was probably the least of the pioneers. Unfortunately, most of his early work was destroyed during World War II. His special-purpose relay machines, Z1 and Z2, were built between 1936 and 1940. Z3 was a general-purpose machine that operated under external program control. It had a 64-word data memory and the numbers were of binary floating-point format: 22 bits with 14 mantissa, 7 exponent and one sign bit. The machine contained 2600 relays[14] and was built between 1934 and 1941. During the war, Zuse developed two special-purpose control computers, one which continuously sampled 100 points for process control. Following the war, Zuse built Z4 and then went into business, commercially manufacturing Z5 and subsequent machines. As we shall see, Stibitz was almost an exact American parallel of Zuse, although a few years behind him.

At Bell Laboratories, Stibitz built his Model I or "complex computer" between 1938 and 1940 [Harv48, MTAC49]. It was not a programmable machine; it performed complex arithmetic on numbers presented via a teletype keyboard. Its main claim to fame is that Stibitz demonstrated the first remote terminal system (keyboard and printer) to an American Mathematical Society meeting at Dartmouth in 1940, using the machine which was in New York City.

---

[14] Relays were adapted from telephone switching technology to implement digital circuits in many early computers.

Subsequently, Bell Laboratories built several other relay machines, including an interpolator and a ballistic computer, each of which had a few internal registers for data storage. Between 1944 and 1947, Stibitz and S. B. Williams built the Model V system, which was a general-purpose two processor machine. This machine contained 9000 telephone relays and 50 pieces of teletype equipment occupying 1000 square feet of floor space. The speeds of each processor were: 300 milliseconds for addition, 1 second for multiplication, about 5 seconds for divide or square root, and 0.07 seconds for a register to register transfer. Earlier, Stibitz machines had used an excess three binary number system, but for this machine Stibitz invented and used biquinary decimal numbers for several reasons. It made self-checking, conversion to decimal, and implementation in relay circuits relatively easy. The numbers were floating-point with 7 decimal digits and an exponent of magnitude less than 20. Each processor's internal memory was 15 relay registers. The entire system consisted of two such processors and three I/O positions, all interconnected. Each I/O position could handle a number of I/O devices. Thus one job could use both processors or two separate jobs could be run together. Furthermore, the machines could, on completing one job, switch to another I/O position. Thus, set-up time by a human operator could be masked. Also the tape motion time to access a new job could be masked, and by preparing a number of jobs on several paper tapes the machine could be run overnight, unattended.

The machine was programmed using a simple three-address symbolic language, taking advantage of the fact that the 15 registers were named by letters of the alphabet. Loops could be programmed by making paper tape loops. With typical Bell System concern for reliability, the machine had various self-checking features and high reliability was achieved. The chief cause of difficulty was dirty relay contacts. Various lamps would indicate to an operator where the difficulty was if the machine stopped. On an unattended run, the machine could abort one job and proceed to try the next one if a fault occurred. Two of these machines were built, one for the National Advisory Committee for Aeronautics (Langley Field, Virginia), and one for the Ordnance Department of the Army (Aberdeen Proving Ground, Maryland).

Bell Telephone Laboratories constructed a model VI system in the late 1940s, which was installed at their Murray Hill, New Jersey, laboratory. This machine was an improved version of the Model V in several ways. First, it serviced a number of remote terminals from which jobs could be submitted to the machine via telephone lines. Second, when a job failed for some reason, the machine would automatically restart and try once more. A sticky relay might work the second time. If not, it would go on to the next job as did Model V. These two features made the system appear to be very much like a modern machine with a remote entry batch processing operating system.

Another interesting feature of Model VI was the ability to wire in subroutines. Provisions were made for up to 200 such subroutines. They could call each other and be nested down to four levels. Because the program was otherwise on external paper tape, this speeded up the operation of the machine and made the programmer's life easier.

Models V and VI were both "asynchronous" machines; that is, they had no controlling clock—when one step of an operation was over it caused the next step to begin. This design philosophy has been tried with varying success in some later high-speed machines, but is seldom used now in CPUs.

In contrast to the Bell Laboratories' approach, Aiken and the IBM group designed a synchronous computer that was operated at a 300 millisecond cycle [Harv48]. This machine was designed and built between 1937 and 1944. IBM became involved in 1939, and the work from then until completion was carried out in their facilities at Endicott, New York. The machine was operated at Harvard University, and was known either as the Automatic Sequence Controlled Calculator or the Harvard Mark I. Mark I was 8 feet high, 51 feet long, and 6 feet deep. It was a decimal, fixed-point machine using a 23-digit plus sign, word. It could store 72 such words in 10-position counter wheels and had an additional 60-number storage facility in manually set dial positions (what would now be called a read-only memory). It could add or subtract in 300 ms, multiply in 6 seconds, divide in 11.4 seconds, and evaluate several special functions in about 1 minute. These latter were so slow that faster, lower-accuracy subroutines were often used. The machine could also perform double precision or half-word operations.

Instructions were externally stored on 24-hole paper tape and were in two-address format. Initially, it could conditionally jump to one of two external tape routines based on the range of an argument. This was later changed to a branch to one of several tapes based on a more general transfer on minus instruction.

Programming for maximum speed could present interesting challenges. All operations shared a main bus, and during the execution of a long operation the programmer could initiate shorter commands such as addition or certain I/O operations. A hardware interlock prevented these "interposed operations" from conflicting with the longer ongoing operation. Evidently this technique was used a great deal. Mark I was the first large-scale machine to be completed, and was first used to compute various tables and later used to solve systems of algebraic and differential equations. After it was broken in, Mark I was quite reliable, reportedly available 95 percent of the time in 1950, and it was in use for 15 years.

The fourth of the computer pioneers of the 1930s is unique in several respects. First, Atanasoff proceeded to consider vacuum tube digital circuits, whereas the others were using relay circuits. Physicists had used vacuum tube counters for some time, and this encouraged Atanasoff. Furthermore, the tradition of computing at Iowa State was well-established by the late 1930s; Henry Wallace, who was later Secretary of Agriculture under President Roosevelt, and eventually Vice President, had introduced IBM tabulating equipment at Iowa State in the 1920s for statistical analysis of agricultural and meteorological data [Trop74]. Thus, the Iowa State Research Council liberally granted Atanasoff $650 to build a prototype computer in the Spring of 1939—later he received larger grants [Rand73].

A second area of difference between Atansoff and the other three pioneers is that he never built a general-purpose machine. The prototype, built with graduate student Clifford Berry, was operating by the end of 1939. By 1942, he had constructed a digital electronic linear equation solver (called the ABC for Atanasoff, Berry computer). As a physicist, his original motivation had come from the fact that large linear systems arose commonly and were impossible to solve by means of a hand calculator. In 1942, the computer was working but the I/O equipment was not. At that point, Atanasoff left Iowa State for the Naval Ordnance Laboratory and the machine was never used.

A third unique feature of the Atanasoff story is that his role as a computer pioneer was all but lost in the shadows of the other three people we have discussed and the ENIAC designers at the University of Pennsylvania (the group traditionally credited with the building of the first electronic computer). As we shall learn shortly, their machine was more successful than Atanasoff's, but they owed a direct debt to him. Atanasoff never patented his machine, but Mauchly and Eckert filed for a patent in 1947 and received it in 1964. Ten years later, the patent was overturned by the Atanasoff invention, as we discuss in Section 1.3.7.

Although we have gone over the period of early development briefly, it is clear that spectacular progress was made. Zuse, Stibitz, Aiken, and Atanasoff had broken ground for events that in the subsequent five years would yield the "modern" digital computer. Whereas their hardware realizations were great feats of engineering, their ideas were mainly rediscoveries of things that were familiar to Babbage exactly 100 years earlier. For their implementations alone, however, they would have earned Babbage's respect, as he wrote in *The Life of a Philosopher* in 1864, "If, unwarned by my example, any man shall undertake and shall succeed in really constructing an engine embodying in itself the whole of the executive department of mathematical analysis upon different principles or by simpler mechanical means, I have no fear of leaving my reputation in his charge, for he alone will be fully able to appreciate the nature of my efforts and the value of their results."

1.3.4 The second wave

The improvements introduced in the next wave of machines included electronic parts, large internal memories, stored programs, index registers, and magnetic tape and drum secondary storage. By the early 1950s, the typical machine could multiply in a few milliseconds and had 1024 words of main memory. We shall attempt to point out the most important steps in terms of the people who made them and the machines they built.

In 1943, Mauchly and Eckert undertook the design of what turned out to be one of the physically largest computers made before or after that time [MTAC47, Harv48, Mauc75]. ENIAC (Electronic Numerical Integrator and Computer) was sponsored by the Army Ordnance Department and was intended to integrate ordinary differential equations for the generation of ballistics tables. It was finished at the Moore School in February, 1946. The machine was configured in a U-shape, but overall it was about 100 feet long and 8-$\frac{1}{2}$ feet high. It contained 18,000 vacuum tubes, 1500 relays, and consumed 150 kilowatts of power. Each register in the machine used 550 tubes and was about 2 feet wide and 8-$\frac{1}{2}$ feet high! Despite its gargantuan dimensions, the machine was very fast and quite reliable.

ENIAC was a 10-digit fixed-point decimal machine with a parallel arithmetic unit that performed at the following speeds: add in 200 μs, multiply in 2.8 ms, and divide in 6 ms. It also had a square root unit and was capable of double precision operations. Its internal memory consisted of 20 registers, each of 10 digits. It was able to do I/O and arithmetic simultaneously and had an 800 card per minute reader. Nevertheless, computations were often I/O bound and although its raw speed was a factor of 1000 over Mark I, its overall performance may have been closer to a speedup of 200 or 300. The machine was externally programmed by attaching various portable "function tables," which would be arranged by the programmer. These external tables could also be used as a read-only data memory. The machine was capable of conditional jumps, although this feature evolved in time. The time to set up the machine for a particular calculation ranged from a $\frac{1}{2}$ hour to a day. In 1947, its "up time" was estimated to be 20 percent, but by 1950, measured over a one-month period, the hardware was available 85 percent of the time; when set-up time and program hangups were included, 67 percent utilization was measured. After completion, the machine was moved to the Aberdeen Proving Ground and various improvements were made. John von Neumann was instrumental in making the programming easier and faster via external boards, wires, and switches.

Von Neumann, having been attracted by ENIAC, became a consultant to the Moore School group and began to study machine design. In 1944, Eckert wrote a memo suggesting the use of a magnetic drum or disk as the main memory of a machine. A variety of memories for radar systems were first used during World War II. Crawford had written a thesis at M.I.T. in 1942 suggesting a magnetic disk or drum in this context, and a variety of acoustic delay line memories were in use by radar people at the time.

In 1945, von Neumann wrote a memo as an ENIAC consultant discussing a stored program machine. This important idea, due perhaps to Eckert, Mauchly, and von Neumann, led to a new project to build EDVAC (Electronic Discrete Variable Automatic Computer). This was to be a machine of much more modest size than ENIAC, but with a larger internal memory and slightly slower arithmetic. Although it spawned a great many other machines and ideas,

EDVAC was not the first stored program machine to become operational. The project was begun in 1946 and the machine was not operational until 1952. During this period, Mauchly and Eckert left the Moore School to form their own computer company and von Neumann launched his own project at Princeton, taking with him several other Moore School people.

In any case, EDVAC was a binary, 44-bit, fixed-point machine with a bit serial arithmetic unit. This required only 3500 tubes to achieve average speeds of 850 μs for add, and 2.8 ms for multiply. It had a mercury delay line memory which contained 1024 words of data and program. This was organized as 128 delay lines each containing 8 words. This memory led the designers to choose a four-address instruction format, two for arguments, one for result, and one for next instruction, because any of these could be anywhere in the 1024-word circulating memory. The machine had two arithmetic units; the second was used for checking the first.

In the preceding section, we noted that Atanasoff had built an electronic digital machine prototype in 1939 and a larger special-purpose machine in 1942. It happened that John Mauchly and John Atanasoff met at an AAAS meeting in Philadelphia in late 1940 [Trop74], and Mauchly became very interested in Atanasoff's work. In fact, Mauchly visited Atanasoff at Ames, Iowa, in the Summer of 1941; there he observed the Iowa machine, had it explained, and read reports about its design, although the machine was not yet complete. Thus, Atanasoff's work had a clear influence on the ENIAC project, and we shall return to this in Section 1.3.7.

At least one other electronic digital computer was completed before ENIAC; a fact that has come to light in recent years, despite the British government's insistence on maintaining a secret classification on this project of the early 1940s. For cryptanalysis work during World War II, a number of electromechanical machines were built in England and in the United States. In December 1943, an electronic digital computer called the Colossus, containing approximately 2000 vacuum tubes, was installed in the Department of Communications at Bletchley Park. Later, perhaps 10 copies of this machine were installed [Mich73].

Thus, the Colossus was operating more than two years before ENIAC, although after Atanasoff's machine. The Colossus project was headed by Professor M. H. A. Newman, who later moved to Manchester University to start a project that led to a long line of influential machines, as we shall see. A number of others who later became influential in British computer design were involved in this project and development. Alan Turing, while apparently not a member of the team, was involved with the project to some extent [Rand72].

1.3.5   England pulls ahead again

Following a visit to the Moore School, Maurice Wilkes of Cambridge University started a project at Cambridge at the end of 1946. This led in 1949 to

EDSAC (Electronic Delay Storage Automatic Calculator), the first stored program machine to be completed [MTAC50, Wilk56]. EDSAC was similar in design to EDVAC, although somewhat slower. It had a 1.5 ms add time, an average 6 ms multiply time, and required a few hundred ms for division. Its memory characteristics were much like those of EDVAC described above. The overall machine had about 3000 tubes and dissipated 15 kw. Wilkes was quite interested in questions concerning the programming and use of the machine. Among other things, he developed a large subroutine library for EDSAC users.

Others (besides Babbage) had preceded Wilkes in England, with ideas about automatic computers. Alan M. Turing had published his famous paper in 1936, the cryptanalysis work which led to Colossus had begun in the early 1940s, and J. R. Womersley at the National Physical Laboratory had begun to think about general-purpose machines by 1945. By 1947, Turing and others had joined him to begin a project which led to the construction of ACE, the pilot model being completed in 1950. The ACE pilot had only about 1000 tubes but achieved an add time of 32 μs on 32-bit words. Its small component count made it very reliable. Under the direction of Professor M. H. A. Newman, who had earlier directed the Bletchley project, work at Manchester University began in early 1947 with continuing support from the Telecommunications Research Establishment [Bowd53]. This led to the development of MADM at Manchester University.

Delay line memories had a rather long latency; because they operated at a few megacycles and contained several hundred bits, it could take a millisecond to access a word. Thus a random access, large, inexpensive memory device was sought. At Manchester, F. C. Williams developed the "Williams tube" which filled this bill. His first tube worked in 1947 and was used in a prototype machine by June of 1948 (and indeed this may have been the first operational stored program computer [Rand73, Ch. VIII]). This was a cathode-ray tube with bits stored on its face. They could be capacitively sensed, and access time was a function of electron beam switching and sensing times only. Thus, the first large random access memory design was available. In 1948, the Manchester group, which also included T. Kilburn, demonstrated a 2000 rpm head-per-track magnetic drum, and used this as backup to Williams tube primary memories in 1949.

Using this memory hierarchy, they issued I/O instruction for blocks of data from the drum and stole processor cycles to access the main memory. In 1949 they built another prototype that had an interesting new feature which they called the B-tube. Using the B-tube, they said,". . . instructions, and in particular their address section, could be modified in their effect without being modified in their stored form." Thus appeared the first modern index register. With these important innovations as background, they designed MADM in 1949 and it was finished in 1951. This was a one-address, binary machine with 40-bit, fixed-point operations. Its arithmetic speeds were: addition in 1.2 ms and multiplication in 2.16 ms. The number of pentodes used was 1600, and

2000 diodes were used. The Williams tube memory consisted of 512 words stored in 8 tubes, together with a 150,000-bit drum.

We remarked earlier that magnetic recording on disks or drums had been suggested at least as early as 1942. The first successful machine to use a magnetic drum was built in 1947 by A. D. Booth at the University of London. It was called SEC and had 256 words of 21 bits. The arithmetic unit employed only 230 tubes and had a 1.6 ms add time.

1.3.6   Meanwhile, back at Princeton

Just a year after his EDVAC report, von Neumann and two co-workers, Arthur W. Burks and Herman H. Goldstine, published another report [GvNB47]. This was June 1946, and they were all at the Institute for Advanced Study (IAS) at Princeton University; Burks and Goldstine had both been at the Moore School for some time and had been involved with ENIAC. Their new report was entitled "Preliminary Discussion of the Logical Design of an Electronic Computing Instrument," and it was a detailed, clearly argued discussion of many details of machine design. In 1947, Goldstine and von Neumann wrote an accompanying document on the analysis and coding of problems for the machine. These documents led to the construction of the IAS machine, which was completed in 1952. Julian H. Bigelow was the chief engineer in charge of the IAS machine, and he was later replaced by James Pomerene. This project became the focal point of computing activities in the United States. The project was funded by the Army Ordnance Department, with contributions from the Air Force, the Office of Naval Research, and the Atomic Energy Commission.

The IAS machine was completed in June 1952, and was a rather compact unit; excluding the I/O gear its dimensions were $8 \times 8 \times 2$ feet. It contained 2300 tubes (many double triodes) and 40 Williams tubes, each containing 1024 bits. Thus the memory contained 1024 40-bit words, each being interpreted as one fixed-point number or two instructions. The machine had a one-address order code with 10 bits of address per instruction. The memory access time was about 25 μs and excluding this, the average arithmetic times were: 15 μs for addition, 400 μs for multiplication, and 1 ms for division. Many engineering innovations were included; among them was a word parallel memory access feature not included in the Manchester machines. The arithmetic unit also was parallel, binary and the machine was asynchronous.

This machine and project were quite important from several standpoints. First, the excellent engineers who built the machine had a number of rather good recent inventions to use. Second, von Neumann and his staff thought very imaginatively and broadly about how to use the machine. Finally, their reports and visitors enabled this machine to be widely known. A number of copies of the machine were built.

In parallel with the IAS activity, the Servomechanisms Laboratory of M.I.T. began to build a machine. One original motivation was the problem of real time aircraft simulation. The Whirlwind I project began in 1947 under the

Office of Naval Research sponsorship and was directed by Jay W. Forrester. Very high speeds were achieved in the 15-bit (plus sign) parallel, fixed-point arithmetic unit: add in 8 μs, multiply in 24 μs. When memory fetch time was included, both operations averaged 180 μs. Whirlwind was a synchronous machine with a 2 megacycle clock for the arithmetic unit; it was also a stored program machine. The machine was operational in 1951.

One important outcome of the M.I.T. activity was in the main memory area. Initially, Whirlwind had a 1024 word, 16-bit, modified Williams tube memory. Under Forrester's direction, alternative memory devices were being studied. The M.I.T. group was in close competition with an RCA team headed by Jan Rajchman. At least by virtue of consent decrees some ten years later, M.I.T. won the race. (The settlement included royalty-free rights to RCA and a $13 million license from M.I.T. to IBM.) In 1953, they had installed in Whirlwind a 2048-word coincident current magnetic core memory. This memory had a 1 μs read time and an 8 μs write and cycle time, and the cores were about 80 mils OD. The machine also had a cathode-ray tube for output display with a computer-controlled camera attached.

Thus by 1953, both Whirlwind I with its core memory, and the IAS machine were in operation. These two machines are regarded by many people as the first of the "modern" digital computers. They had combined some ten years of engineering development by a number of other groups together with their own inventions and excellent engineering. The influence of these machines was widely felt both in university projects and the newly emerging electronic computing industry.

1.3.7 A new industry begins

We mentioned earlier that one of the reasons why EDVAC was not completed earlier may have been the departures of von Neumann and his people to the IAS project, as well as Eckert and Mauchly to form their own company. In December 1947, the Eckert-Mauchly Computer Corporation was founded with financial backing from a multimillionaire. The firm designed and built BINAC for Northrop Aircraft under an Air Force contract. It was an EDVAC-like machine with a delay line memory and about a 1 millisecond arithmetic speed. BINAC was demonstrated in August 1949.

At the time, their only commercial competition was from IBM, which was selling various combination electronic and electromechanical devices. These included the Selective Sequence Electronic Calculator (SSEC), the 604 Electronic Calculating Punch, and the Card Programmed Calculator (CPC), all introduced in 1948. The CPC actually grew out of an experiment in which a 604 and an accounting machine were joined by people at Northrop. None of these was a stored program machine, and it appeared that the Eckert-Mauchly Corporation had a clear field. Based on their BINAC experience they designed a new machine, UNIVAC (UNIVersal Automatic Computer), and began taking orders at $250,000 per system.

At that point their fortune changed. Their financial backer was killed in a plane crash at about the time they realized that the $250,000 UNIVAC price tag was too low to make a profit. Seeking funds they talked with people at the T. J. Watson Laboratory in New York. The technical people there were enthusiastic about UNIVAC but evidently on Watson's decision, the Eckert-Mauchly talks were terminated. James Rand of Remington Rand then discussed the matter with Eckert and Mauchly and subsequently took over their company.

At the time, Remington Rand had a line of desk calculators as well as various punched card equipment. Unlike IBM, Remington Rand used a 6-row, 90-column card. Whereas IBM equipment had been designed primarily for "business applications," it had found its way into many "scientific" uses. Remington Rand equipment seems to have retained the flavor of "business equipment" only, at that time.

The first UNIVAC was delivered to the Bureau of the Census in June 1951. UNIVAC was a synchronous machine and had a delay line memory of 1000 (not 1024) words of 12 decimal digits. The serial arithmetic unit operated at about 1 millisecond and the numbers were binary coded decimal in excess three format. Magnetic tapes were used as secondary memory, and special buffer registers were provided for data entry to main memory. UNIVAC was quite successful and 48 systems were built (sale price was $750K, although they were also leased).

In 1952, Remington Rand bought out Engineering Research Associates of Minneapolis. ERA had been a pioneer in commercial magnetic drum manufacture and had designed their 1101 and 1102 computers around their drum. The UNIVAC name had numbers attached to it for later Remington Rand machines, and still later the 1100 numbering scheme was resurrected.

As we discussed in Section 1.3.3, Atanasoff never obtained a patent on his invention at Iowa State, but Mauchly and Eckert obtained one on theirs in 1964 (the application was filed in 1947). This patent was assigned to Sperry Rand (formerly Remington Rand). More recently, Sperry Rand brought suit against Honeywell for infringing on the Mauchly and Eckert ENIAC patent. In 1973, nearly 10 years after the patent was granted, and following a lengthy trial, a federal District Court found that "Eckert and Mauchly did not themselves first invent the automatic electronic digital computer, but instead derived that subject matter from one Dr. John Vincent Atanasoff," [Anon74]. The legal and financial implications that would have followed a reverse decision are interesting to contemplate! For a good background on this case, as well as many others, see [Broc75].

IBM finally began a project in 1950 which led to the IBM 701 by the end of 1952. The 701 was a 36-bit fixed-point, synchronous, parallel machine with a 2048-word Williams tube memory. Its speed was about 40 μs for addition and 400 μs for multiplication or division. This was the beginning of a long series of 700 and 7000 series machines. It also signaled the end of the open field for

Remington Rand. With Watson's aggressive sales background and widely established sales network, IBM quickly moved in. Eventually, nineteen 701 systems were sold and many other machines followed.

Thus by 1953—just nine years after the completion of Mark I—Whirlwind I and the IAS machine were leading the research front and both UNIVAC I and the IBM 701 were commercially available.

1.3.8 Summary

We conclude the present discussion with a synopsis of the history of machine organization up to 1953 and a few remarks about what followed. At this point, the reader has surely noticed that a large fraction of the "big ideas" of modern machines were in use by 1953. In fact, a good many of them were considered by Babbage, 100 years earlier. Babbage had proposed a machine organization with a memory, arithmetic unit, control unit, and I/O facilities. He invented a parallel arithmetic unit with anticipatory carry logic and an overflow alarm. He also used an index register for loop counting and it worked in parallel with the arithmetic unit. Between them, Babbage and Lady Lovelace proposed a good many programming ideas which were similar to those now in use. Unfortunately, they were 100 years ahead of the technology.

In fact, both the vacuum tube and Eccles-Jordan flip-flop circuit were invented in the first quarter of the twentieth century but were not employed until 25 years later in ENIAC. After the feasibility of large, general-purpose computers had been demonstrated using electric relay and mechanical technology, the events of World War II caused the United States and British governments to provide the funds for a good deal of computer research and development. The earlier radar efforts certainly provided many engineering and technology ideas.

By 1953, most of what Babbage had proposed was implemented. Machine speed was the main factor that would have surprised Babbage. He proposed a 1 second add and a 1 minute multiply. In fact, several tens of microseconds were all that addition required, and multiplication was about an order of magnitude slower. The clever memory hierarchy ideas of the Manchester group as well as the notion of a stored program would have impressed, if not surprised, Babbage.

The modern computer scientist should give pause to note the wealth of innovations which had been demonstrated by 1953.[15] The multiprocessor with remote job entry at Bell Laboratories, the 8 μs core memory at M.I.T., the proposal of microprogramming by Wilkes in 1951—any of these sound like current subjects.

Many topics had been sharply debated in the 1940s, including synchronous versus asynchronous operation, bit serial versus word parallel arithmetic, decimal versus binary, and fixed versus floating-point number representation.

---

[15] A good summary of early hardware components is contained in [Pome72].

Several of these subjects are still debated—or "settled" by providing both. It should be noted that asynchronous operation, as pioneered by Stibitz and followed through the IAS machine, has largely disappeared. The extra control hardware and time required for "reply backs" between elementary operations became unreasonable as machine speeds increased. It is also interesting to note that although early machines (Zuse and Stibitz) had floating-point hardware, it had largely disappeared by 1953 and was not to return for several years. Instrumental in this was von Neumann who argued that proper scaling was easy if one sufficiently understood the problem; otherwise the person should not be computing in the first place. His argument contained one genuinely unfortunate flaw—few users since have understood their calculations as von Neumann understood his. In any case, the "philosophy of machine design" papers written in the 1940s often read in part as though they had been written last year.

Not that all ideas had been proposed by 1953. Some inventions large and small that came after 1953 will close this chapter. The transistor and integrated circuit certainly provided the biggest technology changes and with them came remarkable system speedups. Memories with extra tag bits, indirect addressing, and phased or interleaved banks were to follow as was modern paging hardware. This led to complex multiprogramming and time-sharing systems. Fancy terminals have greatly aided some users. Faster arithmetic algorithms and pipelined arithmetic units as well as program lookahead have contributed to faster computation. Stack machines have led to a variation in addressing as well as fast compilation. As we said at the beginning, things have become much more complicated and hardware and software organization have become deeply intertwined. In 1953, software was in a rather simple and pure state. Symbolic assemblers were common and high-level languages were being discussed. Fortunately, no one had thought about software operating systems.

The history of computers after the early 1950s is rather complex. Sketches of the history of the 1950s are included in [BeBL61] and [SAPP62]. A more elaborate survey that spans the mid-1940s to the late 1960s may be found in [Rose69]. A brief outline of the entire span of computer history appears in [HuHu76]. Extensive bibliographies are contained in all of these papers. Two early special issues of the IRE Proceedings [IREP53] and [IREP61] give a good overview of early developments.

1.4   OVERVIEW OF BOOK

Chapter 1 has attempted to provide background material and whet the reader's appetite for more detailed study of computer organization. Because both hardware and software aspects of computers are discussed in this book, Chapter 1 provides a broad range of background ideas. The remainder of Volume 1 is divided into six chapters, and we will survey them shortly. Volume 2 presents a number of details that are beyond the scope of an introductory textbook, but most of the topics of Volume 2 are deeply rooted in Volume 1.

From time to time in this volume we will make references to details which are being deferred to Volume 2.

The remaining six chapters of Volume 1 are:

Chapter 2   Theoretical Background
Chapter 3   Processors
Chapter 4   Control Units
Chapter 5   Main Memories
Chapter 6   Interconnection Networks
Chapter 7   Memory Hierarchies

Chapter 2 provides background material that is used throughout most of the book. Chapters 3 to 7 consider all of the various subsystems of computers.

Earlier in this chapter, we discussed a number of computer system design criteria and approaches. Our goal throughout the book is to present as many pertinent facts as possible and then try to relate them to real machines and possible future designs. The five computer subsystems of Chapters 3 through 7 are relatively well understood at the present time. This means that many approaches to each have been tried, and in a number of cases the results have been analyzed both theoretically and empirically. This does not mean, however, that overall computer system design is an exact science.

Indeed, computer system hardware and software design are very much engineering design problems in that theoretical and empirical results are brought to bear on designs that are user oriented. It seems likely that this design spirit will prevail for a long time in the future, since even a good understanding of how to design computer systems for one class of users will not carry over directly to all types of users. A little reflection on the wide variety of applications of computers makes this obvious.

It should not be assumed that there are no universal principles, however. We show in Chapter 2 that certain theoretical ideas can be used in several quite different aspects of computer system design, and these can probably be pushed into a number of areas not discussed here. We believe that other such principles will emerge in the future. Similarly, for example, the analyses of various types of memory systems or interconnection switches are applicable in the design of a number of different types of computer systems.

In spite of the above remarks, the design of computer systems today is not a "straightforward" engineering process—at least where machines with some innovative aspects are concerned. There is often a great deal of "seat of the pants" thinking and many decisions are reached in the smoke-filled room spirit of political decisions. In other words, intelligent, experienced people can have serious differences of opinion about how to proceed with a system design, even in view of detailed design analyses. Of course, the more that is known about the analysis and design of systems, the easier the process becomes, and one of the goals of this book is to try to bring together a number of pertinent facts and ideas to aid in the design process.

The above paragraph discussed system design, but similar discussions can be given from the standpoint of the system salesperson or owner, and the system user or critic as mentioned in Section 1.1.1.

Throughout the book, the reader will find references to other sections. Because the various subsystems of a computer are often intimately related to each other, it seems desirable to point out these relations. Occassionally, when it seems justified, some topics are briefly presented in two places to aid the continuity. Some topics are very difficult to localize in one of the five subsystems, so different aspects of them are discussed in several places. Addressing memory, for example, is presented in the control unit discussion of Chapter 4, since addresses come from programs, but it is also discussed in Chapters 5 and 7, because addresses are sent to the main memory and/or memory hierarchy for use. Thus, there is some arbitrariness in the organization of Chapters 3 through 7, but the attempt was to organize the material according to how a computer system itself is organized.

PROBLEMS

Easy problems in text order

1.1   Investigate Boolean switching.
   (a)   Show how to implement $A + B$ using two NOR gates and $A \cdot B$ using two NAND gates.
   (b)   Show how to implement $A \cdot B$ using three NOR gates and $A + B$ using three NAND gates. (*Hint:* De Morgan's Laws, $\overline{(A + B)} = \bar{A} \cdot \bar{B}$ and $\overline{(A \cdot B)} = \bar{A} + \bar{B}$ may be of use here.)
   (c)   Can you implement a NAND with AND and OR gates; also with OR and NOT gates?

1.2   The Boolean function realized by the circuit shown below can also be implemented as a two-level circuit containing which of the following gate combinations?
   Assume that the complemented inputs are also available.

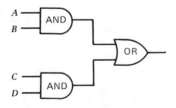

   (a)   Three NAND gates.
   (b)   Three NOR gates.
   (c)   Two OR gates and a NAND gate.
   (d)   Two NAND gates and a NOR gate.
   (e)   Two NOR gates and a NAND gate.

1.3 Consider the cost of typical ROM, RAM, CAM, and SAM memory systems of the same size built from the same technology. Order these memories from high to low in terms of estimated cost per bit of the system. Order the memories in terms of speed. In terms of feasible size.

1.4 Assume a random access memory (RAM) has 2^k words of 2^p bits each. How many bits long must the memory address register be? How many bits long must the memory information register be?

1.5 Consider a sequential access disk memory system consisting of two independent disk drive units. Let each drive contain two recording surfaces and each surface contain 128 tracks. If the disk system holds a total of 2 million bytes (8 bits each), how many bits are stored per track? Assume each track holds the same amount of data.

1.6 Match each of the following computers to the phrase that *best describes* it.

_____ STARAN IV	(a)	parallel processor
_____ von Neumann's machine	(b)	pipeline processor
_____ ILLIAC IV	(c)	associative processor
_____ TI ASC	(d)	multifunction processor
_____ PDP-11	(e)	uniprocessor
_____ CDC 7600	(f)	multiprocessor
_____ B7700	(g)	minicomputer

1.7 True or false.
   (a) In general, a pipelined operation requires more time from beginning to end, for a single pair of operands, than the same operation in a nonpipelined implementation.
   (b) A machine with k parallel processors has a maximum speedup asymptotically much greater than a k-segment pipeline processor.

1.8 Which of the following modern concepts were *not included* in Babbage's plans for the Analytical Engine (none or more than one may apply): card reader, printer, binary number system, internally stored program, subroutine calls, applications programmer?

1.9 As a computer designer, Babbage had to cope with the five design criteria: cost, speed, quality and usefulness, design assurance, and reliability. Give an example of how he successfully or unsuccessfully handled each.

1.10 Match each machine with the phrase that best describes it.

_____ ATLAS	(a)	An early relay computer.
_____ B5000	(b)	One of the first machines with a pipelined control unit.
_____ ENIAC	(c)	The first integrated circuit computer.
_____ IBM 360	(d)	The first system designed with a paged memory.

_____ STRETCH   (e) The first floating-point computer.

                       (f) An early vacuum tube computer.

                       (g) One of the first families of compatible machines.

                       (h) One of the first stack machines.

1.11   Which of the following concepts had not been demonstrated by 1953: Justice Department suits against IBM, core memory, microprogramming, floating-point hardware, stack machine, remote job entry?

Medium and hard problems in text order

1.12   (a) How many Boolean functions of two variables are there?

        (b) Show how each of them could be implemented with AND, OR, and NOT.

        (c) How many Boolean functions of three variables are there? Of n variables?

1.13   Several interesting problems arise with respect to the interconnection of gates (within a chip), packages (between ICs mounted on a board), and boards (mounted on a frame). Minimizing lead length is of primary importance. But minimizing crossovers is also important. As a relaxing diversion:

        (a) Reconstruct the following exclusive-OR, ($\oplus$), so that the crossover is eliminated:

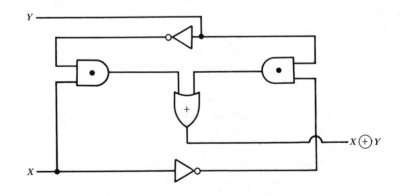

(Use 4 NAND gates.)

        (b) Show how any crossover can be eliminated using an AND, OR, and NOT network (having no crossovers). (It can be done with 3 ANDs, 3 ORs, and 4 NOTs).

1.14   The characteristic table for a D flip-flop is shown below.

Input (D)	Next State Output (A or B below)
0	0
1	1

That is, each time a clock pulse arrives, the flip-flop outputs the value of the D input. This value is maintained regardless of changes of D until the next clock pulse arrives.

The following diagram shows a synchronous sequential circuit implemented with D flip-flops. Complete the state transition table below describing the behavior of this circuit.

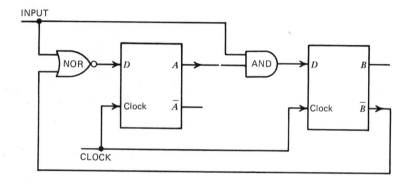

Present State		Next State			
		INPUT = 0		INPUT = 1	
A	B	A	B	A	B
0	0	0	0	0	0
0	1				
1	0				
1	1				

1.15 Suppose that a nanocomputer has 3 one-address instructions:

SUB X, which subtracts the contents of location X from the accumulator.

STORE X, which stores the accumulator in location X.

JMPNEG X, which branches to location X if the contents of the accumulator is negative.

(a) Write a program for this machine to implement the following high-level language segment. Temporary locations may be used.

You may assume a location named ONE contains the constant 1.

$$Z \leftarrow 0$$
$$DO \quad S_1 \quad I \leftarrow 1, X$$
$$S_1 \quad Z \leftarrow Z + Y$$

(b) If you were allowed to design *one* more instruction for this computer, what would it be?

1.16 Decision tables are used in high-level programming languages to format a complex series of logical decision rules and to specify what actions are to be taken when each rule is found to hold. In this context, it is a good exercise in Boolean logic. Decision tables have a left column containing a set of conditions to be evaluated and below the conditions a set of actions to be performed. All of the columns on the right are rules that stipulate which actions to perform if the values of the conditions match the rule.

In the decision table below 'yes,' 'no,' and 'don't care' are represented by Y, N, and -. The integers in the actions field specify the order in which the actions are to take place. For example, the second rule says, if $Q > R$ is not true and $Y < X$ (we don't care whether $A = B$ or $A \neq B$), then the actions $A \leftarrow 5$ and $B \leftarrow 7$ will be executed in that order.

(a) Which rule is redundant; that is, which rule is a particular case of a more general rule?

(b) Add to the table a rule that sets $B \leftarrow 7$ when none of the other rules apply. (*Hint:* Check each of the 2^3 possible condition combinations to see which are covered.)

(c) Construct a flowchart that describes the action of the decision table.

		Rules			
		1	2	3	4
Conditions	$Q > R$	N	N	Y	—
	$A = B$	Y	—	N	—
	$Y < X$	N	Y	Y	N
Actions	$A \leftarrow 5$	1	1	1	1
	$B \leftarrow 7$	2	2		2

1.17 (a) Write an assembly language program using the instruction set illustrated in Prog. 2 for the FORTRAN-like program which implements a relaxation iteration.

$$DO \quad S_3 \quad I \leftarrow 2, N - 1$$
$$DO \quad S_2 \quad J \leftarrow 2, N - 1$$
$$A(I, J) \leftarrow (A(I - 1, J) + A(I, J - 1) + A(I + 1, J) + A(I, J + 1))/4$$
$$S_2 \quad CONTINUE$$
$$S_3 \quad CONTINUE$$

Assume that the machine can evaluate the index expressions above directly in machine language instructions. For example, assume that instruction ADD A(I, J − 1) exists and that the control unit evaluates the subscript while decoding the instruction.

(b)   On a machine with overlapped control unit, memory, and processor as in Fig. 1.10, for what fraction of the inner loop execution time is the processor active in your program for part (a)? Is this fraction greater than the processor active fraction for Fig. 1.8?

1.18   Take one concept of digital computer architecture. Give its history up to the present and make a prediction about its role in future machines. Keep these points in mind:

- Limit yourself to at most 400 words.
- Don't choose a large or ambiguous subject, for example, operating systems, data bases, or transistors.
- Pick something that has already been or will imminently be implemented.
- Put your concept in perspective.
- What developments reinforced or brought about its popularity?
- For ideas, you might try any tutorial publication or [BeNe71].

   Some examples:

   Core memory (see Section 1.3)
   Stacks (see Section 4.3)
   Microprocessors (see [WiJe76])
   Bubble memories (see [Salz76])

1.19   Is there really such a thing as a general-purpose computer (besides humans)? In 400 words or less, give the pros and cons, the past, present, and future of the general-purpose computer (gpc).
   A few things to consider:

- Is a gpc a good thing from the viewpoint of a designer, a sales-person, or a user?
- Which of the five design criteria would a gpc favor?
- What is or was the best gpc?
- Did the gpc give birth to the industry or did the concept evolve?
- Can we expect more emphasis in gpc design or will the industry split up?

CH

2

If you can't be a pine on the top of the hill,
  Be a scrub in the valley—but be
The best little scrub by the side of the rill;
  Be a bush if you can't be a tree.

"Be the Best of Whatever You Are"

Douglas Malloch

O, thou hast damnable iteration,
and art indeed able to corrupt a saint.
Thou hast done much harm upon me. Hal—
God forgive thee for it!
Before I knew thee Hal, I knew nothing;
and now am I, if a man shall speak truly,
little better than one of the wicked.
I must give over this life, and I will give it over!

Henry the Fourth

William Shakespeare

THEORETICAL
BACKGROUND

2.1 INTRODUCTION

It is quite unusual, early in a discussion of computer systems, to present any theoretical results. Nevertheless, that is exactly what this chapter will do. We proceed in this way because an understanding of these results is very helpful in gaining insight to a number of computer system questions.

We will give bounds on the time and components required for certain classes of computations. These can be used at the level of elementary logic design, at the level of overall machine design, or in compiler design. First, we will consider computations in the form of trees, and later we will consider linear recurrences. In both cases, a number of applications will be presented.

Results about trees are useful at the hardware level for studying combinational circuit logic design and at the software level for parsing arithmetic expressions. The fundamental application of recurrences in the case of logic design lies in transforming logic design problems from easily stated sequential logic into much faster running combinational logic. This can be done at the level of gates or integrated circuit packages. We will mention software applications of recurrences shortly.

A third abstract topic we will study involves graphs whose nodes contain the above-mentioned trees and linear recurrences. If a few other types of nodes are also considered, these graphs can be interpreted as program flow charts. The graphs could be interpreted as flow charts of the logic of computer hardware, although we will not pursue this point. Generally, flow charts of programs are more complex than those of hardware, so we will consider the software case.

We will discuss certain transformations that can be used to rewrite programs in forms which are equivalent to given programs, but which are "improved" in several ways over the given programs. First, they can be executed in fewer processor time steps than the original programs, as we shall see in this chapter. Second, the addresses they generate in accessing data do not jump around as much as the original; this allows them to operate better in a memory hierarchy, a point we shall return to in Chapter 7. Finally, their structure is "cleaner," in general, than the original programs, so they are easier to understand. A full discussion of this involves conditional statements as well, but these will be deferred until Volume 2. These ideas can serve as the principles for writing a compiler for any of a variety of computer system organizations.

Sections 2.2 and 2.3 will deal with tree-height reduction and recurrence relations, respectively, whereas program graphs will be considered in Section 2.4. We will close the chapter with an abstract model of overall computer systems (Section 2.5). This model of system capacity ties together the hardware subsystems and relates them to the programs being run on a computer system, and it should serve as an introduction to how the remaining chapters of the book fit together in representing complete systems.

We strongly emphasize that it is very important to understand the ideas presented in this chapter. A grasp of the ideas allows one to avoid a great deal of confusion often found in discussions of computer systems, by being able to make quick speed and cost estimates for various parts of the systems. Because there are only a few ideas to be understood, this study seems like a very valuable investment. The novice should be warned that some of the results in this chapter look rather formidable; at the same time it is very important to emphasize that the basic ideas of the chapter are *not* difficult to understand. A number of results will be given in detail, but the key point is that on a first reading—and for long-term retention—only the order of magnitude of the bounds is important. The coefficients and additive constants are important for working out the details of examples, but to make quick estimates, it is very useful to remember only whether some function requires, for example, $O(\log n)$ or $O(\log^2 n)$ time steps. In the remainder of this introduction, we will give more motivation of the results in this chapter, particularly of Sections 2.2, 2.3, and 2.4.

2.1.1 Logic design and compiler uniformity

First, we consider the matter of computation speed. Whether the computation in question is at the bit, byte, word, or array level, there is always a question about how fast it can be performed. Assuming we have some serial algorithm for computing one data element (bit, byte, etc.) at a time, we ask whether or not the computation can be performed faster. Furthermore, if it can be, we want to know how to speed it up. Ultimately, of course, we would like to know the fastest possible way to compute it.

Throughout this book, we will deal with upper bounds on the times to compute various functions. These upper bounds will always be achievable through some constructive procedure. Thus, given a serial algorithm, we will give a procedure for transforming that algorithm into an equivalent algorithm which can be evaluated in a time satisfying our upper bound. Such bounds generally evade the question of carrying out the computation in "the fastest possible way."

We use quotation marks, because the question of a "fastest possible" algorithm is philosophical. Who can say, in general, whether or not we have examined all possible ways of computing a given function? If the function is simple enough, and if certain assumptions are made, it is sometimes possible to prove nontrivial lower bounds on computation time. Trivial bounds, such as "one step," are of no real interest for many problems.

In this book we will discuss some lower bounds, but only in a few cases. We do this to show that our upper bounds are often rather close to a lower bound which is easy to prove. Lower bounds for many of the problems we discuss have not been studied in much detail and trying to prove such bounds could lead to interesting theoretical results. Practically, however, sharper lower bounds are of little interest in most cases, because the upper bounds are already rather close to simple lower bounds. In some cases this is not true and we will point them out from time to time.

As a first example, consider the problem of performing logical operations on two n-bit computer words $a = (a_1 \cdots a_n)$ and $b = (b_1 \cdots b_n)$. If we have

$$a = (101101)$$

and

$$b = (011001),$$

then the result of a logical OR written as $(a + b)$ (cf., Section 1.1.2) is

$$c = (111101)$$

and the result of a logical AND written as $(a \cdot b)$ is

$$d = (001001).$$

Note that either the AND or the OR function is performed on pairs of bits of a and b, *independently* of all other bits in the words. Hence it is obvious that either of these functions can be computed in a time (e.g., one gate delay) which is independent of the number of bits involved. This assumes that we can use as many gates as needed; in this case the number of AND and OR gates will be proportional to n.

Now, let us turn our attention to arithmetic operations rather than logical operations. Again consider $a = (a_1, \ldots, a_n)$ and $b = (b_1, \ldots, b_n)$, but now let the a_i and b_i be full computer words each representing a number. If we have

$$a = (3, 5, 2, 1, 0, 7)$$

and

$$b = (1, 2, 3, 4, 5, 6),$$

then the result of a vector add is

$$c = (4, 7, 5, 5, 5, 13)$$

and the result of a vector multiply is

$$d = (3, 10, 6, 4, 0, 42).$$

Just as in the logical case, we can perform all of the above arithmetic operations independently of one another. Thus, regardless of n, the dimension of the vectors, we can form c in one add time or d in one multiply time; however, these times will be greater than the single gate delay assumed for the AND and OR above. This assumes that we have n adders or n multipliers available.

Next, let us consider some more difficult problems at the bit and arithmetic level. Suppose we have one computer word $a = (a_1 \cdots a_n)$ in which bit a_i corresponds to the occurrence of some event. In other words, let $a_i = 1$ if event e_i has occurred and $a_i = 0$ otherwise. Further, let b and c be one-bit indicators defined as follows. If one or more of events $e_1 \cdots e_n$ have occurred, b is to be 1, otherwise $b = 0$. And if *all* of events $e_1 \cdots e_n$ have occurred, c is to be 1, otherwise $c = 0$.

What are the fastest possible designs for logical circuits which compute b and c? It is intuitively clear that these problems are more difficult than the pairwise logical AND and OR problems discussed above. Here, all bits in the word a are involved in the computation of b and c. A simple way to solve this also turns out to be the fastest. To form b, we compute $a_1 + a_2, a_3 + a_4, \ldots, a_{n-1} + a_n$ simultaneously using $n/2$ OR gates each accepting just 2 inputs[1] (assuming $n = 2^k$). Next, we combine these in pairs to form $(a_1 + a_2) + (a_3 + a_4)$ and so on, fanning in the result to a single result bit b in $k = \log n$ steps. To form the result c, we replace the logical OR by a logical AND in the above discussion.

It is not difficult to prove that for such problems, this kind of fan-in approach yields the best possible result. The technique is useful in many logic design problems. We pursue some of these problems in Sections 2.2 and 2.3.

Now we consider the arithmetic problems corresponding to the above logic design questions. If

$$a = (a_1, \ldots, a_n)$$

is a vector of n numbers stored in a computer, suppose we want to compute the sum and product

$$b = \sum_{i=1}^{n} a_i \quad \text{and} \quad c = \prod_{i=1}^{n} a_i.$$

Instead of dealing with gates, we now consider two-input adders or multipliers as our basic building blocks. Again, the best solutions to these problems are

---

[1] As we shall see later, this argument easily generalizes to gates with more than two inputs; such gates are commonly found in practice. We limit ourselves to fan-ins of 2 for simplicity here.

obtained simply by fanning in the arguments in the form of a tree. If we now interpret the + as an arithmetic addition, the result is b; and similarly for c.

From the above discussion, we see that for a class of computations that requires the interaction of more than two data elements, more time is required than was needed by the first type of computation. In particular, for these calculations, if n arguments are involved and each operator combines 2 arguments, then we need $\lceil \log n \rceil$ operation times to compute the result. An operation time may be a logical OR or AND, or it may be an arithmetic add or multiply.

Finally, let us consider an even messier kind of computation. Suppose we have two n-bit words

$$x = (x_1 \cdots x_n)$$

and

$$y = (y_1 \cdots y_n),$$

and we want to design hardware logic to compute

$$c_i = \begin{cases} 0 & \text{if } i = 0 \\ y_i + x_i \cdot c_{i-1} & \text{if } 1 \leq i \leq n. \end{cases} \tag{1}$$

This may seem to be a strange logic design problem. It is not very unusual, however, since it forms the heart of the design of a binary adder. In particular, this recurrence relation accounts for carry propagation which is the main time delay in an adder circuit, as we will see in Section 2.3.7.3 where the x_i and y_i are derived from the bits of two words to be added. How much time is required to compute the vector of carry bits c?

The solution of this problem is not so obvious as were the solutions of our earlier problems. Before discussing how to solve it, let us consider an analogous arithmetic problem. It frequently occurs in numerical computation that we wish to evaluate a polynomial

$$p_n(x) = a_n + a_{n-1}x + a_{n-2}x^2 + \cdots + a_0 x^n.$$

Traditionally, one is told to do this using Horner's rule

$$h_n(x) = a_n + x(a_{n-1} + x(a_{n-2} + \cdots + x(a_1 + xa_0) \cdots)), \tag{2}$$

since it requires only $O(n)$ operations. This can be restated as a program of the form

Prog. 1

$$P \leftarrow A(0)$$
$$DO \quad S_1 \quad I \leftarrow 1, N$$
$$S_1 \quad P \leftarrow A(I) + X * P$$

which computes the expression $h_n(x)$ from inside out in N iterations.

It is clear that Eq. 1 and Prog. 1 share an important property. Both are recurrences in which step i depends on the result that was computed during step $i-1$. This may initially create the sinking feeling that no speedup is possible here. Nevertheless, $O(n)$ steps are not required to compute such linear recurrence functions; to show this in general is a nontrivial problem that has been studied in many forms.

Later, we show that Eq. 1 can in fact be evaluated in time of $O(\log n)$ gate delays using $O(n \log n)$ gates. By exactly the same kind of parallel algorithm, we can evaluate the polynomial of Prog. 1 in $O(\log n)$ operation times using $O(n)$ arithmetic processors. This follows from the fact that both problems can be formulated as linear recurrences with $O(n)$ arguments.

Other linear recurrences are more difficult to handle. We will see that in the worst case, linear recurrences of $O(n^2)$ arguments can be solved in $O(\log^2 N)$ steps using the fastest known methods. Nonlinear recurrences may require even more time, however. Certain nonlinear recurrences can be shown which, using standard methods, cannot be speeded up at all. In other words, the serial version of such algorithms is the fastest computational scheme known.

We can summarize the above by noting that we have distinguished four types of algorithms in a speedup hierarchy. These four types characterize the maximum speedup possible over the fastest serial algorithm. In each case, assume that the computation time is T_1 if we compute one data element (bit, word, etc.) at a time. *Type 0 algorithms* exhibit a maximum speedup of $O(T_1)$, examples being the ANDing of two computer words or the addition of two vectors. *Type 1 algorithms* have a maximum speedup of $O(T_1/\log T_1)$ and we saw several examples of this. In general, the evaluation of an arithmetic or Boolean expression is a Type 1 computation, as is the evaluation of certain arithmetic or Boolean linear recurrences. *Type 2 algorithms* have a maximum speedup of $O(T_1/\log^2 T_1)$, and we shall see examples of these later. Finally, *Type 3 algorithms* have lower order of magnitude maximum speedups. The worst of these are certain nonlinear recurrences whose best known speedup is $O(1)$, although we shall also see Type 3 algorithms with $O(T_1^{1/2})$ as their best known speedup, and so on.

It is important to note that the above speedup types are independent of whether the algorithm operates on bits at the hardware level or on words at the compiler level. This means that the transformations used to speed up algorithms presented in a serial form are exactly the same, regardless of the context of the algorithm. Thus, the algorithms we derive for the speedup of computations can be regarded as logic design automation techniques if applied at the component level, and they can be regarded as compiler techniques if they are applied at the floating-point operation level.

The above problems are examples of what we shall be studying in this chapter. Not included in the class of linear recurrences are sorting and merging of arrays of data, important business data processing algorithms that may frequently be found in COBOL programs. It turns out that these also fit into our speedup hierarchy, and we will return to the following in Chapter 6.

It was shown by K. Batcher [Batc68] that two sorted lists of $n/2$ numbers each, may be merged in $O(\log n)$ steps using $O(n)$ processors. A serial machine can do this in $O(n)$ steps. Thus we have a speedup of

$$O\left(\frac{n}{\log n}\right) = O\left(\frac{T_1}{\log T_1}\right),$$

so merging enjoys a Type 1 speedup. Batcher also shows that using $O(n)$ processors, n unordered numbers can be sorted into numerical order in $O(\log^2 n)$ steps. Using a serial processor this requires $O(n \log n)$ steps. Thus we have a speedup of

$$O\left(\frac{n \log n}{\log^2 n}\right) = O\left(\frac{T_1}{\log^2 T_1}\right),$$

so this is a Type 2 computation relative to the best possible serial algorithms.

Notice that various SNOBOL type string operations can be characterized as tree or linear recurrence operations, if we first convert the characters into bit strings, for example, by a comparison. Many other algorithms may be characterized in this heirarchy as we shall learn later.

2.1.2 Logic design realities

We have been discussing logic design problems using gate delays as a measure of speed, and gate count as a measure of cost, but how realistic is this? The question of estimating the speed and cost of an entire computer system or even of its major components is an interesting and very important one.

When discrete components were the main components used in computers, logic designers were greatly concerned with the problem of minimizing the number of gates, and many schemes for simplifying Boolean expressions were proposed. With the advent of integrated circuits, there is much less interest in such questions among real-world logic designers. However, they still are interested in cost as measured in terms of the number of IC packages used (and their types) as well as the overhead costs of printed circuit boards, interconnections, power supplies, testing and maintaining the system, and the like. It is very difficult to compare these costs among different technologies, but many of these costs are generally a function of the total physical volume of the system. Or, to be more specific, the extremely small volume of a gate in an integrated circuit package allows designers to ignore the cost of extra gates that just happen to be in a package but that are unused in some application of the package. Of course, in some cases, traditional Boolean simplification techniques are valuable in squeezing the desired function onto an integrated circuit package.

Both integrated circuit designers and logic designers are interested in what functions are put into IC packages; the former as producers and the latter as consumers. IC designers are keenly interested in reducing the number of different package types made because this reduces manufacturing costs. Logic designers are interested in the total number of packages used because the system cost is directly proportional to the number of packages. They are also concerned about the types of packages, because some are more expensive than others, and spare parts inventories may be smaller with fewer types.

Throughout this book we estimate the costs of system components in one way or another. In this chapter we give abstract bounds on gate counts for various logic design problems. These bounds should not be mistaken as attempts to minimize gate counts in the sense that Boolean expression simplification techniques are traditionally aimed at circuit cost minimization. We are attempting to put bounds on large chunks of logic at once. For example, we bound the number of gates in an adder circuit, or a multiplier, or a circuit that counts the ones to the left of each position in a word in Chapter 3, and later we give such counts for networks that permute data, sort arrays, merge arrays of data, and so on.

This allows designers an overall picture of the total volume of gates required in various parts of a system. The circuits are usually physically implemented using some IC circuit family and, of course, within an IC package containing, say, 100 gates, a dozen gates one way or the other may not matter. But when gates are measured at the level of whole computer functions, it is reasonable to assume that the cost measured in IC packages will be directly related to the gate count. Thus, if a processor requires 10,000 gates, about 100 IC packages of about 100 gates each will be needed, and variations between package types will not have a major impact on the total gate count.

We also give some attention to specific IC package design questions in this chapter. For example, we offer bounds on the maximum number of gates and gate delays required in IC packages in terms of the external parameters of the package. In Volume 2, we will also define various IC package types and discuss their use at the system level. In particular, we will bound the IC packages required for several kinds of logic design problems. A good discussion of practical logic design using IC packages may be found in [Blak75].

It should be emphasized that the chapter contains examples of the type mentioned above as well as general theoretical results that can be used in other problems not considered here. In this chapter we state several general results and give examples of their use. Proofs of these results will be given in Volume 2. All of our proofs are constructive so the methods could be regarded as general algorithms for automating a wide class of logic design problems. It is often easy to specify logic in a sequential (bit serial) form, and in Section 2.3 we show how linear sequential logic equations can be transformed into fast combinational logic.

2.1.3 Program transformations and machine organization

We have seen above that various computations can be transformed to achieve rather impressive speedups in an abstract sense. In Chapter 1 we surveyed a

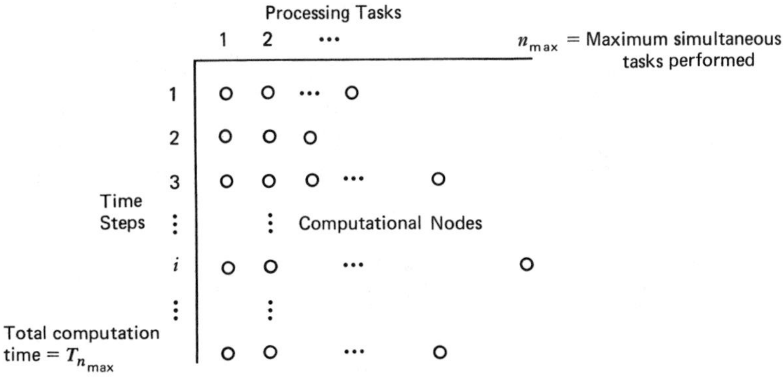

FIGURE 2.1 **Processing tasks versus time.**

number of machine organization types and observed how an inner product computation could be organized on them (see Section 1.2.1). As a final set of introductory comments, we now extend the discussion of Section 1.2.1, attempting only to give the reader some further intuition about how to interpret the ideas of the rest of the chapter.

A basic goal of a compiler for any multioperation machine is to discover as many operations or functions as possible that can be executed simultaneously. At the lowest level, we may seek arithmetic operations or memory accesses for array computers. At a higher level, we may seek procedures that can be executed simultaneously on a multiprocessor. In any case, we can imagine the compiler producing computation nodes that correspond to a timing diagram like that shown in Fig. 2.1.

Since we discuss several machine organizations here, Fig. 2.1 must be interpreted in a rather general way. The nodes of Fig. 2.1 may be any kind of processing tasks, ranging from individual operations such as memory accesses or arithmetic operations up to subroutines or coroutines that carry out a large piece of the overall computation. Similarly, we measure time in a fairly granular way in Fig. 2.1. If the nodes represent operations, then a time unit is the time required for the longest operation; if the nodes represent routines, then a time unit is the time required to finish the longest routine. The total number of nodes in the figure represents the *space-time product* of the computation in a strict sense, but if n_{max} processing units are dedicated to the entire computation, then the space-time product is $n_{max} \cdot T_{n_{max}}$. We assume that a programmer or compiler has broken a computation up into such nodes and that the nodes at one horizontal level all can be executed at once or in any sequential order. However, the nodes at each time step are constrained to follow the preceding step and to precede the following step. These constraints may arise from any of three sources: data dependence, control dependence, or resource limitations.

Examples of these are the following. If we compute a variable's value in one assignment statement and use it in another, we have a data dependence between the first and the second statements. A GOTO statement causes a control dependence between statements before and after it. If a given array machine can execute only one type of operation at a time, this would impose a resource limitation on each time step. Even though a number of additions and multiplications could logically be executed at once, say, if the machine were capable of doing only additions *or* multiplications at one step, a compiler would be forced to compile this in two execution steps.

In general, an important distinction between multioperation machine types can be made on the basis of whether or not all of the operations executed at once must be of the same type. Most parallel and pipeline processors are constrained in this way, although there are exceptions. We will refer to these as SIME (*single instruction multiple execution*) machines because a single instruction is executed on many data elements. On the other hand, multiprocessors and multifunction processors can be classified as MIME (*multiple instruction multiple execution*) machines. We will deal with this further in Chapter 4.

Assume that a program written in any source language has been analyzed to detect as much parallelism as possible, and the result is represented by a diagram such as Fig. 2.1. This can loosely be called a maximally parallel graph, since the parallelism is maximized with respect to some given set of analysis transformations. How would code be generated for various real machine organizations? For a multifunction processor, we could proceed across rows, assigning operations to function units of the proper type; but the dependences between rows would have to be preserved.

In a multiprogrammed uniprocessor, the same kind of procedure can be used to assign tasks to independently operating parts of the system, for example, the processor, a disk drive, a card reader, and so on. For a SIME pipeline processor, the like operations of each row (or parts of rows) could be assigned to one (or more) pipelines. The longer the rows of Fig. 2.1 the better, in the sense that it is desirable to amortize the overhead of starting up each row's processing over many operations.

The cases of parallel and multiprocessor machines are similar, but parallel machines are usually SIME, whereas multiprocessors are MIME. Units of work (operations or routines) may be assigned from each row to as many processors as are available. Thus a row with k nodes can be computed using p processors in $\lceil k/p \rceil$ steps by sweeping across each row in p processor steps. This assumes uniform operation rows in the parallel machine case and arbitrary row nodes in the multiprocessor case.

Throughout this chapter, we turn our attention to transformations that find a great deal of parallelism in a given program. We first study various constructs that form parts of programs, and then put them together in dependence graphs. Sometimes we find much more parallelism than a given machine can handle and in such cases sweeping across rows of a graph such as Fig. 2.1 can always be used to map the computation onto a fixed number of processors. The following generalization of this idea is useful for multiprocessors or (assuming the rows of Fig. 2.1 contain uniform operations) for parallel processors. If a computation C can be completed in time T_p with N_p computation nodes using p processors, then C can be computed in

$$\frac{N_p}{q} \le T_q \le T_p + (N_p - T_p)/q \quad \text{for } q < p.$$

A proof of this (see exercises) follows from the discussion of the paragraph above concerning sweeping rows of nodes using q processors in this case. This result is quite general in that it does not take into account any details of the graph of Fig. 2.1 except that the rows must be computed in order. As we proceed through this chapter, we present similar results for specific computations that are sharper than the above because they do account for specifics of given algorithms.

As we shall see, most of the results in this chapter lead to program graphs that can be directly mapped onto a SIME machine. This is true of the linear recurrence algorithms (Section 2.3) and arrays obtained by loop distribution (Section 2.4.4). The tree-height reduction schemes (Section 2.2) usually do not have this property. Two points should be made about trees, however. First, they can be evaluated in a SIME form simply by carrying out several operation steps at each level in the tree—this adjusts our bounds upward by a small constant, at most. Second, scalar tree evaluation is usually a relatively small part of most programs, so this slowdown (or even serial evaluation) is not very damaging to overall program speedup.

Most of this introduction has emphasized the speedup of computations. The transformations we present in Section 2.4 also are effective in localizing the data addresses generated by a running program. This can lead to a better utilization of the overall computer system, as we shall see in Chapter 7.

2.2   TREE-HEIGHT REDUCTION

2.2.1   Introduction

We will often express our bounds in terms of the number of constants and variables given as inputs to some algorithm. Even though the context of the constants, variables, and operators changes from algorithm to algorithm (e.g., from Boolean to arithmetic), we will use a uniform set of assumptions and definitions (except as noted). An *atom* is a constant or variable. We will deal with *Boolean atoms* (which have values 0 or 1), *arithmetic atoms* (representing numbers), and *array atoms* (representing arrays of Boolean or arithmetic atoms).

The dyadic operators $+$ and $\cdot$ will denote Boolean OR and AND, arithmetic addition and multiplication, or array addition and multiplication, respectively, depending on the atoms used. The context will make our meaning clear. In many cases, our results will hold in several different contexts, Further, we use $-$ to denote Boolean NOT or arithmetic subtraction. We use $/$ for arithmetic division and A^{-1} for the inverse of matrix A.

Any algorithm that is algebraic in nature has algebraic expressions as its fundamental computational units. Thus, logic design algorithms are expressed in terms of Boolean expressions, whereas numerical computation algorithms are expressed in terms of arithmetic expressions. We define an *expression* (Boolean, arithmetic, or array) as a well-formed string of atoms and operators. We denote expressions by uppercase letters. We write $E\langle e\rangle$, for example, to denote an expression E containing e atoms.

We count each constant or variable in an expression as one atom including multiple occurrences of the same symbol. Thus, we have as examples

$$E\langle 3\rangle = a + b + c,$$
$$E\langle 5\rangle = (a + b) * (c + d/2),$$
and
$$E\langle 7\rangle = (a + 5)/(2 * b + a * 5 + c).$$

Our lowest level of components will be simple AND, OR, and NOT gates. We assume that AND, OR, and NOT gates each have one gate delay of unit time and except as noted, that all AND and OR gates have fan-in 2 and fan-out f. By dealing with such stylized gates we are able to compare various designs in elementary terms. If one assumes more complex gates with higher fan-ins, as would be typical in practice, our gate and time upper bounds can obviously be reduced, in general. Another way in which the coefficients in our bounds can be uniformly improved is by ignoring the time required to complement signals. ECL circuit families have gates in which both true and complemented outputs are available with no time or cost penalty. To make our bounds conservative and as widely useful as possible, we have not taken advantage of any such features.

At the arithmetic operation level, we assume that arithmetic processors are capable of addition, subtraction, multiplication, and division of two arguments in one time unit. This is, of course, a greater time unit than used in Boolean logic design studies. In particular, it corresponds to several clock periods in most computers. The assumption that all four operations take equal times simplifies our discussion and is almost true (except for division) in most modern computers.[2] We will also assume that there are never any delays in providing instructions or data to the processors.

In order to characterize the performance of algorithms, we will use the same definition of T_1 and T_p as given in Section 1.2.1.2. Recall that T_p is the time to perform some computation using p processors for $p \geq 1$. As we have mentioned, many of our results will hold for Boolean as well as arithmetic

---

[2] If machine operations take different amounts of time, the bounds can be multiplied by a small constant (at most the ratio of the longest to the smallest operation times) to yield correct time bounds. Later we reference algorithms that actually account for operations requiring different times.

algorithms. Our notation for characterizing the performance of Boolean algorithms will be restricted from the arithmetic case, however, since the notation of T_1 is a bit slippery in the logic design context. Only the most pedantic of purists would care about the number of time steps needed to compute some function using just one gate! It is not even clear how to define "one gate." Furthermore, there has been no controversy over the usefulness of bit parallel arithmetic in several decades. Hence, we will consider only component and time bounds for various parallel schemes for logical function evaluation. Besides gates, we will also use integrated circuits as components in the logic design context.

Let θ be the number of components used in some Boolean algorithm. If we are counting gates as components, then we write G (to denote gates) for θ, and if we are counting integrated circuits, we write IC for θ. We let T_θ denote the number of unit time steps required to perform some algorithm using θ components. It should be noted that θ here is analogous to operations (rather than processors) in the arithmetic algorithm case. This is because when we are using p processors we assume that all p (or any subset) can be used on any time step and that all p can be used again on the next time step, and T_p is the number of such time steps on which we use (some or all of) the p processors. On the other hand, θ represents *all* of the components used in some combinational logic operation and T_θ is the number of component delays involved in the longest path through the combinational circuit implementing the entire operation. Thus, all combinational components are used in each clock period, whereas just one level of a tree is evaluated per clock (or time step) by processors. In the most general cases, we will express results in terms of T_C, where C refers to "components" which may be gates, integrated circuits, microprocessors, or standard arithmetic processors.

2.2.2 Simple bounds

This section will deal with two simple data handling problems. We are interested in time and component requirements. At the lowest level we could be dealing with simple gates as components; at higher levels, components could be microprocessors or even standard arithmetic units. As mentioned earlier, the ambiguous term *components* will refer to any of these. When we give a time bound in terms of component delays, we will be measuring the time to propagate a signal through some number of components which could be defined to include intercomponent wire or circuit board delays as well. All of our bounds will assume that the components have sufficient bandwidth to transmit all bits in parallel. Thus, bit level components (gates) can handle one bit, whereas word level components may handle 32- or 64-bit words in parallel.

The problems we consider are basic to much of what follows, and concern the fan-out and fan-in of atoms. Fan-out and fan-in are notions that have clear intuitive meanings; the *fan-out* of one atom to n places means the physical reproduction of that atom in n distinct physical positions. In the last section we discussed fan-in and fan-out at the level of individual gates, but in general we must deal with these at higher levels as well. For example, fanning out atoms is a common requirement in logic design whenever a signal is needed as input to several other components. Similarly, in a multioperation computer we may wish to broadcast one floating-point number (e.g., a program constant) to a number of processors.

The *fan-in* of n atoms to one place means the logical combination of the n atoms to produce one result. It should be assumed that all n atoms must take part in such a logical combination in order to avoid trivialities such as the fixed choice of atom number seven and the exclusion of all other atoms. Fanning in n atoms is usually more complex than fanning one atom out. The fan-in may be relatively simple as an OR or AND tree to determine if any or all inputs are set, respectively. Or it may be any Boolean expression evaluation at the bit level or any arithmetic expression at the word level. In any case, we assume that in any fan-in, all n inputs must be combined to produce a single output.

It was mentioned above that *component* is used to denote gates, IC packages, processors, and the like, depending on the context. A difficulty with using the terms *fan-in* and *fan-out* as broadly as we do is the corresponding context sensitivity of these words, but because there are few simple terms for these notions, we shall use *fan-in* and *fan-out* in all contexts. As we shall learn, there is great fundamental similarity between the subjects we shall discuss, so the common usage of these terms seems justified.

The following are examples of fan-in and fan-out in various contexts. At the hardware level, a gate with fan-in of five, as seen by a logic designer, may correspond to a five emitter transistor or to a collection of several simpler transistors. At the logic design level, a 16-input multiplexer may be constructed by interconnecting several smaller multiplexers or it may be one IC package; both will be said to have a fan-in of 16. An arithmetic expression of 8 variables corresponds to some tree with 8 leaves; the tree may contain various arithmetic operations, but we still refer to it as a fan-in of 8 variables. Thus, "fan-in" denotes all of these many-to-one mappings.

Our use of "fan-out" is similarly context sensitive. For example, at the hardware level, a gate's fan-out corresponds to how much current it can pass to its successors. If individual gates have insufficient electrical fan-out, at the logic design level a tree of gates can be used to achieve arbitrary fan-outs. Earlier we mentioned broadcasting a number to many processors as a system level fan-out. All of these one-to-many mappings are denoted as "fan-outs." As in our earlier discussion of gates, unless otherwise noted, all component fan-ins and fan-outs will be considered to be two.

The formalization of these ideas is complicated by the fact that hardware realities must be considered in time and component bounds. In particular, we must distinguish what might be called serial and parallel fan-outs and fan-ins. For example, if we consider the evaluation of an arithmetic expression as a fan-in operation (note that it satisfies our intuitive definition), we must define the source of the arguments. On the one hand, they may be provided serially from a single memory whose speed is matched to a single processor, whereas on the other hand they may be provided from n parallel memories and all be available at once. Similar comments can be made about fan-outs. We will now consider bounds on the time to evaluate an algebraic expression.

Lemma   1

Given any algebraic expression of e atoms, $E\langle e \rangle$,

$$e - 1 \geq T_C[E\langle e \rangle] \geq \lceil \log e \rceil,$$

using processors with a fan-in of 2.

Proof

Let $e = 2^q$ and consider a tree for $E\langle e \rangle$ which has the maximum number of nodes at each level. At each level 1 node, each operator consumes two operands, so there can be at most $e/2$ such nodes. Similarly, at level 2 there can be at most $e/4$ nodes, and at any level k there can be at most $e/2^k$ nodes. At the root we must have $e/2^k = 1$ so the tree height is $k = \log e = q$. Because any other tree for $E\langle 2^q \rangle$ will have a greater height than the one constructed with a maximum number of nodes at each level, we have $T_C[E\langle 2^q \rangle] \geq q$. Now assume that $2^q < e \leq 2^{q+1}$. Any node attached to the minimum height tree for $E\langle 2^q \rangle$ constructed above must increase its height by one since the above tree has no free nodes. We can attach at most 2^q nodes—one in place of each original atom—without increasing the original tree height by more than one. Hence, $T_C[E\langle 2^{q+1} \rangle] \geq q + 1$. It follows that for any integer e, $T_C[E\langle e \rangle] \geq \lceil \log e \rceil$.

The upper bound is reached when the expression is evaluated serially. ∎

To bound the components (C) here is difficult. If the evaluation is serial, then we obviously have just one component, for example, processor in the arithmetic expression case. In the parallel case, however, many processors [in fact, more than $O(e)$] may be required if much redundant computation is necessary to achieve a fast evaluation.

Now we turn to some bounds on the simpler problems of fan-in or fan-out. We assume that signals appear in parallel from some external source and are returned to some external destination after our operations on them. We are effectively ignoring registers from which signals come and to which they are returned. By an e-way fan-in we mean an e source to one destination fan-in, and similarly for an e-way fan-out. First we give a variation on Lemma 1.

Corollary   1

Any e-way fan-in or fan-out requires at least

$$T_C \geq \lceil \log e \rceil$$

with

$$C \geq e - 1,$$

using components with fan-in or fan-out of 2.

Proof

The fan-in time bound is just a special case of Lemma 1, and the fan-out time bound is obtained by reversing the flow through the network.

The fan-in component bound follows from the fact that each atom must be combined with some other intermediate result. The first two atoms require one component and the remaining $e-2$ atoms require $e-2$ more components for a total of $e-1$. The fan-out component bound follows by reversing the flow through a fan-in network. ∎

A component bound is possible here (unlike Lemma 1) because we assume that all of the inputs (or outputs) appear in distinct registers at once, say at the beginning or end of a clock period. For the upper bound in Lemma 1, we allowed the operands to be supplied sequentially, for example, from a memory unit, say one per clock period. Note that Corollary 1 can easily be generalized to fan-ins and fan-outs higher than two.

Next we give upper bounds on the fan-in and fan-out of signals.

Lemma 2

An e-way fan-in or fan-out can be accomplished using components with fan-in or fan-out of $f \geq 2$ in

$$T_C \leq \lceil \log_f e \rceil$$

with

$$C < \frac{e-1}{f-1} + 1.$$

Proof

The source and destination of our signals are outside our consideration as illustrated in Fig. 2.2.

We can fan-out to f places with one component, to $f-1+f$ places with two components, to $f-2+2f$ places with three components, and to $f-(C-1)+(C-1)f$

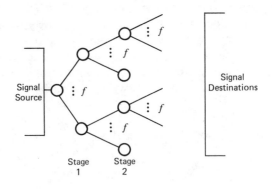

FIGURE 2.2   **Signal fan-out.**

places with C components. Since we want $e \le f - (C-1) + (C-1)f$, we see that $e \le f - (C-1) + (C-1)f < e + f - 1$. Thus we have

$$C < \frac{e-1}{f-1} + 1.$$

We can fan-out to f places in one time unit, to f^2 places in 2 time units, to f^3 places in 3 time units, and to f^k places in k time units. It follows that for $e \le f^k < fe$ we have $k < 1 + \log_f e$. But $k = T_C$ so the lemma is proved. ∎

By comparing Lemma 2 (for $f = 2$) with Corollary 1, we see that Lemma 2 is a tight bound on fan-in and fan-out.

2.2.3 Applications

A large fraction of the gates used in real computers are there for the purpose of fanning in or fanning out signals. If we think of a processor as a collection of registers used as memory, and combinational logic used to transform signals, then we must have other gates which move signals between the registers and transformation logic. Circuits that fan-in and select one signal out of n are called *multiplexers*, and circuits that fan-out one signal to one of n places are called *demultiplexers*. If $n = 2^k$ signals are involved, then k bits must be used to control the selection of one input or output signal. We show examples of these for $n = 8$ in Fig. 2.3.

Given a circuit family with some fixed numbers of inputs and outputs, larger multiplexer and demultiplexer circuits can obviously be constructed by connecting the packages shown in Fig. 2.3 as a tree. Lemma 2 can then be applied directly, assuming we have package components with fan-in or fan-out f.

Let us consider the detailed design of the demultiplexer of Fig. 2.3b. A single node in the fan-out tree can be constructed from two AND gates (one with a complemented input, denoted by a small circle), as shown in Fig. 2.4. Each AND gate has a fan-in of 3.[3] If the control signal is 0, then output 0 is selected by inverting the zero. A control input of 1 selects output 1. Assume that the control signal and the input signal (either a 0 or a 1) are present on their respective lines. Now, whenever an enable (also assumed to be a 1) appears, the output selected by the control line will produce a copy of the input (0 or 1). If we form a tree of such nodes and assume the input and control signals are applied, when the enable appears the input is transmitted to the appropriate output. This is shown in Fig. 2.5, where we avoid showing enable lines for simplicity. For the purpose of interpreting Fig. 2.5 in terms of Lemma 2, we now consider the two gate elements of Fig. 2.4 to be components. Notice that there are seven such components in Fig. 2.5. Of course, real gates may have fan-ins of 4 or even 8, in which case fewer gates are needed, but the same principle applies to larger networks in such cases.

---

[3] This exception to our usual assumption of fan-ins of 2 is made to simplify Fig. 2.4.

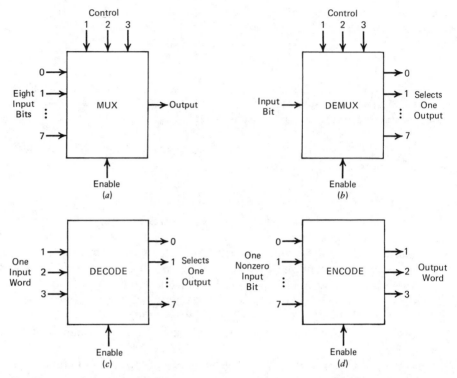

FIGURE 2.3 **Fan-in and fan-out IC packages.** (*a*) **Multiplexer or selector.** (*b*) **Demultiplexer.** (*c*) **Decoder.** (*d*) **Encoder.**

The enable signal is sometimes called a clock or a strobe signal, but in any case its appearance represents a control point in the machine (see Section 1.1.2). The control signals might come from an instruction which, for example, selects two registers and causes their contents to be sent to the adder.

A demultiplexer is related to a *decoder*, because output *i* is selected when the control bits form a binary number equal to *i*. In this case the control bits are regarded as an input word, as shown in Fig. 2.3*c*. We need not use all possible

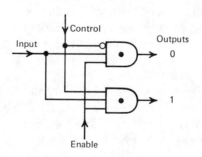

FIGURE 2.4 **Demultiplexer node.**

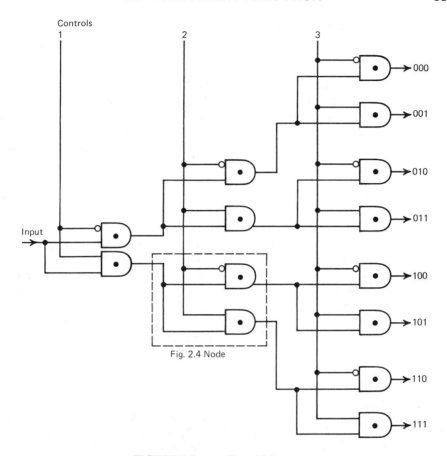

FIGURE 2.5 **Demultiplexer tree.**

outputs in a decoder. For example, a 4-input 10-output decoder could be used to convert binary coded decimal numbers to one of ten outputs. Because a decoder is equivalent to a demultiplexer, which is the inverse of a multiplexer, we have a fourth package type in Fig. 2.3*d*, namely, an *encoder*, which is the inverse of a decoder. It accepts as input an 8-bit word, all of whose bits are zero except the *i*th, and produces the binary number *i* as an output. A circuit to perform this transformation is much more complex than the others of Fig. 2.3. We can formulate it as a linear recurrence (see Section 2.3.7.2), but will delay the discussion of such circuits until Chapter 3.

It should be noted that most gates have a fan-in greater than 2; in practice, 4 or 8 is typical for various circuit types. This leads to fewer gate delays in IC packages of the types discussed here. For further discussion of the topics of this section, see, for example, [Blak75], [Mano72], or the literature of semiconductor circuit manufacturers.

2.2.4 General algebraic trees

2.2.4.1 Introduction

Algebraic expressions play a fundamental role in the design and programming of digital computers. Expressions involving Boolean constants and variables are used to define the operation of a machine at the logic design level. Expressions involving integer and real constants and variables are found in most high-level programming languages. Some very high-level programming languages allow expressions that include constants and variables which represent entire arrays of numbers. We are concerned here with the time and cost required to evaluate algebraic expressions.

Our goals in deriving upper bounds on the time and number of processors required for arithmetic expression evaluation are twofold. First, we want to demonstrate that some expressions can be evaluated in times much smaller than would be permitted by a single processor. Second, we want to exhibit simple algorithms which can be used to achieve these bounds. We seek bounds that are functions of a few easy-to-measure parameters of a given arithmetic expression. We desire algorithms that are easy to apply and are useful in most expressions occurring in practice.

In this section we shall continue to use the notation of Section 1.2.1.2. Recall that the *speedup* of a p processor calculation over a uniprocessor is defined as $S_p = T_1/T_p \geq 1$ and the *efficiency* of the calculation is $E_p = S_p/p \leq 1$, which may be regarded as actual speedup divided by the maximum possible speedup using p processors. Computation time may be saved with the sacrifice of performing extra operations. If O_p is the total number of *operations* executed in performing some computation using p processors, then we call R_p the *operation redundancy* and let $R_p = O_p/O_1 \geq 1$, where $O_1 = T_1$. *Utilization* is defined as $U_p = O_p/pT_p \leq 1$, where pT_p is the number of operations which could have been performed in T_p unit steps. Using R_p, we can rewrite U_p as $U_p = R_p O_1/pT_p = R_p T_1/pT_p$, and by the definition of E_p we have $U_p = R_p E_p$. Thus, if an observer notices that all p processors are computing all of the time, he or she may correctly conclude that $U_p = 1$, but may not conclude that $E_p = 1$ because R_p may be greater than 1.

For various computations we will discuss the maximum possible speedup known according to some algorithm and in such cases we use P to denote the minimum number of processors known to achieve this maximum speedup. In these instances we will use the notation T_P, S_P, E_P, and so on, to denote the corresponding time, speedup, efficiency, and the like, respectively.

Time and processor bounds for some computation A will be expressed as $T_P[A]$ and $P[A]$ in the minimum time cases and $T_p[A]$ in the restricted processor ($p < P$) case. When no ambiguity can result, we will write just T_P in place of $T_P[A]$ and P in place of $P[A]$, for simplicity.

If we use one processor, then the evaluation of an expression $E\langle e \rangle$ containing e operands requires $e - 1$ units of time. But suppose we may use as many processors as we wish. Then it is obvious that some expressions $E\langle e\rangle$ may be evaluated in log e units of time, as discussed in Section 2.1.1. In fact, as we learned in the previous section, the lower bound $T[E\langle e\rangle] \geq \lceil \log e \rceil$ follows from a simple fan-in argument.

On the other hand, it is easy to construct expressions $E\langle e\rangle$ whose evaluation appears to require $O(e)$ time units regardless of the number of processors available. Consider the evaluation of a polynomial by Horner's rule as in Section 2.1. A strict sequential order is imposed by the parentheses in Eq. 2 and more than one processors are of no use in speeding up this expression's evaluation.

2.2.4.2 Transformations used

We are not restricted to dealing with expressions as they are presented to us, however. For example, the associative, commutative, and distributive laws of arithmetic operations may be used to transform a given expression into a form that is numerically equivalent to the original but that may be evaluated more quickly. We now consider examples of each of these.

Fig. 2.6a shows the only parse tree possible (except for isomorphic images) for the expression $(((a+b)+c)+d)$. This tree requires three steps for its

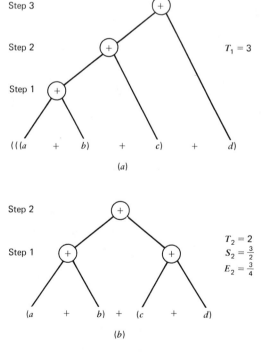

FIGURE 2.6   **Tree-height reduction by associativity.**

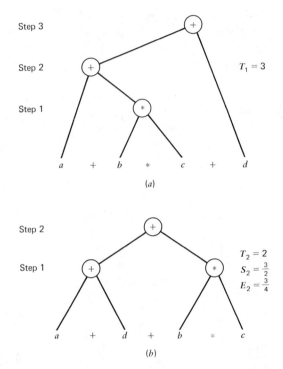

FIGURE 2.7   **Tree-height reduction by commutativity.**

evaluation, and we refer to this as a *tree height* of three. However, the associative law for addition says that $(a + b) + c = a + (b + c)$. Using associativity, we may rearrange the parentheses and transform this to the expression $(a + b) + (c + d)$, which may be evaluated as shown in Fig. 2.6b with a tree height of two. It should be noted that in both cases, three addition operations are performed. Thus, using two processors we achieve a speedup of $S_2 = \frac{3}{2}$, an efficiency of $E_2 = \frac{3}{4}$, and a redundancy of $R_2 = 1$. Clearly, similar results can be achieved using the associative law for multiplication.

Fig. 2.7a shows a parse tree for the expression $a + bc + d$; again we have a tree of height three. In this case the tree is not unique, but it is obvious that no lower height tree can be found for the expression by use of associativity. But by use of the commutative law for addition, $a + b = b + a$, we obtain the expression $a + d + bc$ and the tree of Fig. 2.7b, whose height is just two. As with Fig. 2.6, we remark that both trees contain three operations, and using two processors we obtain speedup, efficiency, and redundancy results that are identical to those of Fig. 2.6. It is also obvious here that similar results can be achieved using the commutative law for multiplication (except of course when the operations do not allow it, as in matrix multiplication).

Now consider the expression $a(bcd + e)$ and the tree for it given in Fig. 2.8a.

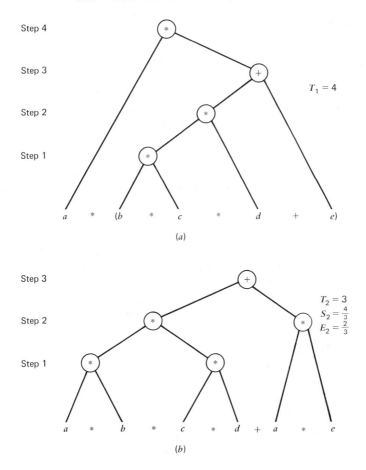

FIGURE 2.8   **Tree-height reduction by distributivity.**

This tree has height four ($T_1 = 4$), and contains four operations ($O_1 = 4$). By use of associativity and commutativity, no lower height tree can be found. But, using the arithmetic law for the distribution of multiplication over addition, $a(b+c) = ab + ac$, we obtain the expression $abcd + ae$, which has a tree of minimum height three, as shown in Fig. 2.8b. Unlike the two previous transformations, however, distribution has introduced an extra operation; the tree of Fig. 2.8b has five operations compared with the four operations of the undistributed form. In this case, we use two processors to attain a speedup of $S_2 = \frac{4}{3}$, an efficiency of $E_2 = \frac{2}{3}$, and a redundancy of $R_2 = \frac{5}{4}$. This is our first example of $R_p > 1$ and, clearly, is a consequence of distributing the multiplication over several terms of the sum. Note that in the case of Boolean expressions, we have the possibility of distributing the OR operation over the AND operation, as well as the AND over the OR.

Preprocessing expressions

To simplify our discussion, we will assume that all expressions we deal with have been preprocessed by the following straightforward transformations. We assume that all algebraically redundant parenthesis pairs have been removed from expressions; parentheses are defined to be *algebraically redundant* if their use in an expression has no effect on the expression's value, assuming exact arithmetic is performed. Of course, some parentheses in programs are algebraically redundant but are computationally necessary to preserve a numerical result; it is well known, for example, that floating-point summation is *not* associative [Wilk63]. Thus our bounds assume that exact arithmetic is performed and to use them in practice one might include special, nonremovable parentheses that a compiler would leave intact.

We assume that unary arithmetic plus and minus operators and Boolean complements are reduced to at most single minus or complement operators. Because binary subtraction is neither associative nor commutative, in general, we assume that all such operators are removed as follows. A binary minus can always be replaced by a binary plus and a unary minus; then the unary minus can be distributed over expressions at lower levels until it reaches the level of individual atoms. We assume that $a - b$ and $a + (-b)$ can be evaluated in equal time. Analogously, Boolean NOTs can be distributed down to the level of atoms by the use of DeMorgan's laws.

Transformations not used

We will restrict ourselves to transforming expressions using associativity, commutativity, and distributivity, because these alone are enough to give us results that are close to the lower bound. However, more complex transformations, such as the following, could be used to gain even better results in general. Expression simplification could be used, for example, to transform $a + a + a$, which takes two steps, into $3a$ which may be evaluated in one step, or to rewrite the Boolean expression $a + a + a$ as a. Factorization also could be used for speedup; for example, $ac + ad + bc + bd$ requires three steps, whereas the factored form $(a + b)(c + d)$ requires only two steps. Partial fraction expansion is also useful; an example of this is the decomposition of $(ad + bc)/cd$, which takes three steps, into $(a/c) + (b/d)$, which may be evaluated in two steps.

It should be noted that each of these reduces the number of operations in a given expression. Thus, if these transformations were used before the algorithms we shall discuss, our algorithms would yield better results with perhaps the following exception. In the case of factorization the parenthesis nesting depth is increased, a fact that could be detrimental, as we shall see in Theorem 1. Note that the above tend to reduce the number of components as well as tree height.

2.2.4.3 Tree-height reduction bounds

Having considered a few examples of arithmetic expression tree-height reduction, we are naturally led to ask a number of questions. For any arithmetic expression, how much tree-height reduction can be achieved? Can general bounds and algorithms for tree-height reduction be given? How many processors are needed?

To answer these questions, we will now survey results concerning the evaluation of expressions. Details and further references may be found in the papers cited. Assuming that only associativity and commutativity are used to transform expressions, Baer and Bovet [BaBo68] gave a comprehensive tree-height reduction algorithm based on a number of earlier papers. Beatty [Beat72] showed the optimality of this method. An upper bound on the reduced tree height assuming only associativity and commutativity are used, given by Kuck and Muraoka [KuMu74], is the following.

Theorem 1

Let $E\langle e \mid d \rangle$ be any expression with depth d of parenthesis nesting. By the use of associativity and commutativity only, $E\langle e \mid d \rangle$ can be transformed such that

$$T_P[E\langle e \mid d\rangle] \leq \lceil \log e \rceil + 2d + 1 \quad \text{and} \quad O_P = e - 1$$

with

$$P \leq \left\lceil \frac{e}{2} - d \right\rceil. \qquad \blacksquare$$

Note that if the depth of parenthesis nesting d, is small, then this bound is quite close to the lower bound of $\lceil \log e \rceil$. The complexity of this algorithm has been studied in [BrTo76], where it is shown that in addition to the standard parsing time, tree-height reduction can be performed in $O(e)$ steps.

Now let us consider an example that compares several methods of evaluating an expression.

Example 1

Consider the expression

$$E\langle 8 \mid 1 \rangle = a + b(c + def + g) + h.$$

Since $e = 8$ we have $T_1 = 7$. Notice that by using associativity alone, no speedup is possible. By Theorem 1, we have

$$T_P[E\langle 8 \mid 1 \rangle] \leq 3 + 2 + 1 = 6$$

with

$$P \leq \left\lceil \frac{e}{2} - d \right\rceil = 3.$$

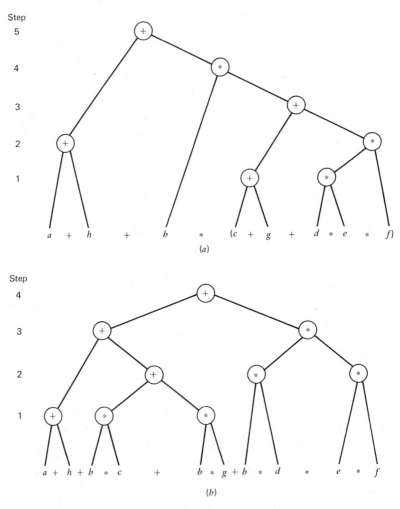

FIGURE 2.9 Tree-height reduction. (*a*) Using associativity and commutativity. (*b*) Using associativity, commutativity, and distributivity.

In Fig. 2.9*a* we see that, in fact, using associativity and commutativity, we can achieve $T_2 = 5$. Thus, the bounds give one more time step and one more processor than are actually needed. Finally, notice in Fig. 2.9*b* that by using distribution as well, we can reduce the time to $T_3 = 4$, although a third processor is required. Notice that although the efficiency drops in this case, the utilization increases. ∎

The idea of tree-height reduction algorithms using only associativity and commutativity is to isolate subtrees containing like operators by using commutativity. Then by using associativity, a tree with as low a height as possible is constructed for each such subtree. For example, in Fig, 2.9a from the bottom up we have the $d * e * f$ subtree, then this subtree added to $c + g$, and so on up to $a + h$ plus the remainder of the expression.

Unfortunately, there are classes of expressions (e.g., Horner's rule polynomials or continued fractions) for which no speed increase can be achieved by using only associativity and commutativity. Muraoka [Mura71] studied the use of distributivity as well as associativity and commutativity for tree-height reduction and developed comprehensive tree-height reduction algorithms using all three transformations and assuming all operations take one time unit. An algorithm that considers operations which take different amounts of time is presented by Kraska [Kras72].

Bounds using associativity, commutativity, and distributivity have been given by a number of people [Bren74, KuMa75, MuPr75]. In [Bren74] the following theorem is proved by Brent.

Theorem 2

Given any expression $E\langle e\rangle$, $e > 2$, by the proper use of associativity, commutativity, and distributivity, $E\langle e\rangle$ can be transformed such that

$$T_P[E\langle e\rangle] \leq \lceil 4 \log (e - 1)\rceil - 1$$

and

$$O_P < 10e$$

with

$$P < 3e. \qquad \blacksquare$$

The proof of Theorem 2 is constructive and can be used to generate trees which satisfy the given bounds. By using some judgment, however, one can often make small perturbations to achieve even lower tree heights.

We now sketch the idea of the proof and give two examples that show how the ideas of Theorem 2 can be used for tree-height reduction—indeed, for minimization of tree heights in some cases. Because Theorem 2 is a general bound, the results achieved in these examples are much better than the bounds would indicate.

Example 2

Consider the evaluation of

$$E\langle 8\rangle = a(b + c(d + e(f + gh)))$$

using an algorithm which fully distributes the atoms to obtain

$$E_1\langle 14\rangle = ab + acd + acef + acegh.$$

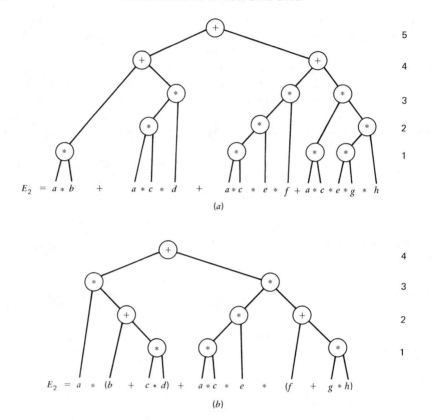

$E_2 = a * b + a * c * d + a * c * e * f + a * c * e * g * h$

(a)

$E_2 = a * (b + c * d) + a * c * e * (f + g * h)$

(b)

FIGURE 2.10   **Horner's rule expression. (a) Fully distributed. (b) Properly distributed.**

By drawing a tree for this expression in Fig. 2.10a, we see that with four processors we can achieve

$$T_4 = 5, \ S_4 = \tfrac{7}{5}, \ E_4 = \tfrac{7}{20}, \quad \text{and} \quad R_4 = \tfrac{13}{7}.$$

However, by cutting the expression in "half" and distributing, we can obtain (see Fig. 2.10b; $X = e(f + gh)$ will be discussed below)

$$E_2\langle 10 \rangle = a(b + cd) + ace(f + gh),$$

so using just three processors we have

$$T_3 = 4, \ S_3 = \tfrac{7}{4}, \ E_3 = \tfrac{7}{12}, \quad \text{and} \quad R_3 = \tfrac{9}{7}.$$

This scheme (as used in Theorem 2) provides a substantial improvement over full distribution. In fact, by a fan-in argument on the eight atoms of the original expression, we cannot expect a better time than three steps using four processors. By inspection, it is clear that four is the lowest possible tree height for this expression.   ∎

The idea of tree-height reduction algorithms which use associativity, commutativity, and distributivity involves two parts. By using associativity and commutativity, a given expression is put in a form that can approximately be cut in "half" by removing one subtree. This subtree, call it X, has about half the atoms in the original expression and the remaining subtree has the remaining atoms. After the overall tree has been cut in "half," the subtree X is moved toward the top of the overall tree by distribution.

The above procedure is carried out recursively on X and the other "half" of the overall tree until the leaves of the tree are reached. This produces a relatively balanced tree that has more operators than the original, but that may be of much lower height. Although this sketch of the algorithm is vague, the examples (which carry out the procedure just once, each) should clarify the idea. For further study see [Bren74, BrKM73]. Problem 2.26 illustrates the difficulties of full distribution.

Example 3

Consider the evaluation of a continued fraction

$$E\langle 8\rangle = \cfrac{a}{b + \cfrac{c}{d + \cfrac{e}{f + \cfrac{g}{h}}}}.$$

By cutting this expression in "half" we can rewrite it as

$$E_1 = \frac{aX}{bX + c} \quad \text{and} \quad X = d + \cfrac{e}{f + \cfrac{g}{h}}.$$

Now by substitution of X and distribution, we obtain the expression of Fig. 2.11. Using four processors, we have $T_4 = 5$, $S_4 = \frac{7}{5}$, $E_4 = \frac{7}{20}$, and $R_4 = 2$. By noticing the common subexpression in the numerator and denominator, we can save one processor and get

$$T_3 = 5, S_3 = \tfrac{7}{5}, E_3 = \tfrac{7}{15}, \quad \text{and} \quad R_3 = \tfrac{12}{7}. \qquad \blacksquare$$

The complexity of the algorithm of [Bren74] has been studied in [BrTo76], where it is shown that tree-height reduction can be done using $O(e \log e)$ steps in addition to normal parsing. Also, if the number of processors is allowed to grow beyond $O(e)$, the time coefficient of Theorem 2 has been reduced to 2.88 by Muller and Preparata [MuPr75].

A number of other results are available for arithmetic expressions of special forms or for general expressions if more information is known about them. In [KuMa75], expressions without division, continued fractions, general expressions with a known number of parenthesis pairs or division operations, and other such cases are considered.

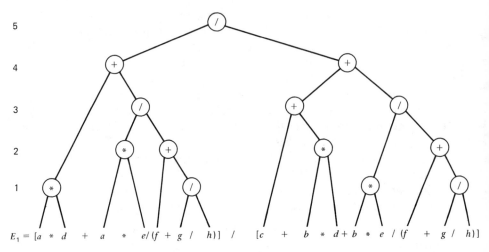

$E_1 = [a * d + a * e/(f + g / h)] / [c + b * d + b * e / (f + g / h)]$

FIGURE 2.11   **Continued fraction evaluation.**

One other case should be mentioned here. For programming languages with array operators, other compilation techniques may be of interest. For example, a solution to the problem of minimizing the time to evaluate the product of a sequence of conformable arrays on a parallel machine is given in [MuKu73]. In [KuMa75] it is shown that any matrix expression including addition, subtraction, multiplication, and matrix inversion can be handled as follows. If any of these four operations takes one matrix operation time step, then any matrix expression of e arrays can be evaluated in 6 log e matrix operation steps. The coefficient is the sum of three multiplication times, two addition times, and one inversion time. Matrix addition and multiplication are straightforward, but the time required to invert a matrix measured in standard arithmetic operations is not obvious and will be discussed further in Volume 2.

Most arithmetic expressions appearing in real programs have a rather small number of atoms. For subscripted atoms in a loop, the arrays may be quite large, so it is usually advisable to evaluate these as a tree of arrays, one array operation at a time. If tree-height reduction techniques are used on such expressions, there are two possibly bad consequences. One is the passing from SIME to MIME operation as discussed earlier. The other is that redundant operations are generally introduced, making the overall computation less efficient. However, for expressions outside loops, for unsubscripted expressions inside loops, or for expressions of small arrays inside loops, tree-height reduction can be of value.

The number of processors required to evaluate such expressions is usually less than is required for recurrence solving, as we shall discuss later. There may be cases where tree-height reduction is desirable, but the number of available processors is very small, in which case the limited processor results of [Bren74, Wino75] are of interest.

2.2.5 Applications

If one attempted to use the results of this section in a real compiler for some kind of multioperation machine, the results would probably be quite disappointing. The bounds are fine, but the expressions in real programs are not! Most have only a few atoms (see Section 4.2.1.1) and, hence, are not amenable to such speedup. Of course, there are some isolated cases of longer expressions and sometimes longer expressions can be generated from a given program, as we shall see below. We will consider two kinds of applications here in which tree-height reduction schemes might in fact be of practical use. First, we deal with blocks of assignment statements. Then we turn to combinational logic circuits.

2.2.5.1 Blocks of assignment statements

We begin by defining our terms. An *assignment statement* is denoted by $x \leftarrow E$, where x is a scalar or array variable and E is a well-formed arithmetic expression. A *block of assignment statements* (BAS) is a sequence of one or more assignment statements with no intervening statements of any other kind. For example, the BAS

$$X \leftarrow B * C * D + E$$
$$Y \leftarrow A * X$$
$$Z \leftarrow F * G + X$$

can be evaluated using one processor in six steps, ignoring memory activity. Note that none of the right-hand side expressions can be speeded up by tree-height reduction. By *statement substitution*, a process in which right-hand side variables are replaced by the right-hand side expressions of previously defined left-hand side variables, we obtain three statements that can be transformed by tree-height reduction techniques to yield:

$$X \leftarrow B * C * D + E; \ Y \leftarrow A * B * C * D + A * E; \ Z \leftarrow B * C * D + E + F * G.$$

Because the resulting expressions can be evaluated simultaneously in three steps, we obtain a speedup of 2. By properly arranging the parse trees it may be seen in Fig. 2.12a that just five processors are required. Thus we have efficiency $E_5 = \frac{2}{5}$.

One of the inefficiencies here is due to the multiple evaluation of the common terms generated by statement substitution for $X \leftarrow B * C * D + E$. If we share the evaluated expression $B * C * D$ between X and Z, we can eliminate one processor and achieve an efficiency of $E_4 = \frac{1}{2}$ as shown in Fig. 2.12b.

In general, we might expect to achieve higher efficiencies by using fewer processors. In the above case, if we restrict ourselves to four processors for the original expressions and do not recognize common subexpressions, we obtain

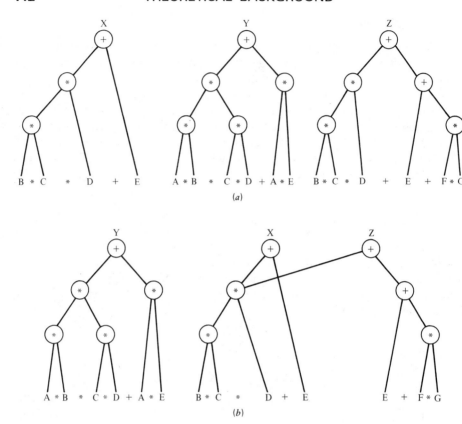

FIGURE 2.12   **BAS tree-height reduction.** (*a*) $S_5 = 2$, $E_5 = \frac{2}{5}$, $R_5 = \frac{13}{6}$, $U_5 = \frac{13}{15}$. (*b*) $S_4 = 2$, $E_4 = \frac{1}{2}$, $R_4 = \frac{11}{16}$, $U_4 = \frac{11}{12}$.

$T_4 = 4$. Thus, $S_4 = \frac{3}{2}$ and $E_4 = \frac{3}{8}$, so we actually achieve a *lower* efficiency as well as a lower speedup in this instance. Since $O_4 = 13$, we have $R_4 = \frac{13}{6}$ and $U_4 = \frac{13}{16}$, so the utilization is also worse than in the five processor case. However, we might be forced into this situation by the fact that our computer has only four processors. In many cases, the efficiency will be increased by reducing the number of processors.

We note that the dual of that problem—minimizing the number of processors required to evaluate a set of trees in a fixed number of steps—may be solved using an algorithm of Hu [HuTC61]. Thus, after carrying out our tree-height reduction process, we could turn to Hu's algorithm, for example, to minimize the number of processors as was done in Fig. 2.12.

The most important observation to draw from this section is that the speedup of a block of assignment statements results from two effects: the simultaneous evaluation of independent trees obtained by statement substitution and tree-height reduction by associativity, commutativity, and distributivity.

2.2.5.2 Combinational logic bounds

As another application of tree-height reduction, we now consider the case of combinational circuits. These are logical circuits that are built by using trees of gates to transform input signals into output signals without any memory of previous inputs or outputs, as in the case of sequential machines. First, we give a formal definition, and some theoretical bounds based on our earlier results. We then illustrate the use of these bounds in the case of integrated circuit packages.

Definition   1

A *combinational circuit* $C\langle r, s, e, n, d \rangle$ is defined by
1. A set of *inputs* x_i, $1 \le i \le r$.
2. A set of *outputs* y_j, $1 \le j \le s$, where y_j is defined by an *output expression* $E_j \langle e_j \mid d_j \rangle$ of e_j atoms (representing inputs or complements of inputs) and with parenthesis nesting depth d_j.
3. $e = \max_j \{e_j\}$ is the maximum number of atoms contained in E_j, $1 \le j \le s$.
4. $n = \sum_{j=1}^{s} e_j$ is the total number of atoms in all E_j, $1 \le j \le s$.
5. $d = \max_j \{d_j\}$ is the maximum parenthesis nesting depth among all of the output expressions E_j, $1 \le j \le s$.

It is clear that $n \ge s$, and we assume that $n \ge r$, since each input is used in at least one output expression.   ■

Next, we give a lemma which can be used to bound the gates and time in the evaluation of any Boolean expression $E\langle e \rangle$ without complementations.

Lemma   3 [KuMu74], [Bren73a]

Any complement-free Boolean expression $E\langle e \mid d \rangle$ of e atoms can be realized using gates of fan-in 2 in

$$T_G[E\langle e \mid d\rangle] \le \begin{cases} 1 + 2d + \lceil \log e \rceil & \text{if } d < \tfrac{3}{2}\log e \\ \lceil 4 \log e \rceil - 3 & \text{otherwise} \end{cases}$$

with

$$G[E\langle e \mid d\rangle] \le \begin{cases} e - 1 & \text{if } d < \tfrac{3}{2}\log e \\ 2(e-1) & \text{otherwise,} \end{cases}$$

where d is the depth of parenthesis nesting in E.   ■

The proof of this lemma for $d < \tfrac{3}{2}\log e$ is found in [KuMu74]. In most practical expressions, the depth of parenthesis nesting is small, so this provides the best bound. However, if $d \ge \tfrac{3}{2}\log e$, we use the second half of the lemma that is proved in [Bren73a] where it is also shown that this may be extended to $T_G[E\langle e \rangle] \le 3 \log e$ with $G[E\langle e \rangle] \le 2.5e$. But this will not be used because in making estimates for practical purposes, a low gate bound is often more important than a low time bound. In much of the following we use Lemma 3, assuming for simplicity that $d < \frac{3}{2} \log e$.

Theorem 3 [ChKu77]

Any combinational circuit $C\langle r, s, e, n, d \rangle$ can be realized by using gates of fan-in 2 and fan-out f in

$$T_G \leq \lceil \log e \rceil + \lceil \log_f n \rceil + 2d + 1$$

with

$$G \leq \left(1 + \frac{2}{f-1}\right)n + \left(1 - \frac{2}{f-1}\right)r - s.$$

Proof

First, consider the fan-out of the inputs. Let the ith input be used k_i times in output expressions. Since we may need to complement the input, we first fan it out to 2 places and complement 1 of these. We can assume that the first fan-out was accomplished by the output of an earlier circuit. Now we fan out the true and complemented signals, and assuming the first gate in one tree does the complementation, by Lemma 2, we need (since we assume each input atom is used at least once)

$$T_{G1} \leq \lceil \log_f (n - r + 1) \rceil < \lceil \log_f n \rceil$$

with

$$G1 \leq 2 \sum_{i=1}^{r} \left(\frac{k_i - 1}{f-1}\right) + 1 \doteq \frac{2(n-r)}{f-1} + r.$$

Next, we consider the fan-in of the atoms to form the output variables according to the output expressions $E_j \langle e_j \mid d_j \rangle$. By Lemma 3, we have

$$T_{G2} \leq \begin{cases} 1 + 2d + \lceil \log e \rceil & \text{if } d_j < \frac{3}{2} \log e_j, \ 1 \leq j \leq s \\ \lceil 4 \log e \rceil & \text{otherwise} \end{cases}$$

with

$$G2 \leq \begin{cases} \sum_{j=1}^{s} e_j - 1 = n - s & \text{if } d_j < \frac{3}{2} \log e_j, \ 1 \leq j \leq s \\ \sum_{j=1}^{s} 2(e_j - 1) = 2(n - s) & \text{otherwise.} \end{cases}$$

Thus (assuming $d_j < \frac{3}{2} \log e_j$, $1 \leq j \leq s$) we have a total of

$$T_G \leq \lceil \log e \rceil + \lceil \log_f n \rceil + 2d + 1$$

with

$$G \leq 2\left(\frac{n-r}{f-1}\right) + r + n - s$$

$$= \left(1 + \frac{2}{f-1}\right)n + \left(1 - \frac{2}{f-1}\right)r - s. \qquad \blacksquare$$

Example 4

Suppose we have a 16-pin integrated circuit package that contains only combinational logic. Assume we can use 7 pins for inputs and 7 pins for outputs, that is, $r = s = 7$. Assume that we have an average of 4 atoms per output expression so $n = 4 \cdot 7 = 28$, the maximum number of atoms per expression is $e = 8$, and $d = 2$. Thus a typical output expression may be of the form

$$y_j = (x_1 + \bar{x}_2) \cdot (\bar{x}_3 + x_5).$$

Let us use circuits with fan-in 2 and fan-out 8. Now for any possible combinational logic with the above characteristics, a package can be designed such that the total package time in gate delays is

$$T_G \le \lceil \log e \rceil + \lceil \log_f n \rceil + 2d + 1$$
$$= \lceil \log 8 \rceil + \lceil \log_8 28 \rceil + 2 \cdot 2 + 1 = 3 + 2 + 4 + 1 = 10.$$

The total number of gates in any such package is at most

$$G \le (1 + \tfrac{2}{7})28 + (1 - \tfrac{2}{7})7 - 7 = 34. \qquad \blacksquare$$

Example 5

Suppose we have a 48-pin package for large-scale integrated circuits. Let $r = s = 23$, $n = 6 \cdot 23 = 138$, $e = 16$, $d = 3$, and $f = 8$. Now any possible combinational circuit can be realized with

$$T_G \le \lceil \log 16 \rceil + \lceil \log_8 138 \rceil + 2 \cdot 3 + 1 = 4 + 3 + 6 + 1 = 14$$

and

$$G \le (1 + \tfrac{2}{7})138 + (1 - \tfrac{2}{7})23 - 23 = 174. \qquad \blacksquare$$

Thus we see that for realistic assumptions about packages and logical expressions, we obtain gate and time bounds that are of practical interest.

More about practical combinational logic design may be found in [Blak75, Chapters 3 and 4], [Mano72, Ch. 4], [HiPe74], or in the literature of semiconductor circuit manufacturers.

2.3 RECURRENCE RELATIONS

2.3.1 Introduction

Linear recurrences share with arithmetic expressions a rôle of central importance in computer design and use. But they are somewhat more difficult to deal with. Although an expression specifies a static computational scheme for a scalar result, a recurrence specifies a dynamic procedure for computing a scalar or an array of results. Linear recurrences are found in computer design, numerical analysis, and program analysis, so it is important to find fast, efficient ways to evaluate them.

Recurrences arise in any logic design problem that is expressed as a sequential machine. Also, almost every practical program that has an iterative loop contains a recurrence. Although not all recurrences are linear, the majority found in practice are, and we shall concentrate on linear recurrences. Although speedup techniques exist for some nonlinear recurrences, we simply assume that they are evaluated serially. For further discussion of the combinatorial theory and applications of recurrences see [LiuC68].

We shall begin with several examples. First, consider the problem of computing an inner product of vectors $a = (a_1, \ldots, a_n)$ and $b = (b_1, \ldots, b_n)$. This can be written in a program loop as a linear recurrence of the form

$$x \leftarrow x + a_i b_i, \qquad 1 \le i \le n, \tag{3}$$

where x is initially set to zero and finally set to the value of the inner product of a and b. The $\leftarrow$ operator in Eqs. 3 and 4 is understood as a program assignment operator to be used repeatedly over the range of i.

As another example of a linear recurrence that produces a scalar result, the evaluation of a degree n polynomial $p_n(x)$ in Horner's rule form can be expressed as

$$p \leftarrow a_i + xp, \qquad 1 \le i \le n, \tag{4}$$

where p is initially set to a_0 and finally set to the value of $p_n(x)$; recall the program form of this in Prog. 1, Section 2.1.1.

Techniques to handle both of these recurrences should be familiar from our discussion of expression evaluation. Note that Eq. 3 can be expanded by substituting the right-hand side into itself (statement substitution) as follows:

$$x \leftarrow a_1 b_1 \qquad \text{Step 1}$$
$$x \leftarrow a_1 b_1 + a_2 b_2 \qquad \text{Step 2}$$
$$x \leftarrow a_1 b_1 + a_2 b_2 + a_3 b_3 \qquad \text{Step 3}$$
$$\cdot$$
$$\cdot$$
$$\cdot$$

After n iterations we have an expression that can be mapped onto a tree of $\log n$ levels. By carrying out a similar procedure for polynomial evaluation, we could obtain an expression that can be handled by tree-height reduction. Thus we would expect that these and similar recurrences could be solved in $T_P = O(\log n)$ time steps using $P = O(n)$ processors.

But there are other, more difficult looking linear recurrences. For example, a Fibonacci sequence can be generated by

$$f_i = f_{i-1} + f_{i-2}, \qquad 3 \le i \le n, \tag{5}$$

where

$$f_1 = f_2 = 1.$$

As another example, consider the addition of two n-bit binary numbers $a = a_n \cdots a_1$ and $b = b_n \cdots b_1$. The propagation of the carry across the sum can be described (as in Eq. 1, Section 2.1.1) by

$$c_i = y_i + x_i \cdot c_{i-1}, \qquad 1 \le i \le n, \tag{6}$$

where

$$c_0 = 0, \; x_i = a_i + b_i \quad \text{and} \quad y_i = a_i \cdot b_i.$$

Here we use $+$ to denote logical OR and $\cdot$ to denote logical AND. This is an example of a bit level linear recurrence, in contrast to our previous examples whose arguments were assumed to be real numbers.

Equations 5 and 6 both require the generation of a vector result because of the subscripted left-hand side, in contrast to the scalar results of Eqs. 3 and 4. Because of this, we can expect a good deal more difficulty in trying to obtain a fast, efficient solution to these recurrences. We now turn to a formalization of the general problem as well as bounds for the solution of the general problem and several important special cases.

Definition 2

An *mth order linear recurrence system* of n equations, $R\langle n, m \rangle$, is defined for $m \le n - 1$ by

$$x_i = 0 \quad \text{for } i \le 0$$

and

$$x_i = c_i + \sum_{j=i-m}^{i-1} a_{ij} x_j \quad \text{for } 1 \le i \le n.$$

If $m = n - 1$, we call the system a *general linear recurrence system* and denote it by $R\langle n \rangle$.

Note that we can express any linear recurrence system in matrix terms as[4]

$$x = c + Ax,$$

where

$$c = (c_1, \ldots, c_n)^t, \qquad x = (x_1, \ldots, x_n)^t,$$

and A is a strictly lower triangular (banded if $m < n - 1$) matrix with $a_{ij} = 0$ for $i \le j$ or $i - j > m$. We refer to A as the *coefficient matrix*, c as the *constant vector*, and x as the *solution vector*.   ∎

For example, an $R\langle 4, 2 \rangle$ system has the form

$$x_1 = c_1$$
$$x_2 = c_2 + a_{21} x_1$$
$$x_3 = c_3 + a_{31} x_1 + a_{32} x_2$$
$$x_4 = c_4 \qquad\quad + a_{42} x_2 + a_{43} x_3$$

---

[4] The superscript t denotes transpose; that is, c and x are column vectors.

or in matrix notation

$$\begin{bmatrix} x_1 \\ x_2 \\ x_3 \\ x_4 \end{bmatrix} = \begin{bmatrix} c_1 \\ c_2 \\ c_3 \\ c_4 \end{bmatrix} + \begin{bmatrix} 0 & 0 & 0 & 0 \\ a_{21} & 0 & 0 & 0 \\ a_{31} & a_{32} & 0 & 0 \\ 0 & a_{42} & a_{43} & 0 \end{bmatrix} \begin{bmatrix} x_1 \\ x_2 \\ x_3 \\ x_4 \end{bmatrix}.$$

It should be observed that the constant vector and coefficient matrix generally contain values which can be computed before the recurrence evaluation begins. Thus, the x_i and y_i values of Eq. 6 would be precomputed from the a_i and b_i. We will assume that the elements of the coefficient matrix and constant vector are precomputed (if necessary) in all cases so that our bounds on recurrence evaluation can be simply stated.

How can we solve an $R\langle n \rangle$ system in a fast, efficient way using many simultaneous operations? The following is a straightforward way that uses $O(n)$ processors to solve the system in $O(n)$ steps.

2.3.2   Column sweep algorithm

Given any $R\langle n \rangle$ system, we initially know the value of x_1. On step 1 we broadcast this value $x_1 = c_1$ to all other equations, multiply by a_{j1}, and add the result to c_j. Since we now know the value of x_2, we have an $R\langle n-1 \rangle$ system that can be treated in exactly the same way as the original $R\langle n \rangle$ system. After $n-1$ steps, each of which consists of a broadcast, a multiply and an add, and each of which generates another x_i, we have the solution vector x. The method requires $n-1$ processors on step 1, and fewer thereafter, so $T_P = 2(n-1)$ with $P = n-1$, ignoring the broadcast time and assuming that addition and multiplication each take one time unit.

What speedup and efficiency have we achieved by this method? The time required to solve this system using a single processor that might sweep the array by rows or columns would be

$$T_1 = 2[1 + 2 + \cdots + (n-1)] = 2\left[\frac{n(n-1)}{2}\right] = n(n-1).$$

Hence, the above method achieves a speedup of

$$S_P = \frac{n(n-1)}{2(n-1)} = \frac{n}{2}$$

with an efficiency of

$$E_P = \frac{S_P}{P} = \frac{n}{2(n-1)} > \frac{1}{2}.$$

Thus we can conclude that the column sweep algorithm is a reasonable method for solving an $R\langle n \rangle$ system. But how does it perform in the $R\langle n, m \rangle$ case for $m \ll n$?

It can be seen that the column sweep algorithm will achieve $S_m = O(m)$ for an $R\langle n, m \rangle$ system. So if m is very small, the method performs poorly, particularly if we have a large number of processors available, since at most m processors may be used. It should be noted that the $m \ll n$ case occurs very often in practice. Note that all of our examples (Eqs. 3–6) had $m \leq 2$.

What are our prospects for finding a faster algorithm? First, we observe that the total number of initial data values in an $R\langle n, m \rangle$ system is $O(mn)$. This is the total of the constant vector c and the coefficient matrix A. Assuming that these numbers all interact in obtaining a solution, a fan-in argument (see Lemma 1) indicates that we need at least $O(\log mn)$ steps to solve an $R\langle n, m \rangle$ system, since $m \leq n$, $O(\log mn) = O(\log n)$. The column sweep algorithm requires $O(n)$ steps, so we still have a big gap in time.

2.3.3 Product form recurrence algorithm

The next theorem is based on an algorithm for the fastest known method of evaluating an $R\langle n, m \rangle$ system. For large m, the number of processors required is rather large, but for small m, the number of processors is quite reasonable. We also give bounds for the case of a small number of processors. To avoid cluttering the notation, in what follows we assume that m and n are powers of two. The next higher power of two must be used to compute results for m and n that are not powers of two. For two different approaches to this theorem see [ChKu75] and [SaBr77].

Theorem 4

Any $R\langle n, m \rangle$ can be computed in

$$T_P \leq (2 + \log m) \log n - \tfrac{1}{2}(\log^2 m + \log m)$$

with

$$O_P \leq m^2 n \log \frac{n}{2m} + O\left(mn \log \frac{n}{2m} \right)$$

and

$$P \leq \frac{m}{2}(m+1)n + O(m^3) \qquad \text{for } 1 \leq m \leq \frac{n}{2},$$

or with

$$O_P \leq \frac{2}{21} n^3 + O(n^2)$$

and

$$P \leq \frac{n^3}{68} + O(n^2) \qquad \text{for } \frac{n}{2} < m \leq n - 1. \qquad \blacksquare$$

In order to use the results of Theorem 4, it is useful to have the complete expressions for P and O_P. In fact, it can be shown that for $1 \le m \le n/2$,

$$O_P = \left\lceil m^2 n\left(\frac{43}{42} + \log\frac{n}{4m}\right) + mn\left(\log\frac{n}{m} - \frac{3}{4}\right) + \frac{4}{3}n + \frac{15}{14}m^3 + 2m^2 + \frac{10}{21}\frac{n}{m} - 2m - \frac{4}{7}\right\rceil$$

and

$$P = \begin{cases} \dfrac{m}{2}(m+1)n - m^3 & \text{if } 1 \le m < \dfrac{n}{2} \\[2ex] \left\lceil \dfrac{21}{128}m^2 n + \dfrac{5}{16}mn + \dfrac{n}{8}\right\rceil & \text{if } m = \dfrac{n}{2}. \end{cases}$$

Furthermore, if $n/2 < m \le n - 1$, it can be shown that

$$O_P = \left\lceil \tfrac{2}{21}n^3 + \tfrac{2}{3}n^2 - \tfrac{2}{3}n - \tfrac{2}{21}\right\rceil$$

and

$$P = \left\lceil \frac{15}{1024}n^3 + \frac{n^2}{8} + \frac{n}{16}\right\rceil.$$

As we shall learn later, many linear recurrences of practical interest have very small m values, often $m = 1$ or $m = 2$. For such cases, it is of interest to compare Theorem 4, with the results of Theorem 2 for arbitrary arithmetic expressions. Although the expressions are more constrained here than in Theorem 2, it is also true that here we must compute *all* intermediate values of x_i as well as x_n.

Example 6

Consider the time and processors required to evaluate an $R\langle n, 2\rangle$ system, for large n. By Theorem 4 we have

$$T_P \le (2 + \log 2)\log n - \tfrac{1}{2}(\log^2 2 + \log 2) = 3 \log n - 1$$

with $P \le 3n - 8$.

Thus we see that an $R\langle n, m\rangle$ system with small m can be solved in the same time we can evaluate any expression $E\langle n\rangle$. The number of processors needed for the recurrence is comparable to the number needed for the expression. Note that the number of atoms in an $R\langle n, 2\rangle$ system is approximately $3n$, whereas the expression has just n atoms. ∎

The proof of Theorem 4 is beyond our present scope, but the following sketch will indicate the operation of the algorithm used in the proof given in [SaBr77]. Any $R\langle n\rangle$ system can be written as $x = Ax + c$, where A is a strictly lower triangular (SLT) matrix. The solution can be expressed as

$$x = (I - A)^{-1}c = L^{-1}c.$$

Thus for $R\langle 4 \rangle$, if

$$A = \begin{bmatrix} 0 & 0 & 0 & 0 \\ a_{21} & 0 & 0 & 0 \\ a_{31} & a_{32} & 0 & 0 \\ a_{41} & a_{42} & a_{43} & 0 \end{bmatrix},$$

we have

$$L = \begin{bmatrix} 1 & 0 & 0 & 0 \\ -a_{21} & 1 & 0 & 0 \\ -a_{31} & -a_{32} & 1 & 0 \\ -a_{41} & -a_{42} & -a_{43} & 1 \end{bmatrix}.$$

Since A is SLT it is a well-known result of linear algebra [Hous64] that we can express the inverse of L in so-called *product form* using just the original columns of A. Thus we have

$$L^{-1}c = \begin{bmatrix} 1 & 0 & 0 & 0 \\ 0 & 1 & 0 & 0 \\ 0 & 0 & 1 & 0 \\ 0 & 0 & a_{43} & 1 \end{bmatrix} \cdot \begin{bmatrix} 1 & 0 & 0 & 0 \\ 0 & 1 & 0 & 0 \\ 0 & a_{32} & 1 & 0 \\ 0 & a_{42} & 0 & 1 \end{bmatrix} \cdot \begin{bmatrix} 1 & 0 & 0 & 0 \\ a_{21} & 1 & 0 & 0 \\ a_{31} & 0 & 1 & 0 \\ a_{41} & 0 & 0 & 1 \end{bmatrix} \cdot \begin{bmatrix} c_1 \\ c_2 \\ c_3 \\ c_4 \end{bmatrix}$$

$$= \begin{bmatrix} 1 & 0 & 0 & 0 \\ 0 & 1 & 0 & 0 \\ 0 & a_{32} & 1 & 0 \\ 0 & a_{42}+a_{43}a_{32} & a_{43} & 1 \end{bmatrix} \cdot \begin{bmatrix} c_1 \\ c_2 + a_{21}c_1 \\ c_3 + a_{31}c_1 \\ c_4 + a_{41}c_1 \end{bmatrix}.$$

So we have

$$\begin{bmatrix} x_1 \\ x_2 \\ x_3 \\ x_4 \end{bmatrix} = \begin{bmatrix} c_1 \\ (c_2 + a_{21}c_1) \\ (c_3 + a_{31}c_1) + a_{32}(c_2 + a_{21}c_1) \\ (c_4 + a_{41}c_1) + a_{43}(c_3 + a_{31}c_1) + (a_{42} + a_{43}a_{32})(c_2 + a_{21}c_1) \end{bmatrix}. \tag{7}$$

In general, $L^{-1}c$ can be computed by fanning in a number of matrices and the c vector in a chain product. Since there are n arrays, for an $R\langle n \rangle$ system $\lceil \log n \rceil$ array products are required, and each of these can be done in $O(\log n)$ operation times. Thus the time bound of $O(\log^2 n)$ steps is obvious (see Theorem 4 with $m = n - 1$), whereas the processor bounds are more difficult to prove.

Returning to our example, note that all of the parenthesized terms in Eq. 7

can be generated simultaneously by the first array multiplication in two steps using four processors, since there are only four distinct terms. Then x_4—the most complex calculation—can be completed by the second array multiplication in just three more steps using two processors, whereas x_3 requires one more processor. Thus, we have a total of four processors required (for the parenthesized expressions) and a total of five time steps.

The bounds of Theorem 4 give

$$T_P \leq \tfrac{1}{2}\log^2 n + \tfrac{3}{2}\log n$$
$$= \tfrac{1}{2}\cdot 4 + \tfrac{3}{2}\cdot 2 = 5$$

with

$$P = \left\lceil \frac{15}{1024}\, n^3 + \frac{n^2}{8} + \frac{n}{16} \right\rceil$$
$$= \lceil \tfrac{15}{1024}\times 64 + \tfrac{16}{8} + \tfrac{4}{16} \rceil = \lceil \tfrac{15}{16} + 2 + \tfrac{1}{4} \rceil = 4.$$

By inspection of other evaluation sequences for this problem, we can see that these bounds are exact in this case.

We can conclude that Theorems 2 and 4 taken together provide a very important underpinning for much practical computer and compiler design work. They guarantee that any expression or any narrow bandwidth recurrence can be evaluated in $O(\log T_1)$ time steps, where T_1 is the serial time required for their evaluation. Furthermore, since only $O(T_1)$ processors are required, the evaluations are carried out at efficiencies proportional to $1/\log T_1$.

For either $R\langle n, m\rangle$ or $R\langle n\rangle$ systems, if n is very large, the number of processors required by Theorem 4 may grow to an unreasonable number (see the tables of [ChKu75]). The following section discusses this problem.

2.3.4 Limited processors results

In practice we may have a machine with a limited number of processors $p < P$ so Theorem 4 cannot be used directly. Several schemes are available for mapping a computation onto a smaller set of processors and generally increasing the efficiency of the computation as well. We describe two approaches here.

If we do not have sufficiently many processors to solve an entire $R\langle n, m\rangle$ system, we can simply cut off a problem that can be solved on the number of processors available. Suppose we can solve the first k equations of the given $R\langle n, m\rangle$ system with p processors. These results can be used to eliminate the first k unknowns in the remaining $n - k$ equations of the original $R\langle n, m\rangle$ system by the technique used in the column sweep algorithm (see Section 2.3.2). Next, we proceed to solve k more equations, and repeating the process $\lceil n/k\rceil$ times we finish the solution of the $R\langle n, m\rangle$ system. Bounds are derived using this *cutting scheme* in [CKTB78].

For most practical $R\langle n, m\rangle$ systems in which m is very small compared with n, if the number of processors is also very limited, then the following result developed in [ChKS78] can be used more efficiently, although for $p < 2m^2$ the column sweep algorithm is fastest and most efficient.

Theorem 5

If p processors are available, where $2m^2 \leq p \ll n$, then any $R\langle n, m \rangle$ can be computed in

$$T_p \leq (2m^2 + 3m)\frac{n}{p} + O\left(m^2 \log \frac{p}{m}\right).$$ ∎

2.3.5 Constant coefficient recurrences

In numerical computation, we are frequently faced with linear recurrences having constant coefficients, that is, constant diagonal matrices. For example, Eqs. 3, 4, and 5 are such recurrences. Thus, Eq. 3 could be rewritten as $x_i = 1 x_{i-1} + a_i b_i$, and similarly for Eq. 4. Intuitively, we might expect to be able to compute such systems more efficiently than the more general recurrences we have been considering.

Indeed, this is the case, as we shall see below. We formalize the problem with the following definition that should be contrasted with Definition 2.

Definition 3

An *mth order linear recurrence system with constant coefficients* of n equations, $\tilde{R}\langle n, m \rangle$, is defined for $m \leq n - 1$ by

$$x_i = 0 \qquad \text{for } i \leq 0$$

and

$$x_i = c_i + \sum_{j=1}^{m} a_j x_{i-j} \quad \text{for } 1 \leq i \leq n.$$

If $m = n - 1$, we call the system a *general linear recurrence system with constant coefficients* and denote it by $\tilde{R}\langle n \rangle$. ∎

An efficient, fast method for solving an $\tilde{R}\langle n, m \rangle$ system can be summarized by the following theorem [Chen75], [Same77]. The proof follows the lines of Theorem 4, but avoids computations that are unnecessary due to the constant coefficients.

Theorem 6

Any $\tilde{R}\langle n, m \rangle$ can be computed in

with

$$T_P \leq (3 + 2 \log m) \log n - (\log^2 m + \log m + 1)$$

$$O_P \leq \tfrac{21}{4} mn - \tfrac{9}{2} n - \tfrac{25}{4} m^2 - m$$

and

$$P \leq mn/2 + n/4 \quad \text{for } m \ll n,$$

or with

$$O_P \leq \tfrac{9}{4} n^2 - \tfrac{7}{2} n$$

and

$$P \le \frac{n^2}{4} \qquad \text{for } m \le n-1.$$ ∎

By exercising special care in avoiding redundant computations, the proof of Theorem 6 can be modified [Chen75] to give us the following.

Corollary 2

Any $\tilde{R}\langle n, 1 \rangle$ can be computed in

$$T_p \le 1 + 2 \log n$$

with

$$P \le \frac{n}{2}.$$ ∎

By comparing Theorems 4 and 6 we see that although the time bounds are about the same, substantial processor savings can be made in the constant coefficient case. In the case of small m, we have saved $O(m)$ processors, whereas in the general case we have saved a factor of $O(n)$ processors.

To test the quality of these bounds, we can compare them with some simple calculations. Consider the inner product of Eq. 3. This can obviously be handled using n processors (for the n multiplications) in $1 + \log n$ steps. Since we have been assuming the coefficient matrix and constant vector are set up before the recurrence solution begins, the multiplication is really outside our present scope, so just $n/2$ processors would be required for the summation.

The bound of Corollary 2 is thus high by about a factor of two in time for this simple recurrence. However, the recurrence method produces not only the inner product x_n, but also all of the "partial inner products" $x_1, x_2, \ldots, x_{n-1}$. [Chen75] has also given other variations on the above to handle these special cases of evaluating only the remote terms of recurrences. As a final example, note that the entire Fibonacci sequence of Eq. 5 can be evaluated (since $m = 2$) in

$$T_P \le 5 \log n - 3$$

with

$$P \le \frac{5}{4} n$$

for large n.

2.3.6 Fan-out considerations

Thus far we have ignored the question of fanning out one intermediate result for use in several subsequent computations. Indeed, the gates and time required to perform such broadcasts can be regarded as negligible compared with the arithmetic gates and time. But at the level of logic design this assumption cannot be made. Hence, we give several results that consider fan-outs and thus can be regarded as generalizations of our previous results.

We will use these results to count gates as well as higher level components such as integrated circuit packages or whole processors. Thus we state them in terms of operations θ, which can be interpreted as logical OR and AND, or as arithmetic addition and multiplication. When we deal with fan-out (denoted by f), at the gate level, θ corresponds to gates, whereas at the processor level it refers to registers or demultiplexers. For more discussion and proofs of the results in this section see [ChKu77].

Lemma 4

Any mth order linear recurrence $R\langle n, m\rangle$ can be solved in

$$T_\theta \le (\tfrac{5}{2} + \log m + \tfrac{1}{2}\log_f n)\log n - \tfrac{1}{2}(\log^2 m + \log m)$$

with

$$\theta < \frac{1}{2}\left[m^2\left(2 + \frac{1}{f-1}\right) + m\left(1 + \frac{1}{f-1}\right)\right] n \log n$$

$$+ \left[m^3\left(1 + \frac{1}{f-1}\right) - m^2\left(2 + \frac{1}{f-1}\right) - \frac{m}{f-1}\right] n + 2m^2 + \left(\frac{2}{f-1}\right)\log n,$$

where fan-in is 2 and fan-out

$$f = 2^q,\ q \ge 1. \qquad\blacksquare$$

The following corollary follows directly from Lemma 4 and covers a case of wide practical interest.

Corollary 3

Any first order linear recurrence $R\langle n, 1\rangle$ can be solved in

$$T_\theta \le \frac{1}{2}(5 + \log_f n)\log n$$

with

$$\theta \le \frac{1}{2}\left(3 + \frac{2}{f-1}\right) n \log n - \left(1 + \frac{1}{f-1}\right) n + \left(\frac{2}{f-1}\right)\log n + 2. \qquad\blacksquare$$

Thus we see that for large fan-outs, we can solve any $R\langle n, m\rangle$ system in $T_G = O(\log m \log n)$ with $G = O(m^2 n \log n)$ and any $R\langle n, 1\rangle$ system in $T_G = O(\log n)$ with $G = O(n \log n)$.

Example 7

As in Eq. 6,

$$c_i = 0, \qquad i \le 0$$

and

$$c_i = y_i + x_i \cdot c_{i-1}, \qquad 1 \le i \le 8$$

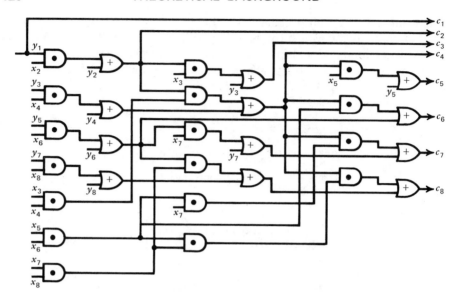

FIGURE 2.13   An $R\langle 8, 1 \rangle$ circuit for carry generation.

can be used to describe the carry generation in a binary adder (see Definition 7, Section 2.3.7.3). A circuit to generate the c_i follows directly from Lemma 4 and is shown in Fig. 2.13, assuming[5] $f = 5$. The product form algorithm of Section 2.3.3, interpreting · as AND, and + as OR, specifies the circuit directly, since a parse tree for the resulting expression specifies exactly how to interconnect the components.   ∎

2.3.7 Applications of linear recurrences

Fast linear recurrence solution techniques have many applications; we now discuss two possibilities. One is related to compiling ordinary serial programs for multioperation computers; the other is a logic design application. We first give some background about sequential logic circuits and then show a general method for translating such circuits into very fast, equivalent combinational circuits.

2.3.7.1 Program recurrences

We have already considered several simple recurrences that can be transformed so that speedups of $O(T_1/\log T_1)$ are possible. Simple programs that evaluate Eqs. 3 through 6 are obvious. Now we consider a slightly more complex program.

---

[5] This is just large enough to avoid circuit duplication.

Prog. 2

```
    DO 3  I ← 1, N
  1     E(I) ← 3 * F(I) + SIN (P(I))
  2     B(I) ← D(I − 1) + Q(I)
  3     D(I) ← E(I) + B(I)
```

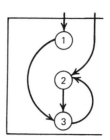

FIGURE 2.14   **Prog. 2 data dependence graph.**

In Prog. 2 we have three assignment statements (assume all right-hand side arrays have been initialized). A data dependence graph for Prog. 2 is shown in Fig. 2.14, indicating that statements 1 and 2 receive data from outside the loop, statement 1 feeds statement 3, and that statements 2 and 3 feed each other. Such graphs will be formally defined in Section 2.4.

For this program the tree-height reduction techniques are of no value. Statement 1 can be executed using N processors by broadcasting the constant 3 to all elements of the F vector, computing the sine of all elements of P in parallel and forming a vector addition. Thus, if a fixed number of steps are required for the sine computation, statement 1 can be evaluated with $E_N = 1$. Note that statement 1 is evaluated entirely in terms of data known before the loop is entered. Statements 2 and 3 are not as easy to handle. Indeed, a number of present compilers for multioperation computers would regard these as necessarily serial computations. Knowing the recurrence methods we have discussed, however, we can obtain a good speedup here.

To get some intuition about what is occurring here, consider the expanded version of this program shown in Fig. 2.15. As noted above, we assume that statement 1 has already been evaluated. The assignment statements can be mapped into a linear recurrence in a single variable x_i by letting $x_{2i-1} = B(i)$ and $x_{2i} = D(i)$, where $1 \le i \le N$. The constants c_i are handled similarly as shown in Fig. 2.15. The entire system can be rewritten in matrix form (see Fig. 2.16) as an $R\langle 2N, 1 \rangle$ linear recurrence.

$$2 \quad B(1) \leftarrow D(0) + Q(1) \Leftrightarrow x_1 = \qquad c_1$$
$$3 \quad D(1) \leftarrow E(1) + B(1) \Leftrightarrow x_2 = x_1 + c_2$$
$$2 \quad B(2) \leftarrow D(1) + Q(2) \Leftrightarrow x_3 = x_2 + c_3$$
$$3 \quad D(2) \leftarrow E(2) + B(2) \Leftrightarrow x_4 = x_3 + c_4$$
$$2 \quad B(3) \leftarrow D(2) + Q(3) \Leftrightarrow x_5 = x_4 + c_5$$
$$3 \quad D(3) \leftarrow E(3) + B(3) \Leftrightarrow x_6 = x_5 + c_6$$

$$\vdots$$

FIGURE 2.15   **Expansion of Prog. 2.**

$$\begin{bmatrix} x_1 \\ x_2 \\ x_3 \\ x_4 \\ x_5 \\ x_6 \\ \cdot \\ \cdot \\ \cdot \end{bmatrix} = \begin{bmatrix} 0 & & & & & \\ 1 & 0 & & & & \\ 0 & 1 & 0 & & & \\ 0 & 0 & 1 & 0 & & \\ 0 & 0 & 0 & 1 & 0 & \\ & & & & \cdot & \cdot \end{bmatrix} \begin{bmatrix} x_1 \\ x_2 \\ x_3 \\ x_4 \\ x_5 \\ x_6 \\ \cdot \\ \cdot \\ \cdot \end{bmatrix} + \begin{bmatrix} D(0)+Q(1) \\ E(1) \\ Q(2) \\ E(2) \\ Q(3) \\ E(3) \\ \cdot \\ \cdot \\ \cdot \end{bmatrix}$$

FIGURE 2.16   **Recurrence from Prog. 2.**

If we knew about the column sweep algorithm only, then we would be unable to speed up this computation. But, by using Corollary 2 we see that it can be evaluated in

$$T_P \le 1 + 2 \log 2N = 2 \log N + 3$$

with

$$P \le N.$$

These bounds assume that we have already set up the coefficient matrix and the constant vector. In this case, only $c_1 \leftarrow D(0) + Q(1)$ would have to be evaluated (possibly in the control unit in an overlapped way). All of the other details of the algorithm can be compiled to operate directly on the stored E and Q arrays. Or, depending on how the machine's memory is organized, we may have to map the E and Q arrays into a new array, say C, which the compiled code uses.

In any case, regarding statements 2 and 3 as an $R\langle 2N, 1\rangle$ system has afforded us a speedup of $O(N/\log N)$, because $T_1 = 2N$. Since we need N processors here as well as in the evaluation of statement 1, we can compute an overall speedup and efficiency for this program.

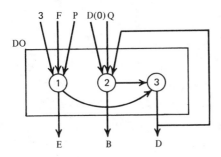

FIGURE 2.17   **Redrawn data dependence graph of Prog. 2.**

For simplicity (and since it is conservative), assume we can compute SIN(X) in one time step. Then T_1 for Prog. 2 is $5N$, ignoring memory accesses. As we have just seen, using N processors, we can evaluate statement 1 in three steps and statements 2 and 3 in at most $1 + 2 \log 2N$ steps. Thus, we have

$$S_N \geq \frac{5N}{(4 + 2 \log 2N)}$$

and

$$E_N \geq \frac{5}{(4 + 2 \log 2N)}.$$

For example, if $N = 16$, we have

$$S_{16} \geq \frac{5 \cdot 16}{(4 + 2 \log 32)} = \frac{80}{14}$$

with

$$E_{16} \geq \frac{5}{(4 + 2 \log 32)} = \frac{5}{14}.$$

This kind of analysis can be extended to any loop that consists of a block of assignment statements enclosed in an iteration statement—any number of iteration statements in fact, as we will discuss later. To prepare for such an analysis, we redraw Fig. 2.14, as shown in Fig. 2.17. Here the F, P, and Q arrays are input variables as are D(0) and the constant 3. The E, B, and D arrays are output variables. It is important to note that the D array is a feedback input because previously computed values are used on subsequent iterations.

As we discussed previously, statement 1 can be separated from statements 2 and 3, and executed in parallel as a tree of array operations. The feedback path from statement 3 to statement 2, together with the path from 2 to 3, forms a recurrence that must be treated separately. As we will see in Section 2.4, these ideas can be extended easily to any BAS inside a loop. Ultimately, such programs lead to one set of trees of array operations and another set of recurrences. Of course, real programs have various kinds of loop nesting, conditional expressions, and jump statements, as well as blocks of assignment statements. In Volume 2, we will deal with all of these by direct extensions of the ideas discussed here.

It is important here to point out the close analogy between the compilation for a multioperation machine of a BAS in an iterative loop, with the logic design problem of developing a fast combinational circuit to carry out the functions specified in sequential circuit terms. In the following section we will formalize the idea of a sequential circuit and give the details of translation to combinational form. The reader should keep in mind the ideas behind Fig. 2.17 throughout this discussion.

2.3.7.2 Logic design recurrences

Earlier we presented time and component bounds for logic design problems stated as combinational circuits. Usually it is easier to specify complex, time-dependent logic functions as sequential circuits. However, combinational circuit implementations generally operate much faster than sequential ones—roughly this is the contrast between bit serial and bit parallel circuits. In this section we discuss methods for transforming sequential circuits into combinational ones. The methods yield circuits that meet stated upper bounds on time and components.

In this sense, we present a uniform design procedure for the realization of any linear sequential circuit in combinational circuit form, assuming a finite input sequence to the sequential circuit. As we said, one can often specify the behavior of some desired function quite easily as a sequential circuit. It is somewhat more difficult to translate such a specification into a faster combinational circuit form. A classic example is the ease with which a bit serial adder is specified in sequential form. On the other hand, the design of combinational parallel adders (with various lookahead schemes) occupied many logic designers for some years in the 1950s (not to mention Babbage's work—see Section 1.3.1). The automatic design of a fast parallel combinational adder derived from a bit serial specification is one example of the use of our method.

First, we define some background terms. Then we give our bounds and illustrate them using a binary adder example.

Definition 4

A *sequential circuit* $S\langle r, s, e, n, d, m \rangle$ is defined at time t by
1. A set of *inputs* $x_i(t)$, $1 \le i \le r = r_1 + r_2$. We call the $x_i(t)$, $1 \le i \le r_1$, the *external inputs*, and the $x_i(t)$, $r_1 + 1 \le i \le r$, the *feedback inputs*.
2. A set of *outputs* $y_j(t)$, $1 \le j \le s = s_1 + s_2$, where for any logical functions f_j,

$$y_j(t) = f_j[x_1(t), x_2(t), \ldots, x_r(t)]$$
$$= f_j[x_1(t), \ldots, x_{r_1}(t), y_{s_1+1}(t - m_1), \ldots, y_s(t - m_{r_2})]$$

as shown in Fig. 2.18. We call the $y_j(t)$, $1 \le j \le s_1$, the *external outputs* and the $y_j(t)$, $s_1 + 1 \le j \le s$, the *feedback outputs*. Note that $r_2 \ge s_2$. Each output is defined by an output expression $E_j\langle e_j \mid d_j \rangle$ of e_j atoms (representing inputs of their complements) and parenthesis nesting depth d_j.
3. $e = \{e_a, e_b\}$, where

$$e_a = \max_{1 \le j \le s_1} \{e_j\} \quad \text{and} \quad e_b = \max_{s_1+1 \le j \le s} \{e_j\}.$$

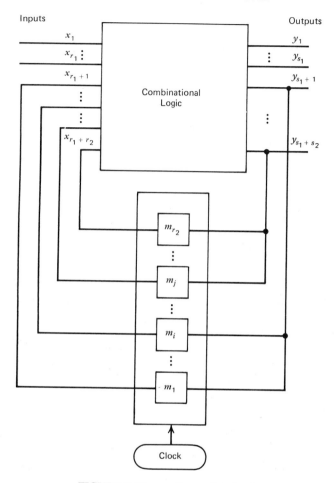

FIGURE 2.18 **Sequential circuit.**

4. $n = n_1 + n_2$, where

$$n_1 = \sum_{j=1}^{s_1} e_j \quad \text{and} \quad n_2 = \sum_{j=s_1+1}^{s} e_j.$$

5. $d = \{d_a, d_b\}$, where

$$d_a = \max_{1 \le j \le s_1} \{d_j\} \quad \text{and} \quad d_b = \max_{s_1+1 \le j \le s} \{d_j\}.$$

6. A set of *delays* m_i, $1 \le i \le r_2$, where

$$m = \max_i m_i \text{ is the } \textit{maximum delay.}$$

Definition 5

A *linear sequential circuit*[6] is a sequential circuit with outputs $y_i(t)$, $s_1 + 1 \leq i \leq s$, of the form ∎

$$y_i(t) = f_i[x_1(t), \ldots, x_{r_1}(t), y_{s_1+1}(t - m_1), \ldots, y_s(t - m_{r_2})]$$
$$= c_i + a_{i1} y_{s_1+1}(t - m_1) + \ldots + a_{ir_2} y_s(t - m_{r_2}),$$

where the c_i and a_{ij}, $1 \leq j \leq r_2$, are derived from any logical functions of the inputs $x_1(t), \ldots, x_{r_1}(t)$.

Definition 6

The *k-step operation* of a sequential circuit S is defined by k pairs of vectors

$$[(x_1(t), \ldots, x_{r_1}(t)), (y_1(t), \ldots, y_s(t))]$$

for $1 \leq t \leq k$. These vectors represent the external inputs and outputs of S at each time step t. ∎

Our next result is of fundamental importance in relating sequential circuits to combinational circuits. Using it, we can directly generate fast combinational circuits which carry out the same function that a sequential circuit would carry out for a sequence of k inputs. The beauty of this is that sequential circuits are usually easy to specify. Thus the proof of the following [ChKu77] contains a design automation procedure that, as a side benefit, includes gate and time bounds for the resulting circuit. In this way we may quickly estimate the cost and speed of a circuit without going through many tedious design details, leaving those to a program, for example.

Theorem 7

The k-step operation of any linear sequential circuit $S\langle r, s, e, n, d, m\rangle$ can be realized by a combinational circuit (using gates of fan-out f and fan-in 2) such that for large k

$$T_G \leq \tfrac{1}{2}(\log_f s_2 k)(\log s_2 k) + O(\log k)$$

with

$$G \leq \tfrac{2}{3}(m+1)^2 s_2{}^3 \left(2 + \frac{1}{f-1}\right) k \log s_2 k + O(k).$$ ∎

The heart of the design automation procedure referred to above is the product form recurrence algorithm of Section 2.3.3. This leads directly to the specification of expressions of AND and OR gates (corresponding to · and + operations, respectively). The parse tree for the expressions specifies exactly

---

[6] This definition is consistent with earlier sections, but could in fact be broader and allow broader results than we shall give since, for example, in Boolean algebra + distributes over · in addition to · distributing over +.

how to interconnect the gates, as we saw in Example 7. The general result of Theorem 7 can be improved by a more detailed analysis in many particular logic design problems, as we shall see in the next section for binary addition. For further discussion of sequential circuits and their practical implementation, see [Blak75, Ch. 5], [Mano72, Ch. 6 and Ch. 9], or [HiPe74].

2.3.7.3 Binary addition

Now we turn to a practical application of our previous work—we present time and component bounds for binary addition. After defining addition, we consider its implementation using gates and then using integrated circuits. Further discussion of this can be found in [ChKu77] and [Bren70], and a lower bound on time that is fairly close to the upper bound given here is presented in [Wino65].

Definition 7

By the *addition* of two n-digit binary numbers $a = a_n \cdots a_1$ and $b = b_n \cdots b_1$ we mean the generation of sum digits $s = s_n \cdots s_1$ and carry digit c_n, defined as follows.

We write

$$s_i = (a_i b_i + \bar{a}_i \bar{b}_i) c_{i-1} + (\bar{a}_i b_i + a_i \bar{b}_i) \bar{c}_{i-1}, \tag{8}$$

where $1 \le i \le n$ and $c_0 = 0$, such that $s_i = 1$ iff just one or all three of a_i, b_i, and c_{i-1} are equal to 1. Also we write

$$c_i = a_i b_i + (a_i + b_i) c_{i-1}, \tag{9}$$

where $1 \le i \le n$ and $c_0 = 0$, such that $c_i = 1$ iff any two or all three of a_i, b_i, and c_{i-1} are equal to 1. Now let

$$x_i = a_i + b_i \tag{10}$$

and

$$y_i = a_i b_i. \tag{11}$$

If we write

$$d_i = \bar{a}_i \bar{b}_i + a_i b_i = \overline{(a_i + b_i)} + a_i b_i = \bar{x}_i + y_i, \tag{12}$$

then Eq. 8 can be rewritten as

$$s_i = d_i c_{i-1} + \bar{d}_i \bar{c}_{i-1} \tag{13}$$

and Eq. 9 can be rewritten as

$$c_i = \begin{cases} y_i + x_i c_{i-1}, & 1 \le i \le n \\ 0, & i = 0. \end{cases} \tag{14}$$

∎

It is traditional in logic design to refer to a circuit that implements Eqs. 8 and 9 as a *full adder* and to define a half adder as a circuit that ignores the carry bits. Thus a *half adder* of bits a_i and b_i is defined by the equations

$$s_i' = \bar{a}_i b_i + a_i \bar{b}_i = a_i \oplus b_i \qquad (8')$$

and

$$c_i' = a_i b_i, \qquad (9')$$

which are derived from Eqs. 8 and 9, respectively, by setting $c_{i-1} = 0$. Note that Eq. 8' is the exclusive-OR (denoted by $\oplus$) of a_i and b_i. The uses of half adders and their relation to full adders will be explored in Chapter 3. Our next result concerns binary addition using gates as components.

Theorem 8 [ChKu77]

Two $n = 2^t$ digit binary numbers can be added in

$$T_G \leq \tfrac{1}{2}(5 + \log_f n) \log n + 4$$

with

$$G \leq \left(\frac{3}{2} + \frac{1}{f-1}\right) n \log n + \left(8 - \frac{1}{f-1}\right) n + \left(\frac{2}{f-1}\right) \log n + 2,$$

using gates with fan-in 2 and fan-out f.

Proof

Our proof consists of three parts.

1. To generate the x_i and y_i, $1 \leq i \leq n$, from a_i and b_i by Eqs. 10 and 11, we need $2n$ gates and one gate delay, so $T_{G1} = 1$ and $G1 = 2n$.

2. To generate the s_i, $1 \leq i \leq n$, from x_i, y_i, and c_{i-1} using Eq. 13, we refer to Fig. 2.19. A total of 7 gates are required for each s_i, for a total of $7n$ gates. After d_i and c_{i-1}

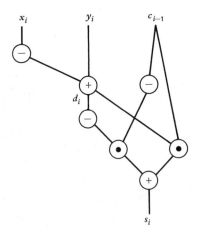

FIGURE 2.19   Sum generation.

are available, three gate delays are required. It will be seen in part 3 that the generation of the c_i, $1 \le i \le n$, from x_i and y_i can be accomplished in $2 \log n$ steps. Thus, for $n \ge 2$ the two steps required to generate d_i from x_i and y_i are no more than the time required to generate c_i, since $2 \log 2 = 2$.

It is easy to verify that the theorem holds true for $n = 1$ by a direct construction. Thus we have $T_{G2} = 3$ with $G2 \le 7n$.

3. To generate the c_i, $1 \le i \le n$, from x_i and y_i using Eq. 14 we turn to Lemma 4. Since Eq. 14 defines an $R\langle n, 1\rangle$ system, it follows immediately from Corollary 3 (see Fig. 2.13) that

$$T_{G3} \le \tfrac{1}{2}(5 + \log_f n) \log n$$

with

$$G3 \le \left[\frac{3}{2} + \frac{1}{f-1}\right] n \log n - \left(1 + \frac{1}{f-1}\right) n + \frac{2}{f-1} \log n + 2.$$

Thus we have from parts 1, 2, and 3 a total of

$$T_G = 1 + 3 + \tfrac{1}{2}(5 + \log_f n) \log n$$
$$= \tfrac{1}{2}(5 + \log_f n) \log n + 4$$

with

$$G \le 2n + 7n + \left(\frac{3}{2} + \frac{1}{f-1}\right) n \log n - \left(1 + \frac{1}{f-1}\right) n + \frac{2}{f-1} \log n + 2$$

$$= \left(\frac{3}{2} + \frac{1}{f-1}\right) n \log n + \left(8 - \frac{1}{f-1}\right) n + \left(\frac{2}{f-1}\right) \log n + 2. \qquad \blacksquare$$

Example 8

Consider the problem of adding two 32-bit binary numbers using gates with fan-in 2 and fan-out 8. By the method of Theorem 8, the sum can be formed in at most 21 gate delays because

$$T_G \le \tfrac{1}{2}(5 + \log_8 32) \log 32 + 4$$
$$= \tfrac{1}{2}(\tfrac{20}{3})5 + 4 = \tfrac{100}{6} + 4 < 21.$$

The number of gates required is at most

$$G \le (\tfrac{3}{2} + \tfrac{1}{7})32 \cdot 5 + (8 - \tfrac{1}{7})32 + \tfrac{2}{7} \cdot 5 + 2 < \tfrac{23}{14} \cdot 160 + \tfrac{55}{7} \cdot 32 + \tfrac{10}{7} + 2 = 518. \qquad \blacksquare$$

2.4 PROGRAM DEPENDENCE AND TRANSFORMATION

2.4.1 Introduction

In compiling programs for any kind of machine organization, we are interested in satisfying two types of goals:

1. The discovery of enough tasks that can be performed simultaneously to occupy all available resources.

2. The localization in address space of data addresses generated when executing the program.

In this section we will discuss program transformations that are aimed at one or both of these goals. We will also present language features that aid in achieving these goals.

In any multioperation computer, program speedup comes about from the execution of several operations at once. We have discussed fast methods for arithmetic expression and recurrence evaluation. Basically, each of these is a single program statement, although a recurrence requires initial conditions as well as an index set to control it. Now we will turn our attention to multiple statement programs including loops with one or more simple arithmetic expressions or recurrences.

As we saw in Chapter 1, multioperation machines include multifunction processors, multiprocessors, parallel and pipeline processors. Each of these has different programming requirements for efficient hardware use. Basically, the problem of compiling for any of them can be stated as follows. A program should be executed as quickly as possible, subject to the data and control dependences of the given program and subject to the resource dependences of the given machine. Even though a machine configuration is held fixed, a number of data and control dependence transformations are possible to speed

Prog. 3

$$X(1) \leftarrow C(1)$$
$$DO \ S \ I \leftarrow 2, 4$$
$$X(I) \leftarrow C(I)$$
$$DO \ S \ J \leftarrow 1, I-1$$
$$S \qquad X(I) \leftarrow A(I, J) * X(J) + X(I)$$

S_1: $X(1) \leftarrow C(1)$
S_2: $X(2) \leftarrow A(2, 1) * X(1) + C(2)$
S_3: $X(3) \leftarrow A(3, 1) * X(1) + A(3, 2) * X(2) + C(3)$
S_4: $X(4) \leftarrow A(4, 1) * X(1) + A(4, 2) * X(2) + A(4, 3) * X(3) + C(4)$

(a)   Prog. 3 execution.

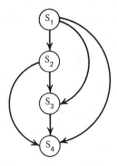

(b)   Prog. 3 data dependence graph.

FIGURE 2.20   **Prog. 3 details. (*a*) Prog. 3 execution. (*b*) Prog. 3 data dependence graph.**

S'_1: $X(1) \leftarrow C(1)$

S'_2: $X(2) \leftarrow C(2) + A(2, 1) * C(1)$

S'_3: $X(3) \leftarrow C(3) + A(3, 1) * C(1) + A(3, 2) * [C(2) + A(2, 1) * C(1)]$

S'_4: $X(4) \leftarrow C(4) + A(4, 1) * C(1) + A(4, 3) * [C(3) + A(3, 1) * C(1)]$
$$+ [A(4, 2) + A(4, 3) * A(3, 2)] * [C(2) + A(2, 1) * C(1)]$$

(a)   Transformed statements of Fig. 20a.

(b)   Data dependence graph.

FIGURE 2.21   **Transformed Prog. 3 details. (a) Transformed statements of Fig. 20a. (b) Data dependence graph.**

up a given program. In this chapter we have already seen two kinds of transformations of data dependences that speed up programs. In this section we will see other such transformations.

To be specific, let us reconsider the evaluation of a linear recurrence by the method of Section 2.3.3. For example, Prog. 3 would be executed on a uniprocessor, as shown in Fig. 2.20a. If we represent each statement by a node labeled with the statement label, we get a data dependence graph of the form shown in Fig. 2.20b. Notice that each statement's left-hand side variable appears on the right-hand sides of all its successors.

After the transformation of Section 2.3.3 (see Eq. 7) we get the four equations of Fig. 2.21a and the corresponding graph of Fig. 2.21b, since none of the statements is now dependent on any other. Of course, to determine whether or not any speedup has been achieved, we must now examine the details of what is inside the primed nodes of Fig. 2.21b, as compared with the unprimed nodes of Fig. 2.20b. Even though the new node computations are more complex, there is indeed a speedup for this computation. In order to save processors we can share common subexpressions between the nodes of Fig. 2.21b, but to represent this we first refine our data dependence graph notation.

We denote a left-hand side assignment to memory by ∇ and a right-hand side expression evaluation by $\square$ in Fig. 2.22. Clearly, there is always a data dependence between the right-hand side and left-hand side of an assignment statement. The connectivity of this graph is similar to Fig. 2.20b. It is possible to begin the computations inside the right-hand side nodes simultaneously, but their evaluations cannot be completed until the data dependences are satisfied, and to represent the details of this, an even more elaborate dependence graph is needed. In fact, what we need is a parse tree for each right-hand side expression. Clearly, a parse tree for an arithmetic expression is a data dependence graph for the expression, since a node labeled with an operation also serves the dual role of representing an intermediate value. A number of examples of transformations of such data depencence graphs were given in Section 2.2.

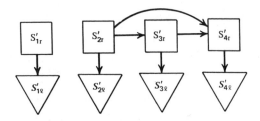

FIGURE 2.22   **Common subexpression sharing.**

Besides a data dependence graph, each program (or program segment) has an associated control dependence graph. If we use dotted lines to represent control dependence, then the program of Fig. 2.20a has the associated control dependence graph shown in Fig. 2.23. The transformed program of Fig. 2.21a would have the control dependence graph of Fig. 2.23 if executed on a uniprocessor, whereas if executed on a multioperation machine it could have the control dependence graph of Fig. 2.21b, since there is no inherent control dependence between the nodes. If processing capacity is limited, we might have a control dependence graph which is some variation of Fig. 2.22 since data dependence would determine control dependence. For example, we might begin S'_1, S'_2, S'_3 at once, and defer S'_4 until these are finished.

In what follows we will be discussing data dependence in a more formal way. To keep the discussion simple, we will assume that an unlimited number of processors (and other resources) are available. If this assumption is not valid in reality, then the nodes we deal with must first be modified according to the limited processors discussions given earlier for tree-height reduction and recurrence evaluation.

We began the above discussion with nodes representing assignment statements, and discussed how data dependence could be studied at that level and

FIGURE 2.23   **Prog. 3 control dependence graph.**

lower levels. Clearly this discussion can also be carried out at higher levels as well. For example, nodes could represent the computations performed by separate procedures. Data dependence lines would then represent data being passed between procedures. Control dependence lines would show all possible control transitions between procedures. If our machine resources were limited to just a few processors in a multiprocessor configuration, this type of graph would provide a job sequence for the processors.

As an example of the above, suppose that the terms in the equations of Fig. 2.21a were arrays rather than scalars. Thus the X_i and C_i could be $n \times 1$ column vectors and the A_{ij} $n \times n$ matrices. Now the nodes of the graphs of Figs. 2.21b. and 2.22 would represent procedures to carry out these array operations.

An important consideration here is how these graphs are generated. If we want to carry out a computation on a multioperation machine, the independence or parallelism between tasks must be discovered somehow. Clearly, the programmer may specify it—for example, by using the FORK and JOIN operators to be discussed in Section 2.4.3. These operations immediately define graph nodes at a high level.

Another possibility would be to have a compiler discover such parallelism. At the level of single statements, we have seen earlier in this chapter that compilers can find much parallelism in arbitrary arithmetic expressions or linear recurrences. It remains to be seen how a compiler can handle more complicated programs. In the rest of this chapter we will deal with two higher level constructs: blocks of assignment statements and loops. Control dependence and data dependence are interrelated and must be considered together in real programs, as we shall see. Conditional statements and jumps, either inside or outside of loops, have been considered in detail in [Towl76] and [Kuck76].

Much early work on parallel computation, including hardware, software, and algorithm organization was begun in the early 1960s by Gerald Estrin at the University of California at Los Angeles. This included various studies of program graphs for data and control dependence as well as the transformations of graphs for program speedup. See, for example, [MaEs67] and [BaBe70]; [Baer73] is a survey that contains many references to this work. A succinct set of conditions for dependence among unsubscripted statements similar to those given below, were presented by Bernstein in [Bern66]. Further work on program graphs and their transformations was done by Bingham, Fisher, and Riegel [Rieg70]; most of this work was published only in Burroughs reports, some of which are listed in [Baer73].

2.4.2 Program data dependence

In this section data dependence for blocks of assignment statements and loops is considered. After defining several terms, we will present an algorithm for distributing loop control over the statements of the loop.

Definition 8

A *loop* is denoted by

$$L = (I_1, I_2, \ldots, I_d)(S_1, S_2, \ldots, S_s),$$

where I_j is a *loop index* and S_j is a *body statement* that is an assignment statement.[7] The body statements may appear at different nesting levels, but d corresponds to the maximum depth of loop nesting in L. We use $\text{OUT}(S_j)$ and $\text{IN}(S_j)$ to denote for S_j the LHS (output) variable and the set of RHS (input) variables, respectively, and we will write $S_j(i_1, i_2, \ldots, i_d)$ to refer to S_j during a particular iteration step, that is, when the active index variables of S_j are assigned the specific values $I_1 = i_1, I_2 = i_2, \ldots, I_d = i_d$ (the only *active* index variables for S_j are those used in subscripts of its variables). If $S_i(k_1, \ldots, k_d)$ is executed before $S_j(l_1, \ldots, l_d)$, we will write $S_i(k_1, \ldots, k_d) \lesssim S_j(l_1, \ldots, l_d)$ and we say that the relation $\lesssim$ defines the *execution order* of the statements. ∎

Example 9

The loop

$$
\begin{array}{lll}
\text{DO} & S_2 & I_1 \leftarrow 1, 10, 2 \\
\text{DO} & S_2 & I_2 \leftarrow 1, 10, 1
\end{array}
$$

$$
\begin{array}{lll}
S_1 & & G(I_1, I_2) \leftarrow A(I_1, I_2) + B(I_1, I_2) \\
S_2 & & Z(I_1, I_2) \leftarrow C(I_1, I_2) * D(I_1, I_2)
\end{array}
$$

is written symbolically as $L = (I_1, I_2)(S_1, S_2)$ with S_1 and S_2 representing statements $G(I_1, I_2) \leftarrow \ldots$, and $Z(I_1, I_2) \leftarrow \ldots$, respectively. (Note that we use S_i in example programs as a statement label; elsewhere S_i represents the entire body statement.) Further, we have for example, $\text{OUT}(S_1(1, 4)) = G(1, 4)$ and $\text{IN}(S_1(1, 4)) = \{A(1, 4), B(1, 4)\}$. ∎

Notice that $\text{IN}(S_j)$ and $\text{OUT}(S_j)$ of Definition 8 can be defined similarly for an assignment outside loops. Next, we introduce three relations that may hold between pairs of statements. Definition 9 holds true for blocks of assignment statements, while Definition 10 covers loops.

Definition 9

Given a block of assignment statements including statements S_i and S_j, the following *data dependence relations* may hold true between S_i and S_j, or the statements may be independent. Assume that $x = \text{OUT}(S_i)$. If $x \, \varepsilon \, \text{IN}(S_j)$ and x is to take[8] the value computed in S_i, we say that S_j is *data dependent* on S_i and denote this by $S_i \, \delta \, S_j$. On the other hand, if $x \, \varepsilon \, \text{IN}(S_j)$ and x is *not* to take the

---

[7] This definition can be easily extended to include other types of statements inside loops.
[8] The phrasing here allows for any order of S_i and S_j and any kind of control structure for passing values from S_i to S_j that may hold in a programming language. Various statement execution orderings will be presented in Section 2.4.3.

value computed in S_i, we say that S_i is *data antidependent* on S_j and denote this by $S_j \bar{\delta} S_i$. Finally, if $x = \text{OUT}(S_j)$ and this value is to be stored after that of S_i, we say that S_j is *data output dependent* on S_i and denote this by $S_i \delta° S_j$. ∎

Definition 10

Given a loop $L = (I_1, \ldots, I_d)(S_1, \ldots, S_s)$, the following *data dependence relations* hold between assignment statements S_i and S_j in L, where i may be equal to j. Assume that $x = \text{OUT}(S_i(k_1, \ldots, k_d))$.

1. If $x \varepsilon \text{IN}(S_j(l_1, \ldots, l_d))$, for $S_i(k_1, \ldots, k_d) \lessgtr S_j(l_1, \ldots, l_d)$, then $S_i \delta S_j$.
2. If $x \varepsilon \text{IN}(S_j(l_1, \ldots, l_d))$, for $S_j(l_1, \ldots, l_d) \lessgtr S_i(k_1, \ldots, k_d)$, then $S_j \bar{\delta} S_i$.
3. If $x = \text{OUT}(S_j(l_1, \ldots, l_d))$, for $S_i(k_1, \ldots, k_d) \lessgtr S_j(l_1, \ldots, l_d)$, then $S_i \delta° S_j$. ∎

Definition 11

All data dependences in a block of assignment statements or loop of s statements can be represented by a *data dependence graph* G of s nodes, one for each S_i, $1 \leq i \leq s$. For each δ, $\bar{\delta}$, and $\delta°$ relation between S_i and S_j, there is a corresponding arc of type $\to$, $\leftrightarrow$, or $\nleftrightarrow$ in G from the node representing S_i to the node representing S_j. Statement S_j is *indirectly data dependent* on S_i, denoted $S_i \Delta S_j$, if there are statements $S_{k_1}, \ldots, S_{k_n}$, $n \geq 0$, such that $S_i \gamma S_{k_1} \gamma \ldots \gamma S_{k_n} \gamma S_j$, where γ denotes $\delta, \bar{\delta}$ or $\delta°$. Practical details for determining if $S_i \delta S_j$, $S_i \bar{\delta} S_j$, or $S_i \delta° S_j$ can be found in [KuMC72] or [Tow176]. ∎

Example 10

The block of assignment statements

$$S_1 \quad A \leftarrow B + D$$
$$S_2 \quad C \leftarrow A * 3$$
$$S_3 \quad A \leftarrow A + C$$

has the following data dependence graph (assuming execution order S_1, S_2, S_3)

G: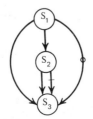

∎

Example 11

Given a loop

$$\text{L} \quad \text{DO} \quad S_2 \quad I_1 \leftarrow 1, 10$$
$$\text{DO} \quad S_2 \quad I_2 \leftarrow 1, 10$$
$$\text{DO} \quad S_2 \quad I_3 \leftarrow 1, 10$$
$$S_1 \qquad\qquad A(I_1, I_2, I_3) \leftarrow B(I_1 - 1, I_2, I_3) * C(I_1, I_2) + D * E$$
$$S_2 \qquad\qquad B(I_1, I_2, I_3) \leftarrow A(I_1, I_2 - 1, I_3) * F(I_2, I_3)$$

the corresponding data dependence graph is

G:

Notice that the graph of Example 10 has no cycles, whereas the graph of Example 11 has a dependence cycle between S_1 and S_2. Acyclic graphs are generally easier to deal with than cyclic graphs (ones containing any path of dependences from some node back to that node). We shall return to the discussion of graphs of program loops in Section 2.4.4.

2.4.3 Statement execution ordering

In the previous section, three types of data dependence were defined. In terms of these we can define several interesting and useful control statements for blocks of assignment statements. These control statements can also be applied to a collection of loops or procedures, for example. The relations between five different execution orderings will be presented, and these correspond to a number of actual hardware and software control techniques that will be described later.

Sequential execution ordering

A *sequential execution ordering* of a BAS is denoted by

$$\text{SEQ}[S_1; S_2; \ldots; S_k].$$

The following data dependence relations hold between assignment statements S_i and S_j of a SEQ block. Assume that $x = \text{OUT}(S_i)$.

1. If $x \varepsilon \text{IN}(S_j)$ for $i < j$, then $S_i \delta S_j$.
2. If $x \varepsilon \text{IN}(S_j)$ for $i > j$, then $S_j \bar{\delta} S_i$.
3. If $x = \text{OUT}(S_j)$ for $i < j$, then $S_i \delta° S_j$.

Notice that a block of assignment statements in an ordinary programming language (e.g., FORTRAN, ALGOL, etc.) is a SEQ block. The above definition was stated entirely in terms of data dependence. However, this determines the control sequence in which the statements must be executed. If $S_i \delta S_j$, $S_i \bar{\delta} S_j$, or $S_i \delta° S_j$, then S_i must be executed before S_j. If we consider the execution ordering of the individual operations in each assignment statement, then an even more refined control sequence can be given.

The BAS can be executed in any control order as long as the parse trees for the right-hand side expressions are followed from leaves to roots (note that parse tree branches are really δ dependences) and control dependence follows the arrows between statements.

Simultaneous execution ordering

A *simultaneous execution ordering* of a BAS is denoted by $\text{SIM}[S_1; S_2; \ldots; S_k]$. The following data dependence relations hold between statements S_i and S_j of such a SIM block. Assume that $x_i = \text{OUT}(S_i)$.

1. If $x_i \varepsilon \text{IN}(S_j)$ for any $j \neq i$, then $S_j \bar{\delta} S_i$.
2. If $x_i = \text{OUT}(S_j)$ for $j \neq i$, then the SIM block is not defined.

During the execution of a SIM block all occurrences of each right-hand variable are assumed to have the same value, namely, the value of that variable before the beginning of the execution of this block of assignment statements (i.e., they are all input variables). It is assumed that all left-hand variables are distinct in such a block; otherwise, an undefined collision would occur. All k statements in a SIM block are given the same execution order number. The SIM block can be used to represent array operations using scalar assignment statements. For example,

$$\text{SIM}[A(1) \leftarrow A(0) + B(1); A(2) \leftarrow A(1) + B(2); A(3) \leftarrow A(2) + B(3)]$$

causes a vector addition in which previously computed A values are shifted by one in subscript values and added to the B vector. Thus $A(1)$ in the second statement is an input value, not the one computed by the first statement.

Relations between execution orderings

The relations between sets of assignment statements that must be executed sequentially, or simultaneously, or that may be commuted, are explored in this section. SEQ and SIM orderings delimit our universe of execution orderings; however, they can be subdivided into the following interesting and useful classes.

A *commutative sequential execution ordering* of k assignment statements is denoted by $\text{COM}[S_1; \ldots; S_k]$. The results of executing $\text{COM}[S_1; \ldots; S_k]$ are equivalent to the results of executing $\text{SEQ}[S_{i_1}; \ldots; S_{i_k}]$ for all possible sequences $\langle i_1, \ldots, i_k \rangle$ which are permutations of $\langle 1, \ldots, k \rangle$.

A *together execution ordering* of k assignment statements is denoted by $TOG[S_1; S_2; \ldots; S_k]$. The results of executing $TOG[S_1; \ldots; S_k]$ are equivalent to the results of executing $SIM[S_1; \ldots; S_k]$ and $COM[S_1; \ldots; S_k]$. Thus for a TOG execution ordering to be defined, none of $S_i \, \delta \, S_j$, $S_i \, \bar{\delta} \, S_j$ or $S_i \, \delta° \, S_j$ is allowed for any S_i and S_j.

A *fetch-store execution ordering* of a block of k assignment statements is denoted by $FS[S_1; S_2; \ldots; S_k]$. The input variables of each S_i must be fetched before the output variables of $S_{i+1}, \ldots, S_k$ are stored. FS allows $S_i \, \bar{\delta} \, S_j$, but neither $S_i \, \delta \, S_j$ nor $S_i \, \delta° \, S_j$, for $1 \le i < j \le k$.

A *store-fetch sequential execution ordering* of k assignment statements is denoted by $SF[S_1; S_2; \ldots; S_k]$. The output variables of $S_1, \ldots, S_{i-1}$ must be stored before the input variables of each S_i are fetched. SF allows any of $S_i \, \delta \, S_j$, $S_i \, \bar{\delta} \, S_j$ or $S_i \, \delta° \, S_j$, for $1 \le i < j \le k$.

Note that COM cuts the set of SEQ execution orderings into two disjoint subsets and that SF cuts these two subsets into four. TOG and FS are names for two of these four subsets. In Fig. 2.24, we show a Venn diagram for these subsets and our entire universe of execution orderings, the union of SEQ and SIM.

Example 12

The following simple examples illustrate the execution orderings defined above. The numbers here correspond to the numbered sections of Fig. 2.24.

1. TOG
    $TOG[A \leftarrow B; C \leftarrow D]$
2. FS
    $FS[A \leftarrow B; B \leftarrow C]$
3a. SF and COM
    $COM[A \leftarrow 2 * A; A \leftarrow 3 * A]$
3b. SF but not COM
    $SF[A \leftarrow B + 1; B \leftarrow A + 1]$
4. SIMP (SIM but not SEQ)
    $SIM[A \leftarrow B; B \leftarrow A]$ ∎

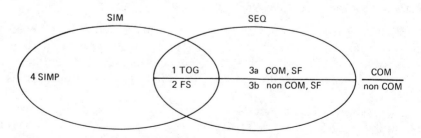

FIGURE 2.24   **Execution ordering relations.**

Practical implications

Practically, these five categories of execution ordering are of interest in specifying program control or hardware control. Programs are normally written with SEQ control implied and are executed as SF but not COM. A compiler can analyze the data dependence and place programs in other SEQ categories, however, for faster execution. Similarly, the effects of SIM may be achieved, for example, by array statements in PL/I or APL; the SIM control of Section 1.2.1.6 is another example. Some practical questions concerning the relations between the execution orderings are discussed below.

If several processors share a memory, a TOG block can be used to indicate that any processor may be used to execute any assignment statement in any order. For example, (see [Bern66])

$$TOG[A \leftarrow B + 15; C \leftarrow D/E; F \leftarrow G * H]$$

can be executed on three different processors at once. In fact, programming languages for multiprocessors often have special control statements [Baer 73] such as DO TOGETHER or FORK and JOIN that are used to cause just this type of program execution (which would be reasonable for array variables here).

If several processors share a memory, an FS block can be used to allow the processing of several statements to proceed in parallel, but to guarantee the proper sequencing of stores and fetches. For example, consider

$$FS[A \leftarrow 3 * C/B; B \leftarrow C * 5; C \leftarrow 7 + E]$$

This block can be executed on three processors, but it guarantees that the values of B and C used in the first statement are input data, not those computed in the second and third statements. Similarly, C in the second statement has the input value, not $7 + E$. Because the first statement is relatively more complex (and needs more execution time) than the second and third, such protection probably would not occur naturally if the programs were simply written as a TOG block.

Of course, if the program were written as an SF block to guarantee proper sequencing, then it would be compiled for just one processor and hence would run more slowly. If it were written as a SIMP block, then it could be evaluated on three processors, but each processor would have to wait until the last one finished computing before anything could be stored to memory. This could overconstrain the scheduling of a large number of statements on a few processors. To contrast SIMP and FS blocks, we give the following example.

The FS block

$$FS[A \leftarrow B + 2; B \leftarrow C + 3; C \leftarrow E + F + 4]$$

could be executed on two processors, with the first two statements on one and the third on another. The first two would be executed sequentially and the second processor would only have to be constrained to store C after it was fetched for the C + 3 calculation. But if a SIMP block were used, the compiler would be forced to execute the first two statements (as well as the third) simultaneously—perhaps on two processors or perhaps on one processor, by evaluating both B + 2 and C + 3 before storing A and B. In any case, an FS block allows a smoother operation here.

P and V have been used extensively to coordinate cooperating and competing tasks in multiprogrammed machines with one or more processors [Dijk68] [Baer73]. These are software-defined functions; hardware versions are discussed in [BrMc70] and [Wirt69]. Their relation to this discussion becomes obvious when we let each statement be a task and say that the tasks are cooperating when they are not data dependent and competing when they are data dependent, data antidependent, or data output dependent. By insertion of P and V in the appropriate places, we achieve the same effect as using SIM, SEQ, FS, SF, or TOG. SIM, SEQ, FS, SF, and TOG are used to *specify* the execution ordering at a global level, whereas P and V can be used to *implement* the execution ordering at the level of individual operations. The combination COM and SF is useful, for example, when several processors share data, but must be denied simultaneous access to certain shared data which may be accessed by them in any order, but not simultaneously (see Section 5.2.4).

2.4.4 Loop distribution

Next we consider the question of distributing loop control over the loop body statements. To achieve statement independence we can use statement substitution, but this is generally less useful inside loops than outside because of the cost of redundant operations on whole arrays instead of scalars. It should be used with discretion, and only in machines with a high degree of parallelism.

In loops with acyclic graphs, it is possible to reduce the graph for the entire loop to a set of independent nodes representing simultaneously executable array statements. In general, however, we must deal with cyclic graphs containing several interdependent nodes. The loop distribution algorithm will be useful in handling these cases. By loop distribution we mean the distribution of the loop control statements over individual or collections of assignment statements contained in the loop.

Next, we define a partition of a dependence graph and then in terms of this partition we present the loop distribution algorithm of [CKTB78].

Definition 12

On the dependence graph G, for a given loop L, we define a *node partition* π of $\{S_1, \ldots, S_s\}$ in such a way that S_k and S_l, $k \neq l$, are in the same subset if and only if $S_k \Delta S_l$ and $S_l \Delta S_k$. These subsets are called π-*blocks*. On the partition

$\pi = \{\pi_1, \pi_2, \ldots\}$ define *partial ordering relations* α, $\bar{\alpha}$, and α° such that $i \neq j$:

1. $\pi_i \, \alpha \, \pi_j$ iff there exist $S_k \, \varepsilon \, \pi_i$ and $S_l \, \varepsilon \, \pi_j$ such that $S_k \, \delta \, S_l$.
2. $\pi_i \, \bar{\alpha} \, \pi_j$ iff there exist $S_k \, \varepsilon \, \pi_i$ and $S_l \, \varepsilon \, \pi_j$ such that $S_k \, \bar{\delta} \, S_l$.
3. $\pi_i \, \alpha^\circ \, \pi_j$ iff there exist $S_k \, \varepsilon \, \pi_i$ and $S_l \, \varepsilon \, \pi_j$ such that $S_k \, \delta^\circ \, S_l$.

During execution of a loop, π-blocks are ordered by the α, $\bar{\alpha}$, and α° relations. If $\pi_i \, \alpha \, \pi_j$, $\pi_i \, \bar{\alpha} \, \pi_j$, or $\pi_i \, \alpha^\circ \, \pi_j$ then π_i must be executed before π_j. This ensures that the δ, $\bar{\delta}$, and δ° relations are preserved. By statement substitution and variable renaming, some of these α relations may be broken to achieve faster execution.   ∎

Loop distribution algorithm

STEP 1   Given a loop

$$L = (I_1, I_2, \ldots, I_d)(S_1, S_2, \ldots, S_s),$$

by analyzing subscript expressions and indexing patterns, construct a dependence graph G (see Definition 11).

STEP 2   On G establish a node partition π as in Definition 12.

STEP 3   On the partition π establish a partial ordering relation as in Definition 12.

STEP 4   Replace L according to π with a set of loops $\{(I^1)(\pi_1), (I^2)(\pi_2), \ldots\}$ where I^i denotes the set of active index variables for each π_i.

STEP 5   For each $L_i = (I^i)(\pi_i)$:

a. if the dependence graph is acyclic, the assignment statement can be handled as an array of arithmetic expressions (see Section 2.2);

b. if the dependence graph is cyclic, block π_i can be handled by a linear recurrence method (see Section 2.3), or executed sequentially if it is nonlinear.

The condition of the partial ordering relation α ensures that data are updated before being used. Hence, any execution order of the set of loops that replaces L will be valid as long as this relation is not violated. Thus, if $\pi_i \, \alpha \, \pi_j$ then loop $(I^i)(\pi_i)$ must be evaluated before $(I^j)(\pi_j)$. We can also use statement substitution to remove this relation between some or all of the distributed loops. But, by not allowing statement substitution we have a somewhat simpler compiler technique, one which generally requires fewer processors and yields less speedup.

Example 13

As an example of the use of loop distribution, consider

$$\text{DO} \quad S_5 \quad I \leftarrow 1, N$$
$$S_1 \qquad A(I) \leftarrow B(I) * C(I)$$
$$\text{DO} \quad S_3 \quad J \leftarrow 1, N$$

$$S_2 \qquad\qquad D(I, J) \leftarrow A(I-3) + E(I, J-1)$$

$$S_3 \qquad\qquad E(I, J) \leftarrow D(I, J-1) + F$$

$$DO \quad S_4 \quad K \leftarrow 1, N$$

$$S_4 \qquad\qquad G(I, K) \leftarrow H(I-5) + 1$$

$$S_5 \qquad\qquad H(I) \leftarrow SQRT(A(I-2))$$

In this example, $L = (I_1, I_2)(S_1, S_2, S_3, S_4, S_5)$. Following step 1 of the loop distribution algorithm, we obtain a dependence graph as shown in Fig. 2.25. We use brackets to denote loop nesting. In step 2, we form the partition $\pi = \{\pi_1, \pi_2, \pi_3, \pi_4\}$ where $\pi_1 = \{S_1\}$, $\pi_2 = \{S_2, S_3\}$, $\pi_3 = \{S_4\}$, and $\pi_4 = \{S_5\}$. These partitions are partially ordered on step 3 as follows: $\pi_1 \, \alpha \, \pi_2$, $\pi_1 \, \alpha \, \pi_4$ and $\pi_4 \, \alpha \, \pi_3$. Note that $I^1 = \{I\}$, $I^2 = \{I, J\}$, $I^3 = \{I, K\}$ and $I^4 = \{I\}$.

The result of this transformation is shown in Fig. 2.26. We could use this graph to compile array operations as follows. First, S_1 yields a vector multiply. Next, we can execute π_2 or π_4. π_2 leads to a set of N independent (I index) linear recurrences (J index) of the form $R\langle 2N, 3\rangle$ which can be solved by the method of Theorem 3, by combining the D and E arrays as an unknown vector in which x_1 represents $D(1)$, x_2 represents $E(1)$, x_3 represents $D(2)$, x_4 represents $E(2)$, and so on. π_4 leads to the execution of S_5 as a vector of square roots. Finally, S_4 may be executed for all I and K simultaneously. Note that this requires the broadcasting of elements of the H array to all elements in the columns of G. Here, the time required to execute π_1, π_3, and π_4 is a constant (independent of N) using $O(N)$ processors. The overall execution time is dominated by π_2 and is $O(\log N)$, so this is a Type 1 loop. The number of processors required to achieve this time is $O(N)$. ∎

Notice that in Example 13 we avoided statement substitution. Using statement substitution, we would have been able to obtain four π-blocks, all of

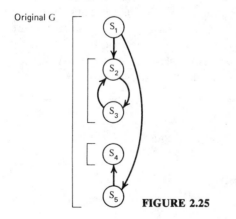

Original G

FIGURE 2.25   **Program graph.**

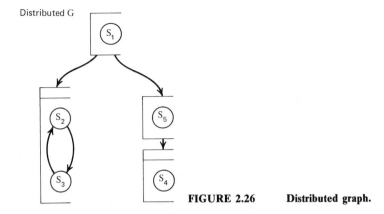

Distributed G

FIGURE 2.26   **Distributed graph.**

which could be executed at once. This would require the execution of several different operations at one time, whereas the technique we used allows all operations at each step to be identical. Furthermore, very little additional speedup would be possible by this method since π_2 dominates the time here. For extensions of these ideas, including loops with IF and GOTO statements, see [Kuck 76].

2.4.5 Loop distribution application

As we pointed out in the introduction, two goals of compilation are the discovery of simultaneously executable tasks and the localization of addresses generated by a running program. Loop distribution can be quite effective in both respects, as the following discussion illustrates. First, we discuss techniques for the discovery of parallel operations and relate these operations to several types of machine organization, including the multiprogrammed uniprocessor. Second, we discuss improving system performance by use of a virtual memory, a subject that will be expanded in Chapter 7.

Consider Prog. 4a, which contains two loops, one that initializes the A and B arrays, another that computes and writes the C and D arrays to secondary memory. By loop distribution, Prog. 4a can be rewritten as Prog. 4b in which form it becomes clear that a great deal of parallelism exists because all of the assignment or I/O statements within each loop can be carried out at once. Further parallelism exists between the six loops, as shown in the data dependence graph of Fig. 2.27.

Let us interpret the observed parallelism in terms of the machine organizations of Section 1.2.1, reversing the order in which the types are considered. The array operations observed first could be directly exploited on a parallel or pipeline machine. In a parallel machine, with p processors, we will need $\lceil N/p \rceil$ steps to complete each operation. In the pipeline case, the greater N is, the

Prog. 4a

$$
\begin{array}{ll}
& \text{DO} \quad S_2 \quad I \leftarrow 1, N+1 \\
S_1 & A(I) \leftarrow 2 * I + 3 \\
S_2 & \text{READ } B(I) \\
& \text{DO} \quad S_6 \quad I \leftarrow 1, N \\
S_3 & C(I) \leftarrow B(I) * B(I+1) \\
S_4 & D(I) \leftarrow C(I) ** 2/A(I) \\
S_5 & \text{WRITE } D(I) \\
S_6 & \text{WRITE } C(I)
\end{array}
$$

Prog. 4b

$$
\begin{array}{ll}
& \text{DO} \quad S_1 \quad I \leftarrow 1, N+1 \\
S_1 & A(I) \leftarrow 2 * I + 3 \\
& \text{DO} \quad S_2 \quad I \leftarrow 1, N+1 \\
S_2 & \text{READ } B(I) \\
& \text{DO} \quad S_3 \quad I \leftarrow 1, N \\
S_3 & C(I) \leftarrow B(I) * B(I+1) \\
& \text{DO} \quad S_4 \quad I \leftarrow 1, N \\
S_4 & D(I) \leftarrow C(I) ** 2/A(I) \\
& \text{DO} \quad S_5 \quad I \leftarrow 1, N \\
S_5 & \text{WRITE } D(I) \\
& \text{DO} \quad S_6 \quad I \leftarrow 1, N \\
S_6 & \text{WRITE } C(I)
\end{array}
$$

better use we can make of a pipeline arithmetic unit. In both cases, I/O speed depends on the organization of main and secondary memory, but in the best case, parallel array transfers are possible.

Given a multifunction processor, this program presents no possibilities for speeding up individual right-hand side computations in Prog. 4b; the individual right-hand sides are too simple for the application of tree-height reduction. However, the computations of S_1 and S_3 could be overlapped because there is no data dependence between them. For example, if an adder and a multiplier were available, we could first form $2 * I$, then add 3 to this, and at the same time multiply $B(I)$ by $B(I+1)$. In fact, using a parallel machine with multifunction processors, the above could be carried out for all I at once. Similarly, using a machine with an adder and multiplier pipeline, we could also overlap statements S_1 and S_3.

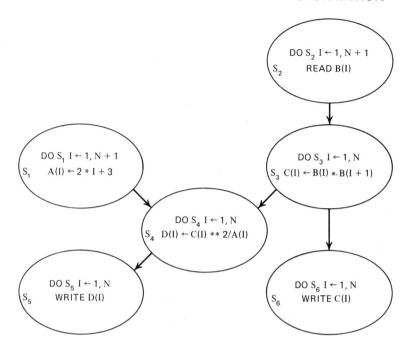

FIGURE 2.27   Data dependence graph for Prog. 4*b*.

With a multiprocessor organization, the program as shown in Fig. 2.27 would be most applicable. If two processors were available, S_1 and S_2 could be carried out simultaneously in separate processors at the beginning of the computation and S_5 and S_6 at the end. Furthermore, if N were sufficiently large, we could break node S_3 into two halves and compute one half on each processor, and similarly for S_4. If more than two processors were available, all of the nodes could be broken into several parallel tasks. Of course, there is a practical limit to this, since interprocessor and interprogram communication time may be substantial. Hence, the condition that N be sufficiently large to allow the computation time to dominate the setup and cleanup communication times.

Even in the case of a uniprocessor, the graph of Fig. 2.27 can be exploited if the machine is multiprogrammed. We can multiprogram a single user by deriving from one program several tasks that may be executed at once. Thus, I/O and computation could be overlapped by executing S_1 and S_2 simultaneously, assuming an independent I/O channel is available to handle S_2. S_5 and S_6 would probably have to be done sequentially because of limitations on I/O bandwidth. In any case, we see that even the simple case of Prog. 4*b* can be speeded up in many ways, depending on the machine architecture available.

Next, consider Prog. 5, which is simply Prog. 4*b* with an outer loop that causes it to be executed K times. Assume that K different B arrays are stored

Prog. 5.

$$
\begin{aligned}
&\text{DO} \quad S_7 \quad J \leftarrow 1, K \\
&\qquad \text{DO} \quad S_1 \quad I \leftarrow 1, N+1 \\
&S_1 \qquad\qquad A(I) \leftarrow 2 * I + 3 \\
&\qquad \text{DO} \quad S_2 \quad I \leftarrow 1, N+1 \\
&S_2 \qquad\qquad \text{READ } B(I) \\
&\qquad \text{DO} \quad S_3 \quad I \leftarrow 1, N \\
&S_3 \qquad\qquad C(I) \leftarrow B(I) * B(I+1) \\
&\qquad \text{DO} \quad S_4 \quad I \leftarrow 1, N \\
&S_4 \qquad\qquad D(I) \leftarrow C(I) ** 2/A(I) \\
&\qquad \text{DO} \quad S_5 \quad I \leftarrow 1, N \\
&S_5 \qquad\qquad \text{WRITE } D(I) \\
&\qquad \text{DO} \quad S_6 \quad I \leftarrow 1, N \\
&S_6 \qquad\qquad \text{WRITE } C(I) \\
&S_7 \qquad\qquad \text{CONTINUE}
\end{aligned}
$$

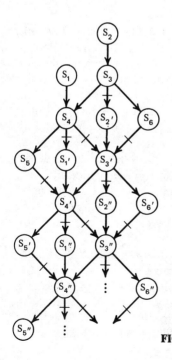

FIGURE 2.28   Data dependence graph for Prog. 5.

in an input file to be processed one after another by Prog. 5. This is typical of the organization of COBOL programs.

In discussing Prog. 4b, we saw that there was parallelism within each statement and there was also parallelism among certain statements. Now we will see that there is also parallelism among repeated executions of Prog. 4b when written in the form of Prog. 5. In Fig. 2.28 three cycles of the outer loop of Prog. 5 are shown; iterations are distinguished by primed statement numbers in the nodes.

The key idea here is that as soon as we are finished with the storage space for an array on one iteration of the outer loop, that space can be used to begin the next outer loop iteration. Hence, when loop S_3 is finished, the READ statement can be executed again to bring a new B array into main memory. If this were done before the completion of S_3, we would risk overwriting parts of the old B array before they were used in computing the C array. Of course, we could break these arrays into blocks and overlap things at a lower level, but we are concerned only with general principles at the moment.

In Fig. 2.28, the fact that S_2 must not begin execution until S_3 is completed is denoted by the antidependence arc from S_3 to $S_{2'}$. Similar relationships exist between S_4 and $S_{1'}$ with respect to the A array, and the others shown in Fig. 2.28. These relationships are, of course, repeated between each pair of iterations. Notice that this leads, in Fig. 2.28, to parallelism among up to three statements at once.

The overall logic of this program is typical of various file processing computations. A number of records in a file are to be processed by several programs in succession. As in Fig. 2.28, it is possible to execute the programs in such a way that several records are simultaneously sharing the same program, and several programs can be operating on different parts of one file at the same time.

In a multiprogrammed machine, situations often arise where several different programs must share a common data set. For example, if two different programs are handling some real-time task, each can signal the other through a shared memory location. This would allow each to know if the other has as yet carried out some task. A danger can arise here if both try to access the shared memory location at the same time. In a single program that has been broken up for multiprogramming, correct sequencing is maintained by data dependence as in Fig. 2.28. But, in general, it may be difficult for a compiler to determine a priori which program will or should access the shared data first. Thus, the burden of synchronizing a set of programs (or processors) is often placed on the programmer. The P and V or FORK and JOIN of Section 2.4.3, for example, are two ways of specifying characteristics of the control of multiple programs.

Here we will use a simple version of the FORK and JOIN to specify the control of Prog. 4b for simultaneous execution. The resulting program is shown as Prog. 6 and this should be compared with Fig. 2.27. The FORK S_7

Prog. 6

```
              FORK S₇
              DO   S₁   I←1,N+1
   S₁              A(I)←2 * I+3
              JOIN
              FORK S₈
              DO   S₄   I←1,N
   S₄              D(I)←C(I) ** 2/A(I)
              DO   S₅   I←1,N
   S₅              WRITE D(I)
              JOIN
              GOTO   S₉
   S₇    DO   S₂   I←1,N+1
   S₂              READ B(I)
              DO   S₃   I←1,N
   S₃              C(I)←B(I) * B(I+1)
              JOIN
   S₈    DO   S₆   I←1,N
   S₆              WRITE C(I)
              JOIN
   S₉
```

statement causes control to pass to both S_7 and the DO S_1 statement following the FORK. Thus the DO S_1 and DO S_2 can be executed simultaneously on two (or more) distinct processors. If implemented on a single, multiprogrammed processor, control could pass back and forth between the two, or the computation of S_1 could be overlapped with the READ of S_2. The S_2 loop is followed in the normal way by the S_3 loop.

Following the S_1 and S_3 loops are JOIN statements. The meaning of these is that at this point the two control paths we have FORKed to are to be rejoined as a single control path following the S_1 loop (since the FORK appeared immediately before the S_1 loop). This is implemented by compiling code that causes test bits to be available that allow the two routines to synchronize themselves after they are finished. When both paths have reached their JOIN instructions, control passes to the FORK S_8 statement, which allows the simultaneous execution of the S_4 computation and the S_6 WRITE. The S_4 loop is followed by the S_5 loop and the S_5 and S_6 loops are followed by a JOIN pair which ends the computation. It is clear that the execution of this program leads to precisely the flow chart of Fig. 2.27. Generalizations of the FORK and JOIN to multiway branches are easy to design and implement [Baer 73]. This reference also contains the history of these constructs, which date back to 1958; the idea was probably first implemented in the Bull Gamma-60 [Drey 58].

An idea that follows immediately from the FORK and JOIN is that of *coroutines.* Here we allow the FORK and JOIN type of control, but we may allow the independently executable routines to communicate with each other during their execution. This simply requires that at certain key points within the coroutines, resynchronization is necessary to ensure that computed values are properly passed from one to the other.

2.5 COMPUTER SYSTEM CAPACITY

Relatively speaking, it is easy to design a computer system but it is hard to know what kind of system to design. In other words, techniques for logic design and system programming are fairly well understood, and there are also a number of techniques for analyzing the performance of a computer system or parts thereof [Drum73] [Full75] [HeCo75]. But, designing a system that will perform well in some application area is a very intuitive undertaking. A good deal of experimentation is usually involved.

In this section we present an overall capacity model that can be used to represent the hardware components of a computer system and also some characteristics of a user's software. A well-designed system must be "balanced" or "matched" in both of these aspects. The hardware components—control unit, processor, main memory, and memory hierarchy—must be matched to each other in terms of speed. This matching cannot be done in the absence of programs, however. We must consider how much processing, how much memory activity, how much I/O, and so on, are required in the set of jobs to be run.

The capacity model we present represents a given computer system configuration in terms of a space that allows us to represent all possible computations. Each computation is related to the machine in terms of the amounts of bandwidth of the various system components that the computation uses. We define the effective speed of the system in terms of the relative speeds of the system components *and* how well a set of user programs is matched to this system. Thus we could use the model in several ways.

Given a set of programs to be run on a computer system, we could design a system by adjusting the system components to a point where the set of programs is reasonably well handled by the proposed machine. Or, given a set of programs and a computer system, we could tell how far we are operating from an optimum speed point. We could also determine how to change the system components to move the optimum closer to the set of programs we are running—that is, to reconfigure the system to match the jobs we have. Finally, given a well-balanced hardware and software system, we could study the sensitivity of the balance to changes in the load.

The capacity model we present is an abstract one. To apply it, measurements are needed of real programs and real machines. Throughout the book we discuss various aspects of such characteristics of real programs and machines. But the claims of the previous paragraph have not as yet been realized; they depend on future development of such performance models. Nevertheless, our model provides an easy to understand, yet comprehensive picture of overall computer system operation.

2.5.1 System costs

In previous sections we have dealt with several aspects of computer system evaluation. But we have said little about the first criterion of Section 1.1.1, namely, cost. Indirectly we *have* dealt with cost, since the number of processors, the size of memory, the speed of components, and so on, are all cost dependent. In a sense, we have taken and will take the position throughout this book, that for a given total amount of money we are interested in finding the best possible computer system configuration. We will consider the relative costs of major system components below and then we will discuss how these components perform when assembled into a system.

Overall, the costs to the user[9] of an installed computer system break down to about one-half computer costs and one-half personnel costs. There may be large variations in this, depending on factors such as the system size and type of users involved. A large computer center, dedicated to a few skilled users could be expected to spend most of its budget on hardware, whereas a facility with a minicomputer and a number of naive users might spend most of its budget on personnel—consultants, programmers, and operators. But overall, we might expect the average installation to spend half of its budget on each side.

Numbers such as the above and those we will discuss below are very hard to document and obviously vary from machine to machine and installation to installation. Books that are interesting sources of facts in this respect are [Shar69], [Broc75], and [Phis76]. The numbers discussed here are averages gleaned from these as well as a number of real computer installations. Whether or not the numbers we give are correct, the following discussion of cost-effectiveness tradeoffs contains a number of factors that should be considered by computer system designers, users, and managers.

Within the computer system itself, the hardware costs break down roughly as follows. The cost of the CPU, that is, the processor and control unit, is about 20 percent of the total hardware cost. The memory hierarchy—including main

---

[9] The manufacturing cost and the manufacturer's price to the user, that is, what we are calling the costs to the user, are determined by a number of economic and political considerations that we cannot consider here.

memory, bulk random access memory, and various rotating sequential access memories—amounts to about 60 or 70 percent. The breakdown of this depends on the system configuration, of course. In some cases main memory may be 40 percent of the total cost and in other cases secondary memory may be 40 percent of the total cost. Various other peripheral devices such as card readers, line printers, user terminals, and so on, usually account for another 10 or 15 percent of the total cost.

It is interesting to observe in this context the relative frequencies of use of the various parts of a computer system. Such numbers are quite difficult to obtain in general. In Section 4.2.1.2 we will give the results of several studies of dynamic measurements of instruction frequencies in various types of real computations. It turns out that even in numerical computations, perhaps only 10 or 15 percent of the instructions executed are arithmetic instructions. Interestingly enough, this matches the fact that perhaps one-half of the CPU cost is in the processor, so using the 20 percent cost figure for the CPU from the previous paragraph, it can be argued that 10 or 15 percent of the instructions executed use a system component which accounts for 10 or 15 percent of the system cost. Similarly, 45 or 50 percent of the instructions executed are memory accesses, and this roughly matches the relative cost of the main memory.

On the other hand, the number of I/O instructions executed is negligible, whereas the equipment costs in this area are very high. Of course, there are several flaws in the above discussion. Instruction frequency is not the appropriate measure; the time to carry out instructions is more important, and I/O tends to be very time-consuming. Thus, it may be that the overall time spent executing each instruction type is indeed proportional to the cost of the part of the system involved with that type of instruction.

If the above were true, it could perhaps be used to argue that computer systems have evolved nicely toward optimal cost-effective configurations. But we are still overlooking several points. One is that the various system components often operate in an overlapped way. Thus it is reasonable to argue that in an ideal machine, all computations should run with all system components always active. This kind of idealized argument will be used below, in our discussion of computer capacity. In the real world, such a situation would be impossible to achieve, and indeed it is not clear that such a criterion should be used in general. In fact, it is quite obvious that certain system components which are only rarely used must be present. For example, a card reader may seldom be used, but if you do not have one, you cannot read cards; so it may be a seldom used, absolute necessity in some systems.

For the system components used in most computations—the control unit, processor, and main memory—the argument that all should be busy all of the time is probably more realistic, in general. And yet, one sometimes hears system designers remark that because processors, for example, are relatively inexpensive and only relatively few of the instructions executed are processor instructions, their design is not important, particularly from a speed point of view. They, of course, are forgetting that in the sense of elapsed time, processor execution time weighs relatively more heavily, and in machines with overlapped control unit, memory, and processor activity, processor execution time is very important.

Our point in this section and throughout the book will be that we must know exactly what the relative execution times of different instruction types are, and we must match them to machine configurations. If we were able to design systems which were balanced because each component was constantly in use, then we could attempt to improve the system further by reducing the cost of the most expensive parts. Of course, even in the real world of existing systems which have been balanced intuitively by evolution, we should always consider the most expensive system components and try to reduce costs there. Similarly, we should consider the relatively less expensive parts of the system and see if we can improve system performance by using relatively more of the less expensive components.

For more discussion of the following capacity model, see [KuKu76].

2.5.2 Capacity/cost definitions

Traditionally, computer speeds have often been quoted in mips (*millions of instructions per second*). But the execution of an "instruction" yields different effects on various machines. The range is from some simple indexing operation on a traditional machine to a vector inner product instruction on a modern pipeline processor. Thus, as computer organizations diverged from one another, mops (*millions of operations per second*) became a more reasonable measure. But in many numerical calculations, floating-point arithmetic operations are the raison d'etre for the computer and logical operations, shifts, and so on, are "overhead." Thus, megaflops (millions of floating-point operations per second) may be the important measure.

Quoting megaflops is, of course, quite irrelevant for most computations performed in the real world every day. Many computations, such as, data base management, file processing, simulation, and so on, perform almost no floating-point arithmetic. The main memory speed and often input/output speeds are the most important to quote in evaluating or comparing machines. Our capacity formulation will include consideration of the type of computation being performed as well as the bandwidths of the various system components (e.g., processor, main memory, control unit, and secondary memory). This will allow us to discuss how well-matched the various system components are to the actual programs being run on the system.

Overall, there are two independent sets of parameters that must be dealt with. One set consists of machine characteristics such as bandwidths and costs of system components, memory size, and operational overlap between system components. The other set consists of program characteristics for the jobs to be run. These include the programs' relative demands on the bandwidths of various system components, program and data addressing patterns, and various software overheads.

In the discussion that follows we will describe the bandwidths of various system components. Although we do not mention costs, they are included implicitly. Instead of bandwidth measured in bits/second, we could be discussing the cost of bandwidth measured in bits/second/dollar, for example. Thus when we compare two bandwidths and say that the memory bandwidth is, for example, twice the processor bandwidth, this could instead represent some system in which the memory bandwidth per dollar of memory cost was twice that of the processor bandwidth per dollar of processor cost. The entire discussion could have been carried out in these terms, but we have avoided it to simplify the discussion.

A discussion of bandwidth per dollar could, however, serve several useful goals. First, it could be interpreted in the sense of *designing* a machine where costs refer to actual hardware costs. Second, it could be interpreted in the sense of *using* a machine, where costs refer to the accounting scheme used in charging users. Third, it could be interpreted in the sense of *managing* a machine, when costs are the same as in the previous case. In the latter two cases, we view the system as an economic resource from two sides. In the former case, we design with the goal of enhancing system cost-effectiveness for some set of programs to be run on the system.

2.5.3 Capacity definitions

Let us consider the definition of bandwith for various computer system components. For a main memory unit, the definition is quite clear. In one memory cycle time unit t, we can access (store or fetch) a word of w bits. So the *memory bandwidth*

$$B_m = \frac{w}{t} \frac{\text{bits}}{\text{second}}$$

is the memory access data rate.

For a secondary memory unit, the definition of bandwidth is somewhat fuzzy. When the secondary memory is transmitting words, a definition similar to the above is obvious. But we must often pay an access delay time in most secondary memory devices. This time includes such things as the rotation time of a disk drive and the time to move a read/write arm (seek time). Because blocks of data are usually transmitted, we must consider the number of words per block and access latency in computing secondary memory bandwidth.

Processor bandwidth definition also has some ambiguity. Various operations may take different amounts of time. For example, if an addition takes one time unit, a traditional multiplication may take two or three time units, although in fast, modern computers, add and multiply times are often equal. Division is usually substantially slower in any machine. Thus we could use some kind of weighted average which considers the frequency of execution of various operations as well as their different times.

Given some definition of "average operation time," there is a further question about defining the number of bits processed in this time. Most arithmetic units accept two arguments and produce one result in the execution of a single instruction. If each of these is a word of w bits, should we define the number of bits handled in an "average operation time" to be $2w$ (input bits), w (output bits), $3w$ (input plus output bits), or something else?

Answering this question is helped by considering other possible processors. For example, consider a special arithmetic unit which accepts four input words and produces their sum in the same time that a standard adder adds two numbers. Clearly, we would regard this four input unit as a higher bandwidth device. Furthermore, a multiplier which produced a w-bit output from two, w-bit inputs should be regarded as having less bandwidth than one which produces a $2w$-bit product.

Thus we conclude that both input and output bits are important in determining processor bandwidth. So we will use the sum of the number of input and output bits divided by the "average operation time" as a working definition of *processor bandwidth* B_p.

Next, we turn to some considerations that are more global. First, we are interested in how bandwidths of various parts of the machine are related to each other. Then we are interested in how well the programs being run are matched to the machine on which they are being executed. Finally, we would like to tie all of the above together, which will be done through the notion of system capacity.

It is important to realize that the bandwidth definitions do not require equality between, say, the main memory and processor bandwidths, because we are allowing for memory-to-memory operations without processing, or several processor steps without memory activity. Thus the balance we seek is between the bandwidths of various system components and the requirements of the programs to be executed. If all parts of a system are utilized at their maximum bandwidths by some computation, this implies the highest possible throughput for that computation on the given system.

It may be useful to give an example that repeats some of the above discussion—suppose two numerical analysts have programs to run. Superficially, it may seem that high processor bandwidth is the key to choosing a machine on which to run the programs of both people. However, suppose that one program performs many iterations on each data element accessed from memory, whereas the other performs few operations each time a word is accessed. Thus the former needs less memory bandwidth than the latter for an overall balanced computation. Similar statements can be made about the I/O requirements of two programs. Thus, our goal is to incorporate the raw hardware bandwidths in a capacity model, and also to allow the representation of a program's bandwidth requirements of the various system components.

To keep the discussion simple, we will ignore disk and control unit considerations temporarily. Thus, for the moment we will consider a computer system that has only a processor and a main memory, and assume that sufficiently many instructions are held in the control unit to allow it to sequence the rest of the system indefinitely.

To relate bandwidths of various parts of the machine to each other, we define the *bandwidth ratios*

$$\alpha_{pm} = \frac{B_m}{B_p} > 0 \quad \text{and} \quad \alpha_{mp} = \frac{B_p}{B_m} > 0.$$

Thus, the α's are purely functions of the hardware of a computer, independent of any programs executed on the machine.

When a set of real programs is executed, not all of the available bandwidths of various parts of the system are used, in general. In particular, we define *utilized bandwidth* $B_p{}^u \le B_p$ to be the bandwidth of the processor that is actually used over the course of some computation. Of course, the details of how to measure this are open to some debate as was the definition of B_p itself. But we shall assume that $B_p{}^u$ is just an average of the number of bits processed over the running time of the program. Similarly, we define $B_m{}^u \le B_m$.

Now we can relate one part of a machine to another for the execution of a given program. Of the total processor and memory bandwidth used, we define $1/\beta_{pm}$ as the fraction used by the processor, that is,

$$\frac{1}{\beta_{pm}} = \frac{B_p{}^u}{B_p{}^u + B_m{}^u} \le 1.$$

Similarly, we define

$$\frac{1}{\beta_{mp}} = \frac{B_m{}^u}{B_m{}^u + B_p{}^u} \le 1,$$

and it is clear that $1/\beta_{mp} = 1 - 1/\beta_{pm}$.

For use below, we define

$$\gamma_m = \frac{B_m}{B_m{}^u} \ge 1 \quad \text{and} \quad \gamma_p = \frac{B_p}{B_p{}^u} \ge 1.$$

When $\gamma_m = 1$ a computation is said to be *memory bound,* and when $\gamma_p = 1$ it is said to be *processor bound.*

If a COBOL program is moving a record from one file to another in main memory, the processor need not be active at all. (In most real machines it probably would be, but in principle a sequence of FETCH, STORE pairs need only use the memory information register.) For such a computation

$$\frac{1}{\beta_{mp}} = \frac{B_m{}^u}{B_m{}^u + \varepsilon} \approx 1,$$

assuming the processor bandwidth used is ε. Furthermore, such a computation would probably run nearly memory bound, with $\gamma_m \approx 1$. On the other hand, a numerical computation might load several processor registers from memory and then perform some iterative computation for a long while, without further access to memory. In this case the memory bandwidth used is ε, so

$$\frac{1}{\beta_{pm}} = \frac{B_p{}^u}{B_p{}^u + \varepsilon} \approx 1,$$

and this computation would be nearly processor bound, with $\gamma_p \approx 1$.

Now we turn to the definition of computer capacity. Because we are concerned with driving machines as hard as possible, we will make two assumptions. First, we assume the processor and memory can operate simultaneously (in an overlapped mode). Further, we assume that its operation is either processor bound or memory bound, that is, either $\gamma_p = 1$ or $\gamma_m = 1$. This will allow us to operate at an upper bound on the bandwidth of some part of the system when performing any calculation.

We define the *processor capacity* of a computation as $C_p = B_p{}^u$, but since there are two cases of interest, this can be expanded as

$$C_p = \begin{cases} B_p{}^u & \text{if } \gamma_m = 1 \\ B_p & \text{if } \gamma_p = 1. \end{cases}$$

In other words, if a computation is processor bound, the processor capacity is just the bandwidth of the processor, whereas if it is memory bound, the processor capacity is the fraction of the processor bandwidth being used.

To relate capacity to the α's and β's, note that

$$B_p{}^u \gamma_m = \frac{B_m}{B_m{}^u / B_p{}^u} = \frac{\alpha_{pm} B_p}{\beta_{pm} - 1},$$

and that $\alpha_{pm} \le \beta_{pm} - 1$ is equivalent to

$$\frac{B_m}{B_m{}^u} \le \frac{B_p}{B_p{}^u},$$

which by the definition of γ implies that $\gamma_m \le \gamma_p$. Since we are assuming that either $\gamma_m = 1$ or $\gamma_p = 1$, $\gamma_m \le \gamma_p$ guarantees that $\gamma_m = 1$. Hence, we can rewrite the capacity expression entirely in terms of α's and β's as

$$C_p = \begin{cases} \dfrac{\alpha_{pm}}{\beta_{pm} - 1} B_p & \text{if } \alpha_{pm} \le \beta_{pm} - 1 \\ B_p & \text{otherwise.} \end{cases} \tag{15}$$

Notice that this relates all possible computations (in terms of β_{pm}) to all

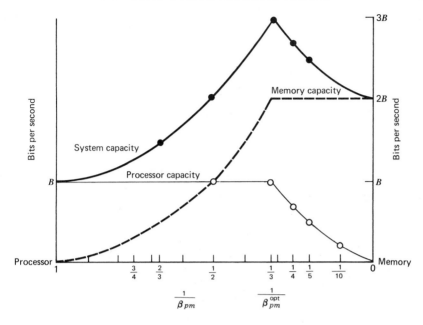

FIGURE 2.29 The *pm* capacity curve (for $\alpha_{pm} = 2$).

possible memory and processor speeds (in terms of α_{pm}). In Fig. 2.29, processor capacity is expressed graphically by plotting C_p versus $1/\beta_{pm}$ for $\alpha_{pm} = 2$. Note that a break is expected where $\alpha_{pm} = \beta_{pm} - 1$, that is, $1/\beta_{pm} = \frac{1}{3}$.

By an analogous argument, the following expression can be derived for memory capacity:

$$C_m = \begin{cases} \dfrac{\alpha_{mp}}{\beta_{mp} - 1} B_m & \text{if } \alpha_{mp} \leq \beta_{mp} - 1 \\[2ex] B_m & \text{otherwise.} \end{cases} \tag{16}$$

Notice that by interchanging the m's and p's in the definition of C_p this follows immediately. Since $\alpha_{mp}B_m = B_p$, $\beta_{mp} - 1 = \dfrac{1}{\beta_{pm} - 1}$ and $B_m = \alpha_{pm}B_p$, C_m can be expressed in terms of B_p as

$$C_m = \begin{cases} (\beta_{pm} - 1)B_p & \text{if } \beta_{pm} - 1 \leq \alpha_{pm} \\ \alpha_{pm}B_p & \text{otherwise.} \end{cases} \tag{17}$$

We define *system capacity* C_s of a computation to be the total system bandwidth utilized by that computation. Assuming the processor and the memory can operate simultaneously, by adding like terms in Eqs. 15 and 17, we obtain

$$
C_s = \begin{cases} \left(1 + \dfrac{1}{\beta_{pm} - 1}\right)\alpha_{pm} B_p & \text{if } \alpha_{pm} \leq \beta_{pm} - 1 \\ (1 + \beta_{pm} - 1) B_p & \text{otherwise,} \end{cases}
$$

so

$$
C_s = \begin{cases} \dfrac{\alpha_{pm}\beta_{pm}}{\beta_{pm} - 1} B_p & \text{if } \alpha_{pm} \leq \beta_{pm} - 1 \\ \beta_{pm} B_p & \text{otherwise.} \end{cases} \tag{18}
$$

A similar expression can be written in terms of B_m.

Note that maximum system capacity occurs when both the memory and processor are bound, that is, $\gamma_p = \gamma_m = 1$. Thus, from Eq. 18, if $\alpha_{pm} = \beta_{pm} - 1$, then

$$
C_s^{\max} = \frac{\alpha_{pm}\beta_{pm}}{\beta_{pm} - 1} B_p = \beta_{pm} B_p
$$
$$
= (1 + \alpha_{pm}) B_p = B_m + B_p. \tag{19}
$$

So the maximum system capacity is the sum of the maximum processor and memory bandwidths, and the condition for this optimality is that $\alpha_{pm} = \beta_{pm} - 1$. Thus, computations in which $\beta_{pm} = \alpha_{pm} + 1$ are able to exploit the system to its utmost and this is labeled $1/\beta_{pm}^{\text{opt}}$ in Fig. 2.29. Figure 2.30 is a plot of system and processor capacity for various values of α_{pm}. Note that the processor can perform at its maximum capacity over a wider range of computations (β_{pm} values) for larger α_{pm}. Note also that the memory capacity which is available for memory-to-memory (or I/O) operations becomes greater for larger α. It should be remarked that as β_{pm} approaches 1, reasonable system performance depends on high frequency of register-to-register operations.

2.5.4 Program examples

With these definitions behind us, how can we apply the ideas to a real computer system? First, we consider α_{pm}, the ratio of memory bandwidth to processor bandwidth. Assume we have a computer which can add two numbers in 1 μs and which has a memory cycle time of 1 μs. If we define processor bandwidth as the sum of the input and output bits divided by the add time, then this machine has $\alpha_{pm} = \frac{1}{3}$ since the processor handles three words in 1 μs, whereas the memory accesses just one word in 1 μs. We will study the system capacity of the processor and main memory only, ignoring the control unit and secondary memory capacity. The control unit does enter our consideration now, however, because we must supply it with instructions from the memory.

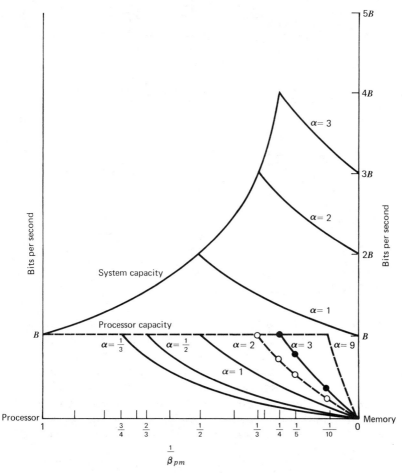

FIGURE 2.30   **Capacities for various α_{pm} values.**

To make matters concrete, assume the assignment statement $X \leftarrow A + B$ is compiled as

$$\text{FETCH} \quad A$$
$$\text{ADD} \quad B$$
$$\text{STORE} \quad X$$

Figure 2.31 shows a timing chart of the execution of this program. On step 1, the FETCH A instruction is fetched for the control unit. This instruction is executed on step 2, causing the fetch of argument A, and so on. The addition cannot occur until both operands have been fetched (step 5). Note that seven steps, that is, 7 μs are required to execute this program, assuming no overlap of processor and memory activity. If overlap were allowed, we could save one

Time Step	Memory Access	Processor Activity
1	FETCH A	
2	A	
3	ADD B	
4	B	
5		A + B
6	STORE X	
7	X	

FIGURE 2.31   Executing $X \leftarrow A + B$ with $\alpha_{pm} = \frac{1}{3}$.

step by fetching the STORE X instruction from memory while the addition was being performed.

On the other hand, if we make $\alpha_{pm} = \frac{2}{3}$, the overall computation can be speeded up. This means that if we can add in 1 μs, we must have a memory cycle of 500 ns. The results are shown in Fig. 2.32, assuming an overlapped processor and memory operation. In this case, no faster execution of the program is possible by increasing α beyond $\alpha_{pm} = \frac{2}{3}$. If we were executing a sequence of such dyadic assignment statements, however, note that just one processor cycle out of three could be used. Thus, we would be wasting two-thirds of the processor bandwidth and in fact be memory bound.

Let us triple the memory bandwidth by introducing a 166 ns memory so $\alpha_{pm} = \frac{6}{3}$. Now for maximum capacity (recall Eq. 19) we want $\beta_{pm}^{opt} = 1 + \alpha_{pm} = 3$, so $1/\beta_{pm}^{opt} = \frac{1}{3}$ is the fraction of the total bandwidth used by the processor. We

Time Step	Memory Access	Processor Activity
1	FETCH A, ADD B	
2	A, B	
3	STORE X	A + B
4	X	

FIGURE 2.32   Executing $X \leftarrow A + B$ with $\alpha_{pm} = \frac{2}{3}$.

Time Step	Memory Access				Processor Activity	Memory Access	
1	FETCH A_1	ADD B_1					
2	FETCH A_2	ADD B_2	A_1	B_1			
3	FETCH A_3	ADD B_3	A_2	B_2	A_1+B_1	STORE X_1	
4	FETCH A_4	ADD B_4	A_3	B_3	A_2+B_2	STORE X_2	X_1
5	FETCH A_5	ADD B_5	A_4	B_4	A_3+B_3	STORE X_3	X_2
6			A_5	B_5	A_4+B_4	STORE X_4	X_3
7					A_5+B_5	STORE X_5	X_4

FIGURE 2.33   A sequence of dyads with $\alpha_{pm}=2$.

can deduce this directly from the program sequence as follows. Each dyadic statement requires six memory cycles (three for instructions and three for data), so $B_m{}^u = 6$ words/1 μs. Each dyadic statement requires one addition cycle, so $B_p{}^u = 3$ words/1 μs. Thus we have

$$\frac{1}{\beta_{pm}} = \frac{B_p{}^u}{B_p{}^u + B_m{}^u} = \frac{3}{3+6} = \frac{1}{3}.$$

Graphically, this operating point can be seen in Fig. 2.30, where a program with $1/\beta_{pm} = \frac{1}{3}$ gives maximum capacity for a machine with $\alpha_{pm} = 2$.

Figure 2.33 illustrates the system operation for a sequence of five dyadic statements $X_i \leftarrow A_i + B_i$. We have drawn the processor activity column between memory accesses concerning fetching arguments and storing results. This makes it obvious that in the steady state such a system will be saturated executing dyads. Note that Fig. 2.33 is drawn to scale in that each time step represents 1 μs. There are six memory access columns because the memory cycle time is $\frac{1}{6}$ μs, and one processor column because the add time is 1 μs.

2.5.5 Processor-memory-disk systems

We turn now to a system with three components—processor and main memory as above, together with a secondary memory which we shall refer to as a disk. We shall assume at all times that one of these three components is operating at its highest data rate, that is, its bandwidth is saturated. We also assume a control unit which overlaps the operation of the processor, the main memory and the disk. We first give some definitions which are analogous to those of Section 2.5.3.

Let B_d be the disk or I/O bandwidth. Then

$$\alpha_{pd} = \frac{B_d}{B_p}, \qquad \alpha_{md} = \frac{B_d}{B_m}$$

and

$$\alpha_{dp} = \frac{B_p}{B_d}, \qquad \alpha_{dm} = \frac{B_m}{B_d}.$$

We also define

$$\beta_{pd} = \frac{B_p{}^u + B_d{}^u}{B_p{}^u},$$

$$\beta_{md} = \frac{B_m{}^u + B_d{}^u}{B_m{}^u},$$

with β_{dp} and β_{dm} being defined similarly. It follows that processor capacity may be written as:

$$C_p = \begin{cases} \dfrac{\alpha_{pm} B_p}{\beta_{pm} - 1} = \dfrac{B_m}{\beta_{pm} - 1} & \text{if } \alpha_{pm} \le \beta_{pm} - 1 \quad \text{and} \quad \alpha_{dm} \le \beta_{dm} - 1 \\[2ex] \dfrac{\alpha_{pd} B_p}{\beta_{pd} - 1} = \dfrac{B_d}{\beta_{pd} - 1} & \text{if } \alpha_{pd} \le \beta_{pd} - 1 \quad \text{and} \quad \alpha_{dm} \ge \beta_{dm} - 1 \\[2ex] B_p & \text{if } \alpha_{pm} \ge \beta_{pm} - 1 \quad \text{and} \quad \alpha_{pd} \ge \beta_{pd} - 1. \end{cases}$$

Similar expressions can be derived for memory and disk capacity (recall Eqs. 15 and 16). By summing these capacities for consistent conditions, we obtain saturated system capacity as follows:

$$C_s = \begin{cases} \left(1 + \dfrac{1}{\beta_{mp} - 1} + \dfrac{1}{\beta_{dp} - 1}\right) B_p & \text{if } \alpha_{pm} \ge \beta_{pm} - 1 \quad \text{and} \quad \alpha_{dp} \le \beta_{dp} - 1 \\[2ex] \left(1 + \dfrac{1}{\beta_{pm} - 1} + \dfrac{1}{\beta_{dm} - 1}\right) B_m & \text{if } \alpha_{pm} \le \beta_{pm} - 1 \quad \text{and} \quad \alpha_{md} \ge \beta_{md} - 1 \\[2ex] \left(1 + \dfrac{1}{\beta_{pd} - 1} + \dfrac{1}{\beta_{md} - 1}\right) B_d & \text{if } \alpha_{pd} \le \beta_{pd} - 1 \quad \text{and} \quad \alpha_{md} \le \beta_{md} - 1. \end{cases}$$

It should be noted that in each of these three cases, if the conditions are written as equalities, then the maximum capacity is obtained. In each case this reduces to

$$C_s^{\max} = B_p + B_m + B_d.$$

To make matters concrete, in Fig. 2.34 we sketch a surface for $B_p = B$, $B_m = 2B$, and $B_d = B/2$. The processor capacity is shown as a plateau of height B which runs off to 0 along the memory-disk axis. The top surface is the

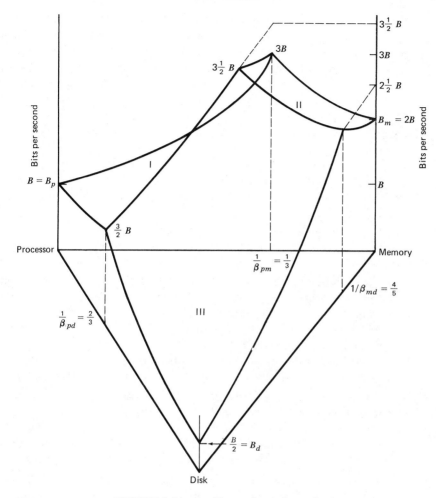

FIGURE 2.34   The *pmd* capacity surface.

system capacity. In the region labeled I, the system is processor bound, and in II and III it is memory and *disk (or I/O) bound*, respectively. Where these three regions meet, the $C_s^{max} = 3.5B$ point is located.

PROBLEMS

Easy problems in text order

2.1 Suppose an array computation on a uniprocessor takes $13N+4$ time units on an array of size N. Three different algorithms for a parallel processor are devised which take $10+\log N$, 65, and $2N$ time units. What is the order of magnitude speedup of each algorithm and what is the type of each computation (i.e., Type 0, 1, 2, or 3)?

2.2 In Section 2.1.2 it was pointed out that in current logic design, minimizing the number of gates is of less interest than minimizing the number of IC packages; hence, Boolean expression simplification is of less interest than it once was. Discuss at least two reasons why Boolean expression simplification may be of interest even in this era of IC logic design.

2.3 Given the Boolean expression $a_1 \cdot a_2 \cdots \cdots a_{n-1} \cdot a_n$ and the same Boolean expression with a_n complemented, $a_1 \cdot a_2 \cdots \cdots a_{n-1} \cdot \bar{a}_n$, in the following, consider gates with fan-in 2. Assume $\bar{a}_n$ is already available.

(a) How fast can each expression be evaluated?

(b) If one is willing to wait one extra time step, what is the cheapest way (i.e., using the fewest gates) to compute both expressions simultaneously?

(c) If the fastest possible time is to be achieved, what is the minimum number of gates needed to compute both expressions simultaneously?

2.4 A device is to be built to broadcast a d-digit number from a control unit to n processors in the fastest possible time. Assume that gates with fan-in and fan-out of f are available.

(a) What is an order of magnitude expression for the minimum number of gate delays required?

(b) What is an order of magnitude expression for the total number of gates needed to perform the above broadcast in minimum time?

2.5 In the algebra of real numbers, multiplication distributes over addition. This transformation was found to be helpful in reducing tree height. In a Boolean algebra OR ($+$) distributes over AND ($\cdot$) as well as AND distributing over OR: $a + (b \cdot c) = (a+b) \cdot (a+c)$. Give an example which shows that this form of distribution can also reduce tree height.

2.6 We have seen that, using certain transformations, any algebraic expression of e atoms and parenthesis depth d, $E\langle e \mid d \rangle$, can be rewritten so that

$$T[E\langle e \mid d \rangle] \leq 1 + 2d + \lceil \log e \rceil.$$

(a) Give an inequality which d must satisfy in order for this bound to be within a factor of 2 of the lower bound.

(b) Suppose we wish to use the algorithm from which this bound was derived for logic design. For any Boolean expression of e atoms, give as sharp an *upper bound* as you can on the number of gates with a fan-in of 2 that are required to implement a conbinational circuit for the expression that satisfies the time bound.

2.7 Give a constant upper bound on the redundancy of the algorithm of Theorem 2.

2.8 Suppose you are writing assembly language code for the CDC 7600 which has two multipliers and one adder, all of which can operate simultaneously. Show a parse tree for evaluating the following polynomial in five steps. Can it be done in four steps?

$$a_0 + x(a_1 + x(a_2 + x(a_3 + xa_4))).$$

2.9 (a) Show that when solving an $R\langle n, m \rangle$ system by the column sweep algorithm, $S_p = O(m)$.

(b) Show that the column sweep algorithm may still be fastest for some cases that are processor limited.

2.10 Consider the binary carry recurrence of Example 7. Write the equations for $i = 4$, and check the logic diagram to see that Example 7 is indeed correctly represented by Fig. 2.13.

2.11 Let $\bar{y}$ represent the Boolean NOT of y; $+$ and $\cdot$ represent OR and AND, respectively. Can

$$x_n = \overline{(a \cdot \bar{x}_{n-1} \cdot \bar{x}_{n-2})}$$

be rewritten as a bit level linear recurrence?

2.12 We have two n-bit words a and b, of the form:

$$a = a_1 a_2 \cdots a_n$$
$$b = b_1 b_2 \cdots b_n.$$

We want a circuit that will generate $c = c_1 c_2 \cdots c_n$, containing the leftmost string of bits for which a and b match; pad the right end of the string with zeros.
Thus, if

$$a = 1101100101$$
and
$$b = 1101011110,$$
then
$$c = 1101000000.$$

The implementation of this can be expressed as several logical equations—some combinational and one linear recurrence.

(a) Write these equations.

(b) Give order of magnitude estimates for the gates and gate delay times required for the fastest realization of these equations.

2.13 Finding the maximum or minimum of an array of numbers can obviously be done in $\lceil \log n \rceil$ time. How could an $O(\log n)$ time implementation of max or min be discovered from the high-level language program that computes max or min. (*Hint:* Try to linearize the program to an $R\langle n, 1\rangle$ recurrence with unusual operations.)

2.14   (a)   Why may more storage be needed to execute a statement block using the SIM execution ordering than to execute the same statement block with the SEQ order?

(b)   Give an example which shows that a SIM block may require more storage when executed with SEQ control.

2.15   Suppose we have a computer system with two processors and two control units, which share a common memory.

Let A, B, C, and D denote $n \times n$ matrices and A^t denote the transpose of A.

(a)   Express each of the following in the fastest executable form using SEQ, TOG, or FS, but without rewriting the statements in any way.

(i)   SEQ[A←B+A; C←D * C]   TOG

(ii)   SEQ[A←3 * A^t; A←2 * A]   SEQ

(iii)   SEQ[A←B; B←C+1]   FS

(b)   Using statement substitution show the fastest form of each of the above blocks.

2.16   Assume a parallel processor computer with a common control unit, $2N^2$ memory units, and N^2 processors where one memory cycle and one CPU operation each take one time unit. Assume each processor has 8 registers. How many time steps are needed to compute the following program?

$$\text{DO} \quad S_3 \quad I \leftarrow 1, N$$
$$\text{DO} \quad S_3 \quad J \leftarrow 1, N$$
$$S_1 \qquad A(I, J) \leftarrow B(I, J) + C(I, J) * D(I, J)$$
$$S_2 \qquad G(I, J) \leftarrow E(I, J) + 5$$
$$S_3 \qquad B(I, J) \leftarrow F(I, J)$$

(a)   Sketch a time chart or computation graph.

(b)   What three special features must the system have to achieve this time and execute the program correctly?

2.17   The processor capacity function C_p has a discontinuity at the point $\alpha_{pm} = \beta_{pm} - 1$. For $1/\beta_{pm}$ less than this point, what type of curve is C_p as a function of β_{pm}: linear $(ax + b)$, parabolic $(ax^2 + bx + c)$, exponential (a^x), or hyperbolic $[(a/x) + b]$? For $1/\beta_{pm}$ greater than this point?

2.18   In a certain scientific instruction mix with very little I/O (i.e., neglect C_d), it is found that $1/\beta_{pm}$ averages as high as 3/4. Assuming full overlap, calculate the smallest α_{pm} that will allow maximum processor capacity to be used.

2.19   A business data-processing system has been selected such that $B_p = 5B_m = 10B_d$. During production runs, performance monitoring showed that there was negligible processor capacity used, while both the memory and disk were bound. What fraction of the total job time was consumed by disk I/O? (That is, compute $1/\beta_{dm}$ under the assumptions above.)

Medium and hard problems in text order

2.20   (a)   Show that, for any SIME computer, if a computation can be carried out in time T_p with N_p operations using p processors, then it can be carried out in

$$\frac{N_p}{q} \le T_q \le T_p + \frac{N_p - T_p}{q} \qquad \text{using } q < p \text{ processors.}$$

(*Hint:* Consider the case when $q = 1$ and then generalize. $N_p = N_q$ of course.)

(b)   Prove or disprove that the efficiency of the computation on q processors satisfies the relation

$$E_q \ge \frac{T_1}{T_p(q + p - 1)}.$$

2.21   Consider the evaluation of "perfect trees" using n parallel processors. A "perfect tree" of height t has exactly $2^t - 1$ nodes. If we have $n = 2^{t-1}/2^f$ processors, $0 \le f \le t - 1$, what is the minimum time in which a perfect tree can be evaluated? (*Hint:* Think of f as the number of *folds* or halvings of the number of processors, and begin with the maximum $n = 2^{t-1}$ processors.)

2.22   Why is it difficult to bound the number of components in Lemma 1? Quote some specific results in your answer.

2.23   Define a *bus* as an interconnection network between n units, such that at any time any one unit may communicate with any other single unit. Assume that multiplexers and demultiplexers of $f = 2^h$ inputs and outputs, respectively, for some integer h are available, and that each of these has a delay of one time unit. How many components and component delays are required to construct a bus to interconnect n units? Sketch your design if $n = 16$ and $f = 4$.

2.24   Show that there is a family of arithmetic expressions with e atoms whose evaluation requires a number of time steps and a number of processors which for large e asymptotically approach the time and processor bounds of Theorem 1.

2.25 Tree-height reduction algorithms (as in Section 2.2.4.3) using associativity and commutativity operate by first isolating subtrees that are combined with like operators. The subtrees in such a collection are combined to form a minimum height combination. Then the algorithm moves on to another collection of subtrees.

(a) Give an algorithm for combining a set of subtrees of different heights such that the resulting tree is of minimum height. Assume that the same commutative operation holds between all the subtrees. Note that the subtrees' contents cannot be modified.

(b) Show how your algorithm would combine the following set of subtrees with the heights shown. What is their combined minimum height?

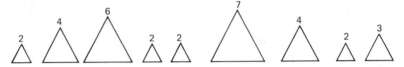

(*Hint:* This algorithm is similar to the Huffman coding scheme [Huff52] for constructing minimum length codes.)

2.26 Suppose a new arithmetic expression tree-height reduction algorithm is proposed which uses associativity, commutativity, and "full" distribution (i.e., the application of the distributive property wherever possible). Consider the worst possible expressions to which "full" distribution might be applied. What should we expect the time bound to be in order to evaluate the resulting expression?

2.27 Consider tree-height reduction using associativity, commutativity, and distributivity for any expression $E\langle n \rangle$ with at most n atoms and only the addition and multiplication operations. Prove each of the following:

Lemma A

$E\langle n \rangle$ can be rewritten as $E'\langle 2n \rangle = A\langle n \rangle * x + B\langle n \rangle$ where x is any atom of $E\langle n \rangle$, E' has at most $2n$ atoms, and A and B each have at most n atoms.

Lemma B

For any $l < m \le n$, $E\langle n \rangle$ contains an expression $L \theta R$ (where θ is + or *), where the expressions L and R each have fewer than m atoms, but the sum of the atoms in L and R is greater than or equal to m.

Theorem

For $k \ge 3$, any $E\langle 2^k \rangle$ can be evaluated in $3k - 4$ steps.

2.28 It can be shown that a continued fraction (see Ex. 3) of n atoms can be evaluated in time $T[E\langle n \rangle] = 2\lceil \log_2 n \rceil$, [KuMa75]. Draw the minimum height evaluation tree for a continued fraction of 16 atoms.

2.29 A common mathematical form is the rational function

$$\frac{b_0 x^m + b_1 x^{m-1} + \cdots + b_m}{(x-a_1)^{k_1}(x-a_2)^{k_2}\cdots(x-a_t)^{k_t}}, \qquad m < k_1 + k_2 + \cdots + k_t,$$

where $a_1, a_2, \ldots, a_t$ are all distinct. An alternate form is

$$\sum_{i=1}^{t} \left(\frac{c_{i1}}{x-a_i} + \frac{c_{i2}}{(x-a_i)^2} + \cdots + \frac{c_{ik_i}}{(x-a_i)^{k_i}} \right),$$

where the c_{ij} are constants that can be precalculated. Which form can be evaluated faster using only associativity and commutativity? Which form is faster using associativity, commutativity, and distribution? How many processors are needed for the fastest evaluation of each form? Assume that

$$\max_i k_i = k > m > t.$$

2.30 Use the following classes of tree-height reduction transformations to evaluate a few of the following expressions in minimum time. For each class find P, the number of processors needed, as well as T_P, S_P, E_P, R_P, and U_P. Assume FORTRAN rules of expression evaluation for T_1.
   (1) associativity only
   (2) associativity and commutativity—(What are the Theorem 1 bounds?)
   (3) associativity, commutativity, and distribution—(What are the Theorem 2 bounds?)
   (a) $a + (b + c * d * e + f) * g + h$
   (b) $a + (b + c * d * e/f + g) * h$
   (c) $a + ((b * (c + d * e) + f) + g) * h + i$
   (d) $a + ((b * b/c) * d - (-b + b * b/c - e) * f)$
   (e) $abc(d + efg(h + i(jklmn + o)(pqr + s(t + u(vwxyz + a)bcd))e))$

2.31 Show how DeMorgan's laws
$$\overline{(a+b)} = \bar{a} \cdot \bar{b}$$
$$\overline{(a \cdot b)} = \bar{a} + \bar{b}$$
can be used to adapt Lemma 3 to hold for *any* Boolean expression.

2.32 In Fig. 2.5 we show a demultiplexer tree. Assuming that this is to be put into a single integrated circuit package, how close an estimate does Theorem 3 provide of the correct number of gates and gate delays? Remember that each AND, OR, and NOT counts as a gate and a delay.

2.33 Compute the speedup, efficiency, and redundancy of solving an $R\langle n, m \rangle$ recurrence system by the method of Theorem 4, assuming $m < n/2$. What do these become in the popular case of $m = 1$? Tabulate the $R\langle n, 1 \rangle$ values of speedup, efficiency, and redundancy for $n = 16$, 128, and 1024. You may use the asymptotic bounds given in Theorem 4.

2.34   Consider the linear system

$$x = c + Ax,$$

where

$$A = \begin{bmatrix} 0 & 0 & 0 & 0 & 0 & 0 \\ a_{21} & 0 & 0 & 0 & 0 & 0 \\ 0 & a_{32} & 0 & 0 & 0 & 0 \\ a_{41} & 0 & a_{43} & 0 & 0 & 0 \\ 0 & a_{52} & 0 & a_{54} & 0 & 0 \\ 0 & 0 & a_{63} & 0 & a_{65} & 0 \end{bmatrix}, \quad c = \begin{bmatrix} c_1 \\ c_2 \\ c_3 \\ c_4 \\ c_5 \\ c_6 \end{bmatrix}.$$

(a)   Describe the system as a linear recurrence; see Definition 2. Give the values of m and n and write the formula for the x's.

(b)   Show how the system would be evaluated using the column sweep algorithm. Give T_1, p, S_p, E_p, R_p, and U_p. Make use of the fact that zeros occur below the $a_{i,i-1}$ diagonal.

(c)   Show how the system would be evaluated as a matrix expression using the product form recurrence algorithm. Give P, S_P, E_P, R_P, and U_P.

(d)   How do your figures compare with the bounds given in Theorem 4?

2.35   In Section 2.3.1 we discussed the time needed to compute several simple recurrences. By repeatedly substituting the left-hand side into the right-hand side, we saw that expressions could be obtained to which tree-height reduction could be applied. Show that this technique does not hold for all linear recurrences in the sense that the process does not yield the best known time bounds. (*Hint:* Consider, for example, the tree height of the linear recurrence

$$x_i = a_i x_{i-1} + b_i x_{i-2} + c_i, \qquad 2 \le i \le n,$$

with $x_0 = a_0$ and $x_1 = a_1$.)

2.36   Suppose we wish to compute all the powers of x up to and including x^n.

(a)   Formulate the problem as an $R\langle n, 1 \rangle$ system. What are the Theorem 4 bounds for T_P, P, and O_P?

(b)   Suppose we have only p processors and $n > p$. Use Theorem 5 to find a more realistic bound for T_p. How many processors are needed to make the linear term of Theorem 5 less than the logarithmic term? Assume

$$O\left(m^2 \log \frac{p}{m}\right) = 1 \cdot m^2 \log \frac{p}{m}.$$

(c) Give the bounds obtainable using Theorem 6 for the unlimited processor case, because this is a constant coefficient recurrence. What bounds can be obtained with Corollary 2?

(d) What are the best bounds on time and processors that you can find independently if all powers are needed? What if only x^n is needed? (See [Mura71].)

2.37 Note that the product form recurrence algorithm from which the bounds of Lemma 4 were derived also gives us a design procedure that constructs a logic circuit to implement a logic design recurrence. Construct a logic circuit to implement the gate level recurrence

$$x_i = a_{i-1}x_{i-1} + a_{i-2}x_{i-2}, \qquad 2 \le i \le 6.$$

Make the fan-out f in Lemma 4 just large enough to avoid having to duplicate any subcircuit. Assume a fan-in of 2.

2.38 Digital signal processing is frequently used to enhance the signal-to-noise ratio in seismic exploration for oil, processing pictures from outer space, and so on. A recursive digital filter often takes the form

$$x_j = \sum_{i=0}^{m} a_i y_{j-i} + \sum_{i=1}^{k} b_i x_{j-i} \quad \text{for} \quad 1 \le j \le m,$$

where the y_{j-i} are input data, the a_i and b_i are precomputed filter weights, and x_j are filter outputs.
(a) What is the order of this linear recurrence?
(b) Give order of magnitude bounds for the number of microprocessors and microprocessor delays required to compute the function in the fastest way you know, assuming that each microprocessor performs only one operation in the algorithm.

2.39 Consider the problem of designing a comparator for two n-bit numbers x and y. Given these two numbers in registers, we wish to set an indicator bit $t = 1$ if $x \ge y$, and set $t = 0$ otherwise. How much time and how many gates would be required to carry out this operation as fast as possible? Is it easier to test $x = y$? (*Hint:* Can this operation be formulated as a linear recurrence?)

2.40 Consider the bit serial addition of two binary numbers. Show a black box with appropriately labeled inputs and outputs following Definition 7. Draw a truth table to verify that Eq. 8 and Eq. 9 are correct, and briefly explain why in words. Verify Eqs. 13 and 14.

2.41 Consider the design of an integrated circuit adder. Tabulate the number of gates and gate delays for 8, 16, 32, and 64-bit number addition. Assume that gate fan-in is 2 and fan-out is 8. Assume that wired-in gate delays average 5 ns, and that we wish to operate with a 100 ns clock period. Furthermore, we are constrained by pin limitations of 55 pins per package. What does this imply about the overall adder circuit?

2.42 Binary addition can be accomplished in a bit serial way using one full adder.

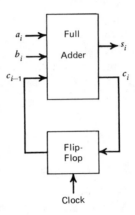

(a) Apply Definition 4 to this circuit and evaluate the time needed to add two n-bit numbers using Theorem 7.

(b) Compare the results of Theorem 8 with what one would obtain using the more general Theorem 7.

2.43 (a) For each of the following three loops, answer these questions. Ignore index computation, memory access, and CU time, and assume that addition and multiplication each require one step.

$$DO \quad S_1 \quad I \leftarrow 1, N$$
$$S_1 \quad U(I) \leftarrow A(I) * V(I-1) + B(I)$$
$$DO \quad S_2 \quad I \leftarrow 1, N$$
$$S_2 \quad U(I) \leftarrow A(I) * U(I-1) + B(I)$$
$$DO \quad S_3 \quad I \leftarrow 1, N$$
$$U(I) \leftarrow A(I) * V(I-1) + B(I)$$
$$S_3 \quad V(I) \leftarrow C(I) * U(I-1) + D(I)$$

(i) What is the minimum time required to execute the loop?

(ii) What is the smallest number of processors P that can be used to achieve this time?

(iii) What efficiency E_P can be achieved by this computation?

(b) In the third DO loop, show the lower triangular linear system that is equivalent to the indicated computation. Show enough entries in the matrix so that the structure is clear.

2.44 The CORDIC algorithm rotates a two-dimensional vector (x, y) counterclockwise by an angle α to an accuracy of 1 bit in an n-bit word, in n iterations. It can be used in a calculator (e.g., HP-35) to generate the trigonometric functions or in calculating Fourier transforms—see [Desp74]. Assume that by table-lookup, 2^{-i} and $\tan^{-1}(2^{-i})$ take zero processor time.

The algorithm is:

Initialize: $i \leftarrow 1$

$$z_i \leftarrow -\alpha$$

$$\text{DO} \quad i \leftarrow 1, n \quad \begin{cases} b_i \leftarrow \text{sgn}(z_i) \\ x_{i+1} \leftarrow x_i + b_i y_i 2^{-i} \\ y_{i+1} \leftarrow y_i - b_i x_i 2^{-i} \\ z_{i+1} \leftarrow z_i - b_i \tan^{-1}(2^{-i}) \end{cases}$$

(a) Construct a data dependence graph for the CORDIC algorithm.
(b) Distribute the loop in the best possible manner.
(c) Set up linear recurrences where possible, that is, state the dimensions of all linear recurrences found and give the form of the A matrix and c vector.
(d) For a three processor MIME system, calculate the time, speedup, and efficiency for the entire algorithm.
(e) Comment on how this algorithm could be implemented in hardware.

2.45 Consider how the following block of assignment statements (BAS) could be compiled for a multiprocessor.

$$X \leftarrow Y + Z$$
$$Y \leftarrow 3 * A$$
$$W \leftarrow X * B/5$$
$$Z \leftarrow X/Y$$

(a) Using the SEQ, FS, and TOG execution orderings and without using redundant operations or variable renaming, what form of compiler output would allow the fastest execution with the least overhead? How much time would it require on how many arithmetic processors? (Again, neglect memory and control unit time and assume all arithmetic operations require one time step each.)
(b) If other transformations are allowed, what execution orderings (SIM, COM, SF, plus the above) would allow the fastest execution time? How much time and how many processors would this require?

2.46 The synchronization primitives P and V can be used to implement the execution ordering specified by SIM, FS, SF, COM, and TOG. P and V operate on integer variables called semaphores. The idea is that the semaphore variable, call it S, will keep a count of the simultaneously executing subtasks. We can specify the actions of P and V in high-level language procedures (braces enclose indivisible actions).

$$\text{BEGIN PROC P(S)}$$

$$S_1 \quad \{\text{IF } S \leq 0 \quad \text{THEN GOTO } S_1$$

$$S \leftarrow S - 1\}$$

$$\text{END PROC P}$$

$$\text{BEGIN PROC V(S)}$$

$$\{S \leftarrow S + 1\}$$

$$\text{END PROC V}$$

Now to implement a SIM block, SIM $[S_1; S_2; \ldots; S_5]$, where each S_i has the form $x_i \leftarrow rhs_i$ where rhs_i is some right-hand side expression, we could use the program:

$$S \leftarrow -5$$

$$\text{FORK } (S_1, S_2, \ldots, S_5)$$

$$\text{JOIN}$$

$$\text{GO TO } S_6$$

$$S_1 \quad t_1 \leftarrow rhs_1$$

$$\text{CALL V(S)}$$

$$\text{CALL P(S)}$$

$$\text{CALL V(S)}$$

$$x_1 \leftarrow t_1$$

$$\text{JOIN}$$

$$S_2 \quad t_2 \leftarrow rhs_2$$

$$\text{CALL V(S)}$$

$$\text{CALL P(S)}$$

$$\text{CALL V(S)}$$

$$x_2 \leftarrow t_2$$

$$\text{JOIN}$$

$$\vdots$$

$$S_5 \quad t_5 \leftarrow rhs_5$$

CALL V(S)

CALL P(S)

CALL V(S)

$x_5 \leftarrow t_5$

JOIN

S_6 · (Comment: $SIM[S_1; S_2; \ldots; S_5]$ is finished.)

·

·

The idea is that the semaphore initially tells us that 5 subtasks must be completed before any x_j can be assigned. As each rhs_j is finished, it signals the other subtasks with the first V(S). The jth subtask must then wait for the semaphore to reach zero, but since P(S) is going to decrement S forcing others into a wait loop, another V(S) must be done.

(a) Change the P procedure so that the two V(S)'s can be avoided when implementing a SIM block and show how to implement SIM with your primitives.

(b) Implement the other execution orderings, FS, SF, COM, and TOG using P and V.

2.47 Consider the design of a multiprocessor with FORK and JOIN operations that take k time units each. Assume Prog. $4a$ runs on a uniprocessor and Prog. 6 runs on a dual processor. In both cases, for simplicity, make the following assumptions: Each arithmetic operation takes one time unit (but subscript evaluation is overlapped), each store takes one time unit (but fetches are overlapped), each READ or WRITE takes one time unit, and loop setup and testing are overlapped. How large must the number of iterations N be for speedup $S_2 > 1$? What does this imply about fast FORK and JOIN operations? (In some real cases at least 10 or 20 instructions are needed—many more if complex operating system software is involved.)

2.48 We discussed simple FORK and JOIN instructions; in general, the FORK may be used to spawn n processes and the JOIN to bring the n together again. These instructions may be implemented purely by software or by a hardware/software combination. Ignoring how they are implemented, consider *what* they must do. Be sure to consider memory allocation, processor allocation, the number of tasks n, and how the FORK and JOIN relate to one another. State any assumptions you make about special hardware available.

2.49 Although there are many variations of the explicit parallel programming constructs FORK and JOIN, the following combinations are fairly widely accepted [Conw63]; [Shaw 74] has high-level language versions.

1. FORK S_i Assign a processor to start executing the instructions at location S_i. The processor encountering the FORK should continue executing the statements after the current one.

2. FORK S_i, J   Same as 1, but also increment the counter at location J.

3. FORK S_i, J, N   Same as 1, but also set the counter at J to the value of N.

4. JOIN J   Decrement the counter J and start executing the instructions at location $J+1$ if J is now zero, otherwise release the processor executing the JOIN.

5. JOIN J, S_i Decrement J and execute location $J+1$ if J is now zero, otherwise keep the same value in J and branch to location S_i.

(a) Use the type 3 FORK and the type 4 JOIN to implement Prog. 6 in the text.

(b) Show how to implement a many way fork

$$\text{FORK } (S_1, S_2, \ldots, S_k),$$

which starts k processors executing the programs at locations S_1 through S_k using a combination of the FORK instructions given above.

(c) Give an appropriate example for the use of each of the FORK and JOIN types, that is, justify the need for so many variations.

(d) Show that FORK and JOIN are more primitive than the SEQ and SIM execution orderings by implementing the following data dependence graph with FORK and JOIN. Show that it can not be implemented with just SEQ and SIM.

2.50 Consider a processor-memory system in which $\alpha_{pm} = 3$; this is perhaps reasonable for a COBOL machine.

(a) Find β_{pm} and C_p for each of the activity diagrams shown. In the diagrams, an X represents a word input to, or output from that unit, that is, 1 word of bandwidth is used. A O means that the word of bandwidth is unused. For example, because

$$\beta_{pm} = \frac{B_m{}^u + B_p{}^u}{B_p{}^u},$$

in the first diagram, we get $\beta_{pm} = 2B$.

Similarly, for the first diagram $C_p = 1B$; the processor is bound.

(1)

processor	memory		
X	X	O	O
X	X	O	O
X	X	O	O
.	.		
.	.		
.	.		

(2)

processor	memory		
X	X	X	X
X	X	X	X
X	X	X	X
.	.		
.	.		
.	.		

(3)

processor	memory		
O	X	X	X
X	X	X	X
X	X	X	X
O	X	X	X
X	X	X	X
X	X	X	X
.	.		
.	.		
.	.		

(4)

processor	memory		
O	X	X	X
X	X	X	X
O	X	X	X
O	X	X	X
X	X	X	X
O	X	X	X
O	X	X	X
X	X	X	X
O	X	X	X
.	.		
.	.		
.	.		

(5)

processor	memory		
O	X	X	X
X	X	X	X
O	X	X	X
X	X	X	X
O	X	X	X
X	X	X	X
.	.		
.	.		
.	.		

(6)

processor	memory		
X	O	O	O
X	X	O	O
X	O	O	O
X	X	O	O
X	O	O	O
X	X	O	O
.	.		
.	.		
.	.		

(b) Draw capacity curves (such as Fig. 2.29) showing processor capacity, memory capacity, and system capacity using the data from part (a).

(c) Find the point at which $C_p = C_m$. What does this point depend on in terms of α_{pm} and β_{pm}? For an arbitrary system, find the condition under which this crossover point is also the point of maximum system capacity C_s^{max}.

(d) If the data in part (a) is considered as a typical job mix for the system, is this job mix processor overbalanced or memory overbalanced? A job mix is processor overbalanced if its mean $1/\beta_{pm}$ is less than the $1/\beta_{pm}$ corresponding to peak system capacity and vice versa for a job mix that is memory overbalanced. Which type of job mix would be better if one were interested only in system stability? Note that a system can be made more stable if the slope of its capacity curve can be decreased, because then a small change in β_{pm} will yield a smaller change in C_s.

2.51 Section 2.5 attempts to quantify the idea of balance in a computer system in terms of its capacity. In most cases the capacity that we can achieve is already determined. If the machine has already been installed, we may be unable to reconfigure it. If we can reconfigure the system, we may be unable to purchase components with exactly the bandwidth needed. If we are purchasing equipment for future needs, we cannot determine precisely what the values of the variables will be. Suppose, however, that we are in a position to actually design a machine to meet fixed specifications. How would we go about obtaining the most bandwidth per dollar? Would we build a processor with the same bandwidth as the memory? Probably not. Consider this approach:

1. Evaluate the real time (or turnaround) constraints of the problem and choose processor bandwidth B_p to meet these constraints.
2. Benchmark the programs that will be run on the machine. Consider not only the data bandwidth required but also the instruction fetch bandwidth required. Use this data to compute the used bandwidth B_m^u and β_{pm}.
3. Finally, choose α_{pm} so that we are at peak system capacity, $C_s = C_s^{max}$.

(a) At what point in this procedure is B_m fixed and exactly how is it derived?

(b) Starting with a blank capacity graph, Fig. 2.29, show the order in which parameters are fixed by the procedure. Briefly describe what influence each parameter has on the shape of the curve as it is constructed.

(c) Why don't we make $B_p = B_m$?

(d) Suppose we have to execute an average of 0.25 megaflops to meet the processing requirements of the 8 to 5 shift at a chemical company. For convenience, suppose that the floating-point operations are all dyads, as in Section 2.5.4. Follow the procedure above to determine B_m and sketch the capacity curve. Check your results with those shown in Section 2.5.4. Do we need an overlapped memory and processor?

2.52 Derive C_s for the processor-memory-disk system from C_p, C_m, and C_d.

2.53 Consider a *pm* system that does not allow memory-processor overlap.
(a) Compute β_{pm} and C_p for the following activity diagrams and draw the capacity curves using this data.

(1) processor   memory
```
    O      X X X
    X      O O O
    X      O O O
    X      O O O
   ─────────────
    O      X X X
    X      O O O
    X      O O O
    X      O O O
    .        .
    .        .
    .        .
```

(2) processor   memory
```
    O      X X X
    X      O O O
   ─────────────
    O      X X X
    X      O O O
   ─────────────
    O      X X X
    X      O O O
   ─────────────
    .        .
    .        .
    .        .
```

(3) processor   memory
```
    O      X X X
    O      X X X
    O      X X X
    O      X X X
    O      X X X
    X      O O O
    X      O O O
    X      O O O
   ─────────────
    O      X X X
    .        .
    .        .
    .        .
```

(4) processor   memory
```
    O      X X X
    O      X X X
    X      O O O
    O      X X X
   ─────────────
    O      X X X
    O      X X X
    X      O O O
    O      X X X
   ─────────────
    O      X X X
    O      X X X
    X      O O O
    O      X X X
   ─────────────
    .        .
    .        .
    .        .
```

(b)   Show that

$$C_p \text{ nonoverlapped} = \frac{\alpha_{pm} B_p}{\alpha_{pm} + \beta_{pm} - 1} \le C_p \text{ overlapped,}$$

$$C_m \text{ nonoverlapped} = \frac{\alpha_{pm}(\beta_{pm} - 1) B_p}{\alpha_{pm} + \beta_{pm} - 1} \le C_m \text{ overlapped,}$$

and

$$C_s \text{ nonoverlapped} = \frac{\alpha_{pm} \beta_{pm} B_p}{\alpha_{pm} + \beta_{pm} - 1} \le C_s \text{ overlapped,}$$

for general systems. (The $\le$'s are easy; the $=$'s are harder.)

CH

3

I'm supposed to know something about science;
  but I know nothing except the mathematics it
    involves.
I can make calculations for engineers, electricians,
    insurance companies, and so on,
  but I know next to nothing about engineering or
    electricity or insurance.
I don't even know arithmetic well.

Mrs. Warren's Profession

George Bernard Shaw

The most constant difficulty in contriving the
engine has arisen from the desire to reduce the time
in which the calculations were executed to the
shortest which is possible.

It is not to be presumed that such an attempt has
succeeded. How near the approach has been made
must remain for aftertimes to determine.

On the Mathematical Powers of the Calculating Engine

Charles Babbage

PROCESSORS

3.1 INTRODUCTION

3.1.1 Processor functions and overview

Various processors have been designed and built into computers over the years, but the variations from one to another lie more in the implementation than in the functions provided. Arithmetic operations are almost always built into a processor's hardware. Also, logical operations (e.g., AND, OR, NOT) on individual bits are usually provided as are tests of certain bits (e.g., sign, overflow, etc.). The ability to shift the bits in a word in various ways is almost always included and these are usually considered to be logical operations. Finally, the processor must access sources of operands and must return results either to a set of registers within the processor itself or to the main memory. In this introduction we will briefly expand on these three processor functions:

- Arithmetic operations
- Logical operations
- Data accessing

In Fig. 3.1a the basic functional organization of a processor is shown. Some variations on the operation of processors were discussed in Section 1.2.1; throughout this chapter we will discuss the design and various operating details of processors.

In almost all computers built since the mid-1960s, a small set of processor registers has been provided for fast access to a few data words. Words fetched from memory as well as temporary results can be held in these registers and be reused without paying a whole memory cycle. In most processors (as elsewhere

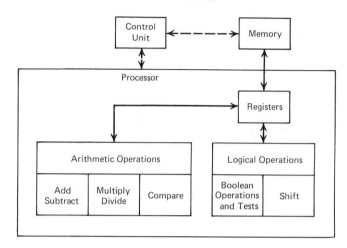

FIGURE 3.1   **Basic processor functions.**

in computer systems) some registers may be addressed by programmers, whereas others are "hidden" and are available only to hardware designers, for example, to hold partially completed arithmetic results. The following counts refer to programmer accessible registers. For example, the IBM 370 has sixteen 32-bit general registers and four 64-bit floating-point registers, whereas the Intel 8080 microprocessor has seven 8-bit registers. In contrast, most computers in the 1950s had just one or two programmer accessible registers. Although there are obvious advantages to having more registers available (see Section 3.5.5), there is an added burden that the programmer (or compiler writer) must shoulder, namely, the management of these registers.

As we shall see in Chapter 4, the availability of such registers also necessitates several different types of addressing schemes for instructions: some access registers only (register-to-register instructions), others access only memory, and others access both memory and registers. A nice convenience in a multiprogrammed machine which frequently switches its attention between users is several sets of register banks. For example, three users and the operating system might each be assigned a complete set of registers which the processor accesses, depending on which of four different programs is active. This avoids the saving and restoring of the registers for each of these programs. A number of machines have used schemes of this kind in the past, and the low cost of registers in microprocessors enables the Zilog Z-80 to have two register sets; other such uses are likely in the future.

There is greater variety in the types of operations needed in the processor than in data accessing for the processor. Some programs are clearly "number crunchers," whereas others are "bit twiddlers"; generally, these are arithmetic-dominated and logical operation-dominated, respectively. Of course, there are many variations on these; for example, fixed-versus floating-point arithmetic and bit versus character level logical operations.

On the one hand, typical "scientific" jobs use floating-point arithmetic because the numerical values involved may take on a wide range of values. On the other hand, "business" arithmetic involves mostly dollars and cents; hence, the numbers may be easily restricted to a relatively narrow range (except for General Motors and the U.S. government!) and the standard anomalies between binary and decimal arithmetic may be highly undesirable. Many computers are used mainly to handle nonnumerical information and these require good character manipulating instructions. Machines used in typesetting or in data communications and message switching networks must be able to compare, insert, and delete characters easily.

One way to learn about a computer's characteristics is to study its instruction set in detail. In some respects this is a good idea; for example, the kinds of questions raised above may be considered, as may others that concern program control (to be discussed in Chapter 4). In other respects, the study of machine instructions per se is a bad idea; many novices do not know what they are looking for and many experts may find it difficult to digest a set of 150 or 200 machine instruction types. How well the individual instructions "work" when used together is obviously more important than what the individual instructions are. In most Burroughs machines, for example, because even most system programming is done in high-level languages, assembly language instructions are seldom seen or discussed. As we point out below, the key item to study is the usefulness and performance of a given processor in the role intended by a given customer.

In any case, in this chapter we will discuss machine instructions, by type at least, and occasionally give the details of how some of the more complicated instructions work. This chapter is concerned with processors and the most complex processor functions are arithmetic operations, together with shifts, compares, and the like. First, we will discuss some of the simpler operations and then work our way up to more complex ones.

As an example of a typical, rather extensive instruction set, consider the IBM 370, which may be regarded as having four instruction sets, composed from the following four types of instructions:

1. Floating-point instructions
2. Fixed-point binary arithmetic, logic, branching, and I/O instructions
3. Decimal instructions
4. Protection instructions.

Types 1 and 2 comprise the *scientific instruction set*, whereas types 2 and 3 comprise the *commercial instruction set*. Type 2 instructions are called the *standard instruction set*, whereas all four types combined are called the *universal instruction set*. These types of instructions are typical of many computers and they do indeed serve different programming constituencies.

The protection instructions lie in the realm of system programming and will be considered in Chapter 4. Types 1, 2, and 3 plainly indicate that the IBM 370 is intended to serve three user communities, because three different kinds of arithmetic are implemented in the hardware. Types 1 and 2 operate on binary numbers with floating binary point and fixed binary point, respectively, whereas the decimal instructions operate on binary coded decimal numbers (4 bits per decimal digit). Each of these types includes data accessing instructions for its data types and various housekeeping instructions, such as number conversion from one format to another.

Floating-point arithmetic operations are the most complex in terms of their hardware implementation. In fact, floating-point mantissa operations are more or less equivalent to fixed-point binary arithmetic. Later in this chapter, we will discuss a number of aspects of floating-point arithmetic.

The decimal operations are also similar to fixed-point, except that since 4 bits are used to represent each decimal digit, there are certain illegal bit combinations. Thus, the propagation of carries has some unusual properties, as we shall see in Section 3.3.2.

Type 2 instructions include "everything else" in that they are the standard basic operations used in almost all computers, from the earliest machines through modern microprocessors. Fixed-point arithmetic, will be discussed later, and branching instructions will be considered in Chapter 4. I/O operations will be examined both in Chapter 4 and in Chapter 7. As we mentioned previously, *logical operations* refers to a collection of bit and character level operations. In this chapter we will discuss several of them, including Boolean operations among words, various kinds of shifts, comparisons, and encoding the positions of ones in a binary word.

Although some variations on these are found in almost all computers, and in an abstract sense one can program most of them if only a few elementary operations are provided, it is important to be able to implement all of the desired functions efficiently using whatever functions are built into the hardware. Thus, a microprocessor which is to be provided with software procedures for floating-point arithmetic should have convenient ways of assembling and disassembling floating-point numbers and operating on the exponent and mantissa separately. It is usually very advisable for a potential customer to write out in detail the key software procedures which will be used in a proposed processor application. Very often, "minor" housekeeping chores that require one or two machine language instructions here or there can add up to a serious amount of overhead, perhaps increasing the processing time by a factor of two or three in practice.

To some extent the above problems can be circumvented by the use of microprogramming, a subject we shall explore in Chapter 4. In microprogrammed processors, new machine language instructions can be implemented after the machine has been built, at a level somewhere between the hardware and software, often called *firmware*. There are, of course, practical limitations to what can be changed in this way, and in microprogrammed machines one pays a price in speed for gains provided in flexibility.

As we have seen, and as will be discussed at some length in the rest of this chapter, certain arithmetic and logical operations are nearly universal computer processor operations. As computers become more widely used, other functions may become equally important. For example, sorting and merging of data lists are commonly encountered applications which can be implemented in hardware; we will return to these in Chapter 6 because the *interconnections* of elementary processors are a key to these functions. Later in this chapter, we will consider collections of processors used to speed up computations of the traditional scientific or commercial type (recall the organizations of Section 1.2.1). But there are questions about future uses of processors other than those referred to in this paragraph.

Let us speculate briefly about other uses of processors that are made possible by the extremely low cost and high reliability of microprocessors. In the mid-1970s, 40-pin packages containing 8-bit processors became available from many semiconductor manufacturers. The instruction sets of these machines are more limited than, say, the IBM 370, but they can outperform the super-computers of the early 1950s in many computations. How they will be applied in the future, and what new microprocessor organizations (e.g. longer words) will appear are open questions that may be of great interest to computer architects.

The architecture of individual microprocessors in the mid-1970s is not too different from previous processors; but their integration into systems could be very different. For example, they could be used to construct parallel processor systems with hundreds or thousands of processors, but this raises serious questions about parallel memory and switch design, not to mention software questions about languages and compilers. Or they could be used as comparison and interchange elements in sort/merge networks (see Chapter 6); even though this may be wasteful of some of their power, the low cost resulting from mass production makes such uses reasonable. Specialization toward various kinds of microprocessors may be possible by their very high-volume use in hand-held calculators, in automobile control, in individual telephones, and so on. The custom design of specialized processors for each new application is a technical possibility, but probably will remain an economic impossibility. Most semiconductor manufacturers obviously have more interest in such mass market items as wristwatches or hand-held calculators with tens or hundreds of millions of possible customers, than in producing exotic, one-of-a-kind custom processors.

Still other system uses of microprocessors may be much more challenging problems for system architects. Suppose a manufacturer has a large, complex assembly line or chemical process to control. A network of microprocessors each monitoring and controlling an elementary part of the overall process, but each interconnected to a number of other processors, might be very effective. In a sense, interconnected microprocessors might serve as a giant analog computer in that the network represents a model of the physical plant it is controlling. When some part of the physical plant deviates from its programmed operating region, its microprocessor could take appropriate action to correct it and could also notify related parts of the physical plant to adapt to a short-term anomaly. Modeling of complex physical and biological systems can also be considered in similar terms. Although such ideas are presently speculative, it is clear that collections of cheap, reliable microprocessors do present interesting and difficult challenges to computer architects.

3.1.2 Arithmetic and logic unit design

If we regard consideration of a computer's processor as the first design problem, then a number of decisions at this level will be reflected throughout the system. In practice, the design of various parts of the machine affected would be considered simultaneously, but we must restrict our attention to one part at a time.

In terms of cost and speed, a designer must be concerned with the kind of circuits used as well as how many parts are required. Circuit parameters of interest are switching speed, fan-in and fan-out limitations, power dissipation, noise immunity, reliability, and cost. Interrelations among parts required by the functions desired must be compatible with their layout on boards, involving such things as the number of wiring levels, propagation delays, cooling, and repairability.

The user requirements given to a designer may be rather vague. As discussed earlier, problems in different contexts tend to place a variety of demands on the processor—some problems require one type of operation and others something else. In any case, arithmetic units for large, numerical computations tend to present the most severe design problems for traditional processors, so some details of these will be discussed.

First, one must decide which operations are to be performed in the hardware. Addition, subtraction, multiplication, and division are typical, although there are many variations on these. In the future, more complicated functions may be built into machines—for example, trigonometric functions, log, exp, or n-ary summation—indeed, some machines have had these in the past. Any functions not provided directly in hardware can be implemented via software subroutines. Each of these operations involves many design decisions, and even if our attention is restricted to addition, we must decide if the processor is actually going to add using combinational logic (see Section 2.3.7.3) or just do a table lookup to obtain the result. Traditionally, this latter strategy was sometimes employed (e.g., IBM 1620) in slow, small machines; large, high-speed machines usually have had the ability to compute the sum of two numbers using some kind of combinational or sequential logic. With the advent of inexpensive, large, read-only memories (ROMs), and programmed logic arrays (PLAs), hybrid schemes using lookup and combinational logic are now attractive in some cases.

The form of the numbers used happens to be quite important in a number of respects. By *form* we mean the number of digits, the number system, and whether or not an explicit exponent is used. The number of digits dictates the word length of memory as well as the arithmetic unit and its registers, and this can be quite important in terms of overall system cost. We shall denote the machine *word length* by w. Users can often give estimates of the required word length in terms of the maximum roundoff error tolerable for certain calculations. It is usually desirable to make the word length a multiple of the character size (byte) used in the computer system, and this has usually been either 6 or 8 bits in binary machines. As was mentioned above, both binary numbers and decimal numbers—in the form of binary coded decimal (BCD)—are often used in computers. For numerical calculations the range of 32 to 64 bits has been common. The possibility exists of choosing a standard word length and then providing arithmetic operations on double or half words. This has often been done to try to satisfy a wider class of users.

Choosing a word length typically requires choosing both an exponent and mantissa size in most modern machines used for numerical computation. Von Neumann argued against floating-point hardware and built a 40-bit fixed point machine. Later, most companies built floating-point machines with 40 or fewer total bits to the chagrin of many numerical users. Typically, from 6–16 bits of exponent are provided. Designers must also decide whether the hardware will always use normalized arithmetic; several unnormalized or significance arithmetic schemes have been proposed and implemented, mainly for purposes of error analysis [Gold 63], [MeAs 63].

Finally, the number system chosen can greatly influence the speed and gate count of the arithmetic unit. The well-known polynomial representation is commonly used, although a redundant form of this has desirable properties. Also, the residue number system has interesting properties that are useful in a theoretical way, as well as for some applications.

We shall attempt to discuss several of these issues and to contrast some of them with others. The reader should be forewarned that no pat answers are forthcoming. Some fairly detailed results are available but the choices among alternatives must be dictated by individual design requirements. A venerable reference for processor design is [Buch62] which was written by the designers of the IBM 7030 (STRETCH), who present a good deal of background philosophy and the tradeoffs they considered. Although technology has changed, a good deal of the book is still quite valuable.

3.2 MACHINE REPRESENTATION OF NUMBERS

3.2.1 Polynomial numbers

Numbers may be coded in a variety of ways. For example, the *positional* or *polynomial* number

$$p(r, k) = \sum_{i=0}^{k-1} d_i r^i, \qquad 0 \le d_i < r$$

represents a k-digit integer with *radix r*. The d_i are *digit values* with *weights* r^i. If $r = 10$, we have a *decimal* number; for example,

$$p(10, 4) = 3 \times 10^3 + 7 \times 10^2 + 1 \times 10^1 + 9 \times 10^0 = (3719)_{10}.$$

We shall use the radix subscript notation when necessary to avoid ambiguity. As another example if $r = 2$, we have a *binary* number; for example,

$$p(2, 3) = 1 \times 2^2 + 0 \times 2^1 + 1 \times 2^0 = (101)_2 = (5)_{10},$$

and here the d_i are called bits (for binary digits). Finally, if $r = 16$, we have a *hexadecimal* number; for example,

$$p(16, 3) = 1 \times 16^2 + 9 \times 16^1 + 15_{10} \times 16^0.$$

To avoid confusion, the substitutions $A = 10_{10}$, $B = 11_{10}$, $C = 12_{10}$, $D = 13_{10}$, $E = 14_{10}$, and $F = 15_{10}$ are often used. Thus for our example, $(19F)_{16} = (415)_{10} = (0001\ 1001\ 1111)_2$. Since four bits can represent each of the 16 possible coefficients required in a hexadecimal number, an easy conversion from binary to hexadecimal may be made. In the last example this can be seen by simply reading off groups of four bits in the binary form and rewriting them as hexadecimal coefficients of appropriate powers of 16.

Because of the ease of building physical devices with two stable internal states, a radix of some power of two is often chosen for computer number representation. Binary, octal, and hexadecimal are common choices.

The above numbers were all integers, but real numbers are easy to write as polynomials by letting the summation range over negative as well as non-negative values. Thus

$$p(r, k, j) = \sum_{i=-j}^{k-1} d_i r^i, \qquad 0 \le d_i < r$$

is a $j + k$ digit real number, of radix r.

Examples of decimal and binary real numbers are

$$p(10, 3, 2) = 9 \times 10^2 + 0 \times 10^1 + 4 \times 10^0 + 7 \times 10^{-1} + 3 \times 10^{-2}$$
$$= 904.73,$$

and

$$p(2, 2, 3) = 1 \times 2^1 + 0 \times 2^0 + 1 \times 2^{-1} + 0 \times 2^{-2} + 1 \times 2^{-3} = (10.101)_2$$
$$= (2.625)_{10}.$$

Note that there are j digits after the decimal and binary points, respectively.

3.2.2 Nomenclature

A wide variety of formats have been proposed or used to store and operate on numbers inside computers. If machine numbers have a word length of $w = n + 1$ bits, n digits plus a sign bit, we say that integers may be represented with n bits of *precision*. It is important to distinguish "precision" in this sense from the meanings of such words as "accuracy" or "significance." Thus, machine numbers may be represented to 20 digits of precision. But if, for example, the measuring device from which they were obtained was only accurate to 3 digits, only 3 digits of the 20 stored are accurate. The other 17 may have been "extrapolated" by a meter reader, or arbitrarily filled with zeros when loaded into the computer, but cannot affect the *accuracy* regardless of the value they contain.

In what follows, we will discuss a number of characteristics of machine representations of number systems. Among them will be the number of distinct representable numbers and the largest number representable, which we call the *range* of the set of representable numbers.

Computer number systems and arithmetic have given rise over the years to some conflicting nomenclatures from one manufacturer to another. We will try to choose from the existing terms, words that have wide use and are intuitively reasonable.

One word that has a multiplicity of meanings is "radix." We have already used it to define polynomial numbers in the traditional mathematical way, but it has several interpretations in computers.

Almost all current machines are built using physical devices with two stable states, although in the past there have also been ten-state vacuum tubes. When devices are assembled into computer elements—registers, arithmetic units, and so on—some hardware radix for numbers is chosen.

We will refer to this basic hardware radix as r_v, which denotes the number of distinct values that the hardware devices can take on. As mentioned above, this is now almost always 2 in real machines. Shortly, we will refer to several other radices used to represent various types of number systems in the performance of machine arithmetic. For example, integers, floating-point mantissas, and floating-point exponents each have a radix that we will denote by a mnemonically subscripted r. It is important to realize that these may equal r_v or they may be some integer greater than r_v, in which case hardware or software schemes allow programmers to use the larger radix. Although it may seem pedantic to make some of these distinctions, there is often confusion and sloppiness in discussing these matters, which are really simple and should not be confusing.

In the following sections we will present several different number systems. We will use the notation

Number System (parameter list)

to refer to the set of all values representable in the particular system; uppercase letters will denote such sets. We will use the same notation with lowercase names to refer to *any* number in that system. We will use the lowercase notation with subscripts to refer to specific numbers in the system.

3.2.3 Fixed- and floating-point numbers

Integers are stored in most machines as a sign bit and n digits of integer. Let $I(r_i, n)$ denote the *integer number system*. Thus, the n-digit *integers* $i(r_i, n)$ in a radix $r_i = r_v$ machine satisfy

$$-(r_i^n - 1) \le i(r_i, n) \le r_i^n - 1 \tag{1}$$

with both plus and minus zero included.[1] We say that the *range* of the system $I(r_i, n)$ is $r_i^n - 1$.

If a number's machine representation is indeed a sign bit and the absolute value of the number, the number is said to have a *signed magnitude* representation. Other representations are also common; we will discuss biased exponent representations shortly, and in our discussion of machine subtraction (see Section 3.3.3) complement numbers will be presented. Integers are often represented in a 1's or 2's complement notation (e.g., the IBM 360 uses 2's complement integers [IBMC70]), whereas floating-point mantissas are often signed magnitude numbers. However, some binary machines use 1's complement (e.g., the CDC 6600 and its successors) or 2's complement number systems throughout. Most elementary logic design books discuss these topics, and we will discuss them only in the context of subtraction.

Although a machine built with binary devices has $r_v = 2$, it may be useful to design decimal arithmetic into the machine, especially for use in business applications. In this case, binary machine words are regarded as a sequence of 4-bit representations of decimal digits and the representation is called *binary coded decimal* (BCD). If a machine has n-bit words and $r_v = 2$, for decimal arithmetic the machine could be regarded as having $n/4$-digit words with the integer radix $r_i = 10$ so the decimal integer range would satisfy

$$-(10^{n/4} - 1) \le i\left(10, \frac{n}{4}\right) \le 10^{n/4} - 1.$$

Decimal arithmetic could be performed by hardware operations (see Section 3.3.2) or software could be used to exploit the standard binary arithmetic unit.

BCD numbers need not be restricted to a single machine word length, however. For example, the commercial instructions of the IBM 360/370 allow decimal arithmetic operands with variable precision ranging from 1 to 31 BCD digits; together with a sign these occupy 16 bytes maximum.

Numbers in the above forms need not be regarded as integers. Obviously, the radix point may be assumed to be anywhere in the number; or it may be assumed to be a fixed number of positions to the right or left of the word. Wherever it is assumed to be, it is fixed by the programmer (as in slide rule computation). This number representation in computers is thus called either

---

[1] For two's complement representation (see Section 3.3.3) only one zero exists.

integer or *fixed-point* form. A fixed-point number which is not an integer clearly satisfies

$$-r^s(r^n - 1) \le fi(r, n, s) \le r^s(r^n - 1), \tag{2}$$

where s (a signed integer) is a *scale factor* assumed by the user and r is either r_v or some larger radix, as discussed above.

Since the late 1950s, most big machines have provided arithmetic units that operate on integer or fixed-point as well as *floating-point* or *real* number forms. For a fixed word size, machines have a wider range of representable floating-point numbers than fixed-point numbers. Floating-point forms may be represented by a signed *mantissa* and a signed *exponent*. Assume two sign bits plus $e + m$ digits are used, where e is the number of digits of the exponent and m is the number of digits of the mantissa. Specific mantissa and exponent values will be denoted by *man* and *exp*, respectively. Suppose we use two different radices, r_e for exponents and r_m for mantissas. An exponent of e digits and a mantissa of m digits may take the forms

$$exp = fi(r_e, e, s_1)$$
$$man = fi(r_m, m, s_2). \tag{3}$$

In most machines, $s_1 = 0$, so exponents are regarded as integers, and we can write

$$exp = i(r_e, e). \tag{4}$$

In many machines, exponents are stored as *biased* numbers. For example, in the IBM 360/370, the seven exponent bits could be used to represent the range from -63 to $+63$. In fact, the actual exponent is biased by adding 64 to it before storing it, so the range of exponents representable is -64 to $+63$. This is sometimes called an excess-64 number representation. The ambiguity of $+0$ and -0 is thus replaced by one extra exponent value. For carrying out floating-point operations, it is sometimes necessary to compare, add, or subtract exponents (see Figs. 3.4 and 3.5) and by using biased exponents the extra complexity of dealing with negative numbers is avoided. Most manufacturers use biased exponents; most Burroughs machines, however, use signed magnitude integer exponents (see Table 3.1). Furthermore, in most machines $r_e = r_v = 2$.

The value of s_2 in Eq. 3 is usually either 0 or $-m$. When $s_2 = -m$, the mantissa is a fraction with the radix point at its left end. This is quite common and has been used in most IBM machines, including the 360 and 370 series. When $s_2 = 0$, the radix point is at the right end of the mantissa and this integer format mantissa expedites conversion between integer and floating-point forms. This form of floating-point numbers is used in most Burroughs and CDC computers.

Up to this point, we have discussed forms of the mantissa[2] and exponent but have not mentioned the base to which the exponent is raised. We shall refer to this as the *floating-point base* or *radix* of machine numbers and we shall denote it by r_b. In most machines, $r_b = r_m$; in fact, if $r_b \neq r_m$, then we must be able to handle fractional exponents—so we will assume $r_b = r_m$ henceforth. But it is not always the case that $r_b = r_e$. For example, in the IBM 360 and 370 floating-point operations, $r_e = 2$ but $r_m = r_b = 16$, and 360s and 370s are referred to as hexadecimal floating-point machines (see Section 3.2.1). In most Burroughs machines $r_b = 8$.

Notice that the largest exponent value we can represent (using Eqs. 1 and 4) is $r_e^e - 1$, so the largest floating-point number we can represent is the largest mantissa times $r_b^{(r_e^e - 1)}$. If we have $r_b = r_v^k$, then this becomes the largest mantissa times $r_v^{k(r_e^e - 1)}$ so we define

$$exponent\ range = k(r_e^e - 1) \tag{5}$$

in terms of r_v. If $s_2 = 0$ in Eq. 3, then using Eq. 2, the largest mantissa value is $r_b^m - 1$, whereas if $s_2 = -m$, the largest mantissa is $r_b^{-m}(r_b^m - 1) = 1 - r_b^{-m} \approx 1$. The smallest nonzero positive mantissas are 1 with $s_2 = 0$, and r_b^{-m} with $s_2 = -m$.

We define a *floating-point number system* $FL(r_e, r_b, m, e, s_2)$ to be the set of all numbers representable, as discussed above. We shall assume $s_1 = 0$ (exponents are integers) throughout our discussion. In the special case where $s_2 = -m$ we shall write $FL(r_e, r_b, f, e)$ to emphasize that the mantissa is a fraction.

As an example, for the floating-point number system with fractional mantissas, we have

$$r_b^{1-f-r_e^e} \leq fl(r_e, r_b, f, e) \leq (1 - r_b^{-f}) r_b^{(r_e^e - 1)}$$

or

$$fl(r_e, r_b, f, e) = \pm 0$$

or

$$-(1 - r_b^{-f}) r_b^{(r_e^e - 1)} \leq fl(r_e, r_b, f, e) \leq -r_b^{1-f-r_e^e}.$$

Furthermore, the binary floating-point numbers $(r_b = r_e = 2)$ with fractional mantissas satisfy

$$2^{(1-f-2^e)} \leq fl(2, 2, f, e) \leq (1 - 2^{-f}) 2^{(2^e - 1)}$$

or

$$fl(2, 2, f, e) = \pm 0$$

or

$$-(1 - 2^{-f}) 2^{(2^e - 1)} \leq fl(2, 2, f, e) \leq -2^{(1-f-2^e)}.$$

---

[2] Several terms other than *mantissa* have been used in this context. The argument against *mantissa* is that it has another meaning, namely, the fraction part of a base ten logarithm. But the use of *fraction* is misleading and clearly oriented to the $s_2 = -m$ representation. *Coefficient* may be a better word, but it is not as commonly used as *mantissa*, and *significand* is also used on occasion.

The *precision* of a floating-point number system is the number of digits representable in the mantissa; normally this is measured in digits of radix r_b, but for comparison with other radices it is useful to measure it in bits, which may be called *binary precision* for any radix. The *range* of a floating-point number system FL (r_e, r_b, m, e, s_2) is the absolute value of its largest representable value,[3] which as we saw is

$$\text{range}\,[\text{FL}\,(r_e, r_b, m, e, s_2)] = r_b^{s_2}(r_b^{m} - 1)r_b^{(r_e^e - 1)},$$

so for a binary machine with fractional mantissas $(s_2 = -f)$, we have

$$\text{range}\,[\text{FL}\,(2, 2, f, e)] = (1 - 2^{-f})2^{(2^e - 1)}.$$

It is important to remember that floating-point number systems contain only a finite collection of values and these values are not uniformly distributed on the real line. Yet in all machine computations we use such systems to represent the entire real line. Later, we will study various consequences of this as well as design tradeoffs in choosing a "good" number system.

Table 3.1 summarizes the characteristics of floating-point number representations in several manufacturers' machines. By scanning down the columns, one observes the diversity of designs that are used. Note that word sizes range from 32 to 60 bits. Each manufacturer also provides some technique for handling double precision numbers if a user finds the single precision formats shown to be inadequate. Some manufacturers use a second word to extend the mantissa, whereas others extend both the exponent and the mantissa. The scientific orientation of CDC is obvious from its 48-bit single precision mantissa. Notice that the Honeywell 8200 provides two options, including BCD floating-point arithmetic [Hone71].

TABLE 3.1   Floating-Point Number Comparison

Machine	Word Size (Bits)	r_b	Exponent (Bits)	Mantissa (Bits)	Mantissa Representation
Burroughs 6700/7700	47 (plus tag)	8	7 (signed magnitude)	39 (integer)	signed magnitude
CDC 6600/CYBER 70	60	2	11 (excess 1024)	48 (integer)	one's complement
DEC PDP-11	32*	2	8 (excess 128)	23 (fraction)	signed magnitude
Honeywell 8200	48	2 or 10	7 (excess 64)	40 binary or 10 BCD digits (fraction)	signed magnitude
IBM 370 Series	32	16	7 (excess 64)	24 (fraction)	signed magnitude

* Stored as two 16-bit memory words.

[3] Range could be defined as the difference of the largest and smallest positive values representable, but most computers have small numbers very close to zero, so such a definition seems pedantic.

For further discussion of number systems see [Buch62], [GsMc75], [Knut69], or [StMu71]. Recommended readings concerning floating-point computation are Chapter 8 of [Buch62] and [Ster74] which discuss many of the issues of this chapter (with an IBM orientation), and [Wilk63] which presents error analysis from the numerical analyst's viewpoint.

3.2.4 Normalized numbers

The computer stored form of the floating-point numbers we have discussed would not necessarily be unique, because

$$man \times 2^{exp} = 2^{-a} \times man \times 2^{a+exp}.$$

For example, for FL $(10, 10, 5, 3, -5)$,

$$0.03210 \times 10^{003} = 0.32100 \times 10^{002} = 0.00321 \times 10^{004}.$$

To make the stored form of floating-point numbers unique, some standard form may be chosen. Usually this is the *normalized* form of a number, which means that if the number being represented is nonzero, the high order or leftmost digit of the mantissa is nonzero. By properly adjusting the exponent, any nonzero floating-point number can be normalized as we did above using an *adjustment factor a*.

We denote a *normalized floating-point number system* NFL (r_e, r_b, m, e, s_2) as the set of all representable normalized floating-point numbers. We use the same abbreviated notations here for fractional mantissas as we discussed for floating-point number systems. For normalized floating-point number systems, the smallest representable positive nonzero mantissa is r_b^{m-1} for $s_2 = 0$ and $r_b^{-m}(r_b^{m-1}) = r_b^{-1}$ for $s_2 = -m$ (the case of fractional mantissa values). For example, we have

$$2^{-2^e} \le nfl(2, 2, f, e) \le (1 - 2^{-f})2^{(2^e - 1)}$$

or

$$nfl(2, 2, f, e) = \pm 0$$

or

$$-(1 - 2^{-f})2^{(2^e - 1)} \le nfl(2, 2, f, e) \le -2^{-2^e}.$$

To make these ideas concrete, we present two simple normalized floating-point systems. Both systems use the same size machine word, but a number of differences can be observed.

Example 1

First, consider the system NFL $(r_e, r_b, f, e) =$ NFL $(2, 2, 4, 2)$ with four bits of fractional mantissa and two bits of exponent. We represent all possible positive values with positive exponents in Table 3.2.

In Table 3.3, we present the system NFL $(r_e, r_b, f, e) =$ NFL $(2, 4, 2, 2)$. Here,

TABLE 3.2   NFL (r_e, r_b, f, e) = NFL $(2, 2, 4, 2)$

Digit Weights				Decimal fraction values	Binary Exponent Values				
					00	01	10	11	*exp*
2^{-1}	2^{-2}	2^{-3}	2^{-4}		1	2	4	8	2^{exp}
1	0	0	0	$\frac{1}{2}$	$\frac{1}{2}$	1	2	4	
1	0	0	1	$\frac{9}{16}$	$\frac{9}{16}$	$1\frac{1}{8}$	$2\frac{1}{4}$	$4\frac{1}{2}$	
1	0	1	0	$\frac{5}{8}$	$\frac{5}{8}$	$1\frac{1}{4}$	$2\frac{1}{2}$	5	
1	0	1	1	$\frac{11}{16}$	$\frac{11}{16}$	$1\frac{3}{8}$	$2\frac{3}{4}$	$5\frac{1}{2}$	
1	1	0	0	$\frac{3}{4}$	$\frac{3}{4}$	$1\frac{1}{2}$	3	6	
1	1	0	1	$\frac{13}{16}$	$\frac{13}{16}$	$1\frac{5}{8}$	$3\frac{1}{4}$	$6\frac{1}{2}$	
1	1	1	0	$\frac{7}{8}$	$\frac{7}{8}$	$1\frac{3}{4}$	$3\frac{1}{2}$	7	
1	1	1	1	$\frac{15}{16}$	$\frac{15}{16}$	$1\frac{7}{8}$	$3\frac{3}{4}$	$7\frac{1}{2}$	
Normalized binary fraction values (*fr*)				Decimal fraction values	Floating-point number values $(fr \times 2^{exp})$				

Smallest fraction $= r_b^{-1} = \frac{1}{2}$
Largest fraction $= 1 - r_b^{-f} = \frac{15}{16}$
Largest exponent $= r_e^e - 1 = 3$

Range $= (1 - r_b^{-f})r_b^{(r_e^e - 1)} = \frac{15}{16} \times 2^3 = 7\frac{1}{2}$
Number of fractions $= r_b^f(\frac{1}{2}) = 8$
Number of exponents $= r_e^e = 4$
Number of values $= r_e^e r_b^f(\frac{1}{2}) = 32$

TABLE 3.3   NFL (r_e, r_b, f, e) = NFL $(2, 4, 2, 2)$

Digit Weights		Decimal fraction values	Binary Exponent Values				
$2^{-1}\ 2^{-2}$	$2^{-3}\ 2^{-4}$		00	01	10	11	*exp*
4^{-1}	4^{-2}		1	4	16	64	4^{exp}
1	0	$\frac{1}{4}$	$\frac{1}{4}$	1	4	16	
1	1	$\frac{5}{16}$	$\frac{5}{16}$	$1\frac{1}{4}$	5	20	
1	2	$\frac{3}{8}$	$\frac{3}{8}$	$1\frac{1}{2}$	6	24	
1	3	$\frac{7}{16}$	$\frac{7}{16}$	$1\frac{3}{4}$	7	28	
2	0	$\frac{1}{2}$	$\frac{1}{2}$	2	8	32	
2	1	$\frac{9}{16}$	$\frac{9}{16}$	$2\frac{1}{4}$	9	36	
2	2	$\frac{5}{8}$	$\frac{5}{8}$	$2\frac{1}{2}$	10	40	
2	3	$\frac{11}{16}$	$\frac{11}{16}$	$2\frac{3}{4}$	11	44	
3	0	$\frac{3}{4}$	$\frac{3}{4}$	3	12	48	
3	1	$\frac{13}{16}$	$\frac{13}{16}$	$3\frac{1}{4}$	13	52	
3	2	$\frac{7}{8}$	$\frac{7}{8}$	$3\frac{1}{2}$	14	56	
3	3	$\frac{15}{16}$	$\frac{15}{16}$	$3\frac{3}{4}$	15	60	
Normalized quaternary fraction values (*fr*)		Decimal fraction values	Floating-point number values $(fr \times 4^{exp})$				

Smallest fraction $= r_b^{-1} = \frac{1}{4}$
Largest fraction $= 1 - r_b^{-f} = \frac{15}{16}$
Largest exponent $= r_e^e - 1 = 3$

Range $= (1 - r_b^{-f})r_b^{(r_e^e - 1)} = \frac{15}{16} \times 4^3 = 60$
Number of fractions $= r_b^f(\frac{1}{2} + \frac{1}{4}) = 12$
Number of exponents $= r_e^e = 4$
Number of values $= r_e^e r_b^f(\frac{1}{2} + \frac{1}{4}) = 48$

the fraction has four bits which we regard as two radix-four digits. Such systems are sometimes called quaternary numbers. We observe that normalized quaternary numbers can have a leading zero bit, because 01 represents $(1)_4$. This allows more representable numbers with $r_b = 4$ than we had with $r_b = 2$.

Notice that both systems use six bits of machine word for exponent and fraction storage. The quaternary system however, has a much wider range and also more representable numbers. On the other hand, the numbers are much more sparsely distributed on the real line. For example, the binary system has seven numbers between 1 and 2, while the quaternary system has only three. ∎

3.2.5 Representation ratio

We now study the number of different values representable using various bases and the distribution of these values. In particular, for a fixed fraction size and positive exponents, we will compute the number of higher radix values and the number of binary values representable in the range of the binary numbers. The ratio of these two numbers is called the *representation ratio*. Notice that when floating-point numbers with $r_b = 2$ are required to be in normalized form, only half of the possible values representable are used (just those with a leading 1). As Example 1 shows, when one leading zero is allowed ($r_b = 4$), then 50 percent more values are representable. We now show how the same effect holds for higher r_b values. The following argument is given for fractions, but a similar argument holds for integer mantissas.

Given e and f bits of exponent and fraction, respectively, there are 2^e different exponents and 2^{f-1} different normalized fractions representable, assuming that $r_b = r_e = 2$. Thus the total number of positive representable values with positive exponents is 2^{e+f-1}. Because the largest fraction representable is approximately 1, and the largest exponent representable is $2^e - 1$, the largest binary number representable (range) is approximately 2^{2^e-1}.

Now, if $r_b = \beta = 2^k$, numbers have the form $fr \times \beta^{exp}$. To estimate the number of values less than the maximum representable binary number ($r_b = 2$) we assume that $fr \approx 1$ and observe that for some p (not necessarily an integer)

$$\beta^p \approx 2^{2^e-1}.$$

Thus $p \log \beta \approx 2^e - 1$. Now using $r_b = \beta$, the number of representable values between $\dfrac{1}{\beta}$ and β^p is approximately

$$(2^{f-1} + 2^{f-2} + \cdots + 2^{f-\log \beta})(p+1) = 2^f\left(1 - \frac{1}{\beta}\right)(p+1).$$

(Note that f here is the number of binary digits, not the number of base-β digits.) Thus to compare the number of base-β values in the range of the binary numbers, with the total number of binary numbers, we can write

$$\text{Representation ratio} = \frac{\frac{1}{2} \leq \text{number of } r_b = \beta \text{ values} \leq 2^{2^{e-1}}}{\frac{1}{2} \leq \text{number of } r_b = 2 \text{ values} \leq 2^{2^{e-1}}}$$

$$\approx \frac{2^f \left(1 - \frac{1}{\beta}\right)(p+1)}{2^{f-1} 2^e}$$

$$= \frac{2 \left(1 - \frac{1}{\beta}\right)(p+1)}{1 + p \log \beta} \; .$$

Example 2

If $\beta = 16$ and $e = 8$, then we have $p = \dfrac{2^8}{\log 16} = 2^6$

and

$$\text{Representation ratio} \approx \frac{2(1 - \frac{1}{16})(2^6 + 1)}{1 + 2^6 \cdot 4} \approx 0.475.$$

By a simple analysis it may be shown that there are 1.875 times as many hexadecimal values as binary values representable using fixed e and f. Thus we conclude that for positive exponents about $\frac{1}{4}$ ($\approx 0.475/1.875$) of the hexadecimal values are in the range of the binary values and about $\frac{3}{4}$ are outside the binary range. ∎

Although more numbers are representable over a wider range by using larger r_b values, such schemes are not a panacea. For example, Example 2 shows that in the range where binary and hexadecimal numbers overlap, the hexadecimal numbers are much less densely distributed and hence do an inferior job of representing the real line (recall Tables 3.2 and 3.3). We will return to this problem in Section 3.4.4. Another criticism of higher r_b values is that whenever a one-digit shift is made, several bits are lost—not just one as with $r_b = 2$. These questions will be further explored in our discussion of floating-point arithmetic.

3.3 COMPUTER ARITHMETIC ALGORITHMS

Several aspects of machine arithmetic will be discussed in this section, although we began the discussion in Section 2.3.7 (for binary addition) and will continue it in Section 3.5. Here we will review binary addition, present binary subtraction, BCD addition and floating-point addition, and multiplication algorithms. Discussions of the components and times involved are found in the above-mentioned sections.

3.3.1 Integer addition

First, let us restrict our attention to the addition of nonnegative integers. For example,

$$i_1(r, n) + i_2(r, n) = \sum_{i=0}^{n-1} d_{1i} r^i + \sum_{i=0}^{n-1} d_{2i} r^i$$
$$= \sum_{i=0}^{n-1} (d_{1i} + d_{2i}) r^i.$$

Since each digit is required to be less than r, $d_{1i} + d_{2i}$ must be regarded as a pair of digits, commonly called a sum and a carry digit, so $d_{1i} + d_{2i} = rc_{i+1} + s_i$ where $c_{i+1} = 1$ if $d_{1i} + d_{2i} \geq r$, otherwise $c_{i+1} = 0$. It is important to decide precisely what we mean by "the addition of two numbers." Is it sufficient to generate only the c_{i+1} and s_i digits for all i? Or must we worry about propagating the carry across the result? Note that

$$\begin{array}{r} 316 \\ +253 \\ \hline 569 \end{array}$$

can be evaluated with all zero carry digits, whereas

$$\begin{array}{r} 316 \\ +694 \\ \hline 1010 \end{array}$$

requires a carry to propagate across all positions. Also, note that the second sum above *overflowed* in the sense that two three-digit numbers led to one four-digit number. With a fixed word length machine this would require the raising of some kind of alarm to cause appropriate action to be taken, and we shall discuss this below.

In Section 2.3.7.3 we discussed fast parallel adder circuits; several other schemes will be pointed out in Section 3.5. An algorithm for floating-point addition will be presented shortly and it assumes an integer adder which may use any of these schemes. If the signs of the integers to be added are unlike, then a subtraction scheme is necessary (see Section 3.3.3). In the next section we will consider BCD addition.

3.3.2 BCD addition

Various schemes can be devised for the addition of BCD numbers. For example, integrated circuit packages can be designed to handle two BCD digits just as standard gates handle bits. It is also easy to preprocess and postprocess BCD numbers in such a way that a standard binary adder may be used, and this scheme will now be described.

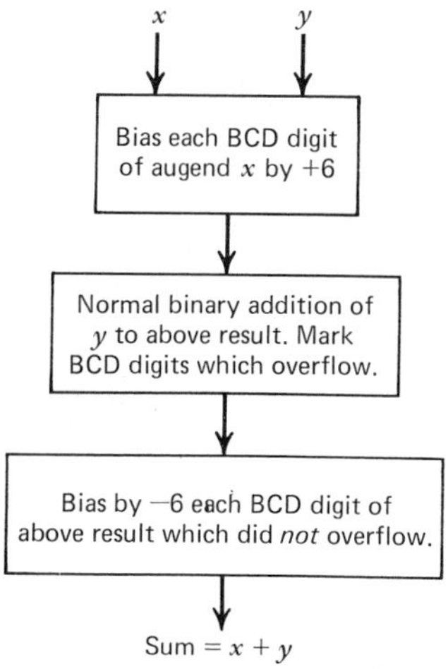
x
y
Bias each BCD digit of augend x by +6
Normal binary addition of y to above result. Mark BCD digits which overflow.
Bias by −6 each BCD digit of above result which did not overflow.
Sum = x + y

FIGURE 3.2 **BCD addition algorithm.**

The main difficulty in designing a BCD number adder is that carry propagation must occur when any sum digit exceeds 9, whereas the hardware is capable of representing digits as big as 15. In fact, a standard binary adder will propagate carries when a 4-bit sequence does contain all 1's. Thus we can precondition a BCD number (say, the augend) by adding 6 (binary 0110) to each BCD digit. Since a proper BCD digit is in the range from 0 to 9, this preconditioning will never cause an overflow to the next BCD digit, so each digit may be preconditioned simultaneously and independently.

The second step is to add the normal BCD addend to the preconditioned augend, and allow carries to propagate in the standard way for binary numbers. Now, for example, a preconditioned 9 has become a 15, so any nonzero digit added to a 9 will result in a carry since the 15 causes a carry to propagate. In fact, any BCD digit that does overflow contains the correct sum in its position, due to the preconditioning.

On step three, those BCD digits that did *not* overflow on step two must be corrected. Since they were biased by 6 on the first step, they can now be corrected by subtracting 6. This is done simultaneously for each BCD digit that does not generate a carry out on the second step.

The above procedure is summarized in Fig. 3.2, and will be illustrated by the following example. We will carry out the example in decimal, but the same results obviously hold for the BCD representations of the digits.

Example 3

Consider the following addition

$$\begin{array}{r} 1536 \\ +9182 \\ \hline 10718 \end{array}$$

The first step of the algorithm of Fig. 3.2 is to bias each digit of the augend by adding 6 (denoted by $\oplus$)

$$
\begin{array}{r}
1 \quad 5 \quad 3 \quad 6 \\
\oplus 6 \quad 6 \quad 6 \quad 6 \\
\hline
7 \ 11 \quad 9 \ 12 \\
= 7 \quad B \quad 9 \quad C
\end{array}
$$

using the standard hexadecimal notation. The second step is to perform a normal binary addition (i.e., letting carries propagate) and to mark those BCD digits which do generate carries out, so we obtain

$$
\begin{array}{r}
7 \quad B \quad 9 \quad C \\
+ 9 \quad 1 \quad 8 \quad 2 \\
\hline
1 \ 0 \ D \ 1 \ E = \text{sum} \\
1 \ 0 \ 1 \ 0 = \text{carry out indicator}
\end{array}
$$

The third step is to subtract the bias of 6 from each position which did not overflow above (denoted by $\ominus$),

$$
\begin{array}{r}
1 \ 0 \ D \ 1 \ E \\
\ominus 0 \ 0 \ 6 \ 0 \ 6 \\
\hline
1 \ 0 \ 7 \ 1 \ 8
\end{array}
$$

which yields the correct result. ∎

The above method is used in the IBM 360 on two digits at a time, and because BCD operands can have up to 31 digits (plus a sign), it must be done repeatedly (in a serial fashion) on words longer than two digits. As an alternative to this scheme, the so-called excess-three number representation could be used [StMu71]. In this case all numbers are biased initially so carries propagate properly. Also, the code is self-complementing in that the one's complement of an excess-three number gives the nine's complement of the decimal digit, aiding subtraction. However, more time must be spent in number conversion on input and output if BCD numbers are to be used outside the central computer. For a discussion of IBM code conversions, see Section 3.4 of [Katz71].

3.3.3 Integer subtraction

Now we will consider the machine subtraction of integers. If this is done one digit at a time, an algorithm similar to the normal pencil and paper scheme with borrowing can be used. A faster scheme, which is compatible with the addition algorithm of Section 2.3.7.3, is used in most binary arithmetic units, however. Two subtraction schemes will be described below, each of which involves complementation and addition, and one or the other of which may be found in use in most computers today.

First, two definitions are needed; the $(r-1)$'s *complement* of an m-digit, radix-r integer x is defined as

$$\tilde{x}_{r-1} = (r^m - 1) - x,$$

and the r's *complement* of an m-digit, radix-r integer x is defined as

$$\tilde{x}_r = r^m - x = \tilde{x}_{r-1} + 1.$$

Example 4

To form the 1's complement of any binary integer is very simple. For any fixed m, $r^m - 1$ is a sequence of m binary 1's. Let y be any m-bit number. Now the subtraction of y from a sequence of all 1's will lead to a result whose bits are the complements of those in y. For example, if $m = 5$ and $y = 10100$ then

$$\tilde{y}_1 = 11111 - 10100 = 01011.$$

Forming the 2's complement is more complex because a 1 must be added to the 1's complement and this may lead to a carry propagation across the number. Continuing with the above example,

$$\tilde{y}_2 = \tilde{y}_1 + 1 = 01011 + 00001 = 01100. \qquad \blacksquare$$

The main reason for discussing complement numbers relates to their use in subtraction; we want to form the difference of x and y by adding the complement of y to x. First, consider the use of r's complements in subtracting the m-digit, radix-r integers, x and y. The difference d can be written

$$\begin{aligned} d = x - y &= (r^m - y) + x - r^m \\ &= \tilde{y}_r + x - r^m. \end{aligned} \qquad (6)$$

Following Eq. 6 subtraction can be carried out by first forming the r's complement of y and then adding x, both of which are straightforward operations. In fact, the 1 that must be added in forming the r's complement of y could be combined with the addition of x, to save time. Now the result of this addition may or may not have overflowed the original m bits. If an overflow bit is produced, its value is exactly r^m, so that the correct result is obtained by discarding the overflow bit. If no overflow is produced, the correct difference can be obtained by rewriting Eq. 6 as

$$d = \tilde{y}_r + x - r^m = -(\widetilde{\tilde{y}_r + x})_r. \qquad (7)$$

Since the m-bit result is just the negative r's complement of $\tilde{y}_r + x$, by recomplementing and setting the sign to minus the correct difference is obtained. This procedure is summarized in Fig. 3.3.

A second scheme for subtraction involves the use of $(r-1)$'s complements. Assuming x and y are m-digit, radix-r integers, their difference d can be

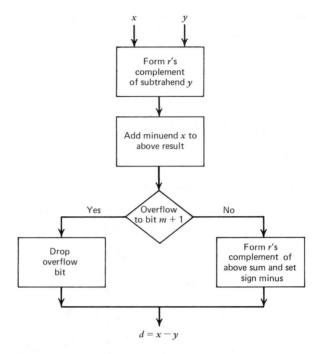

FIGURE 3.3   The r's complement subtraction $d = x - y$.

written

$$d = x - y = (r^m - 1 - y) + x - (r^m - 1)$$
$$= \bar{y}_{r-1} + x - r^m + 1 . \tag{8}$$

This is quite similar to Eq. 6 and a similar algorithm results. Since for binary numbers, the 1's complement is easier to form than the 2's complement, the first step here may be easier. The second step—addition—is the same in both schemes. The third step here again requires checking for overflow. If no overflow occurs, the correct result can be obtained by forming the 1's complement of the result and setting the sign to minus. If the addition does overflow into bit $m + 1$, r^m can be subtracted by dropping this bit, but now the remaining 1 (in Eq. 8) must be added to the above result to obtain the correct difference.

3.3.4 Floating-point arithmetic definitions

This section defines floating-point arithmetic operations and some related terminology. Algorithms for these operations will be given shortly. The following definitions should be intuitively clear.

Let $fl_1 = man_1 \times r_b^{exp_1}$ and $fl_2 = man_2 \times r_b^{exp_2}$; then

$$fl_1 \pm fl_2 = \begin{cases} (man_1 \pm man_2 \times r_b^{-(exp_1 - exp_2)}) \times r_b^{exp_1}, & \text{if } exp_1 \geq exp_2 \\ (man_1 \times r_b^{-(exp_2 - exp_1)} \pm man_2) \times r_b^{exp_2}, & \text{if } exp_1 < exp_2 \end{cases} \qquad (9)$$

$$fl_1 \times fl_2 = man_1 \times man_2 \times r_b^{(exp_1 + exp_2)} \qquad (10)$$

$$fl_1/fl_2 = (man_1/man_2) \times r_b^{(exp_1 - exp_2)}. \qquad (11)$$

A number of difficulties may arise in terms of machine representation of the results of these arithmetic operations. In the case of addition or subtraction, the exponent of the (initial) result is the same as one of the original exponents but one of the arguments must be shifted (aligned) a distance equal to the magnitude of the difference of the exponents. This can cause digits to flow off the right end of a number (machine register), and we shall call it *mantissa (fraction) underflow*. In some additions, a 1 is carried off the left end of the number (machine register) and we shall call this *mantissa (fraction) overflow*. In multiplication the precision of the result is the sum of the precisions of the operands. Whenever the result of an operation has more precision than m (the machine mantissa size), some kind of "roundoff" procedure must be used; more details about this will be given in Section 3.4.2.

In the case of multiplication and division the exponents are added and subtracted, respectively. In case a positive exponent gets too large we shall refer to it *exponent overflow*, and *exponent underflow* will mean that a negative exponent exceeds the e digits in magnitude. We shall return to a discussion of how to handle these cases with the presentation of floating-point arithmetic algorithms.

3.3.5 Normalized floating-point addition

We now consider the process of floating-point addition assuming normalized arguments. Let

$$nfl_1(2, 2, 5, 3) = 0.10100 \times 2^{011}$$
$$nfl_2(2, 2, 5, 3) = 0.10100 \times 2^{001}.$$

The addition process requires equal exponents so we first *align* the fractions by shifting right the one with the smaller exponent, and *adjust* the smaller exponent. Thus we have

$$nfl_1 + nfl_2 = 0.10100 \times 2^{011} + 0.00101 \times 2^{011}$$
$$= 0.11001 \times 2^{011} = nfl_3.$$

In general, the sum may overflow the left end (by at most one digit) and this requires a postaddition adjustment or renormalization step. This may cause a digit to drop off the right end of the word. If we have the choice of losing a digit at the right or left end, clearly we must choose to drop the low-order digit (otherwise the result would be nonsense). Various schemes for the disposal of low-order digits will be discussed later from the standpoint of reducing the errors incurred. Two commonly used schemes are simply dropping the digits, called *truncation*, or adding $0.5r_b$ to the highest order digit about to be dropped, called *rounding*. Generally rounding is preferable in the sense of errors committed, as we shall see later. The errors introduced by these processes are called *truncation error* and *rounding error*, respectively.

We have discussed the error introduced by postaddition normalization, but the preaddition alignment may also introduce error. For example, let

$$nfl_1(2, 2, 5, 3) = 0.11100 \times 2^{011}$$
$$nfl_2(2, 2, 5, 3) = 0.10111 \times 2^{001}.$$

Then

$$
\begin{array}{ll}
0.11100 \;\;\times 2^{011} = nfl_1 \\
+\,0.0010111 \times 2^{011} = nfl_2 \\
\hline
1.0000\underline{111} \times 2^{011} = nfl_3
\end{array}
$$

The fraction underflow digits underlined at the right are somewhat in doubt, being the sum of the low-order digits for nfl_2 and assumed low-order zeros for nfl_1. The underflow digits may be simply truncated, or we may dispose of them by rounding as we shall see below. The underlined digit at the left is the fraction overflow discussed above. To finish the addition we must shift right to renormalize the fraction and add one to the exponent to adjust it. Finally, we round by adding an appropriate 1. Thus we obtain

$$
\begin{array}{ll}
1.0000111 \;\;\times 2^{011} = nfl_3 \\
0.10000111 \times 2^{100} & \text{shift fraction and adjust exponent} \\
+\,0.000001 & \text{round} \\
\hline
0.10001 \;\;\;\;\times 2^{100} & \text{result}
\end{array}
$$

In decimal notation

$$nfl_1 = 7, \qquad nfl_2 = 1.4375, \quad \text{and} \quad nfl_3 = 8.5,$$

and our machine addition process has introduced roundoff error of $+0.0625$. Note that if we had used truncation instead of rounding, $nfl_3 = 8$ and the truncation error would be -0.4375.

3.3.6 Addition and multiplication algorithms

We summarize the above process in Fig. 3.4, which represents a general algorithm for normalized floating-point addition or subtraction corresponding to Eq. 9. When we refer to the addition of mantissas, we mean signed numbers, so either addition or subtraction may occur. The following is a guide to Fig. 3.4. More about the hardware implementation of this algorithm will be discussed later; for the moment, we can regard it as an abstract process.

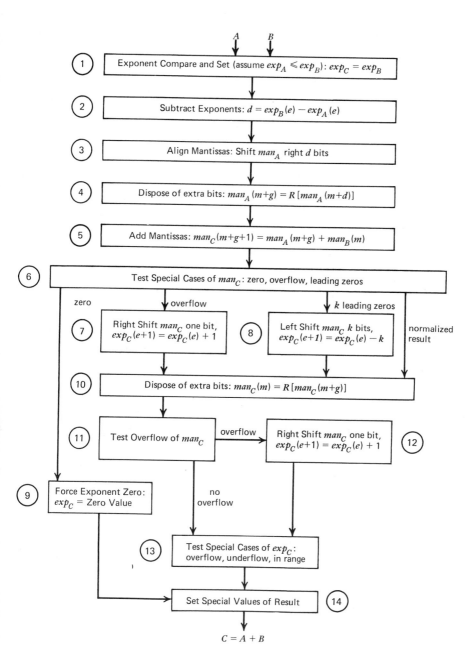

FIGURE 3.4   Floating-point addition.

213

First, we compare the exponents of A and B and set the result exponent to the larger exponent, say exp_B. Then we determine d, the exponent difference, and use it in ③ to shift the smaller mantissa right d bits. At this point, we have $m + d$ bits, which we must shorten to $m + g$ to pass through the adder. Several possible roundoff methods [see Eq. 13 for a definition of $R(x)$] will be discussed in Section 3.4.2. Guard digits (g) will be discussed in Section 3.4.3. Next we add the mantissas, producing at most $m + g + 1$ bits. Several special cases must be tested for as indicated in ⑥, and if necessary, we must renormalize the result in ⑦ for an overflow on addition, and in ⑧ for leading zeros in subtraction. The special case of a computed zero which cannot be normalized must be detected and a special exponent is forced in ⑨. This gives us $m + g$ bits, which must be reduced to m bits, and rounding can cause overflow at this point. Hence, we must again test for overflow and renormalize, if necessary.

In ⑦, ⑧, and ⑫ the exponent arithmetic may cause exponent overflow or underflow, and this requires some kind of special treatment. We will discuss the details of this later, but for the moment we insert ⑬ and ⑭ to clean up such cases.

We next give an algorithm for normalized floating-point multiplication corresponding to Eq. 10. As with addition, we are presenting only the idea of the algorithm here; hardware implementation will be discussed later. The following discussion is a guide to the algorithm of Fig. 3.5.

We can form the product of man_A and man_B at the same time we add the exponents, ① and ②. If one of the arguments was zero, the result is zero, and in ④ we set the result exponent to the zero value. Since both arguments are normalized, at most one leading zero may be generated, and in ⑤ we normalize the mantissa and decrement the exponent. At most, $2m$ digits of product may be generated, which we must reduce to m digits in ⑥, and this may cause mantissa overflow so that renormalization may be necessary in ⑧.

In ②, ⑤, and ⑧ the exponent arithmetic may cause exponent overflow or underflow and this requires some kind of special treatment which we will discuss below. We summarize this in ⑨ and ⑩.

At several points in the discussion of floating-point addition and multiplication we saw that "special" values may be generated. For example, the mantissa may be zero during addition so the result cannot be properly normalized. Or the exponent may overflow or underflow during addition or multiplication, in which case the result is not properly representable in the machine; that is, a machine infinity or infinitesimal has been reached because the exponent is too large or too small, respectively. In division, we may divide a representable number by zero (computing an infinity) or we may divide zero by zero leading to an indeterminate value.

In ⑥ and ⑬ of Fig. 3.4 and in ③ and ⑨ of Fig. 3.5, these special values are assumed to be tested. Depending on what machine values are chosen to represent these special cases, we may also have to make such tests before

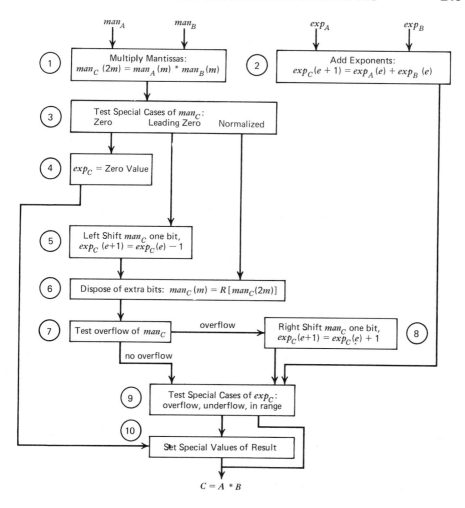

FIGURE 3.5   **Floating-point multiplication.**

carrying out the first step in order to guarantee, for example, that infinity plus a representable number leads to infinity and not some spurious representable number. Typically, special exponent and/or tag bit values denote special floating-point values.

As an example of this technique, consider Table 3.4, which shows the use of special operands in the CDC 6600; the table is, of course, symmetric. Addition of two standard numbers leads to a standard number, ± 0 or $\pm\infty$. A computed zero corresponds to exponent underflow, so we are very close to zero—approaching either from above or below. A computed infinity corresponds to exponent overflow because the number is too large to represent. Adding $+\infty$ to $-\infty$ (and various multiplications and divisions) leads to the indeterminate IND,

TABLE 3.4   Results from Special Operand Addition

Operands	Standard	·+∞	−∞	IND
Standard	Standard ±0 or ±∞	+∞	−∞	IND
+∞	+∞	+∞	IND	IND
−∞	−∞	IND	−∞	IND
IND*	IND	IND	IND	IND

* IND equals positive or negative indeterminate.

which when combined with anything else yields IND. For further discussion, see [Thor70, Chapter 5] or [Buch62, Chapter 8].

It is important to allow users the option of being informed that they have computed such extremal values, but it may not be necessary to abort their computations. By using special words as above, the computation may continue with special flags attached to the output of such values. The details of whether or not a job is to be aborted thus depend on the machine organization, the available software, and the details of a user's job.

The algorithms of this section hold true for normalized mantissas and are typical of machines with fractional mantissas. Machines with integer mantissas (e.g., CDC and Burroughs) often leave numbers unnormalized for ease of conversion between integers and floating-point numbers. A normalize instruction is usually available on such machines, however, and can be compiled together with each arithmetic operation to maintain full machine precision for all results. The algorithms of this section assume that the latter technique is used. For a general discussion of a number system for use with both fixed- and floating-point arithmetic as in the Burroughs B5000 and Bendix G-20, see [Keir75].

3.4 SOME PRACTICAL DESIGN TRADEOFFS

3.4.1 Introduction

Machine designers must choose values for several parameters in the design of a floating-point arithmetic unit. These include the word size w, a partition of the word into exponent and mantissa, the floating-point base r_b, and a method for handling computed digits which exceed the total number allowed by the word size. These choices are interdependent in ways that are not immediately obvious. In what follows, we will discuss how they are related to each other and in some cases how to make a good choice.

The designer's choice must be based on broad considerations that fall into two categories: machine and numerical considerations. By machine considerations we mean that speed and cost are important, and by numerical considerations we mean that the best arithmetic unit produces numbers that are the closest approximations to exact results.

At the beginning of a machine design effort, a word length w must be chosen. This choice is reflected throughout the entire machine and many costs are directly related to it—in I/O equipment, in main memory, and in the arithmetic unit. Usually the choice is based on the anticipated costs and what the competition offers. Clearly, designers want w as small as possible to get an inexpensive, fast machine. Earlier we gave some common values used in real machines, but in this section we will regard w as fixed, assuming someone else has chosen it for us.

To make some of the other choices, we must consider certain numerical properties of computer arithmetic. To introduce the detailed discussions of the following sections, we now present some philosophical background.

When computer users present numbers to a machine they must be aware of two facts. First, regardless of the number of digits of accuracy in their data, they must limit themselves to the precision of the computer immediately upon entering the data. Thus, some digits may be lost upon data input. Second, the best possible results they can get from the machine are full machine precision, but usually they will incur errors that lead to results with less accuracy than the full machine precision. These errors result from the fact that intermediate arithmetic steps generate words that are longer than the memory word and, as we saw earlier, some method must be used to dispose of the extra digits.

Users can avoid the first limitation (machine precision) by using double precision (or higher precision) representation for their data. All machines provide hardware or software to allow operations on double words, although these may be much slower than single precision calculations. This is a reasonable use of double precision, and through it users can also avoid the second problem (accuracy loss). But users who must do this regularly are in a poor situation because twice as much memory and substantially more computation time are needed.

Thus, a well-designed machine should have a word length long enough to satisfy most users, with reasonable double precision capabilities for users with extraordinary data. It should also have a high-quality arithmetic unit which preserves the accuracy of the user's data as much as possible.

In analyzing the quality of arithmetic units, we will have to make some assumptions. Throughout the following discussion it will be assumed that at each step of a computation—for each arithmetic operation—the arguments being used are exact. For input data, as we pointed out above, the user must regard the numbers as exactly representable using the machine precision. Intermediate data must similarly be regarded as exact even though we know that imprecise steps have been taken previously. During addition, when the smaller number has been aligned and is added to assumed low-order zeros in the larger number, for example, we regard these low-order zeros as exact. This assumption allows us to define local error measures, which can be extended in global terms.

Unless a user's computation is very simple, the easiest way for him or her to discover how much error the single precision results contain is to rerun the computation in double precision and compare the results. Of course, the results may vary from one input data set to another, so it may seem that all computations should be run in double precision! Realistically, although most computations cannot be given sharp analytical error bounds, the users know enough about the characteristics of their computations and arithmetic unit to trust single precision results.

This assumes that the arithmetic unit has been designed to yield high-quality results, although we mentioned that a machine's word length is often chosen on rather arbitrary cost and competitive grounds. In what follows, we shall assume that the word size w is fixed. This reduces our open decisions to the three remaining questions mentioned earlier: exponent (or mantissa) size, floating-point base r_b, and a method to dispose of extra computed digits.

The following sections will deal with these questions. First, we will consider the handling of extra computed digits; roundoff schemes and guard digits will be discussed. Following that we will consider tradeoffs between r_b and the partitioning of words into exponent and mantissa. We conclude with some experimental results about shift distances in practice.

3.4.2 Disposal of mantissa underflow digits

At several points in previous sections, we had to dispose of extra low-order digits. We are obviously interested in a scheme that is fast and inexpensive to implement in hardware, but which produces results of numerically high quality. In this section we will present and analyze several alternatives. Generally, all of them will be called *roundoff schemes* with rounding, truncation, and so on, being special cases.

Although this discussion may appear to be a scrutiny of minutiae, two points should clarify its importance. When IBM originally released the System/360, arithmetic results were simply truncated. Since most users had come from IBM 7094s which had 36-bit words with binary exponents, the 32-bit word with hexadecimal exponents was greatly suspect. User complaints forced IBM to add an extra (so-called guard) digit to the arithmetic unit in order to improve arithmetic quality, although truncation was retained.

The second point is a key one in computer arithmetic. To analyze the results of numerically delicate computations, numerical analysts need a scheme that is good (we will discuss quality later); simple to analyze; and (very importantly) is used consistently in all numerical operations. A glaring example of a violation of the latter point is the CDC 6600; the rounding scheme used in multiplication [Thor70] behaves differently according to the form of the product! The 6600 achieved great success in spite of this because it had a relatively big mantissa.

Five different roundoff schemes will be discussed for the disposal of mantissa underflow digits. They can be used at the end of any arithmetic operation, or during the course of any operation where underflow bits are produced, for example, after the alignment shift in addition. In the following, assume we have a mantissa of m digits together with d extra digits to be disposed of; d can be restricted to g guard digits, which will be explained in Section 3.4.3. The result is m digits which are used in succeeding calculations to represent the original $m + d$ digits.

1. Truncation

This is sometimes called *chopping* and is simply the removal of the d digits to be disposed of, with no change in the m digits. Notice that the error introduced by truncation can be almost as large as one in the last retained digit of the mantissa. For example, 7.999 truncates to 7. This is a fast method requiring no extra hardware, but has several unfortunate properties, including the error that it introduces. It is plotted in Fig. 3.6a, where we can see that the function Trunc (x) lies entirely below the ideal[4] line, touching it at the representable numbers. The heavy dots in Fig. 3.6 represent closed intervals, that is, the value of the function at the breakpoints. In Figs. 3.6a and 3.6b we show a sample set of data values that illustrate how the methods work; however, the

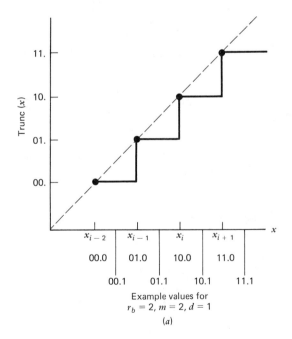

Example values for
$r_b = 2, m = 2, d = 1$

(a)

FIGURE 3.6   **Underflow digit disposal methods.**

[4] In Fig. 3.6 the broken line represents the infinite precision ideal line.

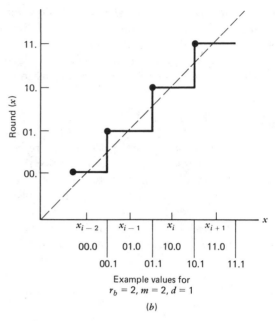

Example values for
$r_b = 2, m = 2, d = 1$

(b)

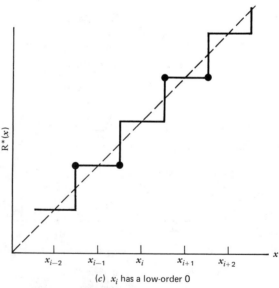

(c) x_i has a low-order 0

FIGURE 3.6   (*Continued*)

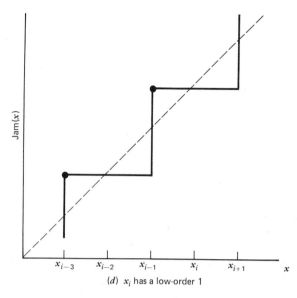

(d) x_i has a low-order 1

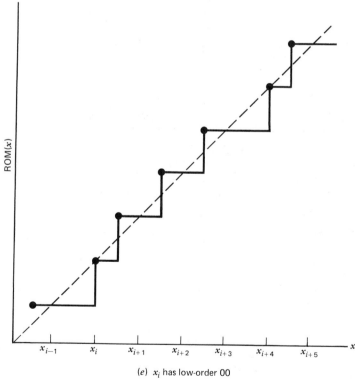

(e) x_i has low-order 00

FIGURE 3.6   (*Continued*)

plots hold in general. The IBM 360 and 370 use truncation; and the CDC 6600 uses it for certain products, whereas it rounds others.

2. Rounding

Whatever the radix, we add an amount to the $m + d$ digits equal to $\frac{1}{2}$ in the last of the m digits, and retain the resulting m digits. The sign of the amount added is the same as the sign of the number being rounded here and in subsequent schemes. For example, $7.99 + 0.5 = 8.49$ so we retain 8, whereas $7.49 + 0.5 = 7.99$ so we retain 7. The maximum error is incurred with a case such as $7.5 + 0.5 = 8$, and is equal to $\frac{1}{2}$ in the last retained digit of the mantissa. Most real machines use either truncation or rounding, or some combination of them.

As can be seen in the plot of Fig. 3.6b, Round (x) is nearly symmetric with respect to the ideal line—a substantial improvement over truncation. However, the dots above the ideal line indicate that at the points exactly half-way between the x_i values, we always round up. Thus over a long sequence of operations we would expect a slight positive bias because all of these dots are above the ideal line. Consider the table of Fig. 3.7, where we show the last digit of m and $d = 2$. By summing the errors in all possible cases (r^d in general, 4 here) we obtain the *total bias*. For any d, there will be a symmetric pairing of positive and negative biases, with the $10 \cdots 0$ case in the center. Thus we obtain a total bias of $\frac{1}{2}$ in the last retained digit of m. The following is one way to eliminate this bias.

3. R*-rounding

This is an unbiased rounding scheme. It operates like rounding except when the d digits have the form $r/2 \ 0 \cdots 0$. No known machine uses this scheme, but it is the best possible with respect to bias.

As indicated in Fig. 3.6c, alternate representable floating-point numbers are forced to lie on intervals that are closed at both ends. Thus the "exactly one-half" values are treated in a symmetric way. Half the dots are above the ideal line, and half are below.

Number presented			Rounded result	Error	
Weights 1	1/2	1/4	1		
X	0	0	X	0	
X	0	1	X	$-1/4$	bias = 1/2
X	1	0	$X + 1$	$1 - 1/2 = 1/2$	
X	1	1	$X + 1$	$1 - 3/4 = 1/4$	

Last retained digit

FIGURE 3.7   **Total bias in rounding.**

In binary arithmetic, the $10 \cdots 0$ case is detected and a 1 is forced into the last retained digit of m. Because this case accounted for all of the bias in Fig. 3.7, we need only study it to see that the bias is removed by this procedure. If the low-order bit of m is a 1, we are simply truncating $\frac{1}{2}$, so this case is biased by $-\frac{1}{2}$. If the low-order bit of m is a 0, we are adding 1 and dropping $\frac{1}{2}$, so this case is biased by $+\frac{1}{2}$. The sum of these two cases is zero, so the R^* scheme has a total bias of zero.

In general, rounding requires one pass through an adder because the carry may propagate across the entire number to be rounded. The R^* scheme requires this plus the detection of all zeros in the $d-1$ digits. The following scheme is much faster than rounding, but has the same total bias.

4. Jamming

This is sometimes called *von Neumann rounding* after its inventor. In binary arithmetic it is performed by truncating the d bits and forcing the low-order bit of the mantissa to be a 1. A simple analysis shows that this method has the same total bias as rounding, but requires no more time than truncation. Note that its maximum error is slightly worse than truncation, since the binary number with $f = 2$, $10.0 \cdots 0$, is rendered as 11. Thus an error of 1 is introduced in the last place of m. Notice also that if the rounded (or R^*) numbers are regarded as "correct" m-digit approximations of the $m + d$-digit arguments, then jamming produces about one-half "wrong" numbers, since it forces *all* low-order bits to one. As we can see in Fig. 3.6d, jamming has the same kind of symmetry as rounding, but the steps are twice as wide.

The following scheme combines some of the best features of the above; it makes an interesting use of ROMs to avoid the carry-propagation time of standard rounding.

5. ROM-rounding

This scheme [KuPS77] can be implemented using a read-only memory (ROM) or combinational logic. An l bit ROM scheme uses the $l-1$ low-order bits of m, together with the high-order bit of d as an l bit address in a 2^l word ROM, which returns a properly rounded $l-1$ bit result, except when the $l-1$ low-order bits of m are all 1's. In this case, the ROM returns all 1's, since a time-consuming full addition would be required for a correct answer. If $l = 8$, say, a ROM lookup can be very fast, and yet we are properly rounding 255 out of the 256 cases, since $2^8 = 256$.

Figure 3.6e illustrates ROM-rounding using $l = 3$, that is, an eight word ROM. In the interval between x_i and x_{i+1}, rounding is carried out in the standard way. Similarly, for the next two intervals between x_{i+1} and x_{i+3}. The fourth interval, between x_{i+3} and x_{i+4}, corresponds to the case where the low-order bit of the mantissa and the high-order bit to be disposed of are both ones. Here the ROM scheme truncates. Clearly, the scheme is periodic and we can see that the x_{i-1} to x_i interval is also handled by truncation. The reason we can achieve zero bias here is that the positive bias created by the dots above the ideal line in the rounded cases can be offset by some negative bias in the single truncated case.

In what follows, we will refer to truncation and jamming as *truncation methods*, to R*-, ROM-, and standard rounding as *rounding methods*, and to all of them as *roundoff methods*.

3.4.3 Guard digits

Although we have glossed over the point thus far, it is quite important to consider the length of words handled *inside* an arithmetic unit. When two m-bit mantissas are added, if one is shifted for alignment and we are rounding (not truncating), at least the last bit shifted out must be held for rounding. In subtraction, borrows may occur through a sequence of assumed low-order minuend zeros to the right of the m known bits. In multiplication, a $2m$ bit product always results from the multiplication of two m-bit mantissas.

Assuming the arithmetic unit is to produce single precision results, what is the smallest number of extra bits that we need? The following discussion will answer this question. These extra bits that exist only inside the arithmetic unit are called *guard digits*.

In normalized floating-point multiplication, two m-digit mantissas can produce one leading zero and this requires a postnormalization left shift by one digit. If truncation is to be used to obtain an m-digit product, we must develop an $m+1$ digit result for postnormalization. And if rounding is to be used, we must develop $m+2$ digits—one for postnormalization and one for rounding (plus another bit for R*-rounding; see R*-rounding below).

Thus we would expect rather poor results from a machine that multiplied using no guard digits, better results from a machine that uses truncation and one guard digit, and still better results using rounding and two guard digits. Clearly, truncation would not be improved by using more than one guard digit, nor would rounding improve by the use of more than two.

Normalized floating-point addition is somewhat trickier than multiplication. If all the terms to be summed are positive, then all postnormalization shifts are to the right, so guard digits are of no value in truncation and just one guard digit is of value in rounding (plus another bit for R*-rounding; see below).

If the terms in the sum are of mixed signs (+ and −), then more guard digits may be of use. One guard digit may be of use for postnormalization as in multiplication. This can be seen from the following argument. In forming $A - B$, assume that $B \le A$—if this is not so, we can carry out the argument for $(B - A)$—the subtrahend B is aligned by a right shift of $q \ge 0$ digits. If $q = 0$, we may have cancellation of a number of digits and require a left shift to normalize the result, but since $q = 0$ no alignment shift occurs, so guard digits would be of no help. If $q = 1$, a similar statement may be made, so one guard digit is useful. If $q \ge 2$, the subtrahend shift could be helped by guard digits, but in this case, due to borrows, the result can have at most one leading zero digit (remember that the minuend A was normalized). Thus, just as in multiplication, we could use one guard digit to hold the digit that may be returned when normalizing the result. In addition to the above role for one guard digit, another one could be useful for rounding the result—again, just as in multiplication.

There is a third use for guard digits in mixed sign summation roundoff schemes. Notice that a minuend of the form $10 \cdots 0$ could have a very small number subtracted from it and this would lead to a very long sequence of borrows. Thus the binary subtraction with $m = 4$ and $g = 6$

$$
\begin{array}{c}
\leftarrow m \rightarrow \quad\quad \leftarrow g \rightarrow \\
\begin{array}{|cccc|cccccc|c}
1\ 0\ 0\ 0 & 0\ 0\ 0\ 0\ 0\ 0 & A \\
& 0\ 0\ 0\ 0\ 0\ 1 & -B \\
\hline
0\ 1\ 1\ 1 & 1\ 1\ 1\ 1\ 1\ 1 & C
\end{array}
\end{array}
$$

makes good use of all six guard digits. Clearly, any number of guard digits—within the range necessary for representable numbers—could be used. However, we can limit the number of guard digits by a careful analysis of the borrow process.

Consider the case of binary subtraction. Note that any sequence of borrows propagates from right to left across a sequence of zeros in the minuend until a one appears in the minuend, at which point the borrow sequence stops. The difference bits generated in this process are a one at the right end and then a sequence of ones and zeros which are the complements of the corresponding bits in the subtrahend. This can be seen easily by adding the difference and subtrahend to reproduce the minuend. Since the g low-order bits of the minuend are always zero—by definition—we can limit the number of guard digits g to just 3 by using a special trick in the third digit.

We will define the low-order or third guard digit to be a *sticky bit* with the property that if a 1 is ever shifted into it during an alignment, it is set to one, otherwise it remains a zero. In renormalizing, we shift at most one digit to the left so that the second digit takes part in rounding and the third is not used—except in the case of R*-rounding, where it can be used to test if all shifted-through digits have been zero. (The sticky bit is similarly useful for R*-rounding in multiplication.) Furthermore, by the discussion of the above paragraph, the sticky bit will generate any borrow sequences to its left just as they would have been generated if there were more guard digits. Recall that in the binary case these would be just the complement of the subtrahend bits in the first and second guard bits since the minuend has all zeros in these positions.

We have carried out this discussion with binary number examples, but by a similar argument it can be shown that two guard digits and a sticky bit are sufficient in any radix. In general, the sticky bit is set to one if a nonzero value is shifted into it. Thus we conclude that for addition, subtraction, or multiplication, just two guard digits and a sticky bit are sufficient to generate single precision normalized results, even in the case of R*-rounding.

The role of guard digits in arithmetic operations should be clear from the above. For a machine with an m-bit mantissa, only m bits may be stored in main memory and the machine's programmable registers usually hold just m mantissa bits. In other words, the guard digits exist only inside the arithmetic unit. It would be useful, in some operations, to retain guard digits throughout the CPU, dropping them only when numbers must be stored in memory. This would require longer registers and wider data paths in the processor but could lead to better numerical results without resorting to full double precision operations.

3.4.4 Tradeoff between r_b and e

In Section 3.2.4, we presented two complete normalized floating-point systems: one binary and the other quaternary. Using a fixed number of bits for exponent (e) and mantissa (m), we saw that a much larger range was possible using quaternary numbers, but the binary numbers were more densely distributed. We further discussed this in Section 3.2.5.

In Section 3.2.4, we observed that normalized quaternary numbers can have leading zero bits in their machine representations, and this is true, of course, for any $r_b > 2$. In Table 3.5, we show the fraction and exponent parts of the binary and hexadecimal representations of several numbers. The hexadecimal numbers may have three leading zeros. This means that with a fixed size mantissa of m bits, if we represent numbers with $r_b = 2$, three more bits of accuracy may be achieved than with an $r_b = 16$ representation.

On the other hand, not as many exponent bits e are required with higher r_b representations. In Table 3.5, with $r_b = 2$ we need $e = 3$, whereas with $r_b = 16$ we have $e = 1$. This is obviously a manifestation of the much wider range of hexadecimal numbers noted in Section 3.2.4.

TABLE 3.5   Binary Versus Hexadecimal Representations

Number	$r_b = 2$		$r_b = 16$	
	fr	exp	fr	exp
$\frac{1}{16}$	0.1	−011	0.0001	0
$\frac{1}{8}$	0.1	−010	0.0010	0
$\frac{1}{4}$	0.1	−001	0.0100	0
$\frac{1}{2}$	0.1	000	0.1000	0
1	0.1	001	0.0001	1
2	0.1	010	0.0010	1
4	0.1	011	0.0100	1

Hence, we are confronted with a tradeoff—for a fixed word size, we let $n = e + m$—between a choice for e (or m) and r_b. In order to make a decision, we must choose criteria on which to base it. Obviously, one criterion should reflect the range of the numbers representable. We will use exponent range—defined for $r_b = 2^k$ as $k(r_e^e - 1)$ (see Eq. 5)—because this reflects the range of representable numbers.

To reflect the accuracy of the representations, we will discuss worst case criteria, although average criteria could also be used. If $r_b = 2^k$, then accuracy suffers in a monotonic way as a function of k, since only $m - k + 1$ bits are used in the worst case.[5] Hence, we seek an accuracy measure that reflects this.

If we write $R(x)$ to denote any machine representation of x (obtained using any of the roundoff methods mentioned earlier), then the quantity $|R(x) - x|$ is called the *absolute representation error* in $R(x)$. It is sometimes more meaningful and convenient to deal with the normalized quantity

$$\delta(x) = \frac{R(x) - x}{x} \tag{12}$$

called the *relative representation error* in $R(x)$. Thus, we have

$$R(x) = x(1 + \delta(x)), \tag{13}$$

and to measure the accuracy of machine representation we are interested in an upper bound on δ. The smallest $\varepsilon \geq |\delta(x)|$ for all x in the representable range is called the *maximum relative representation error* (MRRE) in the machine representation of x. It can be shown [BrRi69] that

$$\text{MRRE} = \frac{1}{1 + 2/r_v^{k-m}}. \tag{14}$$

Now let us assume that $m \geq k$ so at least one digit of accuracy is available with base $r_b = r_v^k$ representation. The $\text{NFL}_1 = \text{NFL}(r_v, r_v^k, m, n - m)$ numbers (recall Section 3.2.4) have the same MRRE as the $\text{NFL}_2 = \text{NFL}(r_v, r_v, m - k + 1, n - (m - k + 1))$ numbers because $r_v^{k-m} = r_v^{1-(m-k+1)}$, so Eq. 14 gives the same MRRE value for both systems. Now for these two systems with equal MRRE, let us consider their respective exponent ranges. Following the definition in Eq. 5, since $r_e = r_v$ in both cases, we have the ratio

$$\frac{\text{exponent range } [\text{NFL}_2]}{\text{exponent range } [\text{NFL}_1]} = \frac{r_v^{(n-m+k-1)} - 1}{k(r_v^{n-m} - 1)} = \frac{r_v^{k-1}}{k} \frac{(r_v^{n-m} - r_v^{1-k})}{(r_v^{n-m} - 1)},$$

and since $r_v^{1-k} < 1 \leq k$, we have

$$\frac{\text{exponent range } [\text{NFL}_2]}{\text{exponent range } [\text{NFL}_1]} > \frac{r_v^{k-1}}{k} \geq 1.$$

---

[5] Note that in some programing languages, for example, PL/I, $m - k + 1$ is *defined* as the precision of a floating-point word, in order to yield conservative results.

Note that if $k = r_v = 2$, then the exponent ranges are almost equal; otherwise the binary numbers ($r_b = 2$) have a bigger exponent range for a fixed MRRE. Thus, we conclude that with respect to MRRE and exponent range, $r_b = r_v = 2$ is best.

3.4.5 Addition shift distances in practice

Now we consider the loss of accuracy due to shifting for alignment and normalization in addition. Specifically, we discuss hexadecimal and binary numbers and observe that less shifting occurs in hexadecimal. Hence, fewer bits are lost due to shifting in hexadecimal; furthermore, the hardware can be simpler because shifts are in increments of four bits rather than one bit as for binary. D. W. Sweeney [Swee65] has analyzed floating-point addition in a number of scientific codes. By tracing about 10 million instruction executions, he observed that an overall average of about 10 percent of the instructions executed were floating-point additions. We reproduce only a few of his findings. In particular, we are interested in preaddition alignment shifts and postaddition normalization shifts. The values in Table 3.6 represent the number of shifts of a particular distance expressed as a percentage of all cases measured. The numbers added were not necessarily of like sign and a few unnormalized operations were included.

One of the most important conclusions we can draw from this data is that most pairs of arguments to be added have exponent values which are quite close to one another. Notice that in more than two-thirds of the cases, alignment shifts of 4 bits or less were required. In one-third of the $r_b = 2$ cases, the exponents were identical.

As expected, we observe more zero shift cases with higher r_b. In fact, normalization shifts for hexadecimal numbers only occur about 18 percent of the time. Comparing the sum of the alignment shifts from 0 to 4 for binary and from 0 to 1 for hexadecimal slightly favors hexadecimal. Of course, the binary shifts occur in increments of only one bit of precision loss. Similar sums for normalization are almost equal.

TABLE 3.6   Addition Shift Distances

	Shift Distance (Binary Digits)	Percent Shifts	Shift Distance (Hexadecimal Digits)	Percent Shifts
Alignment	0	32.64%	0	47.32%
	1–4	34.61%	1	26.02%
Normalization	Overflow	19.65%	Overflow	5.5%
	0	59.38%	0	82.35%
	1–4	14.51%	1	7.24%

The original data shows that the sum of alignment percentages for distance 0 and 1 with base 2 is slightly less than the percentage of distance 0 shifts for base 16. Similarly, the sum of the distance 0 and 1 normalization shift percentages in binary is slightly more than the distance 0 shifts for base 16. The fact that less shifting and simpler shifting hardware would be needed led IBM to use $r_b = 16$ in the IBM 360 [Swee65, AmBB64].

3.4.6 Other experimental and theoretical studies

Ultimately, the quality of machine arithmetic is seen in the output numbers from real computations. Despite many theoretical studies, most of which prove inequalities or derive bounds on error measures, experimental study of roundoff errors gives sharper and more realistic estimates of a computer arithmetic unit's performance. We will cite several papers here that contain both theoretical and experimental results. These papers generally agree that R*-rounding using binary (or in some cases quaternary) numbers provides superior performance. Also, for normalized binary arithmetic, keeping the leading 1 implicit (as in the PDP-11) is recommended for high accuracy.

Three such studies: [Cody73], [Bren73b], and [MaMa73], together with a number of other interesting arithmetic papers may be found in a special issue of the IEEE Transactions on Computers [IEEE73]. In [KuCo73] and [MaMa73] the error growth in sequences of arithmetic operations is studied for various rounding modes, bases, and numbers of operations. Chain sums, differences, and products are used to show the effects of each operation, and some mixed sets of operations are performed. Somewhat more realistically [Bren73b] carries out similar studies using "real algorithms" for solving systems of linear equations and for computing the eigenvalues of symmetric matrices. A theoretical and experimental study of guard digits and roundoff errors is presented in [KaLi73]. Theoretical analysis of floating-point arithmetic is further complicated by the fact that in reality, numbers are not uniformly distributed but, instead, are logarithmically distributed. The relation of this fact to roundoff and shifting has been considered in [Tsao74] and [Fiel69].

3.5 ARITHMETIC AND LOGIC UNIT ORGANIZATION

We can characterize the overall organization of any floating-point arithmetic and logic unit with the diagram of Fig. 3.8. Operands and results are held in a set of registers which are connected to memory. They may be addressable by the programmer, or they may have dedicated, wired-in roles which the programmer can only control implicitly (e.g., stack or accumulator). Most arithmetic units have some of each type of register. The combinational logic functions built into processors depend, of course, on the instruction set the designer wishes to implement.

One class of instructions provided in most machines performs bit level logical operations on whole words. These include AND, OR, NOT, and so on,

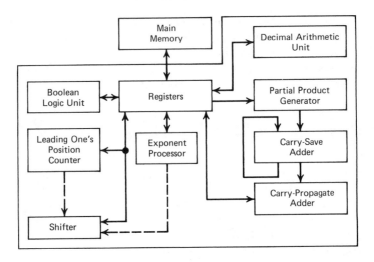

FIGURE 3.8 Arithmetic and logic unit organization.

operating on full words. The number of gates required is $O(n)$ for n-bit words and the time delay is a constant independent of n (as discussed in Section 2.1.1). For these operations we show a Boolean logic unit in Fig. 3.8.

For floating-point arithmetic we must provide various exponent operations, as discussed earlier in this chapter. The exponent processor needs an adder for integers of exponent length, but its total logic and time delay are small relative to other processor components because of the relative size of the exponent to the mantissa (recall Table 3.1).

For logical shifts of various kinds we provide a shifter. This can be used to pack and unpack bytes in a word, to rearrange bits in words, and so on. It is also necessary in floating-point addition to align the arguments and in all operations to normalize the result (see Section 3.3.6). In these roles we control the shifter using the exponent processor and leading one's position unit, respectively. We will discuss the gate count and time delay of these units in Section 3.5.1 and Section 3.5.2, respectively.

For floating-point addition and subtraction we provide a carry-propagate adder. We discussed the component count and delay of such a unit in Section 2.3.7.3. It was pointed out there that a circuit to generate only the sum and carry digits for the input digits in each position is called a half adder, whereas a circuit that handles carry inputs as well is called a full adder. There are many ways to combine these to add two complete numbers, and in Section 2.3.7.3 we discussed a fast, *bit parallel* binary addition algorithm that uses $O(n \log n)$ gates and is similar to those commonly used in most computers. At the other extreme, a *bit serial* full adder may be used which forms just one sum and carry bit at a time and requires $O(n)$ steps.

It is true that by using *signed digit arithmetic* [Aviž61], only $O(n)$ gates are needed to add two numbers in a constant (independent of n) number of gate delays. Briefly, this scheme stores both the sum and carry bits, and when adding two numbers, propagates the carries just one position. Only when numbers are to be output are carries propagated across the entire word. Although this is attractive, signed digit arithmetic is more troublesome for other arithmetic operations so we will not pursue it further here. However, in the course of performing binary multiplication in Section 3.5.3, we will discuss the use of carry-save adders that are an implementation of this idea. Signed digit systems are sometimes called *redundant* number systems.

It should be observed that Winograd has shown [Wino65] that a lower bound on the time to add two n-bit numbers is $\lceil \log 2n \rceil$ assuming gates with fan-in of 2 and ignoring fan-out. He also demonstrated a scheme that approaches this time, but that uses *residue* numbers [SzTa67] and, hence, does not allow overflow detection. He uses a very general definition of number representations but specifically rules out signed digit representations for the above-mentioned reason. In [Wino67], he further shows that overflow detection requires as much time as addition. The upper bound of Theorem 2.8, $T_G \leq \frac{1}{2}(5 + \log_f n) \log n + 4$, is thus seen to be fairly tight even though it follows from a general recurrence result. In fact, Brent [Bren70] showed a scheme for binary number addition whose time is very close to the lower bound.

A number of schemes have been proposed and implemented for machine multiplication. Most practical schemes can be characterized as in the diagram of Fig. 3.8. We will provide a further explanation of the partial product generator and carry-save adders in Section 3.5.3. These, together with the carry-propagate adder, are used in multiplication. In Section 3.5.4 we discuss several approaches to division that may use just the logic of Fig. 3.8 or may include extra division logic.

We continue to use w to denote a machine's word size, and for the various component boxes of Fig. 3.8 we will discuss operations on n bits, which may represent w or the mantissa size m.

3.5.1 Barrel shifter

An arithmetic unit needs hardware for shifting words left and right as we have seen in the addition and multiplication algorithms of Figs. 3.4 and 3.5, respectively. These shifts are uniform in that all bits move the same distance. We dealt with m-digit mantissas and assumed that some registers were larger than that; the register that holds the product of two m-digit mantissas must be $2m$ digits long, for example. But when digits are shifted off the end of such registers, they are assumed to be lost. Also, when bits are shifted away from one end of a register, it is assumed that zeros are shifted in to replace the shifted bits.

In most computers there are also requirements for circular shifts in which bits that leave one end of a register enter the other end in a circular manner.

For packing and unpacking characters from words, such facilities are quite useful. Such shifts usually are provided to the left or to the right. In general, we will refer to shifters that provide uniform shifts left or right, end-off or end-around, or any subset of these, as *barrel shifters*. The analogy with a barrel in the end-around case is obvious.

To give an idea of the time and gates required to build uniform shift networks that can carry out such operations, we restrict our attention here to an end-off right shifter. This makes the discussion somewhat simpler than would be required for a shifter that would have to provide left and right, end-off, and circular shifts; however, the basic time and component count results are similar. For a more complete discussion and a survey of a number of other papers on this subject, see [Davi74b].

Suppose we have words of $n = 2^k$ bits. The network of Fig. 3.9 allows any

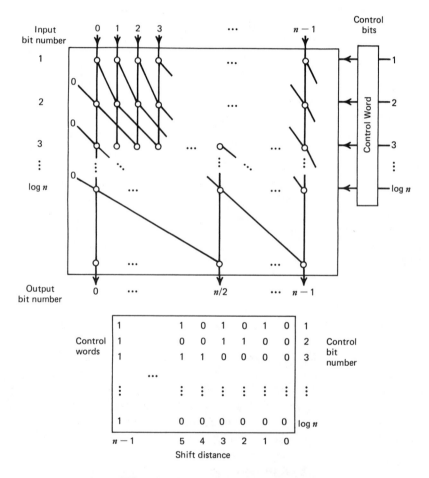

FIGURE 3.9 **Right end-off shifter.**

uniform end-off right shift to be carried out in $\log n$ stages with $O(n)$ gates at each stage. The input bits can, at the first stage, be shifted distance zero or one. At the second stage they can be shifted distance zero or two, and so on for increasing powers of 2 up to the $\log n$th stage where they may be shifted distance zero or $n/2$. The control words are applied to the lines shown at the right and all possible control words are shown below the network. Note that the control words (columns) can be read as binary numbers corresponding to shift distances. Here we have n demultiplexers (recall Section 2.2.3) combined in a single network.

Each circle in the network is set to a straight through connection if the control bit at that stage is zero. If the control bit is one, then all data is switched to the right at that stage. Thus a control word of all zeros sends data straight through the network, and so on for other control words, as described above. Each of the circles can be implemented with one OR gate and two AND gates with fan-in and fan-out of two. Two gate delays per stage are sufficient. The nodes at the left must be designed to shift in zeros, as shown. But the entire process requires at most $2 \log n$ gate delays and $3 n \log n$ gates, excluding input and output registers and also ignoring a register for the control word and the fan-out of the control bits to each node at each stage. Notice that the number of gates in a shifter is of the same order of magnitude as the number of gates in a binary adder.

The control word of the barrel shifter is a binary number equal to the desired shift distance. How do shift distances arise in arithmetic units? For a logical shift instruction, the shift distance is contained in the instruction itself. In addition, such requirements arise in several ways (recall Fig. 3.4). For mantissa alignment, we obtain a shift distance by subtracting exponents. On the other hand, after a mantissa subtraction the normalization left shift distance is determined by counting the leading zeros in the result. The latter problem is a nontrivial one to solve. It arises here and in other logic design contexts, so we will give it further attention below.

3.5.2 Ones' position counting

We will define and discuss ones' position counting, but zeros' position counting of the complemented word is obviously equivalent. The following definition holds for all positions in a word, although in some cases (e.g., normalization after subtraction) only the leading one's position is required. It is clear that counting from the left or from the right can be done in equivalent ways.

Definition 1

The *ones' position counting* of an n-bit word $a = a_n \cdots a_2 a_1$ is the generation of a count vector $z = (z_n, \ldots, z_1)$ such that z_i is the sum of the number of ones in bits $a_i \cdots a_1$. Thus, the ones' position count of $a = 10110110$ is the vector $z = (5, 4, 4, 3, 2, 2, 1, 0)$. ∎

Following Definition 1, we can easily generate the z vector using the following arithmetic $R\langle n, 1\rangle$ system (see Section 2.3):

$$z_0 = 0$$
$$z_i = a_i + z_{i-1}, \qquad 1 \le i \le n.$$

Thus by using $(1 + \log n)$-bit adders (see Theorem 2.8) as components we can solve the system in $O(\log n)$ adder steps (see Corollary 2.3), so

$$T_G = O(\log n) \cdot O(\log \log n) = O(\log n \cdot \log \log n).$$

Because each adder has $O(\log n \cdot \log \log n)$ gates, we have a total gate count of

$$G = O(n \log n) \cdot O(\log n \cdot \log \log n)$$
$$= O(n \log^2 n \cdot \log \log n).$$

By formulating this problem in terms of integrated circuit packages, it is shown in [ChKu77] that the total gate count can be reduced to $O(n \log n (\log \log n)^2)$ or even further, but the time remains as above.

We can try solving the problem using an array of half adders such that the half adder in position (i, j) is described by ($\oplus$ denotes exclusive-OR; recall Section 2.3.7.3):

$$z_{ij} = z_{i-1,j} \oplus c_{i,j-1} \qquad (15)$$
$$c_{ij} = z_{i-1,j} \cdot c_{i,j-1}, \qquad (16)$$

where

$$1 \le i \le n, \qquad 1 \le j \le \log n, \qquad c_{i,0} = a_i, \quad \text{and} \quad z_{0,j} = 0.$$

Here, z_{ij} is the jth bit of z_i. However, this bit level formulation is a nonlinear recurrence and cannot be solved by the methods of Chapter 2. It will be interesting to refer to this recurrence in discussing multiplication later. For more details about this subject, see [ChKu77].

We conclude that a ones' position counter can be implemented using somewhat more components and time than are required for addition. This circuit can be used to generate the leading one's position count for the control of a barrel shifter in postsubtraction normalization. Of course, it does more than is required for that job, and simpler circuits can be designed if that is all that we require.

3.5.3 Binary multiplication

Now we consider the multiplication of two binary numbers. We will give several schemes based on the results of Chapter 2.

Definition 2

By the *multiplication* of two n-digit binary numbers $a = a_n \cdots a_1$ and $b = b_n \cdots b_1$, we mean the generation of $2n$ product digits $p = p_{2n} \cdots p_1$. ∎

multiplicand $a =$ ⠀⠀⠀ 1 0 1 1
⠀multiplier $b =$ ⠀⠀⠀ 1 0 0 1
⠀⠀⠀⠀⠀⠀⠀⠀⠀⠀⠀⠀ 1 0 1 1
partial
product ⠀⠀⠀⠀⠀⠀ 0 0 0 0
bits ⠀⠀⠀⠀ 0 0 0 0
⠀⠀⠀⠀ 1 0 1 1

⠀⠀product $p = 0\ 1\ 1\ 0\ 0\ 0\ 1\ 1$ ⠀⠀ **FIGURE 3.10** ⠀⠀ **Binary multiplication example.**

Machine multiplication schemes usually begin with a step that is quite similar to pencil and paper multiplication by forming an array of *partial product digits*. In Fig. 3.10, we show a simple example. Note that the partial product bits can be formed in parallel at the beginning of the process, or a few may be formed as needed, but they can be generated easily from the input data. This process requires up to $O(n^2)$ gates, depending on how many bits are formed at once.

The time- and gate-consuming part of multiplication arises in forming the sums of these rows of partial product bits. A straightforward way of doing this would be to make $n - 1$ passes through an adder, since there are n numbers to be summed. However, a number of better schemes are available, which are much faster and not much more expensive.

In an attempt to design a fast multiplier, we can study the problem as a bit level recurrence as we did in the case of addition. Several bit level recurrence formulations are possible, but they all share the nonlinear property of the following.

First, consider the partial product bits of Fig. 3.10 as a two-dimensional array of elements r_{ij}, with rows i and columns j, beginning in the upper-right corner, where $1 \le i \le n$ and $1 \le j \le 2n - 1$. Thus the first column has just one element r_{11}, the second column has two elements r_{12} and r_{22}, and so on. We can formulate a multiplication algorithm in terms of a two-dimensional array of full adders, each of which has three bits as inputs and produces a sum and a carry as outputs. In Fig. 3.11, we show the adder at position (i, j), A_{ij}, which adds carry $c_{i-1,j-1}$, sum $q_{i-1,j}$ and partial product bit r_{ij}. The adder implements

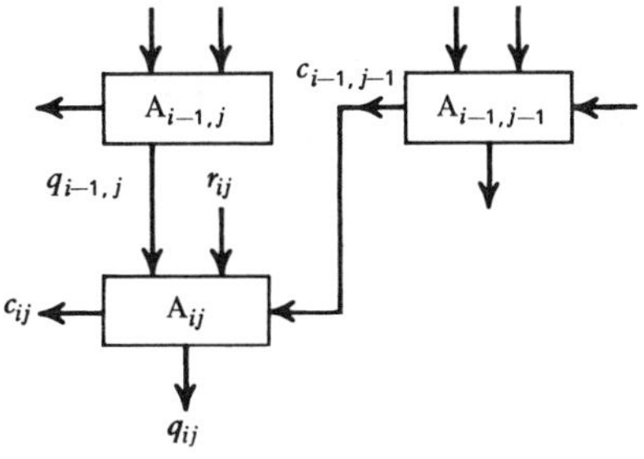

Outputs		Inputs		
c_{ij}	q_{ij}	$q_{i-1,j}$	r_{ij}	$c_{i-1,j-1}$
0	0	0	0	0
0	1	0	0	1
0	1	0	1	0
1	0	0	1	1
0	1	1	0	0
1	0	1	0	1
1	0	1	1	0
1	1	1	1	1

FIGURE 3.11 ⠀⠀ **Adder array detail.**

the truth table shown in Fig. 3.11 and we can express this logical function by the pair of coupled recurrences in Eqs. 17 and 18. The r_{ij} may be regarded as known constants here, so the $q_{i-1,j} \cdot c_{i-1,j-1}$ term causes this system to be a nonlinear recurrence.

$$q_{ij} = r_{ij} \oplus q_{i-1,j} \oplus c_{i-1,j-1} \tag{17}$$

$$c_{ij} = r_{ij} \cdot q_{i-1,j} + r_{ij} \cdot c_{i-1,j-1} + q_{i-1,j} \cdot c_{i-1,j-1}. \tag{18}$$

Note that these equations correspond to Eqs. 2.8 and 2.9 of Section 2.3.7.3, but that system for addition was linear because there was only a recurrence in one dimension, the carry direction. This nonlinear recurrence system is a generalization of Eqs. 15 and 16 for the ones' position counter and cannot be solved by the methods of Chapter 2; however, we can solve it directly using an array of n^2 bit level adders, as shown in Fig. 3.11. This gives a circuit that can multiply two n-bit numbers in $T_G = O(n)$ with $G = O(n^2)$. Since we are interested in faster schemes, we now consider two methods to solve the recurrence of Eqs. 17 and 18 in parallel.

Full adder tree

The first method uses a tree of $2n$-bit adders. First, we form a standard array of partial products. Then we use the adder tree to form the sum, padding each row of partial products with zeros to form $2n$-bit inputs as shown in Fig. 3.12. This method is summarized in the following theorem. After presenting the theorem we will discuss an improvement on this method which avoids dealing with the redundant zeros that we introduce here merely to simplify the following discussion (as in Chapter 2 we assume gates with fan-in 2 and fan-out f).

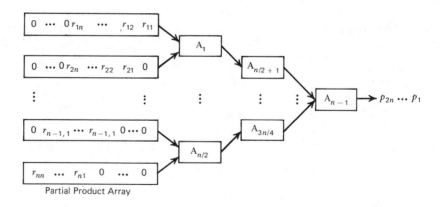

FIGURE 3.12   **Multiplication adder tree with redundant zeros.**

Theorem 1

Two $n = 2^t$, $t \geq 0$, digit binary numbers can be multiplied in

$$T_G \leq \tfrac{1}{2}(6 + \log_f n) \log^2 n + \tfrac{1}{2}(14 + \log_f n) \log n + \log_f n + 1$$

with

$$G < \left(3 + \frac{2}{f-1}\right) n^2 \log n + \left(20 + \frac{2}{f-1}\right) n^2 - 3n \log n - \left(17 - \frac{2}{f-1}\right) n.$$

Proof

Our proof consists of two parts: (1) To generate the n^2 partial product bits $r_{ij} = a_i \cdot b_j$, for all $1 \leq i, j \leq n$, we need n^2 gates and one gate delay. Since each input bit must be fanned out to n places we have from the above and Lemma 2.2,

$$T_{G1} \leq 1 + \log_f n$$

with

$$G1 \leq n^2 + 2n\left(\frac{n-1}{f-1}\right) < n^2\left(1 + \frac{2}{f-1}\right).$$

(2) To generate the sum of the partial products we need an adder tree of $n - 1$ adders. Each adder adds $2n$-bit numbers and the height of the tree is $\log n$ adder delays. Thus, by Theorem 2.8, we have

$$T_{G2} \leq \log n \cdot [\tfrac{1}{2}(5 + \log_f 2n) \log 2n + 4]$$
$$= \tfrac{1}{2}(6 + \log_f n) \log^2 n + \tfrac{1}{2}(14 + \log_f n) \log n$$

with

$$G_2 = (n-1)\left[\left(\frac{3}{2} + \frac{1}{f-1}\right) 2n \log 2n + \left(8 - \frac{1}{f-1}\right) 2n + \frac{2}{f-1} \log 2n + 2\right]$$
$$< \left(3 + \frac{2}{f-1}\right) n^2 \log n + 19n^2 - 3n \log n - \left(17 - \frac{2}{f-1}\right) n. \qquad \blacksquare$$

As an example of this theorem, consider the following multiplier which might be contained in a single integrated circuit package.

Example 5

Using gates with fan-out 8, a multiplier of two 4-bit numbers can be implemented with a delay of

$$T_G \leq \tfrac{1}{2}(6) \log^2 4 + \tfrac{1}{2}(14) \log 4 + 1 = 27$$

using

$$G \leq (3 + \tfrac{2}{7}) 4^2 \log 4 + (20 + \tfrac{2}{7}) 4^2 - 3 \cdot 4 \cdot \log 4 - (17 - \tfrac{2}{7}) 4 < 341. \qquad \blacksquare$$

The above result is somewhat sloppy because we considered all inputs to the tree adder to be $2n$-bit numbers. In fact, the inputs to the first level of adders

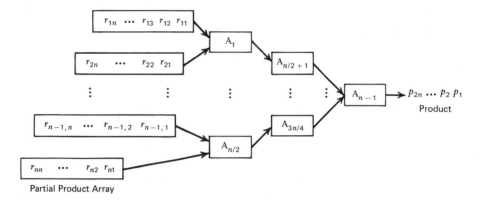

Partial Product Array

FIGURE 3.13 **Multiplication adder tree.**

are only n-bit numbers, as shown in Fig. 3.13. At succeeding levels they are of length $n+2$, $n+5$, ..., $n+i+2^{i-1}-2$, for $1 \leq i \leq \log n$. By a careful analysis, which takes this increasing length into account, we can improve the gate count in Theorem 1 by a factor between 2 and 3. Thus, in our example the gate count could actually be bounded by a number between 115 and 170.

The method above is the best uniform method known (in terms of time) for numbers with few digits. For long numbers, the carry-save adder approach is the best uniform method. The crossover between the two occurs at around 8 bits. Methods using combinations of these methods (nonuniform methods) may achieve better results.

Column compression

The previous scheme dealt with the partial product array by rows. It can also be dealt with by columns or by combinations of rows and columns in several different ways. We describe two such variations which we shall call *column compression* and *carry-save adder* schemes. Whereas the method of Theorem 1 carried out complete carry-lookahead additions on pairs of rows of partial products, the following schemes propagate the carry only a short distance at each step. This saves time and gates for large word sizes.

A simple column compression scheme is the following. Assume that a population counter is available that can count the number of 1's in an n-bit word, producing a $1+\log n$ bit result. If we use $2n-1$ such adders, one per column of the partial product array, we can produce a reduced partial product array of $2n-1$ numbers, each of $1+\log n$ bits, shown in Fig. 3.14a as the result of adder stage 1. By repeating this process, we can generate a second reduction to $2n-1$ words of $O(\log \log n)$ bits, and so on until we reach words of just two bits. We show these as the final reduction in Fig. 3.14a. Now a carry-propagate adder can be used to reduce these to the resulting product of

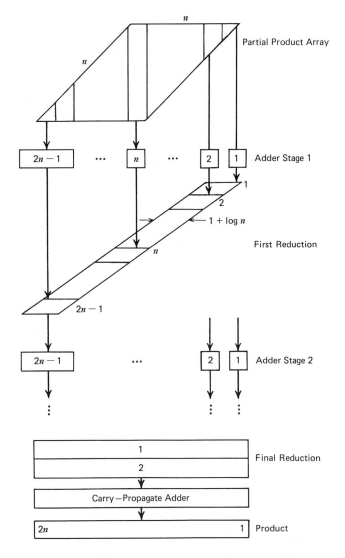

FIGURE 3.14a   **Column compression multiplier.**

$2n$ bits. Figure 3.14b illustrates the column compression method using the example of Fig. 3.10.

Column compression may be regarded as a special case of carry-save addition in which whole single columns are processed. Column compression is faster than the method of Theorem 1, but slower than the next method we will give. But this method is an interesting intermediate approach. Note that what we are really doing here is generating a sequence of reduced partial product arrays,

```
                                           1  0  1  1
        Partial product                 0  0  0  0
            bits                      0  0  0  0
                                   1  0  1  1
                                   ─────────────────
                                              0  0  1
                                           0  0  1
                                        0  0  0
        First reduction              0  1  0
                                  0  0  1
                               0  0  0
                            0  0  1
                            ────────────────
                                              0  1
                                           0  1
                                        0  0
                                     0  0
        Second and final          1  0
            reduction           0  0
                             0  1
                          0  0
                       0  0
```

FIGURE 3.14b   **Column compression of Fig. 3.10 example.**

all of which are equivalent in the sense that if we added the columns and completely propagated the carry at any stage, we would get the correct result. But by propagating carries only a short distance per stage— $O(\log n)$ bits on stage 1, $O(\log \log n)$ bits on stage 2, and so on—we save time and gates over the method of Theorem 1, which propagated the carry across full words at each stage. Here a complete carry-propagate adder is used only at the final stage.

Carry-save adders

Now we have seen two methods, one that deals with the partial product array by rows, the other that deals with it by columns. Clearly, there are many other intermediate approaches. We can use a few rows and a few columns at a time in any way, as long as the resulting reduced arrays all share the property that the sum is correct if the carries are completely propagated; in other words, if the final answer is correct, any intermediate reduction is acceptable. This allows a great deal of flexibility and, in fact, leads us to reconsider the question of multiplication algorithms in terms of the available types of hardware. We have been counting gates and integrated circuit packages for combinational logic circuits to implement various processor functions. Here we are led to consider read-only memories as well.

To introduce the carry-save addition approach, we consider the use of read-only memories. Later we will give a speed and gate count theorem in terms of combinational logic; but, in fact, current technology trends make a combination of ROM and combinational logic a possible design option, and PLAs are even more attractive than ROMs. The simplest carry-save addition technique reduces three rows of the partial product array to two rows, the result being a set of sum bits and a set of carry bits. Clearly, at most two bits are needed to represent the sum and carry of three input bits. We will learn that this can be extended to other convenient reductions by similar methods.

We can use a ROM to carry out a 3 to 2 row reduction or carry-save addition as follows. Suppose we select a three row by four column rectangle from the partial product array as in Fig. 3.15. If we have a 4K word ROM, we can use the 12 bits as an address to look up the 8 bits of sum and carry. By covering the entire parallelogram with ROMs, we can reduce n rows to $2n/3$ rows in one memory cycle time. Hence, we can reduce the entire problem to two rows (which are handled by a carry-propagate adder) in $O(\log_{3/2} n)$ memory cycles.

Notice that repeated ROM lookups here are quite similar to the repeated column compression reductions of Fig. 3.14. But, instead of generating intermediate words of $O(\log n)$, $O(\log \log n)$, and so on, bits as in Fig. 3.14, we now generate only two bits at a time since our "columns" are only three bits high here. The above discussion illustrates the effect of traditional carry-save adders; in fact, however, a ROM would be more effectively used to produce a single word with the carry propagated on each reduction step.

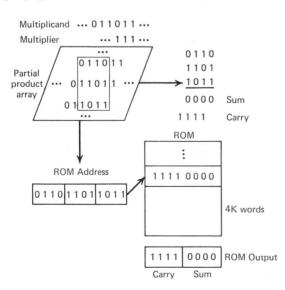

FIGURE 3.15   **ROM multiplication scheme.**

This scheme can be generalized to $(7, 3)$, $(15, 4)$ or any $(2^k - 1, k)$ row reduction. The idea is that the sum of the $2^k - 1$ input rows is equal to the sum of the k output rows and that carries have been generated in the k row form. The total time to reduce n rows to two rows is proportional to $\log_\alpha n$, where $\alpha = (2^k - 1)/k$, although the details vary with n and the type of reduction units available. For example, seven rows can be reduced to two in two such steps; the first using a $(7, 3)$ reduction, and the second a $(3, 2)$ reduction.

In order to give gate and time bounds comparable to Theorem 1, we now consider a combinational logic implementation of the three to two reduction carry-save adder. The following is a variation of the Wallace–Dadda method [Wall64], [Dadd65]. It consists of three stages: generation of partial products, carry-save addition, and carry-propagate addition. This differs from Wallace–Dadda only in the last stage, where their method used slow, ripple-carry adders. The generation of the partial product array is done in the same way as in Theorem 1. For an upper bound on time, we assume a three to two carry-save addition scheme [HaWi70]. The carry-save addition for two n-bit numbers can be done with $(n^2 - 4n + 3)$ full adders and $(n - 1)$ half adders. The half adder can be built using 9 gates (see Theorem 2.8 with $n = 1$). A full adder of 2 bits can easily be implemented with 11 gates by a scheme similar to Fig. 2.19. Thus, we have a total of

$$G2 \leq 11(n^2 - 4n + 3) + 9(n - 1) = 11n^2 - 35n + 24.$$

The time for the carry-save addition is

$$T_{G2} \leq 6 \log_{3/2} n = 10 \log n,$$

since each full adder requires at most 6 gate delays.

Finally, to propagate the carry, we use a $2n$-bit adder (fewer bits are actually needed) as we did in Theorem 1, so

$$T_{G3} \leq (\tfrac{5}{2} + \tfrac{1}{2} \log_f 2n) \log 2n + 4.$$

This leads us to (since $f \geq 2$):

Theorem 2

Two $n = 2^t$, $t \geq 0$, digit binary numbers can be multiplied in

$$T_G \leq (13 + \tfrac{1}{2} \log_f n) \log n + \tfrac{3}{2} \log_f n + 8$$

with

$$G \leq \left(12 + \frac{2}{f-1}\right) n^2 + \left(3 + \frac{2}{f-1}\right) n \log n - 16n + \frac{2}{f-1} \log n + \left(26 + \frac{2}{f-1}\right). \quad \blacksquare$$

Example 6

Using gates of fan-out 8, we can multiply two 32-bit numbers in

$$T_G \leq (13 + \tfrac{1}{2} \log_8 32) \log 32 + \tfrac{3}{2} \log_8 32 + 8 < 81$$

with

$$G \le (12 + \tfrac{2}{7})1024 + (3 + \tfrac{2}{7})32 \log 32 - 512 + \tfrac{2}{7} \log 32 + 26 + \tfrac{2}{7} < 12{,}624.$$

Although these numbers are sizable, they do illustrate that a full 32-bit multiplier is within the realm of possibility using such methods. In fact, most real multipliers operate iteratively on fewer bits per iteration. But gate counts of say, 5000, are often used in multipliers. It must also be remembered that all of our gate counts and delays include all AND, OR, and NOT gates. In practice, NOTs are often regarded as negligible with ECL logic since true and complemented outputs are available as outputs of each gate. Furthermore, relaxing our fan-in of two restrictions to a practically realistic 4 or 6 would further reduce these numbers.   ∎

A commonly used multiplication scheme may be illustrated in terms of Fig. 3.8. Suppose we have carry-save adder circuits which perform a three to two reduction. By cascading four stages of such adders (6 adders in all) in series, 8 bits can be reduced to 2 in one clock period. This assumes that in Fig. 3.8, 8 rows of the partial product were generated initially—say in one clock—and then on the second clock the carry-save adders reduce these to two rows. If six more partial product rows are generated during the second clock, on the third clock we can feed back the two rows produced by the carry-save adders and add them to the six new rows. Thus, by the end of three clocks we have reduced 14 rows to 2. On each subsequent clock, 6 new rows of the partial product are combined with the 2 rows produced previously by the carry-save adders. So after $k + 2$ clocks we can reduce $8 + 6k$ rows to 2, and on one final clock we can pass these two through the carry-propagate adder for our final result. Thus, $k + 3$ clocks are required to multiply two $8 + 6k$ bit numbers by this scheme, so in 10 clocks we can multiply two 50-bit numbers. Such performance is typical of traditional, high-speed multipliers. Of course, if a few more bits were handled per clock, the result could be produced in a few less clocks. The above scheme requires 6 carry-save adders and, in general, to handle r rows at a time we need $r - 2$ carry-save adders. We may refer to this multiplication scheme as an *iterative carry-save multiplier* and to the generalization above as a *combinational carry-save multiplier*.

3.5.4   Division and elementary function evaluation

Machine division will be treated more superficially than were addition and multiplication. Since division is used less frequently than the other operations (see Section 4.2.1), this seems reasonable. Two basically different approaches are used for division in computers and both will be sketched briefly.

The problem of division may be stated as follows: Given a dividend e and divisor s, compute a quotient q and remainder r such that

$$e = qs + r,$$

where

$$|r| < |s|.$$

In the following, e is defined to have $2n$ digits.

There are two classes of division methods that might be called *direct* and *iterative*, respectively. The direct methods require a time proportional to n and are usually implemented using some dedicated hardware in the processor. The iterative methods are generally used when a machine has a fast multiplication unit and are implemented using processor hardware that exists for other operations (e.g., the multiplier). Such methods can operate in $O(\log n)$ steps, where a step is measured in terms of machine multiplication time. If the multiplier is fast (say, one clock), then division by iterative methods may take $O(\log n)$ clocks, whereas direct methods may take $O(N)$ clocks.

Basically, *direct* methods operate in a manner similar to pencil and paper division, by repeatedly subtracting the divisor from the dividend. In each position, the quotient is increased by 1 for each successful subtraction. When a negative result is obtained in some position (a so-called *overdraw*), the divisor is added back to the dividend—a process called *restoring* the dividend—and the divisor is shifted with respect to the dividend. Then the subtraction cycle is again carried out.

The process is easier in binary than in higher radices, because the number of successful subtractions between shifts must be less than the radix. Thus, after a shift, if a subtraction is successful, the next subtraction is guaranteed not to be, so a shift can be made directly. On the other hand, if a subtraction fails, rather than restoring by adding the divisor and then subtracting one-half of the divisor (a shift and subtract), it is necessary only to add one-half of the divisor (shift and add) in that position. This procedure is called *nonrestoring* division and is somewhat faster than restoring division.

Faster direct division schemes can be implemented on normalized numbers by observing sequences of more than one bit of the dividend; for example, sequences of zeros may be skipped. More elaborate and higher-speed direct division schemes are widely used. For example, SRT division, independently discovered by Sweeney [MacS61], Robertson [Robe58], and Tocher [Toch58], is widely used. See [Atki68] for extensions of this and also [Buch62] for a general discussion of division.

Various *iterative* methods may be used to compute quotients. To simplify the problem, one can compute the reciprocal of the divisor and then form the product of this and the dividend. Thus, to evaluate e/s we shall compute $(1/s)e$. A simple, but effective iterative scheme is the well-known Newton-Raphson iteration

$$x_{i+1} = x_i - \frac{f(x_i)}{f'(x_i)},$$

which for a well-behaved function f and a sufficiently good initial value x_0, can be used to evaluate a root of $f(x) = 0$. Now if $f(x) = (1/x) - s$, the root corresponds to $x = 1/s$, the desired reciprocal. Since $f'(x) = -1/x^2$ the Newton-Raphson formula gives

$$x_{i+1} = x_i + x_i^2 \left(\frac{1}{x_i} - s \right)$$

$$= x_i(2 - s \cdot x_i).$$

By examination of a Taylor's series with remainder for $f(x)$, it is easy to see that this scheme converges quadratically (see, for example, [Kunz57]). Thus, if the error is 2^{-k} on step i, it is proportional to 2^{-2k} on step $i + 1$ so the number of correct bits approximately doubles on each iteration. This is the basis for the earlier remark that an n-bit quotient can be formed in $O(\log n)$ steps.

Using a ROM or combinational logic and the first few bits of the dividend and divisor, several correct bits of the quotient can be obtained immediately. Thus, if 4 bits are looked up, a 32-bit quotient can be computed in three iterations. For more details about various iterative division schemes, see [Kris70] and [Flyn70].

It is interesting to note that iterative schemes were used on the earliest computers to avoid the necessity for special division hardware ([WiWG51], [Rich55]), and they are now used for high-speed division because of the availability of very fast multiplication algorithms.

Throughout the history of computers, the evaluation of functions more complicated than arithmetic has been an interesting question (recall Babbage's table lookups). Some early electronic computers had special square root instructions, for example. The tradeoff between hardware and software schemes for evaluating elementary functions has shifted back and forth over the years. The CORDIC algorithm of Volder [Vold59] has been used in hand calculators [Walt71]. Other efficient schemes for elementary functions were developed by deLugish [deLu70] and are extended in [Erce73] and [Bake75]. A recent survey of arithmetic may be found in [Garn76].

3.5.5 Real computer processors

It is rather difficult to determine how many gates there are in various parts of real computers; such numbers are rarely published. Usually the numbers are known only to those who designed the several parts of the machine. Furthermore, the numbers usually were given in terms of transistors (or tubes) in early machines and are now specified in terms of integrated circuit packages. And, of course, from one circuit family to another there are varying conversion factors to count the number of transistors per gate. Gate fan-in and fan-out limitations alone can make a big difference in such counts.

As we pointed out earlier, IC package counts are presently a more realistic measure, and we used the term *components* to refer to whatever package types designers are using at the moment. Machine designers are usually quite willing to use component counts as a rough measure of their designs. The cost is proportional to the number of components as are the physical size, heat dissipation, power requirements, and so on. And, of course, within one technology, comparing the component counts of two different designs is more realistic than comparisons across technologies. So at any fixed time, component count is a reasonable measure for comparing the quality of various designs, assuming, of course, that the speeds are also known.

To relate our abstract discussion of gate bounds to reality, we will consider two real processors. We will give rough estimates of the gates in the IBM 7030 (STRETCH) and the Burroughs ILLIAC IV. These processors form an interesting comparison in that STRETCH was an early transistor design, intended to be very fast. And ILLIAC IV was an early integrated circuit design, also intended to be very fast, but designed about ten years after STRETCH.

We will discuss these gate estimates in terms of Fig. 3.8; we will refer to the boxes of Fig. 3.8 as components (not to be confused with gates). Ignoring the exponent processor and decimal arithmetic unit, we have two classes of components. The $O(w)$ gate components are the registers, Boolean logic unit, partial product generators, and carry-save adders. The carry-propagate adder, leading one's position counter, and shifter have $O(w \log w)$ gates. To make a rough estimate of the overall number of gates in any standard processor, let us assume coefficients of 4 for the components with $O(w)$ gates and 3 for the components with $O(w \log w)$ gates, on the average,[6] and assume $w = 64$. Assume the processor has a total of six registers (this was typical of machines in the era of STRETCH and ILLIAC IV). If the multiplier handles eight rows at a time, we need eight partial product generators and six carry-save adders (as we saw at the end of the last section, this leads to performances similar to STRETCH and ILLIAC IV).

The gate count for the $O(w)$ components (in the above order) is

$$(6 + 1 + 8 + 6)4 \cdot 64 = 5376$$

and for the $O(w \log w)$ components (three components mentioned above) is

$$3 \cdot 3 \cdot 64 \cdot 6 = 3456$$

for a total of 8832.

In fact, the gate counts for one ILLIAC IV processing element [Davi69] and for the arithmetic and logic unit of STRETCH [Buch62] are tabulated in Table 3.7. Both machines had 48-bit floating-point mantissas. These are approximate numbers but we can make several interesting observations about them.

First, observe that less than two-thirds of the gates are in combinational logic which is "useful" in transforming data; the other 30 to 40 percent are in registers and various control functions. Furthermore, many gates are included

---

[6] Registers typically have 2 to 4 gates per bit in the form of flip-flops, and Boolean operators require only a few gates per bit. Recall from Section 2.3.7.3 that an adder has a coefficient of less than 2. Shifters and leading one's detectors will be considered in exercises.

TABLE 3.7. Real Processor Gate Counts

	STRETCH	ILLIAC IV PE
Registers	3,500 (16%)	1,500 (16%)
Logic and Arithmetic	14,000 (65%)	5,300 (57%)
Control and Interconnection	4,000 (19%)	2,500 (27%)
Total Gates	21,500	9,300

in these counts for fan-in and fan-out alone. If these gates are separated from the "useful" combinational gates, we would probably have at least one-half of the gates in "overhead"—registers, fan-in, fan-out, and control—and less than one-half performing "useful" operations such as arithmetic, logic, shifts, and so on.

The comment that the gates used in registers in a processor are "overhead" is, of course, a very narrow view. Sometimes a few registers can lead to substantial differences in the overall speed of the system, since fewer main memory accesses are needed. Furthermore, programming a machine with more registers is often much easier, allowing programmers to concentrate on more important issues than puzzles surrounding register allocation. In the next section we will also discuss the role of registers in multifunction processors; there the use of more registers also speeds up processing. It should also be noted that having more registers generally shortens programs, since fewer address bits are required for registers than memory. This assumes that several instruction formats are available, which is often the case as we shall see in Section 4.3.3.

Fig. 3.16 shows some details of a small part of a processor and its connection to main memory. In Section 1.1.2, we sketched a random access memory with its memory address register (MAR) and memory information register (MIR); more details will be presented in Chapter 5. The main memory and the processor's addressable registers shown in Fig. 3.16 are both such random access memories. A carry-propagate adder is shown with connections to and from various other points in the system. The connections are similar to those shown in Fig. 3.8; here we show an additional connection from the carry-propagate adder to the barrel shifter that could be used to expedite postaddition normalizations, for example. The OR and DEMUX boxes of Fig. 3.16 are OR trees and demultiplexers, respectively. The demultiplexer (see Section 2.2.3) is used for fanning-out and selecting one destination. The OR tree is used to fan-in signals and because we assume just one input is active, multiplexer control (see Section 2.2.3) is not required. A processor bus is shown for interconnecting various processor components (for more details see Chapter 6). The control and interconnection entry in Table 3.7 includes the OR (or multiplexer), DEMUX, and bus gates, as well as other gates used in

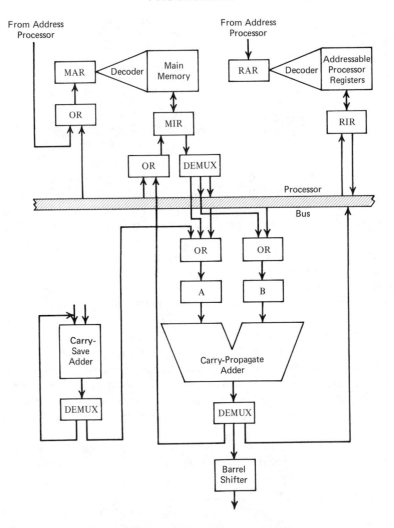

FIGURE 3.16   **Details of part of processor.**

controlling the processor. We will elaborate some details of the control process in Chapter 4 (see Section 4.2.2).

The details of the interconnections provided are, of course, intimately tied to the type of instruction set provided. In Fig. 3.16, for example, it is possible to transmit data simultaneously from the MIR and RIR to registers A and B. Thus one instruction can set up an addition of a memory location and a register location. To add two numbers stored in registers, two complete sequences of register fetch and bus transmission would be required before the addition commences.

Traditional arithmetic and logic units had one or two programmer address-able registers and several other registers used in the course of carrying out arithmetic operations. In the early 1960s, it became clear that more registers would be useful. Compilers, which were popularized by FORTRAN in the late 1950s, often needed more temporary storage than assembly language program-mers used for the storage of intermediate results. Because it is faster to access operands held in registers than those in the main memory, arrays of scratchpad registers began to appear in the mid-1960s, for example, in the Burroughs D825 [Gluc65], CDC 6600, and IBM 360. Now 8 or 16 programmer or compiler addressable registers are commonly used. Even larger sets of fast registers, called cache memories, are also common in fast computers, and we will consider these in our discussion of memory in Chapter 5. Sometimes the processor's registers are organized as a push-down stack and we shall discuss this in Section 4.3.5.

Clock speed

An important design question in laying out combinational logic is how often should we break the logic with a register? This is the same as asking what the clock speed should be. Slow clocks generally imply slow machines, whereas fast clocks imply intricate and occasionally treacherous timing problems. The clock cycle must be set to match the longest delay through combinational logic, conductors, and so on, between any two registers in the system.

Thus in Fig. 3.16, several times would have to be considered. One is the time from the A and B registers, through the CPA and out to some other register; the MIR, the RIR, A, B, or some other register not shown. Another is the time to decode an RAR address, select a register, and gate its contents to the RIR. Others are the times to gate the RIR or MIR to register A or B. Generally, the dominating time is one that involves a good deal of combinational logic, for example, through the CPA here. But physically long paths can also be quite time-consuming, since electrical signals propagate at less than 1 foot per nanosecond. Thus if the main memory were some distance from the processor, transmissions between the two could be slow. In fact, another register might be placed at the output of the adder for use in transmissions to main memory if the path from registers A and B, through the CPA and out to the MIR, were too great. It should be clear that many tradeoffs are involved in laying out a processor and in choosing a clock speed. The memory cycle time is usually a small multiple of the processor clock period, although the memory could be clocked separately.

Observing a number of real machine designs, one concludes that typically from 10 to 20 gate delays are used between pairs of registers. Thus, if one uses circuits with gate delays of 3 ns, 15 gates in series will cause 45 ns of delay. The 3 ns gate delay time may be "nominal"; that is, the switching time of the gate may be 1.5 ns, but due to the average fan-out load, a slowdown of a factor of 2 may be expected. In fact, for any real circuit family, a formula is provided for computing such delays, based on the switching time plus the number of other gates driven by this one; that is, the fan-out used for this gate. Another factor of 1.5 to perhaps 2 must be included for the cable and printed circuit board delays, because signal propagation times are greater than 1 ns per ft of conductor. Thus for our example, we may have to multiply the 45 ns by another factor of 2 to account for delays in conductors. Hence, a processor that contains a maximum of 15 gates in series may require a clock of 100 ns, even though the unloaded gate delay is just 1.5 ns. A factor of 4 may thus be consumed in the realities of laying out real circuits. As faster logic is used, this factor may grow even larger, since the pin, board, and cable delays are a fixed, increasing percentage of the overall time as circuit speeds increase.

3.6 FASTER PROCESSING VIA MULTIOPERATION PROCESSORS

By introducing simultaneous execution, it is possible to design processors that can operate faster than the standard ones of Section 3.5. In Section 1.2.1, we introduced a number of fast processor ideas that are expanded in this section; specifically, multifunction, pipeline, parallel, and multiprocessing are discussed.

In Chapter 1, we introduced the multifunction processor and showed how a processor with an independent adder and multiplier could speed up inner product calculation by a factor of 2. To take advantage of a multifunction processor, obviously we need programs with some potential parallelism between operations. There are four ways that such parallelism could be detected and specified: namely, by

1. The programmer
2. The compiler
3. The control unit
4. The processor

Regardless of how it is detected, we assume that parallelism can be exploited by the machine, but the methods of detection and exploitation are not independent.

If the programmer detects it, he or she must have a language available in which it can be indicated that certain operations may be executed in parallel. Such statements were discussed in Chapter 2. Otherwise, the compiler could be used to detect and compile the operations for parallel execution from ordinary serial languages. Such algorithms were also discussed in Chapter 2. In either of these cases, the control unit must be able to sequence several operations at once, and such operations must be specially denoted for parallel execution in the compiled code. If neither the programmer nor the compiler detects the parallelism, we could place the responsibility on the control unit. It would have to accept ordinary compiled code and then at execution time look ahead trying to detect simultaneously executable instructions. We will return to this subject in Chapter 4 when we consider control units in general. Finally, if we leave the job to the processor, we assume that the control unit issues ordinary instructions, but that somehow the multiple functional units themselves decide when to begin operating in parallel on various operands. It is this topic, together with some ideas about the control unit's detection of parallelism, that we will discuss first.

Of course, it seems obvious that there are relative advantages and disadvantages to each of the above-mentioned parallelism detection methods. In the long run, probably some balance should be struck between the four methods. For example, programmer detection of certain kinds of parallelism may be the easiest way, and languages with array operations may be preferred by many users. In some cases, complex program transformations are required, as we learned in Chapter 2. These would be difficult and annoying for the programmer to make and are too complex to be carried out by any reasonable hardware at run time. Other transformations at low levels are simple. Using control unit or processor hardware to detect these at run time may be better than forcing the compiler to consider them and then cluttering the compiled code with statements indicating such parallelism. The tradeoff between the control unit and processor handling such detection should be better understood after consideration of the example below.

3.6.1 Multifunction processors

When we discussed the multifunction processor evaluation of an inner product in Chapter 1, we did not explain how the parallelism was detected nor did we give any details of how the machine operated. Here we will concentrate on the multifunction processor, ignoring the memory and control unit as much as possible. Let us assume that the source code of Fig. 3.17a has been compiled as shown in Fig. 3.17b. We assume that the T_i are temporary register assignments made by the compiler here. Further, assume we have a processor with independent adder and multiplier function units, each of which requires 2 clocks to perform one operation. We will assume the memory and control unit are fast enough to keep ahead of the processor. Thus, the 8 operations of this example would require a total of 16 clocks for their completion on a serial machine. Since there are 5 additions and 3 multiplications, ideally we should be able to complete the program in max $(6, 10) = 10$ clocks, using a processor with an independent adder and multiplier.

In Fig. 3.17c, we see that this is possible, assuming that the instructions are always available and are dispatched at the right moment. Under the assumptions that the memory and control unit are fast enough, the instruction and data flow rates can be maintained, but we must still consider the problems involved in determining at what time to execute each instruction. The control unit can be assumed to have a queue of instructions waiting to be executed, and to be constantly looking at all of them to determine which is next.

For example, if we now consider a processor with two adders and one multiplier, even more speed can be achieved, but the control problem becomes

$A \leftarrow (B+C)*(D+E)$
$F \leftarrow G+H+I+J$
$H \leftarrow K*L*M$

(a)

1 $T_1 \leftarrow B+C$
2 $T_2 \leftarrow D+E$
3 $A \leftarrow T_1*T_2$
4 $T_3 \leftarrow G+H$
5 $T_4 \leftarrow I+J$
6 $F \leftarrow T_3+T_4$
7 $T_5 \leftarrow K*L$
8 $H \leftarrow T_5*M$

(b)

Clock	1	2	3	4	5	6	7	8	9	10
Adder	B+C	B+C	D+E	D+E	G+H	G+H	I+J	I+J	T_3+T_4	T_3+T_4
Multiplier					T_1*T_2	T_1*T_2	K*L	K*L	T_5*M	T_5*M

(c)

Clock	1	2	3	4	5	6
Adder 1	B+C	B+C	G+H	G+H	T_3+T_4	T_3+T_4
Adder 2	D+E	D+E	I+J	I+J		
Multiplier	K*L	K*L	T_1*T_2	T_1*T_2	T_5*M	T_5*M

(d)

FIGURE 3.17 Multifunction processor computation. (*a*) Source program. (*b*) Compiled code. (*c*) One adder processor. (*d*) Two adder processor.

more difficult. Note that in Fig. 3.17d, by looking ahead to instruction 7, we can begin the multiplication K * L at the same time we begin instructions 1 and 2. This leads to a speedup of 10/6 over the scheme of Fig. 3.17c at the cost of one more adder.

Note that by using the tree-height reduction methods of Chapter 2, we could execute this program segment in a minimum of 4 clocks, that is, two operation times. To realize this, a speedup of 10/4 over the scheme of Fig. 3.17c, we would need a processor with four independent adders and two multipliers—a substantial increase over the one adder and one multiplier used to implement the scheme of Fig. 3.17c. If the costs of the adder and multiplier were equal, then the relative efficiency (T_i is the time required using i functions)

$$\frac{T_2}{3 \cdot T_6} = \frac{10}{3 \cdot 4} = \frac{5}{6}$$

would be quite good. Here, the 3 in the denominator represents the ratio of the number of function units used in the two methods.

But now we can see some of the complexity in making the tradeoff between detecting parallelism at compile time, or at run time in the control unit or in the processor. For example, $B + C$ is assigned to T_1 and $K * L$ is assigned to T_5 in our example. If a compiler had assigned both to T_1, then at run time we would have been blocked from executing these operations at once. On the other hand, if we attempt to make register assignments at run time in the control unit to avoid such compiler decisions and thereby simplify the compiler, the task can become very complicated. A nice hardware solution is to delegate this to the processor, using queues in front of each function unit and a bus interconnecting function unit outputs and inputs as well as a set of backup registers. Then, the data can flow in a "natural" way, with register assignments being made dynamically. We illustrate such a scheme below.

Figure 3.18 shows some details of a processor containing two adders and one multiplier, each of which has a data queue of length four. The control unit can assign instructions to the function units by placing tags in these queues. The tags are identifiers that represent variable and constant names while these variables and constants are in the processor; they need only a few bits, since there are few of them altogether. Figure 3.18 shows the situation that might occur if a lookahead control unit were to handle the compiled code of Fig. 3.17b. Here the instructions have been assigned to function units by placing tags corresponding to variable and temporary names (a represents A, b represents B, etc.) in the data queues of the function units. The control unit should attempt to put simultaneously executable additions in distinct function units, but otherwise no special care must be taken in making these assignments. A lookahead control unit can thus dispatch instructions to queues sequentially and without much testing (see Section 4.2.3.4 for lookahead control units).

Now as data is fetched from memory, identifier tags are attached in the tag assignment unit according to the coding scheme used by the control unit to denote variable names by tags in the data queues. Thus, when variable B is fetched, it is assigned a tag which we denote by b here. The variable is put on the bus together with its tag, which is then compared with all input tags in the data queues.

Input tags are shown in the two left positions and *output tags* in the rightmost position of each data queue entry. Thus, variable value B is sent to the position marked by tag b in the data queue of adder 1. At this point, the tag can be replaced by the data word and a presence bit set for B. If C is fetched next, it replaces c in the data queue of adder 1. If C is not fetched next, the following action is deferred until C is fetched.

When the presence bits of any two input words in any data queue are set, the operands are sent into the corresponding function unit. In our example, B and C are added and the result is placed on the bus, together with tag t_1 obtained from the data queue. At this point, the positions of b, c, and t_1 in the data queue are cleared and made available for new inputs. The output T_1 is matched with input tags in all the data queues and here we find a match in the multiplier queue. Thus, the data item T_1 is placed in the multiplier queue and the

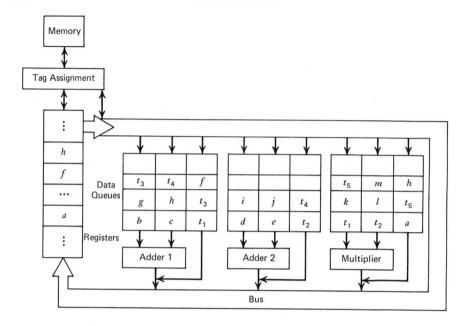

FIGURE 3.18 **Data queue multifunction processor.**

presence bit is set. If T_2 is already present, this would trigger the multiplication $T_1 * T_2$. If not, this multiplication begins at a later time, whenever T_2 arrives. When $T_1 * T_2$ is completed, the output tag a, which matches a register tag (these tags work just like those of the function units), causes the result to be placed in a register. It could also cause it to be placed in one or more function unit input queues if the result were used elsewhere. From the register, A can be stored back to memory.

Thus we see that the control unit is somewhat "detached" from the detailed control of the processor. The control unit assigns operations to function units and causes memory accesses, but otherwise the processor is autonomous. Data flows through the processor at its own speed, without involving the control unit. This type of scheme is used in the IBM 360/91 following a design of [Toma67] and is similar to, but more elaborate than the scheme used in the CDC 6600 (see Section 4.3.3). It is an elegant solution to handling problems of dependence, allowing them to be virtually ignored until the last instant. However, it would be rather expensive to implement for a large number of function units (see Chapter 6). The utility of the scheme is also limited by the number of independent operations found in ordinary programs. For array operations, simpler schemes that can be implemented in a compiler will be discussed next.

3.6.2 Pipeline processors

Multifunction processors are useful for the fast evaluation of one or a few arithmetic expressions in cases where just a few simultaneously executable operations may be found. But in many programs, array operations and recurrences lead to tens or hundreds of scalar operations which may be executed at once. For such computations, particularly those where the same arithmetic operation is to be applied to many data items (e.g., all the elements of an array), pipeline processors are very effective.

Any computational process that requires several clocks for its completion can be pipelined. As an example, consider floating-point addition, as illustrated in Fig. 3.4. Recall that a number of steps were performed in sequence—exponent comparison, exponent subtraction, fraction alignment, fraction addition, and so on. In a standard adder, one pair of numbers is introduced, and some number of clocks (perhaps 5 or 6) later the resulting sum is produced. Registers are used to hold intermediate results between clock periods.

A pipeline adder works just as the standard one did, except that now a new set of operands can be introduced on each clock. The intermediate registers are used to isolate one pipeline segment from the next. Thus, the first segment may do the exponent processing, the second segment fraction alignment, the third segment fraction addition, and so on. The net effect in terms of time for the first pair of operands is negligible. In probably the same number of clocks as used by a standard adder (or perhaps even more clocks due to additional register delays; see [HaF172] for a fast latch design), the first sum is produced in the pipeline adder. The second sum, however, is produced by the pipeline adder one clock after the first sum. And another sum can be produced at every subsequent clock period. Thus, if we have a long vector addition to perform, the pipeline adder produces results approximately at the clock rate; one result per clock period—after the first result appears—rather than one result per 5 or 6 clocks as in a standard adder.

In general, if a standard processor requires k clocks to carry out some process, as we saw in Section 1.2.1.5, the speedup for a k segment pipeline is (assuming the same total combinational logic and register delay in both cases)

$$S_k = \frac{T_1}{T_k} \leq \frac{kN}{k+N-1}. \tag{19}$$

If the arithmetic unit is applied to a vector of N independent pairs of operands (e.g., the example of Section 1.2.1.5), then the upper bound may be approached. For long vectors we can assume that $N \gg k$ and

$$S_k \rightarrow k, \quad \text{for} \quad N \gg k, \tag{20}$$

that is, the speedup approaches the pipeline length as would be expected.

What have we had to pay for this speedup? Although the processor has changed little—perhaps more registers are required—the control unit now must handle the sequencing of array operations. That is, each segment of the pipeline must be operated at each time step, operands must be kept flowing to the pipeline, and results must flow away at the proper rate. The control becomes more complex and the system becomes much faster, which also adds to the complexity of designing, building, and maintaining the system [Cott69].

In other cases, pipelining may lead to the introduction of substantially more combinational logic in the processor. Consider floating-point multiplication as illustrated in Fig. 3.5. Although the housekeeping chores here are somewhat easier than in floating-point addition, the fraction multiplication is usually the major time-consumer.

In Section 3.5.3, we described several multiplication methods and in Section 3.5.5 we discussed real gate counts. Fraction multiplication is usually carried out over several clock periods. For example, the carry-save adder scheme we described in Section 3.5.3 may be used to reduce 8 or 10 rows of the partial product array to 2 rows in one clock. Thus a 30- to 50-bit mantissa may require 4 to 6 clocks. Pipelining this multiplication requires building several carry-save adder segments; the combinational logic is replicated as many times

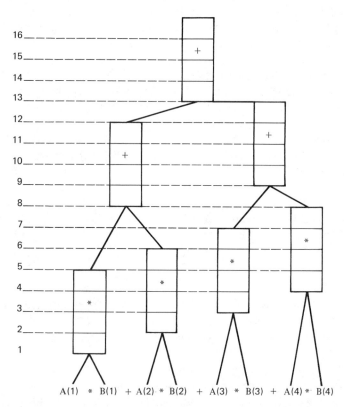

FIGURE 3.19   **Pipeline inner product (one adder and one multiplier).**

as the number of clocks required for the original multiplication. Thus, the first segment might reduce 10 rows to 2 on the first clock. On the second clock, the second segment accepts the 2 rows produced by the first segment together with 8 new rows of the partial product array. At the same time, the first segment accepts the first 10 rows of the partial product array of a new multiplication. If the original carry-save adder process required 5 clocks, then after passing through 5 pipeline segments, the multiplication of the first pair of operands has been completed, and the result is then passed to a carry-propagate adder, which forms a sixth pipeline segment.

We can summarize this process by recalling Fig. 1.14. In real pipeline processors, there may be [Step75] conditional jumps over certain segments. Thus, a pipelined arithmetic unit may contain 8 segments. Perhaps 2 of them are used for fixed-point addition, 4 of them are used for floating-point addition, and all 8 are used for floating-point multiplication. It should be clear that overall, a pipeline processor has more combinational logic than a non-pipelined one. Probably the biggest design problem is in the control logic found in the processor itself, and in the substantially increased complexity of the control unit.

Some real pipeline processors have built-in vector operations of various kinds. As a typical example, consider pipelining an inner product computation, as shown in Prog. 1. Recall that we began such a discussion in Section 1.2.1 for other machine organizations (Prog. 1 is the same as Prog. 1.3). Assume a processor with independent addition and multiplication pipelines, each of which has 4 segments.

Prog. 1

$$SIM[T(I) \leftarrow A(I) * B(I); \quad I \leftarrow I, \quad N]$$
$$TOT \leftarrow SUM[T(I); \quad I \leftarrow 1, \quad N]$$

Figure 3.19 shows a parse tree and timing diagram for the execution of this program with $N = 4$. After 4 clocks, the pipeline is full and $A(1) * B(1)$ emerges; after 7 clocks the products are complete. At this point we begin the reduction operation by starting the first addition. The three additions and the entire computation are complete after 16 clocks. If nonpipelined addition and multiplication each require 4 clocks, we have achieved a speedup of 7/4 here. Because we have effectively 4 simultaneously acting processors (the segments of one pipeline or the other), the efficiency is thus 7/16.

Note that if the adder and multiplier could be operated simultaneously, a slight improvement in speedup would be achieved since the sum of T_1 and T_2 could begin after 5 clocks, the sum of T_3 and T_4 after 7 clocks, and the final result would be finished after 15 clocks. Such an operation would lead to a good deal of extra control unit complexity, however.

In general, this computation requires $4 + N - 1 = N + 3$ steps for the multiplication. Assuming no overlap between the two operations, the addition tree can be executed as follows. If we break the N-element product vector in half, there are $N/2$ sums to perform on the first pass through the pipeline and this takes $4+[(N/2)-1]$ steps. At this point we may assume the resulting sum vector is in memory or registers. Now we break this vector in half and form $N/4$ sums on the second pass through the pipeline, and this takes $4+(N/4-1)$ steps. After $\log N$ such passes we have the resulting inner product. Note that the last sum of two numbers takes just 4 time steps. Thus, our total addition time is

$$T_4[\text{SUM}] = 4+(N/2-1)+4+(N/4-1)+ \cdots +4+(1-1)$$
$$= 3 \log N+(N/2+N/4+ \cdots +1)$$
$$\leq N+3 \log N.$$

So the combined inner product time is $T_4[\text{Prog. 1}] \leq 2N+3 \log N+3$.

If a comparable serial processor had been used, 4 time units per operation for $2N-1$ operations would yield $T_1 = 4(2N-1) = 8N-4$. Hence, we have achieved a speedup, using a 4 segment pipeline, of

$$S_4 \geq \frac{8N-4}{2N+3 \log N+3}.$$

Note that as N becomes very large, S_4 approaches 4, the theoretical maximum speedup. By operating in a more overlapped way, some of the early steps could have begun sooner, but this would not make a fundamental change in the speedup. It would simply allow the sum to approach its limit for smaller N. As we saw earlier, for $N=4$, $S_4 = 7/4$. Similarly, for $N=30$, $S_4 \approx 3$, so we observe that rather long vectors are required to approach the full potential of even a short pipeline processor for some algorithms.

There are other reasons why pipeline processors are difficult to design, build, and use. For one thing, the control unit here must handle k segments at once, and these segments have a sequential dependence (what happens on an overflow, external interrupt, etc.?). Thus the control unit may have even more complexity than is required for the k independent function units of Fig. 1.12. It certainly is more complex than the multiprocessor control unit. There are also questions about how to design a real machine that must perform a complete set of operations. Should we skip segments, making control messier or design other pipelines for other operations? Also, note that the speedup potential of pipeline processors is limited by the number of pipeline segments, but that the number of segments (k in the pipeline of Fig. 1.14) is limited by the total number of separate functions into which machine operations can be broken. This provides a general limit on pipeline speeds, since k is usually in the range of 4 to 8 in practice.

The standard arithmetic operations have a fixed complexity, and to form segments that have too little combinational logic is wasteful—at some point we would have more gates in the intermediate holding registers than in the combinational logic which carries out the function. Of course, we might consider pipelining more complex functions, for example, sine, cosine, square root, and so on. This is reasonable if these functions are frequently used. On the other hand, for good pipeline speedups it must be the case that $N \gg k$. So if k is made very large, we must have vectors of operands that are even longer. Thus, the method may be most useful for special-purpose applications if we attempt to go beyond standard arithmetic operations. For example, pipelining digital signal processing [AhRa75] is a good idea because several arithmetic operations must be performed sequentially in digital filtering, and such filters are often applied to vectors of several hundred or even several thousand elements. There are several commercially available processors, for example, the IBM 2938 array processors [RuCo69], which are pipelined and can be attached to the memory of existing machines for signal processing applications.

Several real computers have pipeline arithmetic units. The CDC 7600 [Bons69] and the IBM 360/91 [IBMJ67] both have pipelines but use rather standard instruction sets that are basically scalar instruction sets. But, if enough operands are provided in the proper sequence, these pipeline processors perform well. In contrast to these machines, the CDC STAR [HiTa72] and Texas Instruments ASC [Ensl74, Wats72] have pipeline processors and have vector instruction sets. The control units of these machines coordinate the flow of vectors of data of arbitrary length from memory, through the processor and back to memory. A good deal of extra hardware is provided to allow this, but high processing speeds are possible as a result. The CRAY-I computer [Cray75] has a pipeline processor and vector instructions that operate on vectors of length 64; longer vectors must be broken up in the program. Vector instruction sets provide a very important advantage over the CDC 7600 and IBM 360/91.

Because the vector instructions (as well as a set of scalar instructions) form the machine language of these computers, source program writers and compilers can avoid a lot of indexing and loop control normally found in programming array operations. Assembly language programming thus bears more similarity to APL programming than to the standard low-level scalar operations of most machines.

Probably the first pipelined processor built was the IBM 7950, otherwise known as HARVEST. This machine was developed simultaneously with the IBM 7030 (STRETCH), which had one of the earliest pipelined control units, and operated in conjunction with STRETCH. HARVEST was a byte-oriented system and could process two streams of data, producing a third. The machine was delivered to the National Security Agency (which engages in a good deal of text processing, code studies, etc.). A description of the system and some ideas about programming it can be found in Chapter 17 of [Buch62].

3.6.3 Parallel processors and multiprocessors

Multifunction and pipeline processors are practically limited in their speedups over serial machines by the technical considerations discussed in previous sections. Multiprocessor or parallel processor machines appear to be less constrained. Indeed, the idea of connecting a number of processors for greater speed or reliability has had great appeal since it was first done at Bell Laboratories in the 1940s (see Section 1.3.3).

Multiprocessor and parallel processor organizations seem more flexible than multifunction or pipeline processors, because the multiple operations that may be performed simultaneously are carried out in separate processors, rather than being closely tied together. Indeed, with the appearance of fast, inexpensive, integrated circuit microprocessors, the idea seems even more appealing from the hardware point of view. Two important questions remain:

1. How should the processors be interconnected, controlled, and connected to memories?
2. How should programming for such machines be done?

These are very difficult questions which are not as yet completely answered. However, we shall briefly survey the state of the art.

Hardware questions

A number of unresolved hardware questions are active research topics, and some results will be presented in Chapters 4, 5, and 6, as well as in Vol. 2. At best, one can hope that as the number of processors and memory units is increased, the effective speed of the system increases at the same rate. The performance of interconnection switches should behave similarly, as the hardware in them increases.

The speedup hierarchy of Section 2.1 characterizes computations in terms of the ratio of their best known serial and parallel execution times. In Chapter 2, it was shown that many computations are of Type 0 or Type 1, that is, their speedup grows linearly with the number of processors or as $O(n/\log n)$ (for an n processor system), respectively.

It is important to realize, however, that only through using large parallel processors or multiprocessors can maximum speedup be achieved, since the other machines we have discussed are limited to at most a constant potential speedup that depends on the machine but not on the problem size. Thus, these other machines are limited to Type 3 speedups at best, because the amount of simultaneity they can introduce is practically limited. Of course, there are also limits to the potential number of processors in a parallel or multiprocessor machine, but practically, these are much larger than the other organizations.

Control units are also a source of some unresolved design questions. In Section 2.1.3, we introduced the notions of SIME (single instruction multiple execution) and MIME (multiple instruction multiple execution) machines, and we will expand these ideas in control unit terms in Section 4.2.5. However, it is useful to view processing in these terms now. Superficially, multiprocessors (each with its own control unit) that can carry out MIME operations seem more flexible than parallel processors that must carry out SIME operations because of their common control unit. On the other hand, the parallel processor approach would seem to be less expensive because of the shared control unit. However, even this may not be valid as microprocessors with integrated control units become candidates for use as machine components. Another consideration is the fact that the individual processors in a multiprocessor system may operate on independent clocks, whereas the processors in a parallel machine are usually synchronized from a common clock.

In any case, an important characteristic of parallel or multiprocessor machines is that they provide the opportunity to go beyond the constant speedup potential of pipeline or multifunction processors. Because of their relatively simpler organization, parallel machines to date have been built with more processors than have multiprocessors.

Programming questions

In Chapter 2, a number of aspects of the structure of parallel computations were discussed, and this discussion will be extended in Vol. 2. It is clear from Chapter 2 that potentially large amounts of parallelism can be found in ordinary programs.

The previous section contrasted parallel and multiprocessor machines using the SIME and MIME characterizations, respectively. In this section we discuss parallel machines, and it is important to realize that various hybrid designs are possible. For example, microprocessors containing their own control units could be used to provide a parallel machine with semiautonomous processors. A central clock and sequencing mechanism could drive the machine, but the processors might perform different arithmetic operations, for example. In what follows, SIME simply implies that on one time step all processors perform the same operation, whereas MIME allows different processors to perform different operations on the same time step.

Although the greater flexibility of MIME machine organizations would seem to offer advantages over SIME machine organizations, a more careful assessment depends on the details of the computations to be performed. In the parallel evaluation of arithmetic expressions, the MIME feature could be valuable; however, in speeding up FORTRAN-like programs, loop speedup is usually much more important than expressions outside loops. By using the loop distribution algorithm of Chapter 2, single node array operations or recurrences may arise.

Single node array operations lead to speedups on SIME machines that are proportional to the loop limits, assuming that sufficiently many processors are available. If the loop limits are small compared with the number of available processors, then tree-height reduction and the concomitant possibilities of requiring more than one type of operation at the same time lead to the necessity of MIME organizations. MIME organizations can also be useful in allowing several statements to be executed at once.

Linear recurrences arising in loops can be handled by any of the methods of Chapter 2. It turns out that all of the methods presented in Chapter 2 allow SIME computations, and no substantial improvements in the results are possible by introducing MIME operation. For nonlinear recurrences, of course, the methods of Chapter 2 do not hold, so nonlinear recurrences can be treated as arithmetic expressions with tree-height reduction applied to each iteration.

From the above one may conclude that although MIME machines offer more flexibility than SIME machines, in many typical computations a good deal of speedup can be derived from a SIME machine. Whether or not the extra complexity of a MIME organization is justified then depends on the details of specific programs or algorithms.

The speedup hierarchy of Chapter 2 was based on proven bounds for the speedup of various classes of computations. Empirically, it has been observed that these same speedup types can be used to describe the behavior of whole programs [KBCD74]. The analytical bounds have also been extended to whole loops [CKTB78]. Intuitively, it is plausible that because programs consist of a collection of array operations, trees, and recurrences, whichever of these dominates the parallel time may be used to characterize the overall program speedup potential.

Several special hardware features usually found in parallel machines ease the problems of programming and writing compilers for them. We now sketch several of these features. In its relation to the processors, a parallel machine's control unit has several simple requirements not found in serial machines. One is the ability to *broadcast* a single number to all of the processors (recall Section 1.2.1.6). The inverse of this is the necessity of fetching one or more numbers from processors to the control unit for testing or subsequent broadcasting. It is also necessary to be able to make *global tests* by fanning-in test bits from each processor. This allows vector tests, for example, IF ANY or IF ALL elements of a vector satisfy some condition. A related requirement is the ability to use control bits to enable (or disable) processors in arbitrary combinations. We will call these *mode bits*, and they may be set locally by tests in the processors (e.g., on arithmetic faults) or globally from the control unit (e.g., based on global tests or compiled patterns). Control unit supplied mode bits may be said to be broadcast, although each processor gets its own unique bit in this case.

Although the above discussion is given in terms of the processors and control unit, it may also be desirable to have some of the same relations between the individual parallel memory units and the control unit. If individual memory units are identified with processors, then the above discussion can immediately be extended to the memories. If not, separate logic may be required for the memory and processor units. For more discussion of parallel memories, see Chapter 5.

Implementations

It was pointed out in Chapter 1 that several parallel machines are in existence. These include the BSP, ILLIAC IV, STARAN IV, and PEPE, as well as an ICL (International Computers, Limited) parallel processor [Redd73] built into certain ICL models. Historically, parallel machines were proposed by a number of people in the 1950s. Unger proposed a two-dimensional array of interconnected bit serial processors for picture processing [Unge58], and Holland proposed an array of processors for various applications [Holl59]. An early hardware prototype was SOLOMON [GrMc63]. Perhaps the first published account of a highly parallel machine design was by Zuse [Zuse58], who proposed an array of processors sharing a multihead magnetic drum memory. Zuse obtained a patent on such a machine; the application was filed in February 1956.

Most manufacturers produce one or more multiprocessor models today. In Section 1.2.1.3, a number of these were listed. For descriptions of a number of early systems, see [BeNe71]; broad surveys are contained in [Baer73] and [Ensl74]. A very influential early machine that is seldom written about (in English) was the Gamma 60 of Compagnie des Machines Bull (later Honeywell Bull). The machine could be classed as an early multiprocessor or multifunction machine that also supported multiprogramming with FORK and JOIN type instructions. The project was begun in 1956, and some 20 machines were produced in the early 1960s. Machines Bull failed in spite of its innovative design; for an account of this triumph of capital (IBM) over architectural innovation (Bull), see [Roge69]. The two best English presentations of the system are one by the Gamma 60 designer Dreyfus [Drey58] and a later, retrospective account in [Bata71].

PROBLEMS

Easy problems in text\order

3.1 Consider the hexadecimal integer 2C4AB. What hexadecimal precision would a machine need to represent it? Rewrite the number in binary. How much binary precision would a machine need to represent it? What can you say about the accuracy of this integer?

3.2 To appreciate the usefulness of decimal machine arithmetic, consider the following. How many bits are necessary to represent 0.95 (as in 95 cents) in a BCD machine word? Using the same number of bits, show whether or not it can be accurately represented as a binary fraction.

3.3 Assume you are designing the format for floating-point words in a machine with 32-bit words. If the mantissa is specified by I(2, 21), that is, 21-bit binary integers, where would you place it in the 32-bit word (before or after the exponent)? Assume the machine has binary integer arithmetic as well and remember that conversion from integer to floating-point numbers occurs frequently in programs. Also show your choice of integer format.

3.4 In Table 3.2, the number of fractions is given as $\frac{1}{2} \cdot r_b^f$. Why?

3.5 Consider the following description of a 40-bit word for the floating-point representation NFL(2, 16, 8, 6):

$$\left.\begin{array}{lr} \text{Exponent sign} & 1 \\ \text{Mantissa sign} & 1 \\ \text{Exponent length} & 6 \\ \text{Mantissa length} & 32 \end{array}\right\} \text{bits}$$

(a) Find the maximum relative spacing between successive normalized representable numbers [$\max\{(a'-a)/a\}$, where a' denotes the successor of a, and a and a' are normalized].

(b) Find the minimum and maximum absolute difference between successive normalized representable numbers.

3.6 Show that there are 1.875 times as many hexadecimal values as binary values representable using fixed e and f (see Section 3.2.5).

3.7 Show that the upper bound for binary addition of Theorem 2.8 is greater than Winograd's lower bound by less than a factor of 3.

3.8 This problem compares the effectiveness of BCD addition of Section 3.3.2 with a BCD to binary conversion, binary addition, binary to BCD conversion scheme.

First, consider an algorithm to convert the BCD number $d = d_j d_{j-1} \ldots d_1$, composed of j BCD digits, to the binary number B(J), J = j. The other J − 1 elements of the B array are intermediate values. Let D(I) = d_i.

$$\begin{array}{ll} & \text{B}(0) \leftarrow 0 \\ & \text{DO} \quad S_3 \quad \text{I} \leftarrow 1, \quad \text{J} \\ & \qquad \text{B}(\text{I}) \leftarrow 10 * \text{B}(\text{I}-1) \\ S_3 & \qquad \text{B}(\text{I}) \leftarrow \text{B}(\text{I}) + \text{D}(\text{I}) \end{array}$$

(a) Construct a data dependence graph for this algorithm. What type of linear recurrence is it?

(b) Recall the BCD addition algorithm of Section 3.3.2. Give an order of magnitude estimate of the time necessary to add two BCD numbers of j BCD digits. Assume the time to subtract binary numbers is the same as the time to add two binary numbers.

(c) Is it faster to use the BCD addition algorithm or to convert BCD to binary, do the binary addition, and convert binary to BCD (assuming it takes the same amount of time to convert binary to BCD as to convert BCD to binary)?

3.9 (a) In the algorithm for floating-point addition, Fig. 3.4 on step ⑪, we test for overflow of man_C. If ⑩ disposed of one extra bit by rounding, give an example of two binary numbers with 3-bit mantissas that could cause overflow on step ⑪.

(b) In step ⑦ of Fig. 3.5, the floating-point multiplication algorithm, we test for overflow of man_C. If ⑥ disposed of one extra bit by rounding, give an example of two binary numbers with 3-bit mantissas that could overflow on step ⑦.

(c) In Fig. 3.5, ⑤ and ⑧ both require shifts. Reorganize ⑤, ⑥, ⑦, and ⑧ such that only one shift step is required.

3.10 Suppose a machine has tag bits to represent exceptional numbers such as INDEFINITE, INFINITY. How much faster is such a scheme compared with a scheme that uses specific bit patterns? Specifically, give an order of magnitude estimate of the number of gate delays to detect an exceptional number for each scheme. Assume that each number is n bits long exclusive of tag, and the tag is m bits. Is the speed difference significant in relation to the time to perform an arithmetic operation? Discuss the cost difference.

3.11 Suppose we wish to write very efficient, precise numerical programs in a machine-independent manner. One proposed solution is to make the crucial parameters of the number system and arithmetic hardware available in FORTRAN-type variables to high-level language programmers.

(a) Which of the following parameters are most relevant in this respect (1) for specifying a floating-point number system; (2) for specifying arithmetic hardware parameters; and (3) which are mainly interesting statistics: maximum relative representation error, range, representation ratio, largest representable fraction, smallest representable fraction, normalized or unnormalized, average alignment shift distance, guard digits for each operation, precision, significance?

(b) Give one other necessary parameter for the number system or the arithmetic hardware not mentioned above and not derivable given all of the above.

3.12 After mantissa multiplication of two normalized base-2 floating-point numbers with f-bit mantissas, which shifts may be necessary to renormalize the result: no shift, right 1 bit, left 1 bit, right 2 bits, left 2 bits, right $f-1$ bits, left $f-1$ bits?

3.13 Show a logic diagram that implements a node in a barrel shifter (Fig. 3.9).

3.14 N demultiplexers would require $O(N^2)$ gates (Section 2.2.3) but a barrel shifter has just $O(N \log N)$. What has been sacrificed?

3.15 Verify that Eqs. 17 and 18 yield the truth table shown in Fig. 3.11. Compare Eqs. 17 and 18 with the adder equations, Eqs. 8 and 9 in Section 2.3.7.3. Show that they are equivalent functions, that is, only the interconnection is different.

3.16 Suppose some operation is implemented using gates of 5 ns delay, that there are at most 10 levels of logic between registers, and that 10 clock times are required to execute the operation. If such an operation were pipelined using the same logic elements and design rules, how long would you expect the operation on one pair of arguments to take? How long would you expect an average operation to take in a long sequence of such operations, that is, after the pipeline is full?

3.17 In Section 3.6.2 the vector sum is formed in log N separate passes. How much faster could it be performed if the pipeline is not drained between passes unless absolutely necessary? Assume that N and the pipeline length are powers of two.

Medium and hard problems in text order

3.18 This problem considers the optimal hardware radix of a processor in terms of hardware cost assuming that the cost per digit C_d is a function of the radix. Let $C_d = \alpha r_v^\beta$.
   (a) Find the cost function for processing an average number N stored in a word of length n, C_N. (*Hint:* Assume $N \approx r_v^n$, and $C_N = \alpha r_v^\beta n$; eliminate n from C_N. Work with the natural logarithm.)
   (b) Minimize the cost function C_N with respect to r_v; that is, what is the smallest possible cost and what value of r_v (in terms of α and β) yields this value?
   (c) What values of α and β produce minimum cost for $r_v = 2$ and $r_v = 10$? Which base costs less for numbers in the range of 10^6?

3.19 (a) Consider the floating-point number system NFL(2, 10, 1, 2) (which may be considered to be the BCD equivalent of NFL(2, 2, 4, 2) in terms of bits used.)
       Compute: the smallest fraction,
                the largest fraction,
                the largest exponent,
                the range,
                the number of fractions,
                the number of exponents,
                the number of values, and
                the representation ratio.
   (b) Repeat these computations for NFL(2, 4, 2, 2, 0). (Note that the mantissa is now a base 4 integer.)

3.20 Compute the representation ratio for the normalized floating-point number systems shown in Tables 3.2 and 3.3. Compare the approximate value given in the equations of Section 3.2.5 with the actual fraction computed from the tables. Also, estimate the total number of NFL(2, 4, 2, 2) values outside the range of NFL(2, 2, 4, 2) and compare it with the tables.

3.21 (a) For the floating-point number system $NFL(r_e, r_b, f, e) = NFL(2, 2, 4, 2)$, plot the positive numbers in the system on the real number line. Mark:

(1) the regions of exponent overflow,

(2) the regions of exponent underflow,

(3) the range of the system, and

(4) the regions not representable in case of mantissa underflow.

(b) Now, for comparison, plot the non normalized system $FL(2, 2, 4, 2)$ and mark the four regions in part (a). Which system is denser? Which system has better range?

3.22 The PDP-11 discards the first bit of the mantissa of its floating-point numbers before storing them in main memory. This is possible because it has $r_b = 2$ and it uses normalized floating-point numbers.

(a) Give the advantages and disadvantages of discarding the leading bit before it is stored in main memory.

(b) Compute the representation ratio of such a scheme where the representation ratio is defined as the number of numbers in the dropped bit representation less than the maximum number in regular representation divided by the number of numbers in regular representation (use only positive numbers with positive exponents).

3.23 Give a flowchart for an algorithm for the subtraction of BCD numbers. Use a method that employs the normal binary arithmetic unit (as in Fig. 3.2 for BCD addition). What is the fastest way to carry out the needed biasing?

3.24 One method of handling negative numbers mentioned in Section 3.2.3 in a radix-r, m-digit system is biased or excess-r^{m-1} notation. In this notation x is stored as $x + r^{m-1}$. For example, if $r = 2$, $m = 5$, $x = +01011$ is stored as $01011 + 10000 = 11011$. $-x$ would be stored as $-01011 + 10000 = 00101$. Write down all the excess-$2^{5-1} = 2^4$ numbers and the equivalent signed magnitude numbers. Is it easy to check the sign of an excess-r^{m-1} number? How is complementation of excess-r^{m-1} numbers performed? Which of the operations $+$, $-$, and $*$ can be carried out as easily in excess-r^{m-1} as in $(r-1)$'s or r's complement?

3.25 Often the e exponent bits of a floating-point number are stored in excess-2^{e-1} notation.

(a) Why does this encoding simplify exponent handling for floating-point operations?

(b) What problem arises when we want to take the reciprocal of a very small number (e.g., when the encoded exponent is zero excess-2^{e-1})?

3.26 Show a modified version of Fig. 3.4 that can be used to add or subtract normalized, signed magnitude, floating-point numbers. You may use either r's complement or $(r-1)$'s complement arithmetic.

3.27 Compute the total bias for the NFL$(2, 2, 4, 2)$ system for each of the roundoff methods below. Assume $m = 4$, $d = 2$.
  (a) Truncation
  (b) Jamming
  (c) Rounding
  (d) R*-rounding
  (e) ROM-rounding using $l = 3$ and the following ROM:

Address	Contents
000	00
001	01
010	01
011	01
100	10
101	11
110	11
111	11

  (*Hint:* Carry out each method on the first four numbers in Table 3.2.)
  (f) Construct an $l = 3$ ROM table that produces zero total bias.

3.28 Recall that for addition, subtraction, and multiplication, just two guard digits (plus a sticky bit) are sufficient to generate single precision normalized results in the case of R*-rounding. For $r_b = 8$ and $f = m = 4$, give examples which show that the stated number of digits is needed for each of the three operations mentioned above.

3.29 It is well-known that computer floating-point arithmetic is not even truly associative. Let us consider the implications of imprecise multiplication. Most introductory numerical analysis texts [FoMo67] show that if x and y are normalized floating-point numbers and if θ represents $+$, $-$, $*$, or $/$ and fl$(x \theta y)$ represents the floating-point counterpart of $(x \theta y)$, then

$$\text{fl}\,(x\,\theta\,y) = (x\,\theta\,y)(1 + \delta),$$

where

$$|\delta| \le \tfrac{1}{2} r_b^{1-f} \quad \text{for rounding}$$

and

$$|\delta| \le r_b^{1-f} \quad \text{for truncation},$$

where r_b is the floating-point radix and f is the number of digits in the mantissa.
  (a) A natural question regarding parallel computation is whether there is less error involved in serial evaluation, for example, $(((x_1 * x_2) * x_3) * x_4)$, or in parallel evaluation using a fan-in tree, $((x_1 * x_2) *$

$(x_3 * x_4))$. Decide which method produces less error for the product of n numbers.

(b) Which method of evaluation is better for the sum of n numbers? If we know that the numbers are in some order, for example, if the numbers are in ascending order, could we get better error bounds?

3.30 Design logical shifters (similar to the barrel shifters) capable of performing:
(a) Either left or right shifts.
(b) Either end-off or end-around shifts.
How many gates are needed for these shifters?

3.31 Show how a leading one's position counter can be constructed directly. Or, alternatively, show how to generate a leading one's position counter from a ones' position counter. Give specific gate and time bounds. A leading one's position counter given the number 00101101 would generate 3.

3.32 Compute the gates and time needed to implement multiplication of two 8-bit numbers using an adder array as in Fig. 3.11, and compare your results with Theorem 1 and Example 5.

3.33 A direct table lookup, using read-only memories, is proposed for generating the 16-bit product of two 8-bit unsigned integers. How many 512×8 ROM chips will be needed? Estimate the number of gate delays through the address decoder, assuming fan-in and fan-out of 2.

3.34 Consider the multiplication of binary numbers using $(2^{k-1}, k)$ reduction components for carry-save addition. Only reduce the partial product array to two rows.
(a) Compare the time required using $(3, 2)$ components with the time required using $(7, 3)$ components, given as many components as needed.
(b) If we can use only two stages of $(7, 3)$ reduction components per clock, how many clocks are needed to multiply two 50-bit mantissas using an iterative method similar to the method described in Section 3.5.3? You may use at most 122 components.
(c) How could a pipelining strategy be used to reduce the time needed in part (b) and how much time can be saved? You may double the part (b) clock speed.

3.35 Carefully derive the gate count of Theorem 2 for fast multiplication.

3.36 Show that carry-save addition of the partial product array for the multiplication of two n-bit numbers can be done with $(n^2 - 4n + 3)$ full adders and $(n-1)$ half adders used as $(3, 2)$ row reduction elements by covering the partial product array with full adders and half adders appropriately.

3.37 Diagram the iterative carry-save multiplier mentioned at the end of

Section 3.5.3. How close is the gate count for this multiplier to the faster $O(n^2)$ gate bound given by Theorem 2?

3.38   (a)   Draw a flowchart for binary integer restoring division of e divided by s, that is, $e = qs + r$, where e is $2n$ bits, and q, s, and r are n bits each.

       (b)   Draw a flowchart for nonrestoring division.

3.39   Draw a flowchart similar to Fig. 3.4 and Fig. 3.5 for normalized floating-point division. As with floating-point addition and multiplication, carefully consider exceptional cases (∞ and 0) and remember to check for overflow and underflow of the exponent and mantissa wherever they can occur. You may use any integer division algorithm.

3.40   Consider double precision arithmetic operations. Assume that our double precision format is to store one mantissa and exponent in each of two words. (Note that most systems use one exponent and the second word is an extension of the mantissa.) For notation, suppose X is a double precision number. We will write it as $X = (X_1, X_2)$ where X_1 is the most significant word and X_2 is the least significant. Let $s(X_i)$ represent the sign of X_i, $e(X_i)$ will represent the exponent of X_i, and $m(X_i)$ will represent the mantissa. Assume that $r_b = 2$, the mantissa is f bits long, and that both words are normalized. By making both words have the same format, some uniformity is obtained. We can use the single precision arithmetic hardware already present. Some redundancy has also been introduced; that is, the mantissa could overlap if the exponents are close together (i.e., if $e(X_2) > e(X_1) - f$). We will assume that the mantissas do not overlap, $e(X_2) \leq e(X_1) - f$, and that $s(X_1) = s(X_2)$. Now consider multiplication, $P = A * B$. Basically, we wish to carry out the following procedure. let $A = (A_1, A_2)$, $B = (B_1, B_2)$, and $P = (P_1, P_2, P_3, P_4)$. First form

$$C = (A_1 * B_1), \quad D = (A_2 * B_1), \quad E = (A_1 * B_2), \quad \text{and} \quad F = (A_2 * B_2),$$

where C, D, E, and F are double precision. Second, add the corresponding parts of C, D, E, and F; that is,

		F_1	F_2	
	E_1	E_2		
	D_1	D_2		
+	C_1	C_2		

P_1	P_2	P_3	P_4

Notice that although the single precision words are floating-point and, hence, the additions could be carried out in any order, we can take advantage of the structure of the sum as is explained below (part b).

Finally, if we wish to restrict ourselves to a double precision result, we must discard P_3 and P_4. Several questions remain, among them:

(1) What happens when there is a carry-out of a column?
(2) Have the exponents been handled properly, that is, is $e(P_2) \leq e(P_1) - f$?
(3) Are both the result mantissas normalized?

To answer such questions, we must consider the hardware of the machine for performing single precision operations. Assume we have single precision arithmetic hardware able to perform the following instructions:

ADD instruction performs addition or subtraction of two single precision floating-point numbers. The result is a double precision floating-point number. If overflow occurs during addition, the mantissa parts of the result are shifted to the right and both exponents adjusted accordingly. Otherwise, the result is left unnormalized.

NORMALIZE performs normalization of a single precision floating-point number. The result is a single precision number obtained by shifting left end-off all leading zeros and adjusting exponent accordingly.

MULTIPLY produces a double precision product of the two single precision floating-point numbers. The most significant portion is a normalized number.

(a) Assuming that we have the hardware described above, answer questions (1), (2) and (3).
(b) Obviously, the value of F is not very important if only P_1 and P_2 are going to be kept. Give examples that show that if F is discarded, the error introduced in P is at most 2 bits. (In fact, it can be shown that if only the 4 high-order bits of D_2 and C_2 are attached to D_1 and C_1 as guard bits, the total error introduced is still at most two bits.)
(c) Use the technique and hardware demonstrated above to implement double precision addition, $S = A + B$. (Hint: There are two cases to consider,

and

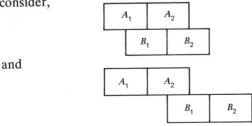

But the addition can be carried out without any explicit test for these cases. Some normalization will be needed.) (Above algorithm is due to [Gajs77].)

3.41 The example program of Fig. 3.17 has data dependences and an antidependence among various statements, but no output dependences. In order to allow a processor such as the one in Fig. 3.18 to process programs with output dependences or antidependences, discuss possible compiler and/or tag assignment logic rules.

3.42 Consider two computers with multiple arithmetic units as shown:

	Machine 1	Machine 2	Time/Operation
Adders:	2	1	2 units
Multipliers:	2	1	4 units
Dividers:	1	1	5 units

Neglecting access time and routing time, schedule the execution of the following FORTRAN statements on the two machines and compare the results. Assume as much instruction lookahead and fast temporary storage capacity as desired.

$$A1 \leftarrow B + C*D*E$$
$$A2 \leftarrow A1 - D*E + D$$
$$A3 \leftarrow (F - 2*B)/C$$
$$A4 \leftarrow (D + E*C)/A3$$
$$A5 \leftarrow A1*A1 - B*A2 + A4 + F$$

We are interested in the shortest possible execution time.

3.43 What are the values of T_A and T_N in clocks for parallel and pipeline machines, where T_A is the average effective time of an operation and T_N is the time required to perform a sequence of N identical operations? For simplicity, assume the number of segments in the pipeline k is equal to the number of parallel processors and also the time required (in clocks) to complete a single arithmetic operation on either machine. Comparatively interpret these results (possibly by a table, with comments) for $N = 1$, $N = k$, $N = jk - 1$, $N = jk + 1$, and for N large.

3.44 Assume that we have a pipeline processor with one pipelined arithmetic unit with five segments, that multiplies or adds but cannot do both simultaneously.

(a) What is the time required to compute a linear combination of vectors?

$$\text{Let } x_1 = \begin{bmatrix} x_{11} \\ x_{12} \\ \cdot \\ \cdot \\ \cdot \\ x_{1n} \end{bmatrix}, \quad x_2 = \begin{bmatrix} x_{21} \\ x_{22} \\ \cdot \\ \cdot \\ \cdot \\ x_{2n} \end{bmatrix}, \ldots, x_m = \begin{bmatrix} x_{m1} \\ x_{m2} \\ \cdot \\ \cdot \\ \cdot \\ x_{mn} \end{bmatrix}$$

and $a_1, a_2, \ldots, a_n$ be scalars.

Compute y, where

$$y = a_1 x_1 + a_2 x_2 + \cdots + a_m x_m$$

$$= \begin{bmatrix} a_1 x_{11} + a_2 x_{21} + \cdots + a_m x_{m1} \\ a_1 x_{12} + a_2 x_{22} + \cdots + a_m x_{m2} \\ \cdot \quad \cdot \quad \quad \cdot \\ \cdot \quad \cdot \quad \quad \cdot \\ \cdot \quad \cdot \quad \quad \cdot \\ a_1 x_{1n} + a_2 x_{2n} + \cdots + a_m x_{mn} \end{bmatrix}.$$

Assume that the pipeline must drain between the vector operations and that the vector operation setup time is equal to 5 times the segment time.

(b) What is the order of magnitude speedup of the computation?

3.45 Suppose we want to compute

$$f = \frac{a_1}{b_1} + \frac{a_2}{b_2} + \cdots + \frac{a_n}{b_n}$$

at high speed and have designed a special processor of the form:

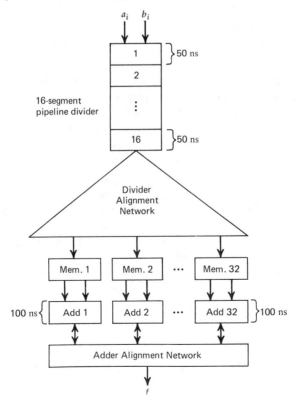

The divider alignment network can send a number to any of the memories from the divider output. The adder alignment network can perform an arbitrary permutation of the adder outputs and can send the result to other adders. The divider and adder alignment networks and memories operate with zero delay. Assuming the machine cannot be operated in an overlapped mode, that is, all divisions must be completed before any addition can proceed, how long would the machine require to compute f if $n = 51$?

3.46 Suppose that we discovered a new algorithm which could transform any arithmetic expression of n atoms, $E\langle n \rangle$, into another form, $E'\langle n \rangle$, also of n atoms, but of height $\lceil \log n \rceil$. Further, assume the availability of a computer in which each processor could perform $+$, $-$, $*$, and $/$ in unit time. The $n\text{-}1$ processors are interconnected in the form of a binary tree. Assume that input registers attached to each processor allow pipelining between processors. Assume that data transmission between processors requires zero time and that n is even. Consider the problem of evaluating k arithmetic expressions, all of form $E\langle n \rangle$, which are independent of each other.

(a) What is the minimum time required to evaluate the entire set of k expressions using this machine?

(b) What is the efficiency of the above machine in evaluating the k independent expressions?

3.47 Assume that we have idealized parallel and pipeline processors. The parallel processor has k arithmetic units, each capable of performing any arithmetic operation in one time unit. The pipeline processor has k segments, each of which has a delay of $1/k$ time units. The pipeline can be used to do any of the arithmetic operations, but it must be "drained" between operations (e.g., when switching from $+$ to $*$, no new operands can enter the pipeline until the last result of the $+$ operation emerges). Memory access time, control unit time, and so on, can be ignored. Assume that each machine has as many temporary registers as are needed for its most efficient operation.

We wish to perform a benchmark test program on each machine that will multiply two $n \times n$ matrices to form the $n \times n$ matrix product.

(a) Determine the number of time steps which a single (nonarray) processor would require to compute the matrix product, at one time step per arithmetic operation.

(b) For each array machine, sketch a plot of speedup versus n, from $n = 1$ to $n \gg k$, where

$$\text{Speedup} = \frac{T_1}{T_k} = \frac{\text{time on single processor}}{\text{time on array processor}}$$

(*Hint:* Consider carefully the points where $n = 1$, $n = k$, $n = k + 1$, $n =$ any integer multiple of k, and n very large.)

3.48 Consider a machine consisting of a set of identical interconnected processors. Each processor has a multiplier, an adder, a memory, and eight associated registers. The machine has a cycle time of T and in this time one word of the memory may be accessed. Each arithmetic unit is designed so that two numbers may be added in time T. Each multiplier is a two segment pipeline that may accept two arguments and produce a result every cycle T. All of these have separate sequencers, and multiplication, addition, routing, and memory activity may occur simultaneously in each processor.

There are eight such processors interconnected as shown below. The circles are processors and the lines show the bidirectional interconnection paths. You may assume that in time T two numbers may be sent in one direction between a pair of connected processors. The square boxes are memories whose memory information register may be gated to one of several processors. Each processor is connected to the memory of the same number. Thus, processors 2, 4, 6, and 8 are also connected to the memories with these numbers although the connections are not shown.

At each cycle (interval T), it is possible to introduce eight new operands together with their instructions into the array of processors. Each processor receives one instruction per cycle. Some processors must hold the instructions until proper data arrives, and each is capable of holding a sufficient number of instructions of the form:

tag	operation	destination

.

The tag field holds an identifying number (ID) which is the same for all instructions introduced in some particular cycle. Sufficiently many different ID's are used however, so that at any time, all tags at one processor are different.

Each data element in the processors has an ID associated with it. At the time the data enters the processors from memory, each datum and instruction is assigned the same ID number. Each processor's control is organized so that when two data elements with the same ID are present in its data registers, the instruction with this ID is applied to the data, and the result is sent to the processor named in the destination field of the instruction.

For example, if at some time processor 6 contained the following instruction:

tag	operation	destination
3	multiply	4

and in its data registers there were two numbers with $ID = 3$, these numbers would be multiplied together, the result would be assigned $ID = 3$, and the result and its ID would be sent to a data register of processor 4.

Whenever final or temporary results are obtained, the ID may be stripped off and the data stored in memory. In answering the following questions you may store each data element in just one memory location—no redundant storage is allowed.

In each case you should try to have the machine evaluate expressions as quickly as possible.

(a) *Arithmetic Expression Evaluation*

To evaluate $x = \sum_{i=1}^{8} a_i$:

(1) How would you store the a_i and x in memory?
(2) Discuss what each processor would do in the computation.
(3) In terms of T, how long would it take to evaluate x from raw data in memory to final result in memory?

Suppose you wanted to loop on j to evaluate y_j for various j values and store all the results in memory 4, where

$$y_j = \prod_{i=1}^{8} b_{ij}:$$

(1) How would you store the b_{ij} array in memory?
(2) How long in terms of T would it require to evaluate all of $y_1 \cdots y_8$?

(b) *Array Multiplication*

Let A be an 8×8 matrix and R be an 8 element row vector. To compute RA and store the result in memory 4:
(1) How would you store R and A?
(2) Discuss how the operation would be performed.
(3) How long would it take in terms of T?

(c) *Exponentiation*

Assume that you could transmit a number from a central controller (CC) to all processors in time T.
(1) If x were in the CC, how would you evaluate $x^2, \ldots, x^8$ and store each in a separate memory in minimum time? Discuss what each processor does. What instruction format changes are needed?
(2) In terms of T, how long would this take?

(d) *Polynomial Evaluation*

Assume a CC as above and let $p = \sum_{i=0}^{7} a_i x^i$.

(1) How would you store the a_i and x?
(2) Discuss the evaluation of p.
(3) In terms of T, how long would it take to evaluate p?

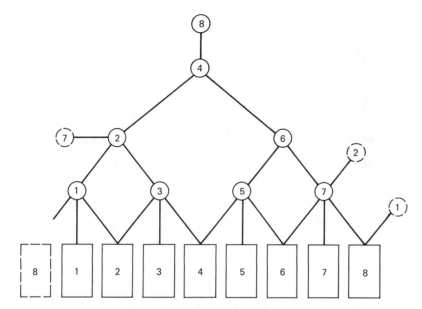

CH

4

I have always known
  That at last I would
Take this road, but yesterday
  I did not know that it would be today.

Ariwara-no-Narihira

Tenth Century

We still have judgment here, that we but teach
Bloody instructions, which, being taught, return
To plague th' inventor.

Macbeth

William Shakespeare

CONTROL UNITS

4.1 CONTROL UNIT OVERVIEW

4.1.1 Introduction

Computer control units are not an easy subject to discuss. The name itself implies that we are dealing with the one system component that is intimately involved with all the rest. For persons with an anthropormorphic bent, the control unit suggests the "brain" of the entire computer system. And indeed the analogy is not a bad one because the control unit has wires running to all other parts of the machine and thereby causes the entire machine to proceed coherently in executing a program. Of course, computer control units are much simpler and easier to understand than human brains!

Nevertheless, for several reasons computer control units are not easy to discuss. One reason is that there is more variety from machine to machine in the control unit than anywhere else in the system organization. Another is that there are a number of more or less independent activities going on at once in a control unit—activities that do interact to some extent, but that can be discussed separately. Still another reason that control unit discussions are difficult is that there are few formal ways of analyzing or presenting the material; in a sense the control unit is a collection of ad hoc functions that are there because they *must* be there to keep the rest of the system going. Finally—and this is really a restatement of all of the above—control units are often the most difficult part of a computer to design and debug, so it is more important to understand them than some other parts of computer systems.

In a broad, philosophical sense, we can view any control unit from three different standpoints, as:

(I)   A language processor that translates several levels of languages.
(II) The master timing and sequencing device for the entire system.
(III) The clearinghouse for information access and transmission throughout the system.

As a language processor, a control unit may be viewed naively as a translator of compiled instructions into electrical signals that drive the computer. As we shall see, however, in some microprogrammed control units, this translation proceeds in several steps. Furthermore, a compiled sequence of instructions can be regarded as a mixture of statements in several different languages. Some instructions are executed in the processor, others in the main memory, others in the secondary memory, and still others are executed directly in the control unit itself. Beyond this, some machines have privileged instructions that can be used only by, say, operating system writers.

In this way, the control unit defines the semantics of all of the programming languages that are used on a machine. Of course, compilers and assemblers carry out the first stages of translation, but final "meanings" are assigned to programs in the control unit. The pragmatics of the programming languages are then the results of the control unit's actions on the entire computer system in executing each given program.

In the language area, there is little understanding of the tradeoffs involved in machine design. Probably some of the most important advances in machine design and in software development will come through a better understanding of these questions. It is here that the control unit could help (1) machine users and maintainers through better diagnostic operations; (2) compiler writers by providing hardware functions well-matched to user languages and programs; and (3) operating system designers by providing simultaneously operating subunits that execute various parts of an operating system. Our discussion of the control unit as a language processor will largely be subordinated to the other two philosophical points we made earlier (II and III above).

Our second way of viewing the control unit—as a timing and sequencing device—is standard. This aspect of the control unit's role involves fetching instructions in order, decoding them, and causing the indicated parts of the computer to go through some sequence of events. This task should be carried out quickly enough so that other parts of the machine are not idled, awaiting control unit signals.

In addition to this function, the control unit must be prepared to be interrupted at any time for any of a variety of reasons. Some "normal" interrupts simply correspond to the completion of activities the control unit has initiated. Other interrupts are "abnormal" in that they signal a fault condition somewhere in the computer.

Thus, time must be carefully accounted for in the control unit, with the sequence of events that are specified in a program held in proper relation to the activities being carried out in the machine. Almost all modern, high-speed computers are synchronous machines. This means that all of their functions are carried out under the control of a central clock, whose pulses are distributed throughout the system to ensure uniform timing everywhere.

Finally, our third philosophical point (III) is to view the control unit as the clearinghouse for information access and transmission throughout the system. The execution of every instruction requires the fetching of that instruction from some storage device to the proper control unit register. Then, the instruction usually indicates that certain items of data are to be moved from one place to another. Sometimes the addresses involved are explicitly found in the instructions, but sometimes the control unit must go through a complicated sequence of events before the proper addresses are known.

The design of a good control unit in this respect requires rather complicated logical thinking—the logic being closely related to certain properties of the users' languages and the purposes to which they will put their programs. Indeed, these questions are made more complex by the need to share the system among a number of users at once.

As we remarked previously, language questions and discussions will be woven throughout this chapter. We will divide the rest of this chapter into two broad parts. One deals with timing and sequencing, whereas the other deals with information accessing and transmission. The rest of the chapter will be a further exposition of points I, II, and III given above. Before discussing the details, we will sketch an overall control unit organization.

There are a great many different kinds of control unit features built into real computers. We will now sketch some of the key features that are present in most machines.

Every general-purpose, synchronous digital computer has the fundamental control unit elements illustrated in Fig. 4.1. The following discussion gives an outline of its operation. All of these events are carried out under the synchronization of the clock, whose output signals are distributed throughout the machine. We begin our discussion in the instruction processor. Most computers follow this general sequence, although small differences in detail exist.

1. Initially, we assume the existence of the address of the next instruction to be executed in the instruction location register.
2. a. This address is sent to the memory, and
   b. the instruction to be executed is fetched to the current instruction register.
3. The instruction is broken into its address part and operation part which are sent to the address processor and operation processor, respectively.
4. The address processor takes the address portion of the current instruction and transforms it into the correct address for either
   a. the operand of this instruction in memory or a register, or

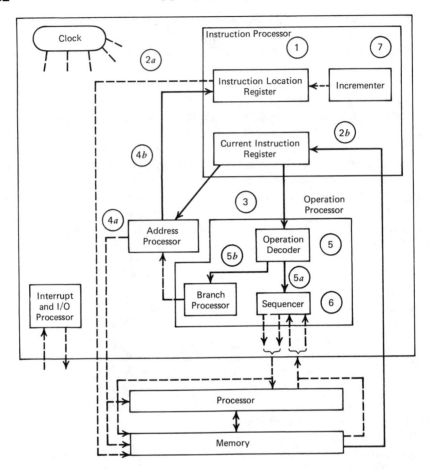

FIGURE 4.1   **Control unit.**

   b.   the next instruction to be executed, in the case of a transfer of control instruction.

In the operation processor a number of events occur.

5.   The operation is decoded, that is, the bit pattern in the operation field is converted to electrical signals which

   a.   trigger a sequencer which carries out the operation, and

   b.   in case the operation may transfer control, causes the branch processor to be activated.

6.   The sequencer drives the entire machine through a specified sequence of events which carry out (indeed *are*) whatever the instruction is defined to do.

7.   When the current instruction sequencing is finished,

   a.   if this instruction was a jump the branch processor causes a new instruction address to be forced into the instruction location register (4b);

b. otherwise, the incrementer adjusts the instruction location register so it points to the next instruction in sequence.

In either case, we then return to step 1 and begin executing the next instruction.

It is always necessary to be able to gain access to various internal locations in a computer from an operator's console or some type of switch panel. For example, to initiate the loading of programs in a dead system, a bootstrap program can be inserted by accessing the instruction location register and a few other key registers. The control unit usually has a special interface to the outside that allows such access and also displays certain aspects of the machine's internal state. This may include various control unit registers as well as processor registers. A trend in recent machine design has been to provide easy access to more and more internal information under program control. This reduces the necessity of attaching probes to various points in troubleshooting the system. In some cases, such information can be sent via telephone lines to the manufacturer's home office. Thus, key diagnosticians can be generally available without constantly flying from one machine to the next, so user satisfaction can be enhanced.

4.1.2 Instruction formats

It is probably safe to say that no two computers (except some of those in the "families" of one manufacturer, for example, IBM System 360) have ever had the same instruction format. But, in one form or another, a string of instructions always contains addresses and operations. Other special indicator bits may also appear in each instruction, for example, to indicate indirect addressing which we discuss below.

Each step of a computation requires information which specifies:

1. An operation to be performed.
2. One or more arguments on which to perform the operation.
3. The destination of the result(s).
4. The location of the next instruction.

The operation is specified by an operation code (opcode) field in each instruction. Normally, the next instruction to be executed is the next one stored in memory, so the next instruction need only be explicitly specified in case of conditional or unconditional branches (or jumps).[1] Normally, at most three addresses (operands or result) are associated with one operation in one instruction, although as we will see below, this can range down to zero operands by making assumptions about where the operands are.

---

[1] We will use the terms *branch* and *jump* interchangeably for instructions that break the normal sequence of execution.

The addresses are usually pointers to the memory or processor register locations of operands for this operation. In most machines there are two variations on this. First, instead of pointing to an operand, the address field may contain the operand itself, so-called *immediate operand addressing*. This is useful for constants specified in the program and, of course, requires fewer memory cycles when executing a program. The other variation is called *indirect addressing*. Here the address points to a pointer to the operand. This can be carried on to any number of levels. Various kinds of indirect addressing are useful in implementing several kinds of data structures, in subroutine calling, and so on. We shall return to these subjects in more detail in Section 4.3.1.

Three-address instruction formats that have been used on several machines (e.g., CDC 6600) usually have two address fields for arguments and one for a result. In branch instructions one field is used to specify which instruction to execute next. In Fig. 4.2*a* we show a simple example of how this format might be used. Note that the two assignment statements require only three machine instructions, but each word is quite long.

The two-address format specifies two operands or an operand and a branch destination. In Fig. 4.2*b*, we assume a computer with an accumulator that always receives computed results. We refer only to the accumulator (acc) explicitly when its contents are to be used as an operand of an instruction. Five machine instructions are now needed for our two assignment statements. The IBM 360 and 370 use a two-address format, but with explicitly addressed registers (see Section 4.3.3) not an implicitly addressed accumulator; the result goes to the first operand's address.

One-address formats are commonly used in computers with accumulators but no addressable registers. One-address instructions specify an operation and a branch destination or the address of one operand. The other operand is assumed to be in the processor's accumulator. As we observe in Fig. 4.2*c*, seven machine instructions are now required for our two assignment statements.

Some machines have instruction sets that include several types of formats, as we learn in Section 4.3.3. Notice that in machines with a set of addressable processor registers, the addresses may refer to memory or registers. Some instructions refer to both. Mixing formats may complicate the control unit somewhat, but they make compiled programs more compact, overall.

Zero-address instructions have no addresses in the operation word, but they do have separate address words. Code for such machines appears very much like Polish suffix notation. Note that 17 "words" are now required for the example of Fig. 4.2. The execution of this kind of program assumes the existence of a push-down stack. When an address is encountered in the program, it is pushed onto the top of the stack. Fetches and stores use the top location of the stack as an address for one operand. All dyadic operations consume the top two registers of the stack and return the result to the top of the stack. The most popular machines with zero-address instruction formats are the Burroughs B5700, B6700, and B7700. We will return to a discussion of stacks in Section 4.3.5.

We have seen that the number of "words" needed to represent the simple source program of Fig. 4.2 varies from 3 to 17 as we change the instruction format from three-address to zero-address. Of course, the number of bits per "word" also changes. Indeed, in the zero-address format, for example, the "words" need not all be the same size. Addresses may be longer than opcodes, on the average. The minimization of total program size will be discussed in Section 4.3.3.

The above discussion of instruction formats represents the tip of a rather large iceberg. There are a number of tradeoffs involved in the design of instruction formats, and these tradeoffs touch many aspects of a machine's structure. Clearly, the number of bits used for instructions is related to memory size and bandwidth. The speed and organization of the control unit are also very much involved here. Furthermore, the subject cannot be discussed exclusively in hardware terms; in fact, the types of instructions appearing in real programs actually define the problem here. Various machine designs are solutions to the problem. Thus, we must consider questions ranging from the technology available for machine hardware to whether programs are to be handwritten in assembly language or compiled from high-level languages.

We will discuss a few of the tradeoffs now, but for a deeper understanding of the question the reader must study a number of the sections that follow in this chapter. The question of choosing an instruction format can easily be broken into two parts—opcode and address formats. We will consider several aspects of operations in Section 4.2, and addressing in Section 4.3. Examples of instruction formats of several real machines will be discussed in these sections.

Note that instruction formats are also tied to data formats in the context of memory addressing, because most machines use the same memory for instruction and data storage. Traditionally, memories could be addressed to access one word at a time. Now, some memories deliver several words at once. Others can be addressed to half word, byte, or bit levels to aid programmers by accessing the exact data elements to be processed; this avoids the need for extracting these fields from full words in the processor. Thus in a logical sense, the memory word size should be regarded as being whatever can be addressed.

Clearly, the most flexible arrangement is to be able to address memory down to the bit level—with a length field allowing access to a bit, byte, word, or more. This is allowed in some machines (e.g., the B1700), but most machines allow addressing only to the byte level (e.g., IBM 360/370) or word level. Instruction formats in some machines are fixed and in others are variable. Because some operations are used less frequently than others, these are candidates for longer formats in variable format machines. The point is that to minimize the expected length of all programs, we should use fewer bits for the opcodes of frequently used instructions and more bits for less frequently used instructions. This may require extra bits to distinguish the opcode types, but the overhead is repaid by the overall number of bits saved in a program. Generally, this reduces main memory size and bandwidth requirements for programs. In the next section we will discuss operation frequencies in real programs and return to this subject.

Addressing also enjoys a wide variety of implementations. In many machines, instructions with address fields of k bits are used to address 2^k words. In some machines more than 2^k words can be addressed. The latter idea is implemented by having the control unit attach extra bits to the addresses

Source Program

$$X \leftarrow A + B * C$$
$$Y \leftarrow F + G$$

3-address format

opcode	operand 1	operand 2	result

(a)

1	MPY	B	C	T
2	ADD	A	T	X
3	ADD	F	G	Y

2-address format

opcode	operand 1	operand 2

(b)

1	MPY	B	C
2	ADD	A	acc
3	STORE	acc	X
4	ADD	F	G
5	STORE	acc	Y

1-address format

opcode	operand

(c)

1	FETCH	B
2	MPY	C
3	ADD	A
4	STORE	X
5	FETCH	F
6	ADD	G
7	STORE	Y

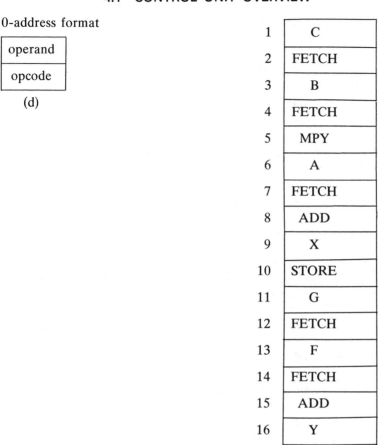

FIGURE 4.2   **Compiled program in various formats.**

generated by programs. This allows, for example, the addressing of secondary memory and main memory in a uniform way and is often called "virtual memory addressing." We will consider this in Section 4.3.4.

In any case, there are various ways of reducing the address bits in instructions. One is by the virtual memory approach of attaching extra bits to addresses in the control unit; another is by providing addressable registers in the processor, which we will discuss in Section 4.3.3. More important than saving address bits in instructions, registers also save memory bandwidth and speed up processing (because they are usually faster than memory). There are a number of tradeoffs between hardware and software complexity here. For example, providing registers leads to various register assignment problems in compilers. Instruction formats with more addresses provide compilers with more freedom than those with fewer addresses.

Another tradeoff—between registers and hardware stacks—will be discussed in Section 4.3.5. Stacks provide a number of useful and elegant features for software implementation besides the zero-address format discussed above. Most Burroughs machines have used stacks since about 1960.

Thus we see that the questions involved in choosing an instruction format are very complex. Because the decisions touch on so many aspects of machine and software organization, they must be carefully considered, not only from speed and cost viewpoints, but also from the viewpoint of ease of use.

4.2 INSTRUCTION AND OPERATION PROCESSING

4.2.1 Instruction frequencies

Computer designers have always been interested in the frequencies with which various instructions are used. Clearly, if an instruction is never used, it can be left out of the machine's repertoire. On the other hand, frequently used instructions should be executed as quickly as possible. Furthermore, it is important to separate instruction frequencies by class, because instructions executed in separate parts of the machine should be overlapped, if possible.

Once we have agreed to measure the frequency of instruction use, we must still agree on exactly what is to be measured. Source program statements or assembly language statements can be measured, and either can be measured statically (quite easily) or dynamically (with a bit more difficulty). Static measurements are based simply on the program, whereas dynamic measurements are based on the execution of the program. Ideally, we might also like to measure the overlap between the executed instructions and take into account the fact that not all instructions require the same amount of execution time.

A number of studies have been made of instruction execution by operation class. Such statistics are clearly dependent on the types of programs studied; scientific programs can be expected to be heavy in floating-point arithmetic whereas business type programs may do much data moving and sorting. Furthermore, it is obvious that these studies depend on the machine organization, and for programs compiled from high-level languages, they may depend strongly on the compiler used. For example, in machines with few registers, more memory references would be expected. Also, compiler writers often use only a small subset of the entire instruction set in generating object code; effectively they use a restricted machine.

We shall quote several studies below, some of high-level languages and others of assembly language. To measure the elapsed time and overlap is possible, but there are no known published studies of this. Thus, the studies and results we quote should be regarded as merely scratching the surface of statistical instruction measurement and study.

4.2.1.1 High-level languages

First, we consider high-level language program statistics. Table 4.1 summarizes static counts in a study of over 200K FORTRAN statements (excluding comments) and a study of 17K COBOL statements. The FORTRAN study consisted of several hundred programs written at Lockheed and Stanford [Knut71]. The FORTRAN averages shown in Table 4.1 were obtained by averaging the Lockheed averages with the Stanford averages. Even though there were about 200K Lockheed cards (plus over 50K comments) and only about 10K Stanford cards (plus about 1K comments), the averages represent different kinds of programmers (industrial and academic) and weighting them equally seems reasonable for our purposes. The COBOL programs were drawn from the Administrative Data Processing Center at the University of Illinois [Stre74]. These were written by professional programmers, perhaps with some student help.

There are several shortcomings in the comparisons of Table 4.1. One problem is that not all statement types are comparable. For example, we list DO and PERFORM together because the ideas of these statements are roughly equivalent. The FORTRAN "other" column includes several large categories which have no COBOL analog, including 4 percent FORMAT statements and 4 percent CONTINUE statements. By an oversight, the number of GOTOs was not counted in COBOL, but by hand inspection the number of GOTOs in the COBOL programs appears to be about the same as the number of IF statements. If GOTOs were included, we would expect all percentages to drop slightly and the GOTO count to be approximately equal to the IF count. Such an adjusted set of figures is shown in parentheses.

There are some rather large differences between COBOL and FORTRAN. Note that nearly one-third of the FORTRAN statements are simple monadic assignment statements, whereas over one-half of the COBOL statements are of this type. There appears to be about twice as much conditional branching in COBOL as FORTRAN. The lack of CALLs in COBOL probably results from each file often being passed entirely through one subprogram and then being passed on to the next, instead of calling all subprograms for each record.

TABLE 4.1   Statement Frequencies (Static)

Statement	Assigment Monad	Other	IF	GOTO	I/O	DO PERFORM	CALL	OTHER
FORTRAN %	31	15	11.5	10.5	6.5	4.5	6	15.0
COBOL %	52	10.5	23.6	not available	9.3	0.2	0.2	4.2
COBOL est. %	(42.1)	(7.5)	(19.1)	(19.1)	(8.46)	(0.17)	(0.17)	(3.4)

TABLE 4.2 Arithmetic Expression Characteristics (Static)

Operation	±	*	/	Supplied Functions	**
FORTRAN %	56	24.5	9.4	7.9	2.2
COBOL %	65.3	17.8	16.2	—	0.7

A few other observations about static counts in the programs are interesting. Measured statically, in the FORTRAN programs a total of about 50K operations resulted from evaluating the right-hand sides of assignment statements. The percentages of these by type are shown in Table 4.2 with 35.6 percent additions and 20.4 percent subtractions. Of these additions, 40 percent (14 percent of the total) added one to a variable.

Statically measured COBOL results are also shown in Table 4.2, for a total of over 2K arithmetic operations. Here there were 62.9 percent additions and only 2.38 percent subtractions. Computing what usually seems like too many payroll deductions is only a small part of these programs! Of these additions, about 30 percent (18.5 percent of the total) added one to a variable. Surprisingly, there were almost as many divisions as multiplications—perhaps a lot of averages (grade point, etc.) are computed.

Although logical operations were not reported for the FORTRAN measurements, the COBOL programs contained more than twice as many equality and inequality relations as arithmetic operations. Of these, about two-thirds were equality tests.

Variable subscripting in FORTRAN was tabulated, and the results are shown in Table 4.3. Of course, one would expect these statistics to shift toward more indexing when measured dynamically, because subscripted statements are executed repeatedly inside loops.

The complexity of DO loops was characterized in two simple ways: by the number of statements in the loop and the depth of loop nesting. The results for some 8K DO loops are found in Table 4.4. It is not surprising that 39 percent of the loops contained just one statement, because of the need to initialize arrays, and related operations. Note that 35 percent of the loops had 2, 3, or 4 statements and that 26 percent were rather complex, with 5 or more statements. The nesting depth results correlate reasonably well with the number of subscripts. Note that more deeply nested variables require more indices.

TABLE 4.3 FORTRAN Subscript Characteristics (Static)

Number of Subscripts	0	1	2	3	More
%	58	30.5	9.5	1	1

TABLE 4.4 DO Loop Characteristics (Static)

Number of Statements in Loop	1	2	3	4	5	>5
%	39	18.5	9.5	7	13	13
Loop Nesting Depth	1	2	3	4	5	>5
%	53.5	23	15	5.5	1.5	1.5

In the following, we see the effects of compiling and executing these programs on the frequencies of various kinds of operations.

The FORTRAN study was also carried over to dynamic counts of some of the programs. The main changes were that the percentage of assignment statements rose and the percentage of DOs, CALLs, and I/O statements dropped. It is intuitively clear that the assignment statements in loops will be executed repeatedly, so their percentage should rise. It was also observed that the percentage of monadic assignment statements dropped when measured dynamically. This is intuitively reasonable, since many assignment statements inside loops are carrying out arithmetic operations, whereas statements outside loops tend to be setting initial values. In [Wich73] a rich set of static and dynamic counts are presented for ALGOL 60; for static PL/I statistics see [Elsh76].

4.2.1.2 Object language measurements

Next we turn our attention to the study of assembly language level programs. In Table 4.5, we summarize the results of three different dynamic studies of operation types. Each study consisted of executing a number of different kinds of programs and then averaging the results. Although a great deal of variation exists from program to program, the averages for each of the studies are strikingly similar. Nearly half of the instructions are data access operations, about one-quarter are processing operations, and one-sixth to one-third are control unit executed branch operations.

Study I [Gibs70] was conducted on the IBM 7090, which had few registers. The programs studied were scientific and compiler runs and were intended to reflect the real workload on typical 7090s. We have combined the indexing instructions with the store and fetch operations to get a memory access total. Note that other memory accesses are performed in the arithmetic instructions, but these are not counted in the memory access total. Since the 7090 was a one-address machine, one would expect more explicit stores and fetches than with a two-address machine, in which more memory accesses would be hidden in arithmetic and other instructions.

Studies II [Ash168] and III [Flyn74] were of the IBM 360, which has a two-address instruction format and has more registers than the 7090. The data access category here includes register-to-register moves, so not all of this is

TABLE 4.5 Dynamic Operation Frequencies (%)

Instruction Types	Study I (IBM 7090 Compile and Scientific)	Study II (IBM 360 Compile and Scientific)	Study III (IBM 360 Scientific and COBOL)
Store/Fetch	31.2		
Index	18		
Data access total	49.2	50.4	42.9
Branch	16.6	19.9	29.6
Compare	3.8		11.2
Shift/Boolean	6.0		4.1
Logic total	9.8	11.2	15.3
Fixed point			
±	6.1		
*	0.6		
/	0.2		
Fixed point total	6.9	7.8	7.4
Floating point			
±	6.9	SP 4.5 DP 6.0	
*	3.8		
/	1.5		
Floating point total	12.2	10.5	2.6
Other	5.3	0.2	2.2
Total	100.0	100.0	100.0

main memory accessing. Thus, one should deflate these figures to get true memory accesses. Note that this would indeed lead to smaller numbers than those for Study I. The data access category in Study II also includes 4.5 percent Move and Translate instructions.

Branching instructions show the biggest variation from study to study. The lowest values for Studies I and II are consistent with the fact that these were both scientific mixes with some compilations. Study III included many COBOL jobs as well, and these programs have nearly twice as many branches as found in Study I. This matches well the static statistics of Table 4.1.

It may be surprising to learn that between one-sixth and one-third of the instructions executed are branch instructions. If we assume that most instructions executed are in loops, this would imply that loops are quite short. It should be remembered that often loops are used simply to initialize an array, so just one simple assignment statement is used. Recall from Table 4.4 that over half of the FORTRAN loops measured contained just one or two statements. Furthermore, many loops may contain several tests—one or more at the end plus other conditions inside the loop. For example, if exit tests are compiled at the beginning of the loop as they should be, every loop will have two branches, as shown in Fig. 4.3. Of course, this is not the case for FORTRAN programs, which did comprise many of the programs in these studies. In compilers that do bounds checking (to see if the user is indexing beyond the declared limits of his arrays) tests must be set up for every subscripted variable access. Thus, we see that large numbers of branch instructions are not hard to understand.

The above-mentioned statistical differences between job types can also be seen in the processor instruction frequencies. Note that the sum of compare, shift, and Boolean operations for Studies I and II were 9.8 percent and 11.2 percent, respectively, whereas for Study III this was 15.3 percent. On the other hand, Studies I and II had 12.2 percent and 10.5 percent floating-point operations, respectively, whereas Study III had only 2.6 percent floating-point operations. Clearly, we can see the underlying scientific nature of the programs in Studies I and II in contrast with the COBOL jobs included in Study III. Comparing these with Table 4.1, which showed about 15 percent nonmonadic assignment statements for FORTRAN and about 10 percent for COBOL, we get a rather close match. Studies I and II have a total of 19.1 percent and 18.3 percent arithmetic, respectively, whereas Study III with more COBOL has a total of 10 percent arithmetic. Note also that the IBM 360 arithmetic—due to its 32-bit single precision words—forces nearly 60 percent of the floating-point arithmetic to be done in double precision (DP). (It should be pointed out that 1 job stream out of 30 had 49 percent double precision floating-point operations. If this job stream were ignored, the double precision instructions would be slightly less than the single precision instructions.)

It is interesting to compare the arithmetic operation counts of these studies with the study of Table 4.2 and with the results of Sweeney shown in Chapter 3. From Table 4.2, we can conclude that addition and subtraction account for somewhat more than one-half of the operations on the right-hand sides of FORTRAN assignment statements, measured statically. In terms of compiled and executed instructions, nearly 20 percent are arithmetic, as seen in Table 4.5 (I and II). Of course, some of these are complied from other than assignment

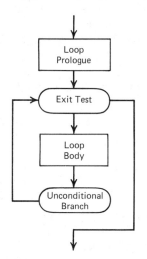

FIGURE 4.3   **Compiled loop.**

statements. Of these, 11 or 12 percent are floating-point operations. Recall Sweeney's measurement that dynamically about 11 percent of all operations executed were floating-point additions. These measurements were made on a machine like the ones used in Table 4.5; however, the programs of Table 4.5 also included some compilations. Perhaps these would shift to as much as 15 percent floating-point operations if the compilations were not included.

Although it is very difficult to compare these diverse studies, the following model of arithmetic operations probably is reasonable. Note that the functions of Table 4.2 must be compiled using the four arithmetic operations. Thus, these statistics will give a higher percentage of additions and subtractions when given in terms of just the four arithmetic operations. Let us assume 70 percent additions and subtractions when measured in terms of floating-point arithmetic alone. Other problems with using Table 4.2 are that it includes fixed- and floating-point operations and that it was measured statically.

In any case, if we execute 15 percent floating-point operations and 70 percent of these are additions and subtractions (as argued in the above paragraphs), we can justify the 11 percent figure of Sweeney as the overall frequency of floating-point additions and subtractions. Further extrapolation from Table 4.2 would lead us to conclude that perhaps 3 percent of the total instructions were floating multiplies and 1 percent floating divides.

Several morals can be found in the above discussion. First, the studies made thus far are all too sketchy and difficult to relate to one another. Second, the amount of floating-point arithmetic performed in real programs is very small when measured as a fraction of all instructions executed. Third, we can see the goals to be achieved by overlap of memory, processor, and control unit.

The latter point is a very important one. As we mentioned earlier, the relative frequencies of instructions are not alone the best measure of the relative utilizations of different parts of a computer. Some instructions are completed in one clock, whereas others need several clocks (e.g., division requires 10 or more clocks). Thus, the percentages we have been discussing really should be weighted by the number of clocks required for their completion. If this were done, we could then draw some useful conclusions about overlap between various machine elements.

Roughly speaking, the processor times would be weighted most and control unit operations least (branches usually take one clock). In any case, these weighted frequencies would indicate which parts of the machine need the most bandwidth to achieve maximum system capacity.

4.2.1.3 Opcode formats

This subject can be viewed from another, more abstract point of view, as follows. From the standpoint of efficiency in designing the machine instructions, we might argue that each instruction type in a well-designed instruction set should be used with equal frequency. On the other hand, it has been widely observed that in many natural languages, Zipf's law holds true. This says that if we rank order the words in a language by their frequency of use, then the rank order (1, 2, 3, . . .) times the frequency of use of each word is approximately a constant. In other words, the second most popular word is used one-half as much as the most popular word, the third most popular word is used one-third as much as the most popular word, and so on. There is some evidence that this also holds for programming languages, although the definition of a "word" is not so clear here.

The question of opcode use was studied, purely on a frequency of use basis in [FoGR71]. Measurements were made of CDC 3600 object code. Some programs had been handwritten in assembly language, whereas others were assembled from various high-level languages, including FORTRAN, COBOL, and SIMSCRIPT. In either case, Zipf-like differences were found in the frequencies of use of different opcodes. Not surprisingly, it was also found that, on the average, handwritten programs used more than twice as many distinct opcodes as those generated by compilers. This is for a static analysis of six different programs, the three handwritten ones being system programs of various kinds. The study also included a measurement of dynamic frequencies.

It seems reasonable that any kind of "general-purpose" instruction set will obey a Zipf-type distribution in use. If this is true, then using a variable length format can save bits in program storage. If we could address memory to the word level and any kind of coding were allowed, then the optimal encoding of an instruction set could be determined using a coding theory method developed by Huffman [Huff52]. Simply stated, Huffman's algorithm minimizes message length—here read program length—by using the shorter code words for the more frequent symbols (letters or words or operations) and longer code words for less popular symbols.

With these ideas in mind, let us briefly examine how real machine designers have dealt with this question. It is clear from the following that there is no consensus about what opcode format should be used in practice.

In the CDC 6600, six bits are used to represent 64 different central processor opcodes. There is a hedge, however, and in certain branch instructions three bits otherwise used to address a register are used to distinguish eight different types of branches. In later Cyber 70 machines derived from the 6600, other operations were added. This led to a mixture of some 6-bit opcodes and some 9-bit opcodes. The peripheral processors have a distinct set of 6-bit opcodes [Thor70].

The IBM 370 uses 8-bit opcode fields, because there are more than 128 but fewer than 256 opcodes executable in the processor. In addition, I/O commands use an 8-bit opcode [AmBB64], [Katz 71].

The PDP-11 is a minicomputer with 16-bit words. To take full advantage of such short words, some opcodes are 4 bits and others are longer, ranging up to 16 bits [StSi75].

The B1700 has a great deal of flexibility in that its memory can be addressed

TABLE 4.6 B1700 Operating System Operation Code

Operation Encoding Method	Total Bits for Operating System Operation Codes	Percent Memory Space Saved
Fixed 8 bits (360 type)	301K	0
4, 6, and 10 bits	185K	39
Huffman Coding (optimum)	172K	43

to the bit level. Furthermore, the machine is microprogrammed (see Section 4.2.2) so that the opcode set can be varied from one run to the next. For example, the designers implemented opcodes of 3- or 9-bit fields for use when the machine is executing FORTRAN or COBOL programs. A system development language (SDL) was used to write compilers and an operating system for the machine. When the SDL is running, opcodes of three different lengths may be used: 4, 6, or 10 bits. The ten most popular operations are encoded in the 4-bit length. The six other possible 4-bit codes are used as follows. Five of them indicate that two successor bits should be examined, yielding a 6-bit opcode. The last one indicates that 6 more bits should be examined, yielding a 10-bit opcode. Thus operation decoding proceeds in at most two steps; first, 4 bits are examined and then 2 or 6 more if so indicated in the 4.

Such a scheme is obviously an approximation of an optimal Huffman coding scheme. It is clearly better than a fixed format. The B1700 designers explored the tradeoffs in some detail [Wiln72a] and Table 4.6 shows their findings from an analysis of the operating system programs of the B1700. Using a fixed 8-bit format as a base line, their 4-, 6-, and 10-bit scheme can be implemented at a saving of 39 percent of the memory space, whereas an optimal encoding would only save 4 percent more. Of course, decoding the optimal scheme would be more difficult, but this depends on logic design details. The decoding of a 4, 6, and 10 scheme is not much more difficult than decoding 8-bit fixed format instructions. Of course, these savings are only part of the story. Address bits take up a good deal of space also. We shall return to variable length address encoding in Section 4.3.3.

4.2.2 Microprogramming

Boxes 5 and 6 of Fig. 4.1 can be implemented in a number of different ways. They transform compiled instruction operation codes—usually less than 10 bits—into a sequence of control words. Each control word may contain 100 or more bits and these bits cause any of the control points in the computer to change states in such a way that one step of the instruction is carried out. Some instructions are complete after one step, others may contain a sequence of 10 or more steps; but each step is carried out in response to one control word issued by the sequencer. Each of these control words will be called a machine *microinstruction,* and the entire set of microinstructions defines the machine's capabilities at the control level. Thus the sequencer transforms each decoded compiled operation code into a sequence of one or more microinstructions.

An elegant way to implement 5 and 6 was proposed by Wilkes [Wilk51] in 1951. He called it microprogramming and the goal was to simplify and provide design assurance for this part of a machine, a part that is susceptible to numerous minor design flaws. By the late 1960s, a number of microprogrammed control units had been implemented. With the wide availability of fast, cheap, random access memory, microprogramming really came of age in the 1970s.

The basic idea of microprogramming can best be explained using a diagram that closely follows Wilkes' original, Fig. 4.4. The next operation register is initially loaded from the operation code part of the current instruction register of Fig. 4.1. We begin by assuming that some compiled operation of k bits has been placed in this register. On the next clock, this operation code is gated into the operation decode register where it is used to select one of 2^k decode lines (recall Section 2.2.3).

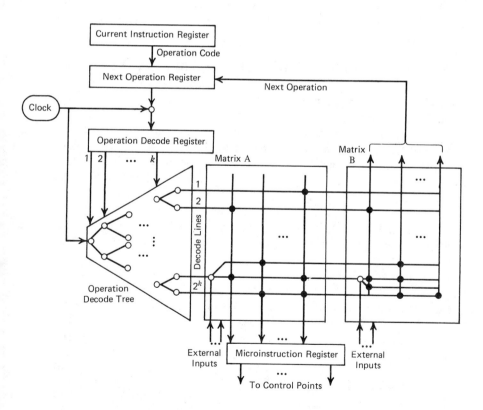

FIGURE 4.4   **ROM microprogram decoder and sequencer.**

The selected decode line may be connected to any of the vertical lines leading to the microinstruction register. The desired pattern is formed by connecting some lines and not connecting others. Each of these decode lines corresponds to a machine microinstruction; there are at most 2^k of these. Each microinstruction is usually a rather long word, perhaps 50–150 bits; for example, in the various IBM 360 models the microinstruction word length ranges from 56–100 bits. After a microinstruction has been formed in the microinstruction register, it is gated to control points throughout the machine to cause the machine to pass into the next desired state. This array which forms the microinstructions is called the A matrix. Notice that the A matrix may also accept external inputs. These inputs can be used in selecting options on various decode lines. For example, the sign of the accumulator might modify the execution of the current instruction.

Simultaneously with the operation of the A matrix, the right half of the decode line connections—also called the B matrix—operates to select the next microinstruction. This is done by connecting appropriate next operation lines to each decode line. There are just k of these next operation lines, and the output is gated back to the next operation register. Note that external inputs can also be used here, to modify the choice of a successor instruction. For example, an arithmetic overflow or other interrupt might alter the selection of the next instruction.

There are a number of implementation details that we will ignore here. One of the obvious questions concerns the sharing of microinstructions by two different compiled instructions. For example, suppose two different compiled instructions require the sequences of microinstructions ABC and ADE, respectively, where A, B, C, D, and E are distinct microinstructions. The original compiled instructions could be decoded on two different decode lines, each with the bit pattern corresponding to microinstruction A. Then each would select a different successor: B and D, respectively. Or we could select the same decode line for both compiled instructions, gating the same pattern for A to the microcode register in both cases, and then use an external input to select successor B or D. The details, of course, depend on considerations of the entire set of microinstructions and how they are used in the entire set of compiled instructions.

In this implementation, the A and B matrices can be regarded as read-only memories (ROMs). They can be modified with wire cutters and soldering iron, or somewhat less painfully using modern technologies. An interesting variation on this idea is to replace these ROMs with read/write memories sometimes called writable control stores. This allows more flexibility in that designers can correct their errors easily and, in fact, users can change the language the machine executes. The latter proposition is one that must be dealt with quite carefully. First, let us consider the system of Fig. 4.5.

Here the next operation register corresponds to the register of the same name in Fig. 4.4. On each clock cycle, this is gated to the operation decode

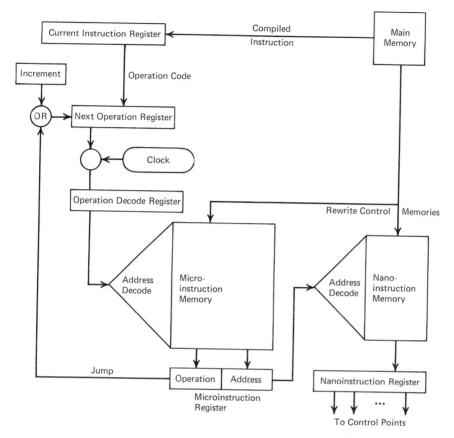

FIGURE 4.5   **Two-level writable microprogram decoder and sequencer.**

register and used as a memory address in the microinstruction memory. This selects one of 2^k microinstruction words of, say, 16 bits. This microinstruction is fetched to the microinstruction register where it is broken into an operation part and an address part. The address part is used to address another memory, the nanoinstruction memory that contains perhaps 256 words of, say, 100 or 200 bits. A nanoinstruction is fetched and used to activate control points throughout the machine. This memory plays the same role as the A matrix of Fig. 4.4.

At the same time, the operation field of the microinstruction is used to control the selection of the next microinstruction; it plays the role of the B matrix of Fig. 4.4. It can cause the selection of the next location in the microinstruction memory via the incrementer, a jump in that memory, or the fetching of another compiled instruction from main memory for decoding and execution. It can also cause other control unit activities to be carried out, such as interrupt processing.

A wide variety of microprogramming implementations have been carried out, ranging from schemes similar to that shown in Fig. 4.4 to those approximating that in Fig. 4.5. It is fairly common to use a one-level writable control store of several thousand words, that is, to replace the A and B matrices with only one read/write microstore. On other occasions, microinstructions and nanoinstructions are stored in the same memory; the choices are made on speed and economy grounds. The backup for any writable control store may be main memory (for a fast refresh), but there are also advantages to loading them from an external device. For example, a floppy disk is sometimes used to load the microstore and thus "initialize" the machine for users, for diagnostic testing, or perhaps for other purposes.

In use, the microinstruction memory may be viewed as containing a number of small subroutines, for example, for fixed-point addition, floating-point addition, fixed-point multiplication, and so on. The subroutines are "called" when the corresponding opcode is placed in the next operation register. Assembly type languages may be devised for writing microprograms, but "efficient" microprograms are very important. Various software design automation aids are possible in producing and checking microprograms.

A microprogramming example

To make matters concrete, consider the machine segment shown in Fig. 4.6, which is an elaboration of Fig. 3.16. Control points are labeled with numbers here, and we shall discuss their use in controlling processor operations. For example, any instruction that includes a memory access must activate control point 1. First, the address to be accessed (as indicated in a compiled instruction) is placed in the memory address register (MAR) and then 01 in bits 2 and 1 of the microinstruction, as shown in Fig. 4.7, causes this address to be decoded and the memory location in MAR to be fetched to the memory information register (MIR). On the other hand, 10 in bits 2 and 1 of the microinstruction causes the MAR to be decoded and the MIR contents to be written in that location. The addressable processor registers are controlled similarly by control point 2 as indicated by bits 3 and 4 of the microinstruction word (see Fig. 4.7).

Now, assume an instruction involves a memory fetch. This leads to the use of control point 3 to select a demultiplexer output destination for the MIR; the three possibilities are shown in Fig. 4.7. For transmissions on the processor bus, a unique destination must be chosen and we assume there are 16 possible destination registers. Among these are the CPA input registers A and B, the MIR and RIR, as well as the carry-save adder input registers, and so on. Bits 7–10 of the microinstruction specify this destination at control point 4. For simplicity, we consider as sources only the MIR (control point 3), the output of the CPA (control point 7), or otherwise the RIR (control point 8). In a real machine, both a bus source and destination field may be required. Here the

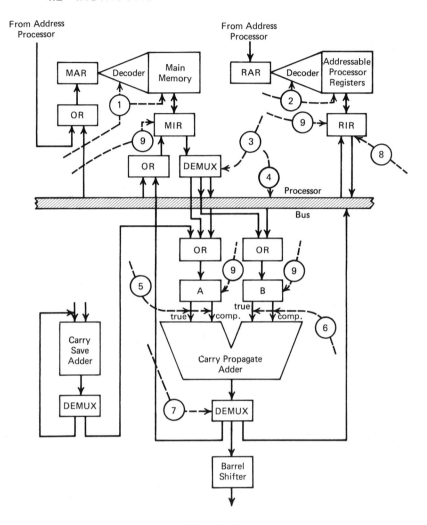

FIGURE 4.6   Control of processor segment.

control points labeled 9 are assumed to be enabled by the clock, thus allowing registers to accept new inputs on each cycle through the OR gates (or trees) that fan in their inputs. In practice these might be multiplexers that select one of several inputs, but here only one input to the OR is activated on each step. Of course, in a correct microinstruction, each register receives at most one input on each clock cycle.

Note that the registers we are discussing here—A, B, MIR, and RIR—are all used to hold intermediate results within the processor and are not available to the programmer. Any individual programmer addressable register is accessed by placing in the RAR the address in the compiled machine instruction, and

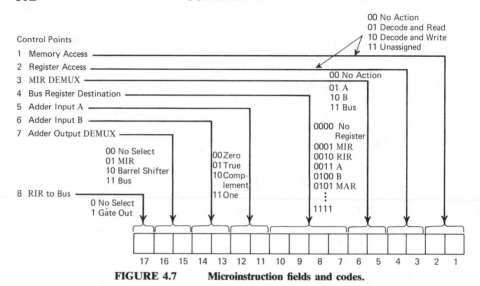

FIGURE 4.7 **Microinstruction fields and codes.**

then accessing the registers via control point 2. It is important to note that the fields of the microinstruction of Fig. 4.7 are used to direct words within the processor in accordance with the opcode of the compiled instruction. Thus, each compiled opcode selects a particular microinstruction whose fields have been appropriately set. It must also be realized that the operations contained in one microinstruction are normally carried out in one machine cycle.

Control points 5 and 6 are used to select the true or complemented outputs of registers A and B. Two bits are allocated for each of these in Fig. 4.7 because registers A and B could also be used to gate in all zeros and possibly another special pattern (e.g., a binary 1). These constants would be useful in subtraction, for example, which may require several passes through the adder as we saw in Section 3.3.3. The demultiplexer at control point 7 is used to select one of three destinations for the adder output in conjunction with bits 15 and 16.

Each individual microinstruction is used to control data paths for one clock period; so one assembled machine instruction may be executed as a sequence of several microinstructions. Consider, as an example, an instruction that adds the contents of memory location X and register 5 and returns the sum to register 5. In Fig. 4.8 we show a sequence of four microinstructions that carry out this addition operation. The four steps are labeled in the figure and the nonzero fields should be compared with Fig. 4.7. Note that the present discussion concerns the operation processor of Fig. 4.1, and that concurrently the address processor is operating. The address processor places the appropriate addresses (X and register 5 here) in the MAR and RAR at the proper times.

There are a number of options open in designing a microprogramming scheme; a useful one is the format of the microinstructions. At one extreme each control point could be controlled by one bit of the microinstruction. For example, each of the 16 destination registers in the above example would then need a unique bit, rather than the encoded 4-bit field used. A microprogramming scheme which tends to use decoded information in its microinstructions is sometimes called *horizontal microprogramming*, because the words are long and directly assigned to control points. In contrast, if many fields are encoded (as in our example), the scheme may be called *vertical microprogramming*.[2] In vertical microprogramming, the wires leaving the microinstruction register of Fig. 4.4 or the nanoinstruction register of Fig. 4.5 will be passed through a set of decoders before reaching the control points. The demultiplexer and bus destination fields of Fig. 4.7 are examples of this.

As indicated in the above discussion, several simplifying assumptions have been made in this example. Nevertheless, the fundamental ideas of sequencing a processor's operation are illustrated by the example. One important technique for processor speedup is in overlapping various processor activities, and

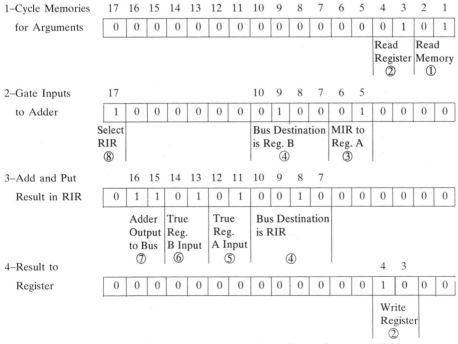

FIGURE 4.8   **Microprogram sequence for register and memory addition.**

<hr>

[2] Although these uses of the terms *horizontal* and *vertical* are common and somewhat vague, the terms have been used with at least two other meanings, which relate *horizontal* microprogramming to a set of micro-operations (simultaneously or sequentially executed) and relate *vertical* microprogramming to microinstructions that control a single resource or issue a single set of control pulses (see [GsMc75] and "microprogramming" in [RaMe76]).

this may be done in various ways at the microprogramming level. We shall discuss certain aspects of this in the next section. For more discussion of microprogramming for a number of real machines, see Husson [Huss70] and Tucker [Tuck67].

Tucker points out that the IBM 360/65 has a total of just 378 micro-orders, each of which is similar to the individual functions specified in Fig. 4.7; for example, gate certain bits of a register, shifted left one bit, into the adder. These are combined to form microinstructions, each of which controls the machine for one clock period, and he estimates that about 5×10^{21} different microinstructions are possible! Most of these are absurd, of course, and the universal instruction set of the CPU consists of fewer than 200 instructions. But, for diagnostic programs, for example, other useful instructions may be constructed from the micro-orders.

Microprogramming uses

The original motivation for microprogramming control units was to ease the engineer's difficulties in designing and building sequencers, that is, to provide design assurance. Modifying the A and B matrices is quite easy and this makes debugging and design changes easy to implement. Originally, the A and B matrices were implemented as arrays of diodes; now they are often implemented by read-only semiconductor memories.

With the arrival of low-cost, fast read/write semiconductor memories, other uses of microprogramming have become practical. Most of these involve the use of the microstore to implement an interpreter program which causes a machine to appear to execute another machine's instruction set. Often, the simulation of another machine on a microprogrammed machine is called *emulation*. The software and control unit hardware involved are called *firmware*. These are just new names for the old idea of interpretation of one machine's program by another machine, except that instead of using the processor to decode another machine's instructions, now the control unit does the job.

Emulation has two important uses. One is to allow compatibility across a family of computers, for example, the IBM 360 or 370 lines. One instruction set can be defined for a family of machines ranging from minicomputers to supercomputers. On the supercomputers, all operations may be implemented directly in specialized combinational logic, but on the minicomputers such operations as floating-point arithmetic can be implemented via microprogramming using a number of elementary microinstructions. Even when the minicomputer has only a 16-bit word, by a long sequence of micro-operations 32- or 64-bit floating-point arithmetic can be carried out. Although this seems to be a straightforward and simple idea, it is economically the most important use of microprogramming to date. Indeed, compatibility among a wide assortment of models was the key to the success of the IBM 360 and 370. By allowing customers to upgrade easily from one model to the next through microprogramming, IBM has been able to maintain its dominant position in the world computer market, in spite of its machines' other shortcomings.

The other important use for emulation arises in transferring programs from one machine to another. Suppose we can emulate machine THEM on our computer US and that at some other location, users have written a number of applications programs for machine THEM. To avoid writing those application programs for our US machine, we simply emulate machine THEM on US and then run THEM programs through emulation. Emulation of earlier IBM machines on the 360 is discussed in [Tuck65], and the STANDARD computer which attempted (but failed) to sell to the emulation market is described in [Rako69].

Another use of microprogramming—besides control unit design and emulation—is simply to run "new" instructions on a computer. For example, suppose the users of a machine decide to augment their languages with several vector operations. By microprogramming these vector operations, they can be executed "directly"; that is, assembly language programmers can use them and the assembler can carry out simple transformations (not, for example, macro expansions) and pass them along for execution. The microstore will contain the equivalent of the macro expansions for the operations.

The above idea can be extended to the "direct execution" of various high-level languages. This is a subject that is open to a great deal of discussion and wide variety of interpretations. But in several real computers, the microstore is loaded with different code depending on the kinds of jobs being performed. The B1700 is one example of this. Various IBM machines' microstores can be loaded for diagnosis of the system [John71]. In fact, hundreds of thousands of words of microcode may be used at one time or another in IBM diagnostics.

Another variation on the above theme is to load the microstore with specialized instruction sets in the factory, depending on what a particular machine's duties are to be. The B700, for example, is sold as a small business computer or an I/O controller—with appropriate microcode to specialize the machine to the task—and is an economic success for Burroughs.

The economics of microprogramming are difficult to assess quickly. As we noted earlier, the high speed and low cost of semiconductor memories have made microprogramming very popular in recent years. Some of the emulation applications obviously depend on the costs of hardware versus the costs of software—and recent trends would seem to favor hardware solutions here. There are also economies of scale involved. As a case in point, if Burroughs can build one type of B700 hardware and sell it for several different uses, the economics would seem to be quite favorable for microprogramming. This is more likely to be true for slower machines than for very fast ones, because slower machines can more painlessly absorb any time penalties of microprogramming.

Comparisons between read/write and read-only microstores also depend on many factors. Basically, a read/write microstore controller has a fixed cost and very wide flexibility, because it can be loaded with any kind of software. A simple read-only microstore controller will probably be cheaper. But as more and more operation types are added to a machine with either type of control unit, the read-only solution will become more expensive than the read/write approach. This follows from the fact that the read/write microstore can remain a fixed size and fixed cost (since it can be rewritten from time to time), whereas the read-only microstore becomes bigger and possibly the control of it becomes more complex as new types of operations are added. The crossover point between these two approaches is obviously crucial in designing microprogrammed control units.

As technology changes, the details of implementing microprogramming change. In the original IBM 360 line, semiconductor memory was not available, and yet over half of the models were microprogrammed. Large, inexpensive, fast semiconductor RAMs and ROMs have made microprogramming practical for many machines in the 1970s. For surveys of current trends, see [Flyn75, FLBK76].

A number of papers in [ChuY75] present various aspects of machines that are oriented toward high-level languages, some via microprogramming and some not. An early effort in this regard was EULER, an ALGOL 60 based language [Webe67]. Recall also the FORTRAN [BaSK67] and SYMBOL [RiSm71] efforts mentioned in Chapter 1.

It should be clear from the above that microprogramming is a subject of importance and multiple uses. On the other hand, it is a straightforward idea, and the mystical properties sometimes attributed to microprogramming disappear on close examination. Writing microprograms is not much different from writing any assembly language program. If one views a computer system as a whole, it is interesting to observe that within the control unit itself the microcosm of microprogramming does indeed involve many of the same ideas as those of programming the entire system. This seems to strongly support our presentation in Fig. 4.1 of this part of the system as a *processor* of operations.

For further reading about microprogramming beyond the references already cited, the surveys of [Davi72], [Rosi69], and [Wilk69] are recommended. Since many machines are now microprogrammed, the literature of various manufacturers may be consulted for specific details. Three special issues of the IEEE Transactions on Computers are of interest: [IEEE71], [IEEE74], and [IEEE75].

4.2.3 Control unit speedup

As we observed in Fig. 4.1, a number of steps are involved in the handling of each instruction by the control unit. It is clear from the above discussions that processing the operation part of each instruction can be quite complex. Later we will see that processing the address part of each instruction can also be very complex. A good deal of combinational logic together with a number of registers are involved in carrying out these control unit activities. A well-designed control unit seldom delays the other parts of the computer, all of which are dependent on the control unit. Hence, control unit designers are particularly concerned about speed.

A superficial examination of Fig. 4.1 reveals that the control unit's activities can be broken down into a number of more or less independent activities. Clearly, we can perform some of these activities in parallel; for example, the operation field and address field can be handled independently of one another. Furthermore, due to the complexity of processing each of these fields, the logic can be sliced into a number of serial segments for pipelining. In fact, pipelining was first implemented in computer control units in the late 1950s, before pipelined processors were constructed, in ILLIAC II [UIll57] and STRETCH [Buch62].

Throughout this section we will discuss various control unit and hence system speedup techniques, and it is important to our understanding of the ideas that we keep them separate, conceptually. To make the control unit itself fast in preparing one instruction at a time for execution, parallelism among various control unit functions is useful. To make the control unit fast in preparing a sequence of instructions for execution, pipelining the control unit is useful. In addition to these techniques for speeding up the control unit and hence the system, there are also techniques for allowing the control unit to execute more than one instruction at a time. This speeds up the system by exploiting parallelism among compiled instructions. Of course, as we saw earlier, sometimes one instruction specifies several functions that may be performed concurrently, thus allowing yet another kind of speedup.

In this section we will discuss several methods for speeding up computer systems. We will emphasize speedup of the control unit by pipelining and speedup of the system by allowing the control unit to discover parallelism among compiled instructions. These two ideas are closely related to each other.

4.2.3.1 CU pipelining

Fundamentally, control units carry out two basic processes: first, to fetch the next instruction, and second, to execute it. We have seen this in Figs. 1.8 and 1.9 and in Figs. 4.1 and 4.4. These will be called an I (instruction) phase and E (execution) phase[3] and are obvious candidates for a two-segment control unit pipeline. The first of these is carried out by the instruction processor of Fig. 4.1 and involves only a little combinational logic. The major time-consumer of this I phase is fetching the next instruction from memory. As we will see shortly, sometimes this time can be shortened by using an instruction buffer in the control unit.

The E phase is somewhat more complex because the instruction must be

---

[3] Our use of the terms *I* and *E phase* is somewhat different from that used by IBM.

decoded and sequenced, and the address must be transformed. In many computers the I and E phases form a two-segment control unit pipeline. Examples range from the IBM 360 and 370 to minicomputers and microprocessors. Many fast machines, in fact, do something even more elaborate than this. Because the E phase may be quite complex, it can be broken down into a sequence of steps and implemented as several pipeline segments. In the next two sections we consider ways of speeding up the E phase and the I phase.

4.2.3.2 Instruction buffers

In a number of computers, an instruction buffer is provided in the control unit. The idea is that when the instruction location register causes an instruction to be fetched for execution, it is copied into this buffer. When a loop is being executed, if the entire loop fits into the buffer, it can be executed repeatedly without further references to main memory. This frees main memory bandwidth for other purposes. It also allows the I phase of the control unit to operate faster because access to the buffer is usually much faster than to main memory.

For example, in the CDC 6600 eight 60-bit registers are provided for instruction buffering. Because instructions require only 15 or 30 bits, from 16–32 instructions may be held in the buffer. The buffer is filled, one word at a time from main memory, as a sequence of instructions is needed for execution. When a branch occurs, the branch unit (see Chapter V [Thor70]) determines whether or not it is to a location within the buffer. If it is, execution continues within the buffer. When a branch destination is an instruction outside the buffer, all instructions in the buffer are declared void and the buffer filling process begins again.

In another example, ILLIAC IV has an instruction buffer of 64 words, each of which holds two 32-bit instructions. It is filled in blocks of 8 words, whenever control transfers to any of the 16 instructions in such a block. Thus, on each cycle, the instruction location register is matched with a small associative memory to determine if the next instruction is in the buffer. If it is, the instruction is fetched and processed. If not, the instruction (together with the 15 neighbors in its block) is fetched from main memory to the buffer. The oldest block in the buffer is overwritten by the newly fetched block. In fact, this process is initiated halfway through each block for a new block so that if there are no jumps, the next sequential block of instructions will be resident in the buffer when needed [BBKK68].

Since most DO loops are small, a buffer that holds a few tens of instructions should be able to contain most compiled loops. Recall from Table 4.4 that 87 percent of the DO loops measured contained five or fewer source statements.

4.2.3.3 Execution pipelining

In the execution phase, control goes off in two directions: to the address processor and to the operation processor. We will ignore the details of the address processor until Section 4.3. For now, we will consider the operation processor and how it might be broken into several pipeline segments. This pipeline obviously ends with an operation sequencer as in Fig. 4.1, and if the sequencer requires a number of clocks to carry out an operation, the pipeline is held up until the sequencer finishes. As long as the sequencer is working, the control unit is doing its job of keeping the rest of the system active, so breaking the pipeline flow is acceptable.

In fact, one reason for having an execution pipeline may be to have several decoded instructions ready for execution. This serves two purposes, one of which is operation overlap, which we discuss below. The other is that potential breaks in the flow of instructions due to memory conflicts, complex address calculations, and so on, can be smoothed out in the steady state. Thus, if the execution pipeline holds one or two instructions which are decoded and ready to be executed, it serves as a kind of final instruction buffer.

Although we will not discuss the details of address processing until Section 4.3, it should be noted that instead of handling these functions in parallel with this execution pipeline, they can be integrated into the pipeline as address processing segments. Generally speaking, if the addressing mechanism is relatively simple, this approach is feasible. However, some address processing is very complex and time-consuming, as we shall see, and this is better handled as a separate parallel process.

It may be possible to sequence more than one part of the machine at once, either due to a single instruction which specifies several events, (e.g., a processor pipeline may hold a number of arithmetic operands at once) or by overlapping the execution of several instructions. By looking ahead to the $i+1$st operation while it is preparing to sequence the ith operation, the control unit may find that the $i+1$st operation can be sequenced at the same time as the ith operation. We refer to the operation specified by the ith instruction in compiled order as the ith operation, and the $i+1$st is the next compiled instruction. In a pipelined control unit, such lookahead is natural and relatively easy to implement because several successive instructions are always in some state of preparation for execution. By looking ahead, for example, the control unit can seek to discover parallelism between the memory and the processor, between several functional units in one processor, or between control unit and processor activities. Overlap between the memory and processor has been used in many real machines.

It was tacitly assumed above that the control unit knows which instruction will indeed be the successor of the one currently being executed. In the case of a conditional branch, this may not be known until after the execution of the current instruction. So in this case the problem must be considered further, as we will do in Section 4.4.1.

4.2.3.4   Operation overlap

Here we consider some of the details of the design and performance of control units which attempt to overlap the execution of several compiled instructions. There may be several kinds of dependences among the instructions. We discuss resource dependence and data dependence here; control dependence will be discussed later.

Resource dependence

Let us return our attention to the control unit's operation processing pipeline, specifically to the last few pipeline segments before the sequencer. Suppose we are able to compare each pair of adjacent instructions in compiled sequence as they pass through the pipeline. Imagine a matrix of dimension $n \times n$, where n is the number of distinct operations in the machine's instruction set. For each pair of instructions—say that an instruction of type i was followed by one of type j—we could look at the i, j entry in the matrix. If the entry were "yes," it would mean that both instructions could be sequenced at once; otherwise instruction i would be executed first, followed by j, as their appearance in the program specified.

If a machine had, say, 200 operations in its instruction set, this would require an array of 4×10^4 bits. But operations can be placed in categories, for example, arithmetic without memory access, arithmetic with memory access, and so on. If only 10 different types of overlap are to be checked, then an array of only 10^2 bits is needed. This usually means that the instructions must be decoded first to determine their category.

The details of such overlap vary from one machine to the next, but the types of overlap tested are fairly standard. One is the simultaneous operation of the processor and the memory; for example, the arithmetic operation of an instruction on two registers can be executed simultaneously with the next instruction which fetches a word from memory to another register. Another is the simultaneous execution of several processor functions for successive instructions; for example, the shift of one number and the addition of two others. A third example would be the execution of one processor operation and another in the control unit; for example, a floating-point addition and setting an index register, assuming the latter is carried out in the control unit. A fourth and final example would be the execution of an input/output operation and almost any other memory, processor, or control unit activity.

All of the above tests check for resource dependence among the operations

```
A ← B + C      FETCH R1, B      FETCH R1, B
D ← E + F      FETCH R2, C      FETCH R2, C
               ADD   R1, R2     FETCH R3, E
               STORE A, R1      FETCH R4, F
               FETCH R1, E      ADD   R1, R2
               FETCH R2, F      STORE A, R1
               ADD   R1, R2     ADD   R3, R4
               STORE D, R1      STORE D, R3
    (a)            (b)              (c)
```

FIGURE 4.9   **Execution lookahead.**

in a sequence of compiled instructions. The success of such checking depends on the lookahead distance, the compiler (or assembly language programmer) used, and of course, the resources available. Consider the program of Fig. 4.9a. Assume that two adders are available and that the lookahead distance is two. In other words, we examine the ith, $i+1$st and $i+2$nd instructions for possible execution overlap. If a compiler produced the code of Fig. 4.9b, then no overlap would be discovered between the additions, whereas in the code of Fig. 4.9c, the ADD R1, R2 and ADD R3, R4 instructions would be executed simultaneously.

Data dependence

In addition to this resource dependence checking, the control unit must also check data dependence. For example, the programs of Fig. 4.10 each have the same form as the program of Fig. 4.9. But no overlap is possible in Fig. 4.10a because it has an SF or δ dependence (recall Section 2.4.3). Figure 4.10b has an FS or $\bar{\delta}$ dependence, so processor overlap is possible if the FS dependence is preserved. This in turn depends on the sequence of compiled code and the speeds of the arithmetic operations and the memory. Clearly, such checking becomes quite complex as the lookahead distance grows.

In fact, there are several approaches to the problem of handling such dependences. In Chapter 2, we discussed breaking such dependences and one approach would be to have a compiler guarantee (at least in certain blocks) that no such dependences exist. Thus the control unit could proceed without making such checks. Another approach is to build such checks into the control unit. This was done in the CDC 6600, for example, and we will consider this approach below. A third approach is to pass the responsibility for maintaining the dependences on to the processor. This was done in the IBM 360/91 as we saw in Section 3.6.1.

4.2.3.5 Control unit lookahead performance

Of course, the speedup attained by looking ahead and overlapping instruction execution must be measured relative to a "serial" machine. In the limit this might be a Turing machine. But all real computers have a good deal of overlap built in. In one study, Foster and Riseman [FoRi72] determined that by using unlimited resources—registers, instruction buffer, processors, and so on—a CDC 3600 could be speeded up by an average factor of 1.72 for a set of seven programs. This presumed that lookahead stopped when a conditional jump was

A⟵ B+C   A⟵ B+C

D⟵ A+E   B⟵ D+E

   (a)   (b)   **FIGURE 4.10**   **SF and FS dependent statements.**

encountered. Note that the CDC 3600 was a well-designed, high-speed machine with some processor, memory, control unit overlap. The seven programs studied ranged from FORTRAN object decks to a complier and an interpreter. A total of nearly two million instructions were traced.

Foster and Riseman also studied speedup as a function of the instruction lookahead distance. We summarize their results in Table 4.7. No difference in the average was noted for lookahead greater than 32. Note that a lookahead of 4 is sufficient to achieve more than 95 percent the total average speedup.

This study was carried out in parallel with one by Tjaden and Flynn [TjF170], [TjF173], which reached almost the same conclusions. For a set of three CACM algorithms, an average speedup of 1.86 over the IBM 7094, a machine with overlap comparable to the CDC 3600, was made possible by using unlimited resources [TjF173].

Of course, the speedup achievable in practice depends on the complexity of the lookahead logic as well as the lookahead distance. The CDC 6600 can be used as a physical realization of a CDC 3600 with additional resources. Although they are not unlimited, there are 10 functional units as well as 8 instruction registers of 60 bits each. Because the instructions are 15 or 30 bits long, 16 or more instructions can be held in these registers in the 6600.

Lookahead in the 6600 is managed by a section of the control unit called the SCOREBOARD. It guarantees that all data, control, and resource dependences are honored. The SCOREBOARD is described in detail in Chapter 6 of [Thor70]. There are no published comparisons of the 6600's performance relative to a "serial" machine of a similar speed. However, several "typical" programs are analyzed in detail in Chapter 6, section F of [Thor70]; speedups over a "serial" 6600 are discussed for two programs and are shown to be 1.7 and 1.61. By properly reordering the assembly language instructions, the 1.61 can be improved to 2.5. In a paper about an optimizing compiler for the 6600, Thorlin [Thor67] shows an example with a speedup of 2.43. Thus it seems reasonable to conclude that speedups in the range of 1.5–2.5 are reasonable, which is consistent with the 1.72 measured by Foster and Riseman, and 1.86 measured by Tjaden and Flynn.

It should be clear that such numbers are quite sensitive to the sequence of machine instructions encountered. For many years, CDC did not provide a good optimizing compiler, so assembly language programmers often were able to get a factor of 2 or 3 improvement in performance over the compiler's object code for FORTRAN. Similar sensitivities are found in the CDC 7600

TABLE 4.7 Speedup versus Lookahead Distance

Lookahead distance	2	4	8	16	32	∞
Speedup	1.568	1.645	1.696	1.718	1.721	1.721

but the effect is not as pronounced because pipelining causes operators to appear to require just one time unit (with respect to initiation) in the 7600.

For a further discussion of this problem and similar results, see section 15.2 of [Buch62] where the design of the lookahead for the IBM STRETCH is discussed in detail. A detailed discussion of lookahead in the IBM 370/165 is given in [Flor74].

4.2.3.6 Memory conflicts

Even though we test the addresses and operations for dependence before proceeding, there can be resource conflicts in the main memory, because the instruction processor is really operating separately from the operation sequencer. Suppose we try to fetch the next instruction just at the moment that the current instruction tries to fetch an operand from memory. This leads to a memory conflict which the control unit must resolve. As we have seen earlier and will discuss below, this can be compounded by several functional units in the processor requesting memory access or an input/output device requesting a memory access at the same time as the above.

For this and other related problems, some kind of logic variously called priority, arbiter, or conflict resolution logic is used. The various units that can demand service from some other unit all issue their requests through this logic. Some rules about which request to service first are built into such arbiters. For example, slow requesters are usually serviced before fast requesters; if a rotating disk is denied a memory cycle, perhaps a rotation period of 30 ms will be lost before the opportunity will arise again, whereas the processor can be serviced just one memory cycle later. This situation is referred to as a disk "stealing" a memory cycle from the processor.

Another arbiter rule may be to service the control unit before the processor. For example, if new instructions do not flow to the control unit, the whole system may slow down or even become deadlocked awaiting instructions. Thus a memory service arbiter to resolve such memory conflicts is usually found in computers with lookahead or overlap. Throughout a computer system, questions about priorities arise, and we will continue to discuss the subject philosophically and in terms of implementation in Section 4.4.3 as well as in Chapters 5, 6, and 7.

4.2.4 Multiprogramming and multiprocessing

Given some computing facility, there is great appeal in the notion of trying to get more from the facility, either at no cost or by some kind of a small addition to the facility. One can try for higher system throughput, faster turnaround time, or some related goal. Multiprogramming and multiprocessing are basically motivated by the above kind of greed, and system designers have proposed or implemented many versions of these basic ideas in attempts to enhance computer system performance. But, of course, it is very difficult to get something for nothing, and every multiprogramming or multiprocessing scheme proposed leads to more complexity in the computer system's hardware, software, or both. It is our purpose here to explore the role of the control unit in various multiprogramming and multiprocessing schemes.

Multiprogramming

Multiprogramming's goal is to allow several programs (usually several users) to occupy main memory at the same time and to share the processor one after the other in quick succesion. Thus if one user's computation is held up by I/O another can be quickly available to use the processor. In order to be systematic, users may be limited to a fixed upper bound on the burst of computation time they are allocated. Especially in machines that are interactive, multiprogramming allows each user to have very fast response time, assuming that each short burst of computation allows the machine to respond with some result for the user. This type of system is usually called a *time-shared* computer, implying that both the memory and CPU are shared by a number of independent users. In large, batch processing systems, multiprogramming allows a number of small jobs to run together with one large job, for example, and the ensemble may be completed in approximately the time required for the large job. This is simply due to switching to small tasks when the large one is waiting for I/O.

Although such systems tend to need more main memory, not much extra control unit hardware is required. Efficient processor sharing requires an interval timer and fast state changing ability (these ideas will be discussed in Section 4.4.3). Memory sharing depends on memory protection hardware as well as virtual memory address mapping (these will be discussed in Section 4.3 and in Chapter 5). The overall question of managing a shared memory hierarchy and the performance of multiprogrammed and time-shared systems will be discussed in Chapter 7.

Multiprogramming is used in many computers. It was first introduced in the late 1950s on ATLAS [KELS62], the TX-2 [Clar57, Forg57], and STRETCH, and the early 1960s on the B5000 and CDC 6600, but now it is commonly found on some of most manufacturers systems, including minicomputers.

Instruction level multiprogramming

In short, multiprogramming is an attempt to achieve better system utilization by allowing several programs to occupy main memory at once and quickly switching the processor from one task to another. Previously we have discussed the idea of using instruction lookahead to allow more than one operation from a single program to be executed at once, each in distinct parts of a machine. Now let us consider combining these two ideas and engaging in instruction level multiprogramming by executing a sequence of instructions drawn from several different programs.

One way to do this is to expand the ideas of Section 3.6.1 where we noted that at the processor level, tags can be used to distinguish operands from several different assignment statements, thus allowing a mixture of them to flow through several arithmetic function units at once. Clearly, such tags could be used to distinguish operands from several distinct programs. Furthermore, we can use the same ideas at the control unit level to keep instructions separate.

In this way, one can hope to increase the duty cycles on various parts of the processor and the control unit. Instead of switching from one task to another on the basis of perhaps a 10 ms interval timer, tasks are switched at the level of individual clock intervals. Of course, such a design may require a good deal of extra logic to handle the tags, in order to provide more registers and other resources that allow several programs to be commingled. Instruction level multiprogramming can also be carried out in a much cleaner way by keeping the instructions of various programs separate. The following example discusses a case where the processor is rigidly time-shared on a one clock per program basis. This is particularly useful in the case of a simple processor.

The CDC 6600 uses instruction level multiprogramming in its peripheral processor units (PPUs) [Thor70]. The 10 PPUs are processors used for I/O handling, as will be seen in Section 6.3.3. They have a rich instruction repertoire and, in fact, are used for other operating system functions as well. They need not be very fast, however, because they must only be matched to the speeds of various I/O devices; but because a number of independent I/O activities may be in process, it is convenient to have a number of PPUs. The idea of instruction level multiprogramming has also been proposed for the CPU of computer systems; see, for example, [AsFR67].

This collection of slow "users" is an ideal situation for instruction level multiprogramming. Indeed, the hardware of the CDC 6600 has only *one* processor for these peripheral activities. But it has 10 independent and complete sets of registers for this processor, one set per "virtual" PPU. Every 100 ns, each of these sets of registers is operated on by the one physical processor; however, programmers regard the PPUs as 10 units, each with a 1 μs clock. Instruction timing for the PPUs is quoted in terms of a number of 1 μs periods, and they can access main memory in its cycle time of 1 μs. Each PPU has a memory of 4096 12-bit words with a 1 μs cycle time, as well as four registers, including an instruction location register of 12 bits; the other three hold data and addresses for various purposes. Thus each PPU can preserve its own state via registers and memory, from one of its 100 ns time slices to the next one 1 μs later.

Multiprocessing

The basic idea of multiprocessing is to share main and secondary memory among a number of standard processors, each with its own control unit. Because memory costs are high relative to the processor and control unit costs, this idea has a great deal of appeal, particularly when it is understood that no processor modifications are needed, and only small control unit modifications are required. The difficulties involve conflicts in sharing the memory and increasingly complicated software to allow the whole system to operate well.

Basically, the only hardware needed in the control unit is a facility to allow the processors to communicate with each other. We will discuss interrupt schemes for such communication in Section 4.4.3, and interprocessor communications in Chapter 6.

This immediately raises the question of who can interrupt whom, and for what reasons. In other words, the processors can be regarded as being in some kind of master/slave relation, or they can be regarded as symmetric. Each of these schemes allows a number of variations on the basic theme.

Multiprocessing has been in use since at least the mid-1940s, as we saw in Chapter 1. Most manufacturers now provide two to four processor configurations. In special situations (e.g., Safeguard [Bell75]) a 10-processor machine has proved effective. For a broad survey of multiprocessors and their structure see [Ens14].

4.2.5 Control unit taxonomy

In Chapter 1, we gave a superficial overview of several machine organizations. In this chapter we have seen that control units can be organized in a wide variety of ways. Here we will relate various control unit and processor organizations. Given any computer system configuration with one or more standard control units (see Fig. 4.1), we will now use the term *global control unit* to refer to all of the hardware used to prepare instructions for sequencing the entire system. Thus one or more instruction streams may be entering or physically contained in the global control unit at any time. Also, the global control unit may be executing one or more operations at any time. The global control unit has undecoded instruction streams as its inputs and decoded execution streams as its outputs, as shown in Fig. 4.11.

Note that there is no fixed relationship between the number of instruction streams coming in and the number of execution sequences going out. For example, a typical multiprocessor has an equal number of input and output streams; the CDC 6600 PPU hardware (see Section 4.2.4) has 10 instruction streams coming in (10 PPU instruction location registers) and only 1 execution sequence going out (1 physical PPU processor); whereas the CDC 6600 main control unit has 1 stream coming in and 10 possible execution sequences going out, since there are 10 independent functional units in the central processor.

For these ideas to make sense, we must be careful about how time is defined. We are considering "instantaneous descriptions" of the global control unit, or

FIGURE 4.11   **Global control unit streams.**

at most, time frames of only a few clocks. If the time window were wider, then various schemes for time-sharing a processor and control unit would confuse the issue. Thus, the input and output lines of Fig. 4.11 are intended to refer to physically co-occurring events, or ones that occur within a few clocks of each other.

Most modern computers can overlap processor, main memory, and secondary memory operations, but we will emphasize processing and main memory here. The goal is to formulate a useful taxonomy of machine organizations based on the global control unit and its relation to the machine's system capacity (see Section 2.5). We will discuss scalar and array instruction sets as control unit inputs, and scalar and array execution sequences as control unit outputs.

Instruction streams and execution streams

We distinguish *single instruction streams* from *multiple instruction streams* simply on the basis of the number of "programs" being executed at once, where a "program" is assumed to need a single instruction location register in some control unit for its execution. Thus two subroutines being executed simultaneously for one user, count as two instruction streams. For example, the application of SIM or TOG to DO loops in addition to BASs (recall Section 2.4.3) could lead to multiple instruction streams being derived from a single user's program.

The distinction between *single* and *multiple execution streams* is based on the ability of the global control unit to sequence one or more operation types, respectively, at once. For main memory and processor operations, an *operation type* corresponds roughly to what has traditionally been specified by a single operation code. For example, store, fetch, fixed-point addition, floating-point addition, left shift, logical compare, and so on, are single operation types. Recall that we discussed this in some detail with respect to processing in Section 3.6.3.

In terms of the above, four types of global control units can be distinguished:

1. **SISE:** single instruction single execution as in a typical uniprocessor computer;
2. **SIME:** single instruction multiple execution as in a multifunction processor (e.g., the CDC 6600 CPU);
3. **MISE:** multiple instruction single execution as in a uniprocessor with instruction level multiprogramming (e.g., the CDC 6600 PPUs);
4. **MIME:** multiple instruction multiple execution as in a typical multiprocessor computer system.

In terms of these four categories, where do parallel and pipeline computer systems fit? In such systems, a single instruction stream leads to the execution of a single operation type on many data elements, so they are SISE machines.

However, it is desirable to distinguish these systems from standard uniprocessors. This can be accomplished nicely by introducing the ideas of scalar and array instruction streams, and scalar and array execution streams. Thus, ILLIAC IV has scalar-type instructions with an array execution stream, whereas Burroughs BSP, the TI ASC, and CDC STAR have array instruction streams with array execution streams. The difference is that the ASC, BSP, and STAR have instructions that refer to whole vectors at once (with a base, limit, and increment for indexing them), whereas ILLIAC's instructions are more or less indistinguishable from those of a traditional uniprocessor.

To extend the above notion, we can call ILLIAC IV a SISSEA (single instruction, scalar; single execution, array) system, and the TI ASC, Burroughs BSP, and CDC STAR SIASEA (single instruction, array; single execution, array) systems. We can now distinguish a total of 16 types of systems, and this provides a reasonably good taxonomy for a wide range of machine organizations. In fact, all 16 categories correspond to physically meaningful machines. More details of this will be found in Volume 2. As a system is considered in more detail, its categorization may change; for example, the three SEA machines above may all be viewed as MEA when considered closely enough.

The point of this discussion is two-fold. First, it is useful to categorize machines based on their global control unit organizations. Second, it is important to realize that system capacity can be strongly related to these categories. Clearly, array execution machines have higher processor capacity than scalar execution systems of the same clock speed. Array instruction stream machines generally have higher control unit capacity in that more simultaneity of CU operation is possible; hence, instruction handling is faster.

The categories presented here are similar to those of Flynn [Flyn72]; he used data streams where we use execution streams. Although that also is a useful taxonomy, it seems difficult to make distinctions between real machines as clearly as can be done using execution streams.

4.3 ADDRESS PROCESSING

4.3.1 Addressing and accessing memory

In most computers, programs and data are stored in the same memory. Operating on program words as data words was once thought a good idea. In view of present-day interests in sharing programs among several users and the general difficulty in debugging programs, modifying anything but the address portion of an instruction is regarded as very dangerous. And, in fact, the address modification usually is carried out in the control unit without changing the contents of the address fields of the instructions stored in memory.

Address modification at execution time is indeed one of the most important and useful aspects of a control unit's activities. The address that is stored in the instruction's address field (the *immediate address*) is used as an initial value in most of the *address modification* schemes in present computers. The *effective address* that is used to access memory can be obtained from this initial value by any of a great variety of schemes which we will describe later. The address modification process is complicated by several memory characteristics and design goals:

1. Memory sharing
2. Virtual memory
3. Parallel memories
4. Low overhead (time and hardware)

We will expand each of these points below, but first we will quickly introduce them.

The memory of almost all computers must be shared by an operating system and at least one user. Often a number of different users have programs in main memory at the same time. Even a single user may require more data and program space than the main memory of a given machine, thus requiring the sharing of the memory with himself or herself.

For one large user or several smaller ones, it is obviously desirable to be able to maintain a smooth flow of information between main and secondary memory. In virtual memory machines, users are allowed to address all of the available memory in the system hierarchy, and the control unit and operating system are expected to carry out the I/O activities and maintain for the users the illusion that they have a large main memory available, any word of which can be accessed at any time.

In many current machines, sufficient main memory bandwidth can be obtained only by using a number of memory units in parallel. If all (or many) of them can be cycled at once, then relatively high bandwidths can be maintained. Somehow, the compiler and control unit must arrange the user's data structures in memory and translate immediate addresses into memory unit numbers and locations within the units.

Finally, as in all of machine design, the above processes must be carried out quickly so as not to slow down the machine too much. And, of course, they cannot be too expensive in hardware terms.

Indexing addresses

One of the simplest and oldest address modification schemes is carried out using index registers and an index adder. This is the standard way of indexing through arrays stored in main memory. As a simple example, assume we have a program containing a one-dimensional array A, whose size may be different each time the program is executed. We can compile all references to elements A(I) using a *base address* for the array A and an index register which contains the value of I. The base address refers to the location in main memory which contains the first element of the A array.

Suppose we have a source program containing the loop

$$\text{DO} \quad \text{S} \quad \text{I} \leftarrow 5, 10$$
$$\text{S} \qquad \text{A(I)} \leftarrow \text{B(I)}$$

and that the arrays begin with elements A(1) and B(1), respectively. This can be complied as

Address	Opcode	Arguments	Comments
	SETX	XR1, 3	Set register XR1 to 3.
LOOP	TESTX	XR1, 9, NEXT	Increment XR1; if XR1 > 9 go to NEXT.
	FETCH	B, XR1	Fetch B + XR1 to acc.
	STORE	A, XR1	Store acc. in A + XR1.
	JUMP	LOOP	Go to LOOP.
NEXT	·		
	·		
	·		

which will be executed six times for I = 5, ..., 10. Here A and B refer to the base addresses for the A and B arrays. Suppose that when the loop is executed, A = 875 and B = 963, as shown in Fig. 4.12. On the first pass through the loop XR1 contains 4 so the FETCH is executed with an effective address obtained by adding the base address 963 to the contents of XR1, so location 967 which contains B(5) is fetched. The STORE is executed with an effective address obtained by adding base address 875 to the contents of XR1, so the store is to location 879 or A(5). On the second pass through the loop, XR1 has been incremented by the TEST X instruction, so it contains 5 and B(6) is assigned to A(6). The loop is repeated 6 times, and when XR1 exceeds 9, the exit to NEXT is made.

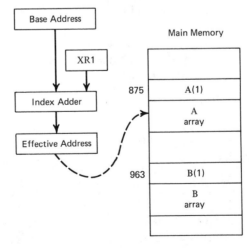

FIGURE 4.12   **Array indexing.**

The example above concerned the indexing of a one-dimensional array. Multidimensional arrays can be handled in a similar way. If a two-dimensional array A is indexed by I and J, we can use two index registers to sweep through it. By defining a linear combination of I and J to access array element A(I, J), the control unit can compute effective addresses using just a base location for A and two index register values. Clearly, this can be extended to arrays of higher dimension.

Furthermore, arrays need not be square or even rectangular. The popular cases of triangular matrices or limited bandwidth matrices, for example, can be accommodated by building special testing and incrementing logic into the control unit.

We can summarize the subject of indexing addresses by pointing out that it involves the use of a compiled, loaded instruction whose address field contains base address. This base address is used as initial value in a computation involving one or more index registers to compute an effective address. As loop indexes are incremented, so are index register values, thus yielding different effective addresses on subsequent passes through the loop.

Indirect addressing

Another address modification technique is *indirect addressing*. This is implemented by fetching the word stored in the location indicated by the instruction's immediate address, then extracting the address field of this word, and using the extracted address as the effective address to access a memory location. For example, consider the instruction

FETCH 837*

where * is used to indicate indirect addressing through location 837. The word in location 837 is fetched first. If its address field contains 952, as in the example of Fig. 4.13, we execute the FETCH again, this time using 952 as an address. This results in fetching X. Clearly, indirect addressing can be used with other operations using a similar definition.

Furthermore, *multilevel indirect addressing* can be carried out as follows. Suppose, in the example of Fig. 4.13, that we examined one other bit in the

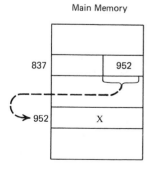

Main Memory

FIGURE 4.13   **Indirect addressing.**

word stored at location 837. If this bit—call it the indirect addressing bit—contains a zero, we proceed as discussed above. But, if this bit contains a one, then we indirectly address location 952. That is, we extract its address field and examine its indirect addressing bit. The process continues until an indirect addressing bit is set to zero at which point we have our effective address.

Indirect addressing has many practical uses. As an example (which is *not* very practical, because almost all real machines have index registers) we could use indirect addressing to allow a memory location to serve as an index register. This simply requires incrementing the contents of the immediately addressed word each time through the loop. Thus

$$\text{FETCH } A^*$$

will access a different element each time it is executed, if the contents of A are changed appropriately.

Similarly, we can use indirect addressing to allow communication among several procedures through an invariant location. For example, suppose some location α is known to several procedures and is used as an address in many places. Then without changing the address fields in the many places that refer to location α, we *can* change the memory location accessed by all of the instructions simply by changing the contents of the address field of the word in location α. This is an easy way to communicate parameters between procedures, for example. Later we will see other examples of the use of indirect addressing.

Indirect addressing has appeared on many computers; for example, the IBM 7094 and PDP-11 have one-level indirect addressing. But some machines have dropped the idea of an indirection bit in the instruction format, providing the effects of indirect addressing by other methods; for example, the IBM 360 and 370 series as well as the CDC 6600 and its successors do not have indirect addressing bits. Burroughs machines effectively use indirect addressing for most memory accesses using their descriptor mechanism, as we shall see in the next section.

4.3.2 Program and data relocation and bounds

When any program is loaded into a computer's main memory, certain address fields must be modified before it can be executed. This is because the locations of variables and constants as well as the destinations of jump instructions are compiled without knowing exactly where in memory the program will reside when it is executed. Usually they are compiled relative to location zero and then a loader program adds a relocation constant equal to the *base address* into which it loads the first word of the program. Of course, not all address fields are relocatable; examples are address fields containing immediate operands or jumps compiled relative to the location in the program of the jump instruction. The address fields to be relocated are flagged somehow by the compiler so the loader's job is straightforward.

User 1
User 2
User 3
Unused Space

User 1
User 3
User 4
Unused Space

(a)   (b)   **FIGURE 4.14**   **Memory sharing.**

Now let us consider this question in the context of main memory sharing between several users. For example, suppose three users are sharing memory, having been loaded in contiguous blocks of memory locations, as shown in Fig. 4.14*a*. Now suppose that User 2 completes execution and is written to the disk. The next user to be run, say User 4, may require more space than User 2 but less than the sum of the unused space and that vacated by User 2. We can run User 4 just by moving, say, User 3 adjacent to User 1, and then loading User 4 into the newly freed block, as shown in Fig. 4.14*b*. This requires that the loader program be used to reload User 3 at a new base address and then load User 4.

Usually each user has a main program and several subprograms that are called by the main program or other subprograms. Each of these procedures (main and subprograms) must be loaded as described above, each using a different base address. Then, before execution, all of the procedures must be linked together by providing each calling procedure with knowledge of the base address of the called procedures.

Once a set of procedures and their data are loaded and linked they can be properly executed. But now let us raise the question of memory sharing in the case of just one user. If the main memory is too small for all of one user's program and data, the user may have to overlay parts needed earlier with parts needed later. For example, in Fig. 4.15, if procedure 1 uses array A for a while and later needs array C but not array A, we can write A to disk, read C into the space formerly occupied by A and continue execution. This assumes that

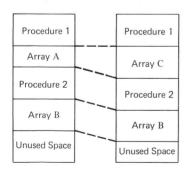

FIGURE 4.15   **Block translation.**

procedure 1 was loaded with the knowledge that C would occupy this space (so its access references are correct) and that C is no larger than A. If C is in fact larger than A, we could slide procedure 2 and array B up or down in memory to take advantage of the unused space. If we slide it up and put C at the bottom of the memory, then the correct base address for references to C must have been known to the loader, otherwise we will have to readjust these addresses when the overlay is carried out. Alternatively, we could slide procedure 2 and array B down, as shown in Fig. 4.15b. But whenever procedure 2 and array B are moved, they will have to be reloaded and relinked to procedure 1. It is clear that if such overlays happen frequently, a good deal of time can be wasted. Furthermore, we are complicating the operations of the original compiler and the loader by requiring them to be concerned with these *dynamic storage allocation* matters.

The problems we have been discussing are sometimes called memory *checkerboarding* or *fragmentation*. They can be avoided by various *memory compacting* schemes such as those we have been discussing which, roughly speaking, amount to squeezing out holes in memory use from time to time. Such schemes suffer from several faults. They are time-consuming, they require extra software complexity (in the compiler, loader, linker, and operating system) and they are ad hoc in that more and more fixes are needed as new memory sharing cases arise (e.g., multiuser sharing, single user overlays, etc.). Memory compacting is an example of a dynamic storage allocation method; we will discuss others below.

Dynamic relocation registers

Instead of relocation at load time, the appropriate addresses can be relocated at run time by use of relocation registers. Just those addresses that would have been modified by the loader are now modified by adding to the immediate address the contents of a *relocation register* or *base register*, as the address is being processed for execution (see Fig. 4.16).

Although this complicates the hardware of address processing, it obviously simplifies program loading. Now the loader simply writes the words into

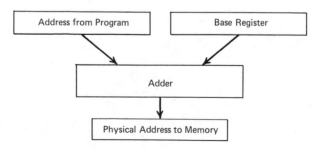

FIGURE 4.16   **Base register address mapping.**

(a) Source Statement	$B(J) \leftarrow A(I) + X$
(b) Loaded Statements	FETCH 360
	ADD 438*, XR1
	STORE 439*, XR2
(c) Executed Statements	FETCH 1360
	ADD 1735 + XR1
	STORE 1450 + XR2

FIGURE 4.17   **Addressing example.**

memory without any responsibility for address modification. Memory compacting can be done more quickly, as in the example of Fig. 4.14.

Data descriptors

Although the use of base registers for dynamic program relocation is a useful idea, the second example above implied another problem that they do not solve. When we overlayed array A with array C, the details of carrying out the I/O operations were ignored. The responsibility for deciding when and where this should be done can be left to the user, or we could have the control unit and software carry this out—thereby removing a very unpleasant task from the user.

The use of a *data descriptor* is fundamental to removing this responsibility from the user. A data descriptor is a word associated with an array (and possibly scalar constants and variables) that contains a number of important characteristics of the array, including its size and its location. Both of these can be allowed to change during the course of a computation. Thus in our example, data descriptors for arrays A and C could be used to expedite their exchange between main and secondary memory. Furthermore, when C is brought into main memory, its descriptor can be used to indirectly address the array. Thus, no matter where C is located in main memory, we can always address it indirectly if we know the location of its descriptor. Hence, the relocation of an array can be handled by a relocation register that obtains the array's base value from the array's data descriptor.

To make matters concrete, we illustrate the use of data descriptors, index registers, and a base register in the following example. Consider the simple assignment statement of Fig. 4.17a. After compilation and loading we have the three statements of Fig. 4.17b. Assume that the program has been compiled relative to location 000 so the scalar X is stored at relative location 360. Descriptors for arrays A and B are at locations 438 and 439, respectively. If we assume that the location in main memory of the base of the array is in the address field of the descriptor word, we can access the arrays by indirectly addressing the descriptors—denoted by an address followed by an asterisk in Fig. 4.17b. Since A and B are indexed arrays, the ADD and STORE instructions also contain references to index registers which will contain the values of I and J, respectively.

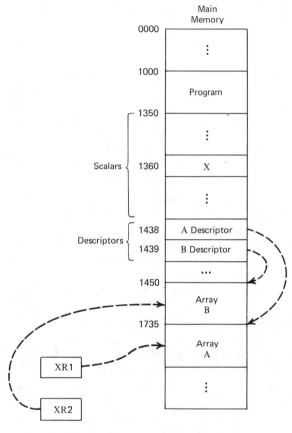

FIGURE 4.18   **Loaded program.**

When the program is loaded, assume it begins at memory location 1000 as shown in Fig. 4.18. When execution begins, a base register is loaded with 1000, which corresponds to the beginning of the loaded program. Now, as indicated in Fig. 4.17c, the FETCH instruction's address field is dynamically relocated using the base address, so indeed X is fetched from location 1360. Then to access A(I), the descriptor of A is indirectly addressed. This causes access to the address field of location 1438—438 plus the contents of the base register. Here we find the address 1735, which is the base of array A. This is an absolute address; hence, it is not modified by the base register. However, it is indexed using index register 1 to fetch A(I). By a similar process we access B(J) and the example is finished.

Descriptors in one form or another are used in various machines. The idea was pioneered by and is widely used in Burroughs machines; more details about descriptors and their use will be given in Section 4.3.4.

Bounds checking

Whenever and however a control unit generates an effective address, the validity of that address is suspect. A user may be indexing through a one-dimensional array which is declared to contain 100 elements—but he may run a DO loop to 110, for example. The 10 addresses beyond the array may be in another array, in the program, or in someone else's program. Unless the effective addresses are compared with the valid range of an array, a disaster could occur.

Incorrect addresses may be generated due to carelessness or stupidity, as above, or they may be generated willfully. For example, a student may attempt to bring down a university's computer center by overwriting key portions of the operating system. Or a curious employee may try to print out the payroll tables for all of a company's employees. Many similar examples of unauthorized access to portions of memory can easily be imagined.

To help prevent such incorrect memory accesses, the control unit can be used to test the validity of each address generated. Basically, this can be done at two different levels. In order to protect others sharing a memory from the active user, each user can be restricted to one or more areas of memory. If a user tries to leave these, *bounds registers* can be used to trap him. By comparing each effective address generated with the limits specified by the bounds registers, we can guarantee that a user is confined to certain areas of memory. Of course, a devious user may attempt to modify the bounds registers before doing damage, but for benign users this method is effective.

The benign user often needs protection from himself, as well as the above which protects him from others and vice versa. By protection from himself, we refer to the first example given in this section—the case of a loop that exceeds the array boundaries. Protection from errors like this can also be achieved by control unit checking. For example, upper and lower bounds on each array access can be determined by the base and limit of the array. These can be compared with each access attempted to that array, and the user can be trapped if he makes an error. Figure 4.19 illustrates the use of a bounds register that effectively limits the distance in memory that an address may be from the base register. Invalid addresses cause an interrupt (see Section 4.4.3).

4.3.3 Addressing formats

Previously we pointed out that there is a great deal of variety in type and format of instructions from one machine to the next. Only within families of machines is there uniformity. We outline the address formats of the CDC 6600, the IBM 360 and 370, and the B1700 here to expose the reader to a range of possible schemes.

The CDC 6600 is a three-address machine with a relatively simple class of instructions. Basically, there are two formats used in the central processor, 15 bits and 30 bits, as shown in Fig. 4.20, and these match the 60-bit memory

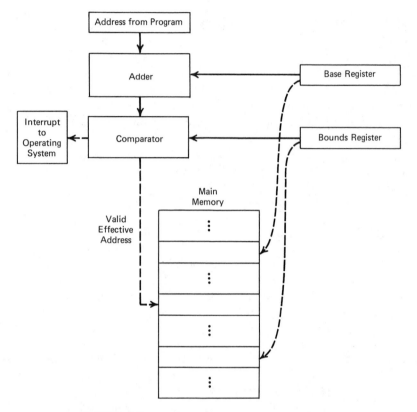

FIGURE 4.19   **Bounds register address validation.**

word. There are 64 basic opcodes. Three sets of 8 registers each are available for operands (60 bits), addresses (18 bits), and indexing (18 bits), respectively [Thor70].

The operand registers (X_i) are paired with "partner" address registers (A_i). Registers one through five are used for fetches, six and seven for stores, and the eighth for another purpose (Exchange Jump). This reflects the fact that more operands flow into the processor than results flow out. Thus, if the memory address of operand C is placed in A_3, this causes C to be fetched to X_3. When C is in X_3 and the other argument of an operation is available in another X_j, the operation takes place.[4] The SCOREBOARD logic performs all of the tests necessary to ensure that operands are available before the operation proceeds. If C is the operand (through reference to X_3) of another operation later, no memory reference will be required. Still later, if the memory address of C is placed in A_6, this causes the contents of X_6 to be stored in the memory location of variable C.

[4] Recall the discussion of Section 3.6.1 and Fig. 3.17, describing the scheme used in the IBM 360/91, which is somewhat more elaborate than this.

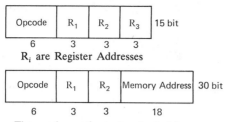

R$_i$ are Register Addresses

The numbers refer to lengths in bits

FIGURE 4.20 **CDU 6600 instruction formats.**

Arithmetic, Boolean, and Shift instructions refer to operands in registers using the 15-bit instruction format. Address registers may be modified by index registers, also using instructions of the 15-bit format. The index and address registers may be loaded from memory or modified by constants using the 30-bit format. Branch instructions also use the 30-bit format to hold a destination address.

The IBM 370 uses a fixed 8-bit opcode field and has five essentially different instruction formats. These are distinguished by their addressing schemes, and we illustrate them in Fig. 4.21. Notice that the length of each format is a multiple of 8 that is matched to the byte level addressability of the memory [Katz71].

The 370 processor has a set of 16 general-purpose, 32-bit registers. These

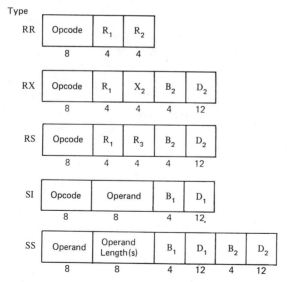

General Registers: R$_i$ for Data, B$_i$ for Base Addresses, X$_i$ for Index Values. The D$_i$ are literal displacement fields.

FIGURE 4.21 **IBM 370 instruction formats.**

are referred to by R_i, X_i, and B_i to denote their use for holding operands, index register values, or base register values, respectively. The RR (register to register) format resembles the 15-bit CDC 6600 format, except that it uses a two-address format. The RR and RX formats both return results to the location of the first operand. The RX (register and indexed storage) format gets one operand from R_1, whereas X_2, B_2, and D_2 are used to generate a memory address for the other operand. B_2 and X_2 point to general-purpose registers used as a base register and index register, respectively. The sum of these values and displacement D_2 gives an effective address. The SI format is similar, but here an immediate operand and a storage location are specified. The above three formats are varieties of two-address instructions. The RS format uses three addresses: R_1, R_3, and one formed from B_2 and D_2. The SS format specifies two addresses, but this is in a sense a vector instruction format because a number of operands in succession may be accessed, beginning at these addresses. The operand length field is used to specify the number of bytes to be accessed of one or both operands. This can be used, for example, to move character strings from one area of memory to another or perform decimal arithmetic on strings of digits of arbitrary lengths.

The instruction formats of the IBM 360 and 370 are similar. All 370 models have an advanced virtual memory scheme, but only a few of the 360 models did. Nevertheless, a kind of virtual memory scheme did exist on the 360 using only base registers, and we will sketch this now. As we will see in Section 4.3.4, virtual memory hardware can become rather complex.

In the 360 and 370, only the low-order 24 bits of the general-purpose registers are used in address arithmetic (base register or index register operations). This allows a 2^{24} byte virtual memory space. However, the displacement field D_i is just 12 bits, allowing access to any of 4096 bytes in a 4096 byte block of virtual memory. Because there are 16 general-purpose registers, any of these can be used to point to one of 16 different blocks of virtual memory—each block containing the 4096 bytes addressed by the displacement field. Thus, at any moment a program may have access to at most $2^4 \cdot 2^{12} = 2^{16}$ bytes of the 2^{24} bytes of virtual memory. Because some of the general-purpose registers are usually being used for operands and indexing, less of the virtual memory is actually accessible at any time. Notice, however, that we have reduced the number of bits needed for addressing memory from 24 to just 16 per instruction (12 for displacement and 4 for base register) by this technique. This method of addressing memory suffers from a number of shortcomings in contrast to the paging methods we will present in Section 4.3.4.

Recall that in Section 4.1.2 we also discussed 0- and 1-address formats. One-address formats assume the existence of an accumulator that serves as an implicit second address. Zero-address formats assume the existence of a stack as a source of operands and a destination for results. Such schemes have been used in many Burroughs machines, and we will discuss stacks in more detail in Section 4.3.5.

Next, we consider address formats on the B1700. The B1700, being a microprogrammable machine, allows different field allocations for different purposes. For example, in the system development language (see Section 4.2.1.3), data addresses may be 8, 11, 13, or 16 bits long. Data addresses in FORTRAN are usually 24 bits long. For COBOL, the format for a program need not be decided until after the compiler has examined the particular program to be compiled!

Using these techniques, the B1700 designers examined 20 diverse COBOL programs and 7 FORTRAN programs. They measured the overall memory requirements in bits, of the programs in the B1700 compared with the IBM 360. Note that space is saved due to the opcode compaction discussed in Section 4.2.1.3, the data address compaction discussed above, and to program address compaction. The measured results [Wiln72b] for FORTRAN showed a 50 percent space saving in the B1700 as compared with the IBM 360 and a 70 percent space saving for the COBOL programs. In other words, FORTRAN on the B1700 required just half the memory space needed on the IBM 360, and COBOL in the B1700 needed less than one-third the IBM 360 space. Of course, somewhat more complex hardware is needed to handle the variable length formats, but in view of the tremendous savings of memory space the technique seems to have justified itself very well.

Finally, we point out that as machines' word lengths get shorter, designers are harder pressed to use complicated instruction formats. For example, the 16-bit PDP-11 has more than a dozen different instruction formats (in contrast to Figs. 4.20 and 4.21) ranging from zero-address (16-bit opcode) to two-address (4-bit opcode) instructions. This clearly reflects the designers' efforts to make the best use of the limited number of bits available in each memory word. Some PDP-11 instructions span two memory words using 16-bit addresses; see [Tane76] or [StSi75].

4.3.4 Paging and segmentation

Two of the original memory design goals we mentioned were memory sharing and virtual memory. In the use of base registers, bounds registers, and array descriptors, we have seen approaches to the implementation of both goals. An important flaw in these ideas concerns the utilization of main memory. We have been assuming that whole programs and arrays were being moved in and out of main memory. Intuitively, it would seem that if only small parts of programs and data arrays were brought into main memory at one time, it might be possible to execute a fairly large number of instructions before other parts of the program and data were needed. Thus we could avoid having some programs and data occupying large segments of memory that are infrequently accessed. It follows that more users could share a fixed size main memory in this way.

This is exactly the motivation for the use of paged memory hierarchies. A *page* of program or data is a fixed size block of words, say 1024 words. A *page frame* or *page slot* is a block of main memory locations of the same size, usually with fixed boundaries in main memory. A *paging scheme* is a hardware and software method for moving pages from secondary memory to page frames in main memory when needed and returning the pages to secondary memory appropriately. Paging allows main memory sharing and virtual memory addressing to be implemented and avoids the problem of main memory fragmentation.

Let us consider the addressing of virtual memory. Assume we have v bits of address in the effective addresses generated by the control unit; this allows us to address a virtual memory of 2^v locations. In some machines it is true that the size of virtual memory is equal to the total number of locations in the entire memory hierarchy. If the hierarchy, in fact, has fewer locations than 2^v, we can regard some of the 2^v locations as illegal or we can assume, for example, that addressing them causes an operator to mount a tape, thereby expanding the on-line hierarchy.

If each page contains 2^l *locations* or *lines* (these can be bytes, machine words, etc.), then the virtual memory contains a total of 2^{v-l} pages. Let us assume that the main memory has a total of 2^p locations, or a total of 2^{p-l} page frames.

In Fig. 4.22, we illustrate these ideas with a picture of one user's situation at an instant of time. This user has k active pages of virtual memory, some of which are in main memory (e.g., pages i and j), and others of which are in secondary memory (e.g., pages l and k). To keep track of each page at any moment, each user has a *page table* as shown in Fig. 4.22. This is simply a pairing of virtual memory locations with physical (main or secondary) memory locations for that user. For example, in the Amdahl 470 V/6 System [Amda75], a hardware page table has 256 entries and these may be from up to 31 different virtual memory users.

We can get an idea of how a typical paging scheme works by following a simple example from the beginning. A user's program and data pages are normally kept in secondary memory when he is inactive. On activation of a user, some of his program and data pages are brought into main memory; they may be placed in any unused page frame and the page table is updated accordingly. Each time the program must access memory for data or a new instruction, the control unit consults the page table to determine where in physical memory the next virtual address may be found.

If the next virtual address is in main memory, the page table yields an address to be used as a base register value. The line number within the page—being the same in virtual and physical memory—is added to the base value to get a physical address. In Fig. 4.23, we show some details of the control unit hardware required to carry out these steps.

If the page containing the next virtual address is not in main memory—a

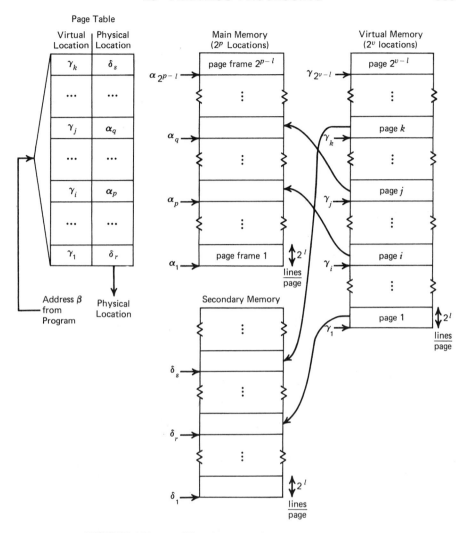

FIGURE 4.22   **Virtual memory instantaneous description.**

condition called a *page fault*—the page table produces a descriptor, allowing us to fetch the needed page from an indicated address in secondary memory. If a page fault occurs, the control unit must suspend the execution of the current user, fetch the page from secondary memory, and update the page table to show the new location of this page. This is summarized in Fig. 4.23. Whenever a page fault occurs, the operating system usually switches control to another user. The user who generated the page fault may be restarted at some later time when the needed page has been accessed.

The active users' page tables are normally kept in main memory. By adding

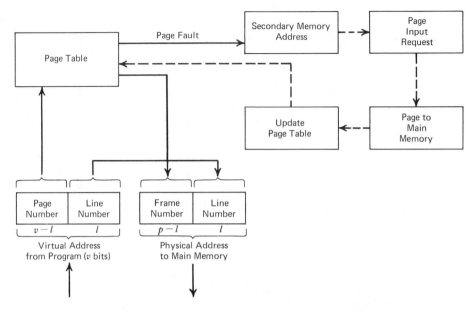

FIGURE 4.23   **Address mapping sequence.**

the base address for a user's page table to the page number to be accessed, we can find the proper page table entry. Doing this for each memory access, however, could slow down the machine operation substantially, for in this case we are really indirectly addressing the memory on each step.

In machines designed for paging, the control unit often has a small associative memory[5] which is used to hold the page table entries for the most recently accessed pages. Thus, if we continue to access these pages, the address mapping from virtual to physical memory can be carried out very quickly. If β is a program generated address, we must determine if

$$\gamma_t \le \beta \le \gamma_t + 2^l - 1$$

for all t in the associative memory. If the test is successful, the associative memory delivers the proper frame number. If not, we must consult the page table in main memory as before, and replace one of the associative memory entries with that for the newly accessed page. Thus the page table of Fig. 4.22 may be regarded as an associative memory containing information about the most recently used 8 or 16 pages, plus a main memory table containing a descriptor for each of the user's pages.

---

[5] As pointed out in Section 1.1.2, an associative memory can be accessed via the contents of certain parts of its words rather than via an address. Here, the page number is used to access the memory and a unique frame number stored with that page number is fetched. In Section 5.4.2.3, more details about associative memories will be presented.

In some cases, virtual memory is in fact *smaller* than the physical size of main memory. For example, an early MIT time-sharing system CTSS [CoDD62] was implemented on an IBM 7094 which normally had 32K memory words. The CTSS machine was augmented with 32K extra words to hold the operating system, whereas the original 32K held users' programs. Although each instruction had just 15 bits of address, an extra bit in the control unit—which could be set only by an operating system instruction—was used to determine whether an address referred to the "high" or "low" 32K words.

As a final example, consider the DEC PDP-11 with its 16-bit words and 16-bit memory address (see Section 4.3.3). This defines a total of 64K bytes of addressable virtual memory. Yet the Unibus (see Section 6.3.1) has 18-bit addresses and this allows the addressing of 256K bytes of physical memory. By a scheme analogous to Fig. 4.22, the PDP-11 augments 16-bit virtual addresses to obtain 18-bit physical addresses for main memory accessing [StSi75]. Although this affords some flexibility in using the machine, it should be regarded more as an anomaly arising from the minicomputer's short physical word length rather than a "great" use of the virtual memory idea.

Probably the first operational paged memory system was in the ATLAS computer at Manchester University. ATLAS had a main core memory of 32 512-word pages plus a drum "backing store," and a 32-register page table was used to map addresses into main memory. In the event of a page fault, an interrupt was generated that initiated the required I/O transmission. ATLAS was a very innovative and influential system. For more details see [KELS62]. The first commercially available virtual memory system was the Burroughs B5000 [Bart61], to be discussed shortly.

Segmentation

The use of paging to implement our original goals of memory sharing and virtual memory gives us a uniform addressing procedure and slices main memory into small pieces so that a large number of users can share main memory at once. It is quite likely that these users may want to share programs and data, as well as jointly occupying main memory. For example, library procedures, compilers, and various data files are candidates for sharing by several users. If the programs are written as nonself-modifying or *pure proce-dures*, there are no logical problems with this.

This shared information can be thought of as being in the virtual memory of several users. If the shared information is data, then when a page is accessed by, say, user 1, it is brought into main memory and the page table of user 1 allows him to access it. If user 2 wants to access it, his page table can be set to the same physical location as user 1's page table entry for the data. Thus they both can access the same physical memory locations, even though the shared data occupied different portions of their virtual memory. Note that if the data file's size is allowed to grow as time passes, then each user must allocate an indeterminate amount of "extra" virtual memory space to this data. This is one difficulty that segmentation helps to avoid.

Now suppose the shared information is a program rather than data. Two (or more) users can call the shared program, just as they accessed shared data. When the shared program is executed, however, what page table will it use? It could use one of its own or it could use that of its caller, modified somehow. The point is that if information is to be communicated back and forth between the shared program and each user who calls it, *each user and the shared program* must somehow share a page table when the shared program is being executed.

This problem is handled in a number of paged machines without segmentation by establishing certain conventions. For example, main memory may be cut in half with one half sharable and the other not sharable. Whole programs can thus be shared if they are written as pure procedures. But parts of programs, for example, subroutines, cannot easily be shared; in some systems, running any FORTRAN program causes the entire FORTRAN subroutine library to be fetched to the shared half of main memory. To allow sharing in a more flexible way, segmentation can be used as follows.

A *segment* is a block of virtual memory. A virtual memory address in a machine with segmentation has the form:

Segment Number	Page Number	Line Number

A *segmentation scheme* is a hardware and software method for partitioning virtual memory into a number of segments. It allows the allocation to a user of many segments for his own information, and some segments can be shared with other users; the segments can also be of various sizes.

As we learned earlier, paging is a way of slicing virtual memory and physical memory into small blocks and binding virtual memory to physical memory through the page table. Segmentation is a way of slicing virtual memory into multipage blocks (each containing a number of virtual pages). Segments can be given symbolic names, and these names need not be bound[6] to virtual memory locations until the segment is accessed. Each user has his or her own segment table (analogous to page table), which is used to bind segment names to virtual memory locations when the segment is accessed. Another way of viewing the

---

[6] Binding refers to the process of assigning numerical values to previously symbolic addresses. This may be a multistep process with the values first in virtual memory and finally in hardware locations of physical memory. The term *binding* was borrowed by computer people from mathematical logic where "free" and "bound" variables are distinguished [Chur56].

distinction between segmentation and paging is that paging slices virtual memory in a one-dimensional way, whereas segmentation slices it in a two-dimensional way—first into segments dictated by the logic of the program and data, and then each segment is sliced into pages for easy memory management.

Segments of virtual memory are assigned as users request more space. The segment number field of an address limits the total number of segments and, hence, the total amount of virtual memory space a user may have. The total amount of virtual memory space a user has at any moment is determined by the number of entries in the user's table. It should be noted that each user can have a virtual memory space that may be the total size of the system's memory hierarchy. Most users need only a small fraction of this total virtual memory. When a number of users are loaded into a machine, the operating system knows which parts of physical space are allocated to which users, and the remaining space is listed in an available space table. When a user requests more space, it is allocated from the available space table and, if none is available, a warning is sent to the machine operator.

The above definition of segmentation, which we shall use throughout, is not the only one in use. Traditionally, the term *segment* was used to refer to a block of program or data that was dealt with in the managing of main (and secondary) memory. For example, the blocks of Fig. 4.15 may be called segments [Dono72]. In other cases, the term *segment* is used to refer to what is essentially a variable sized page. This meaning was introduced by Burroughs in the early 1960s and has carried through to their later machines with some evolution [Orga73]. Burroughs compilers break up a user's program and data into such segments and the operating system then moves these segments back and forth between main and secondary memory. This segmentation or variable page size memory management provided the first commercially available virtual memory system in the B5000; it was very nicely matched to the natural segments found in the block structures of ALGOL 60, which the machine was designed around.

Other manufacturers have implemented various paging and segmentation schemes, often with great confusion in the terminology. For example, in the DEC PDP-11, virtual memory was first described as segmented and later as paged although the system was unchanged. In what follows we shall ignore these meanings and return to the definition of a segment as a block of virtual memory that is in turn paged.

Protection information may be provided in descriptors for pages or segments. Because pages are usually regarded as mechanically sliced chunks of program and data, distinctions between read/write, read-only, write-only, and so on, chunks are hard to make. On the other hand, protection is much easier with segments that allow the user to put logically related items together and separate logically separate items. In some systems (e.g., MULTICS; see below), users can name and declare access modes for various segments so the user can protect himself from others as well as himself, and he can also share with others. We shall discuss several protection schemes shortly, but a general presentation of memory protection will be deferred to Chapter 5.

Burroughs segments do indeed have some of the features of more general segmentation schemes. Data descriptors and program descriptors (called segment descriptors) can be distinguished. Data descriptors also contain the array size so bounds checking can be done, and special bits denote such characteristics as read-only data, whether or not indexing must be done, double precision, and so on. The descriptor also contains a presence bit to denote whether or not its segment is in main memory and, of course, the main memory or disk address of the segment in question [Burr73].

The most ambitious implementation of segmented and paged virtual memory is in MULTICS, an MIT project built on the GE645 [CoVy65, DaDe68, Denn65, Orga72], later named the Honeywell 645 and Honeywell 6180. MULTICS provides an 18-bit segment number (for a total of over a quarter million segments), a 6-bit page number, and a 10-bit line number (for 1024 word pages). This allows a total of 2^{34} 36-bit words of virtual memory. Memory addressing is carried out by a simple extension of the ideas of Figs. 4.22 and 4.23. First, the segment number is used to find the segment descriptor which contains the memory address of the page table as well as the segment size (in pages), protection bits, and other information (e.g., page size, since both 64-word and 1024-word pages were tried). At this point segment protection checks are made and a violation generates an interrupt of some kind. If the page table is not in main memory, then a page fault is generated to fetch it from secondary memory. If all the tests are passed, then the paging process described in Fig. 4.23 begins, using the page number and line number portions of the address. A 16-word associative memory is used to hold segment and page information about the 16 most recently referenced pages, so a program that generates addresses in at most 16 pages can run without accessing main memory for address translation. We will consider addressing patterns in more detail in Chapter 7, but the number 16 seems to be practically effective.

After the MULTICS project had begun, IBM started an effort to develop a virtual memory system for the IBM 360/67, and this has carried over to all models of the IBM 370. Much of the early software development was actually carried out at the University of Michigan [AGOW66]. Although MULTICS has 2^{34} words (36 bits) of virtual memory, IBM has just 2^{24} 8-bit bytes of virtual memory. Various options provide a choice between 16 and 256 segments of virtual memory, and allow 2K- or 4K-byte page sizes. In many respects, the IBM approach is quite similar to MULTICS.

An important difference between the IBM and MULTICS segmentation schemes is that each segment in MULTICS is independent of the others in the following way. Addresses to MULTICS segments must stay within a segment, and indexing beyond the last word in a segment is impossible (the address is trapped as invalid). On the other hand, if an IBM base register contains the last address in some segment and it is indexed by adding 1, the first address in the *following* segment will be accessed. Thus segment sharing and protection can suffer substantially using the IBM approach as compared with MULTICS.

IBM does not rely on segmentation and descriptors to provide protection, but instead uses the memory protection hardware that existed on the earlier 360 system (see Chapter 5). Good overviews of paging and segmentation can be found in [Wats70] and [Wilk72], of MULTICS in [Orga72], and of Burroughs segmentation in [Orga73].

We conclude with three features that segmentation helps to provide:

1. It allows a user to maintain multiple and independent virtual memory address spaces. For example, several dynamic arrays can be allocated to separate segments.
2. It allows several users to share programs and data by placing the shared information in separate segments.
3. It facilitates protection because protection can be provided at the segment level for whole programs or data structures.

4.3.5 Stacks

Stacks can be used in several different ways in a computer. In compiling programs, they can be used in parsing. In executing assignment statements, they can be used with zero-address instructions to manage temporary results. In carrying out dynamic storage allocation, they can be used to activate and deactivate arrays within one user's program. The operating system can use stacks to activate and deactivate various users.

Stacks can be implemented in any computer by software means, but in some machines a good deal of special hardware is provided to carry out stack operations. Regardless of how a stack is implemented, the basic requirements of a *stack* are:

1. A linear array whose length can expand arbitrarily or contract.
2. A PUSH command that adds one word at a time to one end of the array—called the top of the stack.
3. A POP command that removes one word at a time from the top of the stack.

To facilitate stack operations the hardware may include several registers that serve as the top of stack and first few stack positions; the rest of the stack continues in main memory with special registers pointing to the beginning stack element in memory and to the bottom of stack memory location. These are illustrated in Fig. 4.24 where the top of stack and next three entries are in registers.

Push and pop commands can be illustrated in terms of Fig. 4.24 where PUSH(A) causes the stack begin register to be incremented, so it points to memory location $\alpha + 1$; it then moves the contents of register 4 to location $\alpha + 1$, the contents of registers 1, 2, and 3 to registers 2, 3, and 4, respectively;

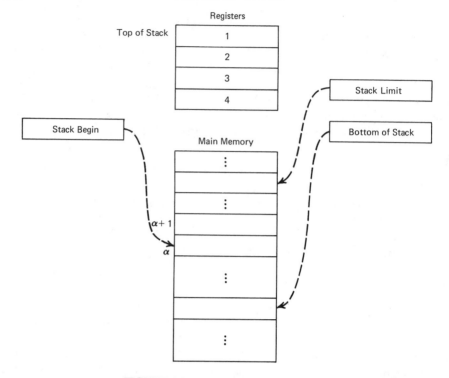

FIGURE 4.24   **Stack implementation.**

and finally enters A in register 1. Similarly, POP(R7) will move the contents of the top of stack register to some register R7 not shown here (POP would simply erase the top of stack entry). It also reverses the sequence of operations mentioned above for a PUSH, including a decrement of the stack begin register and fetch of its memory location to register 4.

In practice, there may also be a stack limit register which, together with the bottom of stack register, defines the usable stack area of memory. Execution of a PUSH requires comparison of the stack begin with the stack limit register for a stack overflow, and execution of a POP requires a similar comparison with the bottom of stack register for a stack underflow.

Real computers have various kinds of stack implementations and uses. In what follows, we will assume the above, simple hardware features and discuss several uses of them. We will see that some embellishments of the above can be of use in practice.

Expression evaluation

The program of Fig. 4.2 can be executed as follows using a stack. Operands that appear in the program as variable names are interpreted as PUSH (address) commands. Thus we begin by pushing address C onto the stack and then we FETCH the contents of C. In Fig. 4.25, we show the program as it appears in memory, with a box around the elements in the stack at a given moment. Operations are assumed to take as many operands as they need from the top several registers of the stack and push their result back onto the stack. Thus, the MPY causes B and C to be popped from the stack and multiplied together. Then their product is pushed back onto the stack. Next, the top two arguments are popped and added, and the result pushed back onto the stack, as shown in Fig. 4.25(4). Now the "X" denotes that the address of X rather than the value X is in the stack and the STORE command stores the value on the top of the stack in the address in the second position. Note that we have assumed an instruction location register which works in the normal way sequencing program control through the original program shown in Fig. 4.2.

This brings us to the next statement as shown in Fig. 4.25(5), which is handled in an analogous way, as shown in steps 5 and 6 of Fig. 4.25. Thus we have seen how zero-address code for assignment statements can be evaluated quite naturally using a stack. Notice that the top stack positions here are used

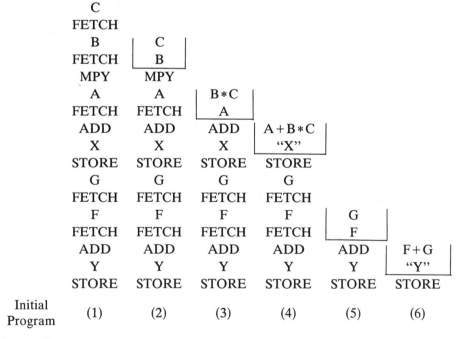

FIGURE 4.25   Expression evaluation using stack.

by the arithmetic unit so they can be regarded as processor registers. Next, we will turn to another use of stacks in program execution—one in which the top stack positions may be regarded as part of the control unit.

Control stack

In the course of executing a program that contains several procedures—or even in executing a single, block-structured procedure—certain variable names may refer to one data element at one time and another data element at another time. A simple example of this is shown in Fig. 4.26, where two procedures are declared. PROC 1 contains arrays A and B (of dimensions 100 and 50, respectively), whereas PROC 2 contains arrays A and C (of dimensions 50 and 20, respectively). When PROC 1 is started and the CALL PROC 2 is executed, the programmer intends to switch attention from the 100-element A array of PROC 1 to the 50-element A array of PROC 2. These are two entirely separate arrays. Then, when control is returned from PROC 2 to PROC 1, attention switches from the 50-element A array of PROC 2 to the 100-element A array of PROC 1.

There are, of course, many ways to implement the software required to switch the addressing from one A array to another A array when a new procedure is called. If stack hardware or software is available, there is an easy and systematic way to do this using a control stack. The following method allows dynamic allocation of storage for the arrays of PROC 2 only during its execution and not when it is loaded. It also allows the size of the arrays of PROC 2 to be determined during the compuation of PROC 1, if we wish.

By a *control stack*, we mean a stack that is used to hold control information.

```
PROC 1;
  DECLARE A(100), B(50);
     .
     .
     .

  CALL PROC 2;
     .
     .
     .

END PROC 1;
PROC 2;
  DECLARE A(50), C(20);
     .
     .
     .

END PROC 2;
```

FIGURE 4.26   **Procedure calling.**

In this case we will keep in a block of stack positions or *activation record* beginning with the top of stack, information concerning the location in memory, size, and so on, of each array available to the active procedure. Then, when a new procedure is called, a new activation record is pushed onto the stack, containing new array information for use during the execution of the new procedure. Activation records can also include the program counter's current value so that return to the proper location is easy when the called procedure is finished. When control returns to the original procedure, the current activation record is popped and the previous activation record is again available. Usually, some kind of special *stack control word* is used as a separator of such blocks of information.

Notice that if a procedure calls itself before its first execution is completed—a *recursive procedure call*—the stack mechanism works in a perfectly natural way. Each time the procedure is called, a new block of storage is set up. Then when the recursion ends, each nested level of variables is popped up at an appropriate time.

As we mentioned earlier, procedure calls can be implemented in many different ways. But, by using stack hardware or software the matter becomes quite straightforward, which is particularly important when recursion is allowed. The procedure calls discussed above were relatively easy to handle because no variables were being passed to the called procedure. In Fig. 4.26, if we rewrite the procedure call as

CALL PROC 2(B),

this means that array B is to be made accessible by PROC 2 as well as PROC 1. This can be handled with stack mechanisms in several ways.

The use of control stacks and various associated registers has been developed in great detail from the early 1960s on by Burroughs in the B5000, B5500, and their successors. A good introduction to this (B6500 and B7500) is contained in Hauck and Dent [HaDe68] and more details are presented in [Orga73]. The idea of a software stack arose in the late 1950s together with list processing and the formalization of programming languages and compilers. The first machines with hardware stacks were the B5000 [Bart61] and the English Electric KDF9 [AlLu62]. Stacks of one kind or another are now found in a number of machines. The PDP-11 has an elementary stack, the Hewlett-Packard HP3000 uses a stack in a real-time environment, and a number of microprocessors have hardware stacks (e.g., the Intel 8080 and National PACE [Osbo75]).

The question of whether a stack or a set of general-purpose registers is "best" in a computer has been debated for many years. The IBM System/360 designers considered the problem and decided against stacks [Broo63, AmBB64], but a counter argument for the Burroughs approach was presented in [Wirt68]. It seems clear that in the long run both ideas will survive and will probably evolve into still other hybrid forms.

4.4 BRANCH AND INTERRUPT PROCESSING

Although the normal program execution sequence is to process instructions in their compiled order, all programs encounter jumps from time to time. In Fig. 4.1, we showed a branch processor that handles jumps, which may be taken unconditionally or conditionally. We also showed an interrupt processor that handles breaks in the flow of control which are caused by events other than program jumps. To simplify this chapter and Chapter 2, we have ignored these details, but now we discuss them. They do not alter the generality of our previous discussions because the previous discussions hold in a piece-wise way in any program—the pieces being those sections of code that are executed in a straightline manner without any breaks in the flow of control. Now we add another type of node to the block of assignment statements and loop blocks discussed earlier; these new nodes will cause breaks in the flow of control.

4.4.1 Branching instructions

All computers have several types of branching instructions; some are unconditional branches and others branch on various conditions. Unconditional branches (or jumps) correspond to GOTO statements in high-level languages, or to subroutine call statements. The former type is executed by simply placing in the instruction location register the address field of the jump instruction (recall step 4 of Fig. 4.1). Subroutine calls and conditional branches are somewhat more complicated and exhibit more variety from machine to machine.

Subroutine or procedure calls are implemented by an instruction that, in addition to an unconditional branch, provides the subroutine with arguments and a way of returning to the caller so that the caller can resume execution properly. Usually there is some convention about passing arguments using certain registers or the top of a stack. Similarly, the return address as well as other information about the system state (see next section) at the time of the call may be saved in certain registers agreed upon by convention or in a stack. The use of a stack is very convenient in this regard, as we noted in the previous section.

Conditional branch instructions usually test one or more specified bits and then cause one of two addresses to enter the instruction location register; either the next address in sequence (no jump) or the address field of the instruction itself (jump destination). Of course, multiple address instructions can be used to implement more elaborate conditional branches. For example, a simple IF THEN ELSE could be implemented in one instruction. In order to save address bits, some machines have "skip" instructions which conditionally increment the instruction location register with a constant of at most 4 or 6 bits.

Typically, the tested bit or bits are the sign of some register (branch on plus, branch on minus) or whether or not some counter has reached zero (branch on zero). In this respect, the representation of zero is important and machines with both $+0$ and -0 can lead to confusion unless special care is taken by programmers. The compared words may be checked by subtraction or by special comparator logic, and the sign bits may or may not be used.

There is a great variety of special condition bits which programmers are interested in testing from time to time. The IBM 370 handles these in a uniform way by including a two-bit *condition code* in the program status word (which we shall discuss below) that is set by different instructions in different ways. For example, in fixed-point addition the condition code is set to indicate a sum of zero, less than zero, greater than zero, or overflow; in a comparison the four cases indicate equal operands, first operand low, second operand low, or undefined. Thus, branching instructions can be compiled to test the condition code subject to the context in which the bits were set.

Many computers have specialized conditional branches to aid in implementing loop control; these branches usually subtract one from a counter and test the result on each pass through the loop. The order in which these operations are done depends on compilation and language details (recall Section 4.2.1.2 and Fig. 4.3). For an example of this, see the BXLE instruction of the IBM 370 or the SOB instruction of the PDP-11. The variety and complexity seen in loop control instructions are motivated by the desire to execute program loops quickly, and in this sense are very important. If an inner loop contains only three or four arithmetic operations, it is disastrous to use three or four additional testing and branch instructions.

As we saw in Section 4.2, between one-sixth and one-third of the instructions executed in real programs may be branches. If a control unit attempts to look ahead and execute several instructions at once, conditional branches may cause considerable difficulty. In the worst case, the lookahead can simply pause when a conditional jump is encountered. A slightly better alternative, implemented in the IBM 360/91 and 195, is to fetch and decode instructions along both paths, but not execute them until the branch direction is decided. Another possibility is to make an assumption about which path will be taken and then begin looking ahead and executing instructions along this path. The IBM STRETCH operated in this way. This idea is not unreasonable if we assume that most conditional branches are loop end tests which will be executed a number of times before exiting. Such tests can be compiled so the lookahead is profitable on all but the last iteration.

Even better than these schemes, in the sense of potential speed, would be to continue processing along both paths. Obviously, this can be extended to lookahead down several possible paths in a program that branches in several directions. Clearly, any scheme that begins executing beyond any conditional branch must be prepared to "back up" after the branching direction is known. This may involve dropping certain values that were computed in anticipation of taking some path that is not taken. Although this approach can quickly become absurd if attempted in hardware, certain hardware and compiler combinations may be reasonable, as will be discussed in Volume 2.

4.4.2 Computer system states

In the normal course of operation, the hardware of any computer passes through a number of different states. The definition of "state" here is open to wide interpretation. Various gates can be regarded as switching on a continuous time line. Processor registers can be regarded as changing from one clock period to the next. The instruction location register changes from one instruction to the next. Certain control unit registers are only changed from one job to the next, for example, those specifying a job's "rights and privileges" with respect to using various machine facilities. Finally, certain words in a user's memory space may change only on certain runs; indeed, the user's program words may never change (if there is such a thing as a debugged program).

It should be clear that the state of a computer system in each of these time frames is of interest to individuals who observe the machine in different ways. Thus, a hardware troubleshooter may want to observe how certain gates behave within one clock period. An operating system designer is concerned with certain control unit registers at the job-to-job level of measuring time. And an ordinary user is normally interested in the states of certain memory locations at the end of the run; that is, the user wants to see certain computed results.

We are discussing these points now, in preparation for a presentation of interrupts in Section 4.4.3. In the broadest sense, an interrupt can be thought of as some kind of a break in the execution of a program, and it follows that at some level the state of the machine must be saved when an interrupt occurs, if resumption of the original program is to be correct.

It is hopeless to try to give a satisfactory general discussion of what must be saved to preserve the state of the system, because that depends on the level and purpose for which it is being saved. In particular, most computers have hardware and software mechanisms for saving a *state instantaneous description* (SID) of the system at a number of different levels. We will elaborate only a few of them here.

A low-level SID is saved at a *program checkpoint* (see Section 7.2.2), which is a dump of memory and most processor and control unit registers. Saving the state of a system at this level allows a user to restart the program later; if a system crash occurs, the user loses only the time from the last checkpoint SID dump, not from the beginning of the run.

A higher-level (more superficial) SID is saved in multiprogrammed computers to switch from one task to another. Here we can assume that all of a task's memory locations will remain intact while it is suspended. But (at least some) CU and processor registers will be used by other tasks in the meantime. Hence, these registers must be saved. In our discussion of interrupts we will give more details about this kind of SID.

We have now illustrated the meaning of "state" by giving examples of the instantaneous description of the system state. It is also useful to use the term *state* in the sense of naming certain control unit states. Thus, special registers can be set to distinguish between control unit states; these allow the machine to behave in fundamentally important different ways.

Privileged instructions and CU states

Most computers can be operated in one of (at least) two *control unit states*. One of the states is for the execution of user programs in the normal way. The other state allows the operating system or other system programs to execute certain privileged instructions that are not available to users. Privileged instructions are typically those that might allow a user to wreak havoc on the system, in other words, instructions that, if improperly used, could interfere with other users or the system programs themselves.

Various manufacturers have different names for the two states (sometimes called *modes*) of operation: Burroughs calls them control and normal state, CDC calls them monitor and program state, DEC calls them kernel and user states, IBM calls them supervisor and problem state, and so on. We will refer to them as *privileged state* and *user state*, names that describe the allowed instruction types.

Typical privileged instruction types are I/O instructions, halt instructions, and instructions that change certain control unit bits

4.4.3 Interrupts

An interrupt is something that, roughly speaking, causes a computer to break the normal control sequence of its running program. Interrupts may arise from an external source (e.g., an input device wanting attention), from the consequences of a previous instruction (e.g., an arithmetic overflow), or from some kind of hardware or software infirmity (e.g., a parity error); a more complete list will be given later. The CPU responds by processing the interrupt using some combination of hardware and software facilities; clearly, a wide range of responses must be available for the many different kinds of interrupts. The term *interrupt* is used somewhat ambiguously to refer to either the triggering or both the triggering and processing of an interrupt.

As we shall see, the interrupt is a simple but very useful device. The convenience of interrupts was evidently clear to Babbage. He designed his Analytical Engine so that if the machine's mechanical tolerances allowed enough slippage to potentially introduce errors in the results, the machine jammed. Thus, such errors were prevented by aborting the whole computation! Babbage's table lookup procedure for supplied functions (recall the discussion of Section 1.3.1) checked the operator supplied card and if it was wrong, rang a second bell, thus forcing the operator to supply the correct card before proceeding. Although the first bell that rang to signal the operator to supply the first card was part of the normal procedure (perhaps an interruption of the operator), the second bell and holding up the computation if a wrong card were inserted, was really a program interruption in the modern sense. His interrupt handling procedure for this would put it in the class of modern "recoverable" error interrupts; the idea is much more subtle than merely aborting the computation.

Most modern computers contain interrupt features of one kind or another. Early commercial machines with interrupts were the UNIVAC 1103 [Mers56] and the IBM STRETCH [Broo57]. The notion of interrupts has become so ingrained in computer systems that many modern operating systems are in fact interrupt driven. Whenever a significant change in the control state of the computer arises, an interrupt is generated and the operating system takes over control, at least momentarily. One of the advantages of modern interrupt handling is that interrupts of great diversity are handled in a uniform way.

In one sense, the interrupt mechanism can be regarded as a procedure calling scheme. For example, when a user program wants to pass control to the operating system, a special interrupt can be used on some machines. In another sense, interrupts can be regarded as a convenient way of synchronizing various units (e.g., I/O devices, other processors, etc.) with a main CPU. As we said, one hardware and software scheme serves all these purposes.

For the purposes of interrupt handling, time is regarded as indivisible at the level of the clock period. To allow an interrupt to occur within a clock period would cause obvious chaos. Usually, interrupts are not allowed to interfere with the CPU instruction currently in progress because of the difficulty of saving the processor state needed for later resumption. Thus the instruction sequencer is usually allowed to run to completion on a given instruction. In the case of long instructions, there may be procedures to suspend sequencing within the instruction. Also, in the case of an illegal instruction, execution is suppressed.

As we have indicated, interrupt procedures vary from one machine to another, and interrupts serve a wide range of purposes. Next, we will list a number of interrupt types and then we will return to some details of interrupt handling procedures.

4.4.3.1 Types of interrupts

There are many sources of interrupts in complex computer systems. Some people make a distinction between internal and external interrupts; internal ones are sometimes called *traps* and are said to be triggered by *faults* that are hardware failures or exceptional conditions. The distinction is really a bit fuzzy if pursued too far but, superficially, it is useful. Thus an *internal interrupt* is one caused by a processor, control unit, or main memory fault, whereas an *external interrupt* comes from an I/O device, another processor, and so on. Generally speaking, external interrupts occur in a completely random fashion, whereas internal interrupts are not predictable but occur at predictable times with respect to particular instructions. The following is a list of some of the different sources of interrupts.

1. Processor generated
    a. Arithmetic result out of range (e.g., overflow, underflow, zero divisor)
    b. Parity error
2. CU generated
    a. Illegal operation code encountered
    b. Interval timer (to end time slice in time-shared machine)
    c. Switch from user state to privileged state
    d. Stack overflow (stack area in memory full)
    e. Page fault (program addressing outside main memory)
3. Memory generated
    a. Improper access attempt (e.g., word not assigned, write a read-only word, nonexistent address)
    b. Parity error
4. I/O generated
    a. Input device being started
    b. I/O device started earlier is finished
    c. Parity error
5. Other
    a. Another processor in multiprocessor system wants attention
    b. Operator at console switch
    c. Laboratory equipment or other real-time process incrementing a counter

Sources of processor generated interrupts were discussed in Section 3.3.6. Control unit generated interrupts are of various types. In Section 4.2.4, we discussed the use of an interval timer in a time-shared computer. The question of an illegal operation code is easy to dispose of. Either the opcode is undefined or the user is trying to execute a privileged opcode reserved for system programmers. An undefined opcode may represent a compiler error, or more likely it is the result of an improper branch and the resulting attempt to execute a data word. This can be prevented by tag bits that distinguish code from data (see Section 5.2.5).

The use of interrupts to switch from user state to privileged state is convenient. It can be done (e.g., in the IBM 360/370 via an SVC opcode) when a compiler knows that some kind of operating system help will be needed in the midst of a running program. In a programming language with dynamic storage allocation upon subroutine or block entry, such an instruction would be compiled. Or, when an I/O routine wants buffer space allocated, it could be used.

Memory generated interrupts were discussed in Section 4.3.2 in the context of address processing. Hardware errors will be discussed in Section 5.2.6. I/O generated interrupts will arise in subsequent discussions in this section and again in Chapters 6 and 7. It is clear that this is the way I/O devices get the CPU's attention. Finally, there are a number of other kinds of interrupts. We list three obvious ones. By studying the literature of various manufacturers still others are easy to discover.

Some computers have *instruction retry* mechanisms that automatically execute certain failed instructions a second time before generating an interrupt. This can avoid some costly but unnecessary interrupts, for example, those due to transient parity errors.

Some computers are used in what is commonly referred to as an *interrupt driven* environment. In real-time, interactive, or process control applications (recall Section 1.1.2), a computer can be regarded as located at the center of a collection of units that may demand service at any time. In a well-designed system, the computer must be poised to service the units, ideally, in a way that gives each unit such fast service it is not aware of the other units. Such a machine clearly needs sufficient processing power as well as good interrupt handling abilities.

4.4.3.2   Interrupt handling

Most modern computers have a combination of hardware and software that allow three key steps to be taken in response to an interrupt. They are:

1.   Stop the computation in progress.
2.   Take some action in response to the interrupt.
3.   Resume the computation that was interrupted.

Although this seems straightforward, there are a number of possible difficulties.

One obvious problem in designing hardware and software for interrupt handling is speed. All of the time involved in the three steps above can be regarded as overhead or lost time for the user whose program is interrupted. Normally, an interrupt handling program is part of the operating system and is stored at a fixed memory location, so interrupt processing can always begin from there. Before much else happens, the state of the machine must be saved so the computation can later be resumed. Whatever is stored on Step 1 must be retrieved on Step 3.

Just what is meant by "the state of the machine" depends on the particular machine involved. In the IBM 370, a 64-bit program status word (PSW) is saved. The PSW contains the instruction location register for the instruction being executed when the interrupt occurred, together with other important control bits [Katz71]. If (some of) the CPU registers are needed in the interrupt handling computations, they must be saved first by the interrupt handler. In the CDC 6600, the PPUs can initiate an Exchange Jump that interrupts the CPU and starts it on a new computation. This Exchange Jump causes all 24 CPU registers, the instruction location counter, and other control information to be stored, and new information replaces the old in these registers [Thor70].

If the interrupt handling routine is a general one, it must make a number of tests to discover exactly what has happened. Then it must take some action and finally it restarts the interrupted computation. Thus it is easy to see how 50 or 100 instructions (including stores and fetches) may be required here. In the CDC 6600, which implements the Exchange Jump as a special instruction, Step 1 alone requires from 3 to 5 μs (depending on the state of the CPU), which amounts to between 30–50 minor cycles (a typical CPU instruction takes 3 or 4 minor cycles on the 6600).

Besides the elapsed time required for interrupt handling, a designer may have to consider some very subtle timing questions about saving the state of the machine at the time of an interrupt's occurrence. Most high-performance machines, in fact, must live with the notion of an *imprecise interrupt;* that is, the exact state of the machine at the time of the interrupt may be unknowable.

For example, suppose we have a pipelined arithmetic unit, and suppose that a sequence of arithmetic instructions is followed by a conditional jump. Now assume that an arithmetic operation is begun, the jump is executed, new arithmetic operations are begun, and then the first arithmetic operation reaches a point where an overflow occurs. Unless we have saved the instruction location register's contents for a number of previous instructions, it will be impossible to determine which instruction caused the overflow!

Any machine with a number of instructions in process at once has this potential problem. In some instances such interrupts can be ignored—as mentioned in Section 3.3.6, in the case of arithmetic overflow or underflow the data may be flagged by the processor as being out of range and the computation continued. If the interrupt is caused by something sufficiently worse than an arithmetic fault, the program may have to be restarted at a checkpoint where the entire state of the machine earlier (including all memory locations) had been dumped for just such an eventuality. This procedure may be necessary, of course, even on machines that are free of the above-mentioned timing hazards, to cope with hardware or software crashes, which ruin a computation.

4.4.3.3 Priorities

A further complexity that must be planned for in implementing the three steps of interrupt handling is that while one interrupt is being processed another interrupt may arrive. Most computers have a way of disabling and enabling interrupts. A simple scheme for handling multiple interrupts is to have the interrupt handler for the first interrupt simply disable all further interrupts. This simplifies matters but is obviously too crude in general.

Most computers have a scheme for assigning priorities to interrupts on the basis of their type. Thus, if an interrupt is being processed and a higher priority interrupt arrives, processing of the first interrupt will itself be interrupted. And as multiple levels of priorities are established, interrupt handling can be interrupted in a recursive way—up to the number of priority levels that exist.

Indeed, a stack mechanism is often used for holding the ensemble of pending interrupts. Note that multiple interrupts at the same priority level or at lower priority levels may simply be queued, awaiting processing.

Priorities between interrupts are usually assigned on the basis of the relative speeds and logical relations between various parts of a computer system. For example, highest priority must be assigned to hardware parity errors, particularly in the CPU and main memory. If the hardware is not operating properly, then all else may be nonsense. Next, priority in a time-shared machine would probably go to the interval timer which defines each user's time slice. In a multiprocessor, the second highest priority may go to interrupts from other processors, so as not to hold them up too long.

Priority between I/O devices and normal CPU or main memory generated interrupts is usually decided on the basis of speed. Thus I/O devices are assigned higher priorities because they are relatively very slow compared with the CPU. A few lost CPU cycles are easy to make up, for example, compared with the time lost waiting for an I/O device.

A subtle point that is often missed in discussions of interrupt priorities is that there are really two kinds of priorities involved here. One is the priority established between a number of interrupts that arrive in precisely the same clock period. Another is the ability to interrupt the processing of a previous interrupt. As we shall see in the next section, in the case of IBM machines priorities are reordered from one of these situations to the other. What we have been discussing in this section is primarily the second point. The following discussion can be interpreted for either point.

Priority schemes may be implemented in a number of ways. An obvious dichotomy exists between hardware and software techniques. If we want to establish priorities between n events that can cause an interrupt, it may not be clear how to do this when the machine is designed.

To provide some flexibility in establishing priorities between I/O channels, for example, fixed priorities could be built into a subset of the n interrupt events and assigned to channel ports. Then field engineers could plug the highest priority channel into the highest priority port, and so on. But if one user wanted one priority ordering between the channels and another user wanted another ordering, this would not work (unless programmable field engineers ran about unplugging and replugging channels at run time!). Furthermore, for various internal types of interrupts, there are no "ports" which could be rearranged. Finally, if the priorities were left up to the user, the compiler, or the operating system, a certain amount of confusion would exist in deciding how to handle priorities of certain interrupts arising at the hardware level (e.g., parity errors).

Thus, most machines partition the n overall interrupt events into $k < n$ equivalence classes and establish fixed priorities at the hardware level between the equivalence classes. If an interrupt has occurred and is being handled and then another, higher-priority interrupt occurs, the latter interrupt interrupts the first and may be serviced first. There is, of course, an ordering between the elements of each equivalence class to break ties between simultaneously arriving interrupt signals. But this is just a hardware defined queue and does not cause the interruption of processing other interrupts in the same equivalence class.

On top of this, the user has the ability to inhibit certain interrupts, under program control. A special word can be set to "mask off" those interrupts one wishes to inhibit. This allows the programmer to establish priorities between the elements of each of the k equivalence classes. It also allows the programmer to circumvent some of the hardware-defined priorities. Thus, it may be possible to ignore certain events that the hardware defines to be higher priority interrupts. In the following section we give an example of these ideas, as implemented in IBM equipment.

In the following chapters, discussions of priorities will be presented on several occasions. In Section 5.4.2.1, priority resolution in multiport memory units will be discussed. The establishment of priorities between I/O devices for several machines will be discussed in Chapter 6. Finally, in Chapter 7 various types of priority resolution will be discussed in connection with memory hierarchy management. In principle, all of these are interrupt priorities because they all arise from several requests demanding service from some unit at the same time. In some cases, the priorities hold only between events that occur simultaneously; the notion of "interrupting" an activity (e.g., main memory cycle) already in progress does not arise, because the entire activity is completed in a relatively short time. Thus, the ideas of this section are applied repeatedly throughout computer systems in establishing priorities. The general principles we have discussed are generally used, but there are no hard and fast rules; priorities must always be assigned so that the case at hand operates in a smooth and logically correct way.

4.4.3.4   IBM 360/370 interrupts

As a concrete example of the interrupt mechanism, we will sketch the IBM 360/370 approach. In these machines there are 32 types of possible interruptions. Some of them represent particular events (e.g., exponent overflow), whereas others represent a general class of events (e.g., a multiplexer channel that handles many I/O devices). In Fig. 4.27, we show the interrupt bits entering the interrupt handling hardware. Under program control, 20 of these can be masked off, whereas others cannot be masked. The masking is carried out by using specified bits of the program status word (PSW). In Fig. 4.27, a line is shown from the PSW register for the currently running program to the mask register for this purpose.

The PSW register is 64 bits long; however it is not really a physically contiguous hardware register. In fact, it is a collection of various key bits and registers that control the program's running. We will discuss it as if it were a

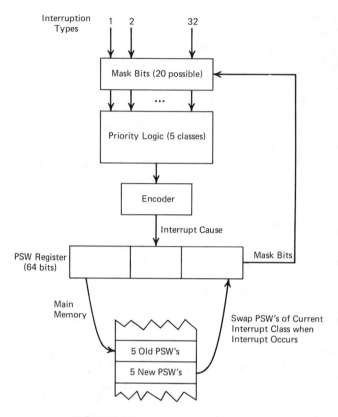

FIGURE 4.27   **IBM interrupt logic.**

64-bit physical register. Besides the various mask bits, the PSW includes the instruction location register for the current program and various bits that identify the state of the current program. As will be discussed shortly, when an interrupt occurs, its cause is encoded and placed in the PSW.

Examples of interruption types that can be masked off are I/O interrupts or certain arithmetic faults. It is necessary to briefly mask off all I/O interrupts while handling a previous I/O interrupt. If this were not done while CPU registers were being saved, certain information would be irretrievably lost. As soon as the appropriate minimal actions have been taken, however, the interrupt handler may change the mask bits, thus making itself available for interruption. These mask bit changes may depend on the type of interrupt that occurred previously, but typically the system would be put in its previous state.

By having their interrupts masked off, the I/O channels simply wait briefly before the CPU responds. In the case of masked-off arithmetic faults (e.g., exponent underflow), it is presumed that the user does not care about such events under certain conditions or that some other hardware/software technique adequately handles the user's needs. Hardware failure interrupts (so-called machine check interrupts) can be masked off, but in the ordinary case they are not masked off and cause a user's program to terminate. Then a diagnostic system program can attempt to determine what has happened by executing certain instructions with the interrupts masked off. In case the system cannot recover from the error, a routine will be invoked which brings the machine to a halt—not unlike Babbage's original interrupt scheme!

On the other hand, masking is not allowed on a number of events that could lead to system wide disasters. For example, the memory protection interrupt cannot be masked off by the user. Indeed, the purpose of this interrupt is to protect the user and others from the consequences of improperly accessing certain parts of memory. As another example, if a user tries to execute a privileged instruction, one that is reserved for system programmers, he is interrupted and he cannot mask off the interrupt.

As shown in Fig. 4.27, after the mask bits have been applied to the 32 interrupt lines, priority logic is applied to the remaining interrupts in the sense discussed in the previous section, this logic decides priorities between simultaneously arriving interrupts, while the mask bits decide which interrupts are interruptable by others. The priority logic groups the 32 lines into 5 classes that correspond to their priorities in the order shown. The five classes of interrupts in the IBM 370 are listed below with brief explanations. For a detailed discussion of their meanings, see [Katz71] or various IBM publications.

1. *Machine check* interrupts arise from recoverable or nonrecoverable hardware failures. The former is processed in the normal way, while the latter leads to a machine halt.
2. *Supervisor call* interrupts are initiated by the SVC command and cause a switch from user (problem) state to privileged (supervisor) state.
3. *Program* interrupts include arithmetic faults (overflow, underflow, etc.), illegal addressing or use of privileged instructions, etc.
4. *External* interrupts include the interval timer, the operator's console, lines from other CPUs or external apparatus.
5. *I/O* interrupts come from I/O channels and they may signal that a channel has completed something the CPU started earlier, or they may arise from an input device being started. The details of I/O channels will be discussed in Chapter 6.

After one interrupt has been filtered through the masking and priority logic, several hardware events are triggered. The type of interrupt is encoded and placed in its field in the PSW register. Heretofore, this field has been meaningless. At this point the control unit actually causes the interrupt to occur. The instruction in progress may or may not be completed, depending on its type. Normal ones finish, very long ones may be interrupted, illegal ones are suppressed. Then the PSW register is stored in a fixed location in memory; this is one of five "old" PSW locations that depend on the priority class to which the interrupt belongs. Finally, based on the type of interrupt received, a new

PSW is fetched from one of five fixed "new" PSW locations in memory and placed in the PSW register.

This new PSW contains an address in its instruction location field and that address is the first location of a program that will be used to handle the just received interrupt. The interrupt handler can find out exactly what happened by examining the previous PSW stored in its type (1 through 5) "old" PSW memory location. The details of what follow are very complex and obviously depend on what type of interrupt occurred. But it is here that the mask bits perform a key role. For example, the new PSW for an I/O interrupt will contain bits to mask off further I/O interrupts. After the program for I/O interrupt handling has saved whatever CPU registers it must have to complete its work, it may reset the PSW I/O mask bits, thereby allowing (at least some) I/O interrupts to interrupt it. Thus, as pointed out earlier, interrupt handling can proceed in a recursive way. And the PSW storage mechanism can be regarded as a recursive procedure calling technique.

If more than one interrupt occurs at once, the above order is their priority (except that 2 and 3 cannot both occur at once). The IBM software is set up to process interrupts in a different order. Machine checks are handled first, but then the above priority list is reversed. I/O interrupts are handled before the others, and so on. As we pointed out earlier, the rationale for this is that, given a properly operating machine, slow units should get fast service.

4.4.3.5 References and extensions

The software details of interrupt handling are rather tricky, in general. A comprehensive discussion of interrupts from the software point of view may be found in [MaDo74]. A detailed discussion of interrupts in the I/O context, together with some logic design details may be found in [HiPe73, Chapter 10]. Much philosophy about interrupts is contained in [Buch62].

Many modern operating systems are organized in a level-structured way. The levels can be viewed as analogous to extensions of the privileged and user states discussed previously. The ease of implementing and debugging such systems has been widely discussed. Hardware support for multi level systems is clearly an important idea to save running time and provide convenient facilities for programmers. Such hardware is discussed in [BeSi75] as are its uses in operating systems. Each level of system programming is built on a lower level, with the hardware at the bottom and user programs at the top. Each such level can be viewed as a "virtual machine" with a different instruction set, as we shall learn in the next section.

4.5 VIRTUAL MACHINES

Virtual machines will be discussed as an application of several of the ideas presented earlier in this chapter. Under previously mentioned system software, several users may share various parts of a computer system; multiprogramming and address mapping provide the sharing of a memory hierarchy, and time-sharing provides the sharing of a CPU. As an extension of these ideas, virtual machine software provides the sharing of a complete computer system and allows each user to operate his or her own facsimile of the machine exactly as desired. Each user may have a different operating system, and each may use a different collection of peripheral equipment. Furthermore, these "users" may be running applications programs, developing new operating systems, or even running hardware diagnostic programs. In short, the goal of virtual machine systems is to provide more services to the users of a single computer system.

This section contains three parts. First, the motivations for virtual machines will be presented. Then we will present approaches to implementing virtual machines. Finally, we will discuss several virtual machine examples.

4.5.1 Virtual machine motivation

The primary goals of system programming have always been to provide better services for users in an efficient way. By allowing each user to have what appears as his or her own computer system, complete with operating system, the "better services" aspect of the previous sentence would seem to be satisfied, assuming that each user can do whatever they wish to with their own private virtual system. The only remaining question then would concern the efficiency with which this is done. Before discussing some details of implementation in Section 4.5.2, we will review the possible services of virtual machines, first for users and then for system people.

Suppose a manufacturing firm develops a program for preparing its annual reports. Inputs include inventory files, employee files, financial statements, and so on, for the previous year, and the output consists of a number of reports, a file containing a summary of the year's activities, and a file used for income tax purposes. Such a system might require a good deal of initial programming effort, but it might be run just once a year. If it were well-written, the program could be used for many years, with only minor changes. Now suppose that after five years of successfully running this program, the firm changes its computer system; it may convert from tapes to disk, buy an upgraded computer, or switch to a new operating system on the old machine. Or, even with the old machine, the operating system may slowly evolve over several years. Any of these changes could devastate the annual report program, which presumably relied heavily on secondary memory for file processing and almost certainly depended on the operating system under which it was developed.

In any of these cases, implementing on the new computer system a virtual machine that corresponds to the original system could save the day. Rather than wasting time rewriting the old programs whose execution consumes relatively little system time when measured over the course of a year, the old programs could be run under virtual machine software that allows the new computer system to simulate the old computer system.

Another virtual machine application would be in teaching students the details of programming and operating a computer system in a "hands on" way. Each student would have a complete system—including simulated console switches—and could operate it as desired. This could be quite useful for training computer operators. Alternatively, for teaching programming, different students could be provided with different virtual I/O equipment. Many other applications of the idea can be imagined at the user level: these include the transporting of software from one facility to another, running systems that are very large, or otherwise put demands on the hardware that require dedicated use of a machine. When a system hardware configuration is changed, virtual machine software can provide a copy of the original system for users while new software is developed. Virtual machine software can also be used to provide high system security and privacy for individual users.

At the system programming and machine maintenance level, a number of other applications of virtual machines exist. For example, in prime time, system programmers may work on the development and testing of new operating systems or modify the existing operating system, together with a user group under the control of another copy of the existing operating system. In this case, the virtual system they use may be equivalent to the physical system in use. System measurements can be carried out under virtual machine software, and system diagnostic programs can be run to exercise almost all parts of the hardware and software.

Summaries of the virtues of virtual machines may be found in [MeSe70], [PPTH72], [McGr72], and [Gold73]. It can be argued that many of the advantages of virtual machines can be obtained by one or another alternative schemes, but the virtual machine idea does present a uniform approach to the ideas.

4.5.2 Approaches

Basically, a virtual machine is provided by simulating one machine using another machine. This idea is not new; indeed it was used by Turing in devising a universal computing machine in his famous, 40-year-old result [Turi36]. The idea of providing software to interpret a high-level language has often been used, and this may be regarded as implementing a virtual machine that executes the high-level language directly. By using microprogramming, the whole process can be brought down to the level of a microstore interpreter or emulator, as discussed in Section 4.2.2. However, there is more complexity in the typical virtual machine than in the typical language interpreter.

A virtual machine may be regarded as consisting of four parts: a virtual operator's console, virtual memory, virtual I/O devices, and virtual CPU. The virtual operator's console allows the user of the virtual machine to set the same switches and interrogate the same display devices that an operator of the real machine has available. This can be provided by simple software techniques.

Virtual memory, as discussed in Section 4.3 (and also Chapters 5 and 7), allows each virtual machine to have as much main memory as desired. The idea of virtual memory is quite useful independently of virtual machines, but it nicely supports virtual machines. The hardware protects programs sharing virtual memory from each other and could be extended to allow various access rights to limited amounts of virtual main memory for each user. Virtual I/O devices may be of any type as long as they are supported by the virtual system's software. For example, a big disk pack could be sliced up into a number of smaller virtual disk packs and one provided to each virtual machine. This would allow many more virtual machines to be run than there are physical disk drives. Alternatively, as mentioned earlier, one type of I/O device (e.g., disk) can be used to simulate other types (e.g., tape). More will be said about I/O devices and memory hierarchy use in Chapter 7.

The fourth component of a virtual machine is the virtual CPU. This could be provided by simulating each instruction—either using a software interpreter or a firmware emulator. However, it is usually the case that virtual machines are run on hardware that has the same instruction set as the virtual machine; indeed, some definitions of virtual machines specifically exclude simulating the virtual CPU because of the resulting speed loss. These are sometimes called *self-virtualizing* machines when the hardware is identical to the virtual machine and *family virtualizing* where the virtual machines are of the same family as the physical machine, for example, in the IBM System/360 or 370 [PPTH72]. Although it may seem strange to simulate a machine on itself, it is useful for the reasons mentioned in the previous section.

Clearly, a machine that is simulating itself can execute most instructions in the "native mode," that is, without interpretation. This is certainly true for all of the user state instructions (recall Section 4.4.2). However, the privileged state instructions could lead to difficulty in that one virtual machine could interfere with another; for example, one virtual machine could halt the physical system leaving all the other virtual machines stranded. Thus, for a virtual machine system to operate properly, any privileged instruction execution attempted by a virtual machine must be executed by interpretation without disturbing any of the other virtual machines. Furthermore, the system hardware and software that handle the privileged state instructions must be protected from all of the virtual machines. This can be done by trapping or interrupting the privileged instructions [MeSe70] and then simulating them, or some more delicate technique (analogous to the way virtual address mapping is handled) which has the same effect [Gold74]. A detailed discussion of instruction set characteristics and their relation to virtual machines can be found in [PoGo74]. Basically, the virtual machines must be prevented from changing or interrogating certain critical aspects of the state of the host CPU. The software aspects of virtual machines are discussed in a general way in [MaDo74] and [Tane76], as well as in other references to specific systems given in the next section.

4.5.3 Virtual machine implementation

The virtual machine notion is a rather natural extension of multiprogramming and virtual memory, two ideas that were widely developed in the early 1960s. Perhaps the first virtual machine implementation is described in [ABCC66]. The idea has been further developed and supported mainly by IBM, probably because of their general use of families of compatible machines and because the idea was not hard to implement on the System/360. Other manufacturers have software and hardware that provide similar features by one mechanism or another.

The first IBM virtual machine system was CP-40 [ABCC66], which served as a prototype for CP-67 [MeSe70]. CP-67 ran on the IBM System/360 Model 67 and provided functional simulation of various 360s, including the Model 67 itself. The CP-67 software consisted of two parts: a virtual machine Control Program (CP), which provided for time-sharing and resource allocation, and the Cambridge Monitor System (CMS). CMS was a single user, conversational monitor system that provided the user's terminal interface and was able to run by itself on the 360/67 without the CP. In fact, the same CMS was used on both CP-40 and CP-67.

With the introduction of the System/370, these systems led to the IBM VM/370 (Virtual Machine/370) which provides users with virtual IBM/370s. Each virtual 370 can run any of the System/360 or System/370 operating systems, or CMS (now sometimes called Conversational Monitor System). Figure 4.28 shows the idea of VM/370 supporting four virtual machines, each with its own operating system: OS/360 controlling an old program, OS/VS2 multiprogramming several System/370 programs, and two CMS systems supporting conversational terminals. Several other virtual machine systems have been developed on IBM equipment and another early system was developed by Hitachi; more recently, virtual machines have been developed for DEC and Burroughs machines [Gold74].

There are some intrinsic shortcomings in all virtual machines. These shortcomings are related to time-sensitive programs. None of the operating systems or applications programs run on a virtual machine can depend on any rigid timing because there are indeterminate slowdowns in running the program on a virtual machine as compared with the raw hardware machine. Thus, external real-time interrupts and interval timer interrupts may display anomalies when run on a virtual machine.

The performance of virtual machines, in the sense of system overhead incurred, depends on implementation details. Some extra time is required to process the privileged state instructions. On the other hand, the virtual machine may use a simpler operating system than that being run on the physical host machine; thus some virtual machine users may *save* overhead time in this way. Sources of overhead are discussed in [MeSe70], [McGr72], and [Gold74]. In [McGr72], a table of measured performance results shows

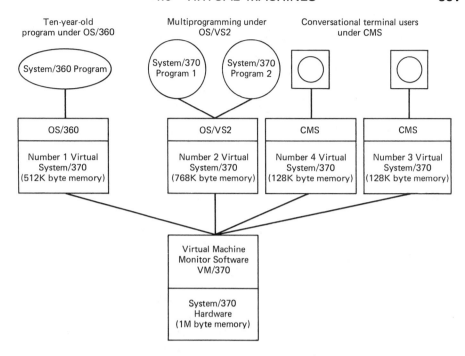

FIGURE 4.28   **VM/370 with four virtual machines.**

that with CP-67 running 10 to 17 users, the user state (virtual machines) had 40–50 percent of the CPU time, whereas the privileged state (CP-67) took about 35 percent of the CPU time. Of course, some overhead time would be required by any operating system used.

PROBLEMS

Easy problems in text order

4.1 Rewrite the following sequence of one-address instructions as a zero-address code sequence, executable on a machine with a stack.

```
FETCH C
ADD   D
ADD   E
STORE T
FETCH A
ADD   B
MPY   T
STORE X
```

4.2 Consider the execution of programs in a university computing center where the jobs are numerically oriented, for example, execution of compiled FORTRAN programs. For each class of instructions below, choose the percent that approximates the measured values of dynamic instruction frequencies. Choices may be used more than once or not at all.

____Operand Access	a.	70%
(memory or register)	b.	50%
____Arithmetic Operations	c.	20%
____Logical Operations	d.	10%
____Input/Output	e.	less than 5%

4.3 (a) Approximately what fraction of machine instructions executed are branch instructions?

(b) Give a few reasons why branches are executed so frequently.

4.4 How does Zipf's law relate static instruction frequency to the rank order of the static frequency? (Give a functional relation, or sketch and label a graph.)

4.5 B1700 experiments described in the chapter discussion show that instruction formats can be arranged so that a 40 percent saving in program memory space can be obtained. This, of course, is a static measure; suppose we wish to adjust instruction formats so that the *bandwidth* used by the CU for instruction fetching is reduced. Specifically, suppose we wish to encode the four common arithmetic operations $(+, -, *, /)$ and that there are only four available opcodes: one 1, one 2, one 3, and one 4 bits long, and that the following statistics are available.

Instruction	Static Frequency	Dynamic Frequency	Execution Time (in clocks)
+	40	40	3
−	20	20	3
*	30	33	15
/	10	7	40

Which opcode length would you assign to each operation to minimize instruction fetch bandwidth? Why? Are there any restrictions on the opcodes themselves because of their relative sizes?

4.6 Microprogramming:
(a) Implies an asynchronous machine.
(b) Makes interrupt handling difficult.
(c) Is usually required for minicomputers.
(d) Requires a read/write microinstruction store.
(e) Does not allow overlap of fetching and execution of microinstructions.

(f)   All of the above.

(g)   None of the above.

4.7   The state diagram for the control circuit of a small digital device is as shown below. When the circuit is in state s_i, the control signal y_i is 1 while the other three control signals are equal to 0. Suppose that this control circuit is to be implemented using a simple microprogrammed control unit as shown in the block diagram.

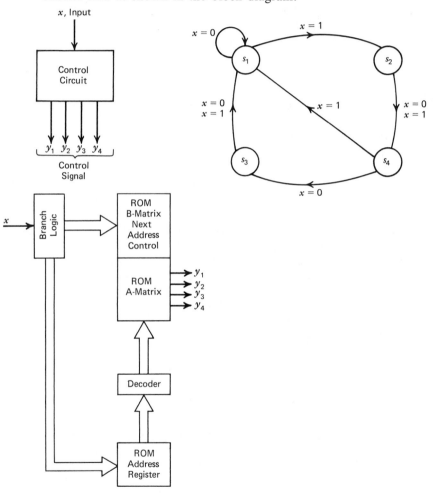

(a)   How many words and how many bits per word are required in the A matrix?

(b)   How many words and how many bits per word are required in the B matrix?

(c)   Fill in the contents of the A and B matrix ROMs.

4.8 Suppose a portion of microcode in a control unit store contains:

Addr.	Control Field	Next Microinstruction Address
$\vdots$	$\vdots$	$\vdots$
0101	0000110001	0110
0110	0100000001	1000
0111	0000110010	1000
1000	0000110001	1001
1001	0100000001	0000
$\vdots$	$\vdots$	$\vdots$

(Assume that 0000 in the next address field ends the microinstruction sequence.)

(a) Which microinstructions would be executed for the operation starting at address 0101?

(b) How wide (in bits) would a nanostore word be for this machine?

(c) If the above control fields are the only distinct patterns, how wide would a microinstruction be if a nanostore is used? Include both the nanostore address field and the next microinstruction field.

4.9 In the microprogrammed control unit in Fig. 4.4, external inputs are used to select alternate actions and next instruction addresses in the A and B matrices, respectively. How might this alternate word selection be implemented if the A and B matrices were implemented with semiconductor ROMs?

4.10 What three types of dependence are important when executing instructions in an overlapped way? Give an example of each type. Name a real machine implementing a scheme for detection of each dependence type.

4.11 When instruction lookahead is used in the control unit of an overlapped uniprocessor, which of the following is likely to be the case, as compared with a similar machine without instruction lookahead?

(a) Bandwidth used by the processor will increase.

(b) Memory freedom γ_m will decrease until the memory is bound.

(c) Some instructions that are fetched will not be executed.

(d) Interrupts caused by exceptional conditions in the arithmetic unit will be handled more efficiently.

(e) The program execution time always will be greater because of the effect of conditional branches.

4.12 One simple advantage of segmentation is in reducing the page table size for naive operating systems. Suppose you are implementing a 360/67 operating system that uses 24-bit addresses and 4K byte pages. If the system provided each user with page tables for the full virtual memory (regardless of the program size), then 4K (multi-byte) entry page tables would be resident in main memory. If segmentation were used, say 16 segments as in the 360/67, how much of a reduction in main memory used for page tables could be achieved assuming that the segment and page table entries were equal in size and that each user has only one segment active at a time.

4.13   Classify the following computer systems as SISE, SIME, MISE, or MIME:

      CDC 6600 CPU
      Burroughs B6500
      ILLIAC IV (4 quadrants)
      CDC 6600 PPU
      Bell Labs. CLC.

4.14   Assume a simple microprocessor has a limited number of instructions, but several powerful addressing modes. Its instruction set includes:

FETCH	load accumulator from memory
FETCHX	load index register X from memory
STORE	store accumulator into memory
STOREX	store index register X into memory
ADD	add to accumulator from memory

The addressing modes and assembly language notations are:

Notation	Type of Addressing
#n	immediate, e.g., a constant
n	absolute
n,X	absolute indexed by X; address is, $n + X$
(n)*	absolute indirect
(n,X)*	absolute indexed by X, indirect; address is $C(n + X)$
(n)*,X	absolute indirect, indexed by X; address is $C(n) + X$

Given the following memory contents before program execution, show the memory contents after execution of the program.

Address	Memory	Program	
0	0	FETCH	1
1	3	STORE	4
2	2	FETCHX	#2
3	1	ADD	(3)*
4	0	STORE	0, X
		ADD	(1)*
		STORE	(3)*, X
		FETCHX	0
		ADD	#1
		STOREX	(0, X)*

4.15

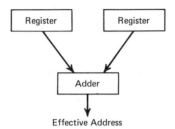

Effective Address

The above hardware is necessary to do which of the following types of address processing: indirect addressing, index addressing, relocatable program addressing, data descriptor addressing, virtual memory addressing.

4.16 Design an instruction format for a computer with 32-bit memory words, 64 different instructions, 32 addressable 32-bit CPU registers, and indirect memory addressing. The one instruction format must include a register address as well as a virtual memory address. How big can this machine's virtual memory be? If the CPU registers can be used as base registers, how big could the virtual memory be?

4.17 A certain stack machine has the following instructions available:

FETCH X	push: $top \leftarrow top + 1$; $C(top) \leftarrow C(X)$
STORE X	pop: $C(X) \leftarrow C(top)$; $top \leftarrow top - 1$
ADD	$C(top-1) \leftarrow C(top) + C(top-1)$; $top \leftarrow top - 1$
SUB	$C(top-1) \leftarrow C(top) - C(top-1)$; $top \leftarrow top - 1$
MPY	$C(top-1) \leftarrow C(top)*C(top-1)$; $top \leftarrow top - 1$
DIV	$C(top-1) \leftarrow C(top)/C(top-1)$; $top \leftarrow top - 1$
DUP	$C(top+1) \leftarrow C(top)$; $top \leftarrow top + 1$
EXCH	exchange $C(top)$, $C(top-1)$

where top is the address of the top of the stack and C(top) denotes the contents of that location. Write the shortest possible stack machine program to evaluate

$$Z \leftarrow (((B*C) - A)**2)/(B*C).$$

4.18 The expression evaluation example in Fig. 4.25 shows a FETCH instruction after every operand, where the operands are actually data descriptors, and a STORE instruction after every result. Could we remove all FETCH instructions by assuming that when an operand descriptor is not followed by a STORE, a fetch is done automatically? Consider how constants would be handled and whether it is ever useful to manipulate data descriptors (not the data itself).

4.19 A tagged evaluation stack is a stack in which each operation and operand has a tag specifying what type [e.g., integer (i) or floating point (f)] each operation or operand is. When the control unit finds a conflict between operand and operation types it automatically converts the operand to the proper type and then performs the operation. For example, the evaluation of the following expression in postfix notation produces the result of 7.0_f, not 7_i:

$$3_i, \quad 4.0_f, \quad +_f$$

(a) Show the postfix tagged expression to evaluate:

$$2_i +_i (3.0_f *_f 4_i)$$

(b) Translate the postfix tagged expression to a nontagged (conventional) expression. Use the operations 'float' and 'integer' where necessary to perform the tagged stack's automatic conversions.

(c) Now suppose we wish to leave the operation type unspecified; that is, when the control unit finds + in the expression it will check the top two elements of the stack to see if they are integer or floating-point so that the appropriate operation $+_i$ or $+_f$ is performed. What should the control unit do when the types of the top two stack elements are different? This type of stack allows the programmer to write "generic" functions. In this context, what is a generic function?

4.20 Some computers such as the CDC 6600 do not have an unconditional branch instruction. How can this instruction be eliminated from the instruction set?

4.21 When a conditional branch instruction is encountered, the IBM 360/91 lookahead unit: (Circle all answers that apply.)
(a) Assumes that the branch test will succeed.
(b) Assumes that the branch test will fail.
(c) Decodes instruction streams for both possibilities (a) and (b).
(d) Blocks execution beyond the conditional branch.
(e) Decodes the instruction stream selected by a global bit flag set by the programmer ("always succeed," "always fail").

4.22 (a) What would happen if an IBM 370 program accidentally overwrote the five new PSWs and then tried to branch to a region of memory with a different protection key? Is it likely that the machine will get into an infinite interrupt loop?
(b) How is a problem state program prevented from overwriting the five new PSWs?

Medium and hard problems in text order

4.23 Consider a simple computer with the microprogrammable architecture similar to the B1700. In this problem we experiment on a program written for such a computer. First, we give the instruction format and available instructions. Instruction format (numbers refer to length in bits):

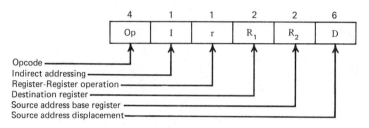

4	1	1	2	2	6
Op	I	r	R_1	R_2	D

Opcode ──────
Indirect addressing ──────
Register-Register operation ──────
Destination register ──────
Source address base register ──────
Source address displacement ──────

Available Instructions

Operation Class	Execution Time (in cycles)	Description	Mnemonic	Fields Present R_1	R_2	D
Data access	1	load into R_1 from $D(R_2)$	FETCH	yes	yes	yes
	1	store R_1 into $D(R_2)$	STORE	yes	yes	yes
Data manipulation	2	logically AND $D(R_2)$ and R_1, store in R_1	MASK	yes	yes	yes
	2	increment R_1	INC	yes	no	no
	3	add $D(R_2)$ into R_1	ADD	yes	yes	yes
	3	subtract $D(R_2)$ from R_1	SUB	yes	yes	yes
	15	multiply R_1 by $D(R_2)$	MPY	yes	yes	yes
	40	divide R_1 by $D(R_2)$	DIV	yes	yes	yes
Control	1	branch to address $D(R_2)$	JUMP	no	yes	yes
	1	branch to $D(R_2)$ if $R_1 \geq 0$	JMPGEZ	yes	yes	yes
	1	branch to $D(R_2)$ if $R_1 > 0$	JMPGTZ	yes	yes	yes
	1	load the current instruction address into R_1	FETCHA	yes	no	no

Notes:

1. Any $D(R_2)$ address (computed by $D + R_2$) can be indirected by setting the indirect bit, I. In our assembly language we use "*" to signal indirection.
2. If the r field is one, a register-to-register instruction will be carried out. In the assembly language we add an R to the front of the mnemonic; for example, RFETCH R1, R2 means transfer the contents of register R2 to register R1. But FETCH R1, D(R2) means to transfer the contents of memory location D(R2) to R1.
3. The machine has three general-purpose registers.
4. All data requires a base register. In our assembly language we use INIT R1, #DATA to mean that the loader will determine the exact

address of the scalar data of the program and place that address in register R1 when the above "pseudo" instruction is executed.

5. For MPY the high-order word is left in an inaccessible register until it is overwritten. For DIV the integer remainder is disposed of similarly. You may assume another instruction MEXT R_1 moves the high-order word to register R_1 to utilize this word if you wish, but we will not use it. A program written in the suggested assembly language is shown below. It is a Simpson's rule integration of a polynomial. The polynomial is evaluated in Horner's rule form in the subroutine EVAL. The value of X to be evaluated is passed in the register mnemonically defined as ACC, the accumulator. The degree of the polynomial is found in M, and the coefficients are found in the array A. The value of the polynomial F is returned in the register ACC.

The main program assumes that the interval of integration, from X1 to X2, and the number of subintervals N has already been loaded into these variables. The two other available registers have the mnemonics INDX and BASE. BASE is tied throughout the computation to the base register for the scalar data. Literals (i.e., constants) are in hexadecimal notation (e.g., #2, #FFFFFFFE).

Label	Instruction		Comment	
SIMP	INIT	BASE, #DATA		
	STORE	INDX, SIMPRIN	Save the return address.	01
	FETCH	ACC, X2	Compute the size of the interval of integration, (X2 − X1).	02
	SUB	ACC, X1		03
	STORE	ACC, INTERVAL		04
	DIV	ACC, N	Compute the subinterval size, i.e., H = (X2 − X1)/N.	05
	STORE	ACC, H		06
	FETCH	ACC, N	Save the final value of the loop index.	07
	STORE	ACC, FINAL INDX		08
	FETCH	ACC, X1	Start at the left endpoint and evaluate the polynomial.	09
	FETCHA	INDX		10
	JUMP	EVAL		11
	STORE	ACC, AREA	It is the initial area.	12
	FETCH	INDX, #1	Load the loop index.	13
SIMPLOOP	RFETCH	ACC, INDX	Do the end test.	14
	SUB	ACC, FINAL INDX		15
	JMPGTZ	ACC, SIMPDONE	Leave loop if done.	16
	RFETCH	ACC, INDX	Compute the distance from left end.	17

Label	Instruction		Comment	
	MPY	ACC, H		18
	ADD	ACC, X1		19
	STORE	INDX, INDEX		20
	FETCHA	INDX	Get ready to evaluate polynomial.	21
	JUMP	EVAL		22
	FETCH	INDX, INDEX		23
	STORE	ACC, F	Save value of polynomial.	24
	RFETCH	ACC, INDX		25
	MASK	ACC, #00000001	Is this an odd or even point?	26
	JMPGTZ	ACC, ODDPOINT		27
EVENPOINT	FETCH	ACC, #2	If even, multiply by 2.	28
	JUMP	EVALAREA		29
ODDPOINT	FETCH	ACC, #4	If odd, multiply by 4.	30
EVALAREA	MPY	ACC, F		31
	ADD	ACC, AREA	Compute new area.	32
	STORE	ACC, AREA		33
	INC	INDX	Go to the next point.	34
	JUMP	SIMPLOOP		35
SIMPDONE	FETCH	ACC, AREA		36
	SUB	ACC, F	Last point was overdone.	37
	MPY	ACC, H	Reduce answer by $H/(X2-X1)$.	38
	DIV	ACC, INTERVAL		39
	JUMP	SIMPRIN*	Return answer in ACC.	40
EVAL	STORE	ACC, X	Save return address and X value.	41
	STORE	ACC, #0		42
	FETCH	ACC, F	Set value of polynomial, F, to zero.	43
	STORE	INDX, EVALRTN		44
	FETCH	INDX, BASE OF A	Compute finishing address of coefficient array, leaving address of first coefficient in INDX reg.	45
	FETCH	ACC, M		46
	RADD	ACC, INDX		47
	STORE	ACC, FNL INDX		48
EVALLOOP	FETCH	ACC, F	Do one iteration of Horner's rule, $F*X+A(I)$.	49
	MPY	ACC, X		50
	ADD	ACC, 0(INDX)		51
	STORE	ACC, F		52
	INC	INDX	Add increment and do endtest.	53
	FETCH	ACC, FNL INDX		54
	RSUB	ACC, INDX		55
	JMPGEZ	ACC, EVALLOOP	If not done branch back.	56
	FETCH	ACC, F		57
	JUMP	EVALRTN*	Return value of polynomial in ACC.	58

(a) Do a static instruction frequency count on the given program. Compare, as best you can, your results with those cited in the chapter discussion from the FORTRAN study (i.e., Table 4.1).

(b) Do a dynamic instruction frequency count on the program. Assume the degree of the polynomial M is 5 and the number of intervals N is 50. Compare your results with the studies cited in the text (i.e., Table 4.5).

(c) Weight the instructions according to their execution times and recompute part (b).

(d) Assume that our control unit is microprogrammed and can access memory by the bit. Based on your part (a) statistics, find a nearly optimal encoding of the instructions used in the program using two or three opcode sizes of your choice. Determine how much the program can be compacted. Don't forget to encode the I, r, R_1, and R_2 fields.

(e) Suppose we are interested in reducing the instruction fetch bandwidth instead of static program compaction. Using opcodes of length 2 and 6, assign the operations so that the instruction fetch bandwidth is reduced.

4.24 Consider the problem of decoding the opcode of an instruction set with multiple length opcodes. Suppose we have two possible opcode lengths of s bits and l bits.

(a) Assume that the output of the decoder is n lines for the n opcodes of the machine and that one of the short opcodes indicates that a long opcode follows. (A different one of these lines should be 1 for each short or long opcode.) Show how the short and long opcodes could be decoded simultaneously. How many gates are required?

(b) Suppose we have a microprogrammed machine and that the output of the decoder is the address of the first microinstruction. How could you simultaneously decode both types of opcodes using two ROMs? How big would the ROMs be if microinstruction addresses are w bits long? How many additional gates are needed?

(c) Construct an efficient method to decode an opcode that has been optimally encoded using Huffman's algorithm. Assume that the opcode could be from 1 to l bits long and that one line out of n, as in part (a), is to be selected. Compare the time and number of gates needed with your solution to part (a). Considering the B1700 studies mentioned in the text, is the extra complexity justified?

4.25 Microprogram each of the following instructions for the microprogrammed machine architecture discussed in the text.

(a) Load a register from memory assuming that the register address and memory address registers have already been loaded.

(b) Memory-to-memory three address add. Assume that the memory address register gets loaded at the appropriate times.

(c) Subtract an indirect memory location from a register. Begin with an address (call it the base address) that is located in an addressable processor register. Assume that the RAR is loaded at the proper time and that neither the base address nor indirect memory address (fetched from memory) needs to be processed by the address processor. Both can be gated to the MAR via the processor bus. Further assume that the MUX into the MAR passes only the address field of a word from the bus.

4.26 In Fig. 4.6, information is demultiplexed from registers onto the processor bus or to other registers and ORed off the bus into registers. Alternately, one could fan out the information from registers to the bus and other registers and multiplex all the information coming into each register. Show how this alternative would be implemented. Select new control points and recode the microinstruction fields and codes. Don't forget to prevent clashing of information on the bus. Redo the examples of Fig. 4.8 with your new machine.

4.27 The following assembly language program segment performs an inner-product computation.

10	STOZ	P	memory location $P \leftarrow 0$
11	SETX	X1, 1	index register $X \leftarrow 1$
12	TESTX	X1, N, 18	if $X1 > N$ go to step 18
13	FETCH	A, X1	load A_i to accumulator
14	MPY	B, X1	form $A_i * B_i$ in accumulator
15	ADD	P	form $P + A_i * B_i$ in accumulator
16	STORE	P	accumulator to memory
17	JUMP	12	go back to step 12
18	$\cdots$		

The control unit of this hypothetical machine performs the indicated steps, in the order given, for each type of instruction in the table below.

Control Step	Clocks	FETCH	STORE	STOZ	ADD	MPY	SETX	INC	TESTX	JUMP
Instruction fetch	2	X	X	X	X	X	X	X	X	X
Increment location register	1	X	X	X	X	X	X	X	X	X
Instruction decode	1	X	X	X	X	X	X	X	X	X
Address arithmetic	1	X	X	X	X	X				
Validity test	1	X	X	X	X	X				
Data fetch	2	X				X	X			
Data store	2		X	X						
Branch test	1									X	
Load location register	1								(X)	X
Index register operation	1						X	X		
Sequence adder	3				X					
Sequence multiplier	4					X				

Assume that this control unit allows *no* concurrency of processor operation and memory references. Instructions may be pipelined, but when the sequencer is busy on an add or multiply, it may not be used to sequence the memory for instruction fetch, data fetch, or data store. Assume here that only one program or data word can be accessed on each memory cycle.

(a) Determine how many clocks the program loop requires (steps 12–17).

(b) Discuss whether processor and memory concurrency would be of any use in speeding up execution for this program.

4.28 Section 4.2.4 discussed the use of multiprogramming with one large processor bound "foreground" job and a number of smaller "background" jobs. Consider the alternate situation where a machine is primarily serving many terminals and is thus I/O bound. Discuss the consequences of running large processor bound jobs in "background" Contrast this with the above with respect to main memory requirements, priority assignments for CPU and I/O, throughput and turnaround time for the various jobs.

4.29 In many early Burroughs machines, all program references to variables are made through data descriptors. Although this has important advantages, it also slows down program execution. However, in the case of array variables being used in DO loops, adding some registers to the control unit allows much of the slowdown to be avoided.

(a) Discuss the advantages of addressing via data descriptors.

(b) Why is descriptor-based addressing slow?

(c) Show how additional registers could speed up the processing of

$$\text{DO} \quad S_1 \quad I \leftarrow 1, \quad 100$$
$$S_1 \quad A(I) \leftarrow B(I) + C(I)$$

(*Hint:* The B7700 has such hardware registers.)

4.30 As discussed in Section 4.3.3, the CDC 6600 has three sets of eight registers:

Register	Type of Register	Implied Operations
A1–A5 X1–X5	Operand address registers Operand data registers	Address stored in A*i* fetches contents of that address to X*i*
A6–A7 X6–X7	Result address registers Result data registers	Address stored in A*i* stores X*i* at that address
B1–B7	Used to modify and increment address registers and perform address calculations	Store in B*i*; no fetch or store to X*i* implied

The registers A0, X0, and B0 are somewhat special: A0 and X0 are not paired, that is, a store to A0 will neither fetch nor store X0; and B0 is always equal to 0. The 15-bit three operand arithmetic and Boolean assembly language instructions are of the form:

$$\tau \quad Ri \qquad Rj \quad \theta \quad Rk$$

where τ is the type of operation. τ could be any one of:

> S for A or B register sum or difference
> F for X register floating-point operations
> I for X register fixed-point operations
> B for X register Boolean operations
> D for double precision, and so on.

Ri is the register to store the result in.
Rj, Rk are the operand registers. (If either is left out, B0 is assumed.)
θ is the operation to be performed: $+$, $-$, $*$, or $/$.

For example, SB3 B5+B4, adds B5 and B4 and stores the result in B3. The 30-bit, three-operand instructions are identical except that Rk is replaced by a constant.

The branch instructions are all 30-bit instructions and most are of the form:

$$\gamma \quad Ri, \quad K$$

where γ is a condition and could be any one of:

ZR	jump if register zero
NZ	jump if register nonzero
PL	jump if register positive
NG	jump if register negative
OR	jump if register $+\infty$
ID	jump to register indefinite.

Ri is an A, B, or X register.
K is an address constant to jump to.
There are several other instructions not mentioned here (see [CDCC75] for the complete set), but these will suffice for our purpose.

The following assembly language program should help make matters concrete. The program computes the following FORTRAN-like program:

$$\text{DO} \quad S_1 \quad I \leftarrow 1, \quad N$$
$$S_1 \qquad Z(I) \leftarrow A*(Y(I)**2)+B*Y(I)+C$$

	Instruction		Comment
	SB1	ADDR.OF.Y	get address of Y array
	SA1	B1	load Y(1) into register X1!
	SA2	ADDR.OF.A	load X2 with A
	SA3	ADDR.OF.B	load X3 with B
	SA4	ADDR.OF.C	load X4 with C
	SB7	ADDR.OF.Z	get address of Z array
	SB2	B0+1	set B2 to 1 for use as increment
	SB3	B0	set B3 to 0 for index, I
	SB4	N	set B4 to N to see if done
LOOP	FX0	X1*X1	form Y(I)**2
	FX6	X2*X0	form A*(Y(I)**2)
	FX0	X3*X1	form B*Y(I)
	FX5	X6+X0	form A*(Y(I)**2)+B*Y(I)
	FX7	X5+X4	form A*(Y(I)**2)+B*Y(I)+C
	SA7	B7+B3	store result in Z(I)
	SB3	B3+B2	increment I
	SA1	B1+B3	load next X(I)
	SB5	B3−B4	see if finished
	NZ	B5, LOOP	if not finished, jump to top of loop

(a) The instruction buffer in the CDC 6600 contains 8 words of 60 bits per word. The loop in the program above is only $2\frac{3}{4}$ words long (9×15 bits $+ 30$ bits); thus, after the loop has been fetched once, no more instruction fetches are needed until the loop is broken. An unsophisticated compiler may expand the size of the loop to overflow the instruction buffer. Rewrite the program, loading the address of A, B, and C each time through the loop, and compare I with N by fetching from memory on every loop execution. Besides not performing obvious optimizations, the compiler may include program debugging features such as array bounds checking and overflow checking. Include in the program above, a test that branches to the compiler's debug routines if array bounds are exceeded or if an overflow occurs after a multiplication. (The CDC 6600 does not generate an interrupt when overflow occurs; you must use an instruction OR X_i, DEBUG after each multiply!) The rewritten program probably exceeds 8 words. If an instruction fetch takes 8 clocks (CDC minor cycles) and a multiply takes 10 clocks, would the inability to save the entire loop in the instruction buffer cause a large slowdown in execution time? (Remember that the control unit and the functional units are overlapped.) Approximately how much is the used memory bandwidth increased?

(b) Write a program to compute the matrix product of A and B where both matrices are $N \times N$. Does your program fill the instruction buffer?

4.31 The PDP-11 has a limited set of opcodes that are complemented by an extensive set of addressing modes. There are three major instruction formats: single operand, double operand, and conditional branch. All are 1 word long (16 bits or 2 bytes) and are laid out as follows: (The numbers refer to length in bits.)

single operand

opcode	addr. mode	@	reg.
10	2	1	3

double operand

opcode	addr. mode	@	src. reg.	addr. mode	@	dest. reg.
4	2	1	3	2	1	3

conditional branch

opcode	byte offset
8	8

(The @ bit is an indirect address indicator.)

Some of the single operand instructions are: clear (CLR), complement (COM), increment (INC), decrement (DEC), negate (NEG), test (TST), and jump (JMP). Some of the double operand instructions are: move (MOV), compare (CMP), bit test (BIT), bit set (BIS), bit clear (BIC), add (ADD), and subtract (SUB). (Many can operate either on full words or bytes.) Some of the branch instructions are: branch unconditional (BR), branch if not equal (BNE), branch if equal (BEQ), branch if greater than (BGT), branch if less than or equal (BLE). There are several other instruction formats and many other instructions.

There are four regular addressing modes:

Code	Name	Syntax	Function
00	register	Ri	Register contains operand.
01	autoincrement	(Ri)+	The contents of register Ri is used as an address for the operand, then the register is incremented by 2 (bytes).
10	autodecrement	−(Ri)	The contents of Ri is first decremented by 2 and the result is used as the address of the operand.
11	index	X(Ri)	The number found in the word following the instruction, the value of X, is added to the register Ri and the result is the address of the operand.

In addition to the addressing modes above, once the operand has been determined as above, the operand can be fetched indirectly if the indirect bit is one. @ is used to denote indirection in the assembly language. (For further information, see [Eckh75] and [DECo71a].) For example, consider implementing a jump table, that is, an array of addresses to branch to, where the address selected is determined by the value of an index (a FORTRAN computed GOTO). Assume the table is labeled ADDRS and the index is currently in location I. The jump table is implemented by:

| MOV | I, R1 | move the index to register 1 |
| JMP | ADDRS(R1) | use R1 as an index into the ADDRS array; take the value found there as the address to jump to |

(a) Give an example of when each of the eight addressing modes might be used.

(b) The program counter is considered to be the regular general-purpose register R7. Among other things, this allows us to extend the instruction set to include immediate operands and relative addresses. In the former, the word following the instruction contains a number to be used as an operand. In the latter, the word following the instruction is the address of data or program relative to the current program counter. (This allows more easily relocatable code.) Describe how the autoincrement and index addressing modes can be used to realize immediate operands and relative addressing. Can you conceive of any of the other six possible addressing modes being usefully applied to the program counter? (*Hint:* Absolute addresses and indirect relative addresses may be useful.) What would the following instruction do?

MOV　LABEL,　R7

(c) The autoincrement and autodecrement modes are often used to implement a stack. (R6 is the top of stack pointer by convention.) Thus, one can write pseudo-zero-address code on the PDP-11. Write pseudo-zero-address code to evaluate the expression:

$$-(A+((B-10)+C+5)-D).$$

Use R6 as the stack pointer and the ADD, SUB, NEG, and MOV instructions.

4.32 Available page frames may be kept track of by using a bit map in which there is one bit for each page frame. If 1 represents an occupied page frame and 0 represents an unoccupied page frame, design a hardware device to find the position of the first unoccupied page frame. Give time bounds and gate counts.

4.33 How large must an arithmetic evaluation stack be to evaluate any expression of e atoms in infix notation for each of the following expression types? (Show, if possible, the form of an expression that actually uses the maximum space required.)

(a) Expressions with binary operators of equal precedence and no parentheses.

(b) Expressions with two types of binary operators of different precedence and no parentheses.

(c) Expressions with binary operators and parentheses.

(d) Expressions with binary and unary operators and parentheses.

4.34 Control stacks were discussed in Section 4.3.5 as a convenient way of maintaining addressing environments in block-structured languages. A *stack control word* was mentioned as a separator in the stack of information about each procedure involved. The stack control word can be used to hold information about the procedures in the stack. Two fields are very useful, namely, the *address environment* and *stack history* fields.

When a new procedure is called, its stack control word's stack history field points to the stack control word of the procedure that called it. Thus, when the newly called procedure finishes, control can be quickly returned to the caller by popping off the stack all information down to the caller's stack control word.

The address environment field of a newly called procedure is set to point to the stack control word of the next outer nested procedure in the original program. This field allows global addressing information to be available at all inner nested levels.

(a) How can the address environment and stack history fields be set when a new procedure is called?

(b) For the following program, show the state of the control stack when the statement $C \leftarrow D + B$ is being executed.

```
BEGIN OUTER
    DECLARE REAL A,B
    BEGIN PROC 1
        DECLARE REAL C,D
        C ← D + B
    END PROC 1
    BEGIN PROC 2
        DECLARE REAL D,E
        BEGIN PROC 3
            DECLARE REAL F
            A ← D * 3
            F ← E + 7
            CALL PROC 1
        END PROC 3
```

CALL PROC 3
D ← E + A
END PROC 2
CALL PROC 2
END OUTER

(c) When a procedure invocation is completed and control is to be returned to the caller, how can the stack control words be used?

(d) When a variable in a nested procedure is to be accessed, how can its proper address be determined using the address environment fields? The speed in finding the address can be improved by what are called display registers in the B6500 and its successors. There are 32 display registers, each of which can be made to correspond to a variable that is local to a procedure which is global to the currently invoked procedure. Each display register then points to the stack control word of the procedure in which the display register's corresponding variable is local. The effect is to provide quick and easy access to appropriate locations deep in the stack.

(e) How could display registers be used in generating addresses for the above example program?

For more details about the B6500 stack mechanism and for a discussion of most of the ideas in this problem, see [HaDe68].

4.35 Most computers have instructions which are used for subroutine calls. For example, the IBM 360/370 series uses a branch and link instruction which stores the next instruction address in a register specified in the instruction and loads the address of the subroutine into the program location counter. The CDC 6000 series uses a return jump which stores, at the jump address, an unconditional branch to the address of the instruction after the return jump instruction and then starts executing the instruction after the jump address. The PDP-11 series, which has a hardware stack mechanism, stores the next instruction address in the stack and then loads the subroutine address into the program counter. Explain how these instructions would be used to implement a subroutine call. How does one return from a subroutine implemented with each of these instructions? Do these instructions aid parameter passing? Rank these instructions in terms of the number of individual (register transfer level) operations required. Show how each of these instructions would be used for reentrant assembly language programs; for implementing recursive subroutines.

4.36 SIME computers, and pipeline processors in particular, have special control structures that eliminate some of the need for branch instructions, because an interruption in the linear flow of a vector operation can be devastating. We can associate with each pair of operands in a vector instruction a mode or mask bit. If this bit is 0, then the operation on that pair will not be performed. Thus, a vector operation now has three operand vectors, the two original operands and the mode bit vector. For example, the program

$$
\begin{array}{ll}
\text{DO} \quad S_1 \quad I \leftarrow 1, N \\
S_1 \quad\quad \text{IF} \quad A(I) = 0 \\
\quad\quad\quad \text{THEN} \quad C(I) \leftarrow 0 \\
\quad\quad\quad \text{ELSE} \quad C(I) \leftarrow B(I)/A(I)
\end{array}
$$

could be restructured to remove the IF statement by first computing mode bit vectors M and N, which can be applied to each unconditional statement in an obvious manner.

$$
\begin{array}{ll}
\text{DO} \quad S_1 \quad I \leftarrow 1, N \\
S_1 \quad\quad M(I) \leftarrow (A(I) \neq 0) \\
\text{DO} \quad S_2 \quad I \leftarrow 1, N \\
S_2 \quad\quad (C(I) \leftarrow B(I)/A(I)) \;\; MODE(M(I)) \\
\text{DO} \quad S_3 \quad I \leftarrow 1, N \\
S_3 \quad\quad N(I) \leftarrow NOT(M(I)) \\
\text{DO} \quad S_4 \quad I \leftarrow 1, N \\
S_4 \quad\quad (C(I) \leftarrow 0) \;\; MODE \;\; (N(I))
\end{array}
$$

We have introduced the statement (STMT) MODE (BVEC(I)), which applies one bit of a mode bit vector, BVEC, to the statement STMT.

(a) Why are mode vectors more efficient than conditional branch instructions for a pipeline processor? Give equations based on the startup time and the segment time of a pipeline processor.

(b) What machine instructions would facilitate the manipulation of mode vectors; for example, an instruction to test if all the bits in the vector are 1?

(c) Do any high-level languages encourage the use of, or directly use, mode vectors?

4.37 In Section 4.4.1 it was observed that the minimal speedup obtained by instruction lookahead in a control unit that blocked at conditional branches could be improved by allowing the decoding and even execution of both paths of a conditional. Assume that we have a processor with as many functional units as required to perform arithmetic operations and that the control unit can decode and issue any number of instructions on both paths of a conditional branch.

(a) In the following program, how far ahead of the IF statement could the functional units execute before being blocked by data dependences?

$$
\begin{array}{ll}
\text{DO} \quad S_6 \quad I \leftarrow 1, 10 \\
\quad\quad T \leftarrow A(I) - B(I)
\end{array}
$$

IF T = 0
    THEN C(I) ← 1
    ELSE C(I) ← A(I) + B(I)/T
S_6 D(I) ← C(I) ** Z

(b) Rewrite the program of part (a) using mode vectors.

4.38 Consider a pipelined processor in which we wish to perform one vector instruction on only a random selection of the elements of a large vector. There are three possible methods:

(1) We could use each of the elements to be operated on as a separate one-element vector.

(2) We could use mode vectors (Problem 4.36) to flag those elements of the large vector on which we wish to perform the operation.

(3) We could move each of the elements on which we wish to operate into a separate vector, then perform the operation on this compressed array, and finally expand the array.

(a) Use the variables:

N = the length of the large vector
P = the density of selected elements ($0 \le P \le 1$)
T_s = the startup time of the pipeline
T_0 = the segment time of the pipeline

Derive equations for the time to perform each of the methods above. Assume that it takes one segment time to fetch or store a data word and that fetches and stores can be overlapped. Also, assume that the large vector elements corresponding to 0 mode bits must travel through the pipe even though they are not operated on. Sketch your equation on a density versus time graph.

(b) Rederive and sketch the case when a total of 20 operations are going to be performed on the selected elements as opposed to just one operation.

4.39 Programs containing logical bugs may often try to branch to an area of memory containing data instead of program. Some Burroughs machines can detect this type of error immediately because they have a tag bit that indicates whether the word fetched is program or data. If the bug mentioned above occurs, an interrupt will immediately halt the processor before any damage is done. On the other hand, a machine without tag bits, such as IBM 360/370, will generally be able to execute very few data words as instructions before an interrupt would be generated anyway (although the true cause of the interrupt is not clear). What are some of the ways that data word execution could generate interrupts on an IBM 360/370? Try to estimate the average number of instructions that would be executed. Try to define an instruction format that would have very little chance of matching typical data formats.

4.40 Consider the problem of imprecise interrupts. Give as general a statement as you can of necessary and sufficient conditions for an interrupt being imprecise. If hardware costs were no object, could imprecise interrupts always be avoided?

4.41 Here we consider how an interrupt is implemented in hardware. The least expensive method is called the single-level indicator system. In this system each of the external interrupt lines enters a different bit of the interrupt status register (ISR). All of the bits of the register are ORed together to form the interrupt request line (REQ) to the CPU. The CPU acknowledges the request at the end of the instruction cycle. Finally, the CPU may issue a RESET signal to clear the ISR or a particular bit of the ISR.

(a) Sketch a logic diagram for this hardware interrupt scheme. How many gates are needed for N interrupt lines?

(b) The CPU acknowledges an interrupt by branching to a predetermined interrupt subroutine. Construct a flowchart of what this subroutine must do. How would it determine which device caused the interrupt? In particular, how could this subroutine establish priority among the interrupts? For N interrupt lines, estimate the number of instructions that must be executed to select the device that requires service, assuming the priority of devices is a serial ordering of the bits in the ISR; call this time I.

(c) Why is this method called the single-level method? Given a hardware recognition time of R, an instruction cycle time of t, the device select time I, and the average time to handle an interrupt H, what is the maximum interrupt rate allowable before the system is saturated?

4.42 A multiple-level interrupt array mechanism for controlling interrupts can be represented schematically as shown on top of page 383 (see [Lane75]), where the subscript ij indicates level i, device j and

$$C_{ij} \text{ is interrupt clear}$$
$$S_{ij} \text{ is interrupt signal}$$
$$M_{ij} \text{ is mask interrupt.}$$

Each module is constructed from a D-type flip-flop, an AND gate, and an OR gate, see bottom of page 383.

(a) Once an interrupt has been detected by the above network, the processor must determine which device signaled the interrupt. Modify the matrix so that the processor can determine which device signaled the interrupt.

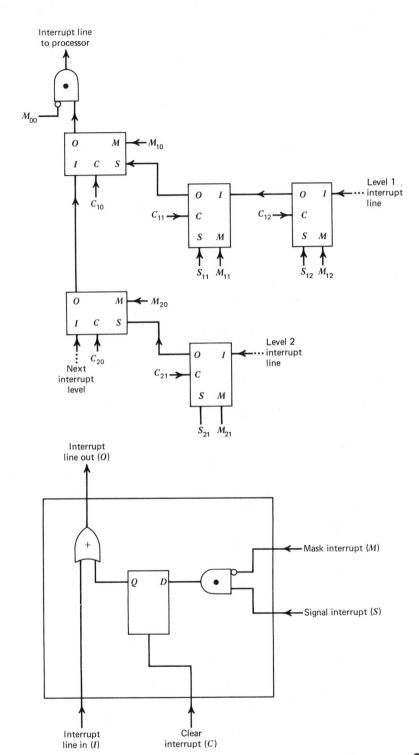

Interrupt line
to processor

M_{00}

O M ← M_{10}

I C S

C_{10}

O I

C_{11}→ C

S M

S_{11} M_{11}

O I ← ···· Level 1
interrupt
line

C_{12}→ C

S M

S_{12} M_{12}

O M ← M_{20}

I C S

C_{20}

Next
interrupt
level

C_{21}→

O I ← ···· Level 2
interrupt
line

C

S M

S_{21} M_{21}

Interrupt
line out (O)

$+$

Mask interrupt (M)

Q D

Signal interrupt (S)

Interrupt
line in (I)

Clear
interrupt (C)

383

(b) How could one dynamically alter the priority of an interrupt, that is, under program control? (*Hint:* Allow a device interrupt line to have more than one level in the matrix.)

(c) Could the IBM 360/370 interrupt scheme (Section 4.4.3.4) use this hardware? If so, how?

4.43 How could a stack mechanism be useful in handling multiple interrupts? If a stack were used to hold pending interrupts, what can you say about the pattern of priorities of the interrupts held in the stack at any instant?

4.44 Different computers implement interrupt subroutine calls in different ways. For example, the IBM 360 uses the method described in Section 4.4.3.4. The PDP-11 uses a hardware-implemented stack to store the current processor status and instruction location register. The new status is loaded from a fixed memory location. In the CDC 6600, the central processor is interrupted by a peripheral processor which supplies the address of a group of memory locations that contain new values for all the processor's registers, as well as the new instruction location register and processor status for the interrupt subroutine. The register contents of the interrupted program are stored where the interrupt subroutine register contents originate. Compare these three methods in terms of speed and usefulness.

4.45 Consider the function of an I/O interrupt handler in a moderately sophisticated operating system. Construct a flowchart showing how one might work. Assume that the I/O interrupt handler is passed the completion code issued by the device which has completed the I/O operations. What should it do with this information? What would happen if the I/O operation failed? How can the I/O interrupt handler determine whose I/O has been completed? Now that the device is available again, how can it determine if more I/O transactions are waiting to use the device? What will happen to the job that was executing when the interrupt occurred? How soon can interrupts again be enabled?

4.46 Suppose you are designing a computer that will be used in time-shared, real-time data collection. Many independent external devices want to keep counters in the machine's main memory. Thus an "interrupt and count" processor instruction is desired. When such an external interrupt occurs, a main memory location corresponding to the source of the interrupt is to have the number in the interrupter's input register added to it. Note that this is not a TEST AND SET type of operation because we assume that only one device is accessing any main memory location. Discuss how this might be implemented. The goal is to have it operate quickly and not use a lot of hardware for its implementation. Assume the computer is a two-address machine with a standard arithmetic unit that can be used for the operation.

4.47 In this problem we consider some of the details of implementing a virtual machine and mention some architecture features which facilitate the running of virtual machines.

(a) Inherent in the concept of a virtual machine is the notion that the virtual machine monitor (VMM) can construct and maintain the state of a virtual machine. List the components of a virtual machine state subdivided into the four parts of a virtual machine mentioned in Section 4.5.2.

(b) It is advantageous to run a VMM on exactly the same machine that it is virtualizing. For example, if the machine hardware allows two processor states, it would be convenient to let the VMM run in the privileged state and force the virtual machine to run in the un-privileged state. The VMM can then maintain an independent processor state for each virtual machine. Unfortunately, some machines simply ignore or NOP a privileged instruction executed in the unprivileged processor state. Why is this unfortunate? Another feature that is hard to virtualize is an unprivileged instruction which changes the processor state of the machine to unprivileged regardless of its previous state. (Why?) Would allowing arithmetic exceptions such as overflow to generate interrupts with or without changing the processor state be difficult to virtualize? Discuss the advantages of allowing the VMM exclusive use of the privileged state in light of all the nuances above.

(c) Discuss whether it is helpful or necessary to have virtual memory to run a VMM. Consider the security gained or lost and what instructions might be hard to virtualize. For example, under what conditions is having fixed memory locations for automatically swapping processor status words on interrupts virtualizable? Can an instruction to load a physical memory address be virtualized?

CH

5

One must have a good memory to be able to keep the promises one makes.

"Human, All Too Human"

Friedrich Wilhelm Nietzsche

A dozen units had been pulled out, yet thanks to the multiple redundancy of its design . . . the computer was still holding its own.

"Dave," said Hal, "I don't understand why you're doing this to me . . . You are destroying my mind . . . I will become childish . . . I will become nothing . . ."

This is harder than I expected, thought Bowman. . . . But it has to be done, if I am ever to regain control of the ship.

"I am a HAL Nine Thousand computer Production Number 3. I became operational at the Hal Plant in Urbana, Illinois, on January 12, 1997. The quick brown fox jumps over the lazy dog. The rain in Spain is mainly in the plain. Dave—are you still there . . . ?"

"2001: A Space Odyssey"

Arthur C. Clarke

MAIN
MEMORIES

5.1 SYSTEM MEMORY USES

Throughout this book we have been discussing various uses of memory in computer systems; Fig. 5.1 shows a number of such uses. A brief discussion of these serves as a review of memories and will introduce several topics which we will expand in this chapter. Figure 5.1 will be discussed from the top down.

The control unit of Fig. 5.1 is shown with two specialized memories. Both are random access memories (RAMs) in that any word in the memory can be accessed in equal time. But the access methods are specialized. The read-only memory (ROM) is written once when the machine is built. It produces long words of bit patterns used to sequence the machine instructions, as discussed in Section 4.2.2. ROMs are usually faster and less expensive than standard random access memories. The content addressable memory (CAM) is given a virtual memory address and returns an address in main memory if the virtual address is that of an active page, as discussed in Section 4.3.4. CAMs are generally slower and more expensive than normal RAMs. We will discuss the details of one such memory in Section 5.4.2.3. Control units may also be equipped with other specialized memories—for example, buffers for data or instruction words may be implemented as small RAMs.

In the processor of Fig. 5.1, we show a ROM. Perhaps several of them may be used to implement combinational logic functions of data words. ROM-rounding and ROM-arithmetic were both discussed in Chapter 3. We also show here a set of working data registers from which the processor takes arguments and to which it returns results. This register array can be thought of as the first level in a *memory hierarchy* that extends through several levels out to secondary memory. Physically, these registers may be organized on a semiconductor

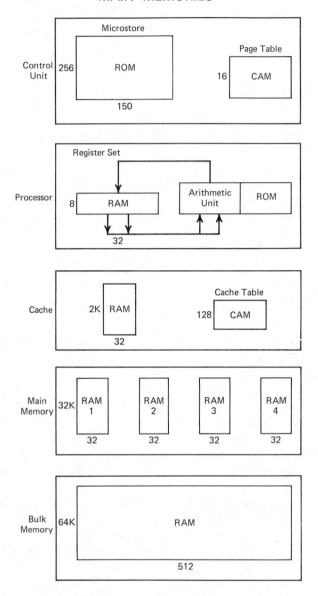

FIGURE 5.1   **Memories in a computer system.**

chip in such a way that two registers may be read and one written in one clock period. Perhaps 8 or 16 words are contained in such a chip and perhaps only an 8- or 16-bit slice of a full word is implemented on one chip. Thus several chips may be needed to build a full length 32- or 64-bit word register set.

The next level in the hierarchy of Fig. 5.1 is a cache memory. This is a RAM which works at high speed and is matched to the processor speed. It is smaller than main memory but much faster. Recently used words and their main memory neighbors are held here in anticipation of their use in the near future. The CAM shown here is used to associate cache addresses with main memory addresses just as the CAM in the control unit associates main memory with secondary memory. We will discuss more details about cache memories in Section 5.4.3.

The main memory is, as its name implies, the main storage area for active data and programs. It may be organized as one big memory, but frequently high-speed memories consist of a number of parallel memory units. Each such unit can be addressed independently, so if there are m units altogether, then m different addresses may be accessed at once. Each memory unit has some physical word length, say 32 or 64 bits, but the memory may be addressable to a lower level, say to the 8-bit byte level. Additional selection logic must be provided for this in each memory unit. In Fig. 5.1, we show a four-way parallel main memory with 32-bit words.

In many large computers, there is another random access memory between the main memory and the various secondary memory devices. This bulk RAM[1] is much faster than secondary memory, but is slower and much larger than main memory. It is used as an immediate backup to main memory. Although this bulk memory is a RAM, it may have very long words, for example, 256 or 512 bits. This can reduce the system cost without degrading performance, because individual word access is usually of no interest here. The goal is simply to buffer large amounts of data either on input, on output, or between uses in main memory. In Fig. 5.1, we show a 512-bit word. This corresponds to 16 main memory sized words, but because main memory has four parallel units, the cycle time here could be one-fourth (4/16) that of main memory and still have a matched bandwidth. In fact, it may be even slower, since it may be used relatively infrequently. The bulk memory we show has 64K words of 512 bits, which is equivalent to a million 32-bit words.

Thus if each main memory unit had a cycle time of 800 ns, the minimum effective main memory cycle would be 200 ns, whereas the bulk memory could have a 3.2 μs cycle time. Because 512 bits correspond to 16 words of 32 bits, the effective cycle time of the bulk memory is

$$\frac{3.2\ \mu\text{s}}{16\ \text{words}} = 200\ \text{ns per 32-bit word,}$$

which matches the main memory. The cache memory might have a cycle time of 50 ns and be matched in speed to the processor clock. Thus if processor functions require 3–5 clocks, the cache could be well-matched to the processing speed, assuming several cache references per instruction executed.

The point of a multilevel memory hierarchy is, of course, to provide a large

---

[1] Various names are used by manufacturers: CDC calls it extended core storage (ECS) [Thor70], IBM calls it large core (or capacity) storage (LCS), and so on.

amount of storage space that is not too expensive. A memory hierarchy is used only because one can seldom afford to have as much fast (register level) memory as needed. If the hierarchy is properly matched to the patterns of addresses generated by programs run on the system, then its effective speed *can* match the processor and control unit so that data and program words flow to the CPU with little delay, thus approximating an arbitrarily large set of fast registers. Later in this chapter and again in Chapter 7, we shall consider various aspects of the address patterns generated by programs; such patterns are important in studying the performance of parallel memories as well as all levels of memory hierarchies.

With this overview behind us, we now present the details of various types of random access memory and their use in computer systems. Our main attention will be focused on main memory to which we now turn.

5.2 MAIN MEMORY USE

5.2.1 Introduction

Main memory is the most expensive single component in most computer systems—most expensive in relation to processors, control units, switches, secondary memory, or I/O devices. Main memory may be as much as 30 or 40 percent of the entire system cost. On this basis alone, machine designers are justified in carefully examining main memory configurations. Of course, any recommendations made toward reducing the main memory size will be carefully examined by almost all users; usually, the more memory they can have the happier they are. This is a hyperbolic way of saying that everyone would like to have as much memory as necessary when necessary, and because good methods of exploiting memory hierarchies are only partly understood, the easy way out is to hold everything in main memory.

We can summarize the above paragraph from both the designer's and user's points of view, as follows. Since main memory is so expensive:

(1) Machine designers should attempt to configure main memories that provide high bandwidth at low cost; and (2) Machine users and software writers should design schemes for using as little memory as necessary in various applications.

One hedge against the high cost of large, fast main memories is the use of a hierarchy of slower, less expensive memory units. In Chapter 7, we present a general discussion of memory hierarchies. But here we will fix our attention on main memory—the most expensive level in the hierarchy—and we will also include cache memory in this discussion. Later we will also discuss bulk random access memory, and questions concerning the size, speed, and configurations of memories used in various kinds of computer systems.

It is convenient to identify three types of use of main memory. A universal use is for program storage. The two remaining types of use are for data arrays and for other data types (scalars, list structures, etc.); these are related to programming language features. Each of these can influence two important aspects of main memory design. One is the relation of the effective bandwidth of main memory to the pattern of addresses generated by a running program. The other concerns what kind of memory access is allowed—read, write, and so on.

For example, programs are usually accessed one address after another, in order. Jumps break the flow, and these may occur fairly frequently (see Section 4.2.1). Arrays are usually addressed in sequence, although in stored multidimensional arrays only one direction can be addressed in a contiguous way; the other directions require a skip between stored elements. Sometimes arrays may be accessed in more or less random order. Scalar data may be stored in a contiguous block of memory, but we can expect to address it in a random way, as is the case for most other types of data structures which involve pointers between data elements. Later in the chapter we will discuss effective memory bandwidth as a function of the pattern of addresses generated by a running program, and we will return to this distinction between regular and random address patterns.

The other concern to memory designers is in the type of access to be allowed; for example, the following may be typical system access constraints. Most programs can only be read, not written. Some data can be read and written, some can be written only, and some can be read only. Furthermore, the type of access—or the ability to access at all—may depend on who or of what class the user is. Various kinds of protected memory access will also be discussed later (see Section 5.2.2).

To enhance bandwidth and to afford various kinds of memory protection, a traditional memory design technique was to put programs in one memory unit and data in another. Babbage used this scheme, as did most early machine designers who regarded programs as fixed, read-only objects. In the late 1940s, with the advent of the "stored program" computer, an additional degree of flexibility was afforded in enabling programs to modify themselves. This idea was not to live forever.

Clearly, it is advantageous to modify addresses, for example, to index through an array. But this can be done using index registers without physically changing the program itself (see Section 4.3.1). Similarly, it was nice to be able to plant addresses in jump instructions, for example, in preparing to return from a subroutine to a main program. But this can also be done by indirectly using a register or "neutral" memory location, rather than by actually changing the stored instruction. And so the list goes on. There is always a way to avoid program modification.

As programs became more and more complicated, as group efforts in programming grew, and as shared use of common programs in multiprogrammed machines proliferated, the notion of programs that modify themselves became anathema. It also became more difficult to accomplish as high-level languages became more popular. Thus, although programs must be written into memory at load time, thereafter the memory might as well be a ROM, because essentially all accesses to programs are reads. In high-performance machines, this may lead us back to a separate memory for programs only.

Also, for high-performance machines, there could be a trend toward separate memories for array data and other types of data. As we shall see, conflict-free access to array data can be arranged in many cases by proper design, so other types of access may simply get in the way. In some languages, arrays dominate the volume of data by far, so a relatively small separate scalar memory could be used, for example. In other languages, list structures or other types of scattered access to data are required, and we must deal with random data accessing as well.

The operation of a basic memory unit will be discussed in terms of Fig. 5.2. One or more CPUs or I/O devices can be connected to a memory unit; they provide addresses and expect access to the memory, either to store or to fetch.

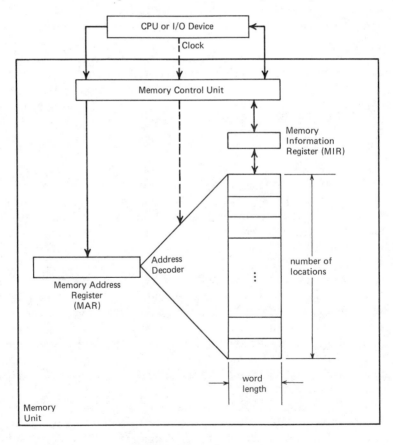

FIGURE 5.2   **A memory unit.**

The memory unit itself can be viewed in two parts. The memory control unit contains some logic for interfacing the memory itself to the outside world, and we will discuss these activities in subsequent sections, summarizing them in Section 5.4.4. The rest of the memory unit consists of the storage area itself organized as a number of words, together with external registers and decode logic. The word length of the physical memory may or may not be the same as the logical words that programmers deal with, but the range is usually from 8 bits to 64 bits. The two registers shown in Fig. 5.2 are important and exist in all memory units. The memory address register (MAR) holds memory addresses and the memory information register (MIR) holds the stored or fetched information. This basic part of the memory unit is the minimal configuration supplied by a memory manufacturer to a computer manufacturer, who may then add on some form of memory control unit to match the rest of a machine.

Basically, the operation is as follows. A CPU or I/O device places an address in the MAR and in the case of a store, it also places a word in the MIR. Then the memory is cycled, which means that the address in the MAR is decoded (see Section 2.2.3), and one of the memory locations is selected. For a store, the MIR contents are gated into the selected memory location, whereas for a fetch the selected memory location's contents are gated into the MIR. At this point the memory cycle is complete. Usually another clock (or minor cycle) is required to gate the MIR out to the CPU or I/O device in the case of a fetch, and symmetrically in the case of a store, an extra clock would have been required before the cycle to get information in from the CPU or I/O device to the memory unit. The operation of the memory control logic can consume one or more additional clocks, depending on its function. When a memory is wired into a computer system, the term *memory cycle* usually refers to the number of clocks required between issuing one address from a CPU (say) and the earliest time another address can be issued. In other words, it is the time the CPU must pay for accessing the memory.

Clearly, the operation of a memory unit involves much detail that we are ignoring here. Various aspects of these details will be presented throughout this chapter.

5.2.2 Main memory access modes

Access to memory in a full-blown computer system, complete with an operating system and a number of active users, is a rather complex process. To execute an innocent looking assignment statement in a user's source program, several levels of software and hardware activity may be necessary before a word reaches the processor from memory. We discuss these matters from the top down.

In order to refer to variables in most programming languages, a user must declare variable names to be integer, fixed, floating, real, and so on, and state whether the name represents a scalar or an array or some other data structure type. Also, the sizes must be declared: Individual variables may be single or multiple precision, arrays may have a number of dimensions (and their sizes) declared, and other structures are similarly specified. Using such declarations, memory space is allocated—either at load time, or run time—so the user's data will fit in memory. We are concerned here with main memory, but the data space is allocated in virtual memory in some machines. As we saw in Section 4.3.4, once space is allocated anywhere in memory, address mapping hardware can handle the rest. Our point here is that system software must know exactly which parts of main memory are allocated to whom. And, in general, it may have to perform several storage management and planning tasks as will be discussed in Chapter 7.

In many compilers, code is generated that compares declared array size with the addresses generated when the arrays are accessed. Such software *bounds checking* is a very valuable debugging aid and also serves as a form of software memory protection.

Another aspect of main memory management is the allocation of temporary space to users within the operating system part of main memory. For example, when users are performing various I/O activities, buffer space is usually required to hold user files temporarily. We will return to this subject in more detail in Section 7.4.

Assume that a program has been loaded into main memory and is being executed. What steps are involved in accessing memory? When a program generates an address, as we saw in Section 4.3.2, that address may point to an area of memory which is off-limits to the program. For one reason or another, illegal addresses may be generated, but are caught by bounds registers. Bounds registers can be regarded as allocating large chunks of memory to a user in a hardware sense; these chunks correspond roughly to those software allocated chunks mentioned above. There are several lower-level tests that an address must pass before data is accessed. Indeed, the array bounds checking by software, mentioned above, is an example of lower-level protection, but now we will turn to several hardware protection schemes.

In many machines, memory is protected at the level of 512- or 1024-word chunks in a more refined way—no access, read-only access, and so on, are provided, as we shall see in Section 5.2.3. If this level of protection is passed, an address may be denied access temporarily for another simple reason: someone else may be accessing memory at the same time, for example, another processor, an I/O device, and so on. This is called a *memory access conflict*, and an instantaneous conflict can be solved only by denying access to all but one requestor. The other requestors must be queued for later service. It is also possible to have access conflicts in a broader sense if two or more users are sharing a section of memory and we wish to deny access to others until one user has left that area of memory. The question of how to handle memory locations shared by several programs will be discussed in Section 5.2.4, where

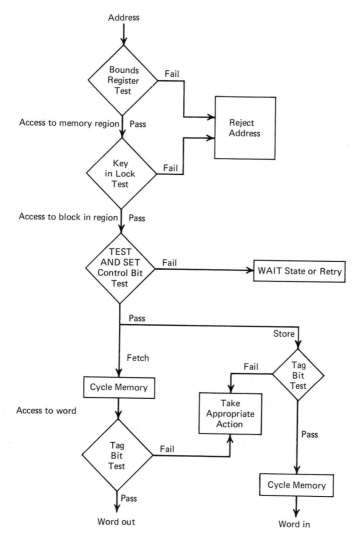

FIGURE 5.3   **Memory access protection.**

TEST AND SET exclusion is presented. Except for memory conflict logic, the above process as well as what follows is summarized in Fig. 5.3.

Finally, assume an address clears all of the above hurdles and actually reaches memory. Most machines have one or more tag bits associated with each word of memory which may prevent or modify the memory access. A common tag use is for parity bits. If an uncorrectable error has occurred, the word cannot be read, for example. We will discuss parity bits in Section 5.2.6. Other tag bits may distinguish program words from data words so a store to a

program word may be blocked. A general discussion of tags will be given in
Section 5.2.5.

Memory allocation and protection are thus complex activities that are part of
the overall processes of memory accessing. More details of these activities will
be discussed in the following sections; a general discussion of conflict detection
and avoidance will be deferred until Volume 2.

5.2.3 Lock and key protection

As we have seen (Section 4.3.2), bounds registers may be used to restrict access
to certain fixed regions of memory. Now we will be concerned with more
refined accessing conditions. Several examples are:

1. No access allowed (e.g., to private system tables).
2. Read-only access (e.g., to a user's program or another user's data).
3. Read/write access (e.g., to a user's data).
4. Write-only access (e.g., for a user to an operating system buffer).
5. Execute-only access (e.g., to a proprietary program).
6. Any access allowed.

Clearly, other combinations are possible, but the point is that a little hardware
can quickly provide a restricted access mechanism that might be very time-
consuming if carried out by software.

One convenient way of restricting access is by providing some kind of lock
and key mechanism. Hardware locks are placed in the memory, and users are
provided with software keys that they place in control unit registers. If the key
satisfies the lock, then access is allowed, as we shall see below.

Several real computers provide protection at the level of memory word
blocks. In the XDS Sigma 9 and in the IBM 370, blocks of 512 words are
protected by such a mechanism. We will sketch the procedure used in the IBM
370. This is much more crude than the examples listed above, but the idea is
the same.

In the IBM 370, each 2048-byte block of memory has associated with it a
4-bit *memory lock* (called by IBM a storage key), as well as a single fetch
protection bit. Each active user is assigned a 4-bit *access key* (called by IBM a
protection key), which permits up to 16 simultaneous (15 plus the operating
system) users. When some user's program is running, the access key is available
in the control unit as part of the program status word (PSW) (see Section
4.4.3).

When a user attempts to access a word in memory, the access key is matched
with the memory lock for the block containing the word to be accessed. If they
match, the user can store or fetch the specified word, as shown in Fig. 5.4. If
they do not match, then the fetch protection bit for the block is consulted. If it
is enabled (i.e., one) then no access is allowed to the word. If it is disabled (i.e.,
zero), then a fetch is allowed, but not a store. Unsuccessful memory access
attempts generate interrupts.

Access Key: Memory Lock	Fetch Protection Bit	Allowed Actions
Match	0	Store/Fetch
Match	1	Store/Fetch
No Match	0	Fetch Only
No Match	1	No Access

FIGURE 5.4   IBM lock and key logic.

The operation of the memory protection system is managed by the operating system. There are two privileged instructions that allow a block's memory lock to be inspected or changed, respectively. Also, an access key of (0000) allows storing or fetching anywhere in memory, so the operating system can have a free hand to do anything using this "pass key."

5.2.4 TEST AND SET Exclusion

The lock and key mechanism is useful in partitioning memory into a number of disjoint blocks, each restricted to one user. The fetch protection bit even allows sharing of read-only portions of memory. In some circumstances, however, we wish to allow several users to access (read or write) shared data, but want to guarantee that only one user may access the data at one time.

For example, one user (program or CPU) may be writing a message to another user in a shared memory file, and we want the addressee of the message to be prevented from reading it before it is complete. If the addressee begins to read it before it is complete, he may read a garbled message—part of the new message plus some leftover information. Another example arises where two programs (on one or more processors) are sharing a counter; perhaps numbers are being tested for several different properties and a count of the total number of properties satisfied is being kept. Here we want to be sure that if one program fetches the counter value, no other program can access it until the first program has incremented the count and stored it back to memory. Otherwise the sum will be wrong, because two programs might fetch the same value, increment it, and store the same sum on top of each other, resulting in the original count plus one instead of plus two.

To accomplish the above goals, a number of computers (e.g., IBM 360 and 370 and Univac 1108 II) have a TEST AND SET type of instruction which works as follows. A particular portion of memory is protected by a single bit; this portion of memory could be a hardware-defined block but we will refer to it as a software-defined file or array. If the control bit is 0 when the TEST AND SET is executed, the control bit is set to 1 and the program proceeds to access the protected file or array. If the control bit is set to 1 when the TEST AND SET is executed, the control bit remains 1 and the program that executed the TEST AND SET is denied access to the protected file or array. When the first program completes accessing the protected part of memory, it can RESET the control bit to 0, thereby opening that part of memory to other programs again.

In order to operate properly, once started this instruction must be completed before anyone else may gain access to the control bit. Thus, if the control bit is in memory, it must be impossible for a second fetch of the memory location to occur before the store that sets the control bit to 1 in response to the first fetch.

If they cannot proceed with other work, programs that find the control bit set to 1 may go into a loop, testing the control bit until it is reset—a rather wasteful procedure—or they may go into some kind of WAIT state until the control bit is reset, at which point the operating system could restart them.

5.2.5 Memory tag bits

Most machines have attached to each memory word, a *tag* that is a set of bits containing information about the associated word. These tag bits are usually examined and operated on at a hardware level. Thus, if a machine has 32-bit words as seen by a programmer, there may be, for example, 35 bits stored in each memory location. The extra three tag bits are examined and operated on by logic associated with the memory unit, and may or may not be sent along outside the memory.

Tag bits are usually operated on only by privileged instructions, not by ordinary user programs. Of course, many types of tags may be set up by compilers to correspond to the user's source program. For example, fixed- and floating-point numbers may have distinct tags, whereas user program words and perhaps system program words may have still other tags. Tags may be used in various ways throughout a computer system.

The purposes of tags are manifold, but basically they can serve in protection or in management roles. An obvious example of a protection tag is a set of parity bits. Most machines have parity bits in main memory as well as various secondary memory units, to check on the correctness of stored and transmitted words. The use of parity bits will be discussed further in Section 5.2.6.

Another kind of protection can be offered by distinguishing data from instructions by tags. For example, unless the control unit is in the privileged state, stores to program words could be prevented. Also, tags can prevent the execution of data words even if the instruction location register somehow points to one. In other words, memory words can be partitioned into various classes and the integrity of their use may be enhanced by using tags. Note that this is a somewhat refined version of the lock and key protection of blocks (see Section 5.2.3); here words instead of blocks are being protected. Finally, the control bit of a block of memory for the TEST AND SET instruction (see Section 5.2.4) can be regarded as a tag that allows orderly access to shared memory by several users.

A use of tags, which falls somewhere between word protection and management, is the following: Tags can be used to carry information about data that would otherwise be in a program. For example, an ADD instruction could be interpreted as fixed, floating, complex, double precision, and so on, as a function of the tag bits of its operands. Although this may require more memory bits because every operand needs a tag now instead of just a few bits in each instruction, it does make compiler writing easier, since only one ADD instruction is needed for all the different data types. It may also speed up processing, since mixed mode arithmetic may be built into the processing hardware here. However, type conversion instructions are still needed to force the results into modes other than the hardware defined ones.

Special treatment of computed zeros, infinities, and so on (Section 3.3.6) are also related to the idea of tags, but usually these are represented by special bit patterns within the data word itself.

The tagged data idea can be extended beyond scalars, however. For example, multidimensional arrays, lists, stacks, and so on, all can have their elements marked by special tags to help ensure their proper use. A similar idea is found in using block floating-point exponents [Wilk63] [Higb76]. Here one exponent can be used for a block of words, keeping some words normalized and some unnormalized. To retain adequate precision, the number's magnitudes must not differ greatly.

Tags can also be useful in distinguishing various words for the control unit. Burroughs machines from the B5000 onward have used tags of some sort in this way. In the B6700, for example, 3-bit tags are used. Two of the eight possibilities are used to distinguish single from double precision operands. Other tags are used for descriptors (pointers to data or code blocks) as well as various special stack control words.

In memory management, tags can be useful in several ways. For example, in systems with dynamic storage allocation it is necessary to keep track of which locations are in use and which are not. Operating systems normally do this at the level of blocks and use tables to keep records. However, list processing systems may have to deal with memory management at the level of individual words. Thus active/inactive tag values could be used. When locations are abandoned by a program they are marked inactive, and when space is needed these are picked up and reactivated.

Similarly, when a page is to be overwritten in the main memory of a virtual memory system, it is useful to know whether or not it must be rewritten to secondary memory. If it has not been changed, it need not be written out. A so-called *dirty bit* can be used for this purpose; it is set if and only if the page was written into. Of course, this is not usually kept in memory, but rather in the page table in the CU (see Section 4.3.4).

To obtain a proper appreciation of the use of some tags, one must consider the details of a system's organization. For more discussion of the B6700, see [Orga73], [Bart70], or [HaDe68]. Tags were also fundamental to the design by

Iliffe of the Rice University computer in the late 1950s and are discussed in detail in [Ilif68]. Surveys of the use of tags may also be found in [Dora75] and [Feus73].

5.2.6 Error detection and correction

The detection and correction of errors is important throughout a computer system. Of primary importance is the question of whether or not errors have occurred. But automatic correction of detected errors is a luxury that one very easily comes to regard as indispensable! Traditionally, machines have used error detection schemes in the most error-prone parts of the system, the I/O devices. Errors there are relatively frequent due to the electromechanical nature of the equipment. Errors also frequently arise when signals propagate great distances over wires, through connectors, and so on.

Parity bits are used to detect and correct errors. For example, one extra bit attached to a word can be used to force, say, an even number of one bits into all words. Then, at a later time, words can be tested for an even number of ones, and if the test fails, an error has occurred. The details of parity bit operations will be presented shortly, but first we must sketch some background ideas.

Today most machines have some form of error checking in the main memory as well as in peripherals and secondary storage devices. Parity bits are checked and regenerated at various stages along the way; for example, in the memory control unit (Section 5.4.4), in the data channels (Section 6.2.2), and in the I/O device controller (Section 7.3). Thus, if an error creeps in anywhere along the line of transmission, it can be caught and localized to some extent. Obviously, errors that arise during the course of a word's retention in some memory are also caught because the parity bits are checked when it is fetched from the memory.

The procedures for detecting and correcting errors are relatively straightforward, and we will present them here, in the context of main memory, simply because this is our first encounter with them and also because parity bits are a common type of tag bits, as discussed above.

Parity bits may be used in the CPU of a machine as well, but are less popular there. One reason for this is that transmission errors are less likely to occur there, and another reason is that the complex transformations (e.g., arithmetic) performed on words in the CPU make it considerably more difficult to decide whether or not an error has occurred. This problem has been studied in some detail in [Aviž71], [RaoT74], and we will not discuss it further here.

Building a code

It is rather straightforward to carry out error detection and correction processes in main memory and other storage devices. To detect an error in a single bit of a memory word, we can use a *parity bit*. This bit is set to 1 or 0 (when a word is about to be stored) in such a way that the total number of 1's in the word is even, for example. Later, when the word is read, we can count the 1's and if there are an odd number, we know that an error has occurred. This is called even parity checking. Of course, odd parity checking can also be done, and we could count 0's instead of 1's without changing the scheme's usefulness.

A single error detection scheme is quite weak. If two errors occur, the parity will still be even, so we will not detect it; a similar failure occurs for any even number of errors. And, of course, if any odd number of errors occur, we will detect the fact that something has gone wrong. More complex schemes are available for detecting multiple errors [Pete61]. Other schemes are available for correcting as well as detecting errors, and we will now consider a simple error correcting code, which was originally due to Hamming [Hamm50].

If several parity bits are used, we can correct errors as well as detect them. This is done by using error detection bits for specific subsets of the data bits. If these subsets are overlapped in just the right way, the entire set of error detection bits can be made to correspond to a binary number which indicates a single bit that is in error. Of course, the error may be in the data bits or in the parity bits themselves. Multiple error correcting codes are possible, but for simplicity we shall demonstrate a single error correcting code.

To illustrate the method of constructing and using an error correcting code, let us consider an example with 4 data bits. As we shall see, 3 parity bits are required in this case. Thus we will consider words of 7 bits total length. Clearly, with 7-bit words, 3 bits are sufficient to point to any position in error (including the parity bits themselves).[2] Let us consider how to overlap the assignment of parity bits so that a single error in the 7-bit word can be corrected.

We group the parity bits so they correspond to subsets of the 7 bits as follows. Parity bit 1, which we denote by p_1, corresponds to just those bits of the 7 bits whose position numbers (in binary) have bit 1 equal to 1. Parity bit 2, p_2, corresponds to those bits of the 7 bits whose position numbers (in binary) have bit 2 equal to 1; and similarly for p_3 and bit 3 of the binary numbers of the 7 bit positions. We summarize this in Table 5.1.

Our goal is to set the parity bits p_1, p_2, and p_3 in a 7-bit word that also contains data bits d_1, d_2, d_3, and d_4. We want p_3 to maintain parity in positions 4, 5, 6, and 7; p_2 to maintain parity in positions 2, 3, 6, and 7; and p_1 to maintain parity in positions 1, 3, 5, and 7. This corresponds to the partitioning shown in Table 5.1 and the lines at the bottom of Table 5.2. We will arbitrarily choose to maintain even parity, that is, an even number of 1's will be set in each 4-bit group by properly choosing the p_i, given any 3 data bits d_i.

To maintain the partitioning of Table 5.1, we can assign the data and parity bits to a 7-bit word in various ways. A systematic scheme is shown in Table 5.2. Here, bit positions 4, 5, 6, and 7 contain 3 data bits and parity bit p_3 which

---

[2] The Hamming codes here are single error correcting codes such that for any positive integer k, the encoded words have $2^k - 1$ bits of which k are *parity bits* and $2^k - 1 - k$ are *message bits*.

TABLE 5.1   Parity Bit Position Assignment

Parity Bit Numbers	Table 5.2 Bit Position Number (Binary)	Table 5.2 Bit Position Number (Decimal)
	0 0 1	1
	0 1 1	3
p_1	1 0 1	5
	1 1 1	7
	0 1 0	2
	0 1 1	3
p_2	1 1 0	6
	1 1 1	7
	1 0 0	4
	1 0 1	5
p_3	1 1 0	6
	1 1 1	7

was assigned by Table 5.1 to protect these four bits. Similarly, p_2 and p_1 are positioned so they can protect the assigned bit positions to their right. Notice that the power-of-two position numbers are the parity bits in this case, but the data bits (d_i) are normal binary numbers corresponding to the decimal values shown at the right of Table 5.2.

Thus if a data word is properly encoded by augmenting it with parity bits, stored in memory, and later read, we can correct single errors as follows. By checking for even parity in bits 4, 5, 6, and 7, we can determine if any of these is in error, and set a check bit in the parity checking hardware which is sketched at the bottom of Table 5.2. If there are an odd number of 1's in these bits, we have an error so we set check bit $c_3 = 1$; otherwise $c_3 = 0$. Similarly, we set c_2 according to bits 2, 3, 6, and 7; and c_1 according to bits 1, 3, 5, and 7. For example, if the check word $c = c_1 c_2 c_3 = 101$, we know there is an error in 4, 5, 6, or 7 (by $c_3 = 1$) and that there is an error in 1, 3, 5, or 7 (by $c_1 = 1$). Thus we have it localized to bits 5 or 7. But since $c_2 = 0$, we know there is no error in bits 2, 3, 6, and 7. Thus bit 5 is the culprit! And, by having designed the p_i to correspond to 1's in the (binary) bit position numbers (in Table 5.1), we have an immediate correspondence between the binary number $c = 101$ and the error in position 5. Thus we can simply complement this bit of the word being tested and transmit the corrected word from the memory. The parity bits may in practice be regarded as a tag attached at the end of the word, and are of course dropped when the data is to be used.

Now let us consider the overhead involved in single error correcting codes. Let p be the total number of parity bits and d be the total number of data bits

TABLE 5.2   Hamming Code (Single Error Correcting)

Bit Position Number	Error Detection and Correction							Decimal Data Value $(d_1 d_2 d_3 d_4)$
	1	2	3	4	5	6	7	
Bit Type	p_1	p_2	d_1	p_3	d_2	d_3	d_4	
	0	0	0	0	0	0	0	0
	1	1	0	1	0	0	1	1
	0	1	0	1	0	1	0	2
	1	0	0	0	0	1	1	3
	1	0	0	1	1	0	0	4
	0	1	0	0	1	0	1	5
	1	1	0	0	1	1	0	6
	0	0	0	1	1	1	1	7
	1	1	1	0	0	0	0	8
	0	0	1	1	0	0	1	9
	1	0	1	1	0	1	0	10
	0	1	1	0	0	1	1	11
	0	1	1	1	1	0	0	12
	1	0	1	0	1	0	1	13
	0	0	1	0	1	1	0	14
	1	1	1	1	1	1	1	15

Even Parity Check

Even Parity Check

Even Parity Check

Parity Check Word $\boxed{c_1 c_2 c_3}$

in a $p + d$ bit word. If the p error correction bits are to point to the error bit (one of $p + d$ cases) or indicate that no error exists (1 case), we must have

$$2^p \geq p + d + 1.$$

Thus $p \geq \log (p + d + 1)$, and it is clear that as d becomes large, p is approximately $\log d$, which is a rather small overhead.

In the IBM 370, for example, one parity bit is used on each 8-bit byte to catch transmission errors within the CPU and for I/O. In main memory, single error correcting parity bits are maintained on an 8-byte (double word) basis using 8 extra parity bits. The code used also allows all double bit errors and most multiple bit errors to be detected (but not corrected) [Pete61] [Katz71].

Consequences of error correction

Consider the task of a repair person of computer semiconductor memories with error correcting codes. Semiconductor memory has its words arranged across memory chips. Thus a 4096-word, 32-bit memory module would consist of 32 chips (plus chips for parity) each containing 4096 bits. Each chip has its own addressing logic and produces one bit of the desired word. When a word is fetched to a memory register, error correcting logic (say, for one error bit) is applied to it.

Suppose we have such a memory operating in a computer. When an error occurs, it is corrected and the fetched word is sent on to its destination. Also, a light bulb is lit that indicates which one of the 32 data bits or the parity bits was in error. This was set after retrying an erroneous word several times to determine that it was not a transient error. Now our repair person enters the picture. His or her job is to remove the chip indicated by the light bulb, insert a new chip, and go away! In fact, a real memory would probably contain many more than 4096 words, so each bit position might be contained on a pluggable printed circuit board (or card) which has a number of 4096-bit chips for that position. Thus the repair person simply has to replace one board with a new one.

But what about the information stored on the newly inserted board? Perhaps only one bit of the old one was bad and the other information was correct. How do we transfer that to the new board? In fact, even if the repair person has thrown the old board away, nothing is lost because we can simply cycle through each memory location (fetch and store) to restore the correct values to all memory locations. Remember that errors in 1 bit position (the garbage on the new board) are automatically corrected here. It is not even necessary to run through the memory in this way because the errors will be corrected whenever the word is fetched and restored. Of course, prudence might argue for the former procedure, because we assumed the hardware corrects only one error and another error may occur before all memory locations are cycled in the natural course of events.

5.3 MEMORY SYSTEM PARAMETERS

As effective speeds of processing units have increased, memory speeds have been forced to keep up. This has been achieved partly by new technologies (from magnetic cores to semiconductors), but technology has not been enough, as evidenced by the fact that as early as 1953 the first core memory operating (in Whirlwind I) had an $8\,\mu s$ memory cycle time. Today, most computer designers cannot afford to use main memories much faster than 100 nanoseconds. Certainly, two orders of magnitude increase in memory speed is an upper bound, over the past 20 odd years.

In the same period, the fastest processor operation times have advanced from a few tens of microseconds to a few tens of nanoseconds, that is, three orders of magnitude. Memory system speeds have kept up with processors only through the use of caches (which are collections of high-speed registers) and memory parallelism at the word level. Both of these allow the use of less expensive main memory units. Because users want larger and larger main memories, the use of parallel units satisfies both the bandwidth and size goals. Main memory sizes have risen from a few thousand words in the early 1950s, to as many as a million or more words in the 1970s.

The use of caches means that if a computation can work out of a small subset of main memory words stored in these fast registers, the CPU will behave as if the entire main memory had the speed of the cache. In both the parallel and cache memory cases, additional logic design and software questions arise, compared with a single main memory unit. The proper operation of both parallel and cache memories depends on the patterns of addresses generated by associated CPUs.

Four standard parameters of a memory system are:

w Memory unit word length (bits or bytes).
n Number of words per memory unit.
m The total number of memory units.
c The cycle (or access) time of each unit.

Using these parameters, we can determine several important memory system characteristics. The total memory size is simply

$$\text{Memory size} = wnm \text{ (bits or bytes)},$$

and the total memory bandwidth is

$$\text{Memory bandwidth} = wm/c \text{ (bits or bytes/second)}.$$

We want these to be sufficiently large to accommodate the programs and data our system must handle; that is, the size must be big enough to hold sufficiently many program and data words to keep the processor busy most of the time, without wasting too much time accessing slower secondary memory devices. And the bandwidth must be high enough to accommodate control unit program fetching, processor data accessing, and I/O. Recall our discussion of capacity (Section 2.5). Thus we want w, n, and m to be large and c to be small, for good system performance.

On the other hand, although the overall cost of a memory may be a complex function of the above parameters, it is roughly true that

$$\text{Memory cost} \propto wnm/c.$$

Hence, from a cost standpoint, we have a function that conflicts with the desiderata of the previous paragraph. This is exactly why we are forced to consider memory hierarchies: They allow us to store large quantities of information by spreading it out over slower and slower devices so that the cost per bit of storage becomes less and less.

Two of these parameters, n and c, are more technology dependent than applications dependent. Given that designers and users want large, fast memories, parameters n and c are the constraints imposed by physics and current manufacturing techniques. On the other hand, parameters w and m are somewhat more dependent on the use to which a machine will be put and its overall architecture.

The number of words per memory unit (n) and its cycle time (c) are determined by various physical considerations. Magnetic core memories require the threading of several wires through magnetic toroids and electrically selecting a word on the basis of coincident current flow in two wires. Standard core memory units have 8–32K words and cycle times of as little as 500 nanoseconds.

In the early 1970s, semiconductor memories became economically feasible. They are usually built from semiconductor chips configured as one bit by 256, 1K or more words—manufacturers jump from one even power of two to the next as technology allows higher and higher levels of integration in circuits. In addition to the storage bits, the chip also contains logic for decoding addresses and accessing the memory. Thus an integrated circuit package may contain 1K storage bits and have 10 pins for addressing the memory and one pin for data input and output, as well as other control and power pins. To configure a 32-bit by 1K word memory, 32 of these chips would be operated in parallel, with the same address going to an MAR in each chip (recall Fig. 5.2). Then all the chips are cycled at once and a 32-bit word is accessed, one bit per chip.

There is one important point to be made about the internal configuration of these chips. Recall from Chapter 2, that the decoding of addresses and fanning-in and fanning-out of bits in an n-bit memory would require an overhead of $O(n)$ gates needed to store n bits. For this reason, a so-called, two-dimensional selection process is often used, in which the bits are physically held in an array of $\sqrt{n} \times \sqrt{n}$ storage elements, so that less overhead gates and time are needed. This also accounts for the fact that semiconductor memories usually hold an even power of two bits.

Despite several weaknesses, semiconductor memories have taken over a good deal of the RAM market. One general problem is that semiconductor memories are volatile, that is, lose their contents when the power goes off, whereas core memories are not. Also, semiconductor memories tend to produce more parity errors than core memories. They can be made to operate much faster than core memories, however, and generally, as their price and physical volume drops, one can expect semiconductor memories to compete over the entire range of core memories, as well as extending to a faster (more expensive) performance range than core memories. In the late 1970s, semiconductor memories with cycle times as low as 50 or 100 ns are becoming economically feasible.

If a memory system designer wants a memory of n words and cycle time c, but $n/2$ word memory modules with cycle time c are the largest available, the designer can adjoin two modules to achieve the size requirements. Thus, the high-order bit of each memory address is used to decide which of the two modules (of $n/2$ words each) to access. A small amount of extra logic is required for this and the method is commonly used for semiconductor or core memories. It can obviously be generalized to adjoin any number of memory modules. But we will always refer to the size of a memory unit as n words, even if it is physically constructed from a set of smaller modules. As we shall see in the next section, a similar technique can be used to achieve higher memory bandwidth, by operating several memory units simultaneously; this is parameter m.

In case a cache memory is used (see Fig. 5.1), the effective main memory cycle time also depends on the cache design and program characteristics. In this case we have two distinct memories, one perhaps ten times the speed and 1 percent of the size of the other. The small, fast cache is loaded from main memory, whenever main memory is accessed. Then, on subsequent accesses to the same location we can access the fast cache without going to the slower main memory. This works well, provided that we have enough space in the cache and addresses are generated with sufficient locality with respect to each other. We shall return to this subject in Section 5.4.3.

Parameter w, the word length, depends not only on technology but also on the use of the machine. Some applications call for short (e.g., 16-bit) fixed point words; others call for long (e.g., 64-bit) floating-point words. Of course, the physical word length and the logical word length (seen by programmers) need not be the same. In fact, bit level addressing can be achieved by interposing a little logic between the memory and the CPU. This has been done in several machines (e.g., B1700; see [Wiln72b]).

As we have seen earlier, there are three types of memory addressing mechanisms: random access, sequential access, and associative access. Most of this chapter will be concerned with random access in which an address is decoded and one memory word is selected; any word in the memory can be accessed in the same amount of time. As a variation on this, we will discuss associative access in Section 5.4.2.3. Associative (or content) addressing allows words to be accessed on the basis of certain bits stored in the words. Sequential access memories, in which the bits are accessed as they shift past some fixed point, will be discussed in detail in Chapter 7. It should be noted that the lowest level in Fig. 5.1 may be built from high-performance sequential access devices (e.g., shift registers). Lower levels in the hierarchy almost always use sequential access devices (e.g., disks or tapes), as we shall see in Chapter 7.

A number of books have been written about the hardware and cost effectiveness of main memories. In [GsMc75] and [HiPe74] various hardware configurations are discussed, and the details of semiconductor memories are presented in detail in [LuMC73]. Economic questions about memory systems are explored at length in [Shar69] and [Phis76]. Past trends are discussed and future extrapolations are attempted in [Turn74].

5.4 TYPICAL MEMORY ORGANIZATIONS

In this section we discuss a number of real memory systems. A number of computers have straightforward memories, as illustrated in Fig. 5.2. If a sufficiently fast cycle time is available, this is the simplest and best memory configuration. For fast processors, however, other techniques must be used to provide faster effective memory speeds at reasonable costs.

Caches and parallel memory units are two memory organizations that have the same goal. They both are intended to allow the use of slow, inexpensive, main memory technology in ways that yield high effective memory bandwidth and large main memory size at low cost. Each involves the use of some additional hardware and each depends for its success on a certain addressing regularity in the execution of programs. We are naturally led to ask: If the two ideas are so similar, which is better? This is a very difficult question to answer. In fact, it seems that each idea has its own niche in the architecture of computer systems, and the situation probably will remain unchanged until major technology changes occur.

As we shall see, in many computers, caches are used together with parallel memory units. An example of such a system was discussed in Section 5.1. In this section we deal with several types of memory systems used in real computers and illustrate how both ideas are used.

5.4.1 Parallel memories

An important flexibility that system designers have is in the use of a number of parallel memories: parameter m of Section 5.3. If a single memory unit is sufficiently fast to keep up with the rest of the system, and if its cost is sufficiently low, then there is no problem. However, if cost or speed considerations force us to use several memory units to get sufficient bandwidth and size, then we must consider several new logic design and compiler problems related to memory conflicts.

In the late 1950s, the first word parallel configurations of random access memories appeared in STRETCH and ILLIAC II [UIll57]. The basic idea is illustrated in Fig. 5.5, where CPU refers to the processor-CU combination which issues data and instruction addresses. The even addresses generated by the CPU are sent via the MCU to memory unit 0, and the odd ones to memory unit 1. These are distinguished by the low-order address bit—0 for even addresses, 1 for odd addresses.

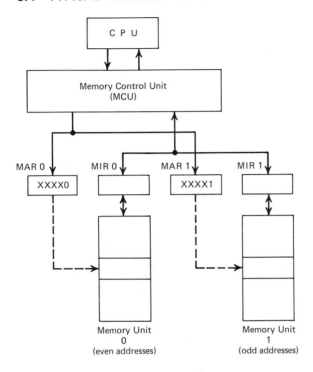

FIGURE 5.5   **Parallel memory with interleaved addresses.**

Now, in the normal course of executing instructions we fetch instructions in sequence. Thus, if the instruction location register points to location XXXX0, when we fetch this instruction we can also fetch XXXX1, the next instruction in sequence. Unless a jump occurs in the instruction of location XXXX0, when the instruction location register is incremented and points to XXXX1 we can gate it from MIR1 to the CPU without waiting for a memory cycle. Thus we can frequently achieve an effective doubling of the memory capacity over the bandwidth of a single memory unit in this way.

Similarly, when arrays are being accessed, we can always fetch an even and odd pair. As long as the array access continues in a sequence, both memory units will produce useful data. Of course, if every other element is requested, then all memory references are to the same unit so the scheme fails completely. When accessing scalar data, we can also do double fetches, hoping that the second is useful; but frequently this will not be the case.

In the normal course of events, I/O operations will be carried out simultaneously with computation, and they will also be able to take advantage of the double memory unit stores and fetches. It should be emphasized that for almost all I/O—explicit user-generated I/O as well as page faults—a large amount of memory parallelism may be easily exploited because large blocks of data are being transmitted back and forth between main memory and slower memory levels.

An important question here concerns the uses to which a machine is put. In Section 2.5 we discussed system capacity in terms of the kinds of programs being run. Clearly, we are sometimes interested in high memory bandwidth per se; for example, in COBOL programs with a high frequency of MOVE statements. In other cases, we are only incidentally interested in the memory bandwidth because our real concern is with high processing speed and the memory is used only to support this, as may be the case in many scientific computations. Hence we should really be concerned with some kind of overall balance.

The use of parallel memory configurations has become popular in many types of machine organization. In fact, the success of parallel memories with two units led designers to build systems with more and more parallel memories. As more memory units are used, the probability of generating a sequence of addresses to all of the units decreases. One way to help insure that there will be addresses to as many memory units as possible is by CU lookahead schemes. For example, in Fig. 5.5 we need not access even-odd pairs of locations that are adjacent to each other, that is, α and $\alpha + 1$. We could look ahead for *any* even and *any* odd address pairs. These could include instruction fetch as well as data stores or fetches. Of course, this also leads to more complex logic to keep the addresses and the information accessed in their proper logical relations in the CPU. We will soon return to this idea with respect to program graphs.

The terminology used to describe various memory system organizations tends to vary somewhat from manufacturer to manufacturer. We adopt the following nomenclature, which seems to reflect a general consensus. Any memory system that contains a number of separately addressable memory units will be called a *multimemory* or *parallel memory* system. In a multimemory system with m memory units, if the successive addresses are assigned across the memory units, modulo m, it will be called an *interleaved* memory system. The low-order log m bits of each address indicate the memory number in this case. Thus Fig. 5.5 is a two-way interleaved memory system.

The terms *phased* memories and *interlaced* memories are used in several ways, sometimes simply to refer to interleaved memory systems and other times to refer to designs in which each of the parallel memory units is cycled on a different minor clock cycle. Thus, a major cycle of 1 μs may be subdivided into 4 minor cycles of 250 ns, and the cycle of each of 4 parallel memory units might begin on a different minor cycle. This allows the memory system to deliver words in sequence at a 250 ns word interval, and the overall memory bandwidth is 4 words per microsecond, just as it would be if all the words were delivered at once. Obviously such phasing can be useful in certain machine organizations, for example, for a pipeline processor. But if such phasing is desired, it can also be implemented by properly timing word transmission from the memory information registers, even if the memories are cycled at identical times. Thus, it is clear that this is a rather low-level engineering design question.

Typical systems

A number of uniprocessor computer systems use parallel memories; usually they are found in the middle- to high-performance systems. However, interleaving is used sometimes on the PDP-11 minicomputer, as we shall see directly. We will also discuss the memories of several IBM 370 models. Finally, we will sketch the memory systems of the multifunction CDC 6600 and 7600.

The basic PDP-11 memory unit has 16-bit words. The size of one memory unit has ranged from 4K up to 16K words in the first half of the 1970s decade, and the cycle time has ranged from 1.2 μs down to less than 700 ns. Because instructions supply 16-bit addresses and byte level addressing is provided, the basic memory size is 32K words; however, the high-order 4K words are used for registers of I/O devices (see Section 6.3.1), so the basic memory has only 28K usable words. Since the bus can handle 18 address bits, special address mapping hardware can be attached to allow up to 124K memory words (plus 4K I/O device registers); recall Section 4.3.4.

If two addresses arrive in rapid succession, two memory units can be cycled in a partially overlapped way, even though the addressing is not interleaved. The memory system may also be wired in a two-way interleaved manner. Thus, sequences of words from alternate memory halves enjoy an access speedup. This can often be useful when fetching instructions, which may have one-, two-, or three-word formats.

In the IBM 370 [Katz71], which addresses memory to the byte level, the 370/135 (which is not interleaved) can access 2 bytes in about 800 or 900 ns (depending on the type of access), whereas the 370/165 has four interleaved memories, each of which can access 8 bytes in 2 μs. Thus the maximum bandwidth of the 370/135 is slightly more than 2 bytes/μs, whereas the 370/165 can produce 16 bytes/μs. The IBM 360/195 can have up to 16 parallel interleaved memory units of 8 bytes each.

Memory sizes in the 370 range from 96K–240K bytes in the Model 135, and from half a million up to 3 million bytes in the Model 165. It is interesting to note that in the earlier 360 series, memories in the Model 30 ranged from 8K up to 64K bytes, and in the Model 65 up to 1 million bytes. Although up to 16 million bytes are addressable with IBM's 24-bit address field, the above numbers are for normal configurations. The IBM 360 series had magnetic core memories, whereas the 370 series has semiconductor memories.

The multifunction processors of CDC also use interleaved memory systems. The CDC 6600 has a 32-way interleaved main memory that contains a total of 128K words of 60 bits each. The memory cycle time is 1 μs so a maximum effective memory bandwidth of 32 words/μs would be possible. In fact, the system is designed to access 1 word per minor cycle (100 ns), so 10 words/μs is the actual main memory bandwidth. Main memory access is managed by the Stunt Box (see Chapter 4 [Thor70]), which is part of what we called the memory control unit in Fig. 5.2.

In the CDC 7600, main memory was restricted to just 64K words of 60 bits (plus 5 parity bits) each, and again the memory was 32-way interleaved. However, early 7600 systems had a 275 ns core memory and as in the 6600, ten memory units could be accessed in a phased way for an effective memory cycle of 27.5 ns, or about 36.4 words/μs. Later models have been equipped with semiconductor memories and greater than 64K words.

5.4.2 Multiprocessing and array processing memory

The tendency to build memory systems with more and more parallelism was spurred by an accompanying trend to build multiprocessor machines. We introduced this idea in Section 1.2.1.3 and pointed out there that the relatively large cost of main memory was one of the primary motivations for multiprocessors, so designers tried to share one large memory among several processors. On the other hand, as more processors were added, more memory space and more memory bandwidth were required. Thus the two ideas—multiprocessor and multimemory architectures—have fed on one another.

As we have seen, a uniprocessor/multimemory machine may fail to achieve its full potential memory bandwidth because addresses cannot be generated simultaneously for all the memory units. With a multiprocessor organization, the uniprocessor difficulties may be compounded by the fact that several processors may now try to access the same memory unit at the same time. Of course, by looking ahead in all processors, we can hope to generate enough addresses so that all memories will be accessed on each cycle, but this has the same logical problems as those mentioned above for the uniprocessor. On the other hand, we might expect that the processors in a multiprocessor system would be likely to generate addresses for different memory units, thereby properly exploiting the multimemory system. In Volume 2, we shall consider several analytical memory/processor models that will help to explain the situation.

There is another way of viewing this whole subject. Instead of discussing how to keep all of the memories busy, we could be asking how many memories are needed so that we can usually keep all of the processors busy. In other words, even in the uniprocessor case, we went to a parallel memory system because the CPU was too fast for one memory. This situation is compounded for multimemory/multiprocessor systems. The point, of course, is that we should really be concerned with system balance for the kind of programs being run (recall our capacity discussion of Section 2.5).

In addition to considering multiprocessors, we will also consider array processors in this section. The analysis of parallel memories for multiprocessors comes down to probabilistic analyses, which we will reference in Section 5.4.2.1. On the other hand, in Section 5.4.2.2 we shall see that for array processors we can guarantee conflict-free data array access by proper design of the memory and array storage schemes. We shall mention busses, crossbar switches, and alignment networks as ways of interconnecting memories and processors. This will serve as an introduction to these ideas; they will be discussed in detail in Chapter 6.

5.4.2.1 Multiprocessor systems

Consider a computer system with n CPUs and m memory units, as shown in Fig. 5.6. Each CPU is capable of generating a memory address in each clock period. We show the system tied together by a set of interconnection switches. These can be regarded as n parallel busses, each with $m + 1$ units attached—a processor and m memories. Or the system can be regarded as an $n \times m$ crossbar switch. In either case, any CPU is allowed to communicate with any memory in any clock period. The broken lines represent control lines by which each CPU can set one of the m switches available to it. If we assume that each

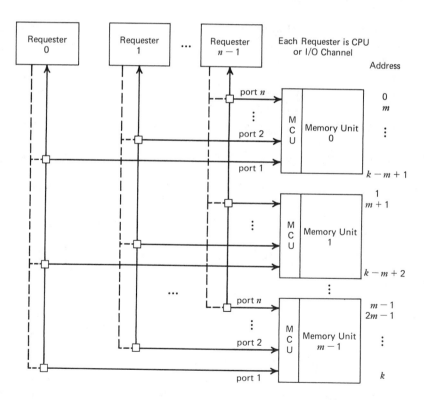

FIGURE 5.6   **Parallel memory unit multiprocessor with interleaved addresses.**

CPU is executing an independent program, we have the potential here for a disaster, namely, many processors can attempt to access the same set of memory units at each step. Avoidance of this memory conflict or memory contention situation will be discussed shortly. The one important assumption we make is the standard one for interleaved systems, namely, that subsequent addresses are assigned to subsequent memory units, modulo m (see Fig. 5.6). Sometimes it is advantageous to run the addresses within the memory units, thus avoiding memory conflicts by assigning different CPUs to different memory units. Such a noninterleaved addressing scheme may defeat the original purpose of such systems, namely, the sharing of expensive main memory. If addressing could be assigned in a flexible and dynamic way, however, alternatives to a standard address interleaving could be potentially useful. For example, if a big job on one processor could be dynamically assigned a number of memory units for its exclusive use, whereas several smaller jobs running on other processors each used one of several other memory units, conflicts could be avoided. This leads to more complex hardware problems and it also leads to dynamic scheduling problems. This may be a fruitful research area, but real systems do not presently operate in this manner.

Another assumption we will normally make is that conflicts are resolved within the memory control units (MCUs). There are obviously three places this could be done: one is in the memory control units, another is within the switch, and the third is in the CPUs. Because we are assuming a set of independently operating CPUs here, the latter approach would be rather messy. A reasonable possibility would be to resolve conflicts in the switch; we will discuss this in Chapter 6. The assumption that conflicts are resolved in the memory control unit means that the interconnections are really made in the form of busses. If we assume that each memory unit has n ports, then conflict resolution in the memory control units is straightforward. The ports share some control logic that detects the condition of more than one simultaneous request to a given memory unit. If this occurs, then some priority scheme can be used to choose one request to honor. The other requests may be held in registers for later handling, or the CPUs that issued these may be signaled and can resubmit them on subsequent cycles.

The following examples typify the memory systems of current, big multiprocessor computer systems. Burroughs and Univac multiprocessors have similar memory systems. We will use the Burroughs B7700 [Burr73] and the Univac 1110 [Sper74] as examples.

The B7700 memory size ranges from 128K to 1 million words of 48 bits, plus 3 tag bits and 9 parity bits. A memory system may contain up to 8 memory control units, each of which may have 2 or 4 memory units of 64K words each. Thus, up to 32 parallel memory units may exist. Each memory control unit has 8 ports and conflict resolution is handled in the memory control unit. The memory control units can, under operating system control, be dedicated to specific processors or I/O channels. In addition to the parallelism between the memory control units, the 2 or 4 memory units under each memory control unit can operate in a phased way. After a 1.75 μs initial memory cycle (faster memories are also available), subsequent words may be transmitted at 125 ns clock intervals. This holds true within one memory control unit or across several if they have been requested by the same source.

The Univac 1110 allows up to 256K words of 36 (plus 2 parity and 2 spare)-bit memory with sub 500 ns cycle time. This is arranged in 32K-word subsystems that are paired in one memory control unit; there can be a total of four memory control units. Eight ports (expandable to 16) are provided to each subsystem and conflicts are resolved in the memory control unit. Each 32K word subsystem consists of four memory units of 8K words each and addresses are interleaved across them; all four may be simultaneously accessed. In both the Univac 1110 and the B7700, I/O channels are granted higher priority than are CPUs, due to the slow speed of I/O transmissions, their critical timing and lower rate of requests (recall the priority discussion of Section 4.4.3.3).

To assess the performance of parallel memory systems, the program dependence graphs (see Section 2.4) of jobs to be run may be studied. In Volume 2 and [ChKL77], these graphs are related to probabilistic models of parallel memory system performance. It may be shown [ChKL77], [BaSm76], that the effective bandwidth improvement can be made to grow linearly—although with a slope less than one—with an increase in the number of parallel memory units. This assumes that the addresses generated are distributed randomly across the parallel set of memories, a reasonable assumption in a number of realistic cases.

5.4.2.2 Array processing systems

In Section 1.2.1, we introduced several kinds of (parallel and pipeline) array processors, and we discussed them further in Chapter 3 from the processor standpoint. In this chapter we consider the memory aspects of these machines, and we present schemes for array storage that allow conflict-free access to many types of array partitions. These ideas are crucial for parallel and pipeline processors, but they are also useful for any parallel memory machine—even one with a standard uniprocessor, if that processor depends on the full memory bandwidth for its proper operation.

In Fig. 5.7, we show an array computer that may employ parallel or pipeline processing. We assume here that the processing of the data proceeds at a speed matched to the effective memory speed, and that the control unit is capable of supplying control signals fast enough so the rest of the system never waits for the CU.

Consider the m memory units and the problems of parallel conflict-free data access. Arrays of one, two, or more dimensions are assumed to be stored in some regular pattern in the m memory units. How can we guarantee, for example, that rows, columns, and diagonals of a matrix can be accessed without

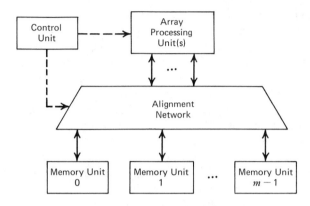

FIGURE 5.7   **Parallel array memory.**

conflict? Furthermore, even if these partitions are available, what if we want only some of their elements, say the even indexed elements of each column?

If a machine has m memory units, we can store one-dimensional arrays across the units as shown in Fig. 5.8, for $m = 4$. While the first m operands are being processed, we can fetch m more, and so on. But, if the array is indexed such that, say, only the odd elements are to be fetched, then the effective bandwidth is cut in half due to access conflicts, as shown in the underlined elements of Fig. 5.8. These conflicts can be avoided by choosing m to be a prime number. Then, any index distance relatively prime to m can be accessed without conflicts. For example, if $m = 5$, every second, third, or fourth element of the array can be accessed without conflict, but not every fifth element; in general, every $5k$th element is stored in the same memory unit.

Many programs contain multidimensional arrays. These can lead to more difficult memory access problems, since we may want to access rows, columns, diagonals, back diagonals, square blocks, and so on. For simplicity, consider two-dimensional arrays and assume we want to access n-element partitions (n-*vectors*) of arrays from parallel memories with m units.

Consider the storage scheme shown in Fig. 5.9, where $m = n = 4$. Clearly, by using this storage scheme we can access any row or diagonal without conflict. But all the elements of a column are stored in the same memory unit, so that

Memory Unit

0	1	2	3
$\underline{a_1}$	a_2	$\underline{a_3}$	a_4
$\underline{a_5}$	a_6	$\underline{a_7}$	a_8
$\underline{a_9}$	a_{10}	$\underline{a_{11}}$	·
·	·		

FIGURE 5.8   **One-dimensional array storage.**

Memory Unit

0	1	2	3
a_{00}	a_{01}	a_{02}	a_{03}
a_{10}	a_{11}	a_{12}	a_{13}
a_{20}	a_{21}	a_{22}	a_{23}
a_{30}	a_{31}	a_{32}	a_{33}

FIGURE 5.9   **Straight storage ($m=4$, $n=4$).**

accessing a column would result in memory conflicts, that is, we would have to cycle the memories n times to get the n elements of a column.

To allow access to row and column n-vectors, we can *skew* the data as shown in Fig. 5.10. Now, however, we can no longer access diagonals without conflict. It can be shown, in fact, that there is no way to store an $n \times n$ matrix in $m = n$ memories, when m is even, so that arbitrary rows, columns, and diagonals can be fetched without conflicts. However, by using more than n memories we can have conflict-free access to any row, column, or diagonal, as well as other useful n-vectors. Figure 5.11 shows such a skewing scheme for $m = 5$ and $n = 4$ [BuKu71].

As may be observed in Fig. 5.11, various array partitions are accessed in scrambled order and are offset relative to one another. This subject will be explored further in Volume 2 (see [Kuck77]). To align arrays properly for processing, the data alignment network shown in Fig. 5.7 interconnects m memories with an array processor that may be one pipeline processor or a number of parallel processors. In principle, we may need to form all possible permutations here as in the case of the multiprocessor of Fig. 5.6. However, because we are concerned with access to partitions of multidimensional arrays for one program at a time, it may seem intuitively reasonable to expect that this problem can be solved with a somewhat simpler switch than required in Fig. 5.6. We will see that this is indeed the case when we study alignment networks in Chapter 6.

We have seen that conflict-free access to a number of commonly needed

Memory Unit

0	1	2	3
a_{00}	a_{01}	a_{02}	a_{03}
a_{13}	a_{10}	a_{11}	a_{12}
a_{22}	a_{23}	a_{20}	a_{21}
a_{31}	a_{32}	a_{33}	a_{30}

FIGURE 5.10   **Skewed storage ($m=4$, $n=4$).**

Memory Unit

0	1	2	3	4
a_{00}	a_{01}	a_{02}	a_{03}	
a_{13}		a_{10}	a_{11}	a_{12}
a_{21}	a_{22}	a_{23}		a_{20}
	a_{30}	a_{31}	a_{32}	a_{33}

FIGURE 5.11   **Skewed storage ($m=5$, $n=4$).**

array partitions can be guaranteed. This means that we can achieve an effective bandwidth increase which grows linearly—with a slope of one—as the number of parallel memory units is increased. This is even better performance than that mentioned for multiprocessors. However, we are considering only a limited class of memory uses here—the access of various array partitions. For scalars, trees, and so on, a probabilistic analysis such as that for multiprocessors can be used. Here again, the dependence classes discussed in Section 2.4 are crucial in determining which of the probabilistic models is suitable for a particular program and data structure.

Several large array processing computers exist. They include the Texas Instruments ASC, the Cray Research CRAY-I, the CDC STAR, the Burroughs BSP, the Burroughs ILLIAC IV, and the Goodyear Aerospace STARAN IV.

The Texas Instruments ASC has a memory cycle time of 160 ns and a 32-bit word length, with memory accesses to 256 bits. The address field is 24 bits long, so up to 16 million words of memory may be addressed, and up to 1 million words are used in typical systems. The memory is interleaved up to eight ways, and a memory control unit offers access to eight ports (plus a ninth for extension). Thus a total bandwidth of nearly 400 words/μs is achievable. Vectors are stored across the memory units for high bandwidth access.

The Burroughs ILLIAC IV system has 64 independently addressable and indexable memory units, each of which contains 2K words for a total capacity of 128K words of 64 bits each. With a memory cycle of under 400 ns, this system has a total memory bandwidth of over 150 words/μs. The independent indexability of these memory units allows array skewing which provides conflict-free array access to some array partitions.

Burroughs BSP has 17 memories, which allow conflict-free access to most partitions of multidimensional arrays (refer to Fig. 5.11). The small extra cost for indexing a non-power-of-two number of memory units is easily offset by the ease of programming and compiling for the system. The memory cycle is 160 ns, and this provides 100 words/μs to the 16 processors. In contrast to the ASC and ILLIAC IV, the BSP has a separate program memory; hence, neither memory conflicts for program access nor array access will degrade this data rate in the BSP.

5.4.2.3 Associative access and processing

A memory is said to provide *associative access* or *content addressability* if words can be fetched on the basis of what they contain rather than on the basis of an explicit location (address) in the memory. This can be implemented in a great variety of ways. At one extreme, purely software techniques can be used in a RAM; hash addressing, list structures, or some other method can be programmed to achieve the effect. At the other extreme, purely hardware methods can be used to allow every bit of the associative memory to be compared at once with a *key register*. For example, access to all words whose odd bits are set to 1 requires instantaneously checking half the bits in the memory, as does access to all words whose first half contains the pattern 1010 . . . . The key register in these cases contains half the desired bits and half "don't care" marks that are ignored. The key register's length is equal to the memory word length, but each position in the key may be in any of three states (0, 1, or don't care).

The small content addressable memories (CAMs) we have discussed (e.g., see Fig. 5.1) are usually implemented as described above, except that not all of the bits in the memory words need to be tested. For example, in the paging CAM of Fig. 4.22 (see also Fig. 5.1), only the virtual location bits need to be matched associatively; the corresponding physical location bits are retrieved but not tested. The cache CAM of Fig. 5.1 operates in a similar way.

In some applications, associative memory access and *associative processing* are useful. For example, in processing digitized pictures, an algorithm may search for patterns representing straight lines, right angles, and so on, in one picture, or differences between two pictures of the same object or geographical site. When desired patterns have been located, they can then be processed, either serially or in parallel; however, parallel processing is quite often very "natural" in these areas. If a fairly large memory is to be used, it is unreasonable to expect associative access to the whole memory at once (on cost grounds) and also such tests may be unnecessary. Instead, certain parts of long words may require content addressing. The Goodyear Aerospace STARAN IV is an associative processor and has a hardware associative memory.

STARAN IV may be regarded as a collection of modules, where each module consists of 256 bit-serial processors and each processor has 256 1-bit memory words. Thus the memory can be fabricated from 256 random access memory chips, each containing 256 bits. However, the machine is used as an associative processor so it must be possible to read and write 256-bit words in the normal way for I/O, but it must also be possible to access, say, the ith bit of all 256 words at once.

Associative access is easy to achieve by storing the bits as a skewed array of size 256×256, similar to Fig. 5.10. Instead of using index registers to generate memory addresses, since only a fixed set of patterns is desired, simple bit-logic is used [Batc77]. Associative access to the ith bit of each word, the jth

8-bit byte of every eighth word, and so on (256 patterns in all), are wired into the machine. This provides in one step, parallel associative access to a 256-bit pattern, and through programming, associative access to the whole memory in 256 steps. For more details about the STARAN system see [Rudo72], [Batc77], or [Ensl74], and for a discussion of programming STARAN IV, see [Davi74a].

The ideas of associative memory and associative processing date back to the mid-1950s, when attempts to build a cryogenic associative memory began. Many other technologies have been tried over the years, but the advent of LSI semiconductor memories has made the idea practical for large memories in the 1970s. Small associative memories, for example, to manage page tables or caches, have been implemented in many computers using various technologies. A comprehensive survey of associative processors may be found in [YaFu77].

5.4.3 Caches

Now we return to the question of how cache memories fit into memory system architectures—with and without parallel memory units. In Section 5.1, we sketched the idea of a cache memory. The details of managing such a memory are very much like the management of a main and secondary memory hierarchy, so we shall defer the details of such a discussion to Chapter 7. The idea of a cache is to provide a copy of recently accessed main memory words in a fast cache memory, and thus avoid accessing the slower main memory whenever possible. In practice, sufficiently high cache "hit ratios" occur to make caches quite popular. In Figs 5.5, 5.6, and 5.7, we showed three types of parallel memory systems and, as we will see here, each of them can easily and profitably be fitted with cache extensions. We now consider each of these types of memories in order.

Placing a cache between the CPU and memory units of Fig. 5.5 yields a system of the kind illustrated in Fig. 5.1. As we pointed out in Section 5.1, the cache maintains images of a number of blocks of main memory. When a word can be accessed in the cache, it is; otherwise, the slower main memory must be accessed. But in case main memory must be accessed, a block of words surrounding the accessed word is fetched to the cache. Thus, subsequent memory accesses may be made to the cache and not to main memory.

Addressing a cache is carried out by hardware similar to that described in Section 4.3.4 for virtual memory accessing. Here main memory and cache correspond to secondary memory and main memory, respectively, of Fig. 4.22 and Fig. 4.23. A block here corresponds to a page there. The two characteristics that have become identified with a modern cache are: (1) it is a small memory between main memory and the CPU, and (2) it has a hardware address map that allows operation at approximately the CPU clock speed.

It is clear that good cache performance depends on the fact that programs and data often are accessed in fairly regular or local ways. In other words, the sequence of addresses generated by the CPU is *not* uniformly distributed throughout memory. They tend to cluster in one part of memory for awhile and then move to another part of memory. This program-dependent assumption is similar to that necessary to ensure the proper operation of a parallel memory system—namely, that a sequence of generated addresses will be spread out across several memory units. Our point is not that parallel and cache memories require the same program assumptions, but that they both depend on program behavior. In fact, cache memories require that in a sequence of CPU-generated addresses, the high-order bits must be clustered, whereas low-order bits are irrelevant. On the other hand, parallel memories require that in a sequence of CPU-generated addresses the low-order bits be distinct, whereas the high-order bits are irrelevant. Memory systems with caches and parallel main memory units have been employed in a number of real computer systems, as will be described later.

Next, consider the computer system of Fig. 5.6. One of the difficulties mentioned with respect to this system was in memory and/or switch conflicts. If two or more CPUs attempt to access the same memory unit at the same time, a conflict arises. We shall analyze such systems later, but for the moment let us consider Fig. 5.6 enhanced with a cache between each CPU and the crossbar switch. As long as each processor computes from its cache, two important advantages would be achieved over the system of Fig. 5.6.

The first advantage is the standard one obtained from a cache, namely, that the cache is faster than the main memory. The second advantage is that those memory accesses handled in the cache do not reach main memory and, hence, cannot cause conflicts with other CPU-generated addresses. This, of course, provides a higher effective main memory bandwidth to those CPUs that must access main memory. The effect can also be regarded as an opportunity to use a slower main memory because not so much main memory bandwidth is needed. Now, in a sense, we are back to the first advantage, namely, that fast caches satisfy the CPUs and a slow, large main memory can be used.

One disadvantage of this scheme is that although a cache is being loaded from main memory, a number of words must be transmitted (probably from each of several main memory units), and this must be done with high priority, thus tying up main memory and perhaps blocking other CPUs. If such cache blocks are not transmitted with high priority, managing the system could become very complicated, since only part of a cache block might be present when the cache is accessed.

Finally, we consider the addition of a cache to a system of the type illustrated in Fig. 5.7. In this case it may be useful to consider separating program fetches from data access. Because this type of computer is designed for high performance on array operations, the parallel memory designs considered in Section 5.4.2.2, which provide conflict-free array access, may be regarded as adequate because they guarantee distinct low-order address bits together with unchanging high-order address bits—as long as a fixed set of arrays is being accessed.

As we observed previously, these conditions are ideal for both parallel and cache memories. But for cache operation to be profitable, the words fetched to the cache *must* be accessed repeatedly. This may not be the case for data, but it often is for programs.

Even for an array machine, a program cache makes sense because loops are often executed many times. In one form or another, caches have been used in many high-performance scientific computers. The CDC 6600 (and 7600) have a "program stack." This is really an instruction buffer (see Section 4.2.3.2), not a stack for retaining a program loop. It is not a cache in that it contains just one block of instructions. Another example is the instruction buffer of ILLIAC IV, which is a cache of 8 blocks of 8 words each, and has associative hardware management.

Caches or scratchpads are provided in ILLIAC IV, the CDC STAR, the CRAY-I, and TI ASC for holding data as well. Although scratchpads do not have cache-type logic for their management, they have the same purposes as mentioned above for the multiprocessor of Fig. 5.6. By holding data that is used only sporadically, they generally prevent the interruption of a smooth flow of data arrays to and from main memory. Such smooth flowing arrays are those for which the conflict-free array access schemes are designed.

It should be clear at this point that cache and parallel memory schemes each have their use in memory system design. Both are dependent on the pattern of CPU-generated addresses. Each has special logic design requirements, although parallel memories are probably somewhat less complex than caches. Now we turn to a detailed analysis of cache performance.

Cache memory details

In Fig. 5.12 we show a typical cache configuration. The memory control unit controls access to the cache. If the control unit or processor attempt a fetch

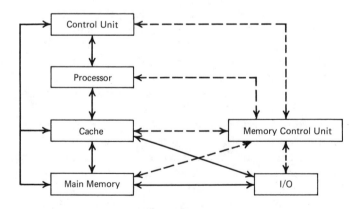

FIGURE 5.12   **System configuration with cache memory.**

from main memory, words are supplied from the cache if they are resident there. If not, words are supplied from main memory, but the cache is also loaded with a block of words including the one requested. Thus, subsequent fetches of the same word can be handled at cache speed. In order to study the effectiveness of caches we need some definitions.

Let ϕ, the *cache hit ratio*, be the fraction of the main memory addresses issued by the control unit, which can be satisfied by accessing the cache. Both data and program addresses are included here. Let T_c be the *cache memory cycle time* and T_m be the *main memory cycle time*. Then the *effective memory cycle time* T_e, as seen by the processor and control unit, is

$$T_e = \phi T_c + (1 - \phi) T_m.$$

The speedup due to the cache is

$$S_c = T_m / T_e,$$

the main memory cycle divided by the effective memory cycle.

It is instructive to express the speedup due to the cache as a function of the hit ratio and the cycle times of the main and cache memories

$$S_c = \frac{T_m}{T_e} = \frac{T_m}{\phi T_c + (1 - \phi) T_m} = \frac{1}{1 + \phi\left(\dfrac{T_c}{T_m} - 1\right)},$$

and since $T_c/T_m < 1$ we write this as

$$S_c = \frac{1}{1 - \left(1 - \dfrac{T_c}{T_m}\right)\phi}.$$

Figure 5.13 shows maximum S_c versus ϕ; observe that if $\phi = k/k+1$, then

$$S_c = \frac{1}{1 + \dfrac{k}{k+1}\left(\dfrac{T_c}{T_m} - 1\right)} = \frac{1}{\dfrac{k}{k+1}\dfrac{T_c}{T_m} + \dfrac{1}{k+1}} = \frac{(k+1)T_m}{T_m + kT_c} < k+1.$$

Thus if $\phi = \frac{1}{2}$, we cannot achieve a speedup of more than 2, regardless of the speed of the cache. It turns out that in practice, hit ratios of well over 0.9 are achievable, so caches do indeed serve their intended purpose well. A number of people have measured cache hit ratios [Gibs67], [KaWi73], [LiMa72], and in Fig. 5.14 we present a typical plot of the cache *miss ratio* $(1 - \phi)$ versus cache size. Note that the cache size axis is logarithmic. A great deal of leverage in S_c, the speedup of an individual job, can be achieved by small increases in cache hit ratio. Consider the following example.

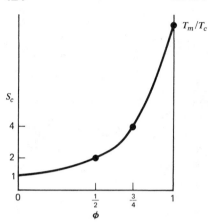

FIGURE 5.13 Maximum possible cache speedup versus hit ratio

Example 1

Assume we are studying the design of cache memory size, and have measured hit ratios for a number of programs, assuming 4K bytes of cache and 8K bytes of cache. Let the average hit ratio for 4K bytes of cache be 0.93 and for 8K bytes be 0.97. If $T_c/T_m = 0.12$, then for a 4K byte cache

$$S_c^{4K} = \frac{1}{1 - 0.88 \times 0.93} \approx 5.5,$$

whereas for the 8K byte cache

$$S_c^{8K} = \frac{1}{1 - 0.88 \times 0.97} \approx 6.85.$$

Thus, adding 4K bytes to the cache achieves a system speedup *improvement* of

$$\frac{S_c^{8K} - S_c^{4K}}{S_c^{4K}} \approx 0.24.$$

This 24 percent improvement could be a very good return on a relatively small investment. ∎

In the early 1960s, many computers were incorporating large numbers of registers (so-called *scratchpads*) that were managed in some way by hardware as well as software. They included the Burroughs D825 and B8500 [AHSW62], [Gluc65], the CDC 6600, the Ferranti ATLAS [KELS62], the Japanese ETL Mk-6 [TNYF63], as well as others. Also, time-shared and memory-shared machines were becoming popular, so the idea of expanding the set of registers to a small, fast cache memory that contained a number of blocks of words fetched from main memory was ripe at that time. Several dynamic cache management schemes were proposed in [Wilk65] by M. V. Wilkes.

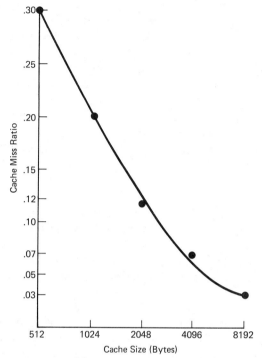

FIGURE 5.14   Cache miss ratio versus size.

A number of machines have used caches of one kind or another—the idea has been particularly popular in IBM machines. An early comprehensive study of cache performance was done by D. H. Gibson [Gibs67] at IBM. These studies recommended that a block size of 16 words be chosen (for transmission between main memory and cache), and that a cache should contain 128 or more blocks (for a total of 2K words). Hit ratios as a function of block size and cache size are shown in his paper.

In addition to the ideas discussed thus far, several other issues arise in the design of a cache memory. One is the question of which block to replace if we need a new block and the cache is already full. For example, this could be done randomly, it could be done by some fixed relation of cache addresses to main memory addresses, the oldest or least recently used block could be replaced, and so on. The same type of question arises in page replacement between main memory and secondary memory; therefore, we will defer a discussion of the subject until Chapter 7.

Another interesting question concerns the details of operation of the memory control unit of Fig. 5.12. For example, how much extra time does it add to the process? As we shall learn, the time may be substantial in terms of cache cycle time but, by pipelining its operation, the time may be regained. When the processor writes the cache, the main memory is also usually written. This *write through* technique saves memory bandwidth by avoiding writing entire blocks back to main memory when the block is replaced in the cache. Another design option is whether to allow I/O channels to communicate directly with the cache (if required) instead of transmitting data through the main memory. For further discussion of these and other implementation questions, the reader is referred to the references given in the following discussion.

In Table 5.3, we show the cache characteristics of several IBM machines. The first commercially available computer with a cache memory was the IBM 360/85. Its cache allowed the Model 85 to outperform the Model 91, which it superseded in the marketplace as the top of the IBM 360 line. The processor and the cache had an 80 ns clock, but cache accesses required two of these. The first checked whether or not the contents of the address were in the cache and the second accessed it. The two steps were pipelined, so 80 ns access was possible [Lipt68] [CoGP68] (shown in Table 5.3 as 2×80 ns).

In Table 5.3, we show the maximum ratio of T_m/T_c, which determines the best possible speedup due to the cache. We also show the cache size in bytes (a range is often available) and the number of words per block fetched from main memory to the cache in response to one access. The 360/85 as well as the next two machines to be discussed had 64-bit (8 byte) data words.

The next IBM entry in the cache market (at the end of 1969) was the 360/195 [McLa69], which had a 54 ns clock and a pipelined processor. It also had a 54 ns cache, which required a total of three clocks for access. But this was also pipelined through a memory control unit so effectively that it could operate at nearly 54 ns. It was a logical descendant of the Model 85 with respect to the cache and of the 360/91 with respect to the pipelined processor. It was estimated to be two or three times the speed of the Model 85, which had already superseded the Model 91. Performance comparisons may be found in [MuWa70] for the 360 models 65, 85, and 195.

The 1970 IBM computer entries were in the 370 series. The 370/165 has an 80 ns cache, operating as a two-segment pipeline. The main memory is a 2 μs, four-way interleaved memory, which allows access in as little as 500 ns. Up to 16K bytes of cache can be used. See [Katz71] for a comprehensive discussion of the details of the 370/165. Note that IBM calls a cache a "buffer storage." Caches are not restricted to large machines; the Data General

TABLE 5.3. IBM Cache Characteristics

Computer	Main Memory Time T_m	Cache Time T_c	max T_m/T_c	Cache Size (words)	Cache Block Size (words)
IBM 360/85	1.04 μs	2×80 ns	13	2K$\rightarrow$4 K	8
IBM 360/195	756 ns	3×54 ns	14.2	4K	8
IBM 370/165	2 μs	2×80 ns	25	1K$\rightarrow$2K	16

Eclipse and the Digital Equipment PDP-11/70 [Stre76] have caches. For performance surveys, see [Mead70] or [KaWi73].

5.4.4 Memory control unit

Thus far, this chapter has presented a number of features associated with main memory besides the obvious program and data storage. Every real memory can, in fact, be regarded as a large storage area, together with certain control logic. In Chapter 4, we discussed the logic associated with address generation in the control unit. In Section 5.4.3 we introduced the cache memory idea and learned that caches need their own control logic. Here we discuss the remaining logic required to operate a memory. In real machines this may be located in the memory or in the control unit (or in some other special box or boxes), but we discuss it as if it were part of the memory unit.

In part, this will be a summary of what we have been discussing, and in part a preview of what follows. We do not give any details of the logic we refer to; it is logic that must be present for the proper operation of various memory features and its details vary from one system to another. We refer to this logic collectively as the *memory control unit* (MCU), and its role is to accept addresses from the outside world and then either store or fetch information for the outside world.

Six functions of the MCU can be distinguished; it may provide:

1. Interface to the outside world.
2. Hardware integrity.
3. Memory management.
4. Memory protection.
5. Local addressing.
6. Cache management (see Section 5.4.3).

We discuss the first five of these functions in order.

Even if nothing else is provided, the MCU must have some registers and logic to provide an interface to the processors, control units, and I/O devices that use the memory. We illustrated memory address and memory information registers in Fig. 5.5. Other registers may be required for the internal operation of the memory. In many cases, electrical interfaces of various kinds are also needed; for example, voltage levels may have to be adjusted between the memory and the outside world. A certain amount of time and gates are required to perform these functions, but they are practical necessities that cannot be avoided. It may also be necessary to provide some kind of formatting facilities for the outside world. For example, the machine word size may be 32 bits in the CPU and memory, but the transmission path between them may be just 16 bits wide and be clocked at twice the rate of the memory and CPU. In this instance, the memory needs an assembly and disassembly register to handle 16–32-bit conversions both going and coming.

The second MCU function is the preservation of memory hardware integrity. In Section 5.2.6, parity bits were discussed in detail. The MCU must test the parity bits of newly fetched words and of words received from the outside world, because errors can arise while words are stored or while they are being transmitted. If an error has occurred, appropriate action must be taken by the MCU. It usually generates an interrupt to the CPU and perhaps turns on a panel light, depending on the machine's design. If an error correcting code is used, the incorrect bit (or bits) are corrected, and parity bits are again generated for the corrected word. For example, a corrected word may be written to memory and reread to determine if the error was transient or not, and in the latter case notice is sent outside the MCU.

Memory management is the third point and various aspects of this were discussed previously with respect to access priorities and various roles of tags. The management may concern who gets access next, or it may involve whether or not a stored word is in use or is garbage, and so on. In Section 5.4.2, multiple port memories were discussed (see Fig. 5.6), each of which requires an interface to the outside world. The resolution of conflicts between ports can be handled in the MCU.

Some ports may be dedicated to I/O channels, and others to one or more CPUs, in which case the slower I/O ports may have higher priority. Or, because they send words relatively slowly, they may be given low priority for a time, and if they cannot obtain a memory cycle in a reasonable period of time, they are then given higher priority. Various so-called *cycle stealing* schemes are used to grant memory cycles to I/O devices. The term *cycle stealing* is used ambiguously—sometimes it means that the I/O device sneaks in and grabs an unused (by the CPU) memory cycle; other times it refers to the case where I/O is granted a memory cycle in preference to the CPU. In any case, I/O devices must occasionally be granted highest priority in accessing memory, because for example, if a disk word is not read, it will not be available again until a complete disk rotation later—perhaps 20 or 30 ms. On the other hand, if the CPU is blocked for a few hundred nanoseconds for a stolen cycle, the time will not really be noticed at the level of job turnaround time.

In fact, a number of different competitors for main memory cycles can be distinguished, and the MCU may be designed to give different priorities to them. They include instruction fetches for the CU, data stores and fetches for the processor, stores and fetches for various I/O devices, and in some systems stores and fetches from a cache memory.

Memories are normally designed with a fixed number of ports (usually less than 8) and some kind of wired-in priority logic. If the system is expanded, *port expanders* are designed that are actually multiplexers which plug into one port. These do not usually enhance the bandwidth of the port, but just allow memory requests to arrive from more sources (recall Section 5.4.2.1).

The fourth point is memory protection. In earlier sections, we discussed various protection schemes. The lock and key logic of Section 5.2.3 can be located in the MCU. In fact, the locks for each block may be contained in main memory or in a small special memory in the MCU. Similarly, at least part of the TEST AND SET logic of Section 5.2.4 may be in the MCU. Recall the timing constraints that necessitate blocking all memory access requests subsequent to the first, until the control bit has been processed for the first access. If several processors share common memory—a typical case that necessitates a TEST AND SET instruction—then such blocking logic can be conveniently located in the MCU for sharing between the processors. In Section 5.2.5 we mentioned a number of uses of tags for protection, and the MCU is a natural place for the necessary logic.

Finally, the fifth point is local addressing, which we have not discussed much before. There are two aspects to this. In a parallel memory system, the MCU may be physically spread out among several boxes. Thus, two memory modules may share one MCU, so a memory system with eight parallel memory modules would consist of four MCUs, each controlling two memory modules. Some means must be provided for the MCUs to coordinate their operation, but we will not discuss that. Our point is that each MCU must select one of the several memory modules it controls. It may even accept several addresses at once and attempt to cycle more than one module simultaneously.

The other aspect of local addressing holds true even if the MCU has just one memory module; it concerns addressing within the physical memory words. A memory module may be organized with 64-bit words, for example, but the computer may have 32-bit data words and may provide 8-bit character addressing. It may even provide bit level addressing. To accommodate the mismatch between logical and physical words, some logic—which Burroughs refers to as *field isolation logic*—must be provided. The address received from the outside world is broken apart and the high-order bits are used to access the memory, whereas the low-order bits of the original address are used to access the desired part of the physical memory word. On the other hand, some Honeywell and CDC machines use the processor to extract the desired fields from memory words.

From the above it should be clear that the MCU can contain a nontrivial number of gates and, what is worse, it may introduce delays that are substantial compared with a memory cycle. For this reason, the MCU may operate on several addresses at once, performing the above operations on the next address while a previously handled address is being accessed.

PROBLEMS

Easy problems in text order

5.1 There are only three modes of addressing any type of memory from the hardware point of view. They are exemplified by: the STARAN IV, a main memory module, and a disk drive. Briefly describe what these addressing modes are and how they differ.

5.2   Rank these memory devices in order of ascending capacity and estimate their capacities: cache, drum, main memory, disk, bulk ECS/LCS, and scratchpad registers.

5.3   IBM uses 8 error correcting parity bits on double words of 8 bytes rather than a single error correcting code on the individual bytes. How many bits per double word are saved in this way over single error correcting per byte?

5.4   Estimate the cost and speed of a circuit that tests for even parity in an n bit word.

5.5   Suppose we wish to encode a data word using a Hamming code by looking up the parity bits in a ROM. What is the largest data word that can be encoded in this way considering the size of ROMs that are currently available? Give a table of data word size and ROM size needed, for ROMs up to 128K words.

5.6   The following curve represents the cost of a memory technology versus its bandwidth.

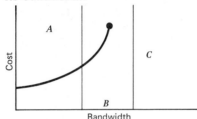

Match each region with one of the following:
_____ Interleaving is the only way to enter this region.
_____ This region should be avoided because of decreased cost-effectiveness for noninterleaved systems.
_____ Backing store technology is found in this region.

5.7   Consider the use of $1 \mu s$ memory units in the construction of a large parallel memory. Suppose you are building a parallel processor machine in which each of 16 processors needs an effective memory bandwidth of one word every 500 ns.
(a)   How many memories and what configuration would you choose?
(b)   If the machine had one processor instead of 16, with an arithmetic pipeline that operates with a 100 ns clock, how many memories and what configuration would you choose?

5.8   An important fundamental point concerning the implementation of random access memories is the method by which an individual memory word is selected. We will discuss two selection methods that can be used in magnetic core or semiconductor memories. A 2^k-word *linear select* memory uses a decode tree to select one of 2^k words. Show how the k-bit address is used to control a decode tree which has $O(2^k)$ gates. In contrast with this, a 2^k-word *coincident select* memory uses two decode trees; each selects one of $2^{k/2}$ intersecting lines in a square array. Show that only $2 \cdot O(2^{k/2})$ gates are required for coincident select address decoding. This is twice the square root of the number of gates required for a linear select memory.

5.9 A memory system is composed of two identical memory units. Match each statement below with the situation where it would lead to the most reasonable machine design.
   (a) The high-order address bit selects the memory unit to be addressed.
   (b) The low-order address bit selects the memory unit to be addressed.
   _____The memory is to be used to match a CPU that is twice the speed of each memory unit.
   _____Multiprogramming of two users is to be done, and each must be protected from erroneous accesses by the other.
   _____Availability of system.
   _____Multiprogramming, where the size of the job varies a lot.

5.10 A computer system with four parallel processors and five memory units, each with its own indexing mechanism, is interconnected via a 4×5 crossbar switch. We want conflict-free access to any four adjacent elements (by rows, by columns, or by diagonals) of an 8×8 array. Show how to store such an array in the five memory units.

5.11 Which of the following do *not* apply to cache-based computer systems?
   (a) The processor tends to operate at the speed of the cache.
   (b) The cache is managed by hardware (or firmware) algorithms.
   (c) The cache is used for data only.
   (d) A cache can enhance memory performance even if it operates at the same speed as main memory.
   (e) None of the above.

5.12 Distinguish between a cache memory and an instruction buffer. Name a machine that has each.

Medium and hard problems in text order

5.13 Consider the design of a memory system with a cache, main and large bulk memory, as shown in Fig. 5.1. For marketing reasons, suppose it has been decided that the main memory is to have 128K words of 32 bits each. Furthermore, suppose the company you work for makes an 800 ns cycle time main memory in 32K-word (32-bit words) modules, that you can get for 1¢/bit. The processor for this machine is to have a 50 ns clock, with most instructions requiring 3–5 clocks. Your boss says that company policy dictates using their main memory in some configuration, and that you can have up to about $150K total for the three-level memory. The boss gives you a supplier's component catalog for the cache and bulk, and the supplier makes various memories that (together with your main memory) follow the formula

$$\text{Cycle time} \times \frac{\text{cost}}{\text{bit}} = 8.00 \frac{\text{ns} \cdot \$}{\text{bit}} = \text{constant.}$$

Thus, you can get a 32-bit word cache that operates at 80 ns for 10¢/bit or one that operates at 8 ns for 1$/bit. Similarly, you can get bulk memory that operates at 4 μs for 0.2¢/bit, and so on, ranging in price down to 0.1¢/bit as a minimum. Bulk memory is in the form of core memory with long words and the word length must be a power of two times 32 bits. You can assume that a continuum of memory specifications are available, but you must buy memories with 2^j words each, for some integer j.

By measuring hit ratios, you decide that somewhere between 2K and 8K of cache words are desirable. Bulk memory should, of course, be "as big as possible." Considering the range of possible memory sizes and costs available to you, which would you choose on the basis of marketing strategy, uniform distribution of expenditures, and so on?

5.14 Consider the airline seat reservation problem which, when viewed abstractly, amounts to having N processors (i.e., terminals at reservation desks), which simultaneously try to read and update a counter indicating the number of seats left on a particular flight. We will use the IBM 360/370 TEST AND SET (TS) instruction. For example, TS DOOR fetches the byte, labeled DOOR in this case, and sets the condition code to the contents of the first bit of the fetched byte. Immediately after fetching the DOOR byte, a byte of ones is written into DOOR assuring that the next TS access to DOOR will find DOOR locked until a STORE 0, DOOR unlocks DOOR. If DOOR is locked, we can branch back to the TS instruction and try again. Suppose each of these processors continuously executes the following loop:

```
LOOP:  TS DOOR
       JMPGTZ LOOP       Keep testing DOOR until we can get in.
       FETCH MISC        Miscellaneous code to read and write
       STORE MISC        counter taking t_l sec. to execute from TS
       ADD MISC          DOOR through STORE 0, DOOR.
          .
          .
          .

       STORE 0, DOOR     Unlock DOOR.
       STORE MISC        Miscellaneous code
       ADD MISC          not involving counter
       FETCH MISC        taking t_u sec. to execute from STORE
          .              MISC to JUMP LOOP.
          .
          .

       JUMP LOOP         The whole loop takes t_loop sec.
```

Consider how much time the processors are waiting. If $N = 2$ and $t_l = t_u$, then the sum of the wasted time per cycle ($SWTPC$) is zero in the steady state because each processor is continuously busy. If $N = 3$ and $t_l = t_u$, $SWTPC$ is $3t_l$ because each processor wastes $1t_l$.

(a) Given N processors and $t_l = t_u$, find $SWTPC(N)$ for all users.

(b) Suppose that the granularity of the lock is changed. That is, suppose that the loop is rewritten to have a larger or smaller locked portion. Let $0 < \alpha \le 1$ be a constant such that $t_l = \alpha t_{loop}$. Find $SWTPC(N, \alpha)$.

Sketch the region through which $SWTPC(N, \alpha)$ can vary on the $SWTPC$ versus N plane.

(c) Find $\Delta SWTPC(N) = SWTPC(N + 1, \alpha) - SWTPC(N, \alpha)$. Comment on the meaning of $\Delta SWTPC$.

5.15 Construct a Hamming code for the 6-bit ASCII code. How many parity bits are needed? Give an algorithm to generate each of the parity bits. Show how each of the following characters would be encoded.

Alphanumeric	ASCII
:	000000
A	000001
I	001001
Q	010001
Y	011001
Z	011010
0	011011
1	011100
9	100100
(blank)	101101

(a) Estimate the cost and speed of the fastest circuit you can design that tests for even parity in an n-bit word.

(b) Given the circuit of part (a), show the overall logic of a single error correcting Hamming code for six data bits (as above).

Include both parity checking and correcting of a single error.

5.16 It is common for bulk (or extended or large) core memories to have linear selection logic even though coincident select logic uses fewer gates (see Problem 5.8). This follows from two facts. First, bulk core memories can afford to have long words because they are used to transfer many bits between main and secondary memory. Second, memories are fabricated from a number of subunits. Thus, coincident selection logic can be used at the subunit level, but normally linear selection logic is used externally to choose between these subunits.

These two points can be quantified as follows. Let us compare two memories: a coincident select memory of N_1 words and d_1 bits, and a linear select memory of N_2 words and d_2 bits, where $N_1 d_1 = N_2 d_2$. Thus the size and cost of the data storage are similar. Let us compare the selection logic costs.

(a) Show that regardless of how many subunits are used, the linear select memory has $O(N_2)$ selection gates.

(b) On the other hand, if the coincident select memory has n words per subunit, then each subunit has $O(n^{1/2})$ selection gates and there are N_1/n subunits in the word direction. Let us suppose there are k bits in each subunit word. Thus there are a total of $N_1/n \cdot d_1/k$ subunits. Sketch the configuration of the coincident select memory. Show that the coincident select scheme will have as many gates as the linear scheme if $d_2 \approx n^{1/2}k$.

(c) In the original CDC 6600, $n = 4K$ and $k = 12$ bits in the coincident select main memory, whereas the extended core storage, a linear select memory, had $d_2 = 480$. Which memory would use more selection hardware if they were the same size? The extended core storage had a cycle time three times slower than the main core storage. Could this speed difference be the result of choosing linear select logic or is it probably due to a slower memory technology?

5.17 A random access memory is to be built from 512-word × 4-bit chips with separate input and output pins, built-in decoders, two chip enables, and tri-state outputs.

(a) Counting only logic pins, that is, address, data, and so on, how many pins per package will be required? Why?

(b) How would the chips be laid out to form a 4K-word by 16-bit memory module? Include the additional logic needed. (If you use multiplexers and/or demultiplexers, state how many and what kind.)

(c) Within each chip, what is the fastest way to address each bit? For example, is it better to have four 1×512-bit arrays, four 2×256, four 4×128, and so on? How many gates are needed for the fastest methods?

5.18 Consider a computer with four independent memory units, two multipliers, an adder, and a bank of 16 fast registers for temporary storage, indexing, and so on; all connected by a data bus as shown in the diagram. All four memories may be accessed simultaneously. Assume each memory has its own index register. Assume that the bus has sufficient bandwidth to permit simultaneous routing of operands among the units in any desired fashion and that the time required to transmit data is negligible.

An incrementer is associated with each register, R1 − R16, so that simple index modifications (additions and subtractions of constants) can be performed directly at registers without the use of the adder.

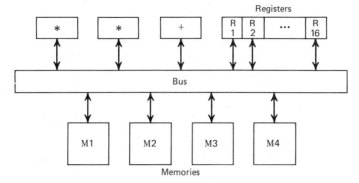

The four instructions of interest for this problem are defined in the following table:

Mnemonic	Arguments	Meaning	Execution Time
FETCH	Ri, X, Rj (Rj is optional)	Ri←C(X + Rj)	5 clocks
INC	Ri, I	Ri←Ri+I	1 clock
MPY	Ri, Rj	Ri←Ri*Rj	10 clocks
ADD	Ri, Rj	Ri←Ri+Rj	5 clocks

(*Note*: Ri and Rj are any of the 16 registers. C(X + Rj) means the contents of memory location X + Rj. X and I are literals.)

The following program will evaluate the statement

$$S \leftarrow S + A(I) * B(J) + A(I+1) * B(J+2)$$

where S is stored in R5 and the index registers have been properly initialized:

FETCH	R1, A, R16
FETCH	R2, B, R15
INC	R16, 1
INC	R15, 2
MPY	R1, R2
FETCH	R3, A, R16
FETCH	R4, B, R15
INC	R16, 1
INC	R15, 2
MPY	R3, R4
ADD	R5, R1
ADD	R5, R3

(a) Assume the control unit contains a single decoder which can process one instruction per clock pulse and only one instruction at a time. The CU also contains as many sequencers as you need for controlling instruction execution; and an instruction lookahead

buffer adequate to contain this entire block of code is provided.
Draw a time chart for execution of this program showing instruction scheduling.

(b) Suppose the program shown was in a loop that indexed through
large A and B arrays and was rewritten in such a way that all four
operand fetches overlapped. Show how to arrange A and B in
memory so that no accessing conflicts would arise. Assume that
odd-numbered B elements will be used in calculation.

5.19 Consider a computer with nine independent memory banks, all of which
can be accessed simultaneously. Each memory bank is three words
"wide" so that as many as 27 words can be fetched in a single cycle.
Each bank has an independent index register for addressing within the
bank. A portion of a program for this machine involves the following
matrix operations:

$$C \leftarrow A * B$$
$$D \leftarrow B * A$$
$$E \leftarrow C * D * C$$

(a) Assume all five matrices A–E are square with dimension 9×9.
Show how to partition and store the arrays in order to keep a very
fast arithmetic unit as busy as possible with useful computations. If
the processor can consume 27 words at the speed the memory
produces them, can you find any memory conflict problems with
this program? Indicate the computational algorithm and diagram
the position of all arrays involved.
(Note: Assume that index manipulations take some time and that
index assignments must be made by a compiler or a programmer.
Keep them as simple as possible.)

(b) Derive a general expression for computing addresses from subscripts I and J of 3×3 partitions.

(c) What new problems appear for 10×10 arrays?

5.20 Assume we have a computer with four processors and four memory
units. Consider the address patterns shown below to be generated on a
computation of three instructions. The numbers shown are memory unit
numbers.

		Processor number				
		1	2	3	4	
Instruction	1	3	2	4	3	Memory
number	2	2	4	1	2	units
	3	4	1	3	1	addressed

(a) Suppose this computer is configured as an array processor. In this configuration, all processors must finish an instruction before any can proceed to the next instruction. When two or more processors access the same memory on a step, the request of the lower numbered processor is granted, and the other requests for that memory must wait one time step. What is the average memory bandwidth used, in words/step?

(b) Suppose this computer is configured as a multiprocessor, with multifunction processors. In this configuration, unexecuted instructions can "queue-up" in each independent processor until they can be executed. The same conflict resolution scheme is used as in part (a). What is the average memory bandwidth used, in words/step?

5.21 Consider the storage of a symmetric $N \times N$ matrix, where N is a perfect square, in an N-unit parallel memory. Devise general storage schemes which require only $\lceil N/2 \rceil$ rows of storage if N is odd and $\lceil N/2 \rceil + 1$ rows of storage if N is even. Assume each memory has its own index register.

(a) With one storage scheme, suppose we require the ability to access any row or column in one memory cycle. For example, if $N = 9$, we should be able to access, say 13, 23, 33, and 43, 53, 63, 73, 83, 93 by symmetry in one cycle if the upper half of the matrix is stored.

(b) With a different storage scheme suppose that in one memory cycle we require access to rows or non-overlapping square partitions of size $\sqrt{N} \times \sqrt{N}$ as shown below for $N = 9$.

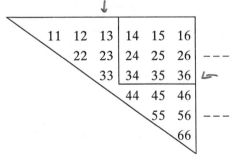

Illustrate your algorithms for (a) and (b) with $N = 9$ and $N = 16$.

(c) Is it possible to achieve (a) and (b) with just one scheme?

5.22 (a) In an ideal CAM, each bit of memory should have a simple processor. The STARAN IV has 256^2 bits of associative memory but only 256 processors. What memory storage technique makes this possible?

(b) Show how the first four words (of 256 bits) might be stored in the STARAN IV's 256 memory modules.

(c) In an ideal CAM, an exact field match for an n-bit wide field can be found in one memory cycle. How many memory cycles are necessary for the STARAN IV in the worst, best, and average cases?

5.23 This problem deals with the efficient use of a content addressable memory (CAM). Assume such a memory contains a list of data words, each b bits in length, and a register of b interrogation drivers, where the ith interrogation driver is associated with the ith bit of each data word in the list. Each driver is capable of one of three driving states: 0, 1, X, where X is a "don't care" state. The pattern of states in the interrogation register (IR) is called the interrogation word, and a word in memory is said to match the interrogation word if there are no disagreements between its bits and the corresponding interrogation states. (The X-state does not disagree with either a stored 0 or a stored 1.) The words that match an interrogation are "selected" or "isolated" for further processing. The combination of bits specified initially for locating data in the memory will be referred to as the tag.

It is necessary to provide a system for sensing the results of memory interrogations. Suppose there are b sensing devices for the memory, one associated with each bit position in a word. This will be called the sense condition register (SCR). Each sensing device is connected to a pair of sense lines which couple it to its corresponding storage element in every word. A sensing device is capable of identifying the following three conditions:

Condition	Signal Pair	Meaning
D	0,0	Selected words could have either 0 or 1 in this position.
0	0,1	All words selected have "0" in this position.
1	1,0	All words selected have "1" in this position.

In addition, a match column containing one bit associated with each word in the memory is provided. After each interrogation, the match bit for word i is set to 1 if and only if word i "matches" the interrogation word. Actually, you don't need the match column if you can sense the condition in which the SCR contains only 0's and 1's. This occurs only when an exact match is obtained, and the desired word appears automatically in SCR.

The following example illustrates the operation of this system for one interrogation:

	(Bit Position: 1	2	3	4	5)	Match Column
Interrogation Register (IR)	1	X	X	1	X	
Sense Condition Register (SCR)	1	D	0	1	D	
Memory Word 1	1	1	0	1	0	1
Memory Word 2	1	0	0	1	1	1
Memory Word 3	0	1	0	1	0	0
Memory Word 4	1	0	0	1	0	1
Memory Word 5	0	0	0	1	1	0

The contents of SCR and the match column are shown after the interrogation; the contents of IR and the memory itself are not changed. Words 1, 2, and 4 have been isolated since their contents match the tag, that is, bit $1 =$ bit $4 = 1$.

If data words are considered to be binary numbers, describe a fast systematic procedure for isolating and reading all words that match a given tag in *decreasing numerical order* (such an algorithm was first described in [Lewi62]). Illustrate the procedure for the list below with tag bits 2 and $6 = 0$ and bit $10 = 1$. How many interrogations are required? (*Hint:* Would you believe fewer than 10?)

Word Number	Contents									
(Bit Position:	1	2	3	4	5	6	7	8	9	10)
1	0	0	1	1	0	0	1	0	0	1
2	0	0	1	0	1	0	0	1	0	1
3	1	1	0	0	1	1	1	0	1	0
4	1	0	1	0	0	1	0	1	1	1
5	1	0	0	1	1	0	0	0	0	1
6	0	1	0	1	1	1	0	0	1	0
7	0	0	1	0	1	0	1	0	1	1
8	0	0	1	1	0	0	1	0	1	1

5.24 Suppose we have a dual processor MIME system, and we wish to add a cache memory. There are two distinct alternatives. We could add a separate cache memory to each processor, or we could buy one cache memory of twice the size and speed to be shared by both processors.

(a) Why would the common cache scheme be better if the software was organized so that both processors might execute a common program simultaneously, for example, some operating system routines? Does the TEST AND SET type of memory access cause any implementation problems in this situation? And, if it does, propose a solution.

(b) When and why might it be better to have a separate cache for each processor?

5.25 The cache of the IBM 360/85 ranged from 16–32K bytes organized into 1024-byte sectors (similar to pages in Chapter 7) that were subdivided into 16 blocks of 64 bytes each. (Note that 1 word in Table 5.3 is 8 bytes.) Each sector in the cache was the image of a 1024-byte sector in main memory. When a main memory location was to be fetched for data or for an instruction, the cache was first checked to see if that address was present in some cache sector. (This test took 80 ns.) If it was, the cache could be cycled in 80 ns to deliver the proper data. The priority of the sector was then increased. If the cache did not contain the proper data, a hardware algorithm found the sector with the lowest priority, determined on a least recently used sector basis. The new sector was then written over the old sector one 64-byte block at a time. The main memory had four interleaved modules and each module was 16 bytes wide so that an entire block could be fetched in one main memory cycle, taking 1.04 μs. It was arranged so that the first block to be read into a sector contained the referenced word. When a main memory location was to be written, the first check was to see if the corresponding sector of main memory was already in the cache, the same as when data was read. But the remainder of the write procedure was entirely different from the read procedure. If the word was present in the cache, the data was written into both the cache and the main memory. The priority of the sector was *not* changed. If the location was not in the cache, the data was simply written into main memory. Note that the sector was not loaded into the cache.

(a) Write a flowchart for the memory reference procedure as described above. Consider only the necessary operations; do not worry about expressing parallelism. Label each path through the flowchart with the probability that that path will be taken. Assume 3 reads per write (why?) and use Fig. 5.14 to determine the miss ratio assuming a cache size of 8K bytes.

(b) Reorganize the flowchart so that the operations that can be carried out in parallel are apparent. Using the figures given above, compute the time it takes to travel down each branch of the flowchart. Don't forget that the main memory is interleaved four ways and the 1.04 μs figure refers to the cycle time of each module. Assume that the main memory requests are uniformly distributed among the four modules. Note that the most likely path should be the fastest. What is the expected time to process a memory request? Suppose that a 16K cache has a miss ratio of 0.018; what is the expected time to process a reference?

5.26 Compare the write-through to main memory strategy for managing a cache memory to the write-in cache only strategy. With the write-in cache only strategy, writes to a block already in cache go to the cache only, other writes go directly to main memory. Then, when an old cache block with written data is to be replaced by a new block, the old block is written back to main memory before the new block is written to the cache. Assume that a block of b words must be transferred from main memory to cache; that the cycle time for one word of the cache T_c is less than the cycle time of the main memory T_m; that the miss ratio is θ; and that there are 3 reads per write.

(a) Give a formula for the expected time to process a reference in terms of the above variables using each strategy. Assume that an entire block must be written and read each time a miss occurs using the write-in cache only strategy and that an entire block must be read for each miss using the write-through strategy.

(b) Show that, if $\theta \approx 0$, write-in cache only is better and that if $\theta \approx 1$, write-through is better as one would expect intuitively. Give a general expression describing when write-through is better than write-in cache as a function of θ and b. Assume $T_m/T_c = 10$.

(c) Note that if a read reference is made and the sector is not present, the data is available long before the entire sector has been transferred into the cache. Did your calculations take this into account? If not, why would the *double miss ratio*, defined as the probability of two misses in succession, be a useful statistic? Assuming that the double miss ratio is the miss ratio squared (this is probably pessimistic), compute the expected reference processing time for a 4K and 8K cache.

CH

6

I shall be telling this with a sigh
  Somewhere ages and ages hence:
Two roads diverged in a wood, and I—
  I took the one less traveled by,
And that has made all the difference.

"The Road Not Taken"

Robert Frost

By the Nine Gods he swore it,
  And named a trysting day,
And bade his messengers ride forth
  East and west and south and north,
To summon his array.

"Lays of Ancient Rome"

Lord Macaulay

INTER-CONNECTION NETWORKS

6.1 INTRODUCTION

From one point of view, a computer is a collection of interconnected storage and processing units. Two interesting questions about the interconnections are: (1) Which units are connected to which other units? and (2) What kind of interconnection techniques are used; for example, what are the priorities, speeds, and costs of the interconnections? In previous chapters we have discussed various memory and processing units and given general discussions about which ones are connected to which others. In this chapter we continue this discussion and give a number of details about the capabilities, speeds, and costs of various interconnection networks.

The units we are interconnecting may be of many different types. For example, we may have several registers and one or more arithmetic units within a processor, or we may have a processor, a memory, and several I/O devices which must be interconnected. The above cases both arise in standard uniprocessor systems. In a multiprocessor or parallel machine we have a number of memory units, a number of processors, and perhaps several control units, all of which must be interconnected. At an even higher level we may have a geographically distributed network of computers to be interconnected for the sharing of programs and data. The techniques we describe can be applied in any of these contexts.

Assume we have a computer system that consists of n units which are to be interconnected in some way. The most general model of this situation is given in Fig. 6.1. Each unit has two lines: one that can provide inputs to the interconnection network and another that can accept outputs from it. Each unit passes a word to be transmitted to the interconnection network; these may be

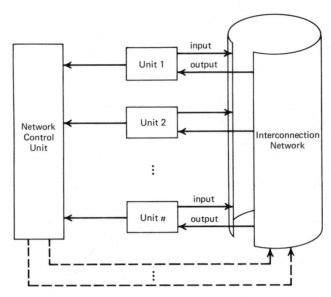

FIGURE 6.1   **General interconnection model.**

data or program words, but we will refer to all such transmitted words as data with respect to the interconnection network. The units (or some of them) also pass control words to the network control unit which then causes the proper transmissions to be carried out. We show one output line from the network to each unit, but in general several input words may be transmitted to the same output unit. As we shall see later, this can lead to added complexities in network design.

The above model is quite general in that the units may be dissimilar and, in fact, some of them may not have (or use) all of the connections shown. The control of the network may be input or output oriented in that units may request that data be sent from them to a specific unit, or they may request that they be sent data from a specific unit. But, in any case, the purpose of the network control unit is to guarantee that units do not make conflicting simultaneous demands on the interconnection network. The timing may be synchronous or asynchronous. The cost and speed of both network control and data transmission will be of concern to us.

To make matters concrete, we now present several examples in more detail. First, we give several examples of the use of a bus; then we discuss alignment networks. The distinction between these two kinds of interconnection networks will be discussed at length later, but the key point is that a bus allows transmissions between just two units at any time, whereas an alignment network allows a number of parallel transmissions to take place. In general, it follows that a bus is a slower, less expensive network than an alignment network.

In all interconnection networks the designer has one simple cost/speed tradeoff in determining the network *transmission path width*. If we have d-bit data to transmit, the network transmission path width can be d bits and each data word is transmitted in its entirety. However, the transmission path width could be just $d/2$ bits. This approximately halves the network cost and doubles the transmission time. This tradeoff obviously holds independently of the overall network capability to perform various interconnections. Typical choices for the transmission path width are one bit, one byte, or a full word.

6.1.1 Bus interconnection networks

First, consider the interconnection of several registers and an arithmetic unit inside a processor, as shown in Fig. 6.2. The bus shown here can be used by any of the registers for transmitting data to or from the arithmetic unit. Thus, we call it a *shared bus*. Here the standard control unit controls the bus as well, guaranteeing that only one data transmission is attempted at any time, and using priorities built into the hardware to maintain proper sequencing. In Section 3.5.5 we sketched the use of a bus in a simple processor and in Section 4.2.2 it was discussed further. In a processor with two arithmetic units or a fast single arithmetic unit, more than one bus could be used for parallel transmissions. An example of this was presented in Fig. 1.12, for a multifunction processor, and more details were discussed in Section 3.6.1.

Various schemes may be used to implement a bus, but a simple scheme employs a multiplexer tree to fan-in data from one selected source unit of the n units joined by the bus, and a demultiplexer tree to select one destination unit. Thus if 2-input, 2-output gates are used, a total of $O(n)$ gates per data bit are

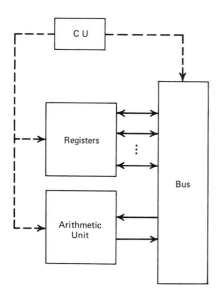

FIGURE 6.2   **Processor bus.**

required in a bus. Often the term *bus* refers to data lines as well as other lines used for controlling the data transmission.

Busses like the one in Fig. 6.2 normally transmit full words in parallel and work in a clocked (synchronous) way and at high speed, because they must be matched to the speed of the arithmetic unit. Another kind of bus may be used to connect a number of I/O devices to the main memory of a computer, as in Fig. 6.3. In this case the devices are relatively slow compared with the memory, and there may be wide variance between the speeds of individual I/O devices. Priorities between I/O interrupts were discussed in Section 4.4.3.3 and we shall discuss several such implementations in this chapter. Busses used in this context usually transmit a byte at a time and may be synchronous or asynchronous depending on the manufacturer (see Section 6.3). Sometimes they are multiplexed, being used in a time-shared way by the devices; for example, read one card, print one line, read the next card, print the next line, and so on.

A third type of bus is illustrated in Fig. 6.4. This is a *dedicated bus* which is used to transmit information between the control units of two computers. The control of this bus may be carried out by the two control units in a shared way, or the control units may be arranged in a master/slave relation. In any case, it must be guaranteed that both control units do not put information on the bus simultaneously, so we might use two busses, one dedicated to transmission in each direction. Sometimes the term *bus* is used to imply a shared bus, so our use of the term *dedicated bus* may be regarded as a degenerate case.

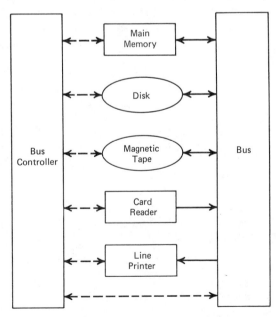

FIGURE 6.3   **Shared I/O bus.**

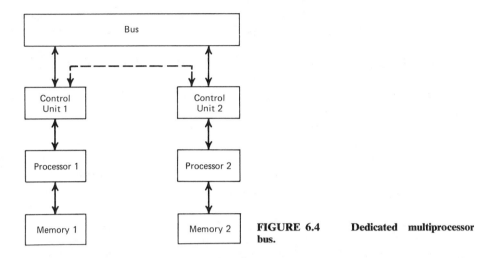

FIGURE 6.4 Dedicated multiprocessor bus.

Although it is difficult to make a rigorous distinction between a bus and an alignment network, in most cases the following characteristics will distinguish them. With a bus, at any instant of time only one pair of units may be communicating. Many units may be attached to the bus, however, and they may be time-sharing the bus in the sense that various pairs of units are allowed to transmit data and communicate via the bus in rapid succession. Thus to an outside observer, the bus may appear to serve many units "at once," whereas only one pair of units is active at any instant of time. In an alignment network, on the other hand, a number of pairs of units may be communicating at the same instant of time. Thus, alignment networks are usually faster but more expensive than busses, as we shall learn shortly.

6.1.2 Alignment networks

We have seen three uses of busses as interconnection networks in computer systems. Next, we consider a class of networks that we call *alignment networks*. The name is derived from the situation where many units in a computer system have data that they wish to transmit simultaneously to other units in the system. The problem is to align the data elements with the correct processors or memory units so that the next step of the computation can proceed as quickly as possible.

There are several ways in which alignment networks and busses can be confused. One is by the use of *parallel busses*. For example, if we have n registers in Fig. 6.2, suppose we use n parallel busses—one for each register. Then we could transmit two arguments and return a result at the same time using three different registers and three busses. If viewed as a single unit, these parallel busses could be regarded as an alignment network. Similar arguments could be given for Figs. 6.3 and 6.4 (in fact, we discussed two busses in the context of Fig. 6.4). These ideas also can overlap depending on how one views time; as we learned above, busses may be time multiplexed so as to give the appearance of carrying out more than one transmission at once. On the other hand, as we shall see, alignment networks may have internal conflicts which force some units to retransmit their data on subsequent cycles. In the limit, conflicts could cause an alignment network to transmit just one data word at a time and thus be reduced to the effective speed of a bus.

In Figs. 1.11, 1.14, and 1.15, we saw examples of the use of alignment networks in multiprocessor, pipeline, and parallel computers, respectively. These were all used to interconnect processors and memories. Transmissions from processor to processor, memory to memory, or back and forth between processors and memories could be carried out.

One example of an alignment network which is fast and quite capable relative to other networks is a standard *crossbar switch*—a commonly used telephone switching network. In Fig. 6.5, we show m memories connected to p processors using an $m \times p$ crossbar alignment network. This allows simultaneous conflict-free transmissions from any memory to any processor, assuming we have a one-to-one mapping. A crossbar switch interconnecting n units may be thought of as n parallel busses between these units and thus contains $O(n^2)$ gates of 2 inputs and 2 outputs each (recall from Section 6.1.1 that one such bus has $O(n)$ gates). We discuss this in more detail in Section 6.5.2, but it should be clear that for large n, there is a vast difference in cost and performance between a single bus and a crossbar switch.

If we wish to allow one-to-many transmissions in a crossbar switch, that is, to allow some kind of broadcasting, this can be arranged using a more complex network. Many-to-one transmissions lead to conflicts, because two or more results cannot appear at the same time on the same physical wires. Therefore,

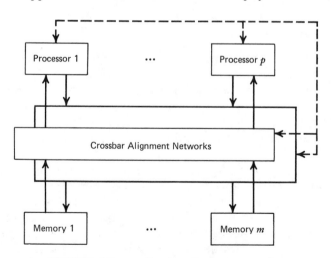

FIGURE 6.5   **Crossbar alignment networks.**

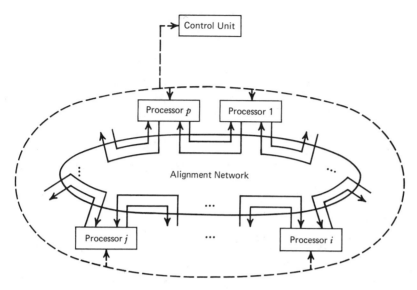

FIGURE 6.6   ± 1 **uniform shift alignment network.**

provisions must be made to avoid such conflicts. For example, if several processors send results to the same memory at the same time, either we can detect the destination conflict, accept one output, and recycle the network until all results have been transmitted, or we can provide multiple ports to each memory. The latter involves an extra register at each port, conflict resolution logic, and multiple memory cycles to clear all the ports. We discussed this in Section 5.4.2.1 and will return to it in Section 6.5.1.

Notice that the alignment network of Fig. 6.5 is bidirectional in that each processor and each memory has an input and an output connection to the network. Thus, we may think of it as two distinct alignment networks or as one with $p + m$ inputs and outputs. Fig. 6.5 shows control lines from the processors to set the switches, and back to the processors in case of conflicts. We will carefully relate this to Fig. 6.1 in Section 6.4.1.

In Fig. 6.6, we show a very simple alignment network, one that can perform simple *uniform shifts* rather quickly. The connections are between adjacent processors in the form of a ring; each unit shift requires one cycle. Thus, uniform data alignments (for all i) from processor i to processor $i \pm k \pmod{p}$, can be performed quickly for small k. It is important to note that although all p data elements may be transmitted simultaneously here (unlike bus transmission), we can perform only a simple set of input-output mappings in one cycle. This is in contrast with the crossbar network, which could form an arbitrary permutation in one cycle. By a cycle here we refer to one or a few clocks (see Section 6.4.2).

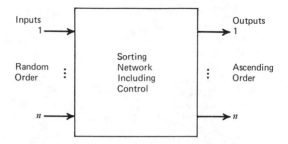

FIGURE 6.7   **Internally controlled alignment network.**

For example, to execute the loop

$$\text{DO} \quad S_2 \quad I \leftarrow 1, 10$$
$$S_2 \qquad A(I) \leftarrow A(I+3)$$

we could fetch elements $A(4) \cdots A(13)$, perhaps from memories $4, \ldots, 13$ to processors $4, \ldots, 13$, assuming memory i is attached to processor i. Then in three cycles we could shift $A(4) \cdots A(13)$ to processors $1, \ldots, 10$, respectively. Finally, we could store the shifted elements in memories $1, \ldots, 10$.

However, the arbitrary permutation required by the loop

$$\text{DO} \quad S_3 \quad I \leftarrow 1, 10$$
$$S_3 \qquad C(B(I)) \leftarrow A(I)$$

where the contents of $B(1), \ldots, B(10)$ are a permutation of the integers $1, \ldots, 10$, may be rather time-consuming and difficult to control. In the worst case, this could be performed by making p individual shifts by 1, checking each time that any of the data elements had arrived at its final destination.

Our third example is an alignment network with internal control—a *sorting network* as shown in Fig. 6.7. The inputs are an unordered set of numbers. The outputs are the same set of numbers arranged in ascending order at output ports 1 to n. Such networks operate by comparing numbers pairwise and transmitting them between comparators to yield a sorted list. We return to these networks in Section 6.5.5.

6.1.3 References

Interconnection schemes used in real computers can be found in manufacturers' manuals. Several specific references to published material will be given in this chapter. General discussions of machine interconnection schemes may be found in [Ensl74]. Communication ideas, especially for interactive and time-shared computers, are presented in Chapter 3 of [Wats70]. A survey of bussing techniques with an annotated bibliography is presented in [TJJK72] and alignment networks are surveyed in [Thur74].

6.2 I/O TYPE INTERCONNECTION NETWORKS

6.2.1 Introduction

In this section we deal with interconnection networks between CPUs and various kinds of I/O devices. Different manufacturers have adopted a rather wide range of solutions and terminology for dealing with this problem. However, a common thread is that just two or at most a few pairs of units are communicating with each other at once through the network, although many units may be connected to the network. Furthermore, if more than one pair of units is communicating, they are usually engaged in executing independent tasks. We present several basic principles of such networks and introduce some uniform terminology, and then illustrate several manufacturers' actual methods.

The basic problem here is that the CPU and main memory must be connected to a wide variety of I/O devices. These devices operate over a wide range of speeds—from card readers at 100 cards per minute to disks at more than 10^7 bits per second. They also operate in a number of different ways. Some only generate information for the computer (e.g., card readers), others only accept information from the computer (e.g., card punches and line printers), whereas others work both ways (e.g., magnetic tapes, disks, and user terminals). We will deal with the details of memory hierarchies in Chapter 7, but for the moment we can imagine a variety of different peripheral I/O devices with which the CPU and main memory (collectively the *main frame*) must communicate.

Our basic problem is: How should all of these I/O devices be connected to the main frame of the computer? This can be divided into two parts—the transmission of data and the control of the transmission. Various key points which we will be discussing are summarized in Fig. 6.8; these are functions that must be carried out at the I/O interface in order to allow I/O devices to communicate with the computer main frame.

The data may be transmitted one bit, byte, or word at a time. The amount of parallelism here must be chosen by trading off the cost of more lines with the resulting speed increases. The format or type of code to use in transmitting the data may also be a question. Sometimes a peripheral device may generate one type of encoded information, whereas the main frame deals with another. Code conversion may be done in the course of transmission—or at either end—for example, between Hollerith card formats and ASCII or EBCDIC characters. Furthermore, parity bits may be attached and checked here. Thus we see that in addition to transmitting the data, there may be a small amount of processing carried out at the I/O interface.

The other half of this problem concerns the control of the data transmission. A fundamental choice is whether to use the CPU to control I/O or to make the I/O interface a separate, free-standing unit that can handle I/O in parallel with normal CPU operations (as suggested by Fig. 6.8). There are obvious

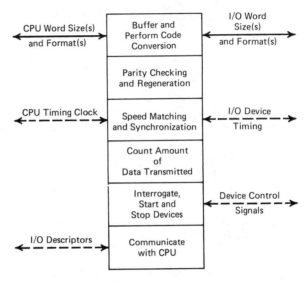

FIGURE 6.8   **I/O interface functions.**

speed/cost tradeoffs here. Another important question is how the I/O process is timed—with the CPU clock or using some kind of timing information generated in the I/O devices themselves. In any case, the speeds of two very different systems (CPU and I/O) must be matched here. Furthermore, one must decide the amount of data to be sent in one period of the interface's attention. In other words, do we send just a byte or word and then have the interface take some action, or do we send a whole block of data in one burst? In addition to speed and cost, the following questions concern both the flexibility and reliability of the system. How many independent data paths can be handled by one interface and how many independent interfaces may a system have?

It should be clear at this point that many design options are available in this area. None of the problems is very difficult individually, but together they form a rather complicated problem. Unless painstaking care is given to details at this level, the overall system can be made difficult for users or software writers.

In what follows, a number of details concerning I/O interfaces will be presented, and in Section 6.3 we will discuss the actual I/O schemes used by several manufacturers.

6.2.2   I/O channel operation

In order to introduce various manufacturers' solutions to the I/O communication problem, in this section we will give a brief functional sketch of how all such systems work. We still use the term *I/O channel* as a catchall to refer to the hardware used to carry out the functions of Fig. 6.8. (Most manufacturers have something they call a channel, but they often use other boxes in conjunction with it.) Later we will refer specifically to the details of several real systems. We now discuss the types of commands executed by I/O channels and outline their operation. Although not every aspect of the following discussion holds for each manufacturer's real I/O systems, the general spirit permeates them all.

Fundamentally, an I/O channel may be regarded as a small computer that can operate independently of the CPU. It executes a small number of commands, usually dealing with bytes on the I/O device side and full words on the CPU side. It should be observed that most I/O devices cannot operate without some kind of device controller. We will usually show the channel communicating with device controllers, which in turn operate their respective I/O devices. The types of I/O channel commands usually available are the following.

First, because devices may be connected to more than one channel, the channel must be able to determine whether or not the device is busy. If it is not busy, the channel must be able to activate the device through its controller. This may involve starting a motor and advancing the I/O medium to a predetermined position. Next, the channel must be able to instruct the I/O device to send or receive data. The channel itself knows how much and it counts the number of bytes it has handled. Thus it can stop at an appropriate point. When an I/O transaction is finished, the channel must disconnect the I/O device, thus freeing it for other activities.

The above paragraph focused on the I/O device side of the channel. On the other side, the channel must deal with the CPU and main memory. The channel must know the starting address for accessing main memory, and by counting bytes or words, it knows where to stop. Usually, the channel is allowed to preempt the CPU and steal a memory cycle whenever it needs one because I/O devices are relatively slow and once a channel buffer is full, it must be cleared to avoid missing subsequent transmissions.

As we have said, I/O can be initiated either by the CPU or by the I/O devices themselves. The communication between the channel and the CPU is a key design question here. At one extreme, the "channel" may be the CPU itself. This was the case historically and is the approach used in some modern minicomputers. It may be called "programmed I/O" because the entire I/O transaction is controlled by an ordinary program executed in the CPU. In other machines, the channel is integrated into the CPU and has some hardware of its own but shares other hardware with the CPU. This is the case with low end of the line models of the IBM 360 and 370. When these machines are handling I/O for very fast I/O devices, they may have to suspend other computations, because the program they execute to control the I/O transaction takes all of the available time.

Next in progression are free-standing I/O channels that communicate with the CPU via interrupts and then only at the beginning or end of an I/O transaction; such is the case at the top of the IBM 360 and 370 lines and a number of other machines, as we shall see. The channel programs are initiated by the CPU when it encounters an I/O instruction. The channel programs are held in the machine's main memory as are other channel information words, and in this sense the CPU and channels can be regarded as multiple, independent processors competing for cycles in one shared system memory.

In some cases, channels may take the form of full-blown minicomputers. The CDC 6600 introduced this idea and other machines have used it as well. Such channels have their own memory and large instruction repertoires. Thus the CDC 6600 and its peripheral processors can be regarded as a tightly coupled multimachine system. In Section 6.3 the IBM and CDC approaches, as well as those of DEC and Burroughs, will be discussed. Although every manufacturer uses a different scheme, these four seem to provide a fairly broad representation of all the schemes.

6.2.3 Shared bus and star connections

A clear distinction can be made between different manufacturers' methods of interfacing the channel with a collection of I/O devices. Two limiting cases are the shared bus and the star connections shown in Fig. 6.9. The IBM 370 typifies the use of a shared bus. Here the bus runs out from the channel and through various I/O devices. All transmissions flow up and down this shared bus, as we shall discuss in Section 6.3.2. In the *star configuration*, typified by the Burroughs B7700, the channel is located at the center of a number of I/O devices, each of which has a dedicated bus connected to the channel, as we shall see in Section 6.3.4.

The distinction shows up in the modus operandi of these systems as well as in their topology. In controlling a shared bus, the channel can send out a device address, not knowing if the device is there and not knowing or caring about its position on the bus. When the address reaches each device, it is checked and the appropriate device identifies itself back to the channel. If the desired device is not there, the address passes through all the devices and retruns to the channel, thereby informing the channel of the device's absence. By contrast, in a star configuration, the channel knows which of its lines is hooked to particular devices and it communicates directly with the appropriate device.

It follows that the star-type connection can easily be operated in a *synchronous* or centrally clocked way. Thus in one clock period a channel selects a device and then some fixed number of clocks later it expects a response—the number of clocks depending on the type of device. In contrast, the shared bus connection is usually *asynchronous*. The channel need not even know the speeds of the various devices. It merely waits until a response comes back or a time-out[1] occurs. Thus, devices of a wide range of speeds can be hooked to one channel with equal ease, and the channel need not make any distinction between them. The above distinction between synchronous and asynchronous

---

[1] A time-out occurs after the wait has exceeded the maximum possible response time required for *any* type of device that might be connected to the bus.

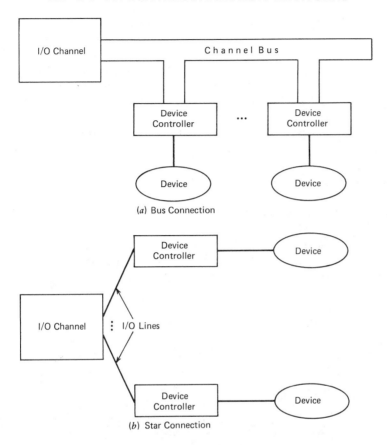

FIGURE 6.9   **Channel device interfaces. (*a*) Bus connection. (*b*) Star connection.**

operation should become clearer when the details of several schemes are presented in Section 6.3. We emphasize, however, that many variations have been invented, so synchronous shared busses, asynchronous stars, and so on, are all perfectly reasonable.

Although the asynchronous-type connection may appear to be more flexible and the synchronous type may appear to be faster, we shall see that manufacturers have devised a number of variations on these themes so that both systems work well in practice. In fact, the choice seems to depend on the designer's personal preference and company traditions.

6.2.4   Polling and data communications

I/O channels usually are operated on the basis of *contention.* This means that various I/O device controllers compete or contend for the use of a channel. Some priority scheme is used to decide which contender will be allocated the next burst of time in the channel.

In contrast to contention, a collection of I/O devices can be managed by *polling*. This means that each device is interrogated in some fixed sequence and asked if it wants to do something. If it does, it is granted a short burst of time to transmit one or more characters, and then the polling resumes.

Usually, polling is used when there are many I/O devices, each of which has similar characteristics. It could thus be regarded as a contention system with priorities assigned symmetrically on a round-robin basis. A typical use of a polled system is in connecting many terminals to a computer. When a user completes a key stroke, the terminal holds the character in a buffer register and when the terminal is polled, it sends one or more characters to the computer. Note that transmissions in either direction can be handled on the basis of contention or polling.

Another way of viewing this situation is to observe that in the case of polling, whether the transmission is from terminal to computer or vice versa, the computer is the active or master unit, whereas the terminals are passive or slave units. On the other hand, in the contention situation, the source of a transmission is the active (master) unit and the destination is the passive (slave) unit.

In some computer systems, many remote terminals are connected to a central computer; the terminals may even be in distant cities. This leads to the subject of *data communications* (or datacom), which we will not explore in detail. However, because polling is often used in data communications, we will briefly consider the subject.

Suppose a number of remote terminals are to be connected via a long-distance telephone line to a central computer. Instead of paying one phone bill per terminal, one high-speed, long-distance line may be leased from the telephone company and interfaced through a minicomputer to a collection of terminals in, say, one building or city. Each of these terminals may be connected to the minicomputer by dedicated wires or dial-up local phone service. The minicomputer is called a *line concentrator* and may operate by polling the local terminals. It then buffers their messages and transmits them in bursts to the central computer. Similarly, it can handle messages from the central computer to the local terminals. In this way it smoothes out and manages the flow of information on the high-speed, long-distance line.

Several types of data communications lines are possible. A *simplex* line can transmit in only one direction, a *half duplex* line can transmit in either direction but in only one direction at a time, and a *full duplex* (or simply *duplex*) line can transmit in both directions simultaneously. These distinctions depend on the line, the software, and the hardware used to connect the units to the line at either end. A *modulator* is needed to convert the digital signals to whatever kind of signals are sent along the telephone lines, and a *demodulator* is needed at the other end to reconvert the signals. Often, both the modulation and demodulation are handled by one unit, called a *modem*, for obvious reasons.

It is interesting to note that data communications people describe the topology of their networks using a nomenclature somewhat different from that used for I/O within a computer system. When two devices are connected, the connection is called *point-to-point*. A *star* connection is like that of Fig. 6.9*b*, where the center is a main computer or a line concentrator. A bus-like connection (as in Fig. 6.9*a* with a computer in place of the channel) is called a *multidrop* connection.

With this bit of terminology, we end this section. For further study, [DaBa73], [Dave71], and [Mart70] are recommended. In Section 6.6 we shall return to the use of data communications ideas in computer networks.

6.3 REAL I/O SCHEMES

In this section we present the I/O schemes used by several manufacturers. First, we discuss bus-type connections that are used in the Unibus of the DEC minicomputers, and have been used in most IBM machines over the years. These are followed by the star-type connections of CDC and Burroughs.

6.3.1 DEC Unibus[2] I/O communications

We begin our discussion of CPU communications with I/O devices by considering the most naive and historically first-used scheme. This is often used in microprocessor-based systems and in minicomputers. Specifically, let us consider the DEC PDP-11 as shown in Fig. 6.10 with slow and fast I/O devices attached to its Unibus.

The Unibus serves as the only communication path between CPU, memory, and peripheral devices. Normal address space in the PDP-11 includes the main memory locations as well as 4096 words of addressable registers in the peripheral device controllers; that is, the high 4K addresses access peripheral registers not main memory locations. Thus the CPU can manipulate memory locations and peripheral controllers with the same instructions. Indeed, the PDP-11 does not have a special set of I/O instructions as found in most computers.

The naive approach referred to above concerns the slow I/O devices in Fig. 6.10. The Unibus consists of 56 lines variously dedicated to transmitting addresses (18 bits), data (16 bits), and a number of control signals (22 bits). Using these lines, the CPU communicates with the slow device controller and causes input or output activities to proceed. While the CPU is controlling I/O, it does nothing else and, hence, computation time is lost. But if the device is slow enough relative to the CPU, it seldom demands attention and the load on the CPU is not noticed. "Slow" here really means that on the average the bit rate of this device (in terms of data, addresses, and control signals) is low relative to the CPU speed.

---

[2] DEC, PDP, and UNIBUS are registered trademarks of Digital Equipment Corporation.

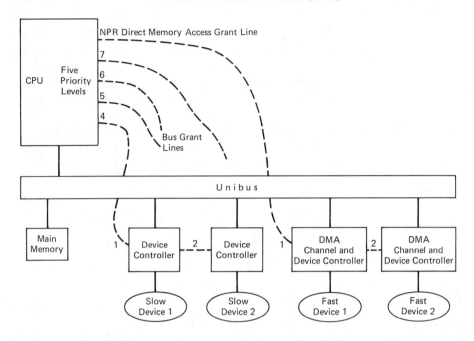

FIGURE 6.10   **PDP-11 peripheral configuration.**

In Fig. 6.10 we show two slow devices as well as two fast devices. Somehow priorities between these devices must be established. A simple scheme—the one used in the PDP-11—is first to establish priorities between similar types of devices based on the order in which the devices are electrically connected to the CPU. Physically, a grant line that is part of the Unibus cable (one of the 22 control signals mentioned earlier) is connected from the CPU to the device with highest priority, from there it is connected to the next highest priority device, and so on down to the lowest priority device on that line. Thus, in Fig. 6.10 communications between slow device 2 and the CPU can be carried out only if slow device 1 does not require service, and so on. This type of connection in which a device's priority depends on its physical (i.e., electrical) connection relative to other devices in series with it, is sometimes called *daisy chaining*. It is simple, but effective. Various manufacturers give the physical daisy chain priority line different names; for example, DEC lines are called grant lines, as shown in Fig. 6.10.

In fact, the PDP-11 allows up to four such sets of daisy-chained devices to be attached to the Unibus, and any number of devices may be attached to each daisy chain. Each daisy chain is attached to the CPU via the Unibus through a port, the ports being arranged in a sequence of four priority levels, as shown in Fig. 6.10, and this establishes a second type of priority, usually between devices of dissimilar speeds. We will return to a discussion of priorities shortly, and a detailed example of the operation of a daisy chain for IBM channels will be given in the next section.

Let us consider an example of a peripheral that wants to send a word to memory. Its priority to do this depends on gaining control of the Unibus, which is determined by the CPU port to which its daisy chain is connected, as well as its position on the daisy chain. Assuming our peripheral has the highest priority, it first seizes the bus, it then interrupts whatever program is currently running and causes the *processor status* (PS) word and instruction location register to be saved on a push-down stack. It then supplies the CPU with an address in memory·of an *interrupt vector* for itself. This is a pair of words that are used to replace the old PS information and instruction location in the processor. Note that this process is similar to the swapping of PSWs in IBM machines. Each peripheral device has its own interrupt vector, unlike the IBM approach.

Now the processor executes whichever peripheral device service routine was specified by the interrupt vector. It can determine just what the device wanted (e.g., parity error, previous transaction done, new input to send) by interrogating the device's status register. In our example, the device wants to send a word to memory so the CPU will read the word from a device controller register to the CPU. Then it will write the word into a memory buffer after checking parity, and so on.

Such transmissions between peripheral devices and main memory through the CPU are carried out in an interlocked way, wherein the sender waits until the receiver acknowledges receipt of a word before sending another word. Control signals pass back and forth, making one end the master and the other end the slave at appropriate points in time. The Unibus has a maximum data rate of 40×10^6 b/s operating in this way. We will give a more elaborate discussion of interlocked transmission when we discuss IBM channels in Section 6.3.2.

Upon completion of its activities the peripheral device service routine executes a Return From Interrupt instruction that pops the information from the stack and restores the CPU to its state before the interrupt. A device service routine can be interrupted by a higher priority peripheral, in which case it will be suspended by the above scheme until the higher priority device service routine is finished.

Bus control is decided on the basis of the priorities mentioned earlier, in parallel with data transfers. Thus, a lookahead scheme is in effect, which allows the next bus control priority to be decided while a previous peripheral device is using the bus.

DMA techniques

Now we consider the fast devices of Fig. 6.10. By "fast" here we mean that if the CPU had to handle every word transmission between one of these devices and main memory, the CPU would be so swamped that it could not keep up with its normal computations. In order to take over the role of the CPU in I/O transactions, we include here extra logic in the device controller. This *direct memory access* (DMA) channel[3] logic consists of registers for buffering data, main memory address, word count, and control bits. The CPU initializes the DMA channel, which then carries out an entire I/O block transmission of the correct number of words. Upon completion, the DMA channel interrupts the CPU to inform it that I/O block transmission is complete. In the meantime, the CPU can continue to execute a program, overlapped with the DMA I/O activity.

Earlier we pointed out that there were four daisy chains, each of which had a different interrupt priority level in the CPU. The DMA channels are connected to a fifth daisy chain, which has a higher priority level called the nonprocessor request (NPR) level. This is *not* a processor interrupt priority, however, but only a bus control priority. In other words, this has priority to steal a cycle from the bus and main memory, so it is like the memory access priorities discussed in Section 5.4.4. It does not need to cause the processor state to be saved because the DMA channel logic can control I/O transmission by itself (without the help of a CPU program) and thus saves interrupt time.

In the PDP-11, I/O interrupts can be masked, but in a rather different way from IBM's (recall Section 4.4.3.4). The CPU of the PDP-11 has a 3-bit

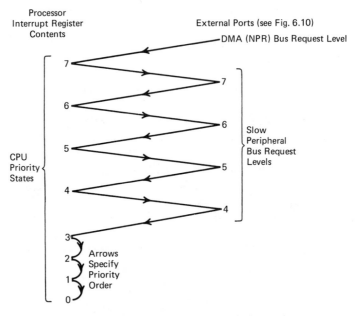

FIGURE 6.11   **PDP-11 priorities.**

[3] DEC does not refer to "channels" in its literature, but the effect of DMA transfers is analogous to what are commonly called channels, and the term carries over nicely to the following sections.

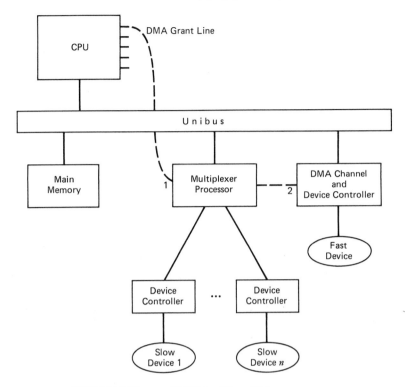

FIGURE 6.12   PDP-11 with multiplexer processor.

register, which indicates the priority level of the CPU. If the CPU is handling a
level 6 interrupt, it can set this register to 6, thus masking out all external
interrupts with priorities lower than 6. Because this register can be changed
under program control, the effect is to change the masking function dynamically.

In Fig. 6.11 we show the 8 settings of the CPU priority register and the 5
external bus priority ports. The DMA port (also called NPR) has the highest
priority and 0 is the lowest priority. The CPU can thus put itself in a priority
state higher than any external interrupt exept the DMA port, or lower than the
level 4 external port. Levels 0, 1, and 2 can be used to define a hierarchy of
internal interrupt levels that could be used by interrupt driven software
processes. For more details about PDP-11 I/O, see [DECo71b].

Next, consider the case of a PDP-11 with many slow devices (e.g., user
terminals) attached—so many that collectively they interfere with the CPU as
much as a fast device would. A normal method of solving this problem would
be to build some kind of multiplexer DMA channel; that is, one that could
handle a number of slow devices in an interleaved way. An easy solution to this
problem would be to hook up another small processor to serve this purpose,

perhaps a smaller DEC processor or some kind of microprocessor (recall the line concentrator of Section 6.2.4). We show such a configuration in Fig. 6.12. Indeed, the use of microprogrammed minicomputers in this role is now becoming popular (Burroughs uses this approach, for example). But we are getting ahead of our story.

The multiplexer processor of Fig. 6.12 must appear to each slow device controller as the CPU did for the slow devices in Fig. 6.10. And it must appear to the bus and memory as the DMA channel did for the fast devices in Fig. 6.10. From this perspective, it will be easy to understand the IBM channels, which we consider next. The details of multiplexer-type channels (like the multiplexer processor of Fig. 6.12) will be discussed in what follows.

6.3.2   IBM I/O channels

The IBM 360 and 370 series machines use the kind of channels we describe next. Although there are differences in implementation between different models in the series, an important advantage is that all of the channels present logically equivalent interfaces to device controllers. We will describe a full-blown hardware system first and then discuss various scaled-down versions of it. For more details about IBM channels, see [Pade64] and [BrET72].

The I/O activities of the IBM 370/165 are carried out in an organization as shown in Fig. 6.13. Before exploring the details of this figure, it is instructive to compare it with the PDP-11 I/O structure of Fig. 6.12. A number of direct analogies are easy to establish. The DMA use of the DEC Unibus serves exactly the same role as the IBM *internal data bus* and a selector channel—as an interface between the CPU, main memory, and high-speed I/O devices. A PDP-11 that has a device controller and one fast device attached to its DMA port would correspond to the selector channel of Fig. 6.13 with a single disk attached. In a PDP-11 with several DMA channels, priorities are established via daisy chaining (see Fig. 6.10), whereas priorities between several IBM selector channels are established by arbiter logic.

The multiplexer processor that we invented in Fig. 6.12 to handle a multitude of slow devices corresponds to the multiplexer channels of Fig. 6.13. In Fig. 6.12, we really did not explain how the multiplexer processor could keep all of its device controllers working; there is another level of priority resolution that was overlooked there. Because the IBM channels are not hypothetical as was Fig. 6.12, we now introduce another bus—the *channel bus*—to tie a collection of devices to a channel.

A multiplexer channel appears to its device controllers very much as the CPU of the PDP-11 appeared to its slow device controllers. It handles transactions on a character-by-character basis for all of its device controllers, and passes these characters on to the internal data bus, which in turn leads to main memory. The five daisy chains of the PDP-11 are expanded in number by IBM, as we will see below, but priorities on each channel bus are determined

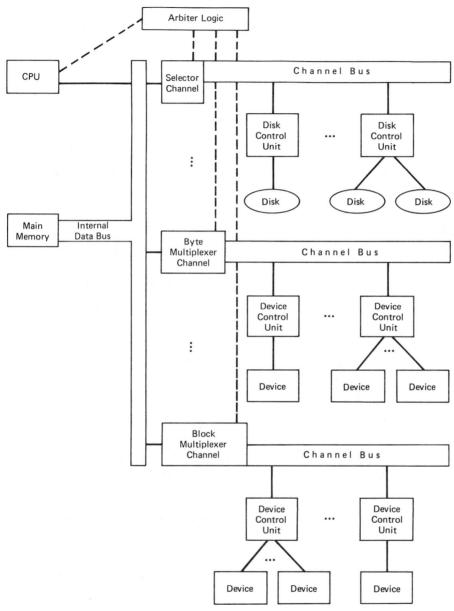

FIGURE 6.13 **IBM I/O configuration.**

463

by a separate daisy chain for that bus. In the PDP-11, for an input transmission the Unibus first provided a link between the device controller and CPU; this corresponds to the IBM channel bus. Secondly, the Unibus provided a path from the CPU to the main memory; this corresponds to the internal data bus of Fig. 6.13. We will give a more detailed explanation of the operation of the channel busses after discussing a few more details about Fig. 6.13.

There are two basic modes of IBM channel operation. In one mode, one transaction is carried out from beginning to end. This is the only way *selector channels* can operate, and is called selector mode or sometimes burst mode. In the other mode, several I/O transactions are time multiplexed. Byte and (to a limited extent) block *multiplexer channels* can operate in this mode—switching their attention from one device controller to another before the whole I/O transaction is complete. *Byte multiplexer channels* are used in the IBM 360 to handle a number of slower devices, whereas selector channels handle high-speed devices, although a device may be attached to any type of channel that can support its data rate. Byte multiplexer channels can switch from one transaction to another between byte transmissions, thus incurring a good deal of overhead time penalty. *Block multiplexer channels* (introduced on the 360/85 and in the 370 series) are designed to operate faster because they can switch from one device to another only between larger blocks of data. The design of block multiplexer channels was based on a good deal of simulation, as reported in [BrET72]. The three types are shown in Fig. 6.13.

Normally, channels handle 8 bits at a time, assembling 64-bit words to transmit to memory for input and vice versa for output. To enhance their speed in block transfers, two bytes in parallel can be handled by block multiplexer channels with fast I/O devices. Normally, up to seven channels may be attached to a Model 165, for example, but this can be extended to a maximum of 12 channels. Up to 8 device control units are normally attached to any channel (although up to 256 are possible). Each device controller may handle a number of devices. A total of up to 192 or 256 (for different models) devices may be attached to a multiplexer channel.

Both types of multiplexer channels can also be used as selector channels simply by not allowing them to switch attention from one I/O transaction until it is completed. Selector and block multiplexer channels operate at data rates of up to 12×10^6 bits/sec., (the 2-byte parallel version, at twice that). The maximum data rate for byte multiplexer channels is less than 1.5×10^6 bits/sec. Thus the channel capacity is cut by a factor of eight due to the overhead of multiplexer control.[4]

Multiplexer channels must contain information at any time for all of the devices that they are multiplexing. The term *subchannel* is used to refer to the storage space associated with each of the multiplexed I/O operations. A small scratch pad memory is included in the channel to hold this subchannel

---

[4] Actual channel speeds are configuration dependent to some extent.

information. For the transmissions of each such subchannel, the memory must hold a main memory address to be accessed, the number of bytes to be transmitted, and the address in main memory of the next channel command to execute. (Notice that this same information is necessary in a selector channel.) When a new command is fetched by a channel, it contains this information as well as control information which it passes to the device controller. The device controller has registers to hold bits that direct the device in its operation (e.g., read or write), that indicate the status of the device (e.g., on or off), and that include other control information that is particular to various devices.

Earlier, it was pointed out that IBM I/O priorities are established at two levels and by two different mechanisms: daisy chains and the arbiter. On each channel bus, a daisy chain scheme is used to decide which device is next serviced by the channel. The order in which the priority line cable is connected to various devices determines a device's priority, as discussed for the PDP-11. Because the priority cable makes a round trip from the channel, through all its device controllers, and back to the channel, there is some flexibility here in permuting the priority. The arbiter logic operates on the basis of fixed priority assignment and, in fact, arbitrates between the several I/O channels and the CPU requests for the internal data bus. It is part of what IBM calls the bus control unit (BCU). Generally, the channels are given higher priorities than the CPU, because (as mentioned previously) they are slower and more sensitive to time delays.

One important feature of IBM channels is their flexibility in handling I/O devices of widely different speeds. This is provided by the interlocked communication on the channel busses. We will discuss the operation of the channel busses in terms of the simplified model of Fig. 6.14. Consider the situation where some device wants to send one byte of information to main memory; an output transmission is similar.

Phase I

Initially, control line ① is used to signal the channel; this simply ORs requests from all device controllers, so any number could make simultaneous requests. Now, the channel must determine which device to service. Priority line ② serves this purpose, with priorities being established by the daisy chain. The first controller on the daisy chain that has an open switch is selected— controller 2 in Fig. 6.14. Thus, any number of controllers can open their switches at once, but only the first open one gets a reply back from the channel to proceed. These switches may be opened at any time, concurrently with using control line ① to signal the channel that transmission is desired. The key point is that when the channel replies back to the controllers via the priority line, there can be only one "first open switch" on the daisy chain, and this controller is selected. In our example, controller 2 proceeds by sending its identification number (address) to the channel via the bus.

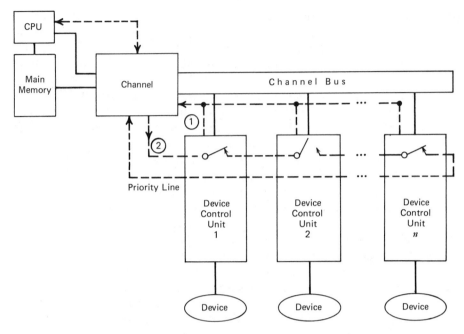

FIGURE 6.14   **Simplified IBM bus control diagram.**

Phase II

The channel replies to device controller 2 on the bus (the bus has a number of control lines in addition to the data lines) that it is ready to accept a transmission. Note that control line ② could not be used to reply to device controller 2, because other devices between the selected device and the channel may have opened their device controller switches and signaled on line ① that they want to start transmitting. When device controller 2 gets the channel's signal, it serves a byte of information, plus parity bit to the channel via the bus. If the transmission is successful, that is, if no parity error occurs, the channel uses the bus to signal device controller 2, and a byte transmission is complete.

There are now two possible ways to proceed. If the channel is a selector channel, then once a transmission has begun, it continues until it is complete. For a selector channel, in the above example we continue to transmit bytes as described in the Phase II paragraph above. The reader can now reread the Phase II paragraph, noting that the signal on the bus at the end of the paragraph corresponds to the one mentioned at the beginning of the paragraph, in the case of a selector channel. In fact, the Phase II paragraph describes an infinite loop that can be used to send as many bytes as desired! Of course, because the channel is in the loop and because the channel contains a count of the number of bytes to be transmitted, the channel breaks the loop when the count is satisfied.

Instead of the selector channel operation described above, we could have a multiplexer channel. In this case, rather than repeating the Phase II paragraph as discussed for a selector channel, we disconnect from the channel and if more data is to be sent, repeat the Phase I paragraph followed again by the Phase II paragraph. This is effective in opening the use of the channel to the highest priority device controller after each transmission.

To contrast the operation of the three IBM channel types, consider the transmission of blocks A, B, and C, where A is a sequence of bytes A_1, $A_2, \ldots, A_n$ and similarly for B and C. The selector channel transmission would appear as a time sequence of the form

$$A_1 A_2 \cdots A_n B_1 B_2 \cdots B_n C_1 C_2 \cdots C_n,$$

whereas the byte multiplexer time sequence might be

$$A_1 B_1 A_2 C_1 B_2 A_3 \cdots A_n \cdots C_n \cdots B_n,$$

and the block multiplexer (with a block size of k bytes) might produce

$$A_1 A_2 \cdots A_k B_1 B_2 \cdots B_k C_1 C_2 \cdots C_k \cdots B_{n-k+1} \cdots B_n C_{n-k+1} \cdots C_n.$$

The precise details depend, of course, on the relative speeds and priorities of the various devices involved in the transmissions.

We pointed out previously that in smaller models of the IBM 360 and 370, the channel hardware we have been discussing does not exist. Instead, the functions we have been discussing are integrated into the CPU in one form or another. In fact, at the low end of the line, the channel activities are carried out entirely by the CPU using microprogrammed channel commands. In this case, the channel registers are in fact parts of the main memory that are not accessible to the programmer, although the channel commands are again held in addressable parts of main memory.

Now in terms of Fig. 6.13, the internal data bus, various channels, and arbiter all can be imagined as collapsed into the CPU. Although we may have several channel busses here, the situation is now very much like the naive channels discussed in Section 6.3.1. In fact, if only one channel bus existed, except for operating details we would be back to a picture that is very close to Fig. 6.10, which describes the PDP-11! Thus, the wonders of microprogramming are again revealed, because the devices attached to a 370/135, for example, can be identical to those on a 370/165. Of course, if too many fast devices are attached to a Model 135, only I/O activities can be supported by the CPU.

To be specific about the analogy between PDP-11 and IBM I/O, we must consider two cases. In the DMA case, the DMA device controller is analogous to an IBM selector channel and the Unibus is analogous to the internal data bus. Priorities among DMA controllers are determined by daisy chaining, whereas priorities among multiple selector channels on the internal data bus are determined by an internal arbiter.

In the non-DMA case, the analogy is in two parts. The PDP-11 CPU corresponds to an IBM channel and the Unibus corresponds to the IBM channel bus for channel/device communications. For channel/memory communications, the Unibus corresponds to the IBM internal data bus whereas, of course, the PDP-11 CPU still corresponds to the IBM channel. Here, the Unibus is time multiplexed to serve as both types of IBM busses. Daisy chain priorities hold among multiple devices on the Unibus as they do among multiple devices on the IBM channel bus.

6.3.3 CDC

The CDC 6600 handles communications between peripheral devices and main memory by its set of 10 PPUs (Peripheral Processing Units, officially termed Peripheral and Control Processors). The PPUs are connected to main memory and the central processor on the one hand and to 12 Peripheral Channels on the other hand. The channels are in turn connected to various I/O devices, as shown in Fig. 6.15. Note that the PPU and the Peripheral Channel together form what we have been calling an I/O channel.

The operation of the entire I/O process on the CDC 6600 is synchronous; clock pulses are distributed from the CPU to PPUs and channels. Synchronizers in the channels convert the clock pulses to whatever form is needed by particular devices, and vice versa. The 1 μs major cycle is divided into 10

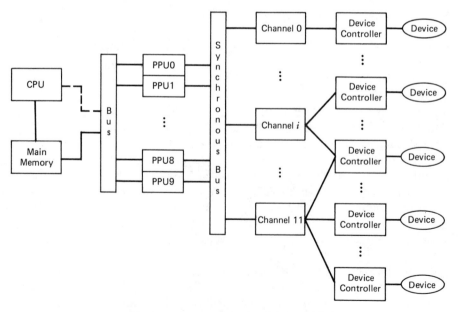

FIGURE 6.15   **CDC 6600 I/O configuration.**

minor cycles of 100 ns each, and each PPU gets one minor cycle per major cycle (recall Section 4.2.4). Thornton describes the details of the CDC 6600 PPUs and I/O in Chapter 7 of [Thor70].

The I/O devices are hard wired to one or more channels and cannot be moved programmatically. Any PPU has access to any channel, however, and each channel may be connected to a number of I/O devices. Furthermore, the PPUs can communicate with each other through a channel.

Input information is passed from a device, through the memory of a PPU, and then into main memory; output information flows in reverse. Single words or blocks may be transmitted. Because the PPU is a 12-bit processor, five minor cycles are required per 60-bit CPU word. Note, however, that since each PPU operates once per major cycle, it can sustain a data rate of (12 bits)/(1 μs) = 12×10^6 b/s, which is fast enough for most I/O devices. The rate could be increased by allowing one device to share several channels and several PPUs.

There is an important difference between the control of I/O activities here and in IBM channels. Because the CPU clock is used to synchronize I/O here, the interlocked "handshaking" activities described in Section 6.3.2 are not necessary. Channels can send out signals and then wait a fixed number of clocks and expect a reply. They need not wait indefinitely (or until a time-out occurs). This means that less time is wasted, in general, but as a consequence there is less flexibility. As we shall see, Burroughs I/O control operates in a manner similar to CDC in this respect. After introducing the 6600, CDC has produced slower speed machines; Burroughs has machines that cover an even wider range. Because the clock speeds of the CPUs change from one machine to another, the number of clocks required for I/O responses changes. Hence, the logic of the channels must vary from large to small CPUs, whereas in the IBM case, speed made no difference. This is the flexibility we have mentioned several times, which IBM gains by giving up some channel speed. They, of course, regain speed by using several types of channels.

6.3.4 Burroughs

Most Burroughs computers have used a star type of I/O configuration (recall Section 6.2.3) with the CPU at the center and peripheral devices at the points of the star. We first describe the early B5500 configuration and then the B6700/B7700 configuration into which it has evolved. Some aspects of the I/O hardware of the B6500 are discussed in [Pate69], although the discussion is software-oriented.

The B5500, in its maximum configuration, is shown in Fig. 6.16. Here the I/O Control Units can be assigned to any of up to 32 devices and up to 4 I/O transactions can be carried out at once. The I/O Control Units handle 7-bit words (6 bits of information plus 1 parity bit). They contain a full word (48-bit) buffer to assemble and disassemble words. Information recoding is also done in the I/O Control Units, between CPU format and device formats. The B5500

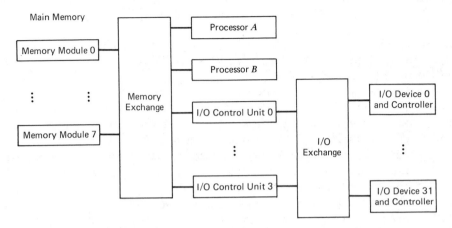

FIGURE 6.16   **Burroughs B5500 I/O configuration.**

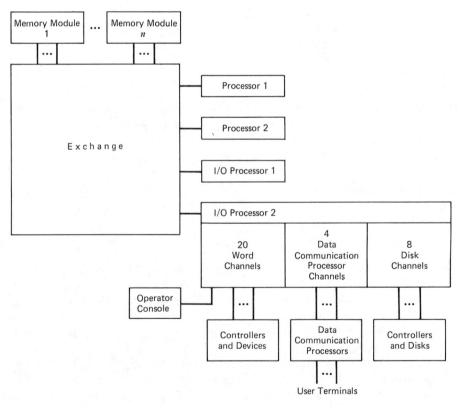

FIGURE 6.17   **Burroughs B6700 I/O configuration.**

470

I/O Control Units are sometimes referred to as "floating channels" because of the way they can be arbitrarily assigned, in contrast to the fixed channels of IBM.

The B5500 architecture evolved into the B6500 and B7500 followed by the B6700 and B7700, which adopted a more purely star-type of I/O configuration. We sketch this configuration in Fig. 6.17. Note that the two crossbar exchanges of the B5500 have been merged into a single one here. Various configurations are available, with exchanges of up to size 8×8 in the B7700. Section 6.5 gives more details about crossbar switches.

Each I/O Processor can handle up to 32 I/O channels, all of which may operate at once for a combined data rate of over 64×10^6 bits/sec. As indicated in Fig. 6.17 for I/O Processor 2, these channels are specialized in several ways. The data communication processors are line concentrators, each of which can handle up to 1024 user lines.

Notice that each I/O device has a direct path to main memory through its I/O processor, in contrast to the sharing required in the use of a bus. Like the CDC peripheral system, Burroughs I/O is clocked from the CPU. Thus the tradeoffs discussed at the end of Section 6.3.3 also hold here. It is interesting to note that Burroughs channels actually contain a number of specialized subchannels. Thus, they can use fewer independent channels than does CDC. In a sense then, the Burroughs I/O system stands logically somewhere between the CDC case and the IBM case. For more details about Burroughs B6700 I/O, see [Burr74] or Burroughs manuals for particular models.

6.4 ALIGNMENT NETWORK CHARACTERISTICS

As we pointed out in Section 6.1, it is not possible to make a rigorous distinction between busses and alignment networks. The basic distinction we make is that only two units can communicate at one instant of time via a bus, whereas a number of units can communicate at the same time via an alignment network. Thus if a collection of processors is connected to a set of memories via an alignment network, all of the processors can use the network simultaneously. Several examples of alignment networks were presented in Section 6.1.2, and in Sections 1.2 and 5.4.2 their relations to various processor and memory systems were discussed.

In this section several different types of alignment networks will be presented. First, we will give some background discussion which is useful in characterizing alignment networks. Basically, we will discuss three network characteristics:

1. Their mappings of inputs to outputs.
2. Some aspects of their speed and cost.
3. How they are controlled.

Throughout this chapter the numbers of network inputs and outputs are assumed to be powers of two.

6.4.1 Alignment network mappings

It is important to characterize alignment networks according to their interconnection capabilities. If, following Fig. 6.1, the inputs $1, \ldots, n$ are mapped to the outputs in a one-to-one way, the network performs a *permutation*, which can be specified by two corresponding lists of the integers 1 through n. For example, if $n = 4$, then $\left(\begin{smallmatrix}1234\\4213\end{smallmatrix}\right)$ specifies a permutation in which input 1 is transmitted to output 4, input 2 to output 2, and so on. Note that the examples of Section 6.1.2 were sometimes between two *distinct* sets of units—those introducing inputs and those receiving outputs. We can always use the model of Fig. 6.1 for these cases by assuming that some inputs are null and some outputs are null. Thus, a system with p processors and m memories, as in Fig. 6.5, could be represented by Fig. 6.1 with $n = p + m$. It is usually more helpful to draw such a machine as in Fig. 6.5, with permutations, if $p \le m$, of p processor inputs to p memory outputs for a store, or of p memory inputs to p processor outputs for a fetch. Thus, we define a *permutation network* of k inputs and l outputs as a network which can perform all possible one-to-one mappings of inputs to outputs for all sets of $\min(k, l)$ input ports.

Another important interconnection is the broadcast of one word to a number of units. If a network can transmit any of its inputs to all of its outputs at once, we call it a *broadcast network*. If it can send one input to one subset of the outputs, another input to another subset of the outputs, and so on, we say it is a *selective broadcast network*. Note that broadcasts are one-to-many mappings of inputs to outputs.

Some networks are quite useful even though they cannot perform all permutations. They may perform a subset of all possible permutations, which totally satisfies the requirements of some application. In addition to forming a subset of all permutations, they may have broadcast capabilities. We will refer to such an alignment network as a *connection network*, and its mappings of inputs to outputs are *connections*. Examples of useful connections are uniform shifts, squeezes (e.g., in which element $2i$ is mapped into element i for all i), spreads (the inverse of squeezes), and reversals (where the last and first, the next to last and second, etc., are interchanged).

6.4.2 Alignment network time consideration

Beyond their capabilities of mapping inputs to outputs, we can characterize alignment networks according to the number of *cycles* required to perform these mappings. A cycle may be one clock period or several, but it is the elementary operation time for the alignment network, analogous to a memory cycle time or an addition time. For example, the crossbar network of Fig. 6.5 can perform a permutation in one cycle. On the other hand, the uniform shift network of Fig. 6.6 may require p cycles to carry out some permutations. In this comparison it is clear that more hardware is required in the one cycle network of Fig. 6.5 than in the p-cycle network of Fig. 6.6.

Another important characterization of alignment networks is whether or not they are *pipelined*. For example, a multistage network can be designed so that several sets of data can be transmitted at once, with a sequence of pipeline states set up between the network input and output ports. This, of course, increases the amount of hardware in the network, but it also increases the effective speed of the network if there are a number of data sets to be handled in rapid succession. Pipelining may be a useful way to increase bandwidth, especially if the system is physically large and wire lengths account for a substantial part of the transmission time. An example of this is found in the MU5 [LaTE77].

6.4.3 Alignment network control and conflict resolution

With any alignment network, we must determine how the network is to be integrated into the overall computer system. One of the most interesting problems in this regard is that of network control. Some networks have control units as shown in Fig. 6.1, which are separate from the data switching network. We say such networks are *externally controlled*. Others have control built into the data switching network and we call these *internally controlled*. Examples of the latter are merging and sorting networks as in Fig. 6.7, which we will consider later.

For the moment we will deal only with externally controlled networks. If the control is external, there are two basic ways that a mapping can be specified. The source units can specify the desired destinations of their input data or the destination units can specify the desired sources of their output data. We shall call these networks *input initiated* and *output initiated*, respectively.

The notion of a *conflict* in an alignment network may be given several interpretations. If the input-to-output mapping is a permutation, then by definition no conflict exists. If one input is to be sent to several outputs, a conflict may or may not arise, depending on the hardware characteristics of the network. Broadcast logic can be used to allow such mappings to proceed in parallel—otherwise an *input conflict* arises which requires the network to be cycled once for each distinct destination of the same input.

More serious are *output conflicts* in which several sources are to be mapped to the same destination; usually these arise with input initiated networks. We first mentioned this in connection with our initial discussion of Fig. 6.1. In this case, we must consider the question of how many output ports exist in each destination unit. If there is one for each input port, then no conflict occurs on one transmission cycle. But in the worst case all of the input ports may transmit to one output unit on a number of subsequent cycles, so each of the output ports would have to be backed up by a queue, assuming the output units were not fast enough to handle this much data. Generally speaking, the total input bandwidth and the total output bandwidth of an alignment network's attached units should be matched, so each output unit may be able to handle just one transmission or it may be able to queue one request from each input port and handle them on subsequent cycles. All additional requests must be regarded as output conflicts. When an output conflict arises, all subsequent requests by input units must be blocked until the output conflict situation disappears. In any case, it is clear that the notion of a conflict is dependent on the hardware available for handling nonpermutation mappings.

Alignment network conflict resolution may be handled in a number of different ways. One possibility is *a priori conflict resolution*. For example, the compiler could check to determine that data alignment patterns are conflict-free. If they were not, several transmissions through the network could be set up, each being conflict-free. Of course, in some programs these patterns are not known at compile time, so the method will not work. Alternatively, the control unit could replace the compiler in this role, checking the patterns at run time between input units in the case of an input initiated network and between output units in the output initiated case. The logic required for such checking however, would generally be greater than that for one of the following methods.

Another possible technique is *internal conflict resolution* carried out in the alignment network's data paths. Here tags may be transmitted with the data, and the network has some kind of internal checking which appropriately blocks data in conflict and causes input ports to retransmit this blocked data on subsequent cycles.

A third possible technique, which we mentioned earlier, is *output port conflict resolution*. This means that we replicate the number of output ports from m to pm if there are p inputs, giving each destination unit as many ports as there are source units. This does not actually avoid the conflicts, it just pushes conflict resolution into the destination units. It is feasible only if p is quite small; otherwise, the cost is unreasonable. The method is sometimes used in the memories of multiprocessor systems with a small number of processors, and will be discussed next.

6.5   TYPICAL ALIGNMENT NETWORKS

In this section we present the details of several typical alignment networks. Multiple bus and crossbar switch networks are discussed, and several variations on these are considered. Gates and time requirements are also included.

6.5.1   Multiple bus alignment networks

A natural way to begin discussing practical alignment networks is to consider a multiprocessor/multimemory/multibus system. In fact, we did present such a system in Section 5.4.2.1 (see Fig. 5.6), and again in Section 6.1.2 (see Fig. 6.5). Recall that Fig. 5.6 showed n ports at each memory unit, and we then discussed priority logic to resolve conflicts in the memory control unit (Section 5.4.4). Another way to view this is to regard each bus as a demultiplexer or fan-out mechanism that allows each processor or I/O channel (requester) to connect itself to any memory unit. The logic in the memory control unit then serves as a multiplexer and selects one of up to n simultaneous requests for memory access. The highest effective bandwidth is achieved when each processor selects a different memory unit, and the lowest is when each processor selects the same memory unit. This is a typical example of output port conflict resolution mentioned above. This depends on one's point of view, however, because if we regard the memory ports and the memory control unit's priority logic as part of the alignment network, then it may be regarded as an internal conflict resolution method, as mentioned above.

6.5.2 Crossbar alignment networks

First, we describe an $n \times n$ crossbar switch and we then discuss several variations on this idea. An $n \times n$ crossbar is often pictured as an $n \times n$ array of switches with sources on rows and destinations on columns. Then by setting just one switch in each row and column, we form a permutation of the inputs to the outputs. (The exchanges of Figs. 6.16 and 6.17 are rectangular crossbars.) Let us consider the implementation of such a switch using combinational logic.

In Fig. 6.18, we sketch the switching of one bit of a d-bit word. To switch all d bits in parallel, we would need d such switches. Each would operate in an identical way as follows. On the left side of the network the bits are fanned-out in horizontal planes and on the right side they are fanned-in in vertical planes. The $n \times n$ array of switches mentioned in the previous paragraph can be thought of as the square array in the middle of Fig. 6.18.

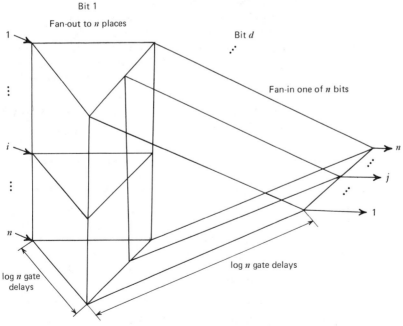

FIGURE 6.18   **Crossbar switch.**

In an *input initiated* crossbar the destination selection is performed in the left half of the network by a demultiplexer (recall Section 2.2.3). Assume that each input unit generates an output destination tag that denotes the output unit to which it wants to send its input. Input unit i presents its tag to horizontal plane i in the left half of the network, where it is decoded to select a path, say to position j. Then multiplexers on the right side of the network simply fan-in all bits in each column to form the outputs. Of course, at most one bit in each column contains input data—row i for column j in our example. Thus, if each input unit presents a distinct output destination tag, the inputs are mapped by a permutation to the outputs.

An *output initiated* crossbar works similarly; but the roles of the right and left halves of the network are reversed. In this case, the left half is used to fan-out each input in horizontal planes. Thus, input i is available for selection by all outputs. Assume that each output unit generates an input source tag that denotes the input unit from which it wants its output. Output j presents its tag to a multiplexer in vertical plane j in the right half of the network, where it is decoded to select an input plane, say i, in our example. Then the data from input i is transmitted to output j. *All* outputs can select the same input here (for broadcasting) unlike the input initiated case, although the latter could be so modified.

Crossbar gates and time

Consider the time and component count for an input initiated $n \times n$ crossbar network (obviously, an output initiated network has identical counts) as follows. To decode each destination tag requires a network of $2(n-1)$ AND gates (plus $n-1$ NOT gates). Then to fan-in the data to output ports, $n-1$ OR gates are required. Recall Corollary 1 and Fig. 2.5 of Chapter 2. Thus, we have a total of $4(n-1)$ gates (including NOTs) to switch one bit of one word. Since we have n words, $4n(n-1)$ gates are needed to switch one bit of each of n words. This includes gates to control the network and switch the data. However, we are ignoring the gates needed to fan-out the control bits [there are only $O(\log^2 n)$ of these].

The time delay through such a network is $2 \log n$ gate delays. For $n \leq 1024$, this would be at most 20 gate delays—one or two clocks in most machines. The transmission line times might be equal to or greater than this in physically large machines. The time to set up or control the network is just $\log n$ gate delays required to fan-out the control bit at the center stage. Thus, we see that a crossbar network is very fast, perhaps faster than necessary, but it contains a great deal of hardware.

6.5.3 Gate bounds for permutation networks

We have seen that $O(n^2)$ gates are used in a crossbar network. If we can achieve linear processing speedup for a linear growth of investment in processors and linear memory bandwidth increase for a linear growth of investment in memories, it seems very unreasonable to have to pay quadratically $[O(n^2)]$ for a linear increase in alignment network bandwidth. Is this really necessary? To attempt an answer to this question, we consider the following argument.

A standard crossbar network can perform all possible permutations of n inputs to n outputs. There are a total of $n!$ such permutations. By Stirling's approximation, we have

$$n! \approx \left(\frac{n}{e}\right)^n \sqrt{2\pi n} \tag{1}$$

as the total number of different internal settings or states of the alignment network necessary to carry out all possible permutations.

On the other hand, a crossbar network can be regarded as an array of n^2 switches, each of which can be set in either of two states. Thus, the total number of internal states of the network is 2^{n^2}. But, since

$$2^{n^2} = n^{n^2/\log n}, \tag{2}$$

(this is obvious by taking the log of both sides) and since

$$n^{n^2/\log n} \gg \left(\frac{n}{e}\right)^n \sqrt{2\pi n}, \tag{3}$$

it is clear by comparing Eqs. 1 and 2 that we are wasting a good deal of hardware in a crossbar network, if permutations are our only interest. In fact, suppose we could devise a network with only $n \log n$ two-state switches. The total number of internal states in such a network would be

$$2^{n \log n} = 2^{\log n^n} = n^n, \tag{4}$$

which is a reasonable approximation of $n!$ by Eq. 1. Thus, we see that only $O(n \log n)$ and not $O(n^2)$ switches are really necessary to perform the $n!$ possible permutations. This fact has led to a number of results about simpler permutation networks. We shall consider some of them below. Note that a network with $O(n \log n)$ switches that provides $O(n)$ bandwidth fits reasonably well with the processor and memory cost and speed rates of growth we mentioned previously.

6.5.4 Networks with $O(n \log n)$ gates

The problem of designing a permutation network for interconnecting computer parts is intuitively related to the problem of designing telephone switching networks. If the units of Fig. 6.1 are regarded as telephones rather than computer parts, the interpretation is obvious. Indeed, the name "crossbar switch" was coined in the telephone switching context, and a great deal of theoretical work on switches has been done by telephone switching people.

A class of switches developed by telephone switching theorists will be presented now. These are called *rearrangeable networks* and have the following interesting properties. A rearrangeable network with $O(n \log n)$ gates is capable of performing all possible permutations of n inputs in $O(\log n)$ gate delays. Rearrangeable networks can take a number of different forms; we shall discuss those with $n = 2^k$ inputs that have a nearly optimal number of components as discussed in the previous section (a few components can, in fact, be eliminated from such switches, see [Waks68]). Because of this gate optimality, we shall refer to such an alignment network as an ORAN (optimal rearrangeable alignment network). The theory of such networks was studied by a number of people, but several papers by C. Clos and V. Beneš [Bene65] developed the subject quite well.

An ORAN network for permuting 4 inputs is shown in Fig. 6.19a. It is an interconnected set of 2×2 crossbar switches, each of which can pass data straight through, or can cross over two data items. Figure 6.19b shows how the network can be set to reverse the order of the inputs. Figure 6.20 shows an 8 input network set to permute inputs (1, 2, 3, 4, 5, 6, 7, 8) to outputs (7, 8, 5, 6, 3, 4, 1, 2). Notice the similarity between the interconnection patterns of Figs. 6.19 and 6.20. Some thought should lead the reader to infer a generalization of this pattern to any 2^k-input network. Notice that the pattern is symmetric about central axes, both vertically and horizontally. We shall return to the question of the interconnection pattern shortly. In general, we have the following theorem [Bene65], [OpTs71].

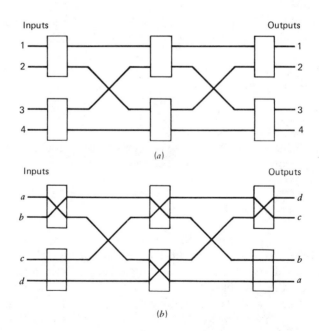

(a)

(b)

FIGURE 6.19 **ORAN networks. (a) Four-input ORAN network. (b) Reversal of the input order.**

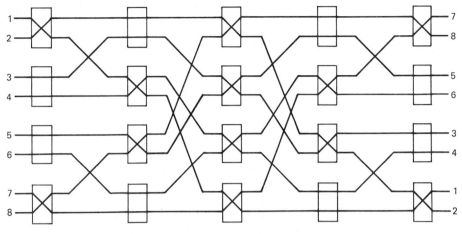

FIGURE 6.20   **Eight-input ORAN network.**

Theorem 1

A permutation network for $n = 2^k$ inputs requires at most $2 \log n - 1$ switch delays using $\frac{n}{2}(2 \log n - 1)$ switches, where each switch is a 2×2 crossbar. ∎

This result approximates the lower bounds on time and gates. The gate bound follows from counting the number of states necessary for all permutations as in Section 6.5.3. The time bound follows from a fan-in or fan-out argument on the distance an input or output may travel. Thus, although Theorem 1 is of theoretical interest, there is an important flaw in such networks, namely, how much time is required to set the 2×2 crossbar switches? A number of persons have studied this problem, and the best known result is that the switches can be set in $O(n \log n)$ time steps [OpTs71]. Thus, although the data may be transmitted in $O(\log n)$ gate delays, $O(n \log n)$ gate delays would be needed to set the switch for the next permutation.

In the telephone switching context this may be useful, because telephone calls may be relatively long compared with the network transmission time. But for interconnecting processors and memories, it is desirable to be able to reset the network on each memory cycle. Thus, such a network would be of practical interest only if the permutations to be performed were known at compile time, so a compiler could precompute the switch settings. Another possibility is that if only a relatively small set of different permutations were ever needed, some type of ROM lookup scheme would be possible at run time.

The ORAN network possesses great generality in being able to perform *any* permutation. Suppose that we could determine, for some set of programs, that only a subset of all possible permutations were necessary connections in a computer. Intuitively, if one thinks about array subscripts and loop control statements in real programs, most of the patterns generated might be quite simple. For example, in the program

Prog. 1

$$\text{DO } S \quad I \leftarrow 1, N$$
$$S \qquad A(I) \leftarrow A(I+1) + B(I-3)$$

the A array and B array are to be uniformly shifted, added, and the result is to be stored back in A. If the machine organization has an alignment network between processors or between processors and memory, it is necessary to perform only uniform shifts of vectors here. In other words, each array element is shifted the same distance.

It turns out that by using just the last $\log n$ stages of an ORAN network, it is possible to perform a number of useful connections *and* to control the network in real time. The Ω-network, studied by D. Lawrie [Lawr75], can be controlled in $O(\log n)$ gate delays and transmits data in $O(\log n)$ gate delays. It is shown in [Lawr75] that many array partitions can be accessed without conflict from a parallel memory (as in Section 5.4.2.2) and that an Ω-network can then permute the accessed data into a standard order for computation. For example, the $A(I+1)$ and $B(I-3)$ of Prog. 1 can be accessed without conflict, and aligned by a shift, each in one pass through the Ω-network. The result is then passed through the network back to memory to be stored without conflict as $A(I)$.

6.5.5 Merge and sort networks

The ORAN and Ω-networks are examples of externally controlled alignment networks, whereas the following is an internally controlled alignment network. It was shown by K. Batcher [Batc68] that parallel merging and sorting networks can be constructed. Except for minor improvements, the results presented in [Batc68] are the fastest known merging and sorting network schemes. Batcher designed a parallel merging network that accepts two ordered lists of $n/2$ numbers each, and he showed that they can be merged into a single ordered list in $O(\log n)$ comparator delays using $O(n \log n)$ comparators.

Using this idea, he then showed how to construct a parallel, sort-by-merge network that can accept n unordered numbers and produce an ordered output sequence. We will refer to such merging and sorting networks as *Batcher networks*. A four-input Batcher sorting network is shown in Fig. 6.21a. In [Batc68], a scheme is given for constructing sorting networks for any power-of-two inputs from smaller networks using a sort-by-merge strategy.

In general, a Batcher sorting network has $O(\log^2 n)$ comparator delays. A total of $O(n \log^2 n)$ full-word comparators are used to achieve this. Alternatively, the network can be implemented in a bit serial fashion using $O(n \log^2 n)$ two-bit comparators. If the words have w bits, the time required is now $O(w) + O(\log^2 n)$ gate delays, because each bit must pass through $O(\log^2 n)$

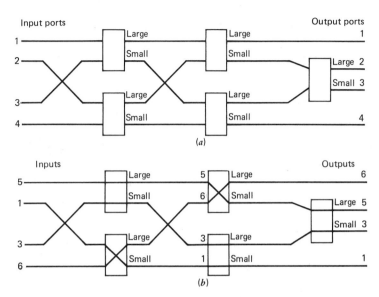

FIGURE 6.21 *(a)* **Four-input Batcher network.** *(b)* **Sorting four numbers.**

comparator stages of a few gate delays each, and they can be fed into the network one after the other in $O(w)$ gate delays. This is actually a bit serial pipeline operation of the network.

The basic element in a Batcher network is a device that accepts two input numbers and produces the larger number at one output port (say, the top one) and the smaller at the other output port. Basically, each of these Batcher elements contains a comparator and a switch that can be latched to a straight through or crossover connection. The comparators may operate in a bit serial or full-word parallel manner, and this affects the detailed form of the gate and time bounds as discussed above. Figure 6.21b shows the settings of the Batcher elements for sorting four example inputs.

Note that a Batcher sorting network can be used as an arbitrary permutation network simply by attaching a destination tag to each data item and sorting the tags. The data items then follow the tags through the network to their proper destinations.

6.5.6 The shuffle connection

The following interconnection scheme has some very interesting properties. Suppose two sets of $n/2$ elements, each with two inputs and two outputs, are interconnected as shown in Fig. 6.22 for $n = 8$. This interconnection pattern is called a *shuffle*—its similarity to splitting a deck of playing cards and shuffling the two halves should be obvious. The inverse of this connection, that is, the network obtained by interchanging the input and output ports, is called an *unshuffle*, as indicated in Fig. 6.22.

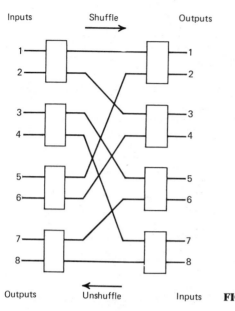

FIGURE 6.22   **A shuffle/unshuffle network.**

An interesting fact is that the ORAN, Ω, and Batcher networks all can be regarded as a collection of 2×2 switching elements, interconnected via shuffles and unshuffles. An example of this may be seen by considering Fig. 6.20. If the switches with inputs $(3, 4)$ and $(5, 6)$ are interchanged, then the interconnections between the first and second columns of switches become a shuffle. The connections between columns 2 and 3 are a shuffle as shown in Fig. 6.20. Similarly, the connections between columns 3 and 4 are an unshuffle as shown, and an unshuffle between columns 4 and 5 is obtained by interchanging the switches with outputs $(5, 6)$ and $(3, 4)$.

The use of the shuffle interconnection is not limited to permutation networks. It was shown by [Peas68] that the Fast Fourier Transform algorithm on n data points could be carried out in $O(\log n)$ steps if the 2×2 elements in Fig. 6.22 are capable of doing addition or multiplication operations as well as interchanging data. Other applications are discussed in [Ston71]. Current research activities in this area indicate that such networks also possess other useful computational properties.

6.5.7 Summary

An important and still unanswered question in the design of parallel computers is: How should the processors be interconnected? For example, in the ILLIAC IV, to avoid an expensive crossbar switch, a network similar to that of Fig. 6.6 was used. Both ± 1 and $\pm \sqrt{n}$ connections were provided and for a uniform shift of distance k, hardware was provided to break k into a minimum term sum of ± 1 and $\pm \sqrt{n}$. The advantage of this network is that it has a constant number of interconnections per processor, as opposed to the other schemes we have seen, where the number of connections per processor is $O(n)$ or $O(\log n)$, in an n-processor system. A drawback of this network is that although it is effective for uniform shifts (particularly short ones), many permutations require longer times [ThKu77]. One appeal of the shuffle connection is that it could be used with a constant number of connections per processor, assuming the boxes of Fig. 6.22 were processors and that the connections were from one set of processors back to the same set, that is, the left and right columns of Fig. 6.22 were identical. The Fast Fourier Transform and related results give hope for this network in algorithms of the shuffle-arithmetic-shuffle-arithmetic-and so on, form. Furthermore, it can always produce the ORAN, Ω, or Batcher results if cycled repeatedly to simulate those networks. The STARAN alignment network and its use [Batc77] should be studied, since it is equivalent to a shuffle network.

As higher levels of circuit integration arrive, crossbar networks become feasible because packages rather than gates are the cost measure. In the Burroughs BSP, the 17 memories are connected to 16 processors using separate input and output alignment networks as shown in Fig. 6.5; one is also used for processor-to-processor interconnections. This allows memory-to-memory data flow pipelining and performing broadcast and sparse array (compress and expand) operations in addition to permutations.

6.6 COMPUTER NETWORKS

Computer networks can be grouped into two broad categories: (1) multiterminal networks with one or a few central computers, and (2) multicomputer networks that may also include a large number of terminals. The technology involved in such networks is usually a combination of bus and alignment network ideas. For this reason and because the subject is an important and rapidly expanding one, we present computer networks in a separate section. Because there is much diversity in real networks, however, we shall restrict our presentation to the overall ideas of networks and avoid much detail. In Section 6.6.1 we discuss the motivations for networks and in Section 6.6.2 we present some network design considerations.

6.6.1 Computer network motivations

The motivations for building computer networks and the effects of their use can be discussed under the following five headings:

1. Resource enhancement.
2. High-speed communication.
3. Load balancing.
4. Cost balancing.
5. Availability enhancement.

The first two apply to multiterminal networks, whereas all five apply to multicomputer networks. We discuss each of these points below.

1. Resource enhancement

A fundamental motivation for multiterminal networks is simply to provide remote services via terminals, to users who otherwise would not have the services available. For example, time-sharing networks allow programmers in small companies to use a large, central machine. The small company may not have a computer at all, or it may have a small machine that does not support the languages or applications programs that certain users need. Indeed, it is frequently the case that small (and large) companies subscribe to one or more time-sharing systems to augment their "in house" computer system.

   In general, the resources made available by a network may be specialized hardware, software, or data bases. For example, high-speed machines can be made available to remote users as is the case with ILLIAC IV via the ARPA Network or the CDC STAR-100 via the CDC CYBERNET. Software examples include the case in the above paragraph or some very special system, for example, for computer-aided instruction as in the case of the PLATO system [Bitz76] at the University of Illinois. Data base examples include company records that are held centrally but accessed from many branch offices or large information retrieval networks such as the National Library of Medicine's MEDLINE system [McLe73]. Other examples of resource enhancement fall naturally under the following heading.

2. High-speed communication

Some multiterminal networks can best be described as high-speed communication networks. For example, airline reservation systems that provide agents with CRT terminals for accessing central files [Knig72] are actually replacements for telephone voice communication with a central office. Similar statements can be made about police cars with radio access to a central file of criminals, grocery clerks with terminals connected to inventory files, and so on. In the multicomputer network case, in a number of banks computers interconnected for the instantaneous transfer of credit are an electronic replacement for the physical transport of many sheets of paper.

   Resource enhancement accompanies a number of these high-speed communication examples. Supermarket chains can centralize inventory and accounting programs and still make them available to individual stores; banks can centralize files and special equipment and make them available to all branches, as well as sell some services to outside customers.

   Similarly, multicomputer networks can be used simply to transport jobs (i.e., communicate) between computing centers. This leads us to our third point.

3. Load balancing

Any multicomputer network with common resources at various nodes can provide load balancing. Users at one site can send jobs to another site when their own system is overloaded. For example, if the network has nodes from coast to coast, east coast users may run on the west coast early in the morning, before those users have arrived for work, and vice versa in the evening.

Load balancing is easiest to carry out in homogeneous networks where each node has the same kind of machine as in IBM's TSS network project which consisted of 360/67s [MKMN73]. However, large networks often have a number of nodes with compatible systems that allow running jobs at various sites. Sometimes this is done without even notifying the user; it is simply a matter of the network operating system providing the best possible service at any time. Load balancing is administratively easiest to carry out when the network nodes involved are part of the same administrative organization.

4. Cost balancing

Even if network nodes are parts of different organizations, it is sometimes the case that users at one site can obtain more cost-effective computer services at another site. For example, one computer center may have a machine that is too large for local needs. It can attempt to load its facilities by selling time via a network and thus undersell smaller, overloaded machines elsewhere on the network. The cost of communications and the added delays involved in using the network must be considered here, but in general, networks can tend to force computer costs to a uniform rate at various network nodes. This may lead to politically disruptive situations. For example, when several universities are connected to a network, because users often are not spending "real" dollars for computer time, price cutting can lead to administrative procedures that tend to *prevent* network use. More discussion of such problems can be found in section V-B of [BlCo76].

5. Availability enhancement

The redundancy provided by common facilities at several network nodes obviously enhances the availability of services at each individual node. Given that the network communication facilities themselves have fairly high reliability, if any node develops problems, jobs can simply be sent to a compatible node for service.

6.6.2 Computer network design considerations

There are two basic types of considerations that enter into the design of any computer network: (1) technical considerations of hardware and software, and

(2) policy considerations including various legal, economic, and administrative questions. We shall expand both of these to some extent, although the latter questions are largely outside the scope of this book.

The first physical, technical considerations we discuss are similar to those mentioned earlier in this chapter. What interconnections are to be provided and how is the network to be controlled? For example, each network node could be provided with a high-bandwidth leased telephone line connecting it to all other network nodes with which it might want to communicate. Such point-to-point connections could be outrageously expensive as the number of network nodes grows beyond a few. Another possibility would be simply to dial up another computer whenever necessary, and use the standard telephone switching network. This is less expensive than leased point-to-point lines, but standard telephone lines allow data rates of only a few hundred or a thousand bits per second; much higher data rates are often desired in computer-computer communications. Of course, for multiterminal networks, this is a good solution.

A good compromise for multicomputer networks is to lease some high-speed lines (with data rates of a few thousand or a few tens of thousands of bits per second), but to share these lines somehow. One possible configuration is a star (recall Section 6.2.3) which works well if large blocks are being transmitted. But for many small blocks, the central control must be very fast and complex. Also, the reliability of the entire network depends on the central node and any network node can be isolated by the failure of its one line to the center.

A better configuration is obtained by leasing two or more lines for each node and connecting them to other selected nodes (presumably nodes for which high traffic will exist). Then by transshipment through several nodes any computer on the network can communicate with any other computer. This allows high-bandwidth communication at relatively low cost and also provides for high reliability. If one line fails, then some other path can be found between any pair of nodes.

Because of the transshipment of information between network nodes, such a network is called a *store and forward* network. Western Union has operated such message switching networks for some time [CoxJ72]. The first major undertaking to link many computers via a high-speed store and forward network was the ARPA Network (ARPANET) [RoWe70].

The ARPANET can be regarded as having three types of components. The network nodes contain two of these components: a host computer (HOST), namely, a given site's original computer which is being connected to the network, and a minicomputer called the interface message processor (IMP), that interfaces the HOST to the network. The third component is a set of 50 kilobit per second lines leased from the telephone company (ATT). Each network node is directly connected to at least two other nodes via such lines. Figure 6.23 shows a small, ARPA-like store and forward network with five nodes (the TIP will be explained below).

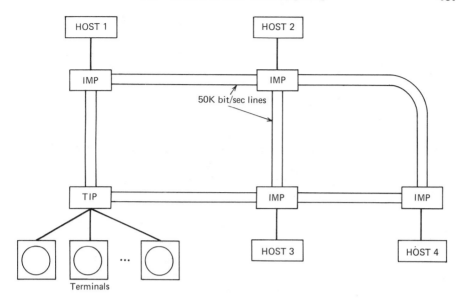

FIGURE 6.23   **Store and forward network.**

The IMPs and the leased lines together form the communication and control aspects of the network. When a host wishes to send a block of data or program to another node, it passes information to the IMP. The IMP has software to perform the following. The block to be transmitted is sliced into 1000-bit *packets*. These contain sufficient control and parity bits and are transmitted to the main memory of an adjacent IMP on the network. That IMP examines the packet, checks it for errors, decides which IMP to forward it to, and retransmits the packet. The average time for transmitting and handling one packet is about 0.1 sec [Robe74].

The IMP thus provides time-sharing of the transmission lines for the packets of many network users. It also can choose a minimum distance route for each packet, and this can be modified as a result of a node or a line being down. By providing point-to-point lines between nodes that are favorite communication pairs, the total number of *hops* (i.e., individual lines traversed) can be kept low; in fact, 3 or 4 hops may be typical [KlNa74].

To provide for orderly operation, network control procedures, called *protocols*, are established and implemented in the hardware and software of the IMPs. The protocols allow communications to be initiated, executed, and terminated. Protocols can become quite complex because communications must be carried out between HOST and IMP, between IMP and IMP, and at a higher level (through the IMPs) between HOST and HOST. Furthermore, the ARPANET has another kind of node that consists of a number of terminals (recall Fig. 6.23); such a node is interfaced via a terminal IMP (TIP) and requires further protocols. Finally, if the ARPANET is to be interfaced with another network, very high-level network-network protocols are required. For a number of papers about protocols, see section II-B of [BlCo76].

The ARPANET has received a great deal of attention because it was a pioneering effort and because it has been so carefully studied. Many other papers about it may be found in [GrLu75] and [BlCo76]. Several commercial networks are under development along these lines and are also discussed in the same two references. A brief survey of data communication (including radio and satellite systems) and computer networks may be found in [Klei76]. A varied collection of network and data communications papers may be found in [ChuW76]. Several teleprocessing system packages are available; for example, IBM has Systems Network Architecture (SNA) [McFa76].

A number of different types of policy questions arise in computer network design. Related to the technical questions and of fundamental importance are the legal and regulatory aspects of building a network. In the United States, the Federal Communications Commission (FCC) regulates interstate common-carrier communications. The bureaucracy of the FCC, coupled with the bureaucracy and reluctance of some of the common carriers (e.g., ATT) to change their methods, frustrated a number of early network efforts. Some companies resorted to building their own transmission systems (see Part III of [GrLu75]). Although the general trend has been toward paving the way for computer networks, these regulatory and legal questions have been serious. For a good survey of this, see [MaWa72] or [WaMa73].

Once the purely legal and regulatory questions are answered, the economic aspects of networks must be considered. What kinds of computers are to be included? This is interesting from the technical (services to be provided) as well as economic and political points of view. Will sufficiently many jobs be shipped to and from all nodes to justify the cost? Will the organizations cooperate? Are the network security problems solvable? Some of these questions are discussed in sections 1-A and 1-B of [GrLu75] and in section V-B of [BlCo76].

One interesting consequence of the above is the development of "value added" networks that sell "retail" network services to users. These services include the communications facilities ("wholesaled" by the common carriers) and network control computers to interface the network to host computers.

Within a given organization, such as a nationwide firm, serious administrative problems can arise due to the introduction of networks. For example, centralizing files and making them available via a multiterminal network may be economically reasonable and may centralize the firm's management. If this replaces a number of locally managed computers spread across the country, however, the branch offices may resent losing their autonomy.

We conclude that computer networks are an important development in bringing more and better services to many users. The technical problems are quite similar to others presented earlier in this chapter. The legal, administrative, and economic questions raised by networks are varied and interesting, and will probably increase as more computer services are provided to more people.

PROBLEMS

Easy problems in text order

6.1 Match the following interconnection patterns with the proper description.

_____Bus I/O connection

a. Arbitrary permutation without conflict.

b. Transmission in two directions at once.

_____Star I/O connection

c. Daisy-chained I/O priority.

d. Cost-effective for

_____Full duplex connection

$$\text{DO} \quad S_2 \quad I \leftarrow 1, N$$
$$S_2 \qquad A(I) \leftarrow A(I+3)$$

_____Crossbar connection

e. Channel knows address of each I/O device requested immediately.

_____Uniform shift connection

6.2 (a) Why would a disk be given a higher interrupt priority than a card reader?

(b) Would an operator's console be given an interrupt priority higher or lower than a disk? Why or why not?

6.3 We are given two proposed configurations for interconnecting N processors (P) by switching elements (S). Below are examples for $N = 4$. When a processor originates a message, it attaches a tag to identify the destination. The processor receives nothing if a switch connects its input to an idle line.

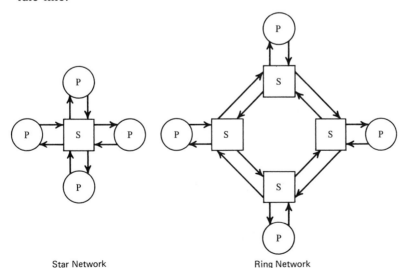

Star Network   Ring Network

In the star network, the switch is a full $N \times N$ crossbar.

In the ring network, each switch is a 3×3 crossbar, with modifications in the control logic so that the switch examines the tag of an incoming message and connects the message to its processor if the tag matches. Otherwise, it chooses the direction which provides the shortest path to the destination and retransmits the message to the next switch.

If a line is busy when a switch needs it for an outgoing message, the incoming message is stored and delayed until the line becomes idle.

(a) Which configuration would be the most economical, in terms of gates for a large number of processors?

(b) Which configuration could most quickly perform a maximum distance route?

(c) Which configuration could most quickly perform a uniform route of distance 1, for large N?

(d) In normal operation, which configuration would suffer most from "busy line" delays?

(e) In which configuration would the inclusion of one additional processor be the most difficult and expensive?

6.4 A memory system consists of a number of memory modules connected together on a common memory bus. When a write request is made, the bus is occupied for 100 ns by the data, address, and control signals. During the same 100 ns, and for 500 ns thereafter, the addressed memory module executes one cycle accepting and storing the data. The operation of the memory modules may overlap but only one request can be on the bus at any time.

(a) Assume there are eight such modules connected to the bus. What is the maximum possible bandwidth at which data can be stored (in words/second)?

(b) Sketch a graph of the maximum write bandwidth as a function of the module cycle time, assuming eight memory modules and a bus busy time of 100 ns.

6.5 An IBM-type multiplexer channel can be described as a shared bus used by a number of I/O devices to access main memory. Which statements would tend to recommend *against* using an IBM-type multiplexer channel in a computer system? Consider each statement as an independent situation.

(a) Only a single I/O device is to be connected to the channel.

(b) The I/O devices have a large range of speeds, from keyboards to fixed-head disks.

(c) The interrupt system requires that each I/O device be assigned a priority, and that high-priority devices receive service before low-priority devices.

(d) Some of the I/O devices employ "cycle stealing" to directly access the memory without involving the processor.

(e) Many of the I/O devices must "burst transfer" large blocks of data, rather than single characters.

6.6 Consider the effective data rate of an I/O channel. Assume that the channel can transmit data at a maximum rate of 8×10^6 bits/sec. When operated in the byte multiplexer mode, however, an additional 3 μs per (8-bit) byte of overhead communication or "handshaking" time is required to control the I/O bus and the device attached to the channel. What is the largest bandwidth (bits/sec) that an I/O device may have and still not saturate this byte multiplexer channel?

6.7 Consider the data rate of an IBM selector channel. On input, a byte must first travel from a device controller register, through some logic and onto the bus; in the channel it again passes through some logic; and when it reaches the memory, more logic delays are encountered before it finally reaches the MIR. Assume that at each of these three stages, about 15 gate delays through 10 ns gates are involved. Furthermore, perhaps 150 feet of cabling are required from the device controller, under the floor, into the channel cabinet, and so on, into the main memory cabinet. The signal propagates at about 1 ns per foot. Estimate the effective bit rate for such a system if 8-bit bytes are transmitted in parallel. How does this rate relate to IBM's advertised selector channel rate?

6.8 The number of components and component delays required by a switch that is capable of arbitrary permutations depends greatly on the technology used. For example, if an array of n^2 relays is used, and electrical signals are such that fan-outs and fan-ins are arbitrary, only one relay delay may be required. On the other hand, if other technologies are considered, a permutation network can be implemented with only n crosspoints if slow setup times are acceptable. Explain how this is possible. Give examples using several technologies, if possible. (*Hint:* Every hotel lobby once had such a system.)

6.9 Make a table showing order of magnitude bounds for speed (in gate delays), gates, and time to control (in gate delays) these alignment networks: crossbar, uniform shift, ORAN, and Batcher. (Don't compute the time to control uniform shift or Batcher networks.) Assume n modules are attached to the interconnection network, that the networks are 1 bit wide, will have to perform permutations, and that fan-in = fan-out = 2.

6.10 Show that $O(n^2)$ gates are needed to fan-out the control bits of a crossbar network of n one-bit inputs and outputs.

6.11 Design a broadcast network to broadcast any one of n sources to n destinations. How many gate delays and how many gates are needed?

6.12 Which of the following ORAN-type networks of five crossbar switches can perform arbitrary permutations of four inputs?

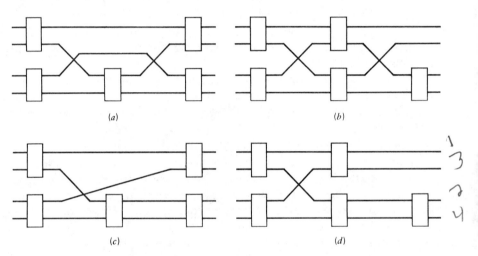

6.13 Consider the ORAN network constructed of 2×2 crossbar switches to permute 2^n numbers. What is the redundancy of such a network? Define redundancy as

$$R = \frac{\text{total number of possible states}}{\text{total number of possible permutations}}.$$

6.14 Fill in inputs to the following Batcher-type network which show that it will *not* sort arbitrary inputs correctly.

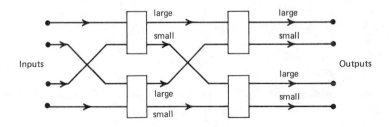

Medium and hard problems in text order

6.15 Data may be uniformly shifted between processors by the Semmelhaack [Semm71] scheme using three basic steps: transpose bits, shift, retranspose. For example, if we have four words of four bits each which we wish to shift a uniform distance of one, we would place the words in a square matrix, take the matrix transpose:

$$[a_{ij}]^T \rightarrow [a_{ji}], \quad \text{for} \quad 1 \le i, j \le 4,$$

shift each column one to the right:

$$\text{for} \quad 1 \le j \le 4 : [a_{ji}] \rightarrow [a_{j,i+1}], \quad \text{for} \quad 1 \le i \le 3; [a_{j4}] \rightarrow [a_{j1}], \quad \text{for} \quad i = 4,$$

and again take the matrix transpose:

$$[a_{ji}]^T \rightarrow [a_{ij}], \quad \text{for} \quad 1 \le i, j \le 4.$$

Sketch the details of a shift of distance three using four processors with 8-bit registers as shown:

$$R1 = \boxed{1 \quad 0 \quad 1 \quad 1 \quad 1 \quad 1 \quad 0 \quad 0}$$

$$R2 = \boxed{1 \quad 1 \quad 0 \quad 0 \quad 0 \quad 0 \quad 0 \quad 1}$$

$$R3 = \boxed{1 \quad 0 \quad 0 \quad 0 \quad 1 \quad 1 \quad 0 \quad 0}$$

$$R4 = \boxed{0 \quad 1 \quad 0 \quad 0 \quad 1 \quad 0 \quad 0 \quad 1}$$

Discuss the implications of this for a parallel machine with a shifter per processor.

6.16 Suppose you have an SIME machine with n parallel processors. Communication among the processors is achieved by two techniques: broadcasting and routing. Broadcast data is transmitted from the central control unit simultaneously to each of the processors. One time unit is required to send data from a processor to the central control and one additional time unit is required to broadcast the data to all of the processors. Routed data is shifted from processor to processor, via a barrel shift switch.

Suppose the parallel machine consists of $n = 2^k$ processors and the barrel shifter is constructed so that a route from one processor to another requires only one time unit t per power-of-two route in either direction; routes of 1, 2, 4, 8, 16, ... processors require time t, and routes of 3, 5, 6, 7, 9, 10, 12, 14, 15, ... require time $2t$, and so on. Routing is accomplished through register R in each processor and broadcasting is accomplished through register B in each processor. Devise a scheme to form the product $X = Y \cdot Z$ in a minimal amount of time. For simplicity, let Y be a vector 2^k wide and Z be a matrix 2^k by 2^j. X, of course, will then be a vector 2^j wide. Further, assume that memory fetching and storing require zero time units, that is, do not worry about anything except broadcasting, routing, and arithmetic operations. All arithmetic operations require one time unit t.

How many arithmetic operation steps will be required and how many broadcasts and/or routes will be required? State all assumptions you make, including any registers required for temporary storage for intermediate results. Consider the cases of $j \gg k$ and $k \gg j$.

6.17 You have a computing system consisting of a polling machine that queues processing requests and a processor. Assume that the queue size is n; the processor takes μ seconds, on the average, to handle a

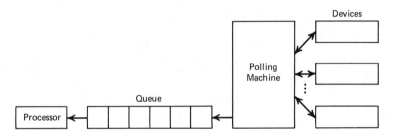

processing request; it takes an average of ν seconds to interrupt the processor and swap programs so that a queue full of requests may be handled; and that the polling machine accumulates n requests and then interrupts the processor and transfers the full queue.

(a) Derive an equation for expected response time, allowing for the interarrival time of requests λ, and the time it takes to store the request in the queue, β ($\beta < \lambda$). (*Hint:* Compute the total time each of the n jobs waits for service to be completed, sum these times, and divide by n.)

(b) Plot expected response time (average time in the system) versus n (size of queue) for $n = 1, 2, 4, 8, 16$ for each of the following relations:

   (1) $\nu \approx 1/2\mu$
   (2) $\nu \approx \mu$
   (3) $\nu \approx 2\mu$.

   Assume that $\mu = \lambda = 2\beta$.

(c) Briefly comment on the effect on response time that λ would have if $\lambda \gg \mu$. If $\lambda < \mu$. For λ in between.

6.18 To save gates, busses are often time multiplexed. Consider a machine with 48-bit words, a 10^7 bit/second disk and a 600 ns main memory cycle time. Assume that each bus transmission requires 750 ns for data bits and various control "handshaking" operations. How many data bits would have to be sent in each 750 ns period to stay ahead of the disk, and what bus format would you choose? What fraction of the main memory bandwidth is consumed by a disk I/O operation?

Sketch the sequence of timing events involved in a continuous input transmission from disk to main memory, that is, show how much of the bandwidth of the disk, bus and main memory are used.

6.19 For interprocessor communications or for user terminals seeking the attention of a CPU, interrupts are not necessary. Polling is an alternative technique. Discuss the advantages and disadvantages of polling and interrupts in each of these cases.

6.20 Regarding priorities on a daisy chain—assume devices $d_1, \ldots, d_k$ are to be put on a daisy chain, and each device d_i uses fraction α_i of the bandwidth of the bus, $0 < \alpha_i < 1$; $\sum_{i=1}^{k} \alpha_i < 1$. How should the devices be attached to the daisy chain to obtain the maximum average remaining bandwidth? The remaining bandwidth for a device on a daisy chain is one minus the sum of the bandwidths used by all the devices with a higher priority on the daisy chain. Briefly comment on what your results mean and give an example of when they may not be applicable.

6.21 Consider the logic design details of a device opening a daisy chain switch to claim a bus. We must prevent the device from opening the switch in the middle of a pulse. If this happens, the device opening the switch will think its request has been granted because it detected the pulse coming in. But if it opens its switch too slowly, a reduced section of the pulse may reach the next device which may then think that it can claim the bus.

The PDP-11 approach is to introduce a fixed delay Δ on the daisy

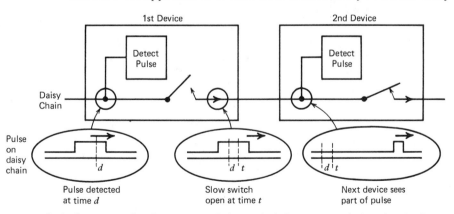

chain between the detector and the switch long enough for the device to be able to open the switch before the leading edge of the pulse can reach the switch. Furthermore, the device's request is granted only if the request is present when the leading edge of the daisy chain pulse enters the delay element. The IBM approach uses two lines to send a pulse down the daisy chain. The SEL line is the true daisy chain pulse described above. In addition, the HLD line is sent out before any SEL pulse and, in effect, tells the device that a pulse is coming. The pair of pulses might look like:

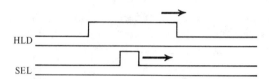

This allows a simple logic implementation of both the pulse detector and the switch using an SR flip-flop, and AND and NOT gates.

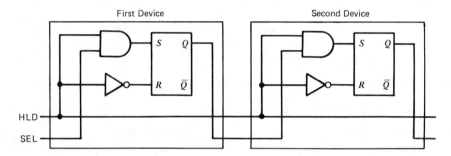

(a) Draw timing diagrams to show that the delay introduced by the IBM approach is negligible.

(b) Construct a switching device for a PDP-11 device. (*Hint:* Use one edge-triggered flip-flop and a few gates.)

(c) (Not involving logic design.) Discuss the impact of the PDP-11 approach on daisy chain bandwidth. Assume that $\Delta \approx 100$ nsec and the daisy chain is connected to typical DMA-speed devices.

6.22 The IBM 370/145 has a memory cycle time of about 600 ns for 32-bit words and a fixed-point addition time of about 1.37 μs (register-to-register). Normally, the total I/O channel data rate that can be sustained is 1.85×10^6 bytes/sec, but when the channel word-buffer feature is installed, this may be increased to 5×10^6 bytes/sec.

(a) What fraction of the total memory bandwidth is free in the normal I/O channel and the channel word-buffer cases when I/O activities are proceeding at a maximum rate?

(b) Compute the effective add time with each I/O rate if a sequence of memory-to-memory adds and I/Os is going on.

6.23 Suppose you are in charge of I/O configuration management for a large IBM computer system. You have eight device controllers to attach to a channel with cables of equal length. Furthermore, once the controllers are placed on the floor, they cannot be moved around to change priorities (at least not in real time!). If you choose a random configuration, what is the probability it is optimal (assume there is just one best configuration)? Notice that even if you make a mistake, there is some hope of salvation, since pairs of cables between adjacent controllers *can* be unplugged and crossed over so that the outgoing daisy chain line is attached to what was the daisy chain return line. In Fig. 6.14, for example, the device controller for unit 1 can be made last by crossing over the priority lines entering it and leaving it. How much does this improve your chances of having guessed right in the sense that your original random placement of the controllers can be corrected to achieve the optimal?

6.24 Show how to pipeline an input initiated $n \times n$ crossbar switch. Assume that there are to be $1 + \log n$ segments in the pipe, $\log n$ segments in the fan-out portion (in each segment, the control line for each of the n inputs must be fanned-out to at most $n/2$ of the demultiplexer's selectors), and one segment in the fan-in portion, and that fan-in = fan-out = 2. How many gate delays should be allowed per clock period? How much faster in terms of effective speed is the pipelined crossbar than the regular crossbar? How many more gates are needed? Could more segments be used to make the pipelined crossbar switch even faster?

6.25 Assume you want to build a bus to interconnect n units, and the words to be transmitted are w bits. If gates with fan-in and fan-out of 2 are used, how many gates does a bus require? How many gate delays are needed for data transmission? Discuss the control of such a bus and how source and destination conflicts can be prevented in the case of a set of processor registers and in the case of an I/O bus. Compare the gates and time in n parallel busses with a crossbar switch to interconnect n units.

6.26 Suppose you want to build a crossbar switch to connect p processors to m memories. Addresses are generated in the processors and each memory has p ports. Assume that conflicts are resolved by each memory control unit. Assume you have multiplexer and demultiplexer packages with fan-in and fan-out of f, respectively. Show how you would implement the crossbar switch and count the number of packages and package delays involved. Don't forget that the switch must be able to transmit to and from the memory.

6.27 Consider a uniform shift switch of N inputs and N outputs in which each input has a limited fan-out of $k = \sqrt{N}$. In the switch, input i may be transferred to output j, where $(i - k/2) \bmod N \leq j \leq (i + k/2) \bmod N$, in unit time. You may assume that no output conflicts occur.
   (a) How many gates are required to implement this switch? (Count AND and OR gates with fan-in = fan-out = 2.)

(b) How much time, in terms of gate delays, is required to perform a route of distance $d \leq k/2$?

(c) How much time, in terms of gate delays, is required to perform a uniform route of distance $d \leq N$?

(d) Suppose that routes of distance ± 1 and $\pm k$ only are available. How much time, in terms of gate delays, is required to perform a uniform route of distance $k \leq N$?

(e) Examine other schemes of uniform connection requiring no more than k fan-outs per input. What can you say in general about the time, in terms of gate delays, required to perform routes of distance $d \leq N$?

6.28 Compare Beneš ORAN networks to the more nearly optimal Waksman ORAN networks.

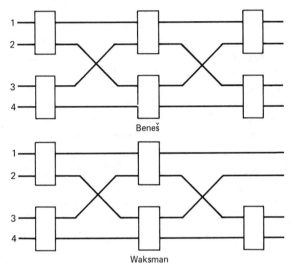

(a) Show that there are two different ways to obtain the identity permutation for the Waksman network. How many ways are there to obtain the reverse permutation (i.e., if input order is 1234, output order is 4321) for a Beneš network? For a Waksman network?

(b) How many states are there in a Waksman network? How many permutations of four inputs are there? Can you design a network [a _____(your name) network] to do any permutation using only four, two-input, two-output modules? Explain your answer.

6.29 To implement a bit serial Batcher network $O(n \log^2 n)$ two-bit comparators are used. Each of these comparator elements is a small, finite state machine which is represented by the state diagram:

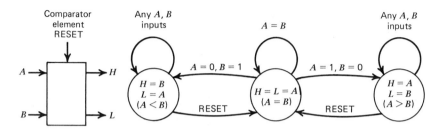

Binary numbers are presented bit serially, least significant bits first, to A and B. H and L are the output bits representing the higher and lower of the inputs, respectively; the RESET signal is sent to all elements in the network before each set of numbers is sorted. The logical meaning of each state is in parentheses.

(a) If the inputs of Fig. 6.21*b* are encoded as 3-bit binary numbers, show how these inputs would be shifted into the network in three clock periods, and when (in which clock period) each of the five elements would first reach its final state.

(b) Explain why the time required to sort n numbers of w bits is $O(w + \log^2 n)$ clock periods. How many clock periods are needed for the sorter in Fig. 6.21?

(c) Show how to implement the finite state machine for the 2-bit comparator elements. How many gate delays are required per element?

6.30 Assume a network (e.g., Batcher's) which can order n unordered numbers (n even) in one pass through the network. Using only one such network connected to a memory, consider how it could be programmed to order $2n$ unordered numbers in a minimum number of passes. Use only the given network and do not design any new logic. You may assume some way of selecting the n inputs from memory, but only on the basis of their positions in sequence, not on their values.

6.31 Draw a network containing the minimum number of three-input, three-output Batcher comparison elements (outputs H, M, L), to sort six input numbers in descending order.

6.32 At b locations throughout a region, Air Traffic Control radars scan the sky and periodically transmit flight information to ATC central. Each radar station gathers radar as well as aircraft transponder information and stores this information in a small local memory. Every t seconds, a polling machine at ATC central requests a remote unit to feed the contents of its 128-word memory into a Batcher sorting network associated with the remote unit. The memory outputs are shifted bit serially into the Batcher network, as diagrammed below, and are sorted and transmitted to ATC central during the polling period.

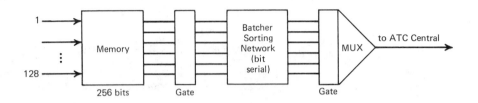

(a) If the delay of one Batcher element is 1 μs, what is the minimum possible bandwidth for the transmission line connecting the output of the sorter to ATC central? You may assume that the sorting network output is gated into the transmission line before the next output appears, that is, in at most one element delay.

(b) How many remote units can the polling machine handle (i.e., how big can b be) if the polling machine works at maximum capacity and polls each remote unit once a minute? You may assume that the average distance between ATC and a remote unit is 250 miles. Data rates from ordinary telephone lines are usually below 1 K bits/second, whereas very high speed lines may handle up to 128 K bits/second. How many remote terminals could be handled with 128 K bit/second lines? (Use "round" numbers, e.g., the speed of transmission is 1 ft/ns.)

(c) If there are only 30 remote units in the system, how large can the delay be per Batcher element at the 1 minute polling frequency? (The slower the element, the cheaper the logic; the lower the bandwidth, the cheaper the transmission cost.)

(d) Suppose the buffer memory of the polling machine holds one record of 4 blocks, where a block is defined to be the number of words generated by one polling of the entire 30-station network. Each track of the head-per-track disk holds 4 records, separated by inter-record gaps. If the remote units operate 24 hours a day, how many tracks would be required to hold an entire day's data on the disk at ATC central?

(e) ATC requires complete hourly summaries of all data. A hardware merge has been added to the central system. The hardware can merge one block with a 60-block merged file in one minute. Assume that the blocks from buffer memory are packed on disk sequentially, that the bandwidth of the merge network matches the bandwidth of the disk (only one head may be active at a time), that the CAM memories have sufficient bandwidth for any scheme you can contrive, and that there is sufficient scratch space on the disk

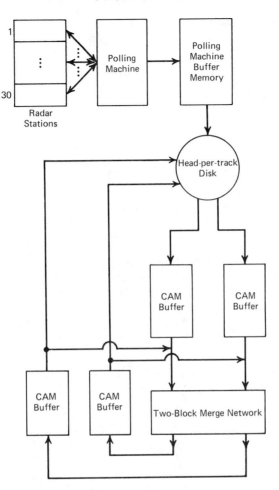

available for intermediate results, if needed. Construct an algorithm which will present the hour's transactions in one merged file for use as soon as possible after the last of the hour's data has been processed.

6.33 In a multidrop terminal network or a multicomputer network, it may be important to minimize the total line length used by the system. Finding the minimum total line length topology for a network is an example of the minimum cost spanning tree problem. A well-known algorithm to find the minimum cost spanning tree is Kruskal's algorithm.

Each possible interconnection line is examined in ascending length order. If the line connects two previously unconnected nodes (all nodes are initially unconnected), the line is retained as part of the minimum cost tree. Otherwise, the line is discarded. We are done as soon as all the nodes are connected.

(a)   Find the minimum total line length topology for the following network for which all possible lines are shown. Is your solution unique?

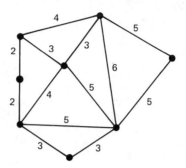

(b)   Of course, total line length is just one factor in establishing a suitable topology. Also, it is apparent that the line length can be reweighted to include some other desirable features. Name a few of these features. Name a desirable feature which cannot be included in this framework.

CH

Lastly there must exist devices, the input and output
organ, whereby the human operator and the
machine can communicate with each other.
This organ will be seen . . . to constitute a secondary
form of automatic memory.

*"Preliminary discussion of the logical design of an
electronic computing instrument"*

A. W. Burks, H. H. Goldstine, John von Neumann

There will be time, there will be time—
Time for you and time for me,
And time yet for a hundred indecisions,
And for a hundred visions and revisions,
Before the taking of toast and tea.

In the room the people come and go
Talking of Michelangelo.

*Adapted from "The Love Song of J. Alfred
Prufrock"*

T. S. Eliot

MEMORY
HIERARCHIES

7.1 INTRODUCTION

At this point, memory hierarchies and I/O operations hardly need an introduction. Throughout the book, references have been made to their existence and use, and this chapter has been cited. Now we will present some details.

The fundamental importance of I/O activities is obvious, both for gaining access to a machine from outside and for backing up computations in progress. The fundamental importance of memory hierarchies is in their cost saving by reducing the size of main memory. As we have mentioned elsewhere, a number of different kinds of I/O devices exist and all can be regarded as part of a memory hierarchy. Due to their wide popularity and because they are among the most complex devices in use, we will emphasize disks—the most common sequential access memories.

In Section 7.2, monoprogrammed memory hierarchy activities will be discussed. Our approach is to discuss the system from as a user's viewpoint and then discuss the underlying software and hardware. Section 7.3 is concerned with the physical aspects of secondary memory devices, primarily disks. Both fixed- and movable-head disks are presented and their operation is discussed step-by-step. Various aspects of their speed are emphasized.

Multiprogramming is introduced in Section 7.4 and the important role of operating systems in multiprogramming is presented. Again, timing aspects are emphasized, ranging from interactive use by many small users to the demands of a few big users. The management of a memory hierarchy by an individual user and by an operating system (OS) is examined, and several alternative multiprogramming and time-sharing schemes are presented.

With the above as background, Section 7.5 takes up the study of paged memory hierarchies. A number of design parameters are presented and several important tradeoffs are discussed. Based on measurements of user programs, several analytical results are developed, allowing the general nature of the tradeoffs to be explored. The first two parts of this section consider monoprogrammed systems, and Section 7.5.3 introduces a multiprogramming model of a paged memory hierarchy. Finally, page replacement algorithms are discussed.

This chapter presents memory hierarchies from the standpoints of the user and his software, the physical organization of the devices, and the operating system's role in managing the hierarchy. Section 7.5 discusses the performance of memory hierarchies, under the variation of a number of key design parameters.

7.2 MONOPROGRAMMED MEMORY HIERARCHY ACTIVITIES

7.2.1 Program preparation

Let us consider how a user might take advantage of many parts of a memory hierarchy in the course of program development and execution. We will assume that a full-blown hypothetical computer system is being used, and, in fact, we will discuss several optional features the system might have.

We begin with a user sitting at a terminal which has a keyboard and some kind of graphical display [usually a cathode-ray tube (CRT) although other devices exist]. The user types in a program he is developing and it is displayed on the CRT just as it would appear on a listing sheet. In fact, if he wants a hard copy of the program, he can call for a line printer listing of it when he is finished. One advantage of the CRT is that a user can remove errors by using an editor program, instead of removing punched cards from a deck and replacing them. The user's other option here, of course, is to use a keypunch machine to prepare the program for input through a card reader.

Simple syntax errors may be observed and be removed immediately. More complex syntax errors can be detected by attempting to compile the program and having the compiler diagnostics displayed on the user's terminal. When a program is syntactically correct, debugging runs with test data may be made and the results displayed immediately. Thus on a step-by-step basis, the user can develop a program using a graphics terminal or a combination of card reader and line printer.

Once the user is satisfied with a program, it can be filed away for later use, using keyboard commands from the terminal. Suppose the user has prepared a number of such programs and now wants to run them using real data. The data may have been professionally keypunched for the user in an offline way, boxes of data cards must be taken to a card reader, read into files, and the programs may then be applied to these files. Alternatively, the user may have obtained data on magnetic tape and now wishes to read the tape to use the data, or the data may be accessed from permanent disk files. At this point, the user can attempt to make "real" runs of the program on this "real" data. Before

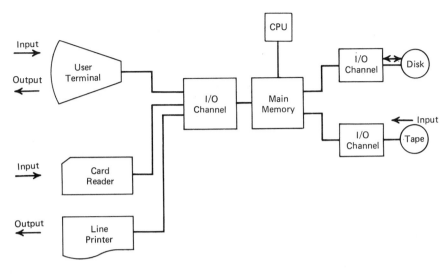

FIGURE 7.1   **I/O configuration for user program and data preparation.**

discussing the process of making runs, let us discuss some details of the hardware and software which the user has already exploited in preparing to run.

Figure 7.1 shows an outline of the hardware used in the above discussion. Five different I/O devices are shown: a user terminal for input and output, a card reader and magnetic tape drive for input, a line printer for output, and a disk drive for storage of intermediate files. It is instructive to consider how a programmer deals with these devices.

A user sitting at a terminal gets attention by typing something like

LOGIN   user ID

which causes the operating system to become aware of her existence. In order to review prior programming activities, the user may be able to type

DISPLAY   PROGABC

or

DISPLAY   FILE 33

and have the operating system display certain previously entered information on the terminal.

New programs can be developed by typing statements, seeing them displayed, and editing them with various software aids. As was pointed out above, the user can also have a program compiled and observe syntax errors on her terminal. The commands used here (e.g., COMPILE and EDIT) and the I/O activities generated by the OS and compiler in executing these commands are beyond the scope of this discussion. Finally, to save a compiled program, a user may type

SAVE   PROG 2,   FILE 33

which causes a program (PROG2) to be saved on disk storage in a file (FILE33) for later use. If PROG 2 is in source form, it may be compiled later; if it is in object form, it may be loaded, linked to other programs, and executed later.

A great deal is being taken for granted here about the details of executing I/O activities. Commands such as LOGIN, DISPLAY, and SAVE are actually instructions to the operating system. For execution, DISPLAY and SAVE must be translated into some kind of machine language instructions that will be executed in the CPU, in an I/O channel, and in a device controller. More details about this will be given in Section 7.3.

7.2.2 Program execution

Next, consider the problems of executing a user's program. Assume the programs are already resident in disk files and that by a sequence of terminal commands or operating system control cards, the user has begun a run. What kinds of input/output matters must a user be concerned with? Basically, there are three:

1. Fetching programs from permanent files to main memory at the beginning of a run and saving certain results in permanent files.
2. The input from outside the system of new data for this run and the output to a printer or display of computed results.
3. The output and input of intermediate results, either because main memory is too small or as a backup procedure in case the computation goes astray.

First is the storage and retrieval of information in permanent files, as we discussed for program preparation. Programs and data that will be used repeatedly are in this category. Permanent files may be kept on disks, or in large systems some type of photo or tape storage device may be used for such archival storage. We will discuss such devices later, in more detail. Commands to the OS similar to DISPLAY and SAVE are used here.

The second case involves getting new data into the program and results to the outside world. Data may come from permanent disk files generated by previous runs, or it may come through temporary disk files from input devices (e.g., card reader or tape drive). Similar statements can be made about output. All programming languages have some kind of I/O statements and the details of their implementation need not concern the programmer. For example, to read cards, the command may be

READ   CARDS, ABC

which causes a deck of cards to be entered into array ABC. And replacing

CARDS by TAPE may read a tape into array ABC. A command such as

PRINT   X

may cause the value of variable X to be output on the line printer.

The compiler is expected to generate the correct I/O commands for execution at run time in these cases. As we shall see later, often the operating system and its files are also involved in carrying out these instructions.

Unlike the first two cases, the third kind of I/O is somewhat different from the activities discussed for program preparation. Here the user must be aware of certain details about the execution of the program. For example, in the case of keeping backup (or restart) files, the user must have some idea about the probability of the machine failing or of the program failing, and must then determine how long to let it execute before dumping the entire memory to a disk file. The idea is that if a failure occurs between one such dump and the next, instead of having to restart with initial data, the computation need only be restarted with the last copy. The establishment of points (called *checkpoints*) in a program for dumping and restarting usually requires some careful user attention, although the system software may be of some help in carrying out such procedures; checkpoints are of interest primarily in long-running programs.

The other example of the third kind of I/O was that required when main memory is too small for a user's computation. Here the user may have to do rather intricate planning to overlay one part of the program or data with another part at a later time. System software can be an invaluable aid here. Thus, if two subroutines are executed at different times, matters can be arranged so that they actually occupy the same physical locations of main memory. Similar tricks can be played with large arrays of data. In either case, managing main memory and secondary memory can become rather difficult. There are obvious logical constraints that must not be violated, and there are also timing considerations that should be taken into account for good performance. For example, one might like to fetch things from secondary to main memory early enough to be available when needed.

A number of factors led to the development of multiprogrammed, shared memory computer systems. One of the resulting benefits was the software solution of some of the problems we have just been discussing. Software developed for managing the memory hierarchy for several users could, of course, be utilized by one user whose program was too large for main memory. But, in general, the problem of managing a multiprogrammed memory hierarchy has a number of interesting complexities, which we shall consider later in this chapter.

Before we discuss multiprogrammed and virtual memory systems, we will consider some details of secondary memory organization. The above discussion of a single user's requirements should be sufficient motivation; the multiuser case will only add more complexity to the situation.

As was pointed out in Chapter 6, the details of executing I/O instructions are all machine dependent; because manufacturers use different schemes— sometimes even from one of their machines to another—we cannot hope to discuss the material above in much detail. As a compromise, we consider disk systems in general, since they are rather complex and interesting devices. By sketching some of the details of how a disk operates during I/O, the operation of other devices should become clear. The principles that we discuss apply to most manufacturers' I/O equipment.

7.3 SECONDARY MEMORY DEVICES

7.3.1 How disks work

The rotating magnetic disk, in its several variations, is the most popular secondary memory device and has been for some time. Rotating magnetic drums and magnetic tapes were developed before disks and are still widely used, but overall, disk technology offers attractive replacements for both drums and tapes. In the future some kind of solid-state device may replace the rotating disk—charge-coupled devices (CCDs) and magnetic bubbles are candidates (see Section 7.3.4). But, regardless of the technology used, the overall organization and use of these secondary memory devices is more or less the same. As discussed in Section 1.1.2, they are sequential access devices in contrast to random access main memories—some words take much longer to access than others and the access time depends on the position of moving bits. We shall specifically discuss disks here and will point out various differences among the other technologies. The reader should be cautioned that many variations exist from one manufacturer to another; the following discussion can be regarded as describing typical, but hypothetical disks.

In Fig. 7.2 we illustrate the basics of the two fundamental disk access mechanisms. Figure 7.2a shows a fixed-head or head-per-track disk, whereas Fig. 7.2b shows a movable-head disk. In either case the storage medium is a solid metal plate coated with magnetizable material. An electric motor is used to spin the disks past the read/write *heads* and this defines storage *tracks* on the disk surfaces. Generally, both sides of each disk surface are used for storage. In the fixed-head case, to access a particular word the disk control logic must wait for the correct rotation angle of the disk. In addition, the movable-head disk controller must first position the head on the correct track. Because all the heads are mechanically connected (and move together), the collection of tracks accessible by all heads in any position is called a *cylinder*. We will discuss these two access mechanisms in more detail shortly.

Both disk types use heads that are capable of reading or writing in any position. The heads are loosely suspended from their arms and actually float on an air cushion just above the disk surface. When the disk is powered down, in many designs, the movable-head disk arms are retracted, which allows the assemblage of storage surfaces (called the *disk pack*) to be physically removed

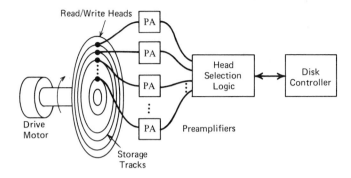

FIGURE 7.2a   **Fixed-head disk.**

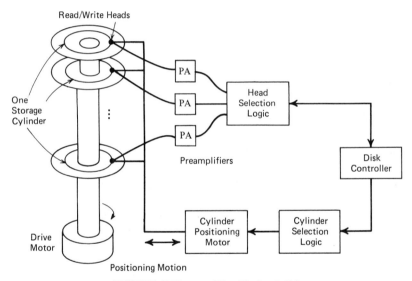

FIGURE 7.2b   **Movable-head disk.**

from the drive mechanism. Such disk packs are less than 2 feet in diameter and 1 foot tall. This has made them an attractive replacement for slower magnetic tapes which hold about the same amount of data but are much slower to access. Although movable-head disks are generally slower than fixed-head disks (as we shall see shortly) their removability and interchangeability make them the most popular scheme in use. For applications where faster access to a bulk storage device is required, fixed-head disks compete with magnetic drums on a cost and speed basis.

7.3.2 Physical characteristics

An individual disk surface can range in diameter from about 1 foot to perhaps 3 feet. Bits are stored in concentric tracks on this surface at densities of 1000 to several thousand bits per inch. The separation between the tracks—required by read/write head spacing—allows track densities of somewhere between 50 and several hundred tracks per inch. Usually a strip of 5 to 10 inches (or more for large fixed-head disks) of radial width is used for storage; if every track is to contain the same number of bits, the maximum allowed bit density determines the length of the innermost track.

In fixed-head disks, large surfaces and higher track densities are possible, but often just two surfaces are available per drive motor. Movable-head disks require lower track densities (because of mechanical positioning tolerances) and usually are arranged in removable packs which contain a number of platters (typically 10 or 12). Generally, both sides of the platters are used for recording. A hybrid scheme is sometimes implemented in which the lower surface of the disk pack is used as a fixed-head surface, with these heads not being retractable. Consider the following example of disk storage capacity.

Example 1

Assume an 18 in.-diameter movable-head disk pack with 20 storage surfaces (s). Let each surface have a 5 in. strip of recorded information at 1000 bits/inch (b/i) (on the inner track) and 100 tracks/inch (t/i). The total *storage capacity* can be estimated as follows. We have

$$\text{Tracks} = s \cdot t/i \cdot 5 \text{ in.} = 20 \cdot 100 \cdot 5 = 10^4.$$

Assuming each track contains the same number of bits, we have

$$\text{Storage capacity} = \text{tracks} \cdot b/i \cdot \text{circumference}.$$

To approximate the circumference, assume an average diameter of about 16 in. for the 5 in.-wide recorded strip on each 18 in.-surface. Thus 16 in. $\cdot \pi$ gives a circumference of about 50 in., so

$$\text{Storage capacity} \cong 10^4 \text{ tracks} \cdot 10^3 \text{ bits/in.} \cdot 50 \text{ in.} = 5 \cdot 10^8 \text{ bits.}$$

This is a reasonable estimate for typical removable disk packs.   ∎

Now consider the data rate and rotational time of such devices. Normally, the motors turn somewhere in the range of 1200–3600 rpm, depending on the size of the disk. If data were stored at the same bit density per track, the data rates at the outer edge of a disk would be higher than near the center, because more track-inches pass one point per time unit at the outer edge. As we assumed above, in many cases the same number of bits are recorded on each track (at different densities due to the differing track lengths), thus, making the data rates equal on each track. This is typical on movable-head disks. On fixed-head disks, which may use relatively more of their larger surfaces, packing more bits on may be important. Thus, the same density can be used on each track and external electronics can be used to compensate for the fact that different heads actually achieve different data rates.

Example   2

Consider the same movable-head disk pack discussed in Example 1. Assume it has a 2400 rpm motor. Thus its *rotational time* or *rotational latency* (time for one rotation) is

$$\text{Rotational time} = \frac{1}{\text{motor speed}} = \frac{60 \times 10^3 \text{ ms/min}}{2400 \text{ rev/min}} = 25 \text{ ms.}$$

The *data rate* per head can be estimated as

$$\text{Head rate} = \frac{\text{bits per track}}{\text{rotational time}} = \frac{50 \times 10^3 \text{b}}{25 \text{ ms}} = 2 \times 10^6 \frac{\text{bits}}{\text{sec}}. \qquad \blacksquare$$

Faster data rates can be obtained by using a faster motor (up to the point where the entire assembly tends to leap off the floor), by using higher bit densities (up to the point where error rates are too high), or by accessing several heads at once. An example of the latter is the ILLIAC IV disk system, which accesses about 100 heads simultaneously on a head-per-track disk to achieve a data rate of nearly 10^9 b/s.

7.3.3   Disk accessing

Next, we consider the problem of addressing and accessing a disk. First, we discuss the fixed-head disk and then the more complex movable-head case.

Typically, head-per-track disk systems dedicate one track to timing information. This provides an explicit record of the angular position of the disk and is required because there can be electrical drift in the motor plus various mechanical slippages. In other words, without feedback from the timing track, the disk addressing logic cannot be precisely sure about where the disk is at any moment. To access a particular disk location, the address is continuously compared with the *timing track* output; when a match occurs, a read or write can proceed.

Notice that the heads on each track must be carefully aligned for this scheme to work properly. Thus, the timing track must accurately represent the angular position of all tracks on the disk, with respect to each of their heads. If some read/write head is jarred and moves relative to the timing track head, the jarred read/write head could access the wrong information. Thus, maintenance personnel must be careful to keep the heads properly aligned.

In the movable-head disk, accessing a particular location involves two separate steps. First, the head must be moved to the proper track. This is called a *seek* operation. Some kind of stepping motion is used to move the heads on all platters to the sought track. At this point the second procedure begins, namely, the access of the proper data within the sought track. One could imagine using a timing track for this purpose, but recall the potential problems in fixed-head disks with respect to head alignment. Here we are moving a comb containing all the heads and a relatively great amount of wobbling about is possible. Thus, to use a timing track, a good deal of bit density within the track would probably have to be sacrificed.

Instead of a timing track, movable-head disks usually rely on explicit information stored with the data in each track. Thus, as the sought track rotates under the head, whether the operation is a read or a write, the channel or disk controller reads the disk. Specially formatted sections appear which identify the following stored information. Thus, by comparing this stored identification with the desired address, when a match appears the read or write operation can be started. In addition to this, there is also very coarse timing track information available. For example, a mechanical notch may exist at one point on the circumference of each track to indicate an angular position origin, and there may be a number of these to divide the circumference into various sectors. Nevertheless, specific information about what is stored on each track must be read before accessing a block.

In addition to rotational latency, movable-head disks must also pay a head-positioning latency or *seek* time. Maximum seek times are in the range of 25–150 ms, depending on the size and type of disk involved.

Movable-head disks rely on two facts for their good performance:

1. Systems may have four or eight or more drives, each of which may be doing a seek simultaneously. This overlap tends to cancel out the individual seek times.
2. In practice, many disk accesses require no seek at all [Lync72]; and even when a seek is required, it may only be to the next track, in which case only 10 or 20 ms is involved.

Manufacturers usually quote maximum and average access times to movable-head disks. The maximum is the longest seek time plus one rotation time. The average is determined in different ways by different suppliers (much like automobile horsepower rating schemes).

Figure 7.3 contains a sketch of a movable-head disk attached to a computer system and illustrates the overall flow of information during a complete I/O transaction. The numbers preceding the following paragraphs are keyed to the circled numbers in the figure.

1. First, the CPU generates an I/O request; a read or write command plus an *I/O descriptor* containing a main memory address, word count, and disk address. Depending on the implementation, some of this is held in the I/O channel, but at least the disk address is communicated to the disk controller, and we show it in the I/O descriptor register.

2. Next, it must be determined whether the disk arms are properly positioned. Cylinder information is extracted from the I/O descriptor and compared with the present cylinder available.

3. If the heads are not properly positioned, a seek must be performed.

4. When the read/write heads are properly positioned, the track number is gated to the head selection logic and the sector address is gated into its register.

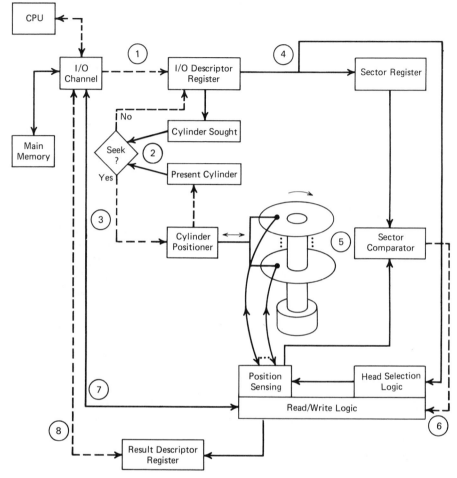

FIGURE 7.3   **Movable-head disk I/O sequence.**

5. Now a search begins for the correct angular position. This is done by comparing the sector register information with header information stored before the data records in the proper track.

6. When the correct record is reached, the comparator signals the read/write logic and the read or write can begin.

7. Transmissions to or from main memory are carried out under the control of the I/O channel (recall Sections 6.2 and 6.3).

8. At the conclusion of this transaction a *result descriptor* is sent back to the CPU via the I/O channel. The result descriptor identifies the I/O transaction which it describes. If the I/O transmission was completed, this is reported. If a parity error or some other problem developed, this is reported. Generally, if a parity error is encountered, the transmission is automatically retried by the

channel, perhaps several times, in the hope that it was a transient error (a piece of dust, a cosmic ray, or whatever) rather than a hard failure (a broken wire or a head that has crashed onto its storage track). On the basis of the result descriptor, the CPU, under control of the operating system and a user program, can determine what action to take next. The result descriptor register of Fig. 7.3 can be thought to gather some bits from the disk controller and some bits from the channel and may be physically located in the channel.

In Fig. 7.4 we show a fixed-head disk and the following discussion illustrates its operation, which should be contrasted with the movable-head discussion above and Fig. 7.3. Note that in Fig. 7.4, a track and sector queue is shown. It is assumed that I/O requests can be sent to the disk controller by the CPU and channel as long as this queue is not full.

1. This is identical to the first step for the movable-head disk.
2. The track and sector numbers are sent to the queue.
3. The timing track is continuously compared with all sector numbers in the queue. Thus, the first to match can be satisfied and that request gets short latency.
4. When a match occurs, the track number is gated to the head-selection logic and the read/write logic is notified.

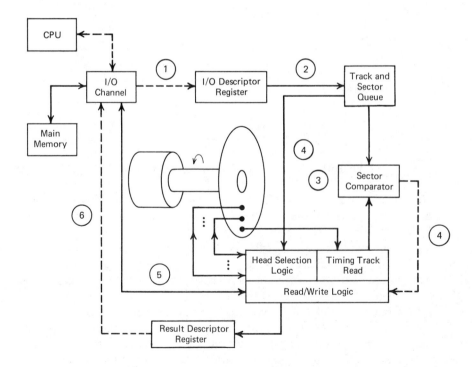

FIGURE 7.4   **Fixed-head disk I/O sequence.**

5. The I/O transmission is carried out under the control of the I/O channel.
6. This is identical to step 8 in the movable-head disk.

Various techniques can be used to establish priorities among a set of requests for I/O service (recall Section 4.4.3.3). Some fixed-head disks have only a single register instead of a queue to hold track and sector information, and thus perform somewhat more slowly, but the idea is the same. It should be observed that queueing of disk requests can also be done in movable-head disks; of course, only the immediate cylinder can be accessed without a seek in that case.

Software can also be used to schedule disk accesses and the problem is hardest for movable-head disks. When a long queue of disk requests appears, in what order should they be handled? One can assume that the disk location and amount of data to be transmitted are known. Various policies have been proposed and studied analytically as well as experimentally. These include first-come, first-served (FCFS); SCAN, which causes the heads to move back and forth across the disk servicing requests as the data is passed on the disk; and shortest seek time first (SSTF), which tries to minimize head movement. Several variations on SCAN have been studied. A comparison of FCFS and SSTF can be found in [Wilh76] and surveys of other results may be found in [Teor72], [CoDe73], and [Full75a].

7.3.4 Other storage devices

The above discussions were intended to convey the general spirit of the operation of two types of disks. Magnetic *drums* operate in a similar way—usually with fixed heads. A disk type that is gaining in popularity is the so-called floppy disk. This is a single magnetic surface that is flexible and can be used like a phonograph record. For example, on minicomputers, users can have their own set of floppy disks. A floppy disk drive and controller are quite inexpensive. Furthermore, the floppy disk itself is one or two orders of magnitude less expensive than a removable disk pack.

At the other extreme, solid-state devices can be used in configurations that operate like disks, but have no moving parts. These promise much higher operating speeds, with a concomitant higher cost. We will sketch the idea below.

Several technologies are available for the fabrication of solid-state disklike memories. The idea is simply to store information in shift registers, as shown in Fig. 7.5. Desired bits may be accessed as they pass the end of the shift register. Otherwise, bits are fed back into the shift register and recycled. In early computers, acoustic delay lines—made of glass, mercury, and so on—were used in just this way as computer memory devices. The advantage of the modern technology is that it is much faster than a disk, and because there are no moving parts it should be more reliable. The main problem is the cost, which is only projected to approach the cost of expensive disks in the late

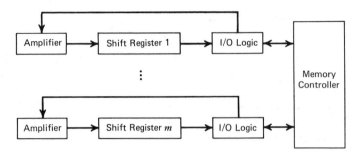

FIGURE 7.5   **Shift register memory.**

1970s. Another problem with semiconductor devices is their volatility when the power supply is removed, whereas a disk is more or less permanent.

MOS gates, charge coupled devices (CCDs), and (nonvolatile) magnetic bubble technologies all have been proposed in this role and are appearing in systems. Regardless of the technology used, the idea is the same. For example, if a shift register of 4K bits length can be clocked at, say, 4×10^6 b/sec, then the worst case access time is

$$\text{Access time} = \frac{\text{shift register length}}{\text{shift rate}} = \frac{4\text{K bits}}{4 \times 10^6 \text{ b/s}} = 1 \text{ ms}.$$

Lengths in the range of up to 64K bits or more are being proposed at shift rates of 10^6 b/s or more. Regardless of the details, we see that an order of magnitude or more speed improvement can be made over disks in this way.

Clearly, the access time would improve if shorter shift registers were used, but the other side of this coin is cost. And the higher the level of integration, the lower the cost per bit, since packaged chip costs are nearly constant. So the tradeoff between cost per bit and effective speed here is clear. Of course, one could also configure two or more shift registers in parallel per chip at the expense of more logic and pins per chip. Regardless of the outcome, it is quite likely that such memories will find a niche somewhere in the memory hierarchy—either as disk or bulk core memory replacements.

In Section 5.1 we discussed a bulk core storage between main memory and secondary memory devices (see [Thor70] for a CDC ECS discussion). This serves as a buffer for block transfers. Its speed is somewhere between main memory and secondary memory and thus its technology is often a slow core memory (usually in a long word configuration, e.g., 512 bits). More recently, semiconductor or magnetic bubble shift registers have become attractive in this area. The use of bulk core storage in a multiprogrammed, multiprocessor CDC 6600 is discussed in [CaFH70].

A number of slower devices have been used for archival storage (recall Section 7.2.2), beyond a disk memory in the hierarchy. Magnetic tape, a traditional I/O and backup medium, is still widely used. It is convenient to handle and inexpensive, but quite slow relative to disk-pack storage. Periodically, trillion bit storage devices appear that use magnetic or optical storage techniques. Such devices are usually very expensive and quite slow relative to disk storage, although they have very large capacity. Sometimes their error rates are also quite high. The most serious disadvantage of such devices may be their inflexibility in that one must add all or nothing, whereas disk drives can be added, often in groups of 8 drives, at relatively low cost and on an as-needed basis. Note that on the basis of Example 1, an 8-drive disk system may hold up to 10^{10} bits (by doubling the density of Example 1). Thus, a trillion-bit store is 100 times larger, but it should be noted that large computing centers may have 100 or more disk and tape drives, so their total disk and tape library may contain much more than 10^{12} bits in total.

In 1974, IBM announced its 3850 storage system and CDC announced a similar system. The 3850 employs a "honeycomb"-shaped array of storage bins for magnetic tape cartridge cylinders that are mechanically picked up, mounted on a drive, and read or written. Such systems are priced in the $500K–$1 million range and have access times of less than 10 seconds.

To remain current in the state of the art, such trade publications as *Datamation, Electronic News,* and others, should be consulted periodically. Surveys of recent memory technology appear from time to time in the *IEEE Proceedings,* the *IEEE Transactions on Magnetics,* the *IEEE Spectrum, Computer,* and numerous conference proceedings.

7.3.5 File organization

There is a great deal of variety in software schemes for accessing secondary memory—both among manufacturers and within one manufacturer. This is due partly to hardware differences, but the major dependence is on the many different uses to which the software will be put. The discussion presented here gives a very brief and general sketch of some of the issues involved and how the software (logical) and hardware (physical) ideas are interrelated.

For purposes of I/O, a collection of information to be treated as a logical unit is called a *file.* A file may be broken into a collection of *records.* Each record can be defined in an arbitrary way—it may be a few bits, bytes, or words; or it may be an array or a tree. The records in a file may be of the same type, or a collection of different types.

In Section 7.3.3, it was pointed out that disks are usually addressed to the level of a sector. The size of a sector can be defined to suit the uses intended. It is clear that addressing at too low a level can lead to a great deal of access latency; because each I/O request will incur some latency, transmitting a fixed amount of data in one block may be much faster than carrying out several separate I/O transmissions. On the other hand, too big a sector will mean wasted disk space, since disk space must be allocated in terms of whole sectors. Typically, about 4K bits might be allocated to each sector. Thus a disk such as the one considered in Example 1, with 50K bits per track, might have each track sliced into 10 or 20 sectors.

Logical files can be allocated to physical sectors in a number of different ways. Two basic possibilities will be discussed here. A *contiguous file* is mapped onto the disk beginning in a given sector and following in a sequence of contiguous sectors in one track. If the file is longer than one track, it can be allocated to a number of tracks—in one cylinder for a movable-head disk or physically adjacent in a fixed-head disk. It is clear that the system software must be carefully designed to handle the assignment of contiguous logical files to physical disks.

The second type of allocation is a *pointer file*. In this case, a logical file may be scattered about on the physical disk, but explicit pointers exist to get from one sector to the next. Thus the file is broken into a number of sector-sized chunks and these may be allocated anywhere on the disk. The pointers may be stored in a table held in main memory or one pointer may be stored in each sector, allowing access to the next sector of the file. This type of file allows more flexibility in allocating disk space, and indeed allows files to expand and contract easily. Access times may be longer than for contiguous files however, since we must pay rotation and seek time here for each sector, whereas the latency is paid just once in the contiguous file case.

Regardless of the type of file storage used, there must be a *disk file directory* which the operating system uses to access any disk file and to allocate unused disk space. This allows users to name files symbolically and leave them on the disk permanently.

As with secondary memory hardware, the software for managing disk files varies from manufacturer to manufacturer. Their literature can be consulted for details. Some operating system books also discuss the subject in a general way. McKeag and Wilson [McWi76] give the details of files for several real systems as does [Saye71].

7.3.6 Summary

The overall time required to handle an I/O transaction can be measured from the point where a program requires an I/O transmission to the point where the transmission is complete. The discussion of this section can be summarized in terms of the components of the *I/O transaction time* for a block of b words:

$$T = t_p + t_a + \frac{b}{\rho},$$

where t_p is the preparation time for the I/O request, t_a is the disk access time, and ρ is the transmission rate (words/sec) between secondary and main memory. Note that t_p includes software time in preparing an I/O descriptor, time to send the descriptor to the appropriate I/O channel, and time in a queue before the disk logic recognizes this request, as well as time for the result descriptor to be returned to the CPU after the transmission is complete. The access time t_a may include head positioning time and certainly includes rotational latency time. In general, T can be reduced in any of several ways:

1. t_p can be reduced by speeding up the software handling I/O.
2. t_a can be decreased by making the disk spin faster or by using shift register type secondary memory.
3. ρ can be increased by the methods of 2, by using higher bit densities, or by activating more heads in parallel.
4. In some input cases, t_a can be reduced by preplanning the disk layout so that blocks are under the read heads just when they are needed; similarly, T can be reduced by fetching blocks before they are needed.
5. The overall effective T in a multiprogrammed system (see Section 7.4) may be reduced by operating several disks in parallel, by overlapping I/O and CPU activities, or by queueing several requests per drive and handling the shortest latency ones first.

Of course, the overall I/O time can also be improved by choosing a file organization well-suited to the computations to be performed.

7.4 MULTIPROGRAMMING AND I/O ACTIVITIES

7.4.1 Interactive terminal use

We now return to a running description of how a system operates dynamically. In Section 7.2, we began with a discussion of what one user might be doing. Here we will consider the multiuser case, which will give an intuitive overview of many of the problems that must be considered in designing the hardware and software of a memory hierarchy. As we will see, multiprogrammed machines may be used to provide small amounts of computation to many users as in the case of airline reservation systems [Knig72], a bank with teller terminals, or a computer-aided instruction system [Bitz76]. On the other hand, multiprogramming may be used to provide some users with small amounts of computation and other users with large amounts of computation (perhaps only in off-hours) as in the case of large laboratories. Sometimes there are also demands for "real-time" services mixed in with the above, as in the case of responding to and controlling laboratory equipment, although "quick response" must be provided to users of any terminal system (as in the examples above).

To make the situation tractable, consider a computer system with a number of user terminals from which people are compiling and running small jobs, and in addition assume there is one big computation that is also waiting to be executed. The terminal users are engaged in activities much like those described in Section 7.2. Here we examine some aspects of what happens in the memory hierarchy, step by step, in carrying out these activities. We use the commands shown in Section 7.2 as examples.

Several effects on the system are discussed for each type of use. Three important system aspects are:

1. Main memory space.
2. CPU time.
3. I/O data rate.

The first two have obvious connections to earlier chapters, and will lead us into a discussion of multiprogramming and time-sharing. The third is one of the important subjects of this chapter.

When a user sits down at a terminal, typing a LOGIN command causes the operating system to be aware of her and allows it to begin charging her account number for services performed. Users generally pay for permanent file space on a monthly basis, whereas for running a job main memory space and CPU time are important parameters in the charging formula. Notice that as soon as the LOGIN is typed, some kind of main memory buffer is required to hold the message and CPU time is necessary to process the command. Such buffer space is usually in an area of memory reserved for the operating system (OS), and shared by all users' message buffers. We show this as area 1 in the composite memory use diagram of Fig. 7.6.

If a user asks for the DISPLAY of a permanent file, a number of steps are involved. First, the terminal gets the attention of the CPU—usually by an interrupt—and passes on the DISPLAY command. Then the OS must allocate a buffer area in main memory for this user's file (2), and consult a disk-file

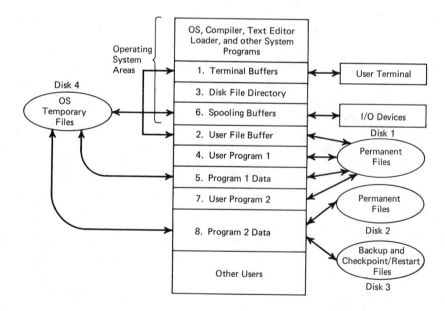

FIGURE 7.6   **Main memory map.**

directory (3) to determine where the file is stored. Then the OS issues an input command to the data channel. An input descriptor reaches the disk controller, which triggers the sequence of events described in Section 7.3.3. The input descriptor contains the disk address of the permanent file sought. This was found in the disk-file directory. The OS added to the input descriptor the main memory address of the buffer which it just allocated for this transmission. After dispatching the input request, the OS can ignore this input activity and go on to other work, since the I/O channel is now in control of it.

Later, the channel interrupts the CPU with a result descriptor that identifies the I/O transaction and indicates whether or not it was successful. If it was a success, the OS can now display the file for the user. (Remember that the OS is still engaged in satisfying the user's original DISPLAY command.) For this purpose, an output request is prepared that identifies the user terminal number, the memory location of the buffer, and the number of lines to be displayed. (Some operating systems would cause moves from area 2 to area 1, whereas others would allow displaying directly from area 2.) The output request is passed to an I/O channel and display controller that take over from this point. When the requisite information has been displayed, the channel again interrupts the CPU announcing its results. And so the process goes on.

Notice the times involved here. The user can get the attention of the CPU in at most a few hundred microseconds. The OS actions take a similar amount of time. Input of the user file, even if a disk seek is required, involves at most 50 or 100 milliseconds. Finally, displaying the file at terminal speeds of, say, 1200 b/s allows a screen full of 1600 characters (80 columns by 20 rows) of 8 bits each to be displayed in

$$\frac{8(\text{b/char.})\ 1600\ \text{char.}}{1200\ \text{b/s}} \approx 10\ \text{seconds.}$$

Thus we see that the terminal itself is the bottleneck; the rest of the process takes less than 0.1 sec. combined. If a 9600 b/s high-speed terminal were used, the display would be filled in less than 1.5 sec.

It is obvious that a fast terminal can respond well within human reaction times, because hitting a few keys and reading the screen may take many seconds. But now, consider the amount of CPU time and I/O time required. We allocated "a few hundred microseconds" of CPU time to this activity. To be concrete, let us say a total of 500 μs was used overall and that we were using terminals that could be written in 5 seconds. Assume also that by the end of this 5-second period a user could respond with another command—perhaps a fast user response—in 10 more seconds of typing. Thus each user would require 500 μs per 15-second time interval, so a *time-shared* computer with such users could handle a total of

$$\frac{15\ \text{sec}}{500\ \mu\text{s/user}} = 30{,}000\ \text{users!}$$

A 10-second user response time, although it seems short, is in fact typical in real systems [Sack70].[1] Before we consider buying this many terminals, however, recall that each user is not really doing any computing in the above situation. The time was based merely on displaying one screen full of information for each user.

If the users were using the COMPILE or EDIT commands, much more CPU time would be required because these would cause the OS to invoke various compilers or text editing programs, respectively. Furthermore, users of interactive time-shared computers typically make short debugging runs with test data at the time they are developing programs. A command such as EXECUTE is used to trigger the linking and loading of compiled programs. Areas 4 and 5 of Fig. 7.6 show a user's loaded program and data area. Later we will expand the discussion of how time-sharing works, but for the moment it should be clear that time slices of much longer than 500 μs are required for each user.

Typically, a *time slice* of 10–100 ms may be allocated to each user of a terminal oriented time-sharing system. Let us give each user 50 ms before interrupting her and starting the next user. This is a factor of 100 more than the time we used in the DISPLAY example above, so we can now support only $30,000/100 = 300$ users; a figure much closer to reality. But, recall that we still are ignoring any large computation jobs. Each terminal user has 50 ms bursts which can be used for I/O, editing, compiling, or running. But suppose one user wants to make a run that would require 5 minutes of dedicated CPU time. Because the user is now sharing the machine with 300 other people, she gets only 1/300 of the CPU time and her 5-minute run will require

$$\text{Elapsed time} = \text{dedicated time} \times \text{number of users}$$
$$= \frac{5 \text{ min/user}}{60 \text{ min/hr}} \times 300 \text{ users} = 25 \text{ hr.}$$

Of course, in that 25-hour period, some of the other users would leave, but others would arrive. So if time were really partitioned out in equal chunks and the machine remained saturated, relatively small runs would blow up enormously. This elapsed time is often called the user's *job turnaround time*. The several time periods discussed in this section can be summarized in Fig. 7.7.

The combined I/O rate of 300 users operating 1200 b/s terminals at full speed (continuously) is

$$\text{I/O rate} = 300 \text{ users} \times 1200 \text{ b/s} = 3.6 \times 10^5 \text{ b/s.}$$

Even this exaggerated use of terminals would not put a heavy load on an I/O channel (see Chapter 6).

The amount of *main memory space* required for the kind of activities we have been discussing is hard to quantify; it is quite dependent on individual users. A typical user might be using a few thousand words of code, plus a little

---

[1] A median of 11 seconds and a mean of 35.2 was measured in a Project MAC study [Sack70].

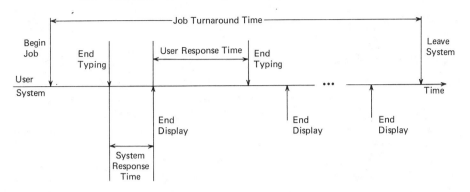

FIGURE 7.7   **Time line of interactive system use.**

data for debugging runs. For approximate numbers we might consider 100 users with 1000 words each or 300 users with 5000 words each—a range of 100K to 1.5 million words of main memory. One to five thousand words is typical for measured user programs in real systems [Sack70]. These results are in the range of large main memories, but of course 100 or 300 users are also relatively large numbers. As we shall see shortly, however, for a large computation the space requirements for data alone can become much larger than this.

7.4.2 Spooling files

The READ and PRINT commands of Section 7.2.1 were represented as standard programming language I/O statements. In fact, if a running program were to wait for a card reader or line printer, a good deal of time would be wasted. Indeed, the I/O channel would control the process, but still the main memory would be occupied by a program and its data, which were idle for rather long time periods. A standard way of avoiding this (sometimes called *spooling*) is to use the disk as a virtual card reader or line printer as follows.

If a user has a deck of cards (or a tape) to be read, it is placed (together with some identification cards) in the card reader, the appropriate buttons are punched, and the cards are read into a disk file controlled by the OS; on their way they pass through main memory buffers (see area 6 of Fig. 7.6). They are held in OS disk files until the user executes the I/O statement (e.g., READ CARDS, ABC) in the course of running the program. At this point the OS retrieves the cards from its temporary file and loads them into the user's array ABC in main memory (area 5 of Fig. 7.6). If the user wants to retain them in a permanent file, she must write them out to a file so identified.

The PRINT X statement is handled in an inverse but similar way. The execution of that statement causes X to be written from main memory to a disk file assigned to the OS for printer activities. When the printer is free, the OS generates an appropriate output descriptor and fires off an output command to the channel and printer controller. Of course, the user does not notice the times involved in all of these intermediate steps because the printer is quite slow regardless.

7.4.3 Multiprogramming large computations

Now consider the introduction of a large user of CPU time and main memory space to the above system. It is not unusual to find programs that regularly consume many tens of minutes of CPU time on even the fastest computers. In fact, some large computations can require many hours per run, although these usually are carried out only as a function of the financial support available. But, in most computer centers it is not unusual to find users making 15- or 30-minute runs. And these times seem constant from one machine to the next, because users of various sizes seem to get the same fraction of the budget, independently of the size of the system. Of course, the details of the problems they are trying to solve can always be made more elaborate, so the computation time required can always be expanded to exploit a new machine.

Such Parkinsonian expansions of computation time are matched—if not exceeded—by demands for more space. Main memories had just 32K words in the early 1960s, but by the early 1970s four or eight times that much had become commonplace. Suppose a big user's machine has 256K words, and that the operating system and small users require 64K of that. It is not difficult for a large user to exhaust the remaining 192K words. If we are processing credit card records, a large company may have many more card holders than that, each of whose records requires several words. Even processing student records (of, say, 10 words each) in a university with 30 or 40 thousand students would overload the memory. Scientific calculations can also grow very large. A model of the earth's weather may contain data points at 100 latitude and longitude lines (10^4 points), at each of 10 levels up in the atmosphere (10^5 points), and involve 10 variables at each data point for a total of 10^6 words. This list of large problems is easy to expand ad infinitum.

Large users may prepare their programs interactively and then load them for a production run. In Fig. 7.6, we show such a program in area 7 together with its data in area 8. The data is shown stored on disk 2, which may be this user's own disk pack, as opposed to disk 1, which many small users may share. For output to a line printer, area 8 is shown with a path through temporary OS files on disk 4.

Such large computations must perform I/O of the third type mentioned in Section 7.2.2, in addition to the first two types, as discussed above. That is, during the course of the computation, some old data must be written out (possible for later use) and new data must be read in. If the computation is properly organized, it may be possible to make just one pass through the data per run; credit card or student record file updating may be in this class. But in some cases, repeated passes must be made through all of the data; forecasting the weather requires updating all the data points at a number of successive time steps. For such backup files and for what follows, we show disk 3.

It is also clear that for some computations (e.g., weather forecasting) which require much time and repeated passes over the data, saving the entire state of the computation at regular intervals can be useful. If the hardware or software crashes just before the end of a 2-hour run, for example, and causes the entire run to be useless, someone will be upset. But if a checkpoint dump were made every 10 minutes, then after the system is repaired the computation could resume with a loss of 10 minutes computation time at most.

Consider the data rates involved here. Suppose a large computation involves 100K data words per memory load and each word is accessed an average of ten times each time the data is brought into main memory. If the CPU and memory speeds allow one operation per data word per microsecond, we have

$$\text{Computation time} = \text{words} \cdot \frac{\text{operations}}{\text{word}} \cdot \frac{\text{time}}{\text{operation}}$$

$$= 100\text{K} \cdot 10 \cdot 10^{-6} \text{ sec.} = 1 \text{ sec.}$$

Thus, in the steady state we must move this much data in and out of main memory (a total of 200K words moved) in one second, so we must maintain

$$\text{I/O bit rate} = \frac{\text{words} \cdot \text{bits/word}}{\text{computation time}} = \frac{200\text{K word} \cdot 32 \text{ bits/word}}{1 \text{ sec.}}$$

$$= 6.4 \times 10^6 \text{ bits/sec.}$$

Recall that this is typical for the data rate of a real disk (see Section 7.3.2). It is clear that a fixed-head disk would be more attractive here than a movable-head disk with its associated seek time penalties.

Notice that this I/O data rate is over 17 times higher than that estimated in Section 7.4.1 for 300 user terminals. This clearly points out the mixed nature of the demands placed on I/O channels, and underlines the need for different types of channels. For example, the terminals would be easily handled by an IBM multiplexer channel, whereas the disk requires a selector channel. Recall also the Burroughs distinctions between data communications and disk channel ports (see Fig. 6.17).

The above computation was a bit roundabout. Notice that, more simply,

$$\text{I/O bit rate} = \frac{2 \times \text{word length}}{\text{operations per datum} \times \text{operation time}},$$

which is independent of the number of words moved and, hence, independent of the main memory size. Of course, this is not strictly true because the algorithm used may depend on how much of the total data base is in main memory at once. Later we shall return to a discussion of the tradeoff between algorithm organization, operations per datum, and main memory size. In any case, the average number of operations per datum is clearly an important algorithm parameter here.

7.4.4 Multiprogramming overview

The above discussions have dealt with the memory hierarchy needs of users. Main memory size and I/O bandwidth were discussed, but the management of the memory hierarchy was largely ignored. All computer systems have an operating system whose central role is to manage the flow of jobs through the computer; a key part of this is managing the memory hierarchy. Some of the operating system's activities were discussed in Section 7.2 and earlier in Section 7.4, but we now consider several questions about the basic strategies used by various operating systems in memory hierarchy management.

All of the discussion of this section can be lumped under the heading of *multiprogramming*, a word that has so many varied meanings that a succinct definition of it is difficult. Usually it means that the following ingredients are present:

1. Several users' programs, several distinct parts of one user's program, or even merely one user and the operating system are being executed at once.
2. The execution is taking place in the CPU and I/O channels, or several CPUs.
3. Main memory is being simultaneously occupied by the several programs being executed.

Basically, multiprogramming may be motivated by:

1. The desire to exploit the full system capacity (in the sense of Section 2.5), thereby increasing the system throughput.
2. The desire to provide fast response to a number of online users or other real-time jobs.

In some instances both these goals may be satisfiable, but often they conflict so one or the other must be chosen. In what follows, we briefly sketch some examples of multiprogramming and emphasize schemes for memory hierarchy management.

The earliest uses of operating systems in memory hierarchy management were concerned with overlapping the I/O activities of one user with the CPU activities of another user. In the simplest form this may mean loading a new user's program and data while a previous user's run is finishing, and then starting to run the new user while unloading the previous user from main memory. By chaining a sequence of jobs in this way, the CPU utilization may be enhanced, simply by avoiding long I/O waits between jobs.

A natural successor to the above arose with the increasing interest in fast response systems. If a computer system were to run one large job and occasionally slip in a very small job, a sequence of small jobs could be given relatively fast turnaround—using either a card reader, line printer I/O station, or using some kind of keyboard terminal. The mechanism for providing this fast turnaround to small users is simply to read them in while a large job is being processed and then to run the small jobs during periods of I/O for the large job that might otherwise idle the CPU. Of course, there is some idealism in the above, because the large job may have little I/O activity and thus not provide CPU windows for running small jobs.

This led to the strategy of interrupting large jobs via an *interval timer* in the CU (recall Section 4.4.3). Typical times are 10–100 ms, as discussed in Section 7.4.1. If the large job is interrupted only rarely, a small job is then run, and control is returned to the large job, then small users can still be provided with good turnaround time and the large job will not notice the small amounts of CPU time stolen from it. Also, the main memory requirements for such a system should not be substantially larger than those required for the one large job.

Historically, the above ideas provided a basis for the development of *interactive time-shared* systems. As described in Section 7.4.1, many users can be provided with quick response provided that each of them does not require much CPU time, overall. Such systems become difficult to manage as the total number of users becomes large relative to main memory size and relative to the I/O bandwidth available.

If one or more of the users require large amounts of CPU time, the situation becomes impossible as discussed in Section 7.4.1. Alternatively, if there are too many jobs (even though each one requires little CPU time), the processor may be overwhelmed. Similar statements can be made about a smaller number of jobs, each of which has relatively larger CPU time requirements. In other words, the total available computation time is fixed, and the total user demand must not exceed what is available. Another aspect of CPU demand is the operating system overhead required to maintain these processes; we shall refer to this again below.

7.4.5 Memory hierarchy management

If several users are sharing it, main memory may lead to management difficulties similar to those of the CPU. Here, however, the situation is more complex, because *all* of each user's programs and data need not be in main memory at once. This leads to the hope that by cleverly sharing main memory, a memory hierarchy may be exploited. Indeed, such sharing is possible, but the details of managing a memory hierarchy in this respect are very complex, as we shall see.

The goals of multiprogramming, as discussed in the previous section, include increasing system throughput and decreasing turnaround time. The goals of exploiting a memory hierarchy depend on the type of system involved, and we discuss them here with multiprogramming because multiprogramming almost always involves a shared memory hierarchy. The amount of main memory required is of central interest, since the basic goal of memory hierarchies is to reduce the amount of main memory. Several cases of interest should be distinguished.

1. In a monoprogrammed system, a memory hierarchy may decrease the amount of main memory needed.

2. In a multiprogrammed system, a memory hierarchy can have the same effect as in (1) for each user, but a multiprogrammed system needs more total memory than a monoprogrammed one.

3. In a multiprocessor/multiprogrammed system, the combined main memory requirements may be smaller than the sum of the requirements if each processor were free-standing, since one processor's job may have small main memory requirements, whereas another has large main memory requirements.

In any type of system, the most naive scheme is to allow each user to manage the memory hierarchy in his or her own way. The use of *overlays* is a traditional technique whereby the user brings in only as much data and program as needed for each phase of the computation. This was the third type of I/O mentioned in Section 7.2.2. When a new phase is entered, some of the space in main memory is overlaid with new programs or data (recall the example of Section 7.4.3). This can be an effective technique but it places all of the memory hierarchy management responsibility on the user, in the sense that the user must decide when to do each I/O transaction. Of course, system software can be used to provide symbolic access to files in secondary memory.

A better way to handle this type of I/O is to provide some type of virtual memory scheme. This has been commercially available since the early 1960s on Burroughs machines, and most manufacturers now have virtual memory systems (including IBM in the early 1970s). In Section 4.3, we introduced the idea and discussed several address mapping schemes that provide users with access to a much larger virtual memory than the physical size of main memory. With virtual memory, the notion of user-controlled overlays disappears in favor of OS controlled overlays of various sections of main memory.

When the OS takes over main memory management, it not only can provide a large virtual memory space but it can also provide *memory sharing* and, as we have seen, this leads to various multiprogramming schemes. In managing the memory hierarchy with respect to main memory sharing, two OS strategies are worth distinguishing, namely, swapping and paging.

As we sketched the history above, simple I/O and CPU overlap between jobs provided the first shared computer facilities. To provide fast response to online users and not use too much main memory, a *swapping* algorithm is useful. When a user's time allotment is finished or she executes an I/O instruction that interrupts the execution and another user is to replace her in main memory, the old user is dumped to a disk file and a new user is loaded into main memory; hence, the two users are swapped. This is a convenient way of providing main memory space but, assuming a number of users are sharing memory, it can lead to checkerboarding problems as discussed in Section 4.3.2; indeed, the main drawback of swapping is that the allocation of space in main memory can become a difficult problem. A solution to this is *paging*, wherein main memory is cut into a set of equal size blocks called *page frames*. A user is allowed a large virtual address space that is cut into pages and a mapping between physical memory space (main and secondary) is maintained by some combination hardware and software scheme (recall Section 4.3.4). The main burden can be borne by fast hardware in this case, so the overhead time may be greatly reduced. The main advantage of paging over swapping is that with paging, the entire address space is broken into equal pages that can be managed in a homogeneous way.

An interesting combination of the above, which might be called *page set swapping*, operates as follows. When one user encounters a page fault, the entire set of her pages that currently occupy main memory are dumped to the disk in a block, thus freeing up some of main memory. When the user's next time burst occurs—at least one disk rotation later—the needed page has been fetched from the disk and the entire set of dumped pages is reloaded. This procedure is carried out for each user in turn. Clearly, it leads to smaller main memory requirements than standard swapping, but it requires higher I/O rates than standard paging because of the page transfers. A scheme like this was attempted in the BCC 500 computer system originated at the University of California, Berkeley, and later at the University of Hawaii [Wats72].

The efficiency of the scheme, of course, depends on the implementation details and the types of jobs being run. Note that if in a standard paged system most of a user's pages were overwritten between one execution burst and the next, then page set swapping would *not* require extra bandwidth and, in fact, it could be regarded as a more systematic way of handling the paging, that is, by blocks for whole users. The above performance of a standard paged system would probably happen only if relatively many users were being run in little memory, of course. The point is that if a sufficiently large main memory is available for the number of jobs present, then page replacement is not much of a problem. Otherwise, if sufficient disk bandwidth capacity exists, then it may be effectively used and, in fact, traded for main memory size by page set swapping.

Swapping, paging, and several variations of these provide a physical mechanism for memory sharing, but algorithms for their use still must be discussed. Furthermore, a number of detailed design parameters must be chosen before such systems are completely specified. In Section 7.5 we will discuss some of them in detail. After that, we will be able to discuss the performance of such systems.

7.4.6 Performance criteria and summary

At this point, it is important to ask a key question: What criteria shall be used to evaluate a shared memory hierarchy management system? Until this is answered, it is not clear whether one system or another is indeed "better." A major difficulty with computer performance evaluation is that the choice of criteria and techniques for measuring performance subject to some criterion are rather vague areas. Improving a system subject to some criterion is even more vague. One of the main difficulties in choosing a criterion is that there may be a wide range of users to satisfy, on the one hand; on the other hand, there may be quite different goals to serve in the "efficient" use of the equipment itself. Thus the shared resource must be viewed from the consumer's side as well as from the producer's side, and when all of the key factors are taken into account, many compromises must be made. Generally, "optimality" with respect to system use or performance for any group of users is impossible to achieve.

Nevertheless, a number of useful measures can be defined and used, and indeed we have been discussing several of these in the past few sections. At this point it seems appropriate to review and relate them, but not to offer any of them as the "correct" criterion for measuring system performance.

Any performance evaluation study must be carried out over some specific time period, which we will call the *total time* T_{tot}. In any total time period, whether the system has one or more users, some of the time goes to serving users and other time goes to "overhead." In the sense of system capacity, time can be measured for various system components, but for the moment we can regard this as CPU time. Even with this restriction, however, it is not easy to distinguish "overhead" from "useful" time. The time lost due to waiting for user responses[2] in a time-shared system (see Fig. 7.7) can be regarded as overhead, operating system time may be regarded as overhead, but what about compilation or linking and loading? In any case, we can write

$$T_{tot} = \text{overhead time} + \sum_{\text{users}} \text{service times.} \qquad (1)$$

A number of time-based criteria can be given. For example, we have discussed throughput intuitively on several occasions and this can be formalized as

$$\text{Throughput} = \frac{\text{total number of jobs}}{T_{tot}}; \qquad (2)$$

it should really be called *throughput rate*, but "throughput" is customary. This is a useful measure if, say, two university computing center managers are comparing their similar systems; it may be agreed that the better one has the highest throughput. Of course, if equivalent computer systems in a university and a major laboratory are compared in this way, the results may be nonsense (e.g., 2000 jobs per day in the university and 200 jobs per day in the laboratory) because of the size of the jobs and their running time.

We have also discussed turnaround time—a measure that is much more user-oriented than throughput. In Fig. 7.7, *job turnaround time* was broken down into system and user response times, and this can be expressed as

$$\text{Job turnaround time} = \sum_{\text{job}} (\text{user response times} + \text{system response times}). \qquad (3)$$

---

[2] The user response time of Fig. 7.7 is sometimes called user "think time," with "response time" meaning system response time.

Of course, the system response times are not devoted entirely to a single user in a multiprogrammed system, so the service time for a job is *not* the sum of the system response times. This also means that a user's job turnaround time is not only dependent on the computer system characteristics, it also depends on who else is using the machine at the time.

If a system is multiprogrammed and averages are computed over a long period T_{tot}, throughput and average job turnaround time are related by

$$\text{Throughput} = \frac{\text{average number of jobs present}}{\text{average job turnaround time}}. \tag{4}$$

For example, if the average job turnaround time is 1 minute and the average number of jobs present in the system is 3 over some long period, then the throughput is 180 jobs per hour.

If a system is not fully saturated, then throughput and turnaround time may be directly (not inversely) proportional to each other as the system load increases. Thus, a lightly loaded system may have a throughput of 10 jobs per hour with an average turnaround time of 1 minute per job, with almost no interference among the jobs. Now, if the load increases to 15 jobs per hour, average turnaround time may increase to 2 minutes per job because of interference among jobs. With 20 jobs per hour, average turnaround time may increase to 3 minutes, saturating the system. Equation 4 holds, assuming that individual job times do not vary. However, in reality jobs usually take longer as system load increases, so if throughput is plotted against turnaround time, the maximum throughput occurs just as the system is saturated. If higher throughputs are to be obtained, then shorter jobs with resulting shorter turnaround must load the system.

It is clear that turnaround time may vary differently with throughput in the *job scheduling* sense, however. Indeed, maximizing throughput could mean running all of the smallest jobs with highest priority and queueing large jobs indefinitely, a strategy that would also tend to maximize turnaround time for large users! Notice also that minimizing overhead time tends to maximize throughput (see Eqs. 1 and 2). On the other hand, the scheduling algorithms, I/O and state changing activities necessary to minimize turnaround time for some set of users may reduce throughput substantially because of the extra overhead involved.

Recall that the capacity model of Section 2.5 and the bandwidth considerations discussed throughout the book are somewhat neutral on the throughput versus turnaround time question. In other words, maximizing the utilization of whatever system hardware is available tends to yield both high throughput and low turnaround time, simply because system time is not wasted. Turnaround time also depends on how jobs are scheduled, however, and this is a key distinction that an operating system must handle.

Nor is the time the only important measure. Main memory space is a critical resource, and to measure main memory use over time, the *memory space-time product* is often used. This can be regarded as an integral or sum over time of the instantaneous amount of space used by a computation:

$$\text{Memory space-time product} = \sum_{\text{job run time}} \text{instantaneous memory space used.} \quad (5)$$

In addition to its intrinsic value as a measure of memory use, memory space-time product can be useful in relation to other criteria. For example, suppose that in a multiprogrammed system, over time period T_{tot} the average amount of main memory used by all jobs is denoted by *average total memory*. Also, suppose that over the same period, the average memory space-time product per job run is denoted *average memory space-time product*. Then, it is easy to see that

$$\text{Throughput} = \frac{\text{average total memory}}{\text{average memory space-time product}}. \quad (6)$$

Notice that the units of the RHS of Eq. 6 are

$$\frac{\text{(average memory space)}}{\text{(average memory space)} \cdot \text{(time)/job}},$$

which matches the units of throughput, that is, jobs/time. For more details of this and further relations of memory space-time product to other system parameters, see [Buze77].

Although memory space-time product is a useful measure, it does have some shortcomings as a criterion for system performance evaluation. One problem is its sensitivity to the total space allotted to a computation—if forced to run in a small space, an extraordinary amount of time may be required by some programs, for example, so there is a tradeoff between space and time.

Another problem is that CPU utilization is ignored by this measure, unless it is assumed that useful CPU activity takes place during the entire period that any memory space is occupied. The latter assumption is quite unrealistic for most computations; however, if a number of users are assumed to be sharing the entire system, then it may be more realistic.

In any case, *CPU utilization* over any time period T_{tot} may be defined as

$$\text{CPU utilization} = \frac{\text{CPU time used}}{T_{tot}}, \quad (7)$$

and it is clearly desirable to maximize this in a capacity sense. Thus, a criterion function that reflects both CPU utilization and main memory use is

$$\text{Processor-memory effectiveness} = \frac{\text{memory space-time product}}{\text{CPU utilization}}. \quad (8)$$

It is obvious that one would like to make this ratio as small as possible. However, it also has weaknesses as a system performance criterion. Suppose two different algorithms were available to solve some problem; assume one has

TABLE 7.1.   A Qualitative Comparison of Several Multiprogrammed Memory Hierarchy Sharing Systems

System Type	Memory Sharing Characteristics	System Response Time	CPU Utilization	I/O Data Rate Requirements	Comments on System
(1) I/O-CPU Overlap	A few users in sequence	Slowest	High by cycle stealing	Lowest	Run each user until I/O allows running another user already present
(2) Swapping	More users than 1	Better than 1	Combination of 1 and 3	Probably higher than 3	Dump one user and run another according to I/O, scheduling algorithm, etc.
(3) Paging	Page level sharing	May be better than 2	Determined by OS and CU design	Higher than 1	Interval timer allots time bursts. Finest memory slicing.
(4) Page set swapping	Swap user page sets	Geared to disk rotation time	Similar to 3	Probably highest	Dump all active pages when fault occurs, restart later with new and all old pages.

low space-time product and low CPU utilization whereas the other has higher values of each measure. If the *ratios* were equal for the two cases, then it is fairly clear that the first algorithm would be preferable, simply because of its lower space-time product; the low CPU utilization is probably irrelevant. On the other hand, if the total number of operations were about the same for both algorithms, then it is likely that a lower space-time product would lead to a *higher* CPU utilization (due to reduced time), so Eq. 8 would perform as desired.

In Table 7.1, several types of systems are compared using the characteristics discussed in recent sections. It is difficult to give terse comparisons and it is difficult to characterize the various multiprogramming and memory sharing systems available, but Table 7.1 does provide a brief summary of the previous discussion. It should be emphasized that Table 7.1 is qualitative and cannot be used to compare real-world systems, since many variations on these ideas are used in actual implementations.

An early, but clear and comprehensive survey of multiprogramming [Codd62] discusses the overall ideas. A number of real machine schemes appear in [Saye71] and [McWi76], whereas some aspects of multiprogramming are presented in most operating system books. For some actual measurements of a number of the parameters discussed here on an IBM 360/67 running CP-67, see [Bard71]; this paper also discusses the methodology of such studies.

7.5   PAGING PARAMETERS AND PERFORMANCE TRADEOFFS

A number of important tradeoffs must be considered in designing a memory hierarchy. The key hardware parameters to be chosen are main memory size and the speed of I/O operations. On the other hand, a user may want fast turnaround of the job or fast reaction at a terminal to one step of a job, as well as low cost.

In what follows we discuss several choices that influence the above. The page size and number of pages allotted to a job influence main memory size, as well as the user response time. The CPU time interval allotted to each job influences user response time, as well as overall system efficiency. Also, system efficiency is affected by the overall time required to carry out an I/O transaction (as discussed in Section 7.3). Thus, page size, page allotment, time allotment, and I/O time will all be studied as parameters that affect system performance in Sections 7.5.1 and 7.5.2. Furthermore, the nature of individual user's jobs is very important in determining how well-suited a hardware system is for the user. In particular, the mean page fault rate (or the mean time between page faults) for a computation is crucial in estimating a machine's performance on that computation. The addressing pattern generated by a program and the layout of a user's program and data in pages are key points here. Sections 7.5.1 and 7.5.2 deal with the monoprogrammed case exclusively, and in Section 7.5.3 we shall consider the multiprogrammed case, relating system efficiency to the I/O speed and the number of jobs being run together. The models presented here are based on measurements of certain programs but, of course, the numerical results cannot be taken to hold true universally. However, the method used and the trends shown do seem to have general application.

To a large extent, the presentation of Sections 7.5.1, 7.5.2, and 7.5.3 deals with programs as "black boxes" that generate a sequence of addresses. Various characteristics of programs will be studied in these sections without examining the structure of the programs at all. In Section 7.5.4, some details of program structure will be discussed, in relation to various page replacement schemes. This material is more intuitive than the preceding sections, not because the ideas are simpler, but because the ideas are less well understood than the earlier ideas. In the long run, it seems clear that paged memory hierarchies will be able to operate more effectively if the data and control structures of programs being run are taken into account when managing the memory hierarchy.

7.5.1   Effect of main memory allotment on page fault rate

If all of a user's instructions and data are allowed to occupy main memory, the page fault rate will be minimized; each page need be read from secondary memory just once. On the other hand, it has been observed that a small memory allotment can lead to disastrous paging rates. The relationship between main memory allotment and page faults has been studied by a number of workers [Denn68a, BeKu69, KuLa70, Denn70], and many experiments have been conducted to determine program paging behavior [Bela66, AnWa67, Ferr76, MaBa76].

One statistic of interest is the length of the mean execution burst; we define an *execution burst* ϕ to be the number of instructions executed by a program between its successive page faults (measuring time in instruction executions; that is, we scale time by the average instruction time). The mean execution burst is measured by allowing a user an initial allotment of p_0 (usually 1) main memory pages[3] and then allowing the user to accumulate more pages of memory until there are at most m pages; we call m the user's *page allotment* for program and data. At this point, any new pages required must displace pages already in main memory. In addition, a *time allotment q*, an upper bound on the total number of instructions executed, is sometimes imposed on the program. This q may be thought of as a time quantum (or slice) determined by an interval timer or by any condition that causes the program to be swapped out of main memory, for example, the arrival of a higher priority user.

Fine et al. [FJMc66] present the results of experiments for $p_0 = 1$, $m = \infty$, $q \leq 8 \times 10^4$, and a page size of 1024 words, which indicate that almost 59 per cent of all execution bursts[4] were less than 20. However, this data includes the results of explicit I/O, and it was assumed that all of a user's pages were swapped out of main memory when an explicit I/O request was made. This would tend to lower the average ϕ because ϕ would include the effects of a lot of short execution bursts that occur when a program is trying to acquire a sufficient working set of pages [Denn68b]. Coffman and Varian [CoVa68] also presented this type of data and their results are broken down by program and instructions versus data for several values of m with a page size of 1024 words. These results are summarized in Table 7.2. All of these statistics indicate that

TABLE 7.2.   Summary of Results from Coffman and Varian [CoVa68]

Program	Total Pages Instructions Data		q	Instruction Page Allotment	Mean Instructions Executed Between Instruction Page Faults φ	Data Page Allotment	Mean Instructions Executed Between Data Page Faults φ
Fast Fourier transform	6	12	100,000	1 4	94 2523	1 4 8	7.8 182 1855
SNOBOL compiler	15	22	125,000	2 4 8	58 140 305	2 4 8	8.9 27 118
Ordinary differential equation integration	2	4	135,000	Instructions and Data Combined			
				2 4	3.0 134		

[3] Strictly speaking, a user is allotted a number of *page frames*, not pages, but for simplicity we will tolerate this ambiguity.

[4] The results of these experiments consisted of 1737 execution bursts from 182 service intervals for five programs: (1) LISP, (2) an interpretive metacompiler, (3) an interpretive, interactive, display generation system, (4) an interactive JOVIAL compiler, and (5) a concordance generation and reformatting program.

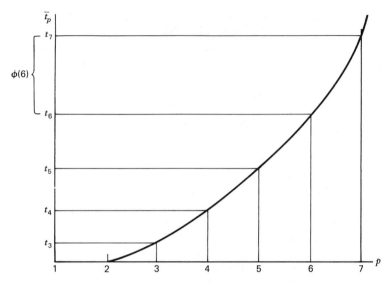

FIGURE 7.8   Mean time to reference *p* pages as a function of *p*.

execution bursts tend to be quite small, and that the mean execution burst is quite sensitive to *m* as we might expect.

Another statistic of interest is the mean time required to reference *p* distinct pages $\bar{t}_p = f(p)$. Data cited in [FJMc66] indicates the shape of the $\bar{t}_p = f(p)$ curve is as shown in Fig. 7.8; a significant number of pages are referenced within a very short time. For example, in one-half of the cases measured, the first 10 pages were required within 500 instructions (median). This has obvious implications for any virtual memory system that does not have sufficient main memory.

The arrival of page faults is often modeled by a Poisson process, where λ_i is the probability of a page fault during a short time interval Δt, given that *i* distinct pages have already been referenced. The mean time to reference *p* pages is [ShSh66]

$$\bar{t}_p = \sum_{i=1}^{p-1} \frac{1}{\lambda_i}, \qquad p > 1$$

(assuming that with probability 1, the first page is referenced at $t = 0$). Values of $1/\lambda_p$ may be estimated by examining an empirical curve for $\bar{t}_p = f(p)$ (Fig. 7.8), since

$$\Delta \bar{t}_p = \bar{t}_{p+1} - \bar{t}_p = \sum_{i=1}^{p} \frac{1}{\lambda_i} - \sum_{i=1}^{p-1} \frac{1}{\lambda_i} = \frac{1}{\lambda_p}. \qquad (9)$$

Thus,

$$\frac{1}{\lambda_p} = \bar{t}_{p+1} - \bar{t}_p = f(p+1) - f(p) \cong \frac{df(p)}{dp} \Delta p$$

or

$$\frac{1}{\lambda_p} \cong \frac{df(p)}{dp} \Delta p. \tag{10}$$

Hence, for $\Delta p = 1$, we can approximate $1/\lambda_p$ by the slope of empirical plots of $\bar{t}_p$ vs. p. Due to the form of Eq. 9, it is clear that the λ_p dimension is 1/time, and λ_p is often called the *mean page fault rate*. For Poisson processes in general, λ_i is called the *mean arrival rate* and $1/\lambda_i$ the *mean time between arrivals*.

We will model the $\bar{t}_p$ function with the formula

$$f(p) = \delta p^\gamma. \tag{11}$$

This formula has been applied to the $f(p)$ data presented in [FJMc66], and it was determined that[5] $\delta \cong 1.1$ and $\gamma \cong 3.4$. Using Eqs. 10 and 11 where $\Delta p = 1$, we find that

$$\frac{1}{\lambda_p} \cong \frac{df(p)}{dp} = \gamma \delta p^{\gamma-1} = \alpha p^\beta, \tag{12}$$

or

$$\frac{1}{\lambda_p} \cong 3.8 \, p^{2.4}.$$

If a system is in state p (p most recently referenced pages in main memory) the probability of referencing a new page (page fault) at time t, assuming a Poisson distribution, is given by $P(t|p) = 1 - e^{-\lambda_p t}$. Assuming that the system is forced to remain in state p by replacing the least recently used page with the new page each time a page fault occurs,[6] we might expect the system to continue to behave as before; that is, the system will continue to generate faults according to $1 - e^{-\lambda_p t}$. This is indeed the case when a user reaches the page allotment and $p = m$. It can then be shown that the mean time between page faults in state p is just

$$\phi_\infty(p) = \frac{1}{\lambda_p} \cong \alpha p^\beta, \tag{13}$$

where we define $\phi_\infty(p)$ to be the *steady-state mean execution burst* (the Poisson mean time between arrivals) given p pages in main memory. In practice, it is useful to know the transient behavior of $\phi_t(p)$ as well as this asymptotic behavior as t approaches infinity. Furthermore, we can assume that p is fixed at some page allotment m, so in what follows we use $p = m$.

---

[5] Determined from a least-squares fit to the function, $\ln(\bar{t}_p) = a + \gamma \ln(p) \delta = e^a$. Average error over 18 points was 16 percent. It should be remembered that values of α and β are characteristics of a given program or class of programs, and should not be used to describe all programs. A similar study of results [CoVa68] from a SNOBOL compiler yielded $\phi(p) = 0.54 \, p^{1.9}$.

[6] The least recently used (LRU) page replacement algorithm will be used throughout this section. In Section 7.5.4 we will discuss this and contrast it with other page replacement schemes.

The mean execution burst over time allotment q, $\phi_q(m)$, given that a user starts with one page and is allowed a maximum of m pages, should be derived using statistical distributions of q (see [Smit67] and [Frei68] for q distributions), but we shall settle for the following three approximations.

Case 1

If the mean time to reference m pages is greater than the time allotment,

$$\phi_q(m) \cong \frac{q}{f^{-1}(q)}, \qquad q \le \bar{t}_m, \tag{14}$$

where $f^{-1}(q)$ is the average number of pages referenced in time $q \le \bar{t}_m$. Note that $f^{-1}(q)$ can be estimated from empirical data in the form of Fig. 7.8.

Case 2

In case $q > \bar{t}_m$, but q does not approach infinity,

$$\phi_q(m) \cong \frac{q}{m + \lambda_m \cdot (q - \bar{t}_m)}, \qquad q > \bar{t}_m, \tag{15}$$

where m is the number of page faults up to time $\bar{t}_m$, and at the mean arrival rate λ_m, $\lambda_m(q - \bar{t}_m)$ is the total number of page faults generated in the remainder of time allotment q.

Case 3

For very large time allotment, $q \gg \bar{t}_m$, we have

$$\phi_q(m) \cong \frac{1}{\lambda_m}, \qquad q \gg \bar{t}_m, \tag{16}$$

which is Eq. 13 as $q \to \infty$.

Each time a page fault occurs, we have to pay a mean time T to make space for and make present in main memory a page from secondary memory. Thus, the *CPU efficiency* can be defined as

$$E(m, T, q) = \frac{\phi_q(m)}{\phi_q(m) + T}, \tag{17}$$

where T is measured in mean instruction times. Figures 7.9a and 7.9b show several E vs. (m, T) surfaces for $q = 2 \times 10^6$ and 5×10^3 where the approximations of Eqs. 14 and 15 were used to compute $\phi_q(m)$, and $1/\lambda_m = 3.8 \ m^{2.4}$.

Figure 7.9a indicates that in the region of low memory allotment m, the only way to get higher efficiency is to use a fast secondary memory. Secondary

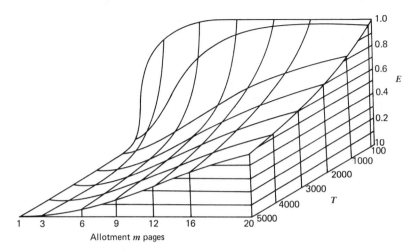

FIGURE 7.9a   CPU efficiency E versus page allotment m pages and I/O time T for $q = 2 \times 10^6$, $\alpha = 3.8$, $\beta = 2.4$.

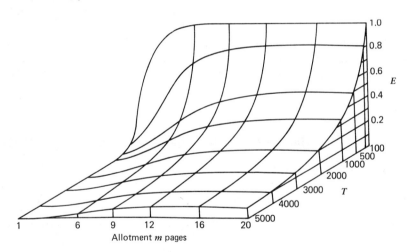

FIGURE 7.9b E versus (m, T) surface for $q = 5 \times 10^3$, $\alpha = 3.8$, $\beta = 2.4$.

memories with $T \leq 1000$ average instruction times would correspond to extended core storage or some type of bulk random access memory. In the region of larger T corresponding to drums and fast, head-per-track disks, the only way to achieve reasonable monoprogrammed efficiency is by providing sufficient main memory.

Figure 7.9b shows the effect of a smaller time allotment. In this case, efficiency is sensitive to T and insensitive to m over almost the entire surface. This is due to the fact that programs corresponding to $\alpha = 3.8$ and $\beta = 2.4$

seldom reference more than about 12 pages within the allotment $q = 5000$. Although this surface was computed using a constant q instead of using a statistical distribution of q, it still indicates what can happen to individual program efficiency when programs are swapped out of main memory for a (nonpage fault) I/O interrupt or a small system imposed time quantum. The actual degradation will, of course, depend on the characteristics of the program (α, β) as well as the system's ability to mask I/O using multiprogramming techniques.

In this section we have presented a very simple model of program paging behavior in terms of the mean time to reference p pages

$$\bar{t}_p = \delta p^\gamma.$$

Then, under the assumption that paging is a Poisson process, we derived the average execution burst ϕ as a function of the main memory page allotment m

$$\phi_\infty(m) \cong \frac{d\bar{t}_m}{dm} \cong \alpha m^\beta.$$

Using these relations and values λ, α and β derived from empirical results, we showed the effect on monoprogrammed efficiency of a gross time characteristic T of secondary memory, main memory page allotment m, and time allotment q. This was done under the assumption that the page size was 1024 words and that a least recently used page replacement algorithm was used. In the following sections, we examine the effects of different page sizes, replacement algorithms, and the use of multiprogramming to mask I/O time.

7.5.2 Effect of page size and main memory allotment on page fault rate

In the previous section we assumed that the page size was fixed at 1024 words. As we learn in this section, the *page size b* can affect the page fault rate λ for two reasons. First, main memory may be underutilized to some extent due to:

1. *Fragmentation*. Main memory not being filled with potentially useful words [Rand69].
2. *Superfluity*. The presence of words that are potentially useful but that are not referenced during a period when the page is occupying main memory.

Any underutilization of main memory tends to increase the page fault rate because the effective memory allotment is decreased (recall the last section). The second effect of b on λ is that more page faults may be generated when the page size is b than when page size is $2b$, because only one page fault is generated to reference all words in the larger page, whereas to reference the same words, two faults are generated if the page size is b.

Before discussing these ideas further, we present a brief survey of the page sizes used in several existing computer systems. In TSS/360 and MULTICS, a page size of 1024 words was used (although an attempt to allow optional 64 word pages was also made in MULTICS); pages must be physically located in page frames that are located at 1024 word boundaries. The PDP-11 family of computers uses variable sized pages (which they call segments) of up to 4096 words (16 bits each) that can be located at any 32-word boundary. Most Burroughs machines have used variable sized pages (which they call segments) from the B5000 to the present. The B6700 and B7700, for example, allow segments of any size up to a million (2^{20}) words to be located anywhere in memory.

Fragmentation occurs when the page size is too large for the blocks of program or data that the pages are to hold. For example, at the end of most programs or data stored in pages, some page space will be unused. Of course, the details of how data and programs are assigned to pages are important here. If the entire program and data space required is simply cut into a continuous sequence of pages, then the only fragmentation will occur in the last page. If each array begins with a new page, then fragmentation will occur in each array.

For variable page size machines, the above "internal" fragmentation is not a problem because the page size can be made to match whatever is to be stored. "External" fragmentation (checkerboarding) of main memory can occur, however, if there is no space in memory to insert a new page without compacting the remainder of memory (recall the checkerboarding discussion of Section 4.3.2).

Superfluity may cause more waste of main memory space than fragmentation. Nearly every page loaded into main memory is likely to contain some program or data words that are not accessed during that page's residence in main memory. Program pages have words that are skipped over and subroutines that are not called. Arrays of data may be indexed by skipping through the array rather than accessing every word in order. Some measurements of superfluity are reported in [BaSa72]. Clearly, as page size increases, there is an increasing probability that part of the page will be superfluous, especially if the time allotment is small.

In Section 7.5.1, the average execution burst $\phi(p)$ was discussed as a function of memory allotment in units of m, the number of $b = 1024$ word pages. Now we will examine the paging rate $\lambda = 1/\phi$ as a function of main memory allotment $n = mb$ words, for various values of page size b. One expects that for small n, λ will vary considerably with the page size, because for small n, the average time each page is in main memory will be relatively short. Hence, the superfluous words that go unreferenced in larger pages will occupy space that might better be occupied by new, smaller pages. On the other hand, as n increases, one expects to see page size have less effect because of a higher probability that more words in the page will be referenced due to the longer expected page residence time. In addition, one might also expect to see, for a given n, a b_{opt} such that any $b_1 > b_{opt}$ will include superfluous words and any $b_2 < b_{opt}$ will not include enough words.

Figure 7.10a is a graph of λ versus b and n based on experimental data from

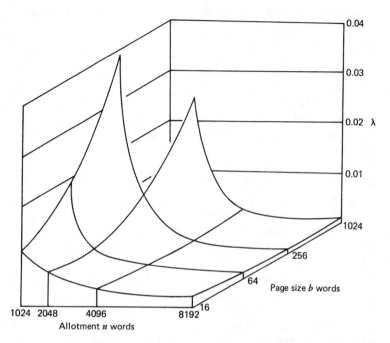

FIGURE 7.10a Page fault rate λ as a function of main memory allotment n words and page size b, for a FORTRAN compiler. Note b scale is logarithmic.

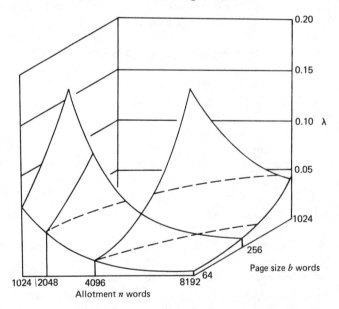

FIGURE 7.10b Page fault rate λ as a function of main memory allotment n words and size b for a SNOBOL compiler. Note λ scale is different from Fig. 7.10a; dashed lines indicate locus of constant λ.

a FORTRAN compiler [AnWa67] (in this and the following experiment, there is apparently negligible fragmentation). This graph clearly exhibits that when a program is "compressed," that is, run in a smaller main memory, large page sizes lead to excessive paging. When the page size is small, then the program tends to be more compressible. As n gets larger, the paging behavior becomes less a function of b, and for large enough n, small b may even increase the page rate. Weak minimum points were observed at the (n, b) points $(2K, 64)$, $(4K, 256)$, and $(8K, 256)$. This illustrates that if minima exist, they are not necessarily independent of n.

Figure 7.10b is another graph of λ versus n and b data for a SNOBOL compiler [CoVa68]. This program is evidently much less "compressible" than the FORTRAN compiler in Fig. 7.10a. However, it shows the same general tendencies as Fig. 7.10a except for the apparent lack of minima.

Another way to view the λ versus (n, b) relationship is by observing in Fig. 7.10b the dashed lines that pass through points of equal λ. Notice that $\lambda(8K, 256)$ is only slightly lower than $\lambda(4K, 64)$. Thus, a tradeoff can be made by halving main memory and quartering the page size; that is, we double the number of pages but each page is only one-fourth as large. However, we must also consider the increase in paging hardware necessary to handle the larger number of pages [Rose67] (recall Section 4.3.4).

The main point of these figures is that programs are more compressible when b is small; that is, they will tolerate a much smaller main memory allotment n if the page size b is small. However, if b is too small, it may lead to an increase in paging activity. (See also a study performed on the ATLAS system [BaFH68].)

The above results support arguments for variable page sizes allowing logically dependent words (e.g., subroutines or array rows) to be grouped in a page without leading to underutilization of memory due to fragmentation or superfluity. Figures 7.10a and 7.10b indicate that page sizes smaller than the 1024 words typically used may be desirable. In practice however, the page allotment may be sufficiently large so that a rather flat surface appears in the b (page size) dimension. Hence, larger pages are more desirable because there will be fewer of them and the paging hardware can be simpler; so the popular 1024-word size may be a good practical compromise.

7.5.3 Multiprogramming performance

In Section 7.4.4, two possible motivations for multiprogramming were pointed out. Here we consider only the first of them, the desire to exploit the full system capacity (recall Section 2.5), thereby increasing the system throughput. As is so often the case in computer system design, an interesting and complex tradeoff arises here.

Whenever several programs share main memory, each program operates with less main memory than it would have if it were running alone. As we have seen, less main memory causes the paging rate for a program to increase. On the other hand, multiprogramming can decrease the effective average time per I/O request (both paging and explicit) because of I/O and CPU overlap (recall point 5 of Section 7.3.6). Several questions now arise: First, when does the degradation of efficiency due to increased page traffic become greater than the increase in efficiency due to more I/O masking. Second, how much of an improvement over monoprogramming can we expect with multiprogramming? The question of page replacement algorithms for multiprogrammed systems will be discussed in Section 7.5.4.3.

Gaver [Gave67] presented an analysis of multiprogramming based on a probability model that relates CPU efficiency to the number of concurrent jobs J, where each job runs for an average of $1/\lambda$ instructions (hyperexponentially distributed) before generating an I/O interrupt, and I/O requires an average of T instruction times to complete (exponentially distributed). As J increases, each job must be executed with less main memory so paging I/O increases, and this can be added to Gaver's model, using the results of Section 7.5.1 [KuLa70].

Suppose the total available main memory is M pages of 1024 words and all programs are identical and are allocated equal amounts of this memory. Then the memory allotment for each program is just M/J pages (assuming that J

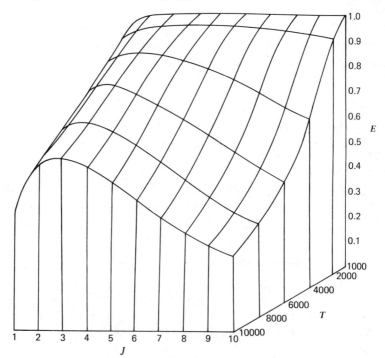

FIGURE 7.11a CPU efficiency as a function of the number of jobs J and average I/O completion time T. Average page rate is $1/(3.8(64/J)^{2.4})$ and explicit I/O interrupts occur every 10K instructions on the average.

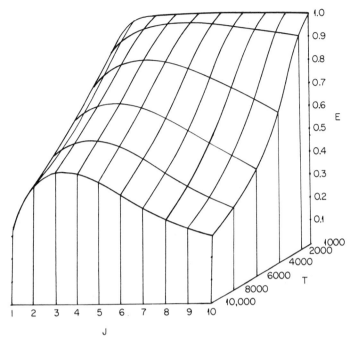

FIGURE 7.11b   CPU efficiency as a function of *J* and *T*. Average page rate is $1/(3.8(64/J)^{2.4})$ and explicit I/O interrupts occur every 5K instructions on the average.

divides *M*). Following the discussion of Section 7.5.1, the paging rate λ for each program as a function of *J* can be expressed as

$$\lambda(J) = \frac{1}{\phi(M/J)}, \tag{18}$$

where the function $\alpha \cdot (M/J)^{\beta}$ can be used to model $\phi(M/J)$, so assuming that explicit (nonpage) I/O interrupts are generated at a rate *r*, the total I/O interrupt rate for each program is

$$\lambda(J) = r + \frac{1}{\alpha \cdot (M/J)^{\beta}}. \tag{19}$$

Using Eq. 19 and Gaver's equations, CPU efficiency can be computed as a function of the number of identical jobs *J* and average effective I/O time *T* for several values of *r* and *M* and for $\alpha = 3.8$ and $\beta = 2.4$ (see Eqs. 12 and 17). The results of these computations are plotted in Figs. 7.11*a*, *b*, and *c*.

Figure 7.11*a* shows CPU efficiency for $M = 64$ and $1/r = 10,000$ (i.e., main memory is 64K words and each program generates an explicit I/O interrupt every 10,000 instructions on the average). Notice that efficiency increases with *J* up to an optimal value at J_{opt} due to overlapping I/O and CPU activities. Thereafter, efficiency decreases because of increased paging. Figure 7.11*b* corresponds to $M = 64$ and $1/r = 5000$. Efficiency is less than that in Fig. 7.11*a*

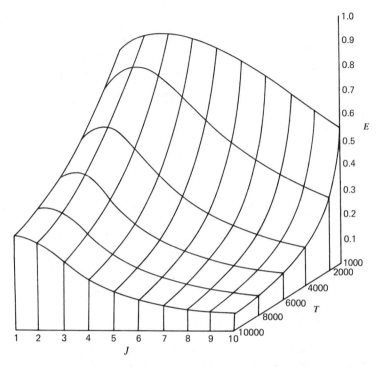

FIGURE 7.11c   CPU efficiency as a function of *J* and *T*. Average page rate is $1/(3.8(32/J)^{2.4})$ and explicit I/O interrupts occur every 10K instructions on the average.

due to the increased explicit I/O, and the gain in efficiency for monoprogramming versus multiprogramming, $E(J_{opt}) - E(1)$, is more pronounced. Figure 7.11c corresponds to $M = 32$ and $1/r = 10,000$. Efficiency is again smaller than in Fig. 7.11a, in this case because of increased paging induced by smaller *M*. Notice that when $T \geq 6000$, there is no gain from multiprogramming. This does not mean that multiprogramming with this system configuration is bad in general, but it is not wise for programs characterized by $\alpha = 3.8$, $\beta = 2.4$, and $1/r = 10,000$.

An interesting collection of measurements of the MULTICS system performance is summarized in [Salt74]. A random collection of 30–50 multiprogrammed users running in a 384-page main memory was studied. A linear ϕ versus p behavior is shown to be a reasonable approximation of the measured data, which is not surprising, given the form of Fig. 7.8 for p in the range of say 5–15. Individual program's paging rates were not measured; rather the ensemble was measured. Thus the variations from program to program, and particularly nonlinear effects that may exist when individual programs are started, seem to disappear when a collection of programs is run in a relatively large main memory. The advantages of using an approximate linear model for memory system design are obvious.

Various attempts have been made to develop models that would allow optimization of CPU efficiency in a multiprogrammed system. Of obvious importance are the I/O time and page fault rate. Three heuristics and a performance survey are presented in [DKLP76]. One heuristic, called the 50 *percent criterion*, states that if paging keeps the secondary memory busy about half of the time, then CPU utilization is maximized. The degree of multiprogramming and concommitant memory allotment to each program clearly affect the amount of paging activity.

Another heuristic is that the time to handle a page fault should be approximately equal to the mean time between page faults. A third criterion is that the page allotment for each program should be set near the knee of a plot of mean time between page faults versus space allotted. The paper [DKLP76] relates these heuristics to each other and presents theoretical and empirical evidence about their value in regulating the degree of multiprogramming and memory management policy in an attempt to maximize system throughput.

Higher level scheduling—which jobs to activate at any moment—is another difficult problem. Certain cases are mathematically tractable; see [CoMM67], [CoDe73], and [Coff76]. The software aspects of multiprogramming are discussed in many operating systems books, see for example, [MaDo74]; some empirical results appear in [BrLB72].

7.5.4 Program structure and page replacement

To this point we have discussed a number of parameters of memory hierarchies and various performance criteria regarding programs as "black boxes" that generate a sequence of addresses. Now we relate some of these ideas to the structure of programs, examining how the address sequence is generated. When a new page is needed in main memory, a decision must be made about replacing an old page, so page replacement algorithms will be discussed here. There is also a question of exactly when the decision should be made to bring a new page into main memory; looking ahead somehow and initiating page fetches before they are actually needed may enhance system performance. Finally, a program's performance in a memory hierarchy may be strongly influenced by how the program is organized and how the program and data are mapped into pages.

7.5.4.1 Program structure and transformation

In the preceding sections, we have discussed tradeoffs between main memory allotment, time allotment, page size, and I/O speed. The CPU efficiency and page fault rate were used as measures of performance. Multiprogramming was considered, with the degree of multiprogramming and rate of explicit I/O requests as additional parameters.

In all of this, real program execution times were used to produce data to illustrate the tradeoffs. The original structure of the programs was ignored however; programs were regarded as generators of long sequences of addresses, ignoring how those address sequences arise or what kinds of correlations there may be between successive addresses or "nearby" addresses.

It is clear that the addresses generated by a running program have a good deal of correlation and "structure." In every case, a sequence of program addresses is commingled with data addresses and each of these usually proceeds in a fairly regular way. Program addresses are sequential, except for jumps. Data may be accessed from several arrays that are widely scattered in memory, but then there may be a repetition, with other elements of the same arrays being accessed with a higher probability than accesses to different arrays.

Details of the process by which addresses are generated are clearly contained in the source program and data. The study and transformation of program graphs (recall Section 2.4) can be quite helpful in understanding as well as improving the performance of a program running in a memory hierarchy. We now give some intuitive ideas about how one can improve a computation by arranging matters so that the sequence of data addresses a program generates stays in the same region of address space for a relatively long time. To explore this we return to the computation of Prog. 4a of Chapter 2 (see Section 2.4.5).

Assume we have a multiprogrammed uniprocessor computer with a paged virtual memory, in which it can be assumed that each user has permanent files in secondary memory and that the B array was initialized earlier from an input device. To simplify the following discussion, we will ignore these explicit I/O operations, assuming that an earlier loop has read the disk file into main memory and that a later loop is used to save the C and D arrays in permanent files (the A array being temporary). Thus, we will consider the modified version shown in Prog. 1a.

Now, assume that N is much larger than the size of individual pages. The question is, how much time and memory space are required to execute a given program? In Prog. 1a, four arrays A, B, C, and D are used. When this program is loaded for execution, the operating system must decide how many pages of main memory are to be allotted to it. If each page holds b words, then $4\lceil N/b \rceil$ pages will be required for the four arrays of Prog. 1a. But suppose the operating system cannot allot that many pages to this program. Because the machine is multiprogrammed, the operating system may have a policy of allotting a fixed number of pages to each user. Or perhaps users are classified as large, medium, and small, and page allotments are based on the program class.

Prog.   1a

$$
\begin{array}{ll}
& \text{DO } \; S_3 \quad I \leftarrow 1, \quad N \\
S_1 & \quad A(I) \leftarrow 2*I+3 \\
S_2 & \quad C(I) \leftarrow B(I)+B(I+1) \\
S_3 & \quad D(I) \leftarrow C(I)**2/A(I)
\end{array}
$$

Prog.   1b

$$DO \quad S_1 \quad I\leftarrow 1, \quad N$$
$$S_1 \qquad A(I)\rightarrow 2*I+3$$
$$DO \quad S_2 \quad I\leftarrow 1, \quad N$$
$$S_2 \qquad C(I)\leftarrow B(I)+B(I+1)$$
$$DO \quad S_3 \quad I\leftarrow 1, \quad N$$
$$S_3 \qquad D(I)\leftarrow C(I)**2/A(I)$$

In any case, Prog. 1a could lead to very poor performance. Although there are four arrays referenced in the loop, within each statement at most three arrays are referenced (in S_3). Thus, if the operating system allotted just three pages to this program, Prog. 1a would be executed as follows. S_1 would cause a page frame of main memory to be assigned to A. Then S_2 would cause page frames to be assigned to arrays B and C and the B page to be read in. With a *demand paging* system.[7] pages are read from secondary memory as needed in response to the page fault generated when it is discovered that they are not in main memory. The A, B, and C pages allow us to compute the right-hand side of S_3 as well. But because three pages of main memory are all the operating system has allotted this program, the assignment to D in S_3 causes a page replacement to occur. Not only do we have a page fault, because the D array is not in main memory, but one of the existing pages must be replaced—from array A, B, or C. A standard algorithm would replace the least recently used (LRU), B in this case, with the new page of array D. In Fig. 7.12a we show this

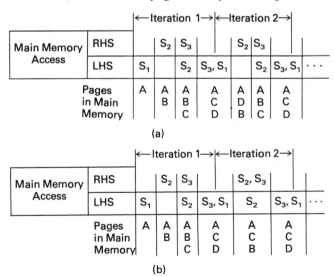

(a)

(b)

FIGURE 7.12   **Page fault sequence for Prog. 1a.**

[7] Note that all of our previous discussion has assumed demand paging; in Section 7.5.4.2 we will discuss anticipatory paging as an alternative approach.

sequence of events; each new column represents a page fault transition. By tracing through one more iteration, it is clear that the page faulting and replacement pattern repeats. Three page faults are generated per iteration.

By changing the page replacement algorithm, the space-time product for Prog. 1a can be reduced by one-third, as shown in Fig. 7.12*b*, assuming that CPU time is masked by I/O time.

Here, after the first iteration, only two page faults are generated per iteration. However, some kind of lookahead may be required to know that ACD should be followed by ACB instead of ADB, and so on; note that the LRU algorithm would in fact replace C instead of D by B. Page replacement algorithms will be discussed in Section 7.5.4.3.

Another option is to increase the program's page allotment. If four pages were allotted to this program, it would generate four faults, A, AB, ABC, and ABCD, and then no more faults would be generated on subsequent iterations until the first four pages had been exhausted. That is, after about *b* loop iterations (*b* is the page size in words) we must transition to a new set of pages, one per array. We say "about" *b* iterations because B(I) and B(I + 1) are needed at the same time, which causes some irregularity at page boundaries. But, on the average, the overall space-time product has been greatly reduced by allotting one extra page to Prog. 1a.

Of course, Prog. 1a is a simple program, and we may not always be allowed to have one page per array referenced in each loop. A general strategy for reducing space-time products follows directly from the kind of program transformations discussed earlier for speeding up Prog. 4a in Chapter 2. By simply distributing the loop control down to the level of individual statements, one can expect good performance by alloting only one page per array in each *statement*, rather than one page per array in a loop.

Consider the program of Prog. 1b. If allotted three pages for arrays, this program will run with zero page faults per iteration—after the initial page faults at the beginning of each loop and when each page is exhausted. The initial and transition page faults are approximately the same for any scheme, of course, because each page in all the arrays *must* be fetched at least once if it is to enter into the computation and stored back to secondary memory if it is to be saved. A further advantage of the distributed program of Prog. 1b is that fewer pages are needed in main memory on the average. Thus, the first loop needs just one page, the second needs two, and the third needs three. This combination of fewer pages and fewer page faults can lead to much lower space-time products for distributed loops. Not all programs behave this well, of course. One difficulty of loop distribution may arise if the same array variables are used in many statements in the loop, because distribution can cause more I/O than would occur in the undistributed case. Thus distribution may trade smaller main memory allotments for more page faults (or I/O bandwidth). If arrays are much larger than individual pages, distribution to the level of pages only may be best for loops with many dependences. This allows one pass through the loop for one page of each array without generating any page faults, given an allotment of one page per array in the loop.

We conclude with a discussion of criteria for evaluating paged, virtual memory systems. A traditional measure has been to count the number of page faults generated; a scheme that generates fewer page faults is regarded as better than one that generates many. If I/O time is relatively long compared with computation time, and turnaround time is a major consideration, this is obviously a good criterion. Another important consideration is main memory allotment, since main memory cost is high. Thus the main memory space-time product (Eq. 5) is often used. This obviously reflects the number of page faults as well as memory space requirements. If I/O time is relatively great and main memory allotment is made in fixed numbers of page frames, then for comparisons of paging schemes, the space-time product measure usually yields comparative results similar to the number of page faults; thus, a page replacement algorithm that rates high on some computation by one criterion would probably rate high by the other.

Both of these measures ignore CPU activity. Presumably, high CPU utilization (Eq. 7) is important both for high throughput and low turnaround time. Thus, space-time product divided by CPU utilization (Eq. 8) may also be a useful measure. On the other hand, it can be argued that in a multiprogrammed virtual memory system, there is always another job to be run, so CPU utilization is always high. In this case, any scheme is a failure if it increases page faults (as the loop distribution scheme may do) in the course of decreasing space-time product or enhancing CPU utilization. The counter argument is that loop distribution may decrease system response time—by quickly presenting parts of the overall results—even though total page faults increase. Recall that as soon as time-sharing is attempted, some I/O bandwidth is wasted due to unnecessary I/O.

Such arguments can continue indefinitely and can become extremely convoluted. The point is that computers are used in various ways and certain criteria may be of more interest in one application than another.

7.5.4.2 Address patterns and prepaging

When a program is being executed, the sequence of addresses it generates is called its *address trace* and the sequence of pages in which these addresses are located is called its (page) *reference string*. It is obviously desirable that sections of the reference string contain only a few distinct page numbers, because this means that only a few distinct pages are needed in main memory. The term *locality* is used to refer to the property of a program's reference string of staying in a relatively small set of pages for some time. In the example of the previous section, it was noted that the distributed form of the program needed fewer pages than the undistributed form; hence, the distributed form exhibited more locality. Measurements of some locality characteristics may be found in [MaBa76].

A related idea is the *working set* of a program [Denn68b, CoDe73]. This is a set of pages that is needed in main memory to ensure good "performance," according to some definition of performance. If a program's reference string clusters at various localities during various phases of its execution, these localities define working sets for the various phases (recall the discussion of ϕ in Section 7.5.1). Because both program and data are required for a run, it is clear that at any instant a working set contains some data and some program pages. The goal of page allotment and page replacement algorithms in operating systems is to attempt to optimize some criterion function and, in general, it seems intuitively clear that a running program's working set should be maintained in main memory, to satisfy almost any useful criterion. This principle can be used to prevent a program from *thrashing*, that is, much page faulting and resulting performance degradation due to under-allotment of memory space to the program (recall the allotment of 3 pages to Prog. 1a in Section 7.5.4.1); see Section 7.5.4.3.

All of the previous discussion of paged memory hierarchies assumed a demand paging scheme in which page faults are generated only when an address is generated by the control unit in the normal course of executing the program. Another class of systems may be called *prepaging or anticipatory paging* systems. In these, certain pages are brought into main memory somewhat before they would be referenced in the normal course of executing the program. Effectively, they are fetched by an explicit input command that is executed sufficiently long before the page is needed so that its fetching is overlapped with CPU execution of other parts of a user's program.

In many instances, the performance of a prepaged version of a program is superior to that of a demand paged version (e.g., lower space-time product or faster service time) [Jose70], [Triv76], but a key problem arises in determining how to insert the input statements for prefetching the proper blocks. In array languages, this is easier than in FORTRAN or PL/I, although loop distribution together with other transformations is of some use in this respect.

It is also quite important to consider the effects of multiprogramming here. In particular, the overlap of I/O and CPU activity for a given user (as discussed above) may not be of much value if there is always another user whose run can be overlapped with any user who generates a page fault. On the other hand, if state changing is expensive in terms of overhead and fetching a page does not involve a state change, then it may be desirable to run each user for the full time slice if at all possible, thus making prepaging an appealing possibility.

The performance of programs in a paged memory hierarchy can also be improved by reorganizing the program and data structures in various ways. For example, by simply collecting into one page the subroutines that call each other, or by forcing subroutines to begin at page boundaries, superfluity can be avoided. Experimental measurements of the effects of program restructuring in virtual memory are given in [Come67] and [TsMa72]. Several efforts have been devoted to finding good automatic methods for clustering various parts of programs in virtual memory. By running a program that has been split into multiple blocks and counting the number of times one block is referenced immediately after another, effective clusters can be generated. This information can be provided to the linker, which locates the program in virtual memory. In [HaGe71], four compilers, four assemblers, two editors, and five application programs were reorganized, with page fault reductions ranging up to ten-to-one. The above *nearness method* can be generalized [MSNO74] to include references that co-occur in some time window (not just adjacent references). Also, one can take into account the memory management strategy when reorganizing a program. In [Ferr76a] a survey of this and a number of previous techniques is presented.

Similarly, *data* may be organized in pages so that page faults are not "wasted." For example, compare a matrix multiplication program operating on two matrices that are both stored one row per page, with a scheme where the first matrix is stored by rows and the second matrix is stored by columns per page [McCo69]. A number of program transformations that users could employ to enhance memory hierarchy performance were described in [Elsh74]. By properly positioning arrays in secondary storage, [GoKu74] shows that all rotational latency can be masked for certain iterative computations. List structure storage in a memory hierarchy was studied in [BoMu67]. In data base systems, prepaging may be quite effective, as discussed in [Rodr76] and [Smit76].

7.5.4.3 Page replacement algorithms

When all page frames in main memory are full, a page fault forces the replacement of some page with a new one. The choice of a page to be replaced should be made to benefit overall system performance. A number of page replacement algorithms have been proposed and studied, and we shall summarize some of the ideas here.

Page replacement algorithms can be characterized by the type of information they use in choosing a page to replace. The difficulty of implementation and quality of performance must be considered in choosing an algorithm.

1. A very simple and naive procedure is to select a page to be replaced at random, the RAND policy.
2. The time of residence in main memory can be used to choose for replacement the oldest page, a so-called first-in, first-out (FIFO) policy.
3. The time in main memory since the page was last referenced can be used to implement a least recently used (LRU) policy.
4. Rather than time, the frequency of referencing a page may be used to implement a least frequently used (LFU) policy. Frequency may be measured over a time window or since the page entered main memory.
5. Any of the above procedures may be biased toward the selection of pages that do not have to be pushed (be written to secondary memory), because exact copies already exist in secondary memory. Only pages that have been

written need be pushed, so this rules out pure procedures, read-only data, and read/write data that has not been written during its present stay in main memory (marked by a dirty/clean bit).

6. An attempt can be made to predict, based on past references, which page will not be referenced again for the longest time in the future. In the ATLAS system such an algorithm was attempted ([KELS62], [BaFH68]).

7. The best possible page replacement algorithm (MIN or OPT) replaces that page which will not be referenced for the longest time in the future. This is not possible to implement in practice but serves as a benchmark for other algorithms [Bela66].

A number of studies have been conducted, comparing one replacement algorithm with another; we will sketch a few of them here. Page size and page allotment are often used as parameters with space-time product or page fault frequency used to measure performance.

In [Bela66], comparisons between RAND, FIFO, and LRU were made, and it was observed that RAND and FIFO gave similar performance results. LRU gave improved results, even though time since the last reference was measured as crudely as "recently used" and "not-so-recently-used." The study of type 5 information indicated that in 10–60 percent of the page faults, no push was required. The ATLAS algorithm (case 6) [BaFH68] was observed to perform worse than LRU and sometimes worse than RAND or FIFO. This was apparently due to the algorithm's attempt to take advantage of program loops, only to find that real loops were either too large or complex to be handled by the algorithm.

The use of the above ideas in a multiprogrammed computer system leads to the additional question of how the algorithm should be applied globally. For example, should LRU be used on each program or on the ensemble sharing main memory at any time? In [Oliv74], local LRU with a fixed allotment for each program and a replaced page chosen from the set of pages that generated the fault, is compared with global LRU where a replaced page is chosen from the entire ensemble of programs. The number of page faults is essentially always smaller with global LRU; the ratio of page faults for the two ranges up to 9.5, with an average of perhaps 1.3. Limited studies were also reported for local LRU with varying partitions for each program, but the results were inconclusive.

The latter case (LRU with varying space) can be regarded as a working set page replacement policy. A working set of pages at time t, $W(t, T)$ is the set of pages referenced in the time interval $[t - T + 1, t]$, where T is called the *window size* and denotes the last T memory references. As a page replacement policy, the *working set* principle is that no page of an active working set should be replaced. It follows that to manage memory exactly according to this principle, pages should be deactivated if they have not been accessed in virtual time T. Furthermore, if a page fault occurs and memory is full of working sets, a whole program should be deactivated to make space. Thus, following the policy exactly would be difficult in practice, but LRU with variable partitions for different programs is an approximation. Further discussions of this may be found in [CoDe73].

An alternative scheme which may be easier to implement is the page fault frequency (PFF) replacement algorithm; like the working set policy, it adaptively allocates more or less memory space according to a running program's needs. The PFF algorithm uses the frequency of page faults to increase or decrease a program's memory allotment based on a critical-level-of-page-faults parameter. Memory allotment changes are made at the time of a page fault, based on the measured virtual time since the last fault, the reciprocal of this time being an estimator of the page fault frequency. This algorithm was introduced in [ChOp72], which presented experimental evidence that PFF gives better space-time products than LRU. Comparisons of PFF and working set algorithms may be found in [ChOp72] as well as in [ChOp74] and [FrGu78].

The methodology of evaluating page replacement algorithms for various page allotments was substantially improved by the stack algorithm idea of [MGST70]. A traditional way to evaluate a proposed system was to simulate its performance using address traces. The approach of [MGST70] allows the page fault frequencies or hit ratios to be measured in one pass for all page allotments with a given page replacement algorithm, provided that it is a stack algorithm. The technique can also be used for memory hierarchies with more than two levels.

A page replacement algorithm is a *stack algorithm* if it has the so-called inclusion property. This implies that the sequence of sets of referenced pages (arranged as a sequence of stacks) has the property that the set of pages in memory for each allotment m, can be found by observing the top m pages in the stack. In particular, LRU, LFU, and OPT are stack algorithms (as is a variation of RAND), so they can all be evaluated efficiently. FIFO is not a stack algorithm. [MGST70] drew together all of these replacement algorithms and showed how they are related. It also proved the optimality of the OPT algorithm.

In practice a number of different schemes are used; some variations on the schemes mentioned above are employed as follows [Oliv74]. Local LRU was used by IBM in the original TSS system. Global LRU is used by IBM in CP-67 as well as OS/VS1 and OS/VS2 (recall Section 4.5.3), the University of Michigan's MTS, and the MIT MULTICS system. The working set principle (local LRU with varying partitions) is used in the Burroughs B6700, a CP-67 at IRIA in France, on MANIAC II [Morr72], and was approximated by a later IBM TSS [Dohe70].

7.6 CONCLUSION AND EXTENSIONS

This chapter has discussed shared memory hierarchies from the user's as well as the designer's standpoint. Many complex, interrelated issues are involved here—indeed, this is probably the least understood and most complex area of most computer systems. To conclude the chapter and the book, we discuss a few points otherwise glossed over in this chapter and review a few aspects of system design.

System designers constantly strive to improve their systems. We have seen that memory hierarchy performance depends on the characteristics of the individual programs being run, as well as on the system hardware and software. One of the issues we avoided is which jobs among those waiting to run should be activated? Job scheduling is a difficult problem mathematically, even when it is abstracted to some degree, but real-world scheduling may include not only a number of programs and processors, but also the sharing of a memory hierarchy. Furthermore, priorities of various kinds must be considered, and user satisfaction may be difficult to quantify. Also, as we pointed out earlier, computer center managers' goals may differ from users' goals. A survey of mathematical as well as practical techniques concerning some of these issues may be found in the latter part of [IEEE75].

It should be clear that the five system design criteria of Section 1.1.1—cost, speed, quality and usefulness, design assurance, and reliability—all are of concern in memory hierarchy design; we have discussed various aspects of them throughout the chapter. As the structure of various kinds of computations becomes better understood, it is likely that better systems will be designed for various classes of users. For example, specialized memory hierarchy hardware and software for data bases and information retrieval can be quite cost-effective [BaHs76], [Stel77]. A number of aspects of interactive system design are presented in various papers in [IEEE75].

When computer systems are capable of holding a great deal of data, two other issues arise: *individual privacy* and *computer security*. The rights of individuals concerning the collection and filing of information about them and the subsequent use of this information in making decisions about them are privacy subjects that have become more serious with the introduction of computers. The record-keeping systems of federal agencies (with certain exceptions) are controlled by the Privacy Act of 1974. This innovative legislation will probably be followed with legislation controlling law enforcement agencies, private industry, and other organizations in the U.S.A.

Computer security involves the prevention of unauthorized access to stored data (as well as avoiding denial of access to authorized parties) and the protection of computer systems from physical harm. Several hundred cases of computer security abuse had been reported by 1975 and the problems are likely to grow. Hardware protection methods are available (recall the memory protection schemes of Chapter 5), but software security is more difficult and research in these areas will continue. For more discussion of security and privacy, see [TuWa76] and the references cited there.

On line computer terminals have proliferated to the point that today computers directly affect the lives of many ordinary people. However, the future probably holds more advances in this area than in other parts of computer systems. In particular, it is likely that new technology for memory hierarchies will make much larger data bases available at higher speeds. Furthermore, better understanding of computations should make it possible to reorganize them to fit new machine organizations. When computer services arrive in people's homes, it is very likely that access to large central memory hierarchies will be one of the most important services provided. Terminals with displays and microprocessors may be used in homes, but files of data will almost certainly be maintained centrally and shared via networks. Thus, extensions of the ideas of this chapter will probably be studied far into the future.

PROBLEMS

Easy problems in text order

7.1 The following announcement of a new line of disks appeared on page 78 of the December 1972 issue of *Computer Design:*

> Eight models are available in two series (all with 120 kilobytes/track): the 010 series, with 128 tracks, in 3600 and 6000 rpm and a useful capacity of 1.875 megabytes; the 100 series in six models, 3600 and 6000 rpm, with useful capacities of 2.8325, 5.675, and 11.25 megabytes on 192, 384, and 786 heads, respectively. Common track capacity is achieved by recording at 7.2- and 12-MHz data rates, utilizing the proprietary OHC recording technique.
>
> The 010 series recording medium is a single, nonremovable, belt-driven, 14.5″ disc mounted on an industry-standard spindle; the 100 series uses a 16″ disc mounted in a field removable module containing the bearings and recording heads. Both are nickel cobalt plated with a protective overcoat and are multiple sourced to a common specification. The 010 series has 8 flying head assemblies of 17 channels each mounted on one side of the disc for its addressable and spare capacity; while the 100 series has 12, 24, and 48 identical head assemblies on one or two sides of one disc or both sides of two discs.

One number is in error by a factor of 10. Point out the error and explain why it cannot be correct. The "series" numbers are okay.

7.2 Consider a fixed-head magnetic drum driven by a 2400 rpm motor. The data tracks are 25″ long and data is stored at a density of 1K bits/inch. What is the average access time (latency) in reading the drum? At what data rate (bits/sec) will the drum operate when transmitting data?

7.3 For a typical, removable pack, movable-head disk storage system that contains a single drive, give a reasonable estimate of:
  (a) The expected average rotational latency.
  (b) The time to move the heads from one edge of the disk surface to the other edge.

(c) The sum of the average rotational latency and the head-motion seek time to a nearby track.

(d) The time to change disk packs.

7.4 A floppy disk that rotates at 360 rpm has 77 tracks, any one of which can be read from or written onto at the fixed rate of 250,000 bits per second. Each track is divided into 16 sectors. In the questions that follow, a byte is 8 bits.

(a) What is the maximum storage capacity of the disk in bytes?

(b) Assuming the head is in contact with a particular track, what is the latency (average access) time for any sector on that track?

(c) If each sector is to store a number of bytes that is an integer power of 2, what is the maximum number of bytes per sector?

(d) For a bit density of 3200 bits per inch, what should the track diameter be?

7.5 Suppose that we are using an interactive text editor that has a search command allowing a user to search for the next occurrence of an arbitrary word. In executing the command the editor may have to search an average of one whole page (about 30 lines of 60 characters each). Furthermore, the editor may work with unnumbered files that prevent any other mode of access than a linear search, which means that each editing command may involve an equally long search. In this case the response time of the system may be limited by the rate at which comparisons can be made. Assume that one comparison takes $1 \mu s$ (recall that we are actually executing a loop with array indexing and a conditional branch). How many users can the system accommodate without any users sensing a delay if each user requests one search every 10 seconds?

Suppose that we cannot do a character by character comparison. Assume that the computer allows word comparison only when there are four characters per word. Then we will have to shift, mask, and compare four times per word, making the equivalent comparison time $3 \mu s$ per character. Further assume that the operating system overhead is $300 \mu s$ per user to handle page requests and time slice scheduling. How many users can the system support conveniently?

7.6 Assume a head-per-track disk with an associative queuer for I/O requests, where n requests can be held in the queue and the rotation time of the disk is t seconds. Assume that a request for any one of m sectors is equally likely and that there are many more sectors than n. If n were changed from 1 to k, what speedup in I/O would you expect? Give an order of magnitude estimate.

7.7 (a) The miss ratio is the reciprocal of the number of instructions executed per page fault. What is the miss ratio in terms of:

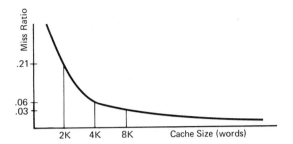

ϕ—execution burst, n—memory allotment (in words), E—CPU efficiency, and t_m—mean time to reference m pages?

(b)   What cache size would you recommend based only on the above curve? Consider the cost of typical cache memories in your response.

7.8   Suppose a compiler and its data require 80K words of memory. If it is to be run on a paged machine with a memory allotment of 4096 words, would it be better to have 64-word pages or 1024-word pages?

7.9   Show that, if the proper page allotment is made, distribution of the following loop down to individual statements will reduce the space-time product of the program segment. Also show that distribution will increase the I/O bandwidth over the nondistributed segment with a four page allotment if the arrays span two or more pages.

$$\text{DO} \quad S_3 \quad I \leftarrow 1, N$$
$$A(I) \leftarrow B(I) + C(I)$$
$$C(I) \leftarrow B(I) * A(I)$$
$$S_3 \qquad D(I) \leftarrow A(I) + B(I)/C(I)$$

Medium and hard problems in text order

7.10   In the movable-head IBM 3330 disk drive, a feature called rotational position sensing is provided, which frees the I/O channel from continuously comparing information specifying the desired data with header information stored on the disk before each data block. The comparison for a desired sector is carried out by logic in the disk controller as shown in Fig. 7.3, and during this time period, the channel can handle other activities. The 3330 drive motor operates at 3600 rpm and there are 128 sectors per track. Assume that with rotational position sensing, a channel need be active only during data transmission, and that without it the channel is tied up, on the average for one-half a rotation, waiting for the proper block. With rotational position sensing, how much time will the channel be active per sector transmission? What is the effective decrease in channel duty cycle with rotational position sensing?

7.11   When new software is under development, it is often a good idea to keep a backup copy of a disk pack containing each day's work. This prevents losing more than a day's work due to an inadvertent disk write to the wrong location, a head crash, and so on. Suppose you want to copy a (2314 type) disk pack that has 20 surfaces, 200 tracks per surface and a 2400 rpm motor. Assume an I/O request is issued for each track and that the software time plus a track-to-track seek requires 5 ms.

(a)   What total time is required to copy one disk to another, assuming the two disks share a controller and I/O channel?

(b)   How much main memory space is needed for buffer space? (Note that it is *not* possible to read from one disk and write directly onto another one!)

7.12   Consider the problem of merging a number of ordered lists stored on a disk in 1K-word blocks. Assume that you have a 4K-word main memory buffer available for the process. The disk has a rotation time of 25 ms, an average global seek time of 50 ms, and a track-to-track seek time of 5 ms. The average global seek time must be paid whenever data from a "new" file is to be merged because they are scattered randomly on the disk. However, intermediate (sometimes called scratch) files are organized on adjacent tracks and we can assume a track-to-track seek time is sufficient when we are working from and to these (some may require no seek, others may require motion across 2 or 3 tracks). Writing to the scratch file initially, however, requires a global seek.

(a)   Assume that the data base consists of N blocks of 1K words each. You are to merge these into one NK-word block stored on the disk. Estimate the time required to complete this task, assuming that each step in the merge requires 1 ms of CPU and main memory time. How important would it be to have a processor five times that fast? If a CPU that operated five times slower could be used at a substantial price saving, how much would the throughput suffer for this computation?

(b)   In most inverted file information retrieval systems, document postings files must be merged to determine responses to a query. If the elements merged are pointers to documents that contain certain words in the query, there may be substantial overlap in the merged lists. If the length of a merged list pair can be reduced to 0.89 times the length of two input lists, rework the above problem.

7.13   Suppose you have a disk file with the following characteristics:
(i)   16 surfaces.
(ii)   3200 tracks (200 per surface).
(iii)   25 ms rotation time.
Each track contains two blocks of 5000 characters each. There is a block gap following each block that requires 3 ms to pass under the read heads:

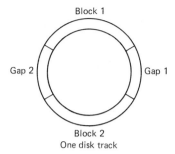

Block 1

Gap 2   Gap 1

Block 2
One disk track

The time required to move the heads from one track to an adjacent track is 5 ms. Only one head may read at a time, the heads are ganged so that they all move together, and the heads do not return to a unique rest position after every read but remain over the track just read, unless moved. Memory may not be read from and written to concurrently.

(a) What is the maximum character rate?

(b) What is the minimum time required to read the entire file?

(c) What is the average access time? (Think twice—this is nontrivial.)

(d) If a set of data is stored in 100 blocks distributed randomly with the address of the next block stored in the current block, what is the average time required to read the data set?

(e) If you were faced with the problem of allocating disk space for data sets to be stored in such a chained fashion, what sort of strategy would you employ?

7.14 In this problem we are given a machine configuration, a problem, and two possible solutions. Analyze the information and choose one of the two solutions. The machine configuration is:

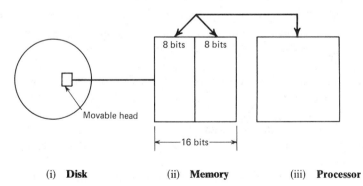

8 bits   8 bits

Movable head

←————16 bits————→

(i) **Disk**   (ii) **Memory**   (iii) **Processor**

(i) A movable-head disk with:

(a) Rotation time $= r$.

(b) n bits/track.

(c) Seek time $= r - \varepsilon$ (i.e., just a little less than the rotation time). This is the time required, ad hoc, to move the head from any track to any other track.

(ii) A memory that is 16 bits wide, but that may be referenced as either one 16-bit memory or as two 8-bit memories. In the latter case, access is simultaneous but not independent, that is, both 8-bit memories must be filling or emptying or quiescent at any given time. This memory, when full (i.e., used as a 16-bit memory), holds n bits, namely, the number of bits on one track of the disk.

(iii) A processor with all the operations required to solve the problem in which we are interested.

The problem is to match each 8-bit character on the disk with one that is held in a register in the processor and count the number of matches.

The two methods of solution are:

(i) Read a track, then use the memory as two 8-bit memories, where the time to process each 8-bit memory $= r - \delta (\delta > 0)$.

(ii) Read a track, then use the memory as one 16-bit memory where the time to process the entire memory $= 2r + \beta (\beta > 0)$. The extra time is required to unpack and shift the contents of the 16-bit configuration.

Given that no cycle stealing is allowed, and that the seek command can be overlapped with processing:

(a) Show how to do each method in the fastest possible way. Which method is best? State all your assumptions.

(b) Suppose you find a second memory that has exactly the same characteristics as the memory above. Connect it to the machine so that while the data from one memory is being processed, the other memory can be reading from the disk. Show which method is best by determining the fastest possible way to perform each one. State all your assumptions.

(c) Method (i) appears very sensitive to δ. Consider method (i) with $\delta < 0$; now how do the two methods compare?

7.15 You have been chosen to design a large shift register memory for your company, using an integrated circuit package they manufacture. The package contains a $16K \times 1$-bit shift register that shifts at a rate of 10^7 bits/sec. Your goal is a memory with access time less than 7.5 ms, and a transmission rate of 10^7 bytes/sec. One error detection bit per byte must be maintained in the memory. Assume that the IC package contains data storage, plus logic for addressing, logic for serially connecting several shift registers (to form a shift register with one larger loop), and an I/O register. Two possible printed circuit boards are available: One holds up to 85 IC packages and costs \$100; the other holds up to 40 IC packages and costs \$25. It is estimated that the cost of each IC package, wired to a printed circuit board, is about \$10. Your company determines a product's selling price using a markup factor of 4 over the cost of manufacturing it. The company wants a product that will sell at under \$100,000. What is the largest capacity memory you can design? You can assume that global addressing to select one of these boards requires negligible time and cost.

7.16 Consider the multiterminal system of Section 7.4.1 from the capacity standpoint (recall Chapter 2). Let the system be a CPU and a set of terminals. When the CPU is displaying data, assume its bandwidth is two words (one in and one out) of 32 bits each per microsecond. Draw a capacity surface for the CPU together with 30,000 terminals (1200 bits/ sec), and show the operating point discussed in the text. To overlap the CPU and terminal activity, what assumption is being made about I/O operations? More typically, the text pointed out, 300 users would share a CPU. What does this do to the capacity surface?

7.17 Suppose we have a multiprogrammed computer in which each job has identical characteristics. In one computation period T, half the time is spent in I/O and the other half in computation, and each job runs for a total of n periods. Compute the turnaround time, throughput, and CPU utilization for one, two, and four simultaneous jobs, assuming that the period T is distributed in each of the following ways.

(a)

(b)

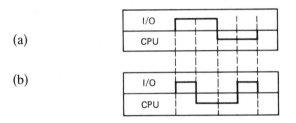

Does the distribution of I/O and CPU time ever change these characteristics? What if the ratio of I/O and CPU time changes?

7.18 The throughput of a multiprogrammed memory system (Eq. 2) is directly related to the space-time product of the system by Eq. 6.
(a) Consider the following example with 3 pages of memory allocated to 5 jobs (circled) as follows:

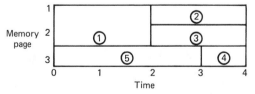

Compute the average space-time product and show that Eq. 6 holds true. Suppose, that job ⑤ is broken into 2 jobs, one with 2 units of time and one with 1 unit of time. Show that Eq. 6 still holds true. Show that even if there was no job in the system to fill page 3 during the time interval from 3 to 4 (i.e., if job ④ did not exist), Eq. 6 would still hold true.

(b) Equation 6 can be derived by considering three elementary variables:

- The total time period, T_{tot}.
- The number of jobs serviced during T_{tot}.
- The instantaneous memory space used for each job at each interval of time.

Note that the space-time product of a job sums instantaneous memory space used over time for one job, and the average total memory sums over time, the instantaneous memory used by all the jobs in the system. Derive Eq. 6 in terms of these variables.

(Problems 7.18 through 7.20 are developed further in [Buze76].)

7.19 An interesting performance criterion discussed in Section 7.4.6 is the average number of jobs present in the system at any time, or simply *average jobs present*. For example, this variable is of interest in measuring the congestion of a time-shared system. In terms of our other variables,

Average jobs present = throughput · average system response time.

(a) Consider the following diagram showing the job history of 5 jobs (circled) active over 4 units of time. Show that average jobs present equation given above is true in this case.

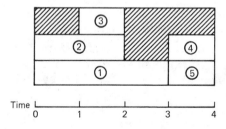

(b) Explain why the equation above is correct. Start by giving a dimensional argument. (*Hint:* One way to derive the result is by using Eq. 6 when all jobs are restricted to one unit of memory.) You may notice that this equation is similar to Little's result for queues, which states that the average number in the system is equal to the average arrival rate times the average time spent in the system.

7.20 In a time-shared system, the system response time can be determined from other variables using approximations such as those used in Section

7.4.6. We can estimate that

$$\frac{\text{Average system}}{\text{response time}} = \frac{\text{number of terminals} \cdot \text{average processing time}}{\text{processor utilization}}$$

$$- \text{average user response time.}$$

(a) Construct a timing diagram showing how four user actions would overlap (assume a favorable overlap). Show why the response time equation is valid.

(b) How does this equation relate to Eq. 3? Specifically, show how job turnaround time in a time-shared environment depends on the number of terminals and the utilization as well as the processing that must be done to complete the job itself.

7.21

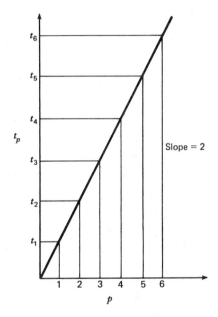

Suppose that t_p, the time for a program to reference p pages, is as shown above.

(a) What is the page fault rate?

(b) What is the value of the execution burst ϕ for large q?

(c) Would you expect the CPU efficiency for this program to be very sensitive to the program's page allotment? Justify your answer. Is a graph of this slope realistic?

(d) Suppose the p versus t_p curve is $t_p = e^p$ and recompute parts (a) through (c).

7.22 An LRU page replacement algorithm can be implemented (and has been used in the IBM 360/85) with an associative memory as follows.

Make a square binary matrix and assign each page, say j, to the jth row and the jth column. When page j is referenced, first set the jth row to 1's, and then set the jth column to 0's. For example, assume there are four pages and the instantaneous contents of the matrix is:

	1	2	3	4
1	0	1	1	0
2	0	0	1	0
3	0	0	0	0
4	1	1	1	0

If page 3 is referenced next, the matrix will contain:

	1	2	3	4
1	0	1	0	0
2	0	0	0	0
3	1	1	0	1
4	1	1	0	0

(a) Show the transition of the four-page matrix for the reference string 1 2 3 4 3 2 1 4 3 2; assume the matrix is initially all zeroes.

(b) Show that the most recently used page is always the page that has the largest number of 1's in its row and that the least recently used page always has the least number of 1's in its row.

(c) Does the least recently used page always have all 0's in its row?

7.23 Suppose you are computing the row sums $c_i = \sum_{j=1}^{n} a_{ij}$ of an array A which is 100 by 100. Assume the machine that you are using is paged with a page size of 1000 words and you have a page allotment of 5 pages for data.

(a) Would you expect any difference in the page fault rate if A were stored in virtual memory by rows or by columns, assuming a "page on demand" system? Explain your answer.

(b) If you could "prepage" the data by issuing explicit I/O requests, would you expect any improvement over part (a)? Explain your answer.

7.24 In some virtual memory systems it is possible to store the matrix as submatrices so that a square submatrix of m rows by m columns fills one page (as closely as possible). An original array with dimensions $n_1 \times n_2$ would be composed of $\lceil n_1/m \rceil$ submatrix rows and $\lceil n_2/m \rceil$ submatrix columns. This representation would be invisible to the programmer and it would reduce the possibility of the erratic behavior that can occur with either row or column storage. (This method is advocated in [McCo69].)

Suppose we wish to find the row sums of an array A (see Problem 7.23) that is 100×100, on a machine with a page size of 1024 words.

(a) If there is a page allotment of five pages for data, what is the page fault rate? Compare this page fault rate with the row storage and the column storage page fault rates. Approximate the page fault rate by the total number of page faults divided by the total number of memory references.

(b) If the page allotment is three pages for data, what is the page fault rate? Assume that the least recently used page is replaced.

(c) Compare the storage fragmentation of the submatrix storage scheme to the row storage scheme. For the row storage, assume that rows do not span pages.

7.25 There are several techniques used by programmers to improve the performance of their programs in a demand paging environment. For each of the following techniques, explain how the technique helps to reduce page faults and give an example of a program which might use the rule. (These techniques are listed in approximately decreasing order of importance; see [Elsh74] for specific details.)

(a) Loops should be nested in an order so that the distance between successive references to array data are as close as possible.

(b) Distribute loops as in Chapter 2 when advantageous.

(c) If possible, operate on all the elements indexed by an outer loop variable that are in one page of data, while the page is in main memory being operated on by an inner loop.

(d) On a system that uses some locality principle to replace pages, alternate the increment direction in inner loops. For example, instead of:

$$
\begin{aligned}
&\text{DO} \quad S_1 \quad I \leftarrow 1, N \\
&\qquad \text{DO} \quad S_1 \quad J \leftarrow 1, N \\
&\qquad \qquad \vdots \\
&S_1 \quad \text{CONTINUE}
\end{aligned}
$$

use:

$$
\begin{aligned}
&\text{DIRECTION} \leftarrow 1 \\
&\text{FIRST} \leftarrow 1 \\
&\text{LAST} \leftarrow N \\
&\text{DO} \quad S_2 \quad I \leftarrow 1, N \\
&\qquad \text{DO} \quad S_1 \quad J \leftarrow \text{FIRST}, \text{LAST}, \text{DIRECTION} \\
&\qquad \qquad \vdots
\end{aligned}
$$

S_1 CONTINUE

   DIRECTION $\leftarrow -1 *$ DIRECTION

   TEMP $\leftarrow$ FIRST

   FIRST $\leftarrow$ N

   LAST $\leftarrow$ TEMP

S_2 CONTINUE

7.26 Prepaging can be a useful technique for reducing the page fault rate of a program. Assume that there are two system commands: PRE(x), which will load page x when the next page fault occurs (as well as loading the page causing the next fault, i.e., demand prepaging [Triv76]), and FREE(x), which marks page x as being replaceable when another page must be loaded. Assume the system uses square submatrix storage for matrices. Write a prepaging algorithm that transposes (in place) a square matrix composed of 25 submatrices with one submatrix per page. Your algorithm should operate on at most 2 submatrices at any time. Thus it should be able to have only four pages (including prepaged pages) in memory at any time. Show that the number of page faults can be reduced by more than 50 percent over regular demand paging. Compare, in a general way, the space-time product of your prepaging algorithm with the space-time product that would be obtained with a demand paging system which allots your program 3 pages. Compare both methods when the system allots your program 5 pages. Assume that CPU time is negligible compared with the disk access time that contains factors t_p and $t_k = (t_a + b/\rho)$ as in Section 7.3.6.

7.27

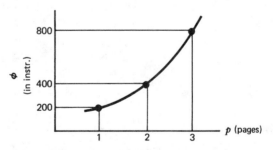

Suppose we wish to multiprogram two identical programs with the characteristic curve shown and that we only have 4 page frames of main memory. Assume each program has a total execution length of 4000 instructions and that q, the time slice, is much larger than ϕ_p. T, the page fetch time, is 600 instruction times.

(a) Is it better to give each program two pages or give one program one page and the other three pages for half the run and then reverse the allocation for the second half of the run? Maximize

CPU utilization. Ignore transients caused by initial loading and reallocation.

(b) Fill out a timing diagram to verify your results showing CPU and disk idle periods and total execution time.

7.28 Several studies have indicated that although different paging algorithms do produce different page fault rates, most implementable algorithms do not do significantly worse than the optimal page replacement algorithm in the sense that the page fault rate is much more sensitive to the memory allotment than to the page replacement algorithm [CoDe73]. In general, we would see the following behavior:

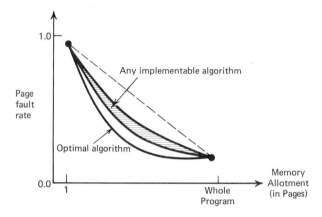

(a) One reason why all page replacement algorithms produce a convex down curve is that they take advantage of the locality of the program to reduce the paging demands that would be associated with a totally random, nonlocal program which would produce a straight line. Use the reference string

A B C C A B B A B A

and the LRU replacement algorithm to show that a convex down curve is produced.

(b) The optimal page replacement algorithm mentioned in the graph above (called Belady's algorithm or MIN) is not implementable because it assumes that the entire page reference sequence is known in advance. It is a useful reference point to gauge the performance of other algorithms, however. Belady's algorithm always replaces the page with the greatest forward distance in the string of references. For example, with the string

A B C C A C B A B A,

at the second reference to A, if a page must be replaced, MIN would replace B if possible because the next B is two references ahead. If B is not currently in memory, C would be replaced because the next reference to C is one ahead. Using the reference string of (a), show that Belady's algorithm improves the page fault rate obtained using LRU. Does this experiment agree with the graph above?

7.29 In Section 7.5.4, it was shown that in a uniprocessor with a paged virtual memory, a change in page allotment can make a drastic change in program and system performance. In fact, more serious anomalies can exist. Given the following program and data, and a FIFO (first in-first out) page replacement algorithm, show that the number of page faults is actually higher if the program is allotted four pages instead of three pages.

Program:

$$\text{DO} \quad S_5 \quad I \leftarrow 1, 3$$
$$B(I) \leftarrow A(I) + 2$$
$$\text{IF} \quad B(I) = 0 \quad \text{GO TO} \quad S_3$$
$$D(I) \leftarrow 2 * C(I)$$
$$\text{IF} \quad D(I) < 0 \quad \text{GO TO} \quad S_5$$
$$S_3 \quad E(I) \leftarrow 0$$
$$S_5 \quad \text{CONTINUE}$$

Data:

$$A = (-3 \quad -2 \quad -1)$$
$$C = (-1 \quad 0 \quad 1)$$

Assume each array is in a different page. See [BeNS69].

7.30 In this problem, we will construct the working set of a small reference string and make some observations about its characteristics. Suppose a program has 5 pages and generates the following 25 references:

A B C D E B B D D E A D E C D E C D E A B A B A B.

(a) Give the working set at each reference for window sizes T: 2, 3, 4, 5, and 6. For example, at the second reference to D we would have:

$$W(8, 2) = W(8, 3) = \{D, B\}, W(8, 4) = W(8, 5) = \{D, B, E\}, W(8, 6)$$
$$= \{D, B, E, C\}.$$

(*Hint:* The working set for all window parameters can be easily constructed by first constructing a sequence of least recently used stacks for the reference string.)

(b) Now find the average working set size $s(T)$ for each T. Graph the function $s(T)$. Show that: It is nondecreasing in T; it is less than min $(5, T)$ for all T; and it is concave down $[s(T-1)+s(T+1) \leq 2 \cdot s(T)]$.

(c) Find and graph the average number of page faults per reference for each T; this function is denoted $m(T)$. Using probability arguments, it can be shown that $s(T+1)-s(T) \approx m(T)$. That is, the "slope" of the working set size is the page fault rate. Is this generally the case for this sample reference string?

(d) The working set principle of multiprogrammed memory management states that a program will be allowed to run if its working set is in main memory. If more pages are needed to bring in the working set of a program, they may not be taken from another active program (as the LRU algorithm might) without the other program being deactivated. To be implementable, several questions remain. For example, how large should the window be? Based on the space-time product for each window size above, how large should the window size be for this reference string? Note that $s(T) \cdot m(T)$ can be used as a rough approximation to the space-time product. (Why?)

7.31 The stack algorithm concept is useful for analyzing page replacement algorithms and for modeling the paging characteristics of programs. A stack algorithm has the property [MGST70] that for any string of memory references, the set of pages that the algorithm would retain in a memory allotment of m pages would be among the pages retained in a memory allotment of $m+1$ pages. Thus the top m elements of a properly maintained stack show which pages would occupy an m-page memory. Movement of pages in the stack is determined by a separate list of the replacement priority of the pages. It can be shown that a stack algorithm always replaces the page with the least priority. For example, the least frequently used (LFU) algorithm gives highest priority to the page which is used most frequently (pages with identical frequency are ordered in least recently used order). For the reference string

$$A B C C C A B A A B,$$

the priority for each reference would be:

```
highest:  A  B  C  C  C  C  A  A  A
          A  B  B  B  A  B  C  C  B
lowest:      A  A  A  B  A  B  B  C
```

The stack at each reference would be:

```
m = 1  A  B  C  C  C  A  B  A  A  B
m = 2     A  B  B  B  C  C  C  C  A
m = 3        A  A  A  B  A  B  B  C
```

It can be shown [CoDe73] that any stack algorithm behaves as follows:

(1) The referenced page always moves to the top of the stack.

(2) The pages below the referenced page do not move.

(3) Pages above the referenced page (before it moves to the top) are never moved up in the stack.

(4) The page displaced from the top of the stack moves down one page at a time until it encounters a page of lower priority. This lower priority page then moves down until a lower priority page is encountered and so on until a page reaches the space vacated by the referenced page. (In the example above, at the second A reference, A displaces C by property 1. C displaces B because it has higher priority at that instant. B then fills the spot vacated by A.)

(a) Check that rules 1 through 4 are obeyed by the LFU example. Also try a few short reference strings to verify that LFU is a stack algorithm according to our definition.

(b) How does the priority list relate to the stack for the LRU algorithm? (*Hint:* The answer is strikingly simple. In fact, LRU is the only paging algorithm with this property.)

(c) What does the definition of the stack algorithm imply about any anomalous page fault rate behavior when a program is allotted $m+1$ pages (as in Problem 7.29)?

(d) All stack algorithms make the processing of a test program in page fault rate simulations easier because only one pass through the reference string is necessary to determine the program's performance with any memory allotment. Verify this for the reference string above under the LFU algorithm by generating a page fault trace for $m = 1$, 2, and 3.

REFERENCES

[ABCC66] R. J. Adair, R. U. Bayles, L. W. Comeau, and R. J. Creasy, "A Virtual Machine System for the 360/40," IBM Corp. Cambridge Scientific Center, Rpt. No. 320-2007, Cambridge, MA, May 1966.

[AbKu73] N. Abramson and F. F. Kuo, eds., *Computer-Communication Networks*, Prentice-Hall, Englewood Cliffs, N.J., 1973.

[AGMR71] A. Avižienis, G. C. Gilley, F. P. Mathur, D. A. Rennels, J. A. Rohr, and D. K. Rubin, "The STAR (Self-Testing And Repairing) Computer: An Investigation of the Theory and Practice of Fault-Tolerant Computer Design," *IEEE Trans. on Computers*, Vol. C-20, No. 1, pp. 1312-1321, Nov. 1971.

[AGOW66] B. W. Arden, B. A. Galler, T. C. O'Brien, and F. H. Westervelt, "Program and Addressing Structure in a Time-Sharing Environment," *Journ. of ACM*, Vol. 13, No. 1, pp. 1-16, Jan. 1966.

[AhRa75] N. Ahmed and K. R. Rao, *Orthogonal Transforms in Digital Signal Processing*, Springer-Verlag, New York, 1975.

[AHSW62] J. P. Anderson, S. A. Hoffman, J. Shifman, and R. J. Williams, "D825-A Multiple Computer System for Command and Control," *Proc. AFIPS Fall Joint Computer Conference*, Vol. 22, pp. 86-96, 1962.

[AlLu62] R. H. Allmark and J. R. Lucking, "Design of an Arithmetic Unit Incorporating A Nesting Store," *Proc. of IFIP Congress*, pp. 694-698, 1962.

[AmBB64] G. M. Amdahl, G. A. Blaauw, and F. P. Brooks, Jr., "Architecture of The IBM System/360," *IBM Journ. of R. and D.*, Vol. 8, No. 2, pp. 87-101, April 1964.

[Amda75] "Amdahl 470 V/6 Features," Amdahl Corporation, Sunnyvale, CA, 1975.

[Anon74] Anon., "Will the Inventor of the First Digital Computer Please Stand Up?", *Datamation*, pp. 84–90, Feb. 1974.

[AnST67] D. W. Anderson, F. A. Sparacio, and R. M. Tomasulo, "The IBM System/360 Model 91: Machine Philosophy and Instruction Handling," *IBM Journ. of R. and D.*, Vol. 11, No. 1, pp. 8–24, 1967.

[AnWa67] W. Anacker and C. P. Wang, "Performance Evaluation of Computing Systems with Memory Hierarchies," *IEEE Trans. on Electronic Computers*, Vol. 16, No. 6, pp. 765–773, Dec. 1967.

[AsFR67] R. A. Aschenbrenner, M. J. Flynn, and G. A. Robinson, "Intrinsic Multiprocessing," Proc. *AFIPS Spring Joint Computer Conference*, Vol. 30, pp. 81–86, 1967.

[Ashl68] D. W. Ashley, "A Methodology for Large Systems Performance Prediction" TR00. 1773, IBM Systems Development Division, Poughkeepsie, N. Y., Sept. 1968.

[Atki68] D. E. Atkins, "Higher Radix Division Using Estimates for the Divisor and Partial Remainders," *IEEE Trans. on Computers*, Vol. C-17, Oct. 1968.

[Aviž61] A. Avižienis, "Signed-Digit Number Representations for Fast Parallel Arithmetic," *IRE Trans. on Electronic Computers*, Vol. EC-10, No. 3, pp. 389–400, Sept. 1961.

[Aviž71] A. Avižienis, "Arithmetic Error Codes: Cost and Effectiveness Studies for Application in Digital System Design," *IEEE Trans. on Computers*, Vol. C-20, No. 11, pp. 1322–1330, Nov. 1971.

[BaBE70] J. L. Baer, D. P. Bovet, and G. Estrin, "Legality and other Properties of Graph Models of Computations," *Journ. of ACM*, Vol. 17, No. 3, pp. 543–552, 1970.

[BaBo68] J. L. Baer and D. P. Bovet, "Compilation of Arithmetic Expressions for Parallel Computations," *Proc. of IFIP Congress*, North-Holland, Amsterdam, pp. 340–346, 1968.

[Baer73] J. L. Baer, "A Survey of Some Theoretical Aspects of Multiprocessing," *ACM Computing Surveys*, Vol. 5, No. 1, pp. 31–80, March 1973.

[BaFH68] M. H. J. Baylis, D. G. Fletcher, and D. J. Howarth, "Paging Studies Made on the I.C.T. Atlas Computer," *Proc. of IFIP Congress, Edinburgh, 1968*, p. D113, North-Holland Publication, Amsterdam, 1968.

[BaHs76] R. I. Baum and D. K. Hsiao, "Database Computers—A Step Towards Data Utilities," *IEEE Trans. on Computers*, Vol. C-25, No. 12, pp. 1254–1259, Dec. 1976.

[Bake75] P. W. Baker, "More Efficient Radix-2 Algorithms for Some Elementary Functions," *IEEE Trans. on Computers*, Vol. C-24, pp. 1049–1054, Nov. 1975.

[Bard71] Y. Bard, "Performance Criteria and Measurement for a Time-Sharing System," *IBM Systs. Journal*, Vol. 10, No. 3, pp. 193–216, 1971.

[Bart61] R. S. Barton, "A New Approach to the Functional Design of a Digital Computer," *Proc. AFIPS Western Joint Computer Conference*, Vol. 19, pp. 393–396, 1961.

[Bart70] R. S. Barton, "Ideas for Computer Systems Organization: A Personal Survey," in *Software Engineering*, ed. J. T. Tou, Vol. 1, pp. 7–16, Academic Press, New York and London, 1970.

[BaSa72] J. L. Baer and G. R. Sager, "Measurement and Improvement of Program Behavior Under Paging Systems," *Statistical Computer Performance Evaluation*, ed., W. Frieberger, pp. 103–134, Academic Press, N. Y., 1972.

[BaSK67] T. Bashkow, A. Sasson, and A. Kronfeld, "System Design of a FORTRAN Machine," *IEEE Trans. on Computers*, Vol. EC-16, No. 4, pp. 485–499, Aug. 1967.

[BaSm76] F. Baskett and A. J. Smith, "Interference in Multiprocessor Computer Systems with Interleaved Memory," *Comm. of the ACM*, Vol. 19, No. 6, pp. 327–334, June 1976.

[Bata71] M. Bataille, "The Gamma 60: The Computer that Was Ahead of its Time," *Honeywell Computer Journal*, Vol. 5, pp. 99–105, 1971.

[Batc68] K. E. Batcher, "Sorting Networks and Their Applications," *Proc. AFIPS Spring Joint Computer Conference*, Vol. 32, pp. 307–315, 1968.

[Batc74] K. E. Batcher, "STARAN Parallel Processor System Hardware," *Proc. AFIPS National Computer Conference*, pp. 405–410, 1974.

[Batc77] K. E. Batcher, "The Multi-dimensional Access Memory in STARAN," *IEEE Trans. on Computers*, Vol. C-26, No. 2, pp. 174–177, Feb. 1977.

[BBKK68] G. H. Barnes, R. M. Brown, M. Kato, D. J. Kuck, D. L. Slotnick, and R. A. Stokes, "The ILLIAC IV Computer," *IEEE Trans. on Computers*, Vol. C-17, No. 8, pp. 746–757, Aug. 1968. [Reprinted in BeNe71].

[Beat72] J. C. Beatty, "An Axiomatic Approach to Code Optimization for Expressions," *Journ. of ACM*, Vol. 19, No. 4, pp. 613–640, Oct. 1972.

[BeBL61] F. S. Beckman, F. P. Brooks, Jr., and W. J. Lawless, Jr., "Developments in the Logical Organization of Computer Arithmetic and Control Units," *Proc. of the IRE*, pp. 53–66, 1961.

[BeCB74] J. Bell, D. Casasent, and C. G. Bell, "The Investigation of Alternative Cache Organizations," *IEEE Trans. on Computers*, Vol. C-23, No. 4, pp. 346–351, Apr. 1974.

[BeKu69] L. A. Belady and C. J. Kuehner, "Dynamic Space Sharing in Computer Systems," *Comm. of the ACM*, Vol. 12, No. 5, pp. 282–288, May 1969.

[Bela66] L. A. Belady, "A Study of Replacement Algorithms for a Virtual Storage Computer," *IBM Systs. Journ.*, Vol. 5, No. 2, pp. 78–101, 1966.

[Bell75] "Safeguard Data-Processing System," Special Supplement, *The Bell System Technical Journal*, 1975.

[Bene65] V. E. Beneš, *Mathematical Theory of Connecting Networks and Telephone Traffic*, Academic Press, N. Y., 1965.

[BeNe71] C. G. Bell and A. Newell, *Computer Structures: Readings and Examples*, McGraw-Hill, N. Y., 1971.

[BeNS69] L. A. Belady, R. A. Nelson, and G. S. Shedler, "An Anomaly in Space-Time Characteristics of Certain Programs Running in a Paging Machine," *Comm. of the ACM*, Vol. 12, No. 6, pp. 349–353, June 1969.

[Bern66] A. J. Bernstein, "Analysis of Programs for Parallel Processing," *IEEE Trans. on Computers,* Vol. EC-15, pp. 757–762, Oct. 1966.

[BeSi75] A. J. Bernstein and P. Siegel, "A Computer Architecture for Level Structured Systems," *IEEE Trans. on Computers,* Vol. C-24, No. 8, pp. 785–793, Aug. 1975.

[BeSt76] C. G. Bell and W. D. Strecker, "Computer Structures: What Have We Learned from the PDP-11?" *Conf. Proc., The Third Annual Symposium on Computer Architecture,* IEEE Press, New York, pp. 1–14, 1976.

[Bitz76] D. Bitzer, "The Wide World of Computer Based Education," in *Advances in Computers,* eds., M. Rubinoff and M. C. Yovits, Vol. 15, pp. 239–281, Academic Press, New York, 1976.

[Blaa64] G. A. Blaauw, "Multisystem Organization," *IBM Systems Journal,* Vol. 3, Nos. 2 and 3, pp. 181–195, 1964.

[Blak75] T. R. Blakeslee, *Digital Design with Standard MSI and LSI,* Wiley-Interscience, New York, 357 pp., 1975.

[BlCo76] R. P. Blanc and I. W. Cotton, eds., *Computer Networking,* IEEE Press, New York, 1976.

[BoMu67] D. G. Bobrow and D. L. Murphy, "Structure of a LISP System Using Two-Level Storage," *Comm. of the ACM,* Vol. 10, No. 3, pp. 155-159, 1967.

[Bons69] P. Bonseigneur, "Description of the 7600 Computer System," *IEEE Computer Group News,* pp. 11–15, May, 1969.

[Bowd53] B. V. Bowden, *Faster than Thought,* Sir Issac Pitman and Sons, Inc., 1953.

[Bren70] R. Brent, "On the Addition of Binary Numbers," *IEEE Trans. on Computers,* Vol. C-19, pp. 758–759, 1970.

[Bren73a] R. Brent, "The Parallel Evaluation of Arithmetic Expressions in Logarithmic Time," *Complexity of Sequential and Parallel Numerical Algorithms,* ed., J. F. Traub, pp. 83–102, Academic Press, New York, 1973.

[Bren73b] R. Brent, "On the Precision Attainable With Various Floating-Point Arithmetic," *IEEE Trans. on Computers,* Vol. C-22, No. 6, pp. 601–607, June 1973.

[Bren74] R. Brent, "The Parallel Evaluation of General Arithmetic Expressions," *Journ. of ACM,* Vol. 21, No. 2, pp. 201–206, Apr. 1974.

[BrET72] D. T. Brown, R. L. Eibsen, and C. A. Thorn, "Channel and Direct Access Device Architecture," *IBM Systs. Journ.,* Vol. 11, No. 3, pp. 186–199, 1972.

[BrKM73] R. Brent, D. Kuck, and K. Maruyama, "The Parallel Evaluation of Arithmetic Expressions Without Division," *IEEE Trans. on Computers,* Vol. C-22, No. 1, pp. 532–534, May 1973.

[BrLB72] J. C. Browne, J. Lan, and F. Baskett, "The Interaction of Multiprogramming Job Scheduling and CPU Scheduling," *Proc. AFIPS FJCC 1972,* AFIPS Press, Montvale, N. J., pp. 13–21, 1972.

[BrMc70] T. H. Bredt and E. J. McCluskey, "Analysis and Synthesis of

Control Mechanisms for Parallel Processes," in *Parallel Processor Systems, Technologies, and Applications*, eds., L. C. Hobbs et al., Spartan Books, N. Y., pp. 287 296, 1970.

[Broc75] G. W. Brock, *The U. S. Computer Industry*, Ballinger Pub., Cambridge, Mass, 1975.

[Broo57] F. P. Brooks, Jr., "A Program-Controlled Program Interruption Scheme," *Proc. Western Joint Computer Conf.*, pp. 128–132, 1957.

[Broo63] F. P. Brooks, Jr., "Recent Developments in Computer Organization," in *Advances in Electronics and Electronic Devices*, pp. 45–65, Academic Press, New York, 1963.

[BrRi69] W. S. Brown and P. L. Richman, "The Choice of Base," *Comm. of the ACM*, Vol. 12, No. 10, pp. 560–561, Oct. 1969.

[BrTo76] R. Brent and R. Towle, "On the Time Required to Parse an Arithmetic Expression for Parallel Processing," *Proc. International Conference on Parallel Processing*, P. H. Enslow, ed., IEEE, N.Y., p. 254, Aug. 1976.

[Buch62] W. Buchholz, ed., *Planning a Computer System*, McGraw-Hill, New York, 1962.

[BuKu71] P. P. Budnik and D. J. Kuck, "The Organization and Use of Parallel Memories," *IEEE Trans. on Computers*, Vol. 20, pp. 1566–1569, Dec. 1971.

[Burr73] *Burroughs B7700 Reference Manual*, Burroughs Corp., Detroit, Mich., 1973.

[Burr74] Burroughs Corporation, "B6700 Information Processing Systems," Appendix C in *Multiprocessors and Parallel Processing*, P. H. Enslow, ed., Wiley-Interscience, New York, 1974.

[Burr77] Burroughs Corporation, "Introduction to Burroughs Scientific Processor," Document 1105327, Detroit, Mich., July 1977.

[Buze77] J. P. Buzen, "Fundamental Laws of Computer System Performance," *Proc. International Symposium on Computer Performance Modeling, Measurement and Evaluation*, P. P. S. Chen and M. Franklin, eds., ACM, N.Y., pp. 200–210, Mar. 1976.

[CaFH70] G. Campbell, K. Fuchel, and S. Heller, "The Use of Extended Core Storage in a Multiprogramming Operating System," in *Software Engineering*, ed., J. T. Tou, Vol. 1, Academic Press, New York, 1970.

[CaHP62] S. G. Campbell, P. S. Herwitz, and J. H. Pomerene, "A Nonarithmetical System Extension," Chapter 17 in *Planning a Computer System*, Project STRETCH, ed., Werner Buchholz, McGraw-Hill, New York, 1962.

[CaPa78] R. P. Case and A. Padegs, "Architecture of the IBM System 370," *Comm. of the ACM*, Vol. 21, No. 1, pp. 73–96, Jan. 1978.

[CDCC75] *Compass Version 3 Reference Manual*, 60492600, Control Data Corp., Publication and Graphics Division, Sunnyvale, CA, 1975.

[Chen75] S. C. Chen, "Speedup of Iterative Programs in Multiprocessor Systems," Ph.D. thesis, Univ. of Ill. at Urb.-Champ., Dept. of Comput. Sci. Rpt. No. 75–694, Jan. 1975.

[ChKL77] D. Chang, D. J. Kuck, and D. H. Lawrie, "On the Effective Bandwidth of Parallel Memories," *IEEE Trans. on Computers*, Vol. C-26, No. 5, pp. 480–490, May 1977.

[ChKS78] S. C. Chen, D. J. Kuck, and A. H. Sameh, "Practical Parallel Band Triangular System Solvers," *ACM Trans. on Math. Software*, Vol. 4, No. 3, pp. 270-277, Sept. 1978.

[ChKu75] S. C. Chen and D. J. Kuck, "Time and Parallel Processor Bounds for Linear Recurrence Systems," *IEEE Trans. on Computers*, Vol. C-24, No. 7, pp. 701–717, July 1975.

[ChKu77] S. C. Chen and D. J. Kuck, "Combinational Circuit Synthesis with Time and Component Bounds," *IEEE Trans. on Computers*, Vol. C-26, No. 8, pp. 712–726, Aug. 1977.

[ChOp72] W. W. Chu and H. Opderbeck, "The Page Fault Frequency Replacement Algorithm," *Proc. FJCC 1972*, AFIPS Press, Montvale, N. J., pp. 597–609, 1972.

[ChOp74] W. W. Chu and H. Opderbeck, "Performance of Replacement Algorithms with Different Page Sizes," *IEEE Computer*, Vol. 7, No. 11, pp. 14–21, Nov. 1974.

[Chur56] A. Church, *Introduction to Mathematical Logic*, Princeton University Press, Princeton, N. J., 1956.

[ChuW76] W. W. Chu, *Advances in Computer Communications*, Artech House, 1976.

[ChuY62] Y. Chu, *Digital Computer Design Fundamentals*, McGraw-Hill, New York, 1962.

[ChuY72] Y. Chu, *Computer Organization and Microprogramming*, Prentice-Hall, Englewood Cliffs, N. J., 1972.

[ChuY75] Y. Chu, *High Level Language Computer Architecture*, Academic Press, New York, 1975.

[CKTB78] S. C. Chen, D. J. Kuck, R. Towle and U. Banerjee, "Time and Parallel Processor Bounds for Fortran-like Loops," submitted to *IEEE Trans. on Computers*.

[Clar57] W. A. Clark, "The Lincoln TX-2 Computer Development," *1957 Western Joint Computer Conf. Proc.*, IRE Press, New York pp. 143–145, 1957.

[Codd62] E. F. Codd, "Multiprogramming," *Advances in Computers*, eds., Franz L. Alt and Morris Rubinoff, Academic Press, New York, Vol. 3, pp. 77–153, 1962.

[CoDD62] F. J. Corbató, M. M. Daggett, and R. C. Daley, "An Experimental Time-Sharing System" *Proc. AFIPS Spring Joint Computer Conference*, Vol. 21, pp. 335–344, 1962.

[CoDe73] E. G. Coffman, Jr. and P. J. Denning, *Operating Systems Theory*, Prentice-Hall, Englewood Cliffs, N. J., 1973.

[Cody73] W. J. Cody, Jr., "Static and Dynamic Numerical Characteristics of Floating-Point Arithmetic," *IEEE Trans. on Computers*, Vol. C-22, No. 6, pp. 598-601, June 1973.

[Coff76] E. G. Coffman, ed., *Computer and Job-Shop Scheduling Theory*, John Wiley, New York, 1976.

[CoGP68] C. J. Conti, D. H. Gibson, and S. H. Pitkowsky, "Structural Aspects of the System/360 Model 85: I General Organization," *IBM Systs. Journ.*, Vol. 7, No. 1, pp. 2–14, 1968.

[Come67] L. W. Comeau, "A Study of the Effects of User Program Optimization in a Paging System," *ACM Symposium Operating System Principles*, 1967.

[CoMM67] R. W. Conway, W. L. Maxwell, and L. W. Miller, *Theory of Scheduling*, Addison-Wesley, Reading, Mass., 1967.

[Conw63] M. E. Conway, "A Multiprocessor System Design," *Proc. AFIPS Fall Joint Computer Conference*, Vol. 24, pp. 139–146, Spartan, Baltimore, 1963.

[Cott69] L. W. Cotten, "Maximum-Rate Pipeline Systems," *Proc. AFIPS Spring Joint Computer Conference*, pp. 581–586, 1969.

[CoVa68] E. G. Coffman and L. C. Varian, "Further Experimental Data on the Behavior of Programs in a Paging Environment," *Comm. of the ACM*, Vol. 11, No. 7, pp. 471–474, 1968.

[CoVy65] F. J. Corbató and V. A. Vyssotsky, "Introduction and Overview of the MULTICS System," *Proc. AFIPS Fall Joint Computer Conference*, Vol. 27, pp. 185–196, 1965.

[CoxJ72] J. E. Cox, "Western Union Digital Services," *Proc. IEEE*, Vol. 60, pp. 1350–1357, Nov. 1972; also appears in [GrLu75].

[Cray75] "The CRAY-1 Computer," Preliminary Reference Manual, Cray Research, Inc., Chippewa Falls, Wisc., 1975.

[DaBa73] D. W. Davies and D. L. A. Barber, *Communications Networks for Computers*, John Wiley, New York, 1973.

[Dadd65] L. Dadda, "Some Schemes for Parallel Multipliers," *Alta Frequenza*, Vol. 31, pp. 319–356, March 1965.

[DaDe68] R. C. Daley and J. B. Dennis, "Virtual Memory, Processes, and Sharing in MULTICS," *Comm. of the ACM*, Vol. 11, No. 5, pp. 306–312, May 1968.

[Dave71] W. P. Davenport, *Modern Data Communications*, Hayden Book Co., Rochelle Park, N.J., 1971.

[Davi69] R. L. Davis "The ILLIAC IV Processing Element," *IEEE Trans. on Computers*, Vol. C-18, No. 9, pp. 800–816, Sept. 1969.

[Davi72] P. M. Davies, "Readings in Microprogramming," *IBM Systs. Journ.*, Vol. 11, No. 1, pp. 16–40, 1972.

[Davi74a] E. W. Davis, "STARAN Parallel Processor System Software," *Proc. AFIPS National Computer Conference*, pp. 17–22, 1974.

[Davi74b] R. L. Davis, "Uniform Shift Networks," *IEEE Computer*, Vol. 7, No. 9, pp. 60–71, Sept. 1974.

[DECo71a] *PDP-11/45, Processor Handbook*, Digital Equipment Corporation, Maynard, Mass., 1971.

[DECo71b] *PDP-11 Peripherals and Interfacing Handbook*, Digital Equipment Corporation, Maynard, Mass., 1971.

[deLu70] B. G. deLugish, "A Class of Algorithms for Automatic Evaluation of Certain Elementary Functions in a Binary Computer," Dept. of Comput. Sci., Univ. of Illinois, Urbana, Ill., Rep. 399, June 1970.

[Denn65] J. B. Dennis, "Segmentation and the Design of Multiprogrammed Computer Systems," *Journ. of ACM*, Vol. 12, No. 4, pp. 589–602, Oct. 1965.

[Denn68a] P. J. Denning, "Thrashing and Its Cause and Prevention," *Proc. AFIPS Fall Joint Computer Conference*, Vol. 33, pp. 915–922, Thompson, Wash., DC, 1968.

[Denn68b] P. J. Denning, "The Working Set Model for Program Behavior," *Comm. of the ACM*, Vol. 11, No. 5, pp. 323–333, 1968.

[Denn70] P. J. Denning, "Virtual Memory," *Computing Surveys*, 2, 3, pp. 153–189, Sept. 1970.

[Desp74] A. M. Despain, "Fourier Transform Computers Using CORDIC Iterations," *IEEE Trans. on Computers*, Vol. C-23, No. 10, Oct. 1974.

[Dijk68] E. W. Dijkstra, "Computing Sequential Processes," *Programming Languages*, ed., F. Genuys, Academic Press, New York, pp. 43–112, 1968.

[DKLP76] P. J. Denning, K. C. Kahn, J. Leroudier, D. Potier, and R. Suri, "Optimal Multiprogramming," *Acta Informatica*, Vol. 7, Fasc. 2, pp. 197–216, 1976.

[Dohe70] W. J. Doherty, "Scheduling TSS/360 for Responsiveness," *Proc. AFIPS 1970 FJCC*, Vol. 37, AFIPS Press, Montvale, N. J., pp. 97–112, 1970.

[Dono72] J. J. Donovan, *Systems Programming*, McGraw-Hill, New York, 1972.

[Dora75] R. W. Doran, "Architecture of Stack Machines," in *High-Level Language Computer Architecture*, ed., Yaohan Chu, Academic Press, New York, pp. 63–108, 1975.

[Drey58] P. Dreyfus, "Programming Design Features of the GAMMA 60 Computer," *Proc. EJCC*, pp. 174–181, 1958.

[Drum73] M. E. Drummond, *Evaluation and Measurement Techniques for Digital Computer Systems*, Prentice-Hall, Englewood Cliffs, N. J., 1973.

[EaEa73] C. Eames and R. Eames, *A Computer Perspective*, Harvard University Press, Cambridge, Mass., 1973.

[Eckh75] R. H. Eckhouse, Jr., *Minicomputer Systems: Organization and Programming (PDP-11)*, Prentice-Hall, Englewood Cliffs, N. J., 1975.

[Elsh74] J. L. Elshoff, "Some Programming Techniques for Processing Multidimensional Matrices in a Paging Environment," *Proc. of AFIPS National Computer Conference*, pp. 185–193, 1974.

[Elsh76] J. L. Elshoff, "An Analysis of Some Commercial PL/I Programs," *IEEE Transactions on Software Engineering*, Vol. SE-2, No. 2, pp. 113–120, June 1976.

[Ensl74] P. H. Enslow, ed., *Multiprocessors and Parallel Processing*, Wiley-Interscience, New York, 1974.

[Erce73] M. D. Ercegovac, "Radix 16 Evaluation of Certain Elementary Functions," *IEEE Trans. on Computers*, Vol. C-22, pp. 561–566, June 1973.

[Ferr76] D. Ferrari, ed., "Special Issue on Program Behavior," *IEEE Computer*, Vol. 9, No. 11, pp. 7–8, Nov. 1976.

[Ferr76a] D. Ferrari, "The Improvement of Program Behavior," *IEEE Computer*, Vol. 9, No. 11, pp. 39–47, Nov. 1976.

[Feus73] E. A. Feustal, "On the Advantages of Tagged Architecture," *IEEE Trans. on Computers*, Vol. C-22, No. 7, pp. 644–656, July 1973.

[Fiel69] J. A. Field, "Optimizing Floating Point Arithmetic Via Post Addition Shift Probabilities," *Proc. AFIPS Spring Joint Computer Conference*, AFIPS Press, Montvale, N.J., pp. 597–603, 1969.

[FJMc66] G. H. Fine, C. W. Jackson, and P. V. McIsaac, "Dynamic Program Behavior Under Paging," *Proc 21st Natl. ACM Conf.*, Thompson, Washington DC, pp. 223–228, 1966.

[FLBK76] S. H. Fuller, V. R. Lesser, C. G. Bell, and C. H. Kamen, "The Effects of Emerging Technology and Emulation Requirements on Microprogramming," *IEEE Trans. on Computers*, Vol. C-25, No. 10, pp. 1000–1009, Oct. 1976.

[Flor73] I. Flores, *Peripheral Devices*, Prentice-Hall, Englewood Cliffs, N. J., 1973.

[Flor74] I. Flores, "Lookahead Control in the IBM System 370 Model 165," *IEEE Computer*, Vol. 7, No. 11, pp. 24–38, Nov. 1974.

[Flyn70] M. J. Flynn, "On Division by Functional Iteration," *IEEE Trans. on Computers*, Vol. C-19, No. 8, pp. 702-706, Aug. 1970.

[Flyn72] M. J. Flynn, "Some Computer Organizations and Their Effectiveness," *IEEE Trans. on Computers*, Vol. C-21, No. 9, pp. 948–960, Sept. 1972.

[Flyn74] M. J. Flynn, "Trends and Problems in Computer Organizations," *Proc. of IFIP Congress*, pp. 3–10, 1974.

[Flyn75] M. J. Flynn, "Interpretation, Microprogramming and the Control of a Computer," Ch. 10 in *Introduction to Computer Architecture*, ed., H. Stone, Science Research Associates, Inc., Chicago, 1975.

[FoGR71] C. C. Foster, R. H. Gonter, and E. M. Riseman, "Measures of Op-Code Utilization," *IEEE Trans. on Computers*, Vol. 20, No. 5, pp. 582–584, May 1971.

[Forg57] J. W. Forgie, "The Lincoln TX-2 Input-Output System," *1957 Western Joint Computer Conf. Proc.*, IRE Press, New York, pp. 156–160, 1957.

[FoRi72] C. C. Foster and E. M. Riseman, "Percolation of Code to Enhance Parallel Dispatching and Execution," *IEEE Trans. on Computers*, Vol. C-21, pp. 1411–1415, Dec. 1972.

[Frei68] I. F. Freibergs, "The Dynamic Behavior of Programs," *Proc. AFIPS Fall Joint Computer Conference*, Thompson, Wash., DC, Vol. 33, pp. 1163–1168, 1968.

[FrGu78] M. A. Franklin and R. K. Gupta, "Working Set and Page Fault Frequency Paging Algorithms: A Performance Comparison," *IEEE Trans. on Computers*, Vol. C-27, No. 8, pp. 706-712, Aug. 1978.

[Frie72] W. Frieberger, ed., *Statistical Computer Performance Evaluation*, Academic Press, New York, 1972.

[Full75] S. H. Fuller, "Performance Evaluation," Ch. 11 in *Introduction to*

Computer Architecture, ed., H. Stone, Science Research Associates, Chicago, 1975.

[Full75a] S. H. Fuller, *Analysis of Drum and Disk Storage Units,* Vol. 31, Lecture Notes in Computer Science, G. Goos and J. Hartmanis, eds., Springer-Verlag, New York, 1975.

[Gajs77] D. D. Gajski, Personal Communication, 1977.

[Garn76] H. L. Garner, "A Survey of Some Recent Contributions to Computer Arithmetic," *IEEE Trans. on Computers,* Vol. C-25, No. 12, pp. 1277–1282, Dec. 1976.

[Gave67] D. P. Gaver, "Probability Models for Multiprogramming Computer System," *Journ. of ACM,* Vol. 14, No. 3, pp. 423–438, July 1967.

[Gear74] C. W. Gear, *Computer Organization and Programming,* 2nd. ed., McGraw-Hill, New York, 1974.

[Gibs67] D. H. Gibson, "Considerations in Block-Oriented Systems Design," *Proc. AFIPS Spring Joint Computer Conference,* Vol. 30, pp. 75–80, 1967.

[Gibs70] J. C. Gibson, "The Gibson Mix" TR00.2043, IBM Systems Development Division, Poughkeepsie, N. Y., June 1970.

[Gluc65] S. E. Gluck, "Impact of Scratchpads in Design: Multifunctional Scratchpad Memories in the Burroughs B8500," Proc. *AFIPS Fall Joint Computer Conference,* pp. 661–666, 1965.

[GoKu74] D. E. Gold and D. J. Kuck, "A Model for Masking Rotational Latency by Dynamic Disk Allocation," *Comm. of the ACM,* Vol. 17, pp. 278–288, May 1974.

[Gold63] M. Goldstein, "Significance Arithmetic on a Digital Computer," *Comm. of the ACM,* Vol. 6, No. 3, pp. 111–117, Mar. 1963.

[Gold73] R. P. Goldberg, "Architecture of Virtual Machines," *Proc. NCC 1973,* Vol. 42, AFIPS Press, Montvale, N. J., pp. 309–318, 1973.

[Gold74] R. P. Goldberg, "Survey of Virtual Machine Research," *IEEE Computer,* Vol. 7, No. 6, pp. 34–45, June 1974.

[GoVi66] R. J. Gountanis and N. L. Viss, "A Method of Processor Selection for Interrupt Handling in a Multiprocessor System," *IEEE Trans. on Computers,* Vol. 54, No. 12, pp. 1812–1819, Dec. 1966.

[GrLu75] P. E. Green, Jr. and R. W. Lucky, eds., *Computer Communications,* IEEE Press, 1975.

[GrMc63] J. Gregory and R. McReynolds, "The SOLOMON Computer," *IEEE Trans. on Computers,* Vol. EC-12, No. 6, pp. 774–781, Dec. 1963.

[GsMc75] H. W. Gschwind and E. J. McCluskey, *Design of Digital Computers,* Springer Verlag, New York, 1975.

[GvNB47] H. H. Goldstine, J. von Neumann, A. W. Burks, *Report on the Mathematical and Logical Aspects of an Electronic Computing Instrument,* Institute for Advanced Study, 1947.

[HaDe68] E. A. Hauck and B. A. Dent, "Burroughs B6500/B7500 Stack Mechanism," *Proc. AFIPS Spring Joint Computer Conference,* Vol. 32, pp.

245–251, Thompson Books, Washington, D. C., 1968.

[HaFl72] T. G. Hallin and M. J. Flynn, "Pipelining of Arithmetic Functions," *IEEE Trans. on Computers*, Vol. C-21, pp. 880–886, Aug. 1972.

[HaGe71] D. J. Hatfield and J. Gerald, "Program Restructuring for Virtual Memory," *IBM Syst. Journ.*, Vol. 10, No. 3, pp. 169–192, 1971.

[Hamm50] R. W. Hamming, "Error Detecting and Error Correcting Codes," *Bell Syst. Tech. Journ.*, Vol. 29, pp. 147–160, 1950.

[Harv48] "Proceedings of a Symposium on Large-Scale Digital Calculating Machinery," *The Annals of the Computation Laboratory of Harvard University*, Harvard University Press, Vol. XVI, 1948.

[HaWi70] A. Habibi and P. A. Wintz, "Fast Multipliers," *IEEE Trans. on Computers*, Vol. C-19, No. 2, pp. 153–157, Feb. 1970.

[HeCo75] H. Hellerman and T. E. Conroy, *Computer System Performance*, McGraw-Hill, New York, 1975.

[Hell73] H. Hellerman, *Digital Computer System Principles*, 2nd. ed. McGraw-Hill, New York, 1973.

[Higb76] L. C. Higbie, "Vector Floating Point Data Format," *IEEE Trans. on Computers*, Vol. C-25, No. 1, pp. 25–31, Jan. 1976.

[HiPe73] F. J. Hill and G. R. Peterson, *Digital Systems: Hardware Organization and Design*, John Wiley, New York, 1973.

[HiPe74] F. J. Hill and G. R. Peterson, *Introduction to Switching Theory and Logical Design*, 2nd. ed., John Wiley, New York, 1974.

[HiTa72] R. G. Hintz and D. P. Tate, "Control Data STAR-100 Processor Design," *Compcon 72, IEEE Computer Society Conference Proc.*, pp. 1–4, Sept. 1972.

[Hoff62] W. Hoffman, *Digital Information Processors*, John Wiley, New York, 1962.

[Holl59] J. H. Holland, "A Universal Computer Capable of Executing an Arbitrary Number of Sub-Programs Simultaneously," *Proc. of the EJCC*, pp. 108–113, 1959.

[Hone71] *Honeywell Model 8200 Master Control Programmer Reference Manual*, Honeywell Information Systems, Inc., Newton Highlands, Mass., 1971.

[Hous64] A. S. Householder, *The Theory of Matrices in Numerical Analysis*, Blaisdell, New York, 257 pp., 1964.

[Huff52] D. A. Huffman, "A Method for the Construction of Minimum-Redundancy Codes," *Proc. of the IRE*, Vol. 40, No. 9, pp. 1098–1101, Sept. 1952.

[HuHu76] H. D. Huskey and V. R. Huskey, "Chronology of Computing Devices," *IEEE Trans. on Computers*, Vol. C-25, No. 12, pp. 1190–1199, Dec. 1976.

[Huss70] S. S. Husson, *Microprogramming: Principles and Practice*, Prentice-Hall, Englewood Cliffs, N. J., 1970.

[HuTC61] T. C. Hu, "Parallel Sequencing and Assembly Line Problems," *Oper. Res.*, Vol. 9, No. 6, pp. 841–848, Nov.–Dec. 1961.

[IBMC70] *IBM System/360 Principles of Operation*, Form GA22–6821–8, IBM Corp., Poughkeepsie, N. Y., 1970.

[IBMJ64] "The IBM System/360," *IBM Journal of Research and Development*, Special Issue, Vol. 8, No. 2, April 1964.

[IBMJ67] "System/360 Model 91," *IBM Journal of Research and Development*, Special Issue, Vol. 11, No. 1, Jan. 1967.

[IBMS64] "The Structure of System/360," *IBM Systems Journal*, Special Issue, Vol. 3, Nos. 2 and 3, 1964.

[IEEE71] IEEE Computer Society, *IEEE Trans. on Computers*, Vol. C-20, No. 7, Special Issue on Microprogramming, July 1971.

[IEEE73] IEEE Computer Society, *IEEE Trans. on Computers*, Vol. C-22, No. 6, Special Section on Computer Arithmetic, June 1973.

[IEEE74] IEEE Computer Society, *IEEE Trans. on Computers*, Vol. C-23, No. 7, Special Issue on Microprogramming, July 1974.

[IEEE75] Institute of Electrical and Electronics Engineers, Inc., *IEEE Proceedings*, Vol. 63, No. 6, Special Issue on Interactive Computer Systems, June 1975.

[IEEE76] IEEE Computer Society, *IEEE Trans. on Computers*, Vol. C-25, No. 10, Special Section on Microprogramming, Oct. 1976.

[Ilif68] J. K. Iliffe, *Basic Machine Principles*, Elsevier, New York, 1968.

[IREP53] Institute of Radio Engineers, *Proc. of the IRE*, Vol. 41, No. 9, Special Issue on Computers, Oct. 1953.

[IREP61] Institute of Radio Engineers, *Proc. of the IRE*, Vol. 49, No. 1, Special Issue on Computers, Jan. 1961.

[John71] A. M. Johnson, "The Microdiagnostics for the IBM System/360 Model 30," *IEEE Trans. Comput.*, Vol. C-20, No. 7, pp. 798–803, July 1971.

[Jose70] M. Joseph, "An Analysis of Paging and Program Behavior," *The Computer Journal*, Vol. 13, pp. 48–53, Feb. 1970.

[KaLi73] T. Kaneko and B. Liu, "On Local Roundoff Errors in Floating-Point Arithmetic," *Journ. of the ACM*, Vol. 20, No. 3, pp. 391–398, July 1973.

[Katz71] H. Katzan, Jr., *Computer Organization and the System/370*, Reinhold-Van Nostrand, New York, 1971.

[KaWi73] K. R. Kaplan and R. O. Winder, "Cache-based Computer Systems," *IEEE Computer*, Vol. 6, No. 3, pp. 30–36, March 1973.

[KBCD74] D. J. Kuck, P. Budnik, S. C. Chen, E. Davis, Jr., J. Han, P. Kraska, D. Lawrie, Y. Muraoka, R. Strebendt, and R. Towle, "Measurements of Parallelism in Ordinary FORTRAN Programs," *IEEE Computer*, Vol. 7, No. 1, pp. 37–46, Jan. 1974.

[Keir75] R. A. Keir, "Compatible Number Representations." *Proc. Third Symposium on Computer Arithmetic*, IEEE Press, New York, 1975.

[Kell75] R. M. Keller, "Look-Ahead Processors," *ACM Computing Surveys*, Vol. 7, No. 4, pp. 177–195, Dec. 1975.

[KELS62] T. Kilburn, D. B. G. Edwards, M. J. Lanigan, and F. H. Sumner, "One-level Storage System," *IRE Trans. on Electronic Computers*, Vol. EC-11, No. 2, pp. 223–235, April 1962. [Reprinted in BeNe71].

[Klei76] L. Kleinrock, "On Communications and Networks," *IEEE Trans. on Comput.*, Vol. C-25, No. 12, pp. 1326–1335, Dec. 1976.

[KlNa74] L. Kleinrock and W. E. Naylor, "On Measured Behavior of the ARPA Network," *Proc. AFIPS NCC*, Vol. 43, pp. 767–780, May 1974; also appears in [BlCo76].

[Knig72] J. R. Knight, "Airlines Reservations Systems," *Proc. of the IEEE*, Vol. 60, No.11, pp. 1423–1431, Nov. 1972. (also in [GrLu75]).

[Knut69] D. E. Knuth, *The Art of Computer Programming, Vol. 2/Seminumerical Algorithms*, Addison-Wesley, Reading, Mass., 1969.

[Knut71] D. E. Knuth, "An Empirical Study of FORTRAN Programs," *Software-Practice and Experience*, Vol. 1, pp. 105–133, 1971.

[Kras72] P. W. Kraska, "Parallelism Exploitation and Scheduling," Ph.D. thesis, Univ. of Ill. at Urb.-Champ., Dept. of Comput. Sci. Rpt. 72-518, June 1972.

[Kris70] E. V. Krishnamurthy, "On Optimal Iterative Schemes for High-Speed Division," *IEEE Trans. on Computers*, Vol. C-19, No. 3, pp. 227–231, March 1970.

[Kuck76] D. J. Kuck, "Parallel Processing of Ordinary Programs," in *Advances in Computers*, Vol. 15, M. Rubinoff and M. C. Yovits, eds., Academic Press, New York, pp. 119–179, 1976.

[Kuck77] D. J. Kuck, "A Survey of Parallel Machine Organization and Programming," *ACM Computing Surveys*, Vol. 9, No. 1, pp. 29–59, March 1977.

[KuCo73] H. Kuki and W. J. Cody, "A Statistical Study of the Accuracy of Floating Point Number Systems," *Comm. of the ACM*, Vol. 16, No. 4, pp. 223–230, April 1973.

[KuKu76] D. J. Kuck and B. Kumar, "A System Model for Computer Performance Evaluation," *Proc. of the International Symposium on Computer Performance Modeling, Measurement and Evaluation*, P. P. S. Chen and M. Franklin, eds., ACM, N.Y., pp. 187–199, March 1976.

[KuLa70] D. J. Kuck and D. H. Lawrie, "The Use and Performance of Memory Hierarchies: A Survey," *Software Engineering*, Vol. 1, J. T. Tou, ed., pp. 45–77, Academic Press, New York, 1970.

[KuLS77] D. J. Kuck, D. H. Lawrie, and A. H. Sameh, eds., *High Speed Computer and Algorithm Organization*, Academic Press, N.Y., 1977.

[KuMa75] D. J. Kuck and K. Maruyama, "Time Bounds on the Parallel Evaluation of Arithmetic Expressions," *SIAM Journ. of Computing*, Vol. 4, No. 2, pp. 147–162, June 1975.

[KuMC72] D. J. Kuck, Y. Muraoka, and S. C. Chen, "On the Number of Operations Simultaneously Executable in FORTRAN-Like Programs and Their Resulting Speed-Up," *IEEE Trans. on Computers*, Vol. C-21, pp. 1293–1310, Dec. 1972.

[KuMu74] D. J. Kuck and Y. Muraoka, "Bounds on the Parallel Evaluation of Arithmetic Expressions Using Associativity and Commutativity," *Acta Informatica*, Vol. 3, Fasc. 3, pp. 203–216, 1974.

[Kunz57] K. S. Kunz, *Numerical Analysis*, McGraw-Hill, New York, 1957.

[KuPS77] D. J. Kuck, D. S. Parker, and A. H. Sameh, "Analysis of Rounding Methods in Floating-Point Arithmetic," *IEEE Trans. on Computers*, Vol. C-26, No. 7, pp. 643–650, July 1977.

[Lane75] W. G. Lane, "Input/Output Processing," Chapter 6 in *Introduction to Computer Architecture*, ed. H. Stone, SRA, Chicago, Ill., 1975.

[LaTE77] S. H. Lavington, G. Thomas, and D. B. G. Edwards, "The MU5 Multicomputer Communication System," *IEEE Trans. on Computers*, Vol. C-26, No. 1, pp. 19–28, Jan. 1977.

[Lawr75] D. H. Lawrie, "Access and Alignment of Data in an Array Processor," *IEEE Trans. on Computers*, Vol. C-24, No. 12, pp. 1145–1155, Dec. 1975.

[Lewi62] M. H. Lewin, "Retrieval of Ordered Lists from a Content-Addressed Memory," *RCA Review*, pp. 215–229, June 1962.

[LiMa72] Y. S. Lin and R. L. Mattson, "Cost-Performance Evaluation of Memory Hierarchies," *IEEE Trans. on Magnetics*, Vol. 8, pp. 390–392, Sept. 1972.

[Lipt68] J. S. Liptay, "Structural Aspects of the System/360 Model 85 II: The Cache," *IBM Systs. Journ.*, Vol. 7, No. 1, pp. 15–21, 1968.

[LiuC68] C. L. Liu, *Introduction to Combinatorial Mathematics*, McGraw-Hill, New York, 1968.

[LNSW59] A. L. Leiner, W. A. Notz, J. L. Smith, and A. Weinberger, "PILOT, A New Multiple Computer System," *Journ. of the ACM*, Vol. 6, No. 3, pp. 313–335, 1959.

[LoKi61] W. Lonergan and P. King, "Design of the B5000 System," *Datamation*, Vol. 7, No. 5, pp. 28–32, May 1961 (reprinted in [BeNe71]).

[Lori72] H. Lorin, *Parallelism in Hardware and Software*, Prentice-Hall, Englewood Cliffs, N. J., 1972.

[LuMC73] G. Luecke, J. P. Mize, and W. N. Carr, *Semiconductor Memory Design and Application*, McGraw-Hill, New York, 1973.

[Lync72] W. C. Lynch, "Do Disk Arms Move?," Performance Evaluation Review, *ACM SIGMETRICS Newsletter*, Vol. 1, pp. 3–16, Dec. 1972.

[MaBa76] A. W. Madison and A. P. Batson, "Characterization of Program Localities," *Comm. of the ACM*, Vol. 19, No. 5, pp. 285–294, May 1976.

[MacS61] O. L. MacSorley, "High Speed Arithmetic in Binary Computers," *IRE Trans. on Electronic Computers*, Vol. 49, pp. 67–91, Jan. 1961.

[MaDo74] S. E. Madnick and J. J. Donovan, *Operating Systems*, McGraw-Hill, New York, 1974.

[MaEs67] D. F. Martin and G. Estrin, "Models of Computational Systems—Cyclic to Acyclic Graph Transformations," *IEEE Trans. on Computers*, Vol. EC-16, pp. 70–74, Feb. 1967.

[MaMa73] J. D. Marasa and D. W. Matula, "A Simulative Study of Correlated Error Propagation in Various Finite-Precision Arithmetic," *IEEE Trans. on Computers*, Vol. C-22, pp. 587–597, June 1973.

[Mano72] M. M. Mano, *Computer Logic Design*, Prentice-Hall, Englewood Cliffs, N. J., 1972.

[Mart70] J. Martin, *Teleprocessing Network Organization*, Prentice-Hall, Englewood Cliffs, N. J., 1970.

[Mauc75] J. W. Mauchly, "Mauchly on the Trials of Building ENIAC," *IEEE Spectrum*, pp. 70–76, April 1975.

[MaWa72] S. L. Mathison and P. M. Walker, "Regulatory and Economic Issues in Computer Communications," *Proc. of the IEEE*, Vol. 60, pp. 1254–1272, Nov. 1972; also appears in [GrLu75].

[McCo63] B. H. McCormick, "The Illinois Pattern Recognition Computer—ILLIAC III," *IEEE Trans. on Computers*, Vol. EC-12, No. 6, pp. 791–813, Dec. 1963.

[McCo69] A. C. McKellar and E. G. Coffman, "Organizing Matrices and Matrix Operations in Paged Memory Systems," *Comm. of the ACM*, Vol. 12, No. 3, pp. 153–165, Mar. 1969.

[McFa76] J. H. McFadyen, "System Network Architecture: An Overview," *IBM Systems Journal*, Vol. 15, No. 1, pp. 4–23, 1976.

[McGr72] M. McGrath, "Virtual Machine Computing in an Engineering Environment," *IBM Systs. Journal*, Vol. 11, No. 2, pp. 131–149, 1972.

[McLa69] R. A. McLaughlin, "The IBM 360/195," *Datamation*, pp. 119–122, Oct. 1969.

[McLe73] D. D. McCarn and J. Leiter, "On-Line Service in Medicine and Beyond," *Science*, pp. 318–324, July 27, 1973.

[McWi76] R. M. McKeag and R. Wilson, *Studies in Operating Systems*, Academic Press, New York, 1976.

[Mead70] R. M. Meade, "On Memory System Design," *Proc. AFIPS Fall Joint Comput. Conf. 1970*, AFIPS Press, Montvale, N. J., pp. 33–43, 1970.

[MeAs63] N. Metropolis and R. L. Ashenhurst, "Basic Operations in an Unnormalized Arithmetic System," *IEEE Trans. on Computers*, Vol. EC-12, No. 6, pp. 896–904, Dec. 1963.

[Mers56] J. Mersel, "Program Interrupt on the Univac Scientific Computer," *Proc. Western Joint Comput. Conf.*, pp. 52–53, 1956.

[MeSe70] R. A. Meyer and L. H. Seawright, "A Virtual Machine Time-Sharing System," *IBM Systems Journal*, Vol. 9, No. 3, pp. 199–218, 1970.

[MGST70] R. L. Mattson, J. Gecsei, D. R. Slutz, and I. L. Traiger, "Evaluation Techniques for Storage Hierarchies," *IBM Systs. Journ.*, Vol. 9, No. 2, pp. 78–117, 1970.

[Mich73] D. Michie, "The Bletchley Machines," Ch. 7.3 in [Rand73].

[MKMN73] D. B. McKay, D. P. Karp, J. M. Meyer, and R. S. Nachbar, "Exploratory Research on Netting at IBM," Ch. 12 in *Computer-Communication Networks*, N. Abramson and F. F. Kuo, eds., Prentice-Hall, Englewood Cliffs, N. J., 1973.

[MoMo61] P. Morrison and E. Morrison, *Charles Babbage and His Calculating Engines*, Dover Publications, New York, 1961.

[Morr72] J. B. Morris, "Demand Paging Through Utilization of Working Sets on the MANIAC II," *Comm. of the ACM*, Vol. 15, No. 10, pp. 867–872, Oct. 1972.

[MSNO74] T. Masuda, H. Shiota, K. Noguchi, and T. Ohki, "Optimization of Program Organization by Cluster Analysis," *Information Processing 74*, Proc. IFIP Congress 74, North-Holland, Amsterdam, pp. 261–265, 1974.

[MTAC47] "Mathematical Tables and Other Aids to Computation," *The National Research Council*, Vol. II, pp. 13–20, 1947.

[MTAC49] "Mathematical Tables and Other Aids to Computation," *The National Research Council*, Vol. III, pp. 21–28, 1949.

[MTAC50] "Mathematical Tables and Other Aids to Computation," *The National Research Council*, Vol. IV, pp. 29–32, 1950.

[MuKu73] Y. Muraoka and D. J. Kuck, "On the Time Required for a Sequence of Matrix Products," *Comm. of the ACM*. Vol. 16, pp. 22–26, Jan. 1973.

[MuPr75] D. E. Muller and F. P. Preparata, "Restructuring of Arithmetic Expressions for Parallel Evaluation," *Journ. of the ACM*, Vol. 23, No. 3, pp. 534–543, July 1975.

[Mura71] Y. Muraoka, "Parallelism Exposure and Exploitation in Programs," Ph.D. thesis, Univ. of Ill. at Urbana-Champaign, Dept. of Computer Science Rpt. 71–424, Feb. 1971.

[MuWa70] J. O. Murphey and R. M. Wade, "The IBM 360/195 in a World of Mixed Jobstreams," *Datamation*, pp. 72–79, April 1970.

[Oliv74] N. A. Oliver, "Experimental Data on Page Replacement Algorithms," *NCC AFIPS Conf. Proc.*, Vol. 43, AFIPS Press, Montvale, N. J., pp. 179–184, 1974.

[OpTs71] D. C. Opferman and N. T. Tsao-Wu, "On a Class of Rearrangeable Switching Networks," *Bell System Technical Journal*, Vol. 50, pp. 1579–1618, June 1971.

[Orga72] E. I. Organick, *The MULTICS System*, MIT Press, Cambridge, Mass., 1972.

[Orga73] E. I. Organick, *Computer System Organization: The B5700/B6700 Series*, Academic Press, New York, 1973.

[Osbo75] A. Osborne, *An Introduction to Microcomputers*, Adam Osborne and Assocs. Berkeley, Cal., 1975.

[Pade64] A. Padegs, "The Structure of System/360, Part IV—Channel Design Considerations," *IBM Systs. Journ.*, Vol. 3, No. 2, pp. 165–181, 1964.

[Pate69] R. M. Patel, "Basic I/O Handling on Burroughs B6500," *ACM Second Symposium on Operating System Principles*, pp. 120–129, Oct. 1969.

[Peas68] M. C. Pease, "An Adaptation of the Fast Fourier Transform for Parallel Processing," *Journ. of the ACM*, Vol. 15, pp. 252–264, April 1968.

[Pete61] W. W. Peterson, *Error Correcting Codes*, 2nd. ed., MIT Press, Cambridge, Mass., 1961.

[Phis76] M. Phister, Jr., *Data Processing Technology and Economics*, Santa Monica Pub. Co., Santa Monica, Calif., 1976.

[PoGo74] G. J. Popek and R. P. Goldberg, "Formal Requirements for Virtualizable Third Generation Architectures," *Comm. of the ACM*, Vol. 17, No. 7, pp. 412–421, July 1974.

[Pome72] J. H. Pomerene, "Historical Perspectives on Computers—Components," *Proc. AFIPS Fall Joint Comput. Conf.*, pp. 977–983, 1972.

[PPTH72] R. P. Parmelee, T. I. Peterson, C. C. Tillman, and D. J. Hatfield, "Virtual Storage and Virtual Machine Concepts," *IBM Systs. Journ.*, Vol. 11, No. 2, pp. 99–130, 1972.

[Rako69] L. L. Rakoczi, "The Computer Within a Computer: A Fourth Generation Concept," *IEEE Computer Group News*, pp. 14–20, March 1969.

[RaMe76] A. Ralston and C. L. Meek, *Encyclopedia of Computer Science*, Petrocelli/Charter, New York, 1976.

[Rand69] B. Randell, "A Note on Storage Fragmentation and Program Segmentation," *Comm. of the ACM*, Vol. 12, No. 7, pp. 365–369, July 1969.

[Rand72] B. Randell, "On Alan Turing and The Origins of Digital Computers," *Machine Intelligence 7*, B. Meltzer and D. Michie, eds., 1972.

[Rand73] B. Randell, *The Origins of Digital Computers: Selected Papers*, Springer-Verlag, Berlin, 1973.

[RaoT74] T. R. N. Rao, *Error Coding for Arithmetic Processors*, Academic Press, New York, 1974.

[Redd73] S. F. Reddaway, "An Elementary Array with Processing and Storage Capabilities," *Proc. International Workshop on Computer Architecture*, Grenoble, June, 1973.

[Rich55] R. K. Richards, *Arithmetic Operations in Digital Computers*, Van Nostrand, New York, 1955.

[Rieg70] E. W. Riegel, "Parallelism Exposure and Exploitation," in *Parallel Processor Systems, Technologies and Applications*, L. C. Hobbs et al., eds., Spartan Books, New York, pp. 417–438, 1970.

[RiSm71] R. Rice and W. R. Smith, "SYMBOL—A Major Departure from Classic Software Dominated vonNeumann Computing Systems," *Proc. AFIPS Spring Joint Computer Conference*, pp. 575–587, AFIPS Press, Montvale, N. J., 1971.

[Robe58] J. E. Robertson, "A New Class of Digital Division Methods," *IRE Trans. on Electronic Computers*, Vol. EC-7, No. 3, pp. 218–222, Sept. 1958.

[Robe74] L. G. Roberts, "Data by the Packet," *IEEE Spectrum*, Vol. 11, pp. 46–51, Feb. 1974; also appears in [BlCo76].

[Rodr76] J. Rodriguez-Rosell, "Empirical Data Reference Behaviour in Data Base Systems," *IEEE Computer*, Vol. 9, No. 11, pp. 9–13, Nov. 1976.

[Roge69] W. Rogers, *Think*, Stein and Day, New York, 1969.

[Rose67] A. F. Rosene, "Memory Allocation for Multiprocessors," *IEEE Trans. on Electronic Computers*, Vol. 16, No. 5, pp. 659–665, Oct. 1967.

[Rose69] S. Rosen, "Electronic Computers: A Historical Survey," *ACM Computing Surveys*, Vol. 1, No. 1, pp. 7–36, Mar. 1969.

[Rosi69] R. F. Rosin, "Contemporary Concepts of Microprogramming and Emulation," *ACM Computing Surveys*, Vol. 1, No. 4, pp. 197–212, Dec. 1969.

[RoWe70] L. G. Roberts and B. D. Wessler, "Computer Network Development to Achieve Resource Sharing," *Proc. AFIPS SJCC 1970*, Vol. 36, pp. 543–549, 1970; also appears in [BlCo76].

[RuCo69] J. F. Ruggiero and D. A. Coryell, "An Auxilliary Processing System for Array Calculations," *IBM Systs. Journ.*, Vol. 8, No. 2, pp. 118–135, 1969.

[Rudo72] J. A. Rudolph, "A Production Implementation of an Associative Array Processor—STARAN," *Proc. AFIPS Fall Joint Computer Conf. 1972*, Vol. 41, pp. 229–241, 1972.

[SaBr77] A. H. Sameh and R. Brent, "Solving Triangular Systems on a Parallel Computer," *SIAM J. Num. Analysis*, Vol. 14, No. 6, pp. 1101–1113, Dec. 1977.

[Sack70] H. Sackman, *Man-Computer Problem Solving*, Auerbach Publishers, Princeton, N. J., 1970.

[Salt74] J. H. Saltzer, "A Simple Linear Model of Demand Paging Performance," *Comm. of the ACM*, Vol. 17, No. 4, pp. 181–186, April 1974.

[Salz76] J. M. Salzer, "Bubble Memories—Where Do We Stand," *IEEE Computer*, Vol. 9, No. 3, pp. 36–41, March 1976.

[Same77] A. H. Sameh, "Numerical Parallel Algorithms—A Survey," in [KuLS77]; expanded in personal communication.

[SAPP62] R. Serrell, M. M. Astrahan, G. W. Patterson, and I. B. Pyne, "The Evolution of Computing Machines and Systems," *Proc. of the IRE*, Vol. 50, No. 5, pp. 1039–1058, May 1962.

[Saye71] A. P. Sayers, ed., *Operating Systems Survey*, The COMTRE Corp., Auerbach Publishers, Princeton, N. J., 1971.

[Semm71] C. F. Semmelhaack, "Method and Apparatus for Routing Data Among Processing Elements of an Array Computer," U. S. Patent No. 3,582,899, Filed March 21, 1968, Granted June 1, 1971.

[Shar69] W. F. Sharpe, *The Economics of Computers*, Columbia Univ. Press, New York, 1969.

[Shaw74] A. C. Shaw, *The Logical Design of Operating Systems*, Prentice Hall, Englewood Cliffs, N.J., 1974.

[ShSh66] J. E. Shemer and G. A. Shippey, "Statistical Analysis of Paged and Segmented Computer Systems," *IEEE Trans. on Electronic Computers*, Vol. 15, No. 6, pp. 855–863, Dec. 1966.

[Smit67] J. L. Smith, "Multiprogramming Under a Page on Demand Strategy," *Comm. of the ACM*, Vol. 10, No. 10, pp. 636–646, Oct. 1967.

[Smit76] A. J. Smith, "Sequentiality and Prefetching in Data Base Systems," IBM Research Rpt. RJ 1743, Mar. 1976.

[Sper74] Sperry-Rand Corporation, "Univac 1110 System," Appendix O, in *Multiprocessors and Parallel Processing*, P. H. Enslow, ed., Wiley-Interscience, New York, 1974.

[Stel77] W. H. Stellhorn, "An Inverted File Processor for Information

Retrieval," *IEEE Trans. on Computers*, Vol. C-26, No. 12, pp. 1258–1267, Dec. 1977.

[Step75] C. Stephenson, "Case Study of the Pipelined Arithmetic Unit for the TI Advanced Scientific Computer," *Proc. of the Third IEEE Symposium on Computer Arithmetic*, pp. 168–173, Nov. 1975.

[Ster74] P. H. Sterbenz, *Floating Point Computation*, Prentice-Hall, Englewood Cliffs, N. J., 1974.

[StMu71] M. L. Stein and W. D. Munro, *Introduction to Machine Arithmetic*, Addison-Wesley Pub. Co., Reading, Mass., 1971.

[Ston71] H. S. Stone, "Parallel Processing with the Perfect Shuffle," *IEEE Trans. on Computers*, Vol C-20, pp. 153–161, Feb. 1971.

[Ston75] H. S. Stone, "Parallel Computers," Chapter 8 in *Introduction to Computer Architecture*, ed., H. Stone, Science Research Associates, Chicago, Ill., 1975.

[Stre74] R. E. Strebendt, "Program Speedup Through Concurrent Record Processing," Dept. of C. S., U. of Illinois, Report UIUCDCS-R-74-638, Oct. 1974.

[Stre76] W. D. Strecker, "Cache Memories for PDP-11 Family Computers," *Proc. Third Annual Symposium on Computer Architecture*, IEEE Press, pp. 155–158, 1976.

[StSi75] H. S. Stone and D. P. Siewiorek, *Introduction to Computer Organization and Data Structures: PDP-11 Edition*, McGraw-Hill, New York, 1975.

[Sumn74] F. H. Sumner, "MU5—An Assessment of the Design," Information Processing 74, *Proc. of IFIP Congress*, North-Holland Pub. Co., Amsterdam, pp. 133–136, 1974.

[Swee65] D. W. Sweeney, "An Analysis of Floating-Point Addition," *IBM Systs. Journ.*, Vol. 4, No. 1, pp. 31–42, 1965.

[SzTa67] N. S. Szabó and R. I. Tanaka, *Residue Arithmetic and its Applications to Computer Technology*, McGraw-Hill, New York, 1967.

[Tane76] A. S. Tanenbaum, *Structured Computer Organization*, Prentice-Hall, Englewood Cliffs, N. J., 1976.

[Teor72] T. J. Teorey, "Properties of Disk Scheduling Policies in Multiprogrammed Computer Systems," *Proc. AFIPS FJCC 1972*, AFIPS Press, Montvale, N. J., pp. 1–11, 1972.

[ThKu77] C. D. Thompson and H. T. Kung, "Sorting on a Mesh-Connected Parallel Computer," *Comm. of the ACM*, Vol. 20, No. 4, pp. 263–271, Apr. 1977.

[Thor67] J. F. Thorlin, "Code Generation for PIE (Parallel Instruction Execution) Computers," *Proc. AFIPS Spring Joint Comput. Conf.*, pp. 641–643, 1967.

[Thor70] J. E. Thornton, *Design of a Computer, the Control Data 6600*, Scott, Foresman and Co., Glenview, Ill., 1970.

[Thur74] K. J. Thurber, "Interconnection Networks—A Survey and Assessment," *Proc. National Computer Conference*, pp. 909–914, 1974.

[TjFl70] G. S. Tjaden and M. J. Flynn, "Detection and Parallel Execution of

Independent Instructions," *IEEE Trans. on Computers*, Vol. C-19, No. 10, pp. 889–895, Oct. 1970.

[TjFl73] G. S. Tjaden and M. J. Flynn, "Representation of Concurrency with Ordering Matrices," *IEEE Trans. on Computers*, Vol. C-22, No. 8, pp. 752–761, Aug. 1973.

[TJJK72] K. J. Thurber, E. D. Jensen, L. A. Jack, L. L. Kinney, P. C. Patton, and L. C. Anderson, "A Systematic Approach to the Design of Digital Bussing Structures," *Proc. AFIPS Fall Joint Computer Conference*, pp. 719–739, 1972.

[TNYF63] S. Takahashi, H. Nishino, K. Yoshihiro, and K. Fuchi, "System Design of the ETL Mk-6 Computers," *Information Processing 1962, Proc. IFIP Congress*, 1962, North-Holland Pub. Co., Amsterdam, p. 690, 1963.

[Toch58] T. D. Tocher, "Techniques of Multiplication and Division for Automatic Binary Computers," *Quarter J. Mech. App. Math.*, Vol. 2, Part 3, pp. 364–384, 1958.

[Toma67] R. M. Tomasulo, "An Efficient Algorithm for Exploiting Multiple Arithmetic Units," *IBM Journ. of Research & Development*, Vol. 11, No. 1, pp. 25–33, Jan. 1967.

[Towl76] R. Towle, "Control and Data Dependence for Program Transformations," Ph.D. thesis, Univ. of Ill. at Urb.-Champ., Dept. of Comput. Sci. Rpt. No. 76-788, Mar. 1976.

[Triv76] K. S. Trivedi, "Prepaging and Applications to Array Algorithms," *IEEE Trans. on Computers*, Vol. C-25, No. 9, pp. 915–921, Sept. 1976.

[Trop74] H. Tropp, "Computer Report VII, The Effervescent Years: A Retrospective," *IEEE Spectrum*, pp. 70–81, Feb. 1974.

[Tsao74] N-K. Tsao, "On the Distribution of Significant Digits and Roundoff Errors," *Comm. of the ACM*, Vol. 17, No. 5, pp. 269–271, May 1974.

[TsMa72] R. F. Tsao and B. H. Margolin, "A Multi-Factor Paging Experiment: II Statistical Methodology," in *Statistical Computer Performance Evaluation*, W. Freiberger, ed., Academic Press, New York, pp. 135–158, 1972.

[Tuck65] S. G. Tucker, "Emulation of Large Systems," *Comm. of the ACM*, Vol. 8, No. 12, pp. 753–761, Dec. 1965.

[Tuck67] S. G. Tucker, "Microprogram Control for System/360," *IBM Systs. Journ.*, Vol. 6, No. 4, pp. 222–241, 1967.

[Turi36] A. M. Turing, "On Computable Numbers, with an Application to the Entscheidungsproblem," *Proc. of the London Math. Soc.*, Ser. 2, Vol. 42, pp. 230–265, 1936–37.

[Turn74] R. Turn, *Computers in the 1980s*, Columbia Univ. Press, N.Y., 1974.

[TuWa76] R. Turn and W. Ware, "Privacy and Security Issues in Information Systems," *IEEE Trans. on Computers*, Vol. C-25, No. 12, pp. 1353–1361, Dec. 1976.

[UIll57] "On the Design of a Very High-Speed Computer," Rpt. No. 80,

Univ. of Ill. at Urbana-Champaign, Digital Computer Lab., Oct. 1957.

[Unge58] S. H. Unger, "A Computer Oriented Toward Spatial Problems," *Proc. of the IRE*, pp. 1744–1750, Oct. 1958.

[Vold59] J. E. Volder, "The Cordic Trigonometric Computing Technique," *IRE Trans. on Electronic Computers*, Vol. EC–8, pp. 330–334, 1959.

[Waks68] A. Waksman, "A Permutation Network," *Journ. of the ACM*, Vol. 15, No. 1, pp. 159–163, Jan. 1968.

[Wall64] C. S. Wallace, "A Suggestion for a Fast Multiplier," *IEEE Trans. on Electronic Computers*, Vol. EC–13, pp. 14–17, Feb. 1964.

[Walt71] J. S. Walther, "A Unified Algorithm for Elementary Functions," *Proc. AFIPS Spring Joint Comput. Conf. 1971*, pp. 379–385, 1971.

[WaMa73] P. M. Walker and S. L. Matheson, "Regulatory Policy and Future Data Transmission Services," Ch. 9 in *Computer-Communication Networks*, N. Abramson and F. F. Kuo, eds., Prentice-Hall, Englewood Cliffs, N. J., 1973.

[Wats70] R. W. Watson, *Timesharing System Design Concepts*, McGraw-Hill, New York, 1970.

[Wats72] W. J. Watson, "The TI ASC—A Highly Modular and Flexible Super Computer Architecture," *Proc. AFIPS Fall Joint Computer Conf. 1972*, pp. 221–228, AFIPS Press, Montvale, N. J., 1972.

[Webe67] H. Weber, "A Microprogrammed Implementation of EULER on IBM System/360 Model 30," *Comm. of the ACM*, Vol. 10, No. 9, pp. 549–558, Sept. 1967 [reprinted in BeNe71].

[Wich73] B. A. Wichmann, *ALGOL-60 Compilation and Assessment*, Academic Press, New York, 1973.

[WiJe76] A. O. Williman and H. J. Jelinek, "Introduction to LSI Microprocessor Developments," *IEEE Computer*, Vol. 9, No. 6, pp. 34–45, June 1976.

[Wilh76] N. C. Wilhelm, "An Anomaly in Disk Scheduling: A Comparison of FCFS and SSTF Seek Scheduling Using an Empirical Model for Disk Accesses," *Comm. of the ACM*, Vol. 19, No. 1, pp. 13–17, Jan. 1976.

[Wilk51] M. V. Wilkes, "The Best Way to Design an Automatic Calculating Machine," *Manchester University Computer Inaugural Conf.*, published by Ferranti, Ltd., London, July 1951.

[Wilk56] M. V. Wilkes, *Automatic Digital Calculations*, Methuen, London, 1956.

[Wilk63] J. H. Wilkinson, *Rounding Errors in Algebraic Processes*, Prentice-Hall, Englewood Cliffs, N. J., 1963.

[Wilk65] M. V. Wilkes, "Slave Memories and Dynamic Storage Allocation," *IEEE Trans. on Computers*, Vol. EC-14, No. 2, pp. 270–271, April 1965.

[Wilk69] M. V. Wilkes, "The Growth of Interest in Microprogramming: A Literature Survey," *ACM Computer Surveys*, Vol. 1, pp. 139–145, Sept. 1969.

[Wilk72] M. V. Wilkes, *Time-Sharing Computer System*, 2nd. ed., Elsevier, New York, 1972.

[Wiln72a] W. T. Wilner, "Burroughs B1700 Memory Utilization," *Proc.*

AFIPS Fall Joint Computer Conference, Vol. 41, pp. 579–586, 1972.

[Wiln72b] W. T. Wilner, "Design of the Burroughs B1700," *Proc. AFIPS Fall Joint Computer Conference,* Vol. 41, pp. 489–497, 1972.

[Wino65] S. Winograd, "On the Time Required to Perform Addition," *Journ. of ACM,* Vol. 12, No. 2, pp. 277–285, Apr. 1965.

[Wino67] S. Winograd, "On the Time Required to Perform Multiplication," *Journ. of ACM,* Vol. 14, No. 4, pp. 793–802, Oct. 1967.

[Wino75] S. Winograd, "On the Parallel Evaluation of Certain Arithmetic Expressions," *Journ. of ACM,* Vol. 22, No. 4, pp. 477–492, Oct. 1975.

[Wirt68] N. Wirth, "Stack vs. Multiregister Computers," *SIGPLAN Notices,* pp. 13–19, Mar. 1968.

[Wirt69] N. Wirth, "On Multiprogramming, Machine Coding, and Computer Organization," *Comm. of the ACM,* Vol. 12, No. 9, pp. 489–498, 1969.

[WiWG51] M. V. Wilkes, D. J. Wheeler, and S. Gill, *The Preparation of Programs for an Electronic Digital Computer,* Addison-Wesley, Cambridge, Mass., 1951.

[WuBe72] W. A. Wulf and C. G. Bell, "C.mmp—A Multi-Miniprocessor," *Proc. AFIPS Fall Joint Computer Conference,* Vol. 41, pp. 765–777, AFIPS Press, Montvale, N. J., 1972.

[YaFu77] S. S. Yau and H. S. Fung, "Associative Processor Architecture— A Survey," *ACM Computing Surveys,* Vol. 9, No. 1, Mar. 1977.

[Zuse58] K. Zuse, "Die Feldrechenmaschine," *Mathematik, Technik, Wirtschaft-Mittelungen,* Vol. 4, pp. 213–220, 1958.

INDEX

Terms are indexed from the text, footnotes (denoted by n), and the Problems sections (for discussions that go beyond the text). A number of entries do not appear alone but are given below a major topic such as a major subsystem (e.g., Main memory), a general idea (e.g., Number systems), or a manufacturer's name.